Foundations of American Education

Second Edition

L. Dean Webb

Arizona State University

Arlene Metha

Arizona State University

K. Forbis Jordan

Arizona State University

Merrill,
an imprint of Prentice Hall

Englewood Cliffs, New Jersey   Columbus, Ohio

Library of Congress Cataloging-in-Publication Data

Webb, L. Dean.
    Foundations of American education/by L. Dean Webb, Arlene Metha,
K. Forbis Jordan. — 2nd ed.
      p.   cm.
    Includes bibliographical references and indexes.
    ISBN 0-02-424974-2
    1. Education—United States.   I. Metha, Arlene.   II. Jordan, K.
Forbis (Kenneth Forbis).   III. Title.
LA217.2.W43 1996
370'.973—dc20   95-4834
                                                              CIP

Cover Photo: © Susan Lapides, 1995
Editor: Debra A. Stollenwerk
Developmental Editor: Linda Ashe Montgomery
Production Editor: Stephen C. Robb
Photo Editor: Anne Vega
Production, Cover and Text Design, Coordination:
    Proof Positive/Farrowlyne Associates, Inc.
Production Manager: Deidra M. Schwartz

This book was set in New Baskerville by Proof Positive/Farrowlyne Associates, Inc. and
was printed and bound by Quebecor Printing/Martinsburg. The cover was printed by
Phoenix Color Corporation.

 © 1996 by Prentice-Hall, Inc.
A Simon & Schuster Company
Englewood Cliffs, New Jersey 07632

Earlier edition © 1992 by Macmillan Publishing Company.

Printed in the United States of America

10 9 8 7 6 5 4 3 2

ISBN: 0-02-424974-2

Prentice-Hall International (UK) Limited, *London*
Prentice-Hall of Australia Pty. Limited, *Sydney*
Prentice-Hall Canada, Inc., *Toronto*
Prentice-Hall Hispanoamericana, S. A., *Mexico*
Prentice-Hall of India Private Limited, *New Delhi*
Prentice-Hall of Japan, Inc., *Tokyo*
Simon & Schuster Asia Pte. Ltd., *Singapore*
Editora Prentice-Hall do Brasil, Ltda., *Rio de Janeiro*

Photo Credits

Preface

The recent interest in education reform has contributed to a renewed emphasis on the critical role of the teacher in American education. As a result of various reforms such as decentralization and site-based decision making, members of this rewarding and challenging profession are having a greater role in making decisions that daily affect their work. The movement toward teaching as a profession is being advanced by the development of national certification programs.

In writing this second edition, our primary goal has been to provide current and useful information that will help persons interested in careers in elementary and secondary education develop an understanding of the historical and philosophical roots of education, current educational structures, recent developments, and projected futures. With this understanding and knowledge, they can make informed decisions about their professional and career goals. There is general agreement about the need for able persons in education; however, the decision to become a teacher should come only after careful deliberation. Before making the decision to enter teaching, individuals need to understand the complexities of the teacher's role, the diverse duties and responsibilities, and the commitment of time and energy required to be a successful teacher.

Orientation of the Text

To help the student develop an understanding of education, this book follows a sequenced presentation of major topics: the historical and philosophical background of education, the relationship between schools and society, the law and its effect on schools, the organization and financing of elementary and secondary schools, the current and evolving process of teaching and learning, the particular challenges of working with diverse populations and at-risk youth, the recent and contemplated changes in the role of the teacher, and projected changes in education. In this interdisciplinary approach, we have given attention to both the theoretical and the applied aspects of education. Our goal has been to prepare a text that includes a balance of past, present, and future applications of education in a context that students will find both readable and challenging.

Interdisciplinary Emphasis

One of the strengths of the text is the extensive use of relevant concepts from the social sciences. Historical materials were used in developing the extensive discussion of the evolution of schooling for the past several centuries. The philosophical roots of education have been identified and discussed. Other disciplines such as sociology, economics, politics of education, political science, public administration, finance, and law have been used to provide an understanding of the current and developing context of education. Research from the field of psychology is used extensively in the discussion of teaching and learning and the future of education.

Theoretical and Applied Aspects of Education

Through the use of current research, we have emphasized the connections between theory and research and the applied world of teaching. Unlike many foundation texts that concentrate primarily on pedagogical knowledge and academic skill domains, this text provides a comprehensive application of research and theory to actual classroom/teaching situations and practice. Through margin notes, special features, and discussion questions, the educational implications of research and theory are reinforced in ways that will be understandable to both practicing and prospective teachers.

New to This Edition

In order to provide *an integrated perspective* this revision:

- Discusses the concurrent pressures for decentralization, national standards, and national goals illustrating the various paradoxes in educational reform

- Raises important questions about the changing role of the teacher and students in the teaching/learning process

- Merges a discussion of governance and finance to explore problems and identify issues related to shared governance and site-based decision making

- Relates real-world experiences of teachers in "Critical Incidents" and "Personal Reflections," which are respective statements and quotations by Teachers of the Year from various states

- Describes the interaction between curriculum and instruction and emerging technological developments

Pedagogical Features

Several features have been designed to help the student use the text for study and review.

Chapter Objectives

The first section in each chapter consists of a series of objectives to be achieved through study and discussion. They may be used as guides for class discussion and also will be a good tool to use in studying and reviewing the material.

Margin Notes and Key Terms

To help you identify and understand key concepts in each chapter, we have included notes in the margins of each chapter. Key terms have been identified in italic type in the text, referenced at the end of each chapter, and defined in a glossary at the end of the book.

Discussion Topics

At the end of each chapter, a series of discussion questions or topics provides an overview of the basic concepts in the chapter. They may be used as oral or written assignments, topics for class discussion, or review topics.

Figures and Tables

Figures and tables have been used to enhance and supplement the text and to add additional content. These visual features give an additional dimension to the chapters and they will help students develop a better understanding of major concepts.

Summary

The key points are presented in a brief summary at the end of each chapter. These can be used as guides for class discussion and in study and review sessions.

Glossary

The glossary at the end of the book defines the terms identified throughout the book. It will help you better understand the key concepts and provides consistent definitions in the use of terms throughout the book.

References

The complete list of references at the end of each chapter provides bibliographic information for all citations. The references can be used in further study to develop a better understanding of specific topics and as beginning points for identifying sources and topics for research papers.

Special Features

Each chapter contains pedagogical features designed to enrich the learning opportunities by including historical notes and discussion stimulators drawn from current and past educational developments, current issues, or applications of educational principles in real-life situations. Special features include the following topics:

- *Critical Incidents* start each chapter with statements by Teachers of the Year from various states about critical incidents from their teaching experiences. These statements from practicing teachers who have received state and national recognition contain examples of the satisfactions and challenges that are a part of the daily life of teaching.

- *Historical Notes* provide background information about specific educational developments that have resulted in changes in education or about individuals who have exerted leadership in some aspect of education. They supplement the other content of the text and illustrate the educational contributions made by various role models.

- *Ask Yourself* features are designed to stimulate reflective thought that will help students develop a better understanding about teaching as a career. They contain a series of questions that expand upon the text and stimulate exploration of specific concepts and issues in greater depth. These enrichment activities can be used by groups of students or by individuals.

- *Controversial Issues* present a dichotomy of arguments, pro and con, about a variety of educational issues. As students reflect on and discuss these controversies, they will have an opportunity to address the range of values and beliefs concerning important educational concepts.

- *Personal Reflections* are direct quotations from Teachers of the Year from various states. They provide focused thoughts and advice based on experiences with students, parents, their peers, and administrators.
    They also will help both the teacher and the students in using the text during the course of the class.

Acknowledgments

The authors wish to recognize the many persons who have contributed to the preparation of both this and the first edition of this text. First, we give special recognition to the teachers and other educators who work each day to provide learning opportunities for the youth of America. Second, we wish to acknowledge the diverse scholars who have provided the past and present record of the development of elementary and secondary education and the researchers and policy analysts who are charting the future. Third, we express our appreciation to our students and professional colleagues for their critical comments and suggestions about ways to improve the first edition. Fourth, we recognize the various persons who supported this second edition.

We extend our special thanks and appreciation for the assistance and guidance of our developmental editor, Linda Montgomery. She guided us, critiqued the first edition, made helpful suggestions, reacted to our suggestions, and provided a good mixture of patience, discipline, and encouragement during development of the manuscript. Special recognition is also extended to the copy editor, Bill Race; the production editor, Steve Robb, who worked closely with us during the final stages of the manuscript; and Debbie Stollenwerk, our editor on the project.

To the various reviewers of the first edition, we extend our sincere thanks for their constructive comments. Their efforts helped us improve the text in this second edition. For their participation, we extend our thanks to Karen D. Carpenter, Coastal Carolina University; Rand L. Bissell, University of Georgia, Athens; Audrey Cohan, Hofstra University; Timothy J, Bergen, Jr., University of South Carolina; and W. Thomas Jamison, Appalachian State University.

L. Dean Webb
Arlene Metha
K. Forbis Jordan

Contents in Brief

Contents

Special Features

Historical Note

Ask Yourself

Controversial Issues

PART ONE

The Teaching Profession

Chapter 1

Status of the Profession

Education is the one investment that means more for our future, because it means the most for our children. . . . The nation will not accept anything less than excellence in education.

President George Bush, State of the Union Address, January 31, 1990

A Critical Incident in My Teaching Career . . .

My role as a teacher was greatly influenced by an incident in my childhood. I came from an extremely dysfunctional home in the 1950s and from a very abusive situation. One night my alcoholic mother hit me and I cut my head open on a very sharp table corner. I went off to bed alone, hungry and crying. I got myself up in the morning and went off to school without any breakfast as usual. I could not get a hairbrush through my hair so I left it just the way it was. My second grade teacher saw me and took me down to the girls' lavatory before school and had me bend over the white sink as she poured cool water through my hair. I saw rusty colored flakes fall into the sink and I remember thinking, "I want to be a teacher just like her when I grow up so I can help kids just like me."

That has been my role, my goal, and my lifelong ambition. Showing love and compassion and teaching children. . . .

Bonnie Lutz
Teacher of the Year, Minnesota

Teaching has been considered by some to be the most noble of the professions. H. G. Wells went so far as to say that "The teacher, whether mother, priest, or schoolmaster, is the real maker of history." Perhaps you are asking yourself, "What is a teacher? What is this profession of teaching all about?" And, perhaps most importantly, "Should I become a teacher?" This chapter presents an overview of the teaching profession. After studying the chapter you should be able to:

- Provide a demographic overview of America's teaching force.
- Discuss the public's views of the schools and the teaching profession.
- Evaluate your motives for becoming a teacher, as well as those commonly cited by others.
- Describe a typical teacher preparation program and the major recommendations that have been made for the reform of teacher education.
- Discuss current issues related to certification, including testing, alternative certification, emergency certification, recertification, and interstate certification.
- Compare projected data related to teacher supply with that projected for demand, and explore the factors contributing to supply and demand.
- Identify the major elements of teacher compensation, including incentive pay and supplemental pay.

The Teacher and Teaching: Definitions

Put most simply, a teacher is one who instructs others. A more formal definition from Good's *Dictionary of Education* (1973) defines a teacher as "a person employed in an official capacity for the purpose of guiding and directing the learning experiences of pupils or students in an educational institution, whether public or private" (p. 586). Teaching is defined in the same work as "the act of instructing in an educational institution" (p. 588). A well-known educator and writer in the field of education, B. O. Smith (1987), provides five definitions of teaching:

1. The descriptive definition of teaching: Defines teaching as imparting knowledge or skill.

2. Teaching as success: Defines teaching as an activity such that X learns what Y teaches. If X does not learn, Y has not taught.

3. Teaching as intentional activity: Defines teaching as intended behavior (i.e., paying attention to what is going on, making diagnoses, changing one's behavior) for which the aim is to induce learning.

4. Teaching as normative behavior: Defines teaching as a family of activities, including training, instructing, indoctrinating, and conditioning.

5. The scientific or technical definition of teaching: Defines teaching by the coordinating propositions; teaching is not explicitly defined, but its meaning is implicated in the sentences where it occurs (e.g., "The teacher gives feedback.").

Perhaps the most provocative definition defines the teacher as an artist and teaching as an art. According to Eisner (1994), teaching can be considered an art from at least four perspectives:

First, it is an art in that teaching can be performed with such skill and grace that, for the student as well as for the teacher, the experience can be justifiably characterized as aesthetic. . . .

Second, teaching is an art in that teachers, like painters, composers, actresses, and dancers, make judgements based largely on qualities that unfold during the course of action. . . . The teacher must "read" the emerging qualities and respond with qualities appropriate to the ends sought. . . .

Third, teaching is an art in that the teacher's activity is not dominated by prescriptions or routines but is influenced by qualities and contingencies that are unpredicted. The teacher must function in an innovative way in order to cope with these contingencies. . . .

Fourth, teaching is an art in that the ends it achieves are often created in the process . . . teaching is a form of human action in which many of the ends achieved are emergent—that is to say, found in the course of interaction with students rather than preconceived and efficiently attained. (pp. 154–155)

To consider teaching an art does not negate the necessity of establishing a scientific basis for the art of teaching and for developing a theoretical framework for teaching that addresses what we know and believe about intelligence, the

Do you believe that teachers are "born, not made"? In your experience as a student, have you been exposed to teachers who were "artists" in the classroom?

conditions of learning, and what defines the effective teacher. The stronger the scientific basis, the greater the potential to improve teaching.

Profile of the Teaching Profession

Whatever definition is used, there is little argument that the teacher is the central element in the educational system. It is of interest to review what we know about the teacher in American society today. Table 1.1 presents some characteristics of public and private teachers.

As indicated in the table, the teaching force is predominantly female and white: only 13.5% of the public school and 7.8% of the private school teaching force is minority. Public school teachers are almost equally divided in terms of degree status: about half have a bachelor's degree and about half have higher

Table 1.1: Selected Characteristics of Public and Private School Teachers, 1991

Teacher Characteristics	Public School Teachers	Private School Teachers
Sex (percent)		
Male	28.1	22.9
Female	71.9	77.1
Race/ethnicity (percent)		
White, non-Hispanic	86.5	92.2
Black, non-Hispanic	8.3	2.7
Hispanic	3.4	3.3
Asian/Pacific Isl.	1.0	1.5
Native American	.8	.4
Average age (years)	41.6	40.3
Highest degree (percent)		
Bachelor's	51.9	61.9
Master's	42.1	27.0
More than master's	5.4	4.7
Average number of students per full-time teacher	16.5	16.1
Average years teaching experience	14.8	12.3
Average salary		
B.A. no experience	$19,913	$15,141
M.A. no experience	21,698	16,511
M.A. 20 yrs. experience	33,199	23,253

Source: U.S. Department of Education, National Center for Education Statistics. (1993). *Schools and staffing in the United States: A statistical profile, 1990–91.* Washington, DC: U.S. Department of Education.

than a bachelor's degree. The degree attainment of public school teachers was higher overall than that of private school teachers. And, while the pupil-teacher ratios for the two groups is almost the same, public school teachers as a whole have more experience than private school teachers and earn more at all degree and experience levels.

The number of teachers and other instructional personnel employed in the public school systems of the United States has grown over the years as enrollments have increased. Table 1.2 gives a historical summary of public elementary and secondary school enrollments; number of instructional staff; and number of teachers, librarians, and other nonsupervisory staff. As can be seen, in the years since 1950 the total number of teachers, librarians, and other nonsupervisory staff more than doubled. The growth in staff reflects not only enrollment increases, but the steady reduction in pupil-teacher ratios, legislation requiring increased services and specialized personnel, and the increased utilization of teacher aides, librarians, guidance counselors, and other instructional support personnel.

Why Become a Teacher?

There are many reasons why an individual might choose a career in teaching. Very few teachers would be able to identify a single reason for entering the profession. Many were positively influenced by former teachers. For others an important reason might be a practical consideration such as job security, or something as forthright as the fact that their first career choices were blocked

Table 1.2: Historical Summary of Public Elementary and Secondary School Statistics: United States, 1869–70 to 1991–92

	1869–70	1879–80	1889–90	1899–1900	1909–10	1919–20
Total enrollment (in thousands)	6,872	9,867	12,723	15,503	17,814	21,578
Total instructional staff (in thousands)	—	—	—	—	—	678
Total teachers, librarians and other nonsupervisory staff (in thousands)	201	287	364	423	523	657
Men	78	123	126	127	110	93
Women	123	164	238	296	413	585

(i.e., they didn't make it into medical school or into professional sports). Others may be attracted by the long summer vacations or a schedule that allows them to spend more time with their families. A less positive reason might be that teaching is a good temporary job while waiting to prepare for or be accepted into another career.

All of the above are indeed motives for becoming a teacher, but they are not the primary motives. Over the years, numerous researchers have asked teachers what attracted them to the profession. The three reasons given most consistently are (1) a caring for and desire to work with young people; (2) a desire to make a contribution to society; and (3) an interest in a certain field and an excitement in sharing it with others.

The reasons one has for becoming a teacher have a significant effect on the ultimate satisfaction one finds in the job. For this reason, Herbert Kohl (1976), elementary school teacher and well-known educator, suggests that prospective teachers question themselves about what they expect to gain from or give to teaching. Several sets of questions suggested by Kohl to guide you in this inquiry are found on page 8.

Satisfactions and Dissatisfactions With Teaching

Just as each individual has his or her motives for becoming a teacher, each individual will find certain aspects of the position satisfying and certain aspects dis-

1929–30	1939–40	1949–50	1959–60	1969–70	1979–80	1989–90	1991–92
25,678	25,434	25,112	36,087	45,550	41,651	40,543	42,047
880	912	963	1,457	2,286	2,406	2,986	3,104
843	875	920	1,393	2,195	2,300	2,860	2,975
140	195	196	404	711	782	—	—
703	681	724	989	1,484	1,518	—	—

Source: U.S. Department of Education, National Center for Education Statistics. (1994). *Digest of educational statistics, 1994* (Table 39). Washington, DC: U.S. Government Printing Office.

Ask Yourself:
Do I Want To Be a Teacher?

1. What reasons do you have for wanting to teach? Are they all negative (e.g., because the schools are oppressive, or because I need a job and working as a teacher is more respectable than working as a cab driver or salesperson)? What are the positive reasons for wanting to teach? Is there any pleasure to be gained from teaching? Knowledge? Power?

2. Why do you want to spend so much time with young people? Do you feel more comfortable with children? Have you spent much time with children recently, or are you mostly fantasizing how they would behave? Are you afraid of adults? Intimidated by adult company? Fed up with the competition and coldness of business and the university?

3. What do you want from the children? Do you want them to do well on tests? Learn particular subject matter? Like each other? Like you? How much do you need to have students like you? Are you afraid to criticize them or set limits on their behavior because they might be angry with you? Do you consider yourself one of the kids? Is there any difference in your mind between your role and that of your prospective students?

4. What do you know that you can teach to or share with your students?

5. With what age youngster do you feel the greatest affinity or are you most comfortable with?

6. Do you have any sex-based motives for wanting to work with young people? Do you want to enable them to become the boy or girl you could never be? For example, to free the girls of the image of prettiness and quietness and encourage them to run and fight, mess about with science and get lost in the abstraction of math? Or to encourage boys to write poetry, play with dolls, let their fantasies come out, and not feel abnormal if they enjoy reading, acting, or listening to music?

7. What kind of young people do you want to work with?

8. What kind of school should you teach in?

9. How comfortable would you be teaching in a multiracial or multicultural setting? Do you feel capable of working with a culturally diverse student population?

---

satisfying. In fact, it is possible that a particular aspect may be both satisfying and dissatisfying. Long summer vacations are satisfiers, but the reduced salary is a dissatisfier. Working with children can be both satisfying and frustrating. Although each individual will find his or her own satisfactions and dissatisfactions with teaching, it is of interest to look at what practicing teachers have identified as the satisfactions or attractions of teaching, as well as the dissatisfactions or challenges of teaching. Prospective teachers in particular need to know and prepare for what they will encounter when they enter the classroom.

The Satisfactions of Teaching

We have already mentioned what teachers most often identify as the major satisfactions of teaching: the joy of working with children, the feeling that you are making a difference in the life of the individual student and the larger society. Teachers often talk about the sense of accomplishment they feel and the reward it brings when they watch children learn and progress. In recent years teachers have also mentioned rising salaries as a satisfier. As will be discussed later in this chapter, in the last decade not only have teacher salaries risen at a faster rate than inflation, the indirect compensation they receive in the form of fringe benefits has also improved significantly.

Many teachers find the autonomy they exercise in their classroom and the control they have over their own time to be attractions. For others it would be the opportunity to have a lifelong association with their subject field. And for yet others the security of the position and the feeling of comraderie and cooperation they share with their colleagues are important attractions. Teaching is one of the few professions where competition is virtually nonexistent. Lastly, indeed, many teachers would list extended vacations as a strong attraction of teaching.

The Dissatisfactions of Teaching

The greatest dissatisfactions teachers feel are those that are related to the conditions that impact on their effectiveness and those over which they feel they have little or no control. The dissatisfactions most often identified by teachers are lack of support from parents; lack of discipline; high pupil-teacher ratios; not being involved in decisions about the curriculum, textbooks, or schedules; inadequate resources; and isolation.

A U. S. Department of Education (1993b) survey found that teachers perceive the lack of parental involvement to be the single most serious problem of the schools. The lack of discipline in the schools has also consistently been cited as one of the major challenges faced by teachers. High pupil-teacher ratios increase teachers' frustrations in trying to meet the individual needs of all students: if the class is composed of a wide range of student ability levels the frustration is compounded. And, while teachers feel they are in the best position to recognize the needs of their students, often they are excluded from participation in the decision making process regarding these decisions. Fortunately, an increasing number of districts nationwide are adopting site-based management (see Chapter 13), allowing teachers a greater role in the decisions that affect their professional lives. Inadequate resources, the constant bane of teachers, inhibit the ability of teachers to meet the needs of individual students and prepare all students for higher levels of educational attainment or successful participation in the workforce. Lastly, as Goodlad (1984) and others have discussed, teachers often experience a profound sense of isolation. Contact with other adults is limited to lunchtime or the faculty lounge during the preparation period. Little opportunity is provided for discussion of professional issues.

Perhaps the ultimate indication of teacher job satisfaction or dissatisfaction is whether, given the opportunity to make the decision again, a person would become a teacher. A U.S. Department of Education (1993b) survey that asked teachers this very question found that 66% of public school teachers and 77% of private school teachers said they "certainly" or "probably" would. Slightly lesser percentages (61% and 71%) agreed that teaching had more advantages than disadvantages. Another positive finding was that only 3% of public and private school teachers said they definitely planned to leave teaching. However, a

Metropolitan Life survey of second year teachers found that 19% said they were "very likely" of "fairly likely" to leave the teaching profession in the next five years. The most important reasons given for leaving were: lack of support or help for students from parents and lack of support from school administration, each ranked as the most important factor by 18% of the respondents. These were followed closely by the need or desire to make more money (16%), and to a lesser extent, the belief that the social problems faced by students make teaching too difficult (7%), the availability of jobs (6%), and raising a family (5%) (Harris, 1992).

Avenues to the Profession

There are a number of ways to become a teacher. The most traditional is to complete a four-year baccalaureate teacher education program. At some institutions, undergraduates majoring in fields other than education are able to accumulate enough teacher education credits to qualify for certification. An extended, or five-year preservice, teacher education program has been implemented at a number of institutions. These programs typically emphasize field experiences and most award a master's degree upon completion. For the increasing number of individuals who have non-education college degrees and want to enter the profession the two options are (1) enrolling as a post-baccalaureate student and taking only enough courses to obtain a teaching certificate, or (2) enrolling in a master's degree program leading to teacher certification. In the next section we will review teacher education programs, the most common avenue into the profession.

Teacher Preparation

Program Characteristics

The formal education of teachers takes place in about 1,200 different departments, schools, or colleges of education in the United States. Teacher education programs usually consist of four areas: (1) a general studies requirement, (2) the major and minor areas of specialization, (3) a professional studies component, and (4) a student teaching experience. The general studies or liberal arts portion of the program, as well as the academic major portion, are generally similar to those required of other students at the college or university. The professional studies component usually consists of courses in teaching methods, curriculum, historical and philosophical foundations, and educational psychology.

How do you determine your preference for elementary or secondary teaching?

Preparation programs for elementary school teachers are somewhat different from those for secondary school teachers. Depending on the organization of the institution, students completing preparation programs for secondary school teachers may have a major in education or a major in the subject field to be taught. The number of hours in the major will usually constitute two-thirds of the hours taken in the upper division, with the other one-third in the professional education sequence, namely foundations, educational psychology, one or more discipline specific methods courses, and student teaching. Some variations, though not usually significant, may exist for the preparation of secondary vocational education, physical education, and art teachers (Goodlad, 1994).

Although a growing number of institutions require that students preparing to be elementary school teachers have a minor in a content area, elementary education is considered their major. They are not expected to be subject matter specialists, but must be prepared to teach the full range of subject matter studied in the self-contained elementary classroom. Consequently, they commonly take courses that cover both the content thought desirable for teachers to know and the methods for teaching reading, science, math, social studies, language arts, and so on (Goodlad, 1994).

Student teaching is required for certification in all states. The student teaching component varies in length from five weeks to one semester. Typically, the student teacher is assigned to a cooperating teacher selected because of his or her reputation as an "expert" teacher. A college or university professor is assigned to supervise the student teaching experience and makes periodic observations and visitations with the student and the cooperating teacher. During the student teaching experience the student gradually assumes greater responsibility for instruction under the guidance of the cooperating teacher. While the amount of time the student teacher actually spends teaching may vary considerably, in part a function of the demonstrated ability of the student teacher and in part a function of the nature of the classroom, the average student teacher will spend about 60% of his or her time on teaching. The remaining time is spent on observation, record keeping, and assisting in various classroom activities. The student teaching experience, designed to provide students the opportunity to put into practice what they have learned in the classroom, is consistently rated by teachers as the most important part of their preparation program.

Figure 1.1 graphically depicts the typical preparation programs for elementary and secondary teachers and gives the percentage of each program devoted to each area. As indicated, the general studies and student teaching requirements are approximately the same for both programs; they differ in the percentage of time spent in professional studies and in other academic studies. Overall, secondary education students average 10 semester hours more to complete their program than elementary majors.

Prior to the internship or student teaching experience, teacher preparation programs normally include *field or clinical experiences* designed to give students more firsthand experiences in the classroom. Such experiences commonly include classroom observation, tutoring and small group instruction, or various noninstructional tasks. Typically, special education students spend 166 clock hours in field experience, early childhood and elementary students 140 hours, and secondary education students 90 hours (Galluzzo & Arends, 1989). When added to the average of 360 hours reportedly spent in student teaching, today's teacher education student is receiving significantly more clinical experiences than those trained even a decade ago.

Figure 1.1: Elementary and Secondary Education Program Requirements

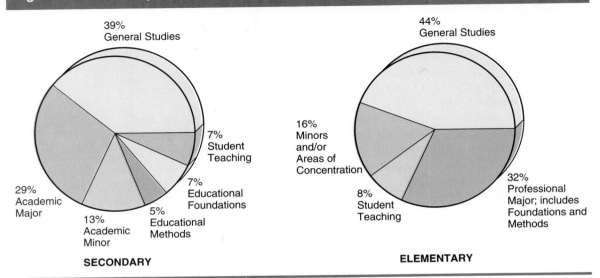

39%
General Studies

7%
Student
Teaching

7%
Educational
Foundations

29%
Academic
Major

5%
Educational
Methods

13%
Academic
Minor

SECONDARY

44%
General Studies

16%
Minors
and/or
Areas of
Concentration

32%
Professional
Major; includes
Foundations and
Methods

8%
Student
Teaching

ELEMENTARY

Admission

How do the admission requirements to the teacher education program at your institution compare to those for admission to other professional programs?

Despite the public perception that "those who can't, teach," teacher education candidates compare favorably with other undergraduates and admission to the teacher education program at most colleges and universities is as competitive, or even more competitive, than admission to other undergraduate programs. Data collected by the American Association of College of Teacher Education (AACTE) found that the SAT and ACT scores of teacher education students compare favorably with other undergraduate students. Additionally, the typical teacher education student was rated in the top 30% of his or her high school graduating class (Galluzzo & Arends, 1989).

Admission to most teacher education programs requires an interview, completion of a general studies/liberal arts requirement, and attainment of a designated minimum grade point average. Institutions accredited by the National Council for Accreditation of Teacher Education (NCATE) are required to establish 2.5 as the minimum grade point average for admission, and many have established higher admission requirements. In addition to meeting these requirements, 32 states require students to pass a test prior to admission to the teacher education program. The most commonly used instruments are the Pre-Professional Skills Test and a similar instrument, the California Basic Education Skills Test, both published by the Educational Testing Service (U. S. Department of Education, 1994).

Minority Participation

Minority teachers are needed in the schools for a variety of reasons, perhaps the most important being their presence as role models. These models "help young children develop an appreciation for diversity, and cultural difference. Without visible examples of diversity, broadened thinking and experience are not only out of sight, but unfortunately out of mind" (Bass de Martinez, 1988, p. 13). Yet one of the major concerns of teacher preparation programs today is that fewer minority students are entering the programs. What once was one of the few professions open to minorities must now compete with all the professions for capable minority students. For example, a study of black students entering college in Ohio found that less than 7% chose education as a major, compared to 57% who chose business (Meadows, et. al, 1991).

The decline in minority enrollments is especially distressing because it has been occurring at the same time that minority enrollments in the public schools have been increasing. It has been predicted that by the year 2000, 50% of the students in our nation's schools will be minorities. Yet, as we have seen, minorities make up only 13.5% of the current teaching force, a figure which is projected to decline to 5% by the end of the century (Otuya, 1988). "This means an average student who might be exposed to forty teachers during his or her public school career can at best expect to be exposed to only two minority teachers" (Nicklos & Brown, 1989, p. 146).

Increasingly, students are given the opportunity to gain clinical experience in the classroom, often beginning with their first professional teacher education course.

Strategies for Increasing Diversity

In an attempt to address the critical shortage of minority teachers, educators and policy makers at the local, state, and national levels have initiated a number of programs aimed at both eliminating obstacles to participation and recruitment. Strategies aimed at removing obstacles to participation include recruitment fairs, increasing scholarship and loan programs, increasing support services and retention efforts, and ensuring that testing and evaluation programs minimize the influences of race and ethnicity on entry to the profession.

A number of the recruitment programs are aimed at junior and senior high school students. A few of these, such as the Calvin Coolidge High School in Washington, D.C., and the Austin High School for the Teaching Professions in Houston, are magnet schools that offer a college preparatory program for students interested in becoming teachers. Most programs targeting junior or senior high school students are operated by colleges or universities who cooperate with local schools to provide on-campus and in-school experiences for interested students. Such programs often provide financial aid, support services, and, in some cases, transferable credits that may be taken while in high school.

An increasingly popular recruitment strategy operated as a joint venture between a college or university and local school districts is the "grow your own" program for teacher aides. Under the typical program the teacher aides continue in their regular jobs, taking courses after school, on the weekend, and during the summer. Some districts provide the aides one day off with pay to attend classes. Tuition is often at a reduced rate or paid for by the district. And, perhaps most important, graduates are guaranteed employment in the district.

Reform in Teacher Education: Recommendations and Responses

Are you aware of any changes that have been made in the teacher education program at your institution as a result of the "calls for reform?"

Calls for the reform of teacher education in the United States are not a new phenomenon. Such calls have occurred on an almost cyclical basis:

> Reforms were demanded in the 1950s, when poor teacher preparation caught a portion of the blame for America falling behind in the space race with the Soviets. During the 1960s the humanistic movement in education was born, and reform was once again generated. The decade of the 1970s witnessed a reform movement spawned by a backlash against the humanistic period, while the 1980s "Second Wave of Reform" appears to have been fueled by failures in the international economic race. (Klausmeier, 1990, p. 23)

While calls for reform of teacher education may not be new, there are several things about the most recent calls that set them apart from the past and also contribute to the active response they have generated. First is their numbers and the broad base of the reformers. During the 1980s almost 50 reform proposals, directed in whole or in part at teacher education were published by various blue-ribbon commissions, corporations, foundations, and governmental and educational organizations, as well as by nationally known and respected scholars.

Second, these reform proposals have gained more political and public support than those in the past. The public is not only concerned about the quality of the educational programs in the public schools, but about the quality of the teaching force. According to a NCATE survey, one-quarter of the public believes that teachers are not adequately trained to meet the challenge of improving student performance (Wise, 1994).

While the recommendations coming from the various reports and papers often varied in their focus, several clear themes emerged:

1. Teacher education programs should be lengthened.

2. Greater emphasis should be given to the teaching field: teachers need to know their subjects.

3. The liberal arts component of the curriculum should be strengthened.

4. The professional curriculum should occupy a proportionately lesser share of the overall curriculum and should be based on teaching and learning theory and what we know about effective teachers and schools.

5. Admission, performance, and exit standards should be raised.

The projected demographics of student populations support the pressing need for preparing greater numbers of minority teachers.

In the following sections we will address these recommendations in more detail, as well as the response of colleges and departments of education to them.

Length of Program

An important recommendation of several reports is that teacher education programs should be at least five years in length. The rationale for this recommendation, as the Carnegie Forum on Education and the Economy (1986) report, *A Nation Prepared: Teachers for the 21st Century,* explains, is that four years of college is not enough time for the prospective teacher to master the subjects to be taught and gain the skills to teach them. Consequently, both the Carnegie Forum report and the 1986 report of the Holmes Group (a consortium of deans of colleges and chief academic officers at approximately 100 research universities), *Tomorrow's Teachers: A Report of the Holmes Group,* recommended abolishing the undergraduate teacher education major and requiring a bachelor's degree as a prerequisite for the professional study of teaching. At the completion of a minimum of a year of professional study the student would be awarded a master's degree. The 1985 report of the National Commission on Excellence in Teacher Education (NCETE), *A Call for Change in Teacher Education,* as well as numerous other reform reports, while not necessarily calling for the abolition of undergraduate teacher education, presume that adequate preparation of teachers would require a more lengthy program than currently exists in most colleges of education. Lastly, Goodlad (1994) has recommended a five-year program leading to both a bachlor's degree in general studies after four years and a professional bachelor's degree in pedagogy or education and a certificate of completion at the end of five years.

The positive response to this recommendation has been greatest among Holmes Group members. Several member institutions have shifted their professional preparation programs almost entirely to the graduate level. However, even within the Holmes Group this recommendation has not been widely implemented. At most institutions, eliminating a major undergraduate program such as teacher education would have far reaching consequences. And, at the hundreds of four-year institutions that train teachers, such a change would be virtually impossible to accomplish.

Program Content

A major focus of all the reports is on the actual content of teacher education programs. The most common complaint seemed to be that voiced by perhaps the most publicized of all the reform reports, *A Nation at Risk:* "The teacher-preparation curriculum is weighted heavily with courses in 'educational methods' at the expense of courses in subjects to be taught" (National Commission of Excellence in Education, 1983, p. 22). A consistent theme is that teachers must be knowledgeable in the content of the subjects they are to teach. Accordingly, a common recommendation is to reduce the professional curriculum and to have secondary education students have a major in an academic discipline and elementary education students have "an extended liberal arts program in the content areas of the elementary education school, as well as specialization in child development with particular emphasis on language development and thinking" (NCETE, 1985, p. 12).

A second major recommendation related to program content is that the liberal arts component of the curriculum be strengthened. The NCETE proposed that "teachers should have a liberal education equivalent to that of the best-educated members of their community . . . that teachers should know and understand the intellectual and practical content from which school curricula are drawn . . . that teachers should have both the skills to teach and the knowledge of the research and experimental bases for those skills" (NCETE, 1985, pp. 14–15).

The response to these recommendations has been mixed. About two-thirds of the colleges responding to an AACTE survey conducted more than a decade after the calls for reform began said that they had been able to obtain "substantial involvement" of the liberal arts faculty in teacher preparation. However, only about half said that they had strengthened the liberal arts requirement for teacher education students (AACTE, 1992). This is not to say that the liberal arts requirement is not strong at most colleges and universities and that teacher education students are not getting a "liberal arts education equivalent to that of the best educated members of the community." Indeed, perhaps one of the reasons why some institutions had not taken action was they were confident that their liberal arts requirement already met this criterion.

The Professional Preparation Program

Another major concern of the reform reports relates to program content in the professional curriculum. The Carnegie Forum, for example, speaks of a need to develop a new professional curriculum based on systematic knowledge of teaching. The NCETE (1985) report recommends that the professional program prepare teachers to select and present content and use teaching strategies appropriate to the student's ability and developmental levels; teach difficult subjects; observe and diagnose the performance of students from varying cultural and ethnic needs, and individualize instruction accordingly; use the results of research on teacher and school effectiveness; integrate technology with effective teaching practices to promote higher order thinking, problem solving, and conceptual and social learning; and relate the ideas and facts learned in advanced academic courses to those that are appropriate to teach in elementary, middle, and high schools.

Several other reports have recommended the development of a "core of essential courses" that would focus on teaching and learning theory and would include research on teaching. Consequently, one of the major identifiable trends in teacher preparation today is the effort to document the knowledge bases for teacher preparation (Cruickshank & Cruz, 1989). Almost 80% of the colleges in the AACTE (1992) study said they had already implemented or were studying the integration of "more of a scientific basis for teaching and learning into the teacher education curriculum."

A number of the reports, especially the more recent ones, recommend increasing the clinical experiences provided in the professional preparation program. For example, the reform proposal of the National Education Association (1982), *Excellence in Our Schools,* recommended that clinical experiences be integrated into the entire teacher education program beginning with the first course. The master in teaching degree proposed in the Carnegie report includes internship and programs, each lasting nine months. And, both the Carnegie report and the report of the Holmes Group go so far as to suggest the establishment of "clinical schools" or "professional development schools" that would serve the same function in education as do teaching hospitals in medicine.

Responses to the recommendations related to enhancing the clinical experiences provided teacher education students have been both positive and widespread. A full 71% of the colleges in the AACTE study said they had improved their formal partnerships with K–12 schools (to facilitate clinical experiences as well as other activities), and another 16% had them under study. Moreover, the vast majority of the action had taken place within the last five years (AACTE, 1992).

Admission, Performance, and Exit Standards

How do the liberal arts requirements for the teacher education program at your institution compare to those of other professional programs?

Many of the reports included recommendations related to admission, performance, and exit standards for the teacher preparation program. Various recommendations were made, including making more careful selection of candidates, raising g.p.a. entrance requirements, and requiring candidates to pass skills tests. For example, the National Commission for Excellence in Education (1985) recommended that during the selection and training process three thorough reviews of the student's program be made. And, the Holmes Group recommended that prospective teachers be required to pass a written test in each subject to be taught.

It is in this area of recommendations that the most demonstrable action has been taken. State legislatures and boards of education have mandated various entry, exit, or certification requirements, the most common being the passage of an examination (see section on Competency Testing). In addition, the AACTE survey also found that the recommendation "having rigorous admission standards for entry into teacher education" had been acted on the most of 11 reform items coming out of the major reform reports, and "having clearly specified exit standards for teacher candidates" was ranked second in terms of extent of action (AACTE, 1992).

Teacher Certification

Successful completion of a teacher training program does not automatically qualify an individual to teach. To become qualified for teaching, administrative, and many other positions in the public schools and many private schools, an individual must acquire a valid certificate or license from the state where they wish to practice. The *certification* or licensure requirement is intended to ensure that the holder has met established state standards and is therefore qualified for employment in the area specified on the certificate. The certification process is administered by the state education agency. The certificate can be obtained in one of two ways: assessment by the state agency of the candidate's transcripts and experiences against a particular set of course and experience requirements, or, more typically, the "approved program approach." In this case, candidates who have graduated from a teacher preparation program approved by the state to prepare teachers are automatically certified upon graduation (Zimpher, 1987). The certificate, when issued, may be good for life, or more commonly, must be renewed every three to five years.

While specific state certification requirements may vary, they typically include a college degree (all states require a bachelor's degree as a minimum), recommendation of a college or employer, minimum credit hours in designated curricular areas, a student teaching experience, evidence of specific job experience, "good moral character," attainment of a minimum age, United States citizenship, the signing of a loyalty oath affirming support of the government, and, in recent years, the passing of a state prescribed competency exam.

Competency Testing

The number of states requiring some form of competency testing as a requisite for initial certification has increased dramatically in the past decade, from 13 in 1980 to 43 in 1990 (U.S. Department of Education, 1994). The increase in the testing of teachers grew out of the reform movement and the debate over the quality of education and the quality of the teaching force. Testing for certification was seen as a necessary accountability measure to ensure that prospective teachers are qualified to enter the classroom. The most commonly used instruments are the National Teacher Examination (NTE) and state-developed tests. Testing is in one or more of four areas: basic skills, professional knowledge, content knowledge, and in-class observation.

A major concern that has been voiced in regard to the precertification testing of teachers is the adverse impact on minorities. The results of teacher testing indicate the pass rate for blacks and Hispanics is disproportionately lower than that for whites. A study of states that require prospective or practicing teachers to pass some form of competency test found the pass rate for blacks ranged from 15% to 50%, for Hispanics the range was 39% to 65%, and for whites 71% to 90% (Farrell, 1990).

Alternative Certification Programs

In response to the shortage of qualified teachers in some teaching areas, 36 states have adopted *alternative certification* programs to certify candidates who have subject-matter competence without completion of a formal teacher preparation program (AACTE, 1994). These programs hope to attract to the teaching profession qualified recent college graduates or persons with at least a bachelor's degree from other professions who may voluntarily wish to re-career or who have been the victims of layoffs and downsizing in the private sector or the military. As a result of the end of the Cold War as many as 250,000 military personnel will enter the civilian labor force by 1995 (Littleton & Holcomb, 1994). Although many programs were originally intended to address the shortages in math and science, most are open to those with majors in any teaching field.

Alternative certification programs may be offered through the hiring school district, a college or university, or a partnership of the two. The typical alternative certification program includes (1) a rigorous selection process to ensure the selection of qualified applicants, (2) preservice training in the philosophical, historical, and sociological foundations, methodology, classroom management, and

Alternative certification programs provide professionals outside of education the opportunity to recareer into teaching.

human development, and (3) a structured, yearlong internship that includes the guidance of a mentor teacher (Littleton & Holcomb, 1994). Studies of alternative certification programs have found little difference in command of subject matter between those completing alternative certification programs and those completing traditional teacher education programs. However, an equal number of studies have found that alternatively certified teachers may lack the pedagogical skills that, along with subject matter expertise, are necessary for effective instruction. One positive finding is that alternative certification programs tend to attract more men and minorities than traditional teacher education programs, as well as persons with a greater disposition toward working in urban areas (Stoddart, 1993).

Emergency Certification

Forty-nine states have some provision for granting *emergency or temporary certificates* to persons who do not meet the requirements for regular certification when districts cannot employ fully qualified teachers. Emergency certificates are issued with the presumption that the recipient teacher will obtain the credentials or will be replaced by a regularly certified teacher. In every state, before the emergency certificate is granted the vacancy must be confirmed by the district or state superintendent (AACTE, 1994). While the spread of alternative certification programs has reduced the rate at which emergency certificates are issued, nationwide tens of thousands are issued each year. In the 1991–92 school year, California alone issued almost 10,000 emergency certificates (Neumann, 1994).

Have you completed a precertification examination? Do you believe the examination made a fair estimate of your knowledge and skills?

Unlike alternative certification, emergency certification does not require any professional education training prior to the assumption of teaching duties and normally does not require the passage of a subject matter test (although some states do require the passage of a basic skills test). Many professional educators question the ethics and safety of hiring untrained persons to teach: What other state-licensed profession would issue "emergency" certificates to untrained persons? Many others point out the disturbing inequity that emergency certified teachers are disproportionately employed by inner city, low-income schools with predominately minority populations. However, despite the call of the American Association of Colleges of Teacher Education to halt the issuance of emergency certificates, it seems unlikely that the practice will be abandoned any time in the near future (Neuman, 1994).

Recertification

Acquiring certification once does not mean that a teacher is certified for life. One of the reform efforts a number of states have adopted in an attempt to upgrade the quality of the teaching force is to raise the requirements for the recertification of experienced teachers. To obtain recertification a teacher is typically required to earn a specified number of continuing education credits (CEUs) which may be earned by taking approved college courses, by attending workshops, in-service training, or other acceptable activities. In three states (Texas, Arkansas, and Georgia) passage of a competency test is required for recertification.

Interstate/National Certification

A matter of concern related to state certification for any profession is whether the certification granted by one state will be recognized by another. The increasing mobility of teachers has encouraged state certification authorities to establish *interstate reciprocity*, which allows teachers who are certified in one state to be eligible for certification in another. It is to the advantage of each state to facilitate the employment of qualified educators and to increase the availability of educational personnel, not to establish barriers to employment. To this end, 32 states, the District of Columbia, and the overseas dependents schools have entered into Interstate Certification Agreement Contracts to permit certification reciprocity.

What are the personal requirements for certification in your state or the state in which you plan to teach?

The prospect for some form of national certification has been enhanced by the efforts of the National Board for Professional Teaching Standards to not only develop professional standards for teaching (discussed in Chapter 2), but to develop certification in more than 30 fields. Certification in six fields is to be finished by the 1996–97 school year. Teachers with three years teaching experience and holding a state teaching license, upon payment of a $975 fee, can start the certification process. The process involves preparing a professional portfolio and coming to one of the board's assessment centers for two days of examination and performance assessment. If the candidate is successful, he or she is deemed *board certified,* a term commonly used in other professions. Such certification is public acknowledgement that the teacher possesses not only the requisite knowledge but the demonstrated ability to teach in the areas or level of certification specified. A major incentive for teachers to undertake this process is that several states are offering financial rewards or other incentives to teachers who receive board certification (Harrington-Lueker, 1994; Richardson, 1994).

Teacher Supply and Demand

Reasons for Demand

Following a decade or more of teacher surpluses, the demand for teachers began to increase in the mid-1980s. The demand for additional teachers has resulted primarily from increases in enrollment. As shown in Table 1.3, by the year 1998 a total of 218,000 new teachers will be needed to fill the nation's classrooms. And, with public and private school enrollments projected to continue to increase into the first decade of the twenty-first century, the demand for new teachers is expected to remain strong through the turn of the century, reaching 225,000 in 2001.

Teacher attrition, reduced pupil-teacher ratios, and increased requirements for high school graduation have also contributed to the demand for additional teachers. Teacher attrition is a serious problem. Significant numbers of the current teaching force are becoming eligible for retirement. And, as previously noted, many others are considering leaving the teaching field. The continued lowering of pupil-teacher ratios has also contributed to an increased demand for teachers. Pupil-teacher ratios in the public schools have declined from 20.6 at the elementary level and 17.2 at the secondary level in 1979, to 19.0 and 15.4

Table 1.3: Trends in the Demand for New-Hiring of Classroom Teachers in Public Elementary and Secondary Schools, 1991–2001		
Fall of Year	Projected Demand for More Teachers (in thousands)		
	Total	Elementary	Secondary
1991	201	105	96
1992	190	95	95
1993	210	103	107
1994	208	100	108
1995	209	112	107
1996	217	108	109
1997	220	108	112
1998	218	110	108
1999	223	111	112
2000	227	114	113
2001	225	112	113

Source: U.S. Department of Education, National Center for Education Statistics. (1990). *Projection of education statistics to the year 2001, an update* (Tables 35 and 36). Washington, DC: U.S. Government Printing Office.

respectively in 1993, and are projected to decline to 18.8 and 15.1 by the year 2004 (U.S. Department of Education, 1993c). Lastly, each of the major reform reports addressing the public schools has recommended increased coursework for high school graduation, thereby requiring additional teachers.

The Supply Side

While the demand for teachers is expected to increase, the projected supply of new teachers is not expected to be sufficient to meet the demand, and a teacher shortage is projected by many. The supply of new teachers is a function of (1) the number of college graduates entering teaching, (2) the number of former teachers, and (3) the number of "trained but never served" teachers in the workforce. Despite the fact that enrollments in colleges and universities increased significantly in the 1980s, this has not resulted in any significant increase in the number of bachelor's degrees awarded in education. However, there has been some increase in the number of noneducation graduates entering teaching. In fact, the percentage of newly qualified teachers who were not education majors increased from 29% to 41% between 1985 and 1991 (U.S. Department of Education, 1993a). The number of returning teachers and the number of individuals who were trained as teachers but never entered the profession is far greater than the number of students preparing to teach. One of the major unknown factors in projecting teacher supply and demand is what percentage of these individuals would enter teaching if salaries and working conditions were improved and the status of the profession were enhanced.

If noneducation graduates can prepare for teaching in one year of study, why can't education graduates also be prepared in one year?

While a shortage of teachers is expected nationwide, supply and demand will vary among states, school districts, and disciplines. States in the South and West with growing populations will have a greater demand for teachers. For example, Florida officials anticipate 10,000 public school vacancies per year to the year 2010 (Drummond, 1994). Inner-city and rural districts will also experience teacher shortages. Shortages are also expected in such fields as special education, foreign languages, bilingual education, art, music, physics, mathematics, gifted and talented, and physical sciences.

Salary and Other Compensation

Historically, teachers' salaries have not only lagged behind those of other professionals with comparable training and responsibility, but behind those of many of the technical and semiskilled occupations. However, with renewed public interest in the quality of education, teacher compensation has generally improved. Beginning in 1986 teacher salaries increased at a higher rate than inflation. Figure 1.2 depicts the trend in average annual salaries of teachers since 1960 in both current and constant dollars (adjusted for inflation). Since 1980 the average teacher's salary has increased 21% in 1993 constant dollars. In 1993 the average salary was $35,873.

The specific salary a teacher will receive depends upon a number of factors including supply and demand, union activity, the prevailing wage rate in neighboring districts, and perhaps most importantly, the wealth of the district (or state) as determined by the tax base. School districts with a higher assessed value

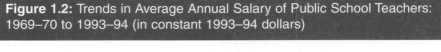

Figure 1.2: Trends in Average Annual Salary of Public School Teachers: 1969–70 to 1993–94 (in constant 1993–94 dollars)

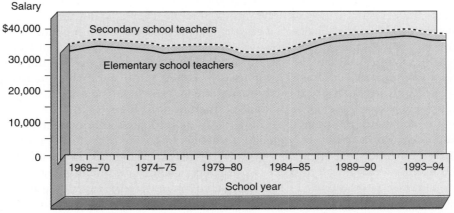

Source: U.S. Department of Education, National Center for Education Statistics. (1994). *The Digest of Education Statistics.* (p. 48). Washington, DC: U.S. Department of Education.

of property per pupil will typically pay higher salaries than those with lesser assessed value of property-per-pupil. However, many poor districts, in terms of assessed valuation, have chosen to levy higher tax rates and are able to pay competitive salaries.

Salary Schedules[1]

More than 90% of teacher salary schedules across the nation are based on the *single salary schedule* format. The single salary schedule pays equivalent salaries for equivalent preparation and experience. The trend toward the adoption of a single salary schedule for teachers began in the first quarter of the twentieth century, and before the end of the third quarter had come to dominate direct compensation. The position system it replaced based salaries on positions within the school system (elementary teacher, secondary teacher, librarian, counselor, etc.). The single salary schedule has not always been favored by teachers' groups, but it is popular with boards of education because it is easy to understand and to administer.

There are two basic dimensions to the single salary schedule: a *horizontal dimension* made up of columns that correspond to levels of academic preparation (e.g., bachelor's degree, master's degree, master's degree plus 30 hours, doctorate degree), and a *vertical dimension* of rows of "steps" that correspond to the years of teaching experience. There is no standard number of columns or rows in a teacher's salary schedule, although there are usually more rows than columns so that the schedule tends to form a vertical matrix (see Table 1.4).

Initial Placement

The initial vertical placement of a new teacher on a specific vertical step on a scale is determined by several factors, the most common of which is previous teaching experience. To receive credit for any previous years of teaching the teacher usually must have taught for 75% of the school year. Most school districts place a limit on the number of years of teaching experience credited toward initial placement on the salary schedule. Factors that bear on this decision are whether the experience is in or out of the district and in or out of the state.

Other factors that are considered in making the initial placement on the schedule are credit for related experience, credit for military service, and credit for other experience. Some districts recognize related experience such as public library experience for librarians or recreational experience for physical educators. Others grant full or partial credit for military service or for experience in the Peace Corps, VISTA, or the National Teachers Corps.

Advancement

Horizontal advancement across columns in a salary schedule is dependent upon earned academic credit beyond the bachelor's degree. Vertical advancement from one step to the next within the scale is normally automatic after a stipulated period of time, usually one year, although longer periods may be required for

1. Discussion in this section is largely based on Educational Research Service. (1987). *Methods of scheduling salaries for teachers.* Arlington, VA: Educational Research Service.

Table 1.4: Mesa Unified School District Teachers/Nurses Salary Schedule

1994–1995 Years Experience	Range Line	1 B.A.	2 B.A. 15	3 B.A. 30	4 B.A. + 45 or M.A.
	Step				
0	3	24,055	24,829	25,603	26,377
1	4	24,751	25,525	26,299	27,073
2	5	25,679	26,453	27,227	28,001
3	6	26,615	27,389	28,163	28,937
4	7	27,350	28,348	29,122	29,896
5	8		29,743	30,517	31,291
	9		30,567	31,912	32,686
	10			33,788	34,562
	11			34,723	36,438
	12				38,314
	13				39,374
	14				
	15				
	Longevity A				
	Longevity B				
	Longevity C				

advancement to the higher steps. Although teachers' groups have continued to advocate automatic advancement, in an increasing number of districts certain restrictions are being placed on vertical advancement. For example, advancement at specified points may be made contingent on (1) the attainment of additional units of academic credit or completion of in-service training programs; (2) satisfactory performance or merit.

To provide for teachers who have reached the maximum number of steps in a particular scale, some salary schedules also provide for supermaximum or long-term service increments beyond the highest step in the scale. Whereas in most instances the awarding of this increment is based solely on the attainment of a specific number of years' experience above the highest number recognized on the schedule, in some cases a performance or merit evaluation is required before the award is made.

Incentive Pay Plans

The 1980s saw heightened concern about the quality of the teaching force. Concern centered around not only the performance of practicing teachers but the fact that various studies showed that teaching was not attracting the "best and brightest." Several of the reform reports recommended that teachers be paid for recognized performance rather than solely on the basis of experience or acade-

5 M.A. 15	6 M.A. 30	7 M.A. + 45 or Ed.S.	8 M.A. 60	9 M.A. + 75 Ed. D. Ph. D.
27,151	27,925	28,699	29,473	30,247
27,847	28,621	29,395	30,169	30,943
28,775	29,549	30,323	31,097	31,871
29,711	30,485	31,259	32,033	32,807
30,670	31,444	32,218	32,992	33,766
32,065	32,839	33,613	34,387	35,161
33,460	34,234	35,008	35,782	36,556
35,336	36,110	36,884	37,658	38,432
37,212	37,986	38,760	39,534	40,308
39,088	39,862	40,636	41,410	42,184
41,266	42,040	42,814	43,588	44,362
42,408	43,204	45,199	45,973	46,747
		46,451	47,246	48,040
		47,380	48,191	49,001
		48,309	49,136	49,962
		49,238	50,081	50,922

Source: Mesa, Arizona Public Schools, 1994–1995.

mic credentials. School districts across the country came under increased pressure to improve the performance of their teachers. Teacher incentive plans have been perceived as a strategy that will both attract and retain good teachers as well as motivate them to greater performance. However, although the general public and the major administrators' organizations in education have voiced support for performance-based pay, the NEA and teachers as a whole have been opposed. Nonetheless, by 1994 about half the states were funding various forms of teacher incentive programs (Cornett & Gaines, 1994).

Incentive pay plans are of two basic types: performance based programs in which differential pay is awarded to individuals with the same job description on the basis of their performance, and differential staffing programs that in effect pay teachers more for different kinds or amounts of work (e.g., master/mentor teacher plans or career ladder plans). Programs of the latter type are discussed in the following chapter. Discussion here will focus on performance-based plans.

Performance-based programs may be based on the performance of the individual teacher or the performance of the school as a whole. Merit pay programs, which predate the single salary schedule in their use, are the most common form of the individual performance-based program. While merit pay programs have been around for a long time, the experience of many school districts with merit pay has been more negative than positive. This is no doubt in large part a result of the incentives often being too small to really make a difference, that too few teachers received awards, and that the teaching staff was not involved in the development of the program. As a result of their negative experiences many school districts abandoned the merit pay programs. In numerous other districts they are operating successfully. The major arguments for and against merit pay are presented in the Controversial Issue presented on page 29.

The typical performance-based pay plan involves an evaluation conducted by the principal with teacher input into the process. The St. Louis suburb of Ladue, Missouri, has one of the oldest plans still in operation. Under its plan, merit pay is based on evaluation points assigned by the principal, although a teacher committee recommends the criteria for evaluation. Each teacher may receive up to 15 points annually, with each point being worth $300. The average evaluation is 10 points, worth $3,000 in merit pay.

Performance-based programs that reward individual schools for the improved performance of their schools are in operation in six states—Georgia, Indiana, Kentucky, North Carolina, South Carolina, and Texas—and similar plans are being proposed in several others. In Indiana, schools can receive cash awards if they show improvement in at least two of four areas (performance on the state progress exam, language arts test scores, mathematics test scores, and attendance rates). In Georgia, schools that accomplish the performance objectives that have been submitted to and approved by the Georgia Department of Education are eligible for awards that may be used as the school faculty decides. Among the options are salary bonuses and program improvement. Funding for 1995 has been requested at $2,000 per certified staff member in the eligible schools (Gaines & Cornett, 1994).

Compensation for Supplemental Activities

In addition to their base salary, approximately one-third of the public school teaching force receives compensation during the school year for supplemental activities such as coaching, student activity sponsorship, or evening classes. Another 17% receive summer supplemental salary (U.S. Department of Education, 1993). At one time extracurricular activities were considered normal duties that teachers had to assume as part of their work. In the 1950s, as teacher salaries began to lose ground in a rising economy and as many teachers sought to supplement their incomes by working second jobs, teachers' organizations became more aggressive in seeking additional compensation for time spent in extracurricular activities (Greene, 1971). Now it is common practice for districts to provide supplemental pay for extracurricular assignments. As indicated by the listing in Table 1.5, supplements are paid for a variety of extracurricular activities.

Salaries for Administrative and Support Personnel

Many teachers begin their educational careers in the classroom and then move into administrative or supervisory positions or into positions such as counselor or librarian. Most of these positions are 10–12 month positions and command significantly higher salaries, even on a monthly basis, than classroom teachers. As

Have the financial benefits of the teaching profession entered into your decision to become a teacher?

Controversial Issues:
Merit Pay

Several of the reform reports of the 1980s advocated merit pay for the teachers—the part or all of the teacher's pay be based on performance. However while the public supports the practice, teachers, as a whole do not support merit pay. The reasons often given in favor of or against merit pay are:

Reasons For

1. Merit pay would reward good teachers and provide the incentive for them to stay in education.

2. The public would be more willing to support the schools if they knew that teachers were paid according to merit.

3. Rewarding performance is consistent with the standard applied to other workers and professions.

4. Teachers would be encouraged to improve their performance and students would be the beneficiaries.

Reasons Against

1. There is little agreement about what is good teaching or how it should be evaluated.

2. Evaluation systems are often subjective and potentially inequitable.

3. Competition creates morale problems for people doing the same job.

4. Research has identified the ingredients of effective teaching, none of which are directly linked to merit pay.

Why do you oppose or favor merit pay? Are you familiar with a school system where merit pay is in operation? What effect has merit pay had on education in that system?

---

the data on Table 1.6 indicate, the average salary of superintendents in 1993–94 was $87,717. Superintendents in districts with over 25,000 enrollment often earn a salary of over $100,000 per year. Principals, the administrators closest to the teacher, earn 156% to 178% of the average salary of classroom teachers. However, it must be noted that most administrative and supervisory positions do require higher levels of educational preparation and experience than is required of classroom teachers.

Indirect Compensation: Employee Benefits and Services

Indirect compensation, commonly referred to as fringe benefits, is an important part of any teacher's compensation package and cost the district an average of 30% of wages. Indirect compensation can be classified as either employee benefits or employee services. Many benefits, including health and life insurance, long-term disability protection, payment of professional employment-related expenses, and leaves with pay (sick leave, personal leave, sabbatical leave), are voluntarily provided by the school district. Although voluntary, almost all school districts provide medical insurance (96%), and 71% provide life insurance. In addition, a growing number of districts (53% in 1987–88, 70% in 1990–91) pro-

Table 1.5: Supplements for Athletic and Nonathletic Extracurricular Activities as Percentage of Teachers' Salaries, 1991

Activity	Percentage of Teachers' Salaries
Athletic trainer	9.30
Senior high head football coach	8.76
Director of athletics	8.61
Senior high band director	7.87
Senior high head basketball coach	7.72
Senior high head wrestling coach	6.63
Senior high head track coach	6.36
Senior high head baseball coach	5.88
Senior high head hockey coach	5.87
Senior high head swimming coach	5.60
Senior high head gymnastics coach	5.46
Senior high head volleyball coach	5.41
Senior high director of music	5.37
Senior high head soccer coach	5.23
Senior high chorus director	4.42
Senior high head cross country coach	4.40
Senior high head cheerleading coach	4.39
Senior high head tennis coach	4.31
Junior high head football coach	4.30
Senior high dramatic director	4.00
Senior high head golf coach	3.99
Senior high orchestra director	3.93
Junior high band director	3.91
Junior high head basketball coach	3.81
Debate advisor	3.69
Yearbook advisor	3.64
Speech advisor	3.57
Senior high drill team director	3.50
Junior high head wrestling coach	3.43
Junior high head track coach	3.29
Junior high head volleyball coach	3.15
Senior high newspaper advisor	3.07
Senior high student council advisor	2.90
Junior high orchestra director	2.75
Junior high chorus director	2.59
Junior high cheerleading coach	2.31
Junior high dramatics director	2.29
Senior high class sponsor	2.29

Source: Seymour, M. L. (1991). *Extra pay for extra duties of teachers,* Fifth Edition. Arlington, VA: Educational Research Service.

Table 1.6: Mean Salaries Paid Personnel in Selected Positions in the Public Schools, 1993–94

Superintendents (Contract Salary)	$87,717
Deputy/Associate Superintendents	78,672
Assistant Superintendents	72, 701
Directors, Managers, Coordinators, and Supervisors for:	
Finance and Business	59,997
Instructional Services	64,676
Public Relations/Information	52,366
Staff Personnel Services	63,690
Other Areas	54,689
Subject Area Supervisors	52,837
Other Central-Office Administrative and Professional Staff	45,473
Principals	
Elementary	56,906
Junior High/Middle School	60,651
High School	64,993
Assistant Principals	
Elementary	47,057
Junior High/Middle School	51,518
High School	54,170
Classroom Teachers	36,531
Counselors	41,355
Librarians	39,319
School Nurses	30,630

Source: Educational Research Service. (1994). *Salaries paid professional personnel in public schools, 1993–94,* Part 2. Arlington, VA: Educational Research Service.

vide "in-kind benefits, including housing, free or reduced-price lunch, transportation, and tuition reimbursement" (U.S. Department of Education, 1993b).

Certain other benefits, namely Social Security, worker's compensation, and retirement plans, are required by law. In most states retirement benefits are financed jointly by teacher and public contributions. In several states, in an attempt to increase compensation but not increase state aid to education, school districts pay not only the employer's share toward retirement, but also the employee's share. This benefit has great appeal to employees because it has a significant impact on net income while not increasing gross taxable income. Consequently, in an increasing number of school districts this provision has become a popular item for negotiation.

Employee services are not required by law but "enable the employee to enjoy a better lifestyle or to meet social or personal obligations while minimizing employment-related cost" (Henderson, 1985, p. 434). Employee services include such items as credit unions, counseling, child care, or social and recreational programs.

Do you have any interest in becoming involved in any extracurricular activities? Which?

Professional Reflections

"Teaching is a seamless process of becoming and growing."

M. Ignacio Timajero, Teacher of the Year, Texas

"If you do not have a genuine love for children, choose another profession."

Sheba Brown, Teacher of the Year, Mississippi

"Ask yourself every day. Why did I become a teacher? Who will I make a difference to today? How will my students remember me and what I taught them?"

Richard K. Bojak, Teacher of the Year, Utah

How the Public Views the Schools and Teaching

Each year the public's perceptions of the schools and issues related to the schools is assessed by the *Gallup Poll of the Public's Attitudes Toward the Public Schools*. The poll "has become a barometer, closely watched and debated each year by educators and policymakers" (U.S. Department of Education, 1991, p. 82). In 1994, the Gallup Poll results indicated that 44% of the public surveyed gave their local schools grades of A or B, a slightly higher proportion than the mean of the previous decade, but about the same proportion as when the survey began two decades ago. Table 1.7 shows the ratings given to schools in the nation as a whole, to the local schools, and to the local public school attended by the

Table 1.7: Ratings Given the Public Schools, 1994

Ratings	Nation's Public Schools	Public School Parents	Nonpublic School Parents	Local Public School	Public School of Oldest Child
A&B	22	19	18	44	70
A	2	2	4	9	28
B	20	17	14	35	42
C	49	48	45	30	22
D	17	22	23	14	6
Fail	6	4	6	7	1
Don't know	6	7	8	5	1

Source: Elam, S. M., Rose, L. C., & Gallup, A. M. (1994). The 26th annual Phi Delta Kappa/Gallup poll of the public's attitudes toward the public schools. *Phi Delta Kappan, 76*, 45.

respondent's oldest child. As was true in every past poll, the more respondents know about the school, the more likely they are to give a higher rating: raters gave local public schools in their community higher ratings than the schools nationally, and the school attended by their child was likely to be rated higher than those in the entire community. In addition, parents with children in public schools rate them higher than those with children in private schools.

One of the strongest indicators of the perception held of any profession is whether people want their children to enter it. The 1993 Gallup Poll asked parents if they would like to have their child take up teaching as a career. The results showed a significant increase over the last decade in the popularity of teaching as a profession. In the 1993 survey, 67% of respondents would like their child to take up teaching as a profession, compared to 45% a decade earlier (Elam, Rose, & Gallup, 1993).

Summary

There are as many definitions of *teacher* as there are reasons for becoming a teacher. It is important that those considering the profession evaluate their perceptions and expectations of teaching and their motives for considering teaching as their chosen profession.

After a period of serious criticism of the teaching profession and teacher preparation, the status of the profession appears to be improving. There is still a shortage of minority teachers, but more and more bright and talented individuals are entering the teaching profession, either through traditional baccalaureate programs or through the growing number of alternative certification programs. These programs have responded to the recommendations of various reform reports and have raised admission standards and taken steps to improve quality. And a greater percentage of the practicing teaching force reports being satisfied with teaching as a career.

As the current demand for teachers intensifies, various proposals for differential compensation have been made in an effort to attract qualified individuals into teaching. The next chapter discusses other efforts to make teaching more attractive by increasing professionalization and reviews other professional opportunities available to teachers.

Key Terms

Alternative certification
Board certified
Certification
Emergency (temporary) certificate
Field (clinical) experience
Incentive pay
Indirect compensation
Single salary schedule

Discussion Questions

1. Was there any single event or experience that motivated you to choose teaching as a career? In an incident such as that described at the beginning of the chapter, in addition to attending to the physical needs of the child, what are the professional and legal responsibilities of the teacher?

2. What is your perception of what a teacher is and does?

3. What are the advantages and disadvantages of teaching as a career? Have you considered teaching as a career? If yes, what motivated you to prepare to become a teacher?

4. What strategies should be used to attract more top-quality students into teaching?

5. Should people be required to complete a teacher training program to become a teacher? Should there be any minimum requirements?

6. The public has increasingly expressed support for the competency testing of teachers. In your opinion, should prospective teachers be required to pass a competency test?

7. The public has also shown increasing support for merit pay for teachers. What are the pros and cons of merit pay? To what extent are financial incentives likely to improve job performance?

References

American Association of Colleges of Teacher Education (AACTE). (1992). *Teaching teachers: Facts & figures.* Washington, DC: AACTE.

AACTE. (1994). *Teacher education policy in the states: A 50-state survey of legislative and administrative actions.* Washington, DC: AACTE.

Bass de Martinez, B. (1988). Political and reform agendas' impact on the supply of black teachers. *Journal of Teacher Education, 38,* 10–13.

Carnegie Forum on Education and the Economy. (1986). *A nation prepared: Teachers for the 21st century.* Washington, DC: Carnegie Forum.

Cornett, L. M., & Gaines, G. F. (1994). *Reflecting on ten years of incentive programs.* Atlanta: Southern Regional Educational Board, Career Ladder Clearinghouse.

Cruickshank, D. R., & Cruz, J., Jr. (1989). Trends in teacher preparation. *Journal of Teacher Education, 40*(3), 49–56.

Drummond, S. (1994, June 8). Outlook for new teachers in job market rosy. *Education Week,* 5.

Eisner, E. W. (1994). *The educational imagination,* (3rd ed.) New York: Macmillan.

Elam, S. M., Rose, L. C., Gallup, A. M. (1993). The 25th annual Gallup poll of the public's attitudes toward the public schools. *Phi Delta Kappan, 72,* 140.

Farrell, E. J. (1990). On the growing shortage of Black and Hispanic teachers. *English Journal, 79*(1), 39–46

Gaines, G. F., & Cornett, L. M. (1994). *Survey of state actions.* Atlanta: Southern Regional Education Board, Career Ladder Clearinghouse.

Galluzzo, G. R., & Arends, R. I. (1989). The RATE Project: A Profile of Teacher Education Institutions. *Journal of Teacher Education, 40*(4), 56–58.

Good, C. V. (Ed.). (1973). *The dictionary of education.* New York: McGraw-Hill.

Goodlad, J. I. (1994). *Education renewal: Better teachers, better schools.* San Francisco: Jossey-Bass.

Goodlad, J. I. (1984). *A place called school.* New York: McGraw-Hill.

Greene, J. E. (1971). *School personnel administration.* New York: Chilton Book Company.

Harris, L. & Associates, Inc. (1992). *The Metropolitan Life survey of the American teacher 1992.* New York: Metropolitan Life Insurance Co.

Harrington-Lucker, D. (1994). Certification: Teachers at the top of their profession. *American School Board Journal, 181*(6), 24.

Henderson, R. I. (1985). *Compensation management: Rewarding performance* (4th ed.). Reston, VA: Reston Publishing.

Holmes Group. (1986). *Tomorrow's teachers: A report of the Holmes Group.* East Lansing: Holmes Group.

Klausmeier, R. L., Jr. (1990). Four decades of calls for reform of teacher education: the 1950s through the 1980s. *Teacher Education Quarterly, 17*(4), 23–64.

Kohl, H. R. (1976). *On teaching.* New York: Schocken Books.

Littleton, M., Holcomb, J. (1994). New routes to the classroom. *American School Board Journal, 181* (5), 37–39.

Meadows, F. B., Jr., Anglin, L. W., Barton, L., Hamilton, A., Padak, N., & Padak, G. (1991). A response to the shortage of African-American and minority teachers. In E. J. Middleton, F. Bickel, H. Barnard, E. J. Masom, & R. P. Fons (Eds.), *The impact of nationwide school reform on the recruitment and retention of minorities.* Lexington, KY: University of Kentucky.

Murray, F. B. (1986). Goals for the reform of teacher education: An executive summary of the Holmes Group report. *Phi Delta Kappan, 68,* 28–32.

National Commission on Excellence in Education. (1983). *A nation at risk: The imperative for educational reform.* Washington, DC: U.S. Government Printing Office.

National Commission on Excellence in Teacher Education. (1985). *A call for change in teacher education.* Washington, DC: AACTE.

National Education Association. (1982). *Excellence in our schools.* Washington, DC: National Education Association.

Neumann, R. A. (1944). Reconsidering emergency teaching certificates and alternative certification programs as responses to teacher shortages. *Urban Education, 29,* 89–108.

Nicklos, L. B. & Brown, W. S. (1989). Recruiting minorities into the teaching profession: An educational imperative. *Educational Horizons, 67,* 146.

Otuya, E., Jr. (1988). Supply and demand of minority teachers. *ERIC Digest, Clearinghouse on Teacher Education.* Washington, DC: AACTE.

Richardson, J. (1994, September 7). States offer incentives to teachers seeking national board certification. *Education Week,* 14.

Smith, B. O. (1987). Definitions of teaching. In M. J. Durkin (Ed.), *The international encyclopedia of teacher education.* New York: Pergammon Books.

State of the States. (1993). *Executive Educator, 15,* A24–A31.

Stoddart, T. (1993). Who is prepared to teach in urban schools? *Education and Urban Society, 26,* 29–48.

U. S. Department of Education, National Center for Education Statistics. (1991). *The condition of education 1991.* Washington, DC: U. S. Department of Education.

U. S. Department of Education, National Center for Education Statistics. (1993a). *New teachers in the job market, 1991 update.* Washington, DC: U. S. Department of Education.

U. S. Department of Education, National Center for Education Statistics. (1993b). *Schools and staffing in the United States: A statistical profile, 1990–91.* Washington, DC: U.S. Department of Education.

U. S. Department of Education, National Center for Education Statistics. (1993c). *Projections of education statistics to 2004.* Washington, DC: U. S. Department of Education.

U. S. Department of Education, National Center for Education Statistics. (1994). *Digest of education statistics.* Washington, DC: U. S. Department of Education.

Wise, A. E. (1994). Teaching the teachers. *American School Board Journal, 181*(6), 22–23, 25.

Zimpher, N. L. (1987). Certification and licensing of teachers. In M. J. Durkin (Ed.), *International encyclopedia of teaching and teacher education.* New York: Pergamon Books.

Chapter 2

Development of the Profession

A teacher who is attempting to teach without inspiring the child to learn is hammering on a cold iron.

Horace Mann (1796–1859)

A Critical Incident in My Teaching Career . . .

I hated school in the early grades and went to school with a stomachache most of the time. At a very young age, I knew in my inner being that there had to be a better way to do "this." Then along came my fifth grade teacher, a high school teacher for whom there was not an opening and had therefore been assigned to our fifth grade. She changed my life, my opinion of education, and consequently my direction.

She treated us like people . . . and talked with us not down to us. She opened doors of learning for me in a way that had not been done before. Calm, nicely dressed, and highly organized, she made learning exciting for me. . . .

Bonnie Smith,
Teacher of the Year, North Dakota

Teaching is a complex and challenging occupation. The extent to which it is a profession is a point of continuing controversy. In a recent analysis of the complexity of the work and knowledge required of over 60 jobs ranging from fast food worker to surgeon, Rowan (1994) stated that teaching is complex work that requires high levels of general education and specific preparation. These findings are consistent with the current interest in promoting the further professionalization of teaching. However, a profession is composed of its individual members, and the extent to which teaching becomes accepted among the professions will be determined by the cumulative commitment and activities of individual teachers. As you read and discuss this chapter and the related activities, consider the following outcome objectives and their impact on you as a potential teacher.

- Evaluate the duties of elementary and secondary school teachers in terms of the recognized criteria for a profession.
- Identify the factors that should be considered in teacher evaluations.
- Compare the license renewal requirements in your state with the career development requirements in a typical local school district.
- Differentiate between teacher licenses and teacher certificates.
- Identify the programs and services provided by the major teacher organizations in your state and local school districts.
- Describe the programs and services provided by the professional organization for your teaching field.

Teaching as a Profession

Is teaching a profession? Many references are made to the "profession of teaching," but the actual status of teachers continues to be a matter of discussion and debate. Few would contend that teaching has attained the status of medicine or law, but some might argue that teaching as an occupation compares favorably with the ministry, accounting, engineering, and similar professions.

Elementary and secondary school teaching is one of the most challenging and stimulating occupations, but teachers encounter a wide range of expectations such as the following in their day-to-day work:

- planning activities

- guiding student learning in the classroom

- keeping records

- providing necessary reports

- maintaining adequate information about students

- communicating with parents

Within the past several years, various factors have contributed to an increase in the status of teachers. Some of them are:

1. Standards for teacher education programs have been raised.

2. State licensing requirements have been increased.

3. Additional use has been made of entry-level examinations for teachers.

4. Professional certification programs are being implemented.

5. Teaching has come to be viewed as a career rather than an interim occupation.

What satisfactions do you think you will derive from being a teacher?

Changes like these have increased satisfaction with teaching as a career and have contributed to a growing recognition of teaching as a profession.

Responses on a national survey to several questions about teacher satisfaction are shown in Figure 2.1. There has been some improvement since the mid-to-late 1980s in the extent to which teachers feel respected by society and a greater shift in how teachers feel about their salaries. The improvements in respect and salary appear to have influenced the willingness of a greater percentage of teachers to advise a young person to pursue a career in teaching. The percentage of teachers expressing satisfaction with teaching increased by 7% over the period 1985 to 1989. In a 1993 national survey, 93% of the public school teachers reported that they believed the quality of education in their school was either *excellent* or *pretty good* (Leitman & Binns, 1993).

Figure 2.1: Indicators of Teacher Satisfaction

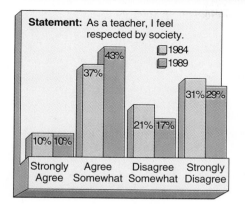

Statement: As a teacher, I feel respected by society.

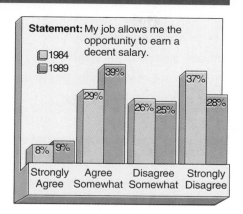

Statement: My job allows me the opportunity to earn a decent salary.

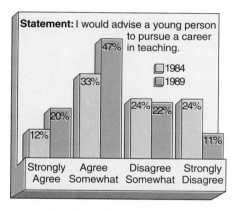

Statement: I would advise a young person to pursue a career in teaching.

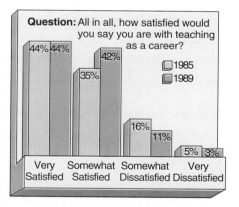

Question: All in all, how satisfied would you say you are with teaching as a career?

Source: Harris, L., Kagay, M., & Leichenko, S. (1989). *The American teacher.* New York: Metropolitan Life Insurance Co. Reprinted with permission.

Requirements of a Profession

Teachers may have improved their status and made progress in a variety of ways, but many observers still question whether teaching meets the recognized criteria for a *profession.* Definitions of a profession vary from short, simple statements to lengthy, complex descriptions; the following simplified definition is from a basic source book for education: "An occupation involving relatively long and specialized preparation on the level of higher education and governed by its own code of ethics" (Good, 1973).

More complex criteria for classifying an occupation as a profession are presented in Figure 2.2. The summary criteria discussed in this chapter include advanced knowledge and specialized preparation, provision of essential services

---

Figure 2.2: Criteria for Classifying an Occupation as a Professional

According to the National Labor Relations Act, the occupation must:

- Be an intellectual endeavor
- Involve discretion and judgment
- Have an output that cannot be standardized
- Require advanced knowledge
- Require a prolonged period of specialized study

In addition, the American Association of Colleges of Teacher Education calls for:

- Provision of essential services to society
- Decision making in providing services
- Organization into one or more professional societies for the purpose of socialization and promotion of the profession.
- Autonomy in the actual day-to-day work
- Agreed upon performance standards
- Relative freedom from direct supervision

---

to society, exercise of discretion, autonomy and freedom from direct supervision, standardized output and performance standards, code of professional standards, and professional organizations.

Advanced Knowledge and Specialized Preparation

Although teaching requires a period of specialized study, policy makers and members of the academic community do not agree on the course of study that produces a teacher or the order in which the courses should be taken. For instance, several education reform reports advocate that professional education courses be delayed until completion of general education and academic major requirements, or even until after completion of the baccalaureate degree. Other reports suggest that college graduates with no professional education courses should be permitted to serve as intern teachers, but with a higher level of supervision than that traditionally provided for beginning teachers. Recent developments in teacher certification and accreditation programs likely will affect preparation programs and expedite the professionalization of teaching (Wise, 1994).

Many teacher educators also now believe that a specific body of knowledge can be identified that is necessary and appropriate for the education of teachers. Admission standards for teacher education programs have been raised, as have course requirements. However, until that specific body of knowledge or specialized field of study has been clearly articulated and implemented, teaching does not appear to meet this basic criterion of a profession.

Provision of Essential Services to Society

Academic observers may not agree that teaching has attained the status of a profession, but the public perception suggests that teachers provide an essential service to society. Although the public and the teachers may not always agree about the exact nature of this service, the importance of education in a democratic society has always been recognized: "If a nation expects to be ignorant and free in a state of civilization, it expects what never was and never will be." This often quoted statement by Thomas Jefferson reinforces the importance of education to the preservation of the nation. Teachers play a critical role in the educational process.

The Exercise of Discretion

Given the relative isolation of individual classrooms and the variety of decisions that a teacher must make during the typical school day, teachers routinely exercise discretion and judgment in providing services to their students. However, teachers are not free agents. They function in an educational environment that is larger than an individual classroom, constrained by school policies and regulations, adopted curriculum guides, and state requirements. Such district-wide concerns as scope and sequence of instruction must be considered. The typical teacher has a group of students for a period of one year, but the educational experiences in that classroom during the year will influence the learning patterns of those students over a period of years. Thus, it would appear that teachers' decisions should be in harmony with the school district's overall plan and policies.

Autonomy and Freedom from Direct Supervision

Teachers have a relatively high degree of autonomy in their actual day-to-day work, and the degree of direct supervision is rather limited. However, when compared with independent, fee-charging professionals, teachers have less autonomy and freedom. Teachers function in the social setting of a school with other teachers. The culture of the school requires a degree of structure and interaction among both teachers and students. In addition, parents and taxpayers have an interest in ensuring that teachers act like responsible professionals. Some degree of supervision is necessary to provide the desired assurances.

Standardized Output and Performance Standards

There appears to be near-universal acceptance of the concept of individual differences among students; however, some of the recent school reform proposals appear to assume that the work of teachers can be standardized and uniformly measured. The latter issue has emerged in discussions about proposals related to merit pay, master teachers, career ladders, and related teacher evaluation issues. Critical questions in implementing these proposals include what to consider in reviewing a teacher's performance, and whether the performance review team is to include practicing members of the profession or only school administrators.

Should teacher pay be based on student performance?

Code of Professional Standards

An additional unresolved issue in determining whether teaching meets the criteria of a profession is whether practicing teachers are to assume responsibility for policing their peers and enforcing a code of professional standards. The alternative is for teachers to be monitored or policed by a public agency, typically at the state level. Such bodies usually are referred to as professional practices boards or commissions. Their purpose is to take appropriate disciplinary action against teachers following a review of reports of questionable professional conduct. A number of states have these bodies, but only a relative small number of teachers have had their professional performance reviewed by the profession or by these bodies.

Professional Organizations

Teaching appears to meet this criterion of a profession because of the two national organizations for teachers—the National Education Association and the American Federation of Teachers—and a full range of specialized subject matter organizations. These bodies serve the functions of socialization and promotion of the profession. Questions might be raised, however, about the extent to which these organizations have developed programs to enhance the profession and to transmit and enhance skills and knowledge throughout the teacher's career.

Unresolved Questions

Previous observations suggest that some questions about the professional status of teachers remain unresolved. Consistent themes in the education reform reports include:

- increased preservice requirements

- higher standards for entrance and continued service

- greater emphasis on career advancements for teachers

These admonitions suggest that the various reform groups were applying at least one of the traditional criteria for a profession in their statements about the expectations of teachers. This level of recognition lends credibility to the concept of teaching as a profession.

When compared with the recognized professions, there are some ways in which public school teaching is different. Typically, a recipient of a professional service may choose which person will provide the service. In contrast, parents or students often have little choice in the assignment of a teacher. An additional criterion is that many of the professions certify the competencies of their members. Teaching appears to be moving in this direction with the creation of the National Board for Professional Teaching Standards (Barringer, 1993). Currently, states have licensing requirements that serve as minimum standards for teachers, but emergency licenses are issued when teacher shortages develop.

From a different perspective and simply stated, discussions about the professionalism of teaching often center on pay, higher admission standards, quality preparation, continuing education, and good working conditions. Related concerns include adequate supplies and equipment, opportunities to interact with colleagues, and reasonable latitude in making decisions. These changes cannot be achieved immediately, but they can have a significant cumulative effect. Even though each of these is important, they do not define the profession nor are they the primary motive for the high level of interest in professionalizing teaching. Rather, the major reason for the professionalization of teaching is to increase the probability that students will be well educated (Brandt, 1993; Darling-Hammond & Wise, 1992).

The Professionalization of Teaching

Great strides in the professionalization of teachers have been made in the past several decades. In the first half of this century, many preparation programs for teachers provided initial licensing after successful completion of a few weeks of summer school following high school graduation. As discussed in Chapter 1, current programs typically involve intensive, structured four- and five-year preparation; these programs conclude with the awarding of a bachelor's or a master's degree. Other evidence of the increased professionalization of teaching may be found in the development of professional standards, teacher competency testing, increased opportunities for professional development, and the adoption of codes of professional standards.

As an illustration of the continuing national interest in the professionalization of teaching, the Rockefeller and Carnegie Foundations have recently funded a new national commission to make recommendations for teacher improvement and development. This group will focus its efforts on teacher development as a way to improve schools; ways to help teachers implement the new standards and use new knowledge about teaching and learning; and ways to connect teacher education, licensing, certification, and accreditation (Richardson, 1994).

Development of Professional Standards

The school reform movement provided new impetus to the interest in developing professional standards for teachers. In the 1980s, various school reform groups, including the Carnegie Forum on Education and the Economy and the Holmes Group, have called for higher standards for teachers and the development of a national teacher certification process. These efforts contributed to the creation of the National Board for Professional Teaching Standards in 1987 (Bradley, 1994).

One model for national teacher certification is found in the medical specialty groups through which medical doctors are granted special professional recognition by their peers when they meet prescribed standards. In discussions about the development of a national certification program for teachers, some confusion has arisen because of a misunderstanding of the technical differences between teacher certification and teacher licensing.

Historically, a person fulfilled the legal requirements to teach when a college or university certified to the appropriate state agency that the person had completed the required teacher education coursework and field experiences. The state licensing body then granted a license to teach to the person. These licenses, often referred to as teaching certificates, are issued for a specified period and may be renewed upon satisfactory teaching experience and completion of additional coursework or continuing education units.

The concept of a professional teacher certificate issued by the National Board for Professional Standards is different. Certificates would be issued to those teachers who sought certification, whose performance merited special recognition, and who had demonstrated a commitment to teaching as a career. Certification would be voluntary rather than compulsory. As opposed to the teaching license that is issued by a state agency, certificates would be awarded by voluntary, nongovernmental certification boards that have no formal legal authority. The current references to state-issued teaching certificates would be replaced by a state licensing process for teachers. Even though the activities are technically separate, developments in teacher certification and licensing are beginning to interact with accreditation of teacher education programs. As these efforts come together, the professionalization of teaching will become a reality (Wise, 1994).

The major teachers' organizations participated in the creation of the National Board for Professional Teaching Standards. The Board has 63 members, the majority of whom are teachers. This voluntary group is developing and field testing a system for adopting standards and awarding certificates to practicing teachers. Teachers seeking certification will be required to submit documentation of successful experience to a state or national board consisting of professional educators. Rather than paper and pencil tests, documentation will be through portfolios that include exemplary lessons, samples of student work, testimony from colleagues, and videotapes of classroom activities (Bradley, 1994).

Competency Testing of Practicing Teachers

Competency testing of practicing teachers is designed to screen out of the teaching force those persons who are deficient in basic skills and knowledge. Proposals for such testing normally anticipate that the testing program will be a requirement for recertification. Required in only a small number of states, this practice is the subject of considerable controversy. Issues are related to contentions that:

- Retesting to determine competency is not required of other occupations such as the legal or medical professions.

- Competency in the classroom cannot be determined by pencil and paper tests.

- The current tests may have a discriminatory impact on minority teachers.

The national teachers' organizations have been skeptical about the benefits of competency tests for teachers and especially for experienced teachers. Both organizations have raised questions about the discriminatory effects of testing elementary and secondary school teachers and not testing other service providers such as doctors, nurses, social workers, and attorneys. The NEA has been strongly opposed to testing current teachers, but the AFT has been supportive of testing current teachers under certain conditions.

Quality vs. Quantity

As discussed in Chapter 1, in the 1980s various observers of American education raised questions about the quality and quantity of elementary and secondary school teachers. Issues of quality have been related to the abilities, competencies, and preparation of current and future teachers. Issues of quantity have been related to the relationship between the projected supply of teachers and the estimated vacancies in the schools.

Quality and quantity concerns interact because higher quality requirements, or increased standards for teachers, may affect the quantity of persons eligible to enter teaching or the willingness of current teachers to remain in teaching. One position is that higher standards will shrink the pool of aspirants; an opposite position is that higher standards will contribute to a higher level of prestige for teaching and result in more able college students pursuing teaching as a career.

Another concern about quality is the relative ability of practicing teachers. No one knows what effect the recent state and national interest in higher standards for schools will have on the continued quality of the teaching staff. The increased standards may contribute to a higher status for teaching and education, or higher standards may be viewed as an encroachment on the freedom of the teacher. If the former is the case, experienced quality teachers may be more likely to remain in teaching, and higher quality students may be attracted to teaching. If the higher standards are difficult to attain, some experienced teachers may desert the classroom in favor of other occupations.

Changes in societal and individual perceptions of teaching as a career may also influence the career decisions of a major reservoir of teaching talent not currently in the teaching force. Many concerns about the staffing of schools would be alleviated if the pool of persons who are graduates of teacher education programs but are not currently teaching should decide to enter the field. Several factors, such as changes in the nation's economic conditions and employment market, school enrollment increases, and improved working conditions and financial rewards for teachers, could result in an increased demand for teachers and greater interest in teaching as a career (Fox, 1987; Leftwich, 1994).

Teacher Evaluation

Teachers are evaluated in a variety of ways. Students, parents, fellow teachers, and administrators have been evaluating teachers since the opening of the first school. Unfortunately, evaluation procedures often have been informal, unsystematic, and based on randomly gathered anecdotal information. For these reasons, considerable progress has been made in identifying the goals of the activity and developing formal teacher evaluation procedures.

The theoretical purpose of any local school district's formal teacher evaluation program is to improve the teaching and learning conditions by improving the overall performance of the teachers in the school district. The two most common evaluation procedures used to accomplish this are:

- systematic gathering and reporting of information about the performance of an individual teacher for the purpose of helping the teacher improve performance

- providing information that can be used in making decisions about retention or dismissal of the teacher

The optimal result of the teacher evaluation program is to help the practicing teacher improve classroom performance.

The school reform movement in the 1980s drew additional attention to teacher evaluation. A common theme in the various reform reports was the need to improve the performance of practicing teachers through the designation of master teachers, creation of career ladder programs, and development of merit pay systems. Each proposal assumed that an objective evaluation system would be used to determine which teachers would receive the additional compensation and recognition, and also that teacher performance could be enhanced by developing and implementing improved teacher evaluation procedures.

Any discussion of the evaluation of teachers eventually centers around a series of what, how, and who questions. As illustrated below, these questions vary in their complexity.

Should teachers be retested on a regular basis to ensure that they are current in their field?

What to Evaluate?

The first task is to identify what is to be evaluated and to provide the person being evaluated with this information. Common courtesy dictates that the person being evaluated be informed as to the evidence, or information, to be gathered in the evaluation process. Yet this may be the most difficult task in the evaluation process. The challenge is to identify the components of the evaluation and the behaviors and information that are to be observed, secured, and recorded during the evaluation process. A major difficulty is that the "what" question cannot be answered until the observable elements have been identified. The concept of teaching as a profession assumes more than the identification of behaviors or practices indicative of "good teaching" by school administrators or outside experts. There must also be development of some degree of consensus between the person being evaluated and that person's professional peers.

How to Conduct the Evaluation?

The second task is to ensure that the person being evaluated understands how the evaluation information is to be gathered, including the procedures and criteria to be used. This involves a determination of the types of information to be provided by the teacher, the number of classroom observations, the process for making the assessment, and the methods to be used in informing the teacher as to the relative level of performance.

Another concern in this second task is the process that will be used in making decisions about the content, design, and implementation of the evaluation program. By reviewing the participants in the evaluation process, a teacher can determine both the strength of the local teachers' organization and the administrative philosophy of the school district. Involvement and participation suggest positive attributes that should contribute to an overall supportive and positive instructional climate in the school district. Confrontation and lack of involvement likely will be further evidenced in a lack of professional respect and isolation between teachers and administrators.

Who Does the Evaluation?

The third task is to identify the person(s) who will conduct the evaluation. One facet of the "who" task is related to the role of the profession in evaluating its own members—teachers evaluating teachers. A second facet of the "who" task is the role of the immediate supervisor or building principal in visiting, observing, and communicating with teachers concerning the relative quality of their performance and the steps that should be taken to improve it. A third facet of the "who" task is the extent to which the evaluation team should include the school district's central office administrators and teachers from both inside and outside the school district.

Currently, the major interests are that evaluations be:

- conducted in a more systematic manner

- based on criteria related to acceptable levels of classroom performance as a teacher

- based on an adequate number of observations

Depending on the procedures, quality of communication, and human relations skills found in a school district, the evaluation system can contribute to either an increase or a decline in teacher morale and performance.

Professional Development

Completion of the teacher preparation program does not mean that a person has mastered all that one needs to know in order to be an effective teacher. In fact, most observers recognize that teachers need to develop professionally by continuing to learn about the process of teaching and their subject areas as long as they are in the profession.

An increasing number of avenues for personal and *professional development* are open to teachers. Many choose to join the professional organization most closely related to their teaching field. This membership provides access to professional materials, but the most critical benefit probably will be the contacts with other teachers, offering the possibilities for a professional peer support network. Other methods of growth might include the development of a personal professional library and an independent study program.

An alternative professional development program, a more structured approach, is to enroll in an advanced degree program in a college or university. The challenge of this approach is to develop an individualized program and select components that will improve competencies, as well as meet degree requirements.

As a new teacher, what will you expect from the teacher evaluation process?

Observation and evaluation by peers and administrators have become an integral part of the organized efforts to improve teacher performance and enhance the learning opportunities for students.

Professional Ethics

Various professions have codes of ethics that serve as standards for behavior of members of the profession. Codes of ethics do not have the status of law, but indicate the aspirations of members of the profession and provide standards by which to judge conduct. In some instances, the professional organization monitors and enforces the code of ethics for its membership. In others, a public agency may assume the monitoring and enforcement role. Reporting of noncompliance can come from a variety of sources including professional peers, clients, supervisors, and the public at large.

The NEA has adopted a code of ethics for the education profession. The NEA Code of Ethics, presented in detail in Figure 2.3, contains two sections: commitment to students and commitment to the profession. The student section notes the expectations of fair, equitable, and nondiscriminatory treatment of students. The section on commitment to the profession contains standards of personal conduct in the performance of professional duties and relationships to others.

In an earlier era, codes of conduct for teachers were adopted by local school boards. These codes often were related to personal as well as professional con-

Figure 2.3: Code of Ethics of the Education Profession

Preamble

The educator, believing in the worth and dignity of each human being, recognizes the supreme importance of the pursuit of truth, devotion to excellence, and the nurture of democratic principles. Essential to these goals is the protection of freedom to learn and to teach and the guarantee of equal educational opportunity for all. The educator accepts the responsibility to adhere to the highest ethical standards.

The educator recognizes the magnitude of the responsibility inherent in the teaching process. The desire for the respect and confidence of one's colleagues, of students, of parents, and of the members of the community provides the incentive to attain and maintain the highest possible degree of ethical conduct. The *Code of Ethics of the Education Profession* indicates the aspiration of all educators and provides standards by which to judge conduct.

The remedies specified by the NEA and/or its affiliates for the violation of any provision of this *Code* shall be exclusive and no such provision shall be enforceable in any form other than one specifically designated by the NEA or its affiliates.

Principle I: Commitment to the Student

The educator strives to help each student realize his or her potential as a worthy and effective member of society. The educator therefore works to stimulate the spirit of inquiry, the acquisition of knowledge and understanding, and the thoughtful formulation of worthy goals.

In fulfillment of the obligation to the student, the educator—

1. Shall not unreasonably restrain the student from independent action in the pursuit of learning.

2. Shall not unreasonably deny the student access to various points of view.

3. Shall not deliberately suppress or distort subject matter relevant to the student's progress.

4. Shall make reasonable effort to protect the student from conditions harmful to learning or to health and safety.

5. Shall not intentionally expose the student to embarrassment or disparagement.

6. Shall not on the basis of race, color, creed, sex, national origin, marital status, political or religious beliefs, family, social or cultural background, or sexual orientation unfairly—

    a. Exclude any student from participation in any program

    b. Deny benefits to any student

    c. Grant any advantage to any student

7. Shall not use professional relationships with students for private advantages.

8. Shall not disclose information about students obtained in the course of professional service, unless disclosure serves a compelling purpose or is required by law.

Figure 2.3: *continued*

Principle II: Commitment to the Profession
The education profession is vested by the public with a trust and responsibility requiring the highest ideals of professional service.

In the belief that the quality of the services of the education profession directly influences the nation and its citizens, the educator shall exert every effort to raise professional standards, to promote a climate that encourages the exercise of professional judgement, to achieve conditions which attract persons worthy of the trust to careers in education, and to assist in preventing the practice of the profession by unqualified persons.

In fulfillment of the obligation to the profession, the educator—

1. Shall not in an application for a professional position deliberately make a false statement or fail to disclose a material fact related to competency and qualifications.

2. Shall not misrepresent his/her professional qualifications.

3. Shall not assist any entry into the profession of a person known to be unqualified in respect to character, education, or other relevant attribute.

4. Shall not knowingly make a false statement concerning the qualifications of a candidate for a profession position.

5. Shall not assist a non-educator in the unauthorized practice of teaching.

6. Shall not disclose information about colleagues obtained in the course of professional service unless disclosure serves a compelling professional purpose or is required by law.

7. Shall not knowingly make false or malicious statements about a colleague.

8. Shall not accept any gratuity, gift, or favor that might impair or appear to influence professional decisions or actions.

Source: NEA Handbook, Washington, DC: National Education Association, 1986–87.

duct, regulating such things as marital status, style of clothing, and places in the community that were "off limits" to teachers. In those days, failure to abide by the requirements was used as justification for dismissal or other punitive action against the teacher. The requirements of yesteryear are quite different from the current concept of codes of ethics that focus on professional conduct. Responsibility for enforcement now resides with the profession rather than with a local school district's governing body.

Career Development

Traditional career opportunities in teaching probably were more accurately defined as career opportunities in education. Elementary and secondary school

Figure 2.4: Sample Career Ladder (Tennessee)

MASTER TEACHERS

Achieved after a series of observations by a team of outside evaluators (master teachers and other experienced educators) after at least five years as a senior teacher

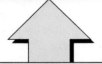

SENIOR TEACHERS

Educators remain at this level for a minimum of five years

PROFESSIONAL TEACHERS

After showing satisfactory performance as a beginning teacher, performs at this level for at least three years

BEGINNING TEACHERS

Classified as apprentice teachers for a period ranging from three to five years

teaching was often viewed as a necessary entry-level experience before one became a school administrator or college professor in the humanities, sciences, or professional education. Changes in teacher salary schedules and teachers' roles have improved professional opportunities and rewards. As a result, persons are encouraged to consider elementary and secondary school teaching as a life career.

Career Ladders

Various states included the *career ladder* concept in their school reform programs in the 1980s. Rochester, New York, Charlotte, North Carolina, and the states of Arizona and Tennessee have adopted career ladder programs. Reasons for implementing the programs include making teaching more attractive as a career and promoting quality control of the profession (McPartland & Fessler, 1992). (See Figure 2.4 for Tennessee's Career Ladder Program.) This concept assumes different forms such as status titles, pay levels, and lengths of contract for teachers at different levels. At the first level the beginning, or apprentice, teacher might receive an entry-level salary with minimal increases. At the end of the three- to five-year apprenticeship, if the person were retained, promotion would be made to the second level.

The second-level professional teacher would receive a higher base salary with additional annual step increases. A person would stay at this level for a minimum of three years if performance were satisfactory, but might stay at this level for a career.

The third-level senior teacher would receive a higher base salary with additional annual step increases. A person would stay at this level for a minimum of five years if performance were satisfactory, and could stay at this level for a career if there were no aspirations to become a master teacher. Most of a district's experienced teachers might be in this group.

If a person desired to attain the fourth level of master teacher, an application and dossier would have to be submitted to a committee of administrators and master teachers. The process would include visitations and classroom observations by this committee and administrators from other school districts. Members of the team would recommend whether the person should be designated a master teacher. Master teachers on a career ladder usually would have a full-year contract and would be involved in various types of curriculum development work during the months when school is not in session. The decision to seek the status of master teacher is voluntary; a teacher can continue to teach indefinitely without attaining the classification of master teacher.

Master Teacher Concept

In addition to the use of the term in the context of career ladders, the concept of the *master teacher* has been used in other less structured ways. In some instances, the master teacher might be given special status, pay, and recognition, but would remain in the classroom as a role model for other teachers. In others, the master teacher might be released from a portion of the regular classroom assignment to work with other teachers in a supportive, nonsupervisory role. Such activities may involve classroom observations and suggestions for improvement, or leadership roles in curriculum development activities.

The key consideration is that the master teacher would have the opportunity to continue as a classroom teacher for most of the time, but would be provided with other professional tasks. These tasks can be personally and professionally rewarding as well as beneficial to the school and other teachers. Opportunities to participate in professional activities outside the classroom contribute to a sense of professional renewal and provide recognition of competency.

Mentoring

The formal and informal relationships that an experienced teacher develops with beginning teachers provide one illustration of professionalization; these relationships often are referred to as peer socialization or *mentoring* (Little, 1993). Such interactions can contribute to the growth of the experienced teacher and be invaluable sources of information and support for the beginning teacher. In contrast to other professions in which an entry-level employee often enters as a junior member of a team consisting of persons with a range of experience, the beginning teacher typically is assigned a classroom of students in an elementary school or a series of classes in a secondary school and is expected to assume the same responsibilities as an experienced teacher.

The concept of mentoring usually involves the development of a support relationship between a beginner and an experienced teacher. The mentor provides basic information about the operation of the school, as well as advice,

Experienced and beginning teachers can work together in a mentoring relationship or a "buddy" system and share experiences to improve student and teacher performance.

counsel, and support that the beginner may seek when confronted with problems. The goal of such programs is to establish a relationship and an initial professional contact that will develop into a collegial relationship.

In a national survey of teachers, the concept of mentor teacher was viewed favorably by 82% of the teachers familiar with the concept. Possible reasons for support include teachers' perceptions that the mentor teacher would provide some help in the day-to-day task of teaching, a reduction of the isolation experienced by the novice teacher, and expanded possibilities of career advancement as a teacher (Harris, Kagay, & Leichenko, 1989).

Self-Renewal

The routine of teaching is tempered by the excitement of new students arriving each semester or school year. However, the continuing pressures of the classroom and the possibilities of teaching the same grade level or the same subject for several decades can have a depressing effect on even the most enthusiastic person. Traditionally, self-renewal has been viewed as the responsibility of the individual teacher; however, experience suggests that school districts can benefit from the development of joint self-renewal or professional renewal efforts with teachers (McLaughlin, Pfeifer, Swanson-Owens, & Yee, 1986).

Local school districts use a variety of approaches to address the teacher "burnout" problem. Among the renewal programs available in various school districts across the country are:

- sabbaticals for advanced study

- periodic change of school or teaching assignment

- attendance at workshops or professional conferences

- visitation programs

Another option involves providing teachers with alternative assignments in curriculum or staff development programs. The purpose of such programs is to recognize outstanding teachers who receive a break from the classroom while continuing to engage in professionally challenging experiences of benefit to the local school district.

Teachers' Organizations

One of the new teacher's initial decisions is the degree of commitment to teaching as a profession. Teachers often find themselves confronted with the choice of which and how many organizations to join. They may affiliate with one of the national teachers' organizations and also with organizations whose focus is on a particular subject or educational specialty.

Affiliation is an indication of the commitment to teaching as a profession and as a career. In some districts, there may be only one active teacher organization; in others, the new teacher may have the opportunity to choose among two or more organizations. Not only will there likely be the opportunity to join a local organization, but the teacher will also have the opportunity to join a state and national organization. The dilemma does not end with the general organization; specialized local and national subject matter organizations related to the teaching area also exist. The challenge is to choose carefully among the options and make the choices that will benefit you most as you begin your teaching career. An important consideration may be a person's level of commitment to the organization and its program or the extent to which the person intends to become involved in the organization's activities.

National Teachers' Organizations

The National Education Association is the larger of the two national teachers' organizations. Its members are found in all types of school districts. In contrast, the American Federation of Teachers has fewer total members, and its activities are concentrated in the nation's urban areas. The membership of both organizations includes professional educators other than classroom teachers, and some persons hold memberships in both organizations. The NEA's membership is estimated to be about 2 million; the AFT's membership has been estimated at more than 500,000.

For almost 100 years, the NEA was the umbrella organization for higher as well as elementary and secondary educators. (See the Historical Note on p. 58 for a short history of the NEA.) Various teacher specialty and administrator organizations were under the NEA umbrella, and individuals held memberships in the specialty group and the overarching organization. Until the 1960s, leadership roles in the NEA and its state affiliates often were held by school superintendents and higher education personnel. Starting in the 1960s, elementary and secondary school classroom teachers assumed the leadership roles. The administrator organizations became independent of the NEA, and teachers became a greater portion of the organization's membership. The organization's program now focuses more on services to teachers and state and local teacher organizations.

In contrast, teachers always have provided the leadership for the AFT. Although the organization has included building principals among its members, central office administrators have been viewed as district management and considered to be in an adversarial relationship with teachers.

Each organization provides a variety of professional development activities and services for its members. Publications include national research reports, a journal for members (*Today's Education* [NEA] and *Changing Education* [AFT]), and a variety of handbooks and related documents. Most of these publications are oriented toward improving teacher performance and working conditions, or providing source information about the status of American education. Both organizations conduct annual conferences at the state and national levels and provide a variety of workshop training activities related to either professional or organizational development.

Representatives of both the NEA and the AFT have served on several of the school reform commissions. In their participation in the reform reports, the primary goals of both organizations have been to enhance the professional status

What was the most active national teachers' organization in the school you attended? Were you aware that your teachers were active in their organizations?

Historical Note:
The Birth of Teachers' Unions

In 1857, teachers' organizations from 10 states joined to form the National Teachers Association (NTA). In 1870, the NTA merged with the American Normal School Association and the National Association of School Superintendents to form the National Education Association (NEA). Although the NEA was concerned with broad educational issues, at the beginning it was dominated primarily by college presidents and school superintendents and had no division for classroom teachers. The organization did not concern itself with teacher welfare. Further, the NEA leaders would not have thought that such action was professional. At this point, the NEA was in no sense a labor union.

The first teachers' labor union was the Chicago Teachers Federation (CTF), formed in 1897. In 1902, the CTF affiliated with the Chicago Federation of Labor. This action was condemned by the Chicago school board. The CTF eventually severed the tie when it lost a battle against the school board's arbitrary decision against union membership. Even with this setback, the CTF continued to grow. In New York City, another union, the Interborough Association of Women Teachers, claimed 12,000 members in the early 1900s. This was the largest local teachers' union in the country. Unions also were formed in many other cities as teachers sought to follow the lead of the growing labor union movement and improve their working conditions through organizational representation and membership.

and working conditions of teachers and to create a more positive attitude toward teachers and education.

Action at the State Level

In addition to their national headquarters and national programs, each national teacher organization has units at the state level and in local school districts. The NEA has been more active at the state level; the organization has served as an advocate for teacher tenure and certification statutes, revisions in state school finance programs, initiation of federal aid for education, and related educational improvements. The AFT also supports many similar activities, but the general perception has been that the AFT's strength has been concentrated in the organizational units at the local school district level.

Action at the Local Level

Both organizations have encouraged teachers to negotiate salaries and working conditions with local school district administrators and school boards. The AFT has been bargaining virtually since its creation; the NEA started major collective bargaining initiatives in this area in the 1960s. During the intervening years, in most of the states, teachers have become actively involved in formal and informal negotiations with school boards. In some states the negotiations are voluntary; in others, school boards are required by state law to enter into a contract with the local teachers' organizations about salaries and working conditions. The result has been an increase in the control and input that teachers have over conditions related to their pay and conditions of employment.

Professional Reflections

". . . teaching is not a job, it's a lifestyle."

Anne Jolly, Teacher of the Year, Alabama

"Typically, we teachers surrender responsibility for improving and developing ourselves to the administration. It is not solely their domain or responsibility. Cooperation and collaboration among teachers are powerful and effective tools for growth and development."

Lynn Rylander Kaufman, Teacher of the Year, Nebraska

Subject Matter Organizations for Teachers

In addition to the general organizations for all teachers, professional organizations have been formed for each discipline. Professional development activities provided by the subject matter organizations typically include a publication program and conferences and workshops for members. These subject matter organizations are independent of the U.S. Department of Education, state educational agencies, and local school districts. They are less prone to be politically active than the two national umbrella organizations for all teachers, but they do influence teachers' positions toward education reform proposals (Little, 1993).

Some specialized organizations such as the Council for Exceptional Children (CEC) include as their members parents and interested citizens as well as professional educators; others, such as the National Conference of Teachers of English (NCTE), the National Council for Teachers of Mathematics (NCTM), the National Council for the Social Studies (NCSS), and the National Science Teachers Association (NSTA), draw their members from teachers at all levels of education. These groups typically do not become involved in direct discussions with school officials about working conditions of teachers; however, they may adopt statements of principles about total teaching load, textbook selection procedures, and selection and use of instructional materials. In this way, the specialized organizations do assume an advocacy role for changes in state or federal legislation related to their teaching area. These groups assumed active leadership roles in the development of the national curriculum goals and standards (Diegmueller, 1994).

Examples of other organizations oriented to specific support roles in the schools include the American Library Association (ALA) and the American Association for Counseling and Development (AACD). A broader-based organization is the Association for Supervision and Curriculum Development (ASCD), which includes teachers, administrators, and college professors. Specialized organizations for school district central office personnel and building principals include the American Association of School Administrators (AASA), the National Association of Secondary School Principals (NASSP), and the National Association of Elementary School Principals (NAESP). With some exceptions, these groups tend to be stronger at the state and national levels. For example,

Teachers gather at national meetings to share ideas and address national educational issues.

both the National Association of Secondary School Principals and the American Association of School Administrators recently have initiated assessment programs to improve the personal and professional knowledge and skills of administrators.

Teachers' Organizations and Public Policy Issues

Both the NEA and the AFT assume an active role in promoting various federal education programs to improve elementary and secondary education. In addition, most of the subject matter organizations also have representatives who provide advice and counsel to Congress and the U.S. Department of Education on legislation, regulations, and administrative procedures. The Council for Exceptional Children has had a continuing interest in the passage and implementation of both state and federal legislation related to education of the handicapped. The National Science Teachers Association and the National Council for Teachers of Mathematics supported federal legislation to improve elementary and secondary school instruction in science and mathematics. Many educational interest groups also were involved in the recent reauthorization of federal elementary and secondary education programs for educationally disadvantaged and at-risk youth.

Summary

The status of teaching as a profession remains unclear. Although the standards have been raised, the changes may not be sufficient to qualify teaching as a profession. In the past decade, progress has been made toward the professionalization of teachers. New certification standards under development could alter the current licensing procedures. To ensure that new teachers possess basic skills, competency testing has been adopted by over 30 states. Some states use the National Teachers Examination or other national examinations, and other states have developed their own examinations (Boydston, 1994). Advances have been made in procedures for evaluating teachers, and local school districts are providing increased opportunities for professional development.

The effect of efforts to reform education on teacher quality and quantity is not known. Higher standards may drive out teachers or may attract more as the reputation of the profession increases. The tradition of teaching being viewed as a stepping stone to careers in administration and higher education is being replaced by teaching being seen as a career in itself. As job rewards have increased, other changes in working conditions have made teaching more attractive. The expansion of practices such as the career ladder concept, master teaching programs, and opportunities for self-renewal contribute to maintaining and fostering the positive aspects of the profession.

In Chapter 3, you will have the opportunity to step back and reflect on the historical origins of Western educational thought and practice. You will also see their influence on the educational process and profession of today.

Key Terms

Career ladder
Competency testing
Master teacher
Mentoring
Profession
Professional development

Discussion Questions

 1. In the incident at the beginning of the chapter Bonnie Smith said that her fifth grade teacher "treated us like people." What does it mean to treat students like people? What steps can you take as a teacher to be more sensitive to the needs of your students? How can you help students raise their self-esteem? As a teacher, how do your dress and personal conduct affect your students?

2. In what ways does teaching differ from professions such as law, medicine, and accounting?

3. What is the current status of the efforts to start a national certification program for teachers?

4. What are the provisions for collective bargaining for teachers in your state?

5. What responsibility does the beginning teacher have for continued professional development? What are the professional development requirements for teachers in school districts with which you are familiar?

6. What types of tests must a person pass before becoming a teacher in the state in which you intend to seek employment?

7. What steps are taken to monitor the extent to which teachers comply with codes of ethics in school districts with which you are familiar?

8. What reasons might there be for not joining a professional organization?

References

Barringer, M. (1993). How the national board builds professionalism. *Educational Leadership, 50* (6), 18–22.

Boydston, J. E. (1994). *Teacher certification requirements in all 50 states, 1994–95,* 12th ed. Sebring, FL: Teacher Certification Publications.

Bradley, A. (1994, April 20). Pioneers in professionalism. *Education Week, 13* 18–27.

Brandt, R. (1993). What do you mean, "professional"? *Educational Leadership, 50*(6), 5.

Darling-Hammond, L., & Wise, A. (1992). Teacher professionalism. *Encyclopedia of Educational Research.* New York: McMillan, 1359–1366.

Diegmueller, K. (1994, September 27). Standards-setters hope to publish best sellers. *Education Week,* 1, 15.

Eaton, W. E. (1975). *The American Federation of Teachers, 1916–61.* Carbondale, IL: Southern Illinois University Press.

Fox, J. N. (1987). The supply of U.S. teachers. In K. Alexander & D. H. Monk (Eds.), *Attracting and compensating America's teachers* (pp. 49–68). Cambridge, MA: Ballinger.

Good, C. V. (Ed.). (1973). *Dictionary of education.* New York: McGraw-Hill.

Harris, L., Kagay, M., & Leichenko, S. (1989). *The American teacher.* New York: Metropolitan Life Insurance Co.

Howsam, R. B., et al. (1985). *Educating a profession.* Washington, DC: American Association of Colleges of Teacher Education.

Jordan, K. F. (1987). Teacher education recommendations in the school reform reports. In K. Alexander & D. H. Monk (Eds.), *Attracting and compensating America's teachers* (pp. 21–47). Cambridge, MA: Ballinger.

Leftwich, K. (1994). Job outlook 2005: Where to find the good jobs. *Vocational Education Journal, 69*(7), 27–29.

Leitman, R., & Binns, K. (1993). *The American teacher: Violence in America's public schools.* New York: Metropolitan Life Insurance Co.

Little, J. W. (1993). Teachers' professional development and education reform. *Educational Evaluation and Policy Analysis, 15,* 129–151.

McLaughlin, M. W., Pfeifer, R. S., Swanson-Owens, D., & Yee, S. (1986). Why teachers won't teach. *Phi Delta Kappan, 67,* 420–426.

McPartland, J. M., & Fessler, R. (1992). Staffing Patterns. *Encyclopedia of Educational Research, (4)* New York: McMillan, 1252–1258.

National Labor Relations Act. (1991). 29 USC 160, Section 2.

Richardson, J. (1994, November 23). 2 foundations create national panel on teaching. *Education Week,* 3.

Rowan, B. (1994). Comparing teachers' work with work in other occupations: Notes on the professional status of teaching. *Educational Researcher, 23,*(6), 4–17, 21.

U.S. Department of Education, National Center for Education Statistics. (1986). *The condition of education 1986.* Washington, DC: U.S. Government Printing Office.

U.S. Department of Education, National Center for Education Statistics. (1987). *The condition of education 1987.* Washington, DC: U.S. Government Printing Office.

Wise, A. (1994). Professionalism and standards: A "unified system of quality assurance." *Education Week,* 48, 37.

PART TWO

Historical Foundations of Education

Chapter 3

American Education: European Heritage and Colonial Experience

Only the educated are free.

Plato

A Critical Incident in My Teaching Career . . .

One day a junior high student returned a library book that was filthy. I began to reprimand him. He put his hand on the book and said, "Why, that book is not dirty." When I looked at his hands, I realized that to him the book was not dirty. His hand looked as if it had not been washed in weeks. I learned that he and his family carried all their water (in a bucket) for a distance of more than a mile.

I learned not to judge students unless I know the circumstances from which they come. I fur-

ther learned that many things in our school experiences are relative to other experiences we have. A child's experiences determine how he views himself and his world. I also learned that students are not dirty (bad). Overt actions may appear to be so, but in light of real evil, most students are good.

Mary E. Fortenberry
Teacher of the Year, Texas

When the courts consider cases that involve interpretation of the Constitution or specific laws, they often review historical records and consider the context of the time to try to determine the intent of the lawmakers. Similarly, studying the history of education helps educators to understand the development of educational thought and practice and to evaluate present educational institutions, theories, and practices in the light of past successes and failures. To help you develop insights into the European and colonial background of American education presented in this chapter, keep the following learning objectives in mind:

- Contrast Spartan and Athenian education.
- Compare Aristotle's and Plato's educational philosophies.
- Explain the contribution of Quintilian to the development of European educational thought and practice.
- Describe the impact of the Reformation on the provision of education.

- Identify the contributions of Bacon, Comenius, Locke, Rousseau, Pestalozzi, Herbart, and Froebel to current educational practice.
- Describe the curriculum in the elementary and secondary schools and the forces that shaped it.
- Compare education in the New England, Middle Atlantic, and Southern colonies.

European Background of American Education

Education in Ancient Societies

The oldest known schools were those of Sumer, an area lying between the Tigris and Euphrates rivers in Mesopotamia. They date from the third millennium B.C. Most of these schools were connected with a temple and taught writing and some calculations. The Sumerian language was not alphabetic, but consisted of 600 or more characters. Writing was done on clay tablets called cuneiform tablets, so a school was called the Tablet House or *edubba*.

Although the first known schools were in Sumer, the Greeks are considered the first real educators in the Western world, "for they were the first western peoples to think seriously and profoundly about educating the young, the first to ask what education is, what it is for, and how children and men should be educated" (Castle, 1967, p. 11). However, while the Greeks were interested in education, they were not all in agreement as to what form it should take. For example, the content and approach to education in the two principal city-states, Sparta and Athens, were quite different.

Education in Sparta

Sparta was predominantly a military state, and education reflected Spartan life. The maintenance of military strength was the most important goal of the government. The welfare of the individual came second to the welfare of the state, life was regimented by the state, and severe limits were placed on individual freedoms. Creative or strictly intellectual pursuits were discouraged. The aim of the educational system was to inculcate patriotism and the ideal of the sacrifice of the individual to the state, as well as to develop and train physically fit and courageous warriors.

At the age of seven boys were enrolled in state military companies where they lived in public barracks and ate at common tables. Training was concerned with cultivating the four great virtues: prudence, temperance, fortitude, and obedience. A system of exercise and games, becoming more military as the boys got older, was designed to make them obey commands, endure hardships, and be successful in battle. Dance and music were taught, but they too involved military and moral themes. Only minimal attention was given to reading and writing.

Girls in Sparta received no formal education. They were trained at home by their mothers in the ideals of the state and housewifery. They were also organized by troops and engaged in competitive sports. Their physical training was so that they might produce strong sons for the state.

Education in Athens

Where Sparta was renowned for its military preeminence, Athens was a democracy that held the individual in the highest regard. There was no compulsory

Military education remains a viable educational option in the United States.

education in Athens, except for two years beginning at age 18 when military training was required of all males. Schools in Athens were private and were restricted to those who could afford the fees.

Education in Athens prior to 479 B.C. (the defeat of Sparta), referred to as "the old education," consisted of sending boys aged 7 to 14 to several schools: the *didascaleum* or music school; the home or building of the *grammatistes* for the study of reading, writing, and arithmetic; and the *palestra* for physical education. After age 14 formal education stopped, although some youth continued their education at the *gymnasia* where more severe physical training, somewhat military in nature, was received. From age 18 to 20 military, public, and religious service was required of all young men; upon completion full citizenship was granted. The aim of educating males in the Athenian state was to prepare a cultivated, well mannered, physically fit and agile individual ready for participation in Athenian citizenship.

The traditional view of the education of girls in Athens is that they only received instruction at home. Yet archaeological evidence seems to point to a different conclusion. Various pottery and statues depict girls going to school (e.g., a girl holding a tablet in one hand and a purse containing her astragals in the other), as well as reading, writing, and engaging in sports. However, it is uncertain how widespread these practices were (Beck, 1964).

What parallels do you see between modern educational systems and those of Sparta and Athens?

Sophists.   The "new Greek education" (post–479 B.C.) continued much the same at the elementary level. At the secondary level, however, a new element was introduced—the Sophists, traveling teachers who charged admission to their popular lectures. Many of them were foreigners lured to Athens by its reputation and its success in defeating the Persians. Among the Sophists were the *skeptics,* who did not value knowledge for its own sake and therefore taught practical skills, especially the art of persuasion, which had easy application to public life. Other Sophists were the *rhetoricians,* who were concerned with the use of words in terms of plausibility, expedience, and political or legal success (Bowen, 1972). Their critics, including Plato, charged that they "brought to Athens a divesting spirit of critical rejection of the traditional beliefs and attitudes" and that behind their claim to teach the art of rhetoric "lay the presumption that success in public life, to be defined in terms of power, was more or less the supreme achievement possible to man" (Barrow, 1976, p. 14).

In the absence of a legal profession, some Sophists developed the practice of logography, the writing of speeches, which their clients could deliver in courts of law. Sets of speeches and handbooks on rhetoric were sold. Schools of rhetoric grew in size and number. Two of the more famous Sophists were Gorgras, a renowned orator who in his seventies was still enthralling the audience at the Olympic Games of 407 B.C., and Protagoras. The latter was considered to be so brilliant that he could charge a student as much as $10,000. Even Plato esteemed Protagoras as a man of sterling quality. Protagoras is considered the father of European grammar and philosophy (Meyer, 1972).

Socrates (469–399 B.C.).   Socrates accepted as his starting point the Sophists' position that man is the measure of all things. However, in contrast to the Sophists, he did not commercialize his teaching and accepted no fees. He also disagreed with the use of knowledge merely to achieve success or gain power, but believed that knowledge was ethically and morally important to all men. According to Socrates, knowledge was virtue. He also believed knowledge was eternal and universal.

To Socrates, the purpose of education was not to perfect the art of rhetoric, but to develop in the individual his inherent knowledge and to perfect the ability to reason. Socrates believed that education and society were inextricably related: society was only as good as its schools. If education succeeded in producing good citizens, then society would be strong and good.

Can you recall an example of the application of the Socratic Method in your own educational experience?

Socratic Method.   Socrates employed a dialectical teaching method that has come to be known as the *Socratic Method* and is similar to the inquiry method practiced today. Using this method Socrates would first demolish false or shaky opinions or assumptions held by the student while disclaiming any knowledge himself. Then, through a questioning process based on the student's experiences, and analyzing the consequences of responses, he led the student to a better understanding of the problem. Finally, he brought the student to a discovery of general ideas or concepts that could be applied to new problems.

"What is courage?" he would casually ask a soldier.
"Courage is holding your ground when things get rough."

"But supposing strategy required that you give way?"

"Well, in that case you wouldn't hold—that would be silly."

"Then you agree that courage is neither holding or giving way."

"I guess so. I don't know."

"Well, I don't know either. Maybe it might be just using your head. What do you say to that?"

"Yes—that's it; using your head, that's what it is."

"Then shall we say, at least tentatively, that courage is presence of mind—sound judgment in time of stress?"

"Yes." (Meyer, 1972, p. 26)

Plato (427–347 B.C.). Socrates' most famous pupil was Plato. Plato founded the Academy, a school of higher learning that admitted both males and females. Fees were not charged, but donations were accepted. As a teacher Plato practiced a variety of methods. Sometimes he employed the Socratic Method. At other times he assigned individual exercises and problems. Sometimes he lectured, though according to Meyer (1972), he was too technical and lecturing was reportedly not his best performance. Plato's theory of education is most clearly put forward in *The Republic* and the *Laws*. In *The Republic* Plato begins by accepting Socrates' premise that "knowledge is virtue." He then expounds on the nature of knowledge and lays out the framework for both a political and social system, including an educational system. Plato believed that the state should operate the educational system. The aim of the schools was to discover and de-velop the abilities of the individual, to aid the individual in discovering the knowledge of truth that is within each of us, and to prepare the individual for his or her role in society. The curriculum was to include reading, especially the classics, writing, mathematics, and logic. Plato also emphasized the physical aspects of education. However, games and sports, as well as music, were important not for the purpose of entertainment but to improve the soul and achieve moral excellence.

Although Plato advocated universal education, he presumed that few possessed the capacity to reach its final stages. Those who passed the successive selection tests and reached the highest levels of wisdom and devotion to the state were to rule the state—the philosopher was to be king (Good & Teller, 1969). Education, then, is the means by which one arrives at the ultimate good. In the process it promotes the happiness and fulfillment of the individual (because he is sorted into the social office to which he is most fitted), as well as the good of the state. Plato's belief in leadership by the most intelligent has been espoused by countless since, including some of the founders of our nation. His belief in unchanging ideas and absolute truths has earned him the title of "the Father of Idealism."

Aristotle (384–322 B.C.). Aristotle was Plato's most famous student. For 20 years he studied and taught at the Academy. However, as the picture at the beginning of this chapter aptly reminds us, although the two agreed on many issues, they differed in some important respects. In the picture Plato is shown pointing heavenward as Aristotle points earthward. And that, metaphorically, was the main difference between them: Plato was the idealist, the lover of the metaphysical; Aristotle was a realist, the more scientific of the two (Winn & Jacks, 1967). If

Plato's concern for the idea served as the basis for Idealism, Aristotle provided the basis for Realism.

It is probably fair to say that Aristotle has had more of an impact on education than either Socrates or Plato, perhaps because he gave the most systematic attention to it. Like Plato he believed in the importance of reason. However, unlike Plato he dismissed "mere intellectual ponderings as insufficient to the advancement of knowledge. What was needed in addition was a diligent and unsparing scrutiny of all observable phenomena" (Meyer, 1972, p. 32). Aristotle is credited with the introduction of the scientific method of inquiry. He systematically classified all branches of existing knowledge and was the first to teach logic as a formal discipline. He believed that reality was to be found in an objective order.

Whereas Plato believed that knowledge is a virtue in itself and that wisdom is good, Aristotle maintained that goodness or virtue rests on deeds, not knowledge. He further maintained that man is a rational being and that the most important activity a man can do is to use his intellect fully. By doing so he attains happiness and accumulates knowledge.

Like Plato, Aristotle believed in the importance of education to the functioning of society and that education should be provided by the state; unlike Plato, he did not believe in educating girls. The aim of education, he felt, is the achievement of the highest possible happiness of the individual by the development of the intellect through the cultivating of habits and the specific use of inductive and deductive reasoning (Bowen, 1972). An additional aim is to produce the good person and good citizen. "The good person should have goodness of intellect which may be achieved by instruction, and goodness of character attained through conditioning of the control of habits" (Gillett, 1966, p. 36).

Last, Aristotle believed that there was a common core of knowledge that was basic to education, which included reading, writing, music, and physical education. This belief in a "core" of knowledge has prevailed through the centuries and is the basis for the core course requirement in American schools and colleges today.

Education in Rome

The Roman conquest of Greece in the second century B.C. brought thousands of Greek slaves to Rome and brought Romans into contact with Greece and its culture. The educational theories of the Greeks had a great impact on the Romans, and by the end of the first century they dominated Roman education. The formal Roman school system that evolved (and which influenced education throughout Europe for centuries) was composed of the elementary school, known as the *ludus,* and the secondary school or grammar school. At the ludus children aged 7 to 12 were taught reading, writing, and accounting. Girls could attend the ludus, but usually that was as far as their education extended. *Grammar schools* were attended by upper class boys aged 12 to 16 who learned grammar (either Greek or Latin) and literature. From age 16 to 20 boys attended the school of rhetoric where they were instructed in grammar, rhetoric, dialectic, music, arithmetic, geometry, and astronomy. Universities were founded during the early years of the Roman Empire. Philosophy, law, mathematics, medicine, architecture, and rhetoric were the principal subjects taught.

Quintilian (35–95 A.D.).   The most noteworthy Roman educator was Quintilian. His influence on Roman schooling has had a subsequent impact on education through the centuries. Quintilian was so respected that he was made a senator and was the first known endowed (state-supported) professor (Wilkins, 1914). His *Institutio Oratoria (Education of the Orator),* published in 95 A.D., is considered to be "the most thorough, systematic and scientific treatment of education to be found in classical literature, whether Greek or Roman" (Monroe, 1939, p. 450).

Quintilian believed education should be concerned with a person's whole intellectual and moral nature, and should have as its goal the production of the effective moral man in practical life (Monroe, 1939). Accordingly, in addition to instruction in grammar and rhetoric, Quintilian recommended a broad literary education that included music, astronomy, geometry, and philosophy. Such an education was to take place in the schools, preferably the public schools, not at home with private tutors as had been the earlier practice in Rome. Public (i.e., group) education, he maintained, provided the opportunity for emulation, friendships, and learning from the successes and failures of others. Progressive for his time, Quintilian (Monroe, 1939) disapproved of corporal punishment:

> first because it is a disgrace . . . and in reality . . . an affront; secondly, because if a boy's disposition be so abject as not to be amended by reproof, he will be hardened . . . (by) stripes. Besides, after you have coerced a boy with stripes, how will you treat him when he becomes a young man, to whom such terror cannot be held out? (pp. 466–467)

The "Ask Yourself" on page 74 will help you examine your position on corporal punishment in the schools.

In many other respects Quintilian's views seem remarkably modern. Recognizing that "study depends on the good will of the student, a quality that cannot be secured by compulsion," Quintilian supported holidays because "relaxation brings greater energy to study, and also games because it is the nature of young things to play" (Castle, 1967, p. 138). He believed in the importance of early training to child development. Of the proper methods of early instruction Quintilian said: "Let his instruction be an amusement to him; let him be questioned and praised; and let him never feel pleased that he does not know a thing . . . let his powers be called forth by rewards, such as that age prizes" (Monroe, 1939, p. 455). He also maintained that children should not be introduced to specific subject matter until they are mature enough to master it. Last, Quintilian emphasized the importance of recognizing individual differences when prescribing the curriculum. He charged the teacher to "ascertain first of all, when a boy is entrusted to him, his ability and disposition . . . when a tutor has observed these indications, let him consider how the mind of his pupil is to be managed" (Monroe, 1939, p. 465).

The Roman system of education spread throughout western Europe. The schools of medieval Europe retained the standard curriculum of the Roman schools: grammar, rhetoric, logic, mathematics, geometry, music, and astronomy. And Latin has remained the language of the scholar until recent times. Figure 3.1 provides an overview of education in Sparta, Athens, and Rome.

In what ways are the educational ideas of Quintilian relevant today?

Ask Yourself:
Does Corporal Punishment Have a Place in the Schools?

Quintilian vehemently opposed corporal punishment. The U.S. Supreme Court has said that corporal punishment does not violate the Constitution. Still, a number of states have abolished corporal punishment in the schools. In others, the decision to administer corporal punishment and the procedure to be followed in its administration have been delegated to local school districts. What is your position on corporal punishment? Ask yourself the following questions:

1. Does corporal punishment serve as a deterrent to undesirable behavior?

2. If it is practiced, for what infractions should it be reserved?

3. Who should administer it?

4. Should a teacher or administrator who administers excessive corporal punishment be held liable to prosecution under child abuse statutes?

5. Would you administer corporal punishment if required by the district? (If, for example, district policy stated that after three unexcused tardies to any one class, the student is to be given three swats by the teacher of the class.)

6. If struck by a student, how would you respond?

Education in the Middle Ages

The period between the end of the Roman Empire (476 A.D.) and the fourteenth century is known as the Middle Ages. The Germanic tribes that conquered the Romans appropriated not only their land but much of their culture and their Catholic religion. The Roman Catholic Church became the dominant force in society and in education. By the end of the sixth century public education had all but disappeared, and what remained took place under the auspices of the church. At the secondary level, monastic schools, originally established to train the clergy, educated boys in the established disciplines of the Roman schools. Theology was studied by those preparing for the priesthood. One important function of the monastic schools was preserving and copying manuscripts. Had it not been for the monastic schools, many of the ancient manuscripts we have today would have been lost.

Alcuin and the Palace School

Another type of school, the palace school, was established by the Emperor Charlemagne (742–814). Charlemagne brought one of the most revered scholars and teachers of his age, Alcuin of York (England), to his court to establish a school. Through Alcuin's efforts, the school became an important force in education in Europe. Charlemagne and all the members of his family studied at the school, and many future teachers, writers, and scholars were trained there.

During this time the curriculum consisted of what was called the *seven liberal arts,* which included the *trivium* (grammar, rhetoric, and logic) and the

Figure 3.1: Education in Ancient Societies

EDUCATION IN SPARTA

- Goal of education: to promote patriotism and train warriors
- Welfare of individual secondary to the welfare of the state
- Curriculum emphasized exercise and games, military training, dance and music
- Schools: military schools

EDUCATION IN ATHENS

- Goal of education: to prepare the well-rounded individual for participation in citizenship
- Emphasis on the development of reason

- Curriculum: reading, writing, mathematics, logic, physical education, music, and drama
- Schools: didascaleum (music school); grammatistes (reading, writing, and arithmetic);

EDUCATION IN ROME

- Goal of education: to develop the intellectual and moral citizen
- Emphasis on education for citizenship
- Curriculum: reading, writing, arithmetic, grammar, literature, music, rhetoric, astronomy, geometry, and philosophy
- Schools: ludus (elementary); grammar school (secondary); schools of rhetoric (from age 16-20); universities

CONTRIBUTION TO WESTERN EDUCATION

- Recognition of importance of physical and moral training

- Concept of liberal education
- The Socratic method as a teaching method
- Importance of reason/the scientific method

- Roman curriculum and organization adopted throughout Europe
- Recognition of individual differences
- Recognition of importance of play and relaxation

quadrivium (arithmetic, geometry, music, and astronomy; see Figure 3.2). The term "liberal arts," if not the exact subjects, is still used today to describe that portion of the college curriculum that is not concerned with technical or professional studies.

Thomas Aquinas (1225–1274)

The most important scholar and philosopher of the Middle Ages was the Dominican monk St. Thomas Aquinas. His philosophy, called *scholasticism* or Thomism, is the foundation of Roman Catholic education. Aquinas was able to reconcile religion with the rediscovered ancient philosophies, particularly the

Figure 3.2: Tower of Knowledge, Showing Stages of Medieval Education

Source: Reisch, G. (1504). *Margarita Philosophica* (2nd ed.). Argentinae (Strassbourg): Johannes Schottus.

rationalism of Aristotle. He believed that human beings possess both a spiritual nature, the soul, and a physical nature, the body. He also maintained that man is a rational being and that through the deductive process of rational analysis man can arrive at truth. When reason fails, man must rely on faith. Thus reason supports what man knows by faith: reason and faith are complementary sources of truth. In accordance with this philosophy, the schools were to teach both the principles of the faith and rational philosophy. The curriculum was to contain both theology and the liberal arts.

The Medieval Universities

During the later Middle Ages, as the Crusades opened Europe to other parts of the world and as many of the Greek masterpieces were rediscovered, there was an intellectual revival that manifested itself not only in scholasticism but in the establishment of several of the world's great universities. The University of Salerno, established in 1050 A.D., specialized in medicine; the University of Bologna (1113 A.D.) in law; the University of Paris (1160 A.D.) in theology; and Oxford University (1349 A.D.) in liberal arts and theology. By the end of the Middle Ages some 80 universities were in existence (Meyer, 1972). Some, such as the University of Paris, grew out of a cathedral school, in this case, Notre-Dame. Others evolved from associations called *universitas,* which were chartered corporations of teachers and students, organized for their protection against interference from secular or religious authorities.

At first, most universities did not have buildings of their own but occupied rented space. The curriculum at the undergraduate level followed the seven liberal arts. Classes started soon after sunrise. The mode of instruction was lecture in Latin, with the teacher usually reading from a text he had written. Student guilds or unions, commonplace at the time, ventured to tell the professors how fast to speak. At Bologna the students wanted to get full value for their fees and required the professors to speak very fast. By contrast, the Parisian students insisted on a leisurely pace and when the authorities ordered some acceleration, the students not only "howled and clamored" but threatened to go on strike (Meyer, 1972). More exciting than the lectures were the *disputations* at which students presented and debated opposing intellectual positions. The disputations also served to prepare students for the much dreaded day when they would defend their theses. The Historical Note on page 78 provides a brief glimpse of the life of the university student in medieval times. Note the differences and similarities with today.

If the student guild or union were in effect today, what changes might it recommend for undergraduate education?

Of all the institutions that have survived from medieval times to the present, with the exception of the Catholic Church, the university bears the closest resemblance to its ancient ancestors. As it was then, it is still an organization of students and professors dedicated to the pursuit of knowledge. It still grants the medieval degrees: the bachelor's, the master's, and the doctorate. In most universities students are still required to study a given curriculum, and if they seek the doctorate, are required to write a thesis or dissertation and to defend it publicly. The gowns worn at academic ceremonies today are patterned after those worn by our medieval ancestors. And deans, rectors, and chancellors still exist, though their duties have changed (Meyer, 1972).

Historical Note:
Life of the Medieval University Student

Although academic life was rigorous, students had many privileges. They were exempt from military service and from paying taxes. A student who shaved his head and assumed a few other burdens became one of the clerical class and was allowed some of the benefits associated with it. For example, if he broke what would be considered civil law he was tried under church law, not civil law. However, in keeping with his clerical status the student was required to be celibate. If he did stray, he could continue with his studies, but lost his privileges and could receive no degree.

Medieval students were not without vices. Taverns often surrounded the universities and at the taverns were women and gambling. More seriously, students at Oxford were said to roam the streets at night, assaulting all who passed. In Rome the students went from tavern to tavern committing assault and robbery. At Leipzig they were fined for throwing stones at professors, and at Paris they were excommunicated for shooting dice on the altars of Notre-Dame.

Although these acts were the exceptions rather than the rule, such actions, as well as the attitude of the students, who held townspeople in low regard, were sufficient to lead to open hostilities between "town" and "gown." Some separation exists between town and gown in many university communities today, perhaps a legacy from our medieval ancestors.

Source: Based on accounts in Meyer, A. E. (1972). *An educational history of the western world.* New York: McGraw-Hill Book Company.

Education During the Renaissance

The Renaissance began in the fourteenth century and reached its high point in the fifteenth century. It is so called because it represented a *renaissance* or rebirth of interest in the humanist aspects of Greek and Latin thought. When Constantinople fell to the Muslims in 1453 many Byzantine scholars came to Italy, bringing with them the works of classical antiquity that had been forgotten in the West, most notably Quintilian's *Education of the Orator.* The influence of this treatise, great as it had been in imperial Rome, was even greater in the Renaissance (Woodward, 1906). Quintilian was viewed as the prime authority on Roman educational ideals. It is symbolic of the respect given Quintilian that Erasmus, the most noted educator of the Renaissance, should apologize for touching on the aims or methods of teaching "seeing that Quintilian has said in effect the last word on the matter" (Woodward, 1906, p. 10).

During the Middle Ages the Catholic Church was dominant and emphasis was on the hereafter. In the fourteenth and fifteenth centuries the increase in trade and commerce, the increase in science and technology, the growth of the Italian city-states, and the rise of a new aristocracy whose wealth came from trade and banking brought an end to the old social, economic, and political order and in so doing brought a greater concern for the here than the hereafter.

Humanism

The dominant philosophy of the Renaissance was *humanism.* Rejecting scholasticism and the model of the cleric as the educated man, the humanists considered the educated man to be the man of learning described in the classics. The first products of the Renaissance in education can be seen in the famous *court schools* operated by Vittorino da Feltre at Mantua from 1423 to 1446 and by Guarino da Verona at Ferrara from 1429 to 1469. Like the school of Alcuin in the ninth century, they were connected to the courts of reigning families. Like many modern preparatory boarding schools, they housed boys aged 8 or 10 to age 20. They emphasized what Woodward called the "doctrine of courtesy"—the manners, grace, and dignity of the antique culture (Woodward, 1906). At the court schools, a humanist curriculum was taught that included not only the seven liberal arts, but reading, writing, and speaking in Latin; study of the Greek classics; and, for the first time, the study of history. Following the teachings of Quintilian, games and play were also emphasized, individual differences were recognized, and punishment was discouraged. The goal was to produce the well-rounded, liberally educated *courtier*—the ideal personality of the Renaissance.

Erasmuas (1466–1536)

The foremost humanist of the Renaissance was Desiderius Erasmus of the Netherlands. Although Erasmus was not a prolific writer, what he wrote was full of charm and wit, and as a result was widely read. His *Colloquies,* textbooks on Latin style, also contained instruction in religion and morals and were among the most important textbooks of his time. In *Upon the Method of Right Instruction* he proposed the systematic training of teachers. His views on pedagogy are found in his treatise *Of the First Liberal Education of Children.* It contained much that had been advanced by Quintilian: the abolition of corporal punishment, the value of play and games, and the necessity of understanding the student's individual needs and abilities. Erasmus was also one of the first educators to understand the importance of politeness. "Erasmus knew perfectly well that politeness has a moral side, that it is not a matter of pure convention, but that it proceeds from the inner disposition of a well-ordered soul. So he assigns it an important place in education" (Laurie, 1968, p. 56).

The educational program of Erasmus was characteristic of the humanist school, which can be described as:

> return to the ancients; classical tongues to be studied in the sources, and no longer in barbarous manuals; rhetorical exercises to be substituted for useless and obscure dialectic; the study of nature to animate and vivify literary studies; the largest possible diffusion of human knowledge without distinction of age or sex. (Laurie, 1968, p. 55)

Education During the Reformation

That period of history known as the Reformation formally began in 1517 when an Augustinian monk and professor of religion named Martin Luther nailed his *Ninety-five Theses,* questioning the authority of the Catholic Church, to the door of the court church in Wittenberg, Germany. In the years that followed, a religious revolution swept the European continent, resulting in a century of war and reformation of the Church. Those who protested the authority (and abuses) of the Church came to be known as Protestants. The invention of the printing press enabled them to spread their doctrine rapidly.

Speculate on the impact of the invention of the printing press on education.

Vernacular Schools

In disavowing the authority of the Church the Protestant reformers stressed the authority of the Bible over that of the Church. They also stressed the responsibility of each man for his own salvation. Therefore it was necessary that each person be able to read the Scriptures and, as a corollary, to be educated. The initial product of this belief was the establishment of *vernacular schools* —primary or elementary schools that offered instruction in the mother tongue or "vernacular" and a basic curriculum of reading, writing, mathematics, and religion.

Vernacular schools were established throughout Germany by Philip Melanchthon and Johann Bugenhagen following Luther's teachings. Melanchthon in particular is noted for his advocacy of universal elementary education and has been called the "Schoolmaster of Germany." Elementary schools also began to appear in other Protestant strongholds, especially those that followed the teachings of John Calvin, such as in the Netherlands, in Scotland, and in the canton of Geneva (Switzerland), where Calvin established a theocratic dictatorship.

Luther (1483–1546)

Martin Luther believed that every child should have a free and compulsory elementary education. Education should be supported by the state and the state should have the authority and responsibility to control the curriculum, the textbooks, and the instruction in the schools. His *Letters to the Mayors and Aldermen of All Cities of Germany in Behalf of Christian Schools* stressed the spiritual, economic, and political benefits of education. The curriculum was to include classical languages, which were to be learned by practice. Grammar, mathematics, science, history, physical education, music, and didactics were all considered important. Theology was taught, and study of Protestant doctrines was accomplished through the catechism (a question and answer drill).

Although formal schooling was important to the establishment of a "priesthood of believers," Luther thought such public instruction should occupy only part of the day. At least one or two hours a day should be spent at home in vocational training, preparing for an occupation through an apprenticeship. Secondary schools, designed primarily as preparatory schools for the clergy, taught Hebrew as well as the classical languages, rhetoric, dialectic, history, mathematics, science, music, and gymnastics. A university education, whose purpose was seen as providing training for higher service in the government or the Church, was available only to those young men who demonstrated exceptional intellectual abilities.

Calvin (1509–1564)

John Calvin's views on education were very similar to those of Luther. He too stressed the necessity of a universal, compulsory, state-supported education that would not only enable all individuals to read the Bible themselves and thereby attain salvation, but would profit the state through the contributions of an educated citizenry. The school was also seen as a place for religious indoctrination. Calvin also supported a two-track educational system consisting of common schools for the masses, and secondary schools teaching the classical, humanist curriculum for the preparation of the leaders of church and state. Calvin's influence was widespread, especially in the colonies of the New World.

The Reformation in England

In contrast to what was taking place on the continent, the Protestant Reformation in England did not lead to an increase in the number of schools, but to a decrease. When Henry VIII broke with the Catholic Church and closed the Catholic monasteries, the monastic schools were also closed. Under Elizabeth I such schools as existed were placed under the regulation of the Anglican Church. The few secondary (Latin grammar) schools that continued to exist were established by a town council or by an individual benefactor and were narrow and sectarian in nature. Uniform textbooks were required throughout the country, the curriculum was rigid, and discipline was severe.

Calvinism spread to England. The English Calvinists, called Puritans, aspired to reform or purify the Anglican Church, which had maintained much of the structure of the Catholic Church. Persecuted for their efforts and seeking religious freedom, the Puritans were important in the settlement of the American colonies.

The Jesuits

While the Reformation was taking place outside the Catholic Church, a Counter-Reformation in the Church resulted in the formation of the Society of Jesus, or Jesuits, by Ignatius of Loyola (1491–1556). The Jesuits became a teaching order and were instrumental in the establishment of a number of secondary schools and universities throughout Europe. Their major contribution to education was in the training of teachers. They established, perhaps for the first time in history, a specific plan for the selection, training, and supervision of teachers.

Which of the major colleges and universities in the United States were founded and are operated by the Jesuits?

Later European Educational Thought

The Reformation not only opened the door to the questioning of religious dogma and superstition, but to investigation of the laws of nature. The Reformation gave way to the Age of Enlightenment or Reason, so called because of the great reliance placed on reason and scientific inquiry. Philosophers and scholars of the period believed that observation and scientific inquiry were the avenues to the discovery of the "natural laws" that dictated the orderly operation of the universe.

Bacon (1561–1626)

Francis Bacon, an English philosopher, was central to this movement. He was also important to education because of the emphasis he placed on scientific inquiry rather than on accepting previously derived hypotheses of deductive logic or the writings of the past. He emphasized the need for education to develop what today is termed "critical thinking skills." The Utopia described in his *The New Atlantis* envisioned a research university not inconsistent with modern ideas.

Comenius (1592–1670)

Bacon had a major influence on Jan Amos Comenius, a Moravian bishop. Like Bacon he was a proponent of what is termed *sense realism,* which is the belief that learning must come through the senses. Accordingly, education must allow children to observe for themselves and experience by doing. Children can best learn to write by writing, to talk by talking, to sing by singing, and to reason by reasoning. The notion of sensory learning was later expanded by Locke, Rousseau, and Pestalozzi.

Like Bacon, Comenius believed in the scientific method and an ordered universe that could be discovered through reason. He proposed a set of teaching methods based on these beliefs that incorporated both the deductive method and whatever instructional method was most appropriate for the specific developmental stage of the child. Comenius is said to be the first educator to propose a theory of child growth and development.

Comenius proposed that teaching be straightforward and simple and proceed from the concrete to the abstract, that it deal with things before symbols, and that it have practical application. He affirmed Quintilian's beliefs in regard to individual differences, motivation, and corporal punishment. Finally, he believed in a general learning, *paideia,* which should be possessed by all educated persons.

Comenius is also known for his Latin textbooks, which were used throughout Europe. The texts were very popular, not only because they attempted to teach Latin through the use of the vernacular, but because they were among the first textbooks to contain illustrations.

Comenius has had a profound effect on Western education through his influence on the thinking of such educational leaders as Horace Mann, John Dewey, Robert Hutchins, and Mortimer Adler. Mortimer Adler's dedication to *The Paideia Program: An Educational Syllabus* (1984) reads:

> To
> John Amos Comenius
> Who, more than 300 years ago
> envisaged the educational ideal that
> *The Paideia Program* aims to realize
> before the end of this century.

Locke (1632–1704)

Although the English philosopher John Locke is best known for his political theories, which served as the basis for the American and French constitutions, he also had a profound influence on education. He held views very similar to others in the school of sensory reasoning. Locke taught the *tabula rasa* concept of the human mind, which says that we come into the world with our minds a blank slate. We then learn through sensation. "A sound mind in a sound body is a short but full description of a happy state in the world" are his first words in *Some Thoughts Concerning Education* (Axtell, 1968, p. 114). The sound body needs fresh air, recreation, exercise, and good hygiene. The sound mind, like the sound body, needs exercise and discipline. The curriculum he recommended included, beyond the three Rs, history, geography, ethics, philosophy, science, and conversational foreign languages, especially French. **Mathematics was also empha-sized, not to make the scholar a mathematician, but to make him a reasonable man.** Locke believed the goal of education was to create the moral, practical individual who could participate effectively in the governing process.

Rousseau (1712–1778)

In the later eighteenth century an educational movement called *naturalism* developed. Its emphasis on freedom and the individual formed the basis for modern educational theory and practice. The forerunner of the movement was Jean-Jacques Rousseau. Like Locke, Rousseau is perhaps best remembered for his political theories. His book *Social Contract* had a strong influence on the thinking of those involved in both the French and American revolutions. Although he was never an educator, Rousseau expounded a theory and philoso-phy of education that influenced many educators, including John Dewey and the progressive educators of a century or more later. Rousseau has also been called the "father of modern child psychology" (Mayer, 1973).

Like Comenius, Rousseau believed in stages of children's growth and devel-opment and in the educational necessity of adapting instruction to the various stages. His major thoughts on education are contained in his novel *Emile,* which puts forward the ideal education for a youth named Emile. He contends that the child is inherently good and that it is society that corrupts the natural goodness of man. Like Locke he was concerned with the physical growth and health of the child. The education of Emile is to be child-centered, concerned with develop-ing his natural abilities. He is to learn by his senses through direct experience and is not to be punished. Emile's education is to progress as he is ready and as his interests motivate him. Finally, he is taught a trade in order to prepare him for an occupation in life.

How does Rousseau's belief in the inherent goodness of the child compare to the doctrine of original sin?

Pestalozzi (1746–1827)

Johann Heinrich Pestalozzi was a Swiss educator who put Rousseau's ideas into practice. Pestalozzi has had a profound impact on education throughout much of the Western world. The Prussian government sent teachers to be instructed by him, and educators came from all over the world, including the United States, to observe and study his methods. He was made a citizen of the French Republic and knighted by the czar of Russia. Horace Mann and Henry Barnard came under his influence. Edward A. Sheldon, superintendent of schools in Oswego, New York, established a teacher training school at Oswego in 1861 that followed Pestalozzi's methods.

Pestalozzi's philosophy of education incorporated the child-centered, sen-sory experience principles of Rousseau. He believed with Rousseau in the nat-ural goodness of human nature and the corrupting influence of society. He also supported Rousseau's idea of individual differences in "readiness" to learn. His belief in the development of the total child to his or her maximum potential has been given its greatest recognition in the movement for the education of the dis-advantaged during the second half of the twentieth century.

Perhaps more than Rousseau, Pestalozzi recognized the importance of human emotions in the learning process. It was important, he believed, that the child be given feelings of self-respect and emotional security. It also was important that the teacher treat students with love. In fact, it can be said that the ideal of love governs Pestalozzi's educational philosophy. Pestalozzi was especially fond of poor children and did everything in his power to improve their condition (Mayer, 1973).

Like Comenius, Pestalozzi believed that instruction must begin with the concrete and proceed to the abstract. Materials should be presented slowly, in developmental order from simple to complex, from known to unknown. The *object lesson* centers on concrete materials within the child's experience, involves discussion and oral presentation, and replaces rote learning. For example, "in an arithmetic lesson dealing with the number 'three,' the child should handle three objects, then progress from sight and touch to abstract concepts of number and the idea contained in the word 'three'" (Gillett, 1966, p. 218).

Herbart (1776–1841)

One of the Prussian educators who studied under Pestalozzi was Johann Friedrich Herbart. Herbart believed that the aim of education should be the development of moral character. His pedagogical theory included three key concepts: *interest, apperception,* and *correlation.* Instruction can only be successful if it arouses interest. Interests are derived from both nature and society, and thus the curriculum should include both the natural and social sciences. All new material presented to the child is interpreted in terms of past experiences by the process of apperception. Additionally, ideas are reinforced and organized in the mind by the process of correlation (Gillett, 1966).

Herbart maintained that any suitable material could be learned if presented systematically. The five steps in the Herbartian methodology included:

1. *Preparation*—preparing the student to receive the new material by arousing interest or recalling past material or experiences

2. *Presentation*—presenting the new material

3. *Association*—combining old and new ideas

4. *Generalization*—formulating general ideas or principles

5. *Application*—applying the ideas or principles to new situations

Herbart's ideas had a significant influence on American education. The National Herbartian Society, founded in 1892, 10 years later became the National Society of the Scientific Study of Education. Herbart made the study of educational psychology of paramount importance. He demonstrated the significance of methodology in instruction. But, perhaps most importantly, his greatness "lies in his faith that education ultimately could become a science" (Mayer, 1973, p. 282).

Froebel (1782–1852)

Friedrich Froebel was the third member of what Gillett (1966) called the nineteenth century's "famous pedagogical triumvirate" that broke with subject-centered instruction and created a new concern for the child. Froebel is known

The child-centered philosophy of Pestalozzi influenced education practice throughout the Western world.

for the establishment in 1837 of the first kindergarten and for providing the theoretical basis for early childhood education. Although Froebel accepted many of Pestalozzi's ideas associated with child-centeredness, Froebel was more concerned with activity than Pestalozzi, but less concerned with observation. According to Froebel, the primary aim of the school should be self-development through self-expression. Self-expression took place through games, singing, or any number of creative and spontaneous activities, which were to be part of an *activity curriculum.* Froebel was also concerned with the development of creativity in children. He viewed the classroom as a miniature society in which children learned social cooperation.

Froebel developed highly stylized materials that were mass produced and used throughout the world. They were designed to aid self-expression and bring

The learning of social cooperation and playing creatively with objects are important in early childhood education according to Froebel.

Recall your own experience in the primary grades. To what extent was your educational experience similar to Froebel's activity curriculum?

out the "divine effluence" (the fundamental unity of all nature with God) within each child. *Mother and Nursery Songs* was a collection of songs, poems, pictures, instructions, games, and suggested activities designed for instruction of the young at home (Gillett, 1966). In the kindergarten, *gifts* and *occupations* were used. The gifts were play objects that did not change their form (e.g., wooden spheres or cubes), symbols of the fundamentals of nature. The occupations were materials used in creative construction or design activities whose shape changed in use (e.g., clay or paper). Used together they were said to ensure the progressive self-development of the child.

One of Froebel's pupils, Margaretha Schurz, opened the first kindergarten in the United States in Watertown, Wisconsin. John Dewey adopted many of Froebel's principles and used them in his famous laboratory school at the University of Chicago. Today, the kindergarten is recognized for its importance in the educational process and as a socializing force. It is the cornerstone of our educational system.

Table 3.1 gives an overview of the educational theories we have discussed and their influence on Western education.

Table 3.1: Western European Educational Thought, 1200 A.D.–1850 A.D.

Theorist	Educational Theories	Influence on Western Education
Aquinas (1225–1274)	Human beings possess both a spiritual and a physical nature. Man is a rational being. Faith and reasons are complementary sources of truth.	Provided basis for Roman Catholic education.
Erasmus (1466–1536)	The liberally educated man is one educated in the seven liberal arts, steeped in the classics and in rhetoric. Systematic training of teachers is needed. Follower of Quintilian.	Advanced the need for the systematic training of teachers and a humanistic pedagogy. Promoted the importance of politeness in education.
Luther (1483–1546)	Education is necessary for religious instruction, the preparation of religious leaders, and the economic well-being of the state. Education should include vocational training.	Provided support for concept of free and compulsory elementary education. Promoted concept of universal literacy.
Calvin (1509–1564)	Education serves both the religious and political establishment: elementary schools for the masses where they could learn to read the Bible and thereby attain salvation; secondary schools to prepare the leaders of church and state.	Concept of two-track system and emphasis on literacy influenced education in New England and ultimately the entire nation.
Bacon (1561–1626)	Education should advance scientific inquiry. Understanding of an ordered universe comes through reason.	Provided major rationale for the development of critical thinking skills. Proposed the concept of a research university.
Comenius (1592–1670)	Learning must come through the senses. Education must allow the child to reason by doing. There is a general body of knowledge (*paideia*) that should be possessed by all.	Provided theory of child growth and development. Concept of *paideia* profoundly influenced numerous Western educational leaders.
Locke (1632–1704)	Children enter the world with their minds like a blank slate (*tabula rasa*). The goal of education is to promote the development of reason and morality.	Provided philosophical basis for American and French revolutions. Provided support for the concept of the reasonable man and the ability and necessity for the reasonable man to participate in the governing process.

Table 3.1: *continued*

Theorist	Educational Theories	Influence on Western Education
Rousseau (1712–1778)	Major proponent of naturalism, which emphasized individual freedom. The child is inherently good. Children's growth and development goes through stages, which necessitates adaptation of instruction. Education should be concerned with the development of the child's natural abilities.	Naturalism provided basis for modern educational theory and practice. Father of modern child psychology.
Pestalozzi (1746–1827)	Education should be child-centered and based on sensory experience. The individual differences of each child must be considered in assessing readiness to learn. Each child should be developed to his or her maximum potential. Ideal of love emphasized the importance of emotion in the learning process. Instruction should begin with the concrete and proceed to the abstract.	Concept of maximum development of each child provided support for education of the disadvantaged. Pestalozzian methods exported throughout Europe and to the United States, one of the earliest theories of instruction formally taught to teachers.
Herbart (1776–1841)	The aim of education should be the development of moral character. Any material can be learned if presented systematically: preparation, presentation, association, generalization, and application. Instruction must arouse interest to be successful. Education is a science.	Elevated the study of educational psychology. Demonstrated the significance of methodology in instruction. Advanced the concept that education is a science and can be studied scientifically.
Froebel (1782–1852)	The aim of education should be to ensure self-development through self-expression. Self-expression takes place through an activity curriculum. The school should promote creativity and bring out "divine effluence" within each child.	Established first kindergarten. Provided theoretical basis for early childhood education.

Education in Colonial America

The English, the predominant settlers of the American colonies, had the greatest influence on the educational system that emerged in the colonies, but the French and Spanish also played a role. The French empire once spread from Canada to Louisiana. French priests, particularly the Jesuits, followed explorers and fur traders into the wilderness to convert and educate the Native Americans. The Catholic influence on education, which can still be seen today in cities as far apart as Quebec and New Orleans, can be traced to the French Jesuits and to orders of teaching nuns.

The Spanish empire was no less vast, containing at various times the entire Southwest, Florida, and California. Spanish Catholic priests, especially the Franciscans, also followed the explorers and sought to convert and educate the Native Americans. Their vast array of missions stretched throughout the Southwest and into California. The missions often included schools where Native Americans were taught not only the Spanish language but agricultural and vocational skills.

English Settlement

The first English settlement in North America was at Jamestown (Virginia) in 1607. In 1620, the Pilgrims, a group of Separatist Puritans (Protestants who wanted not only to purify but to separate from the Church of England), settled at Plymouth (Massachusetts). Ten years later a group of nonseparatist Puritans founded the Massachusetts Bay Colony. This colony became a focal point of migration and other New England colonies (Rhode Island, New Haven [Connecticut], New Hampshire, Maine) developed from this base (Cohen, 1974). Many of the colonists who came to the New World were filled with a sense of religious commitment, largely Protestant, which shaped their views on life and education. However, settlers in different regions developed varying conceptions of society and education (Gutek, 1991). These variations are explored in the following sections.

Education in the New England Colonies

According to Cubberley (1934), the Puritans who settled New England "contributed most that was of value for our future educational development" (p. 14). The New England colonists sustained a vigorous emphasis on education even in the hostile new environment. In fact, by 1700 the colonies could boast of literacy rates that were often superior to those in England (Cohen, 1974).

Initially, the Puritans attempted to follow English practice regarding the establishment and support of schools by relying on private benefactors and limiting the role of the state. However, the general absence of wealthy Puritan migrants soon led to the abandonment of this practice and, because of fears that parents were neglecting the education of their children, to a more direct role for the state (Cohen, 1974).

First Education Laws

The Massachusetts Law of 1642 ordered the selectmen of each town to ascertain whether parents and masters (of apprentices) were, in fact, providing for the education of their children. The selectmen were also to determine what the child was being taught. The child of any parent or master who failed to meet his obligation could be apprenticed to a new master who would be required to fulfill the law. Although the law neither specified schools nor required attendance, it is said to have established the principle of compulsory education. Five years later, the Education Law of 1647 ordered every township of 50 households to provide a teacher to teach reading and writing, and all townships of 100 or more households to establish a grammar school. Although there was no uniform compliance nor administration of these laws, they show how important education was to the Puritans and demonstrate their belief in the necessity of a literate citizenry for the functioning of a political society. The laws also served as models for other colonies and are considered the first education laws in America.

Religious Influence

How do the basic purposes of education in Colonial America compare with those of today?

In New England, as in the other colonies, the institutions of secular government, including education, were closely aligned with the dominant religious group. The Puritans brought with them many of the educational views of the Reformation, namely that education was necessary for religious instruction and salvation, as well as for good citizenship. As the Massachusetts Law of 1642 explained, there was a need to ensure the ability of children "to read and understand the principles of religion and the capital laws of this country." This purpose is also evidenced by the first words of the Massachusetts Education Law of 1647, also called the "old Deluder Satan Law": "It being one chief project of that old deluder, Satan, to keep men from knowledge of the Scriptures." The founding of Harvard College in 1636 was also based on religious motives—to ensure that there would be an educated ministry for the colony. Fearful that there would be no replacements for the ministers who first came with them, the colonists dreaded "to leave an illiterate Ministry to the churches, when our present Ministers should lie in the Dust" (Cubberley, 1934, p. 13).

Elementary School

The New England colonists not only shared Calvin's view of the aim of education, they also adopted the two-track system advocated by Calvin and other scholars of the Reformation. Town schools and *dame schools* were established to educate the children of the common folk in elementary reading, writing, and mathematics. The dame schools were held in the kitchen or living room of a neighborhood woman, often a widow, usually a person with minimal education herself, who received a modest fee for her efforts. So-called "writing" or "reading schools" were concerned with the teaching of these disciplines and also were operated on a fee basis. *Charity* or *pauper schools* were operated for the children of the poor who could not afford to attend other schools.

Education was also made available as a result of the apprenticeship system whereby a child was apprenticed to a master to learn a trade. In addition, the master was required by the terms of the indenture to ensure that the apprentice received a basic education. For some children this was the avenue by which they learned what little reading and writing they knew.

Instruction in the schools was primarily religious and authoritarian. Students learned their basic lessons from the *hornbook*, so called because the material was written on a sheet of parchment, placed on a wooden board, and covered with a thin sheath of cow's horn for protection (see Figure 3.3). The board had a handle with a hole in it so it could be strung around the child's neck.

The New England Primer

The *New England Primer* was used with slightly older children. The primer is an excellent example of the interrelationship between education and religion. Although different editions of the primer varied somewhat in the 150 years of its publication, which began in 1690, it usually featured an alphabet and spelling guide, followed by one of the things that made the primer famous—24 little pictures with alphabetical rhymes as illustrated in Figure 3.4.

The primer also included the Lord's Prayer, the Creed, the Ten Commandments, a listing of the books of the Bible, and a list of numbers from 1 to 100, using both Arabic and Roman numerals. Another prominent feature of the primer was a poem, the exhortation of John Rogers to his children, from John Foxe's *Book of Martyrs,* with a picture of the martyr burning at the stake as his wife and children look on. The primer ended with a shortened version of the Puritan catechism (Ford, 1962).

Figure 3.3: Hornbook of the Eighteenth Century

Source: Littlefield, G. E. (1965). *Early Schools and School-Books of New England* (p. 111). New York: Russell & Russell, Inc. Reprinted with permission.

Figure 3.4: An Alphabet Including Both Religious and Secular Jingles

In *Adam's* Fall
We Sinned all.

Thy Life to Mend
This *Book* Attend.

The *Cat* doth play
And after flay.

A *Dog* will bite
A *Thief* at night.

An *Eagles* flight
Is out of fight.

The Idle *Fool*
Is whipt at School.

As runs the *Glafs*
Mans life doth pafs.

My *Book* and *Heart*
Shall never part.

Job feels the Rod
Yet blefles GOD.

Our *K I N G* the good
No man of blood.

The *Lion* bold
The *Lamb* doth hold.

The *Moon* gives light
In time of night.

Nightingales fing
In Time of Spring.

The *Royal Oak*
it was the Tree
That fav'd His
Royal Majeftie.

Peter denies
His Lord and cries.

Queen *Efther* comes
in Royal State
To Save the JEWS
from difmal Fate

Rachol doth mourn
For her firft born.

Samuel anoints
Whom God appoints.

Time cuts down all
Both great and fmall.

Uriah'sbeauteousWife
Made *David* feek his
Life.

Whales in the Sea
God's Voice obey.

Xerxes the great did die,
And fo muft you & I,

Youth forward flips
Death foonest nips.

Zacheus he
Did climb the Tree
His Lord to fee,

Source: Ford, P. L. (Ed.). (1962). *The New England Primer.* New York: Teachers College Press.

Secondary Grammar Schools

Secondary grammar schools existed for the further education of the male children of the well-to-do. They also served as preparatory schools for the university where the leaders of the church and political affairs were to be trained and which required proficiency in Latin and Greek for admission. The Boston Latin School, established in 1635, became the model for similar schools throughout New England.

Education at the grammar school was quite different from that at the dame or town school. The emphasis was on Latin, with some Greek and occasionally Hebrew. Other disciplines included those necessary for the education of the Renaissance concept of the educated man. The course of study in the grammar school lasted fairly intensively for six to seven years, although students "tended to withdraw and return, depending on familial need and circumstances; and since school was conducted on a year-round basis and instruction organized around particular texts, it was fairly simple for a student to resume study after a period of absence" (Cremin, 1970, p. 186).

University Curriculum

The curriculum of the university in the early colonial period was also based on the classically oriented pattern of English universities. As Cohen (1974) described it:

> The undergraduate courses revolved around the traditional Trivium and Quadrivium but without musical studies, the Three Philosophies (Metaphysics, Ethics, Natural Science), and Greek, Hebrew, and a chronological study of ancient history. As in English universities logic and rhetoric were the basic subjects in the curriculum. . . . Compositions, orations, and disputations were given the same careful scrutiny as at English universities. (p. 66)

Education in New England During the Later Colonial Period

Social and Economic Changes.   The Age of the Enlightenment or Age of Reason that swept the Western world in the seventeenth century had found its way to the shores of the American colonies by the eighteenth century. As in Europe, it brought greater concern for independent rationality, a repudiation of supernatural explanations of phenomena, and a greater questioning of traditional dogma. At the same time that the Enlightenment was sweeping the colonies, the population of the colonies increased rapidly, and its economy outgrew its localized base of farming and fishing. Trade and commerce increased and a new mercantile gentry emerged (Cohen, 1974). The mercantile activities of the new middle class called for a freer environment and increased religious toleration.

Changes in Education: Birth of the Academy.   It was inevitable that the educational system would change to meet the needs of the intellectual, economic, and social order. The writing and dame schools began to give way to town schools. The curriculum at the elementary level, while still dominated by reading and writing, placed greater importance on arithmetic than before. Greater concern was also shown for practical and vocational training at both the elementary and secondary levels.

Many grammar schools, however, refused to change their classical curricula. As a result, numerous *academies* and private venture schools sprang up in the larger towns, teaching subjects useful in trade and commerce. If the prestigious Boston Latin School would not teach mathematics, there were others who would. The newspapers of the time were filled with advertisements for these schools. One such 1723 advertisement appearing in New York City read:

> There is a school in New York, in the Broad Street, near the Exchange, where Mr. John Walton, late of Yale College, Teacheth Reading, Writing, Arethmatick, whole Numbers and Fractions, Vulgar and Decimal, The Mariners Art, Plain and Mercators Way; Also Geometry, Surveying, the Latin Tongue, the Greek and Hebrew Grammers, Ethicks, Rhetorick, Logick, Natural Philosophy and Metaphysicks, all or any of them for a Reasonable Price. The School from the first of October till the first of March will be tended in the Evening. If any Gentlemen in the Country are disposed to send their Sons to the said School, if they apply themselves to the Master he will immediately procure suitable Entertainment for them, very Cheap. Also if any Young Gentlemen of the City will please to come in the Evening and make some Tryal of the Liberal Arts, they may have the opportunity of Learning the same things which are commonly Taught in Colledges. (Seybolt, cited in Rippa, 1988, p. 66)

Which would you prefer to attend, the Boston Latin School or Mr. Walton's school? Why?

Growth of Colleges.   During this period several colleges were founded in the New England colonies: Collegiate School, now Yale University, in 1701; the College of Rhode Island, now Brown University, in 1764; and Dartmouth College in 1769. The colleges of this era also reflected the growing secularism of the society. This was manifested in a broadened curricula. In 1722 Harvard established its first professorship in secular subjects—mathematics and natural philosophy. By 1760 the scientific subjects accounted for 20% of the student's time. Another manifestation of the growing secularism was the change in graduates' careers. Theology remained the most popular career, but an increasing number of graduates were turning to law, medicine, trade, or commerce as the New England colleges became centers of independence, stimulation, and social usefulness (Cohen, 1974).

Education in the Middle Colonies

The New England colonies had been settled primarily by English colonists who shared the same language, traditions, and religion. The settlers of the middle colonies (New York, New Jersey, Pennsylvania, Delaware) came from a variety of national and religious backgrounds. Most had fled Europe because of religious persecution and were generally more distrusting of secular authority than the New England colonists. Thus, while the schools in the middle colonies were as religious in character as those in New England, because of the diverse religious backgrounds it was not possible for the government in any colony to agree on the establishment of any one system of state-supported schools, and it fell to each denomination to establish its own schools. The consequence of this pattern of pluralistic, parochial schooling was the absence of any basis for the establishment of a system of public schools or any basis for state support or regulation of the schools.

New York

The colony of New Netherlands was established in 1621 by the Dutch. Initially, New Netherlands was similar to the New England colonies. Schools were supported by the Dutch West India Company and were operated by the Dutch Reformed Church. After the colony was seized by the British and became the royal colony of New York (1674), state responsibility and support was withdrawn, and except for a few towns that maintained their own schools, formal schooling became a private concern. Education at the elementary level was by private tutors for the upper class, private venture schools for the middle class, and denominational schools for the lower class.

Most notable of the denominational schools were those operated by a missionary society of the Church of England, the Society for the Propagation of the Gospel in Foreign Parts (SPG). The apprenticeship system also was very strong in New York and provided the means by which some children gained an elementary education. However, since few towns established their own schools and the provision of education was principally left to the will or ability of parents to send their children to private or denominational schools, the illiteracy rate was high (Cohen, 1974).

Education at the secondary level was even more exclusively private or parochial. The private venture secondary schools were few in number and questionable in quality.

Higher education was absent for any but the few who could afford to leave the colony. It was not until 1754 that the first institution of higher education, Kings College, now Columbia University, opened in the colony.

New Jersey

As in New York, education in New Jersey was primarily private and denominational. The religious diversification was great, and each of the sects—Dutch Reformed, Puritan, Quaker, German Lutheran, Baptist, Scotch-Irish Presbyterian—established its own schools. The SPG also operated schools for the poor. A few towns, mainly those in the eastern region settled by the Puritans, established town schools. Secondary education was limited. Because of the primarily rural, agrarian economy, the private venture secondary schools found in the other middle colonies were lacking. However, the proximity to New York and Philadelphia did provide access to their secondary institutions for those who could afford it (Cohen, 1974).

It is in the realm of higher education that the colony of New Jersey most distinguished itself. Prior to the revolution it had founded more colleges than any other colony: the College of New Jersey, now Princeton University, in 1746; and Queens College, now Rutgers University, in 1766.

Pennsylvania

The Pennsylvania colony was founded in 1681 by a Quaker, William Penn. The Quakers, or Society of Friends, were very tolerant of other religions; consequently, a number of different religious groups or sects settled in Pennsylvania. William Penn advocated free public education, and the Pennsylvania Assembly enacted a law in 1683 providing that all children be instructed in reading and writing and be taught "some useful trade or skill." Yet the colony did not develop a system of free public education, primarily because of the great diversity among the settlers. A few community-supported schools were established, but as in the other middle colonies, formal education was primarily a private or denominational affair.

However, the major difference between this Middle Atlantic colony and the others was that the various denominations did, in fact, establish a fairly widespread system of schools in Pennsylvania. The SPG founded a number of charity schools, including a school for black children in Philadelphia. The Moravians also established a number of elementary schools, including the first nursery school in the colonies, and were active in efforts to Christianize and educate the Native Americans. They devised a written script for several Native-American languages and translated the Bible and other religious materials into these languages. In their pedagogical practices they were influenced by the Moravian bishop Jan Amos Comenius (Gutek, 1991).

The Quakers were the most significant denomination in terms of educational endeavors. They believed that all were created equal under God, a principle that led not only to the education of both sexes and to the free admission of the poor, but to the education of blacks and Native Americans. A school for black children was established in Philadelphia as early as 1700. Schools were also established at the secondary level by the various denominations. The Moravians established a boarding school for girls at Bethlehem, one of the first in the colonies. Since the Quakers do not have a ministry, they were not as interested in the establishment of secondary schools leading to that vocation. In their secondary schools they emphasized practical knowledge rather than the classical curriculum studied at most secondary schools at that time.

A number of private secondary schools were opened during the later colonial period, many offering such practical subjects as navigation, gauging, accounting, geometry, trigonometry, surveying, French, and Spanish. Among them was Benjamin Franklin's Philadelphia Academy, opened in 1751.

Benjamin Franklin (1706–1790)

Franklin was strongly influenced by the writings of John Locke and was a proponent of practical education. In his *Proposals Relating to the Education of Youth in Pennsylvania* he laid out the plan for a school in which English was to be the medium of instruction rather than Latin. This break with tradition was important, for in effect it proposed that vernacular English could be the language of the educated person. Franklin also proposed that students be taught "those Things that are likely to be most useful and most ornamental. Regard being had to the several Professions which they are intended" (Gillett, 1969, p. 138).

From this statement of principle Franklin went on to detail the specific subject matter:

> All should be taught "to write a fair hand" and "something of drawing"; arithmetic, accounts, geometry, and astronomy; English grammar out of Tillotson, Addison, Pope, Sidney, Trenchard, and Gordon; the writing of essays and letters; rhetoric, history, geography, and ethics; natural history and gardening; and the history of commerce and principles of mechanics. Instruction should include visits to neighboring farms, opportunities for natural observations, experiments with scientific

apparatus, and physical exercise. And the whole should be suffused with a quest for benignity of mind, which Franklin saw as the foundation of good breeding and a spirit of service, which he regarded as "the great aim and end of all learning." (Cremin, 1970, p. 376)

As time passed, Franklin's academy gave less emphasis to the practical studies and came to more closely resemble the Latin grammar school. Before he died Franklin declared the academy a failure as measured against his initial intent (Cremin, 1970).

Founding of the University of Pennsylvania.   Franklin was also instrumental in the founding in 1753 of the College of Philadelphia, now the University of Pennsylvania. Unlike its sister institutions, the College of Philadelphia was nonsectarian in origin (although it later came under Anglican control). The curriculum of the college was perhaps more progressive than at other institutions. Students were allowed a voice in the election of courses, and the curriculum emphasized not only the classics but mathematics, philosophy, and the natural and social sciences. A medical school was established in connection with the college. The college appointed as the first professor of chemistry in the colonies Dr. Benjamin Rush (Cohen, 1974), one of the signers of the Declaration of Independence, a noted physician, and the father of American psychiatry.

Delaware

Delaware, founded in 1638 as a Swedish colony, New Sweden, fell under Dutch control in 1655, then under the rule of the English with their conquest of New Netherlands. Education in Delaware was greatly influenced by Pennsylvania. Pennsylvania's general abandonment of the responsibility for the provision of education to private or denominational groups after 1683 was followed in Delaware. Although a number of elementary schools were established in the colony, the level of literacy remained low. During the colonial period, formal secondary level instruction was available on a very limited basis and no institution of higher education was established (Cohen, 1974).

Which states today have the highest concentration of denominational schools? How has this changed since colonial times?

Education in the Southern Colonies

Social and Economic Systems

The Southern colonies (Maryland, Virginia, the Carolinas, and Georgia) differed in significant ways from the New England and Middle Atlantic colonies. The Southern colonies were royal colonies administered by governors responsible directly to the king. The prevailing view was that it was the responsibility of parents to educate their children, not the government. Consequently, no legislation was enacted requiring local governments to establish or support schools. And, where religious dissatisfaction was the principal motivation for the settling of New England, the reason for settlement of the Southern colonies, where the Church of England was the established church, was primarily economic.

Rather than small farms and commerce, the economy of the Southern colonies was based on the plantation and slave system. The plantation system created distinct classes dominated by the aristocratic plantation owners. The relatively small population of the Southern colonies was widely dispersed. This factor limited the growth of any public or universal system of education.

Elementary and Secondary Education

As a result of the social and economic structure of the Southern colonies, educational opportunities were largely determined by social position. The children of the plantation owners and the wealthy commercial classes in the Tidewater cities received their education from private tutors or at private Latin grammar schools before being sent to a university. In the early colonial period it was common for the children of the plantation aristocracy to be sent to England to receive their secondary or, more often, their university education. However, this practice was on the decline by the later colonial period (Cohen, 1974; Gutek, 1991).

For the majority of the other classes the only education available was at the elementary level, informally through the apprenticeship system or formally at endowed (free) schools, charity schools, denominational schools, "old field schools," or private venture schools. Virginia was the most active of the Southern colonies in attempting to ensure the education of apprenticed children, especially orphaned children. Often this education took place in so-called "workhouse" schools.

The endowed or free schools were few in number and actually were not free except to a small number of poor boys. The charity schools were primarily those operated by the SPG. The influence of the SPG in the Southern colonies was significant and represented "the nearest approach to a public school organization found in the South before the Revolution" (Cohen, 1974, p. 129). Schools operated by other denominations were also established in the Southern colonies. In some rural areas where other schooling was not available, several small planters or farmers might build a schoolhouse on an abandoned tobacco field. These "old field schools" generally charged a fee and offered only the most basic education. Private venture elementary schools were found in some of the largest cities.

At the secondary level, except for the private venture schools, only a very small number of schools existed. And even the number of private venture schools was limited. As a result of the public neglect of education, the overall educational level of the Southern colonies was below that of most of the Northern colonies, especially those in New England.

Higher Education: The College of William and Mary

The only institution of higher education established in the South prior to the Revolutionary War was the College of William and Mary, established in 1693 to train ministers for the Church of England. Like Harvard, its sister institution in New England and the only older institution of higher education in the colonies, it also originally offered the traditional curriculum. But, by the first quarter of the eighteenth century, it began to broaden its curriculum. In fact, one educational historian states that by 1779 its curriculum was probably the most advanced in the United States (Cohen, 1974).

Figure 3.5 presents an overview of education in colonial America.

Figure 3.5: Education in Colonial America

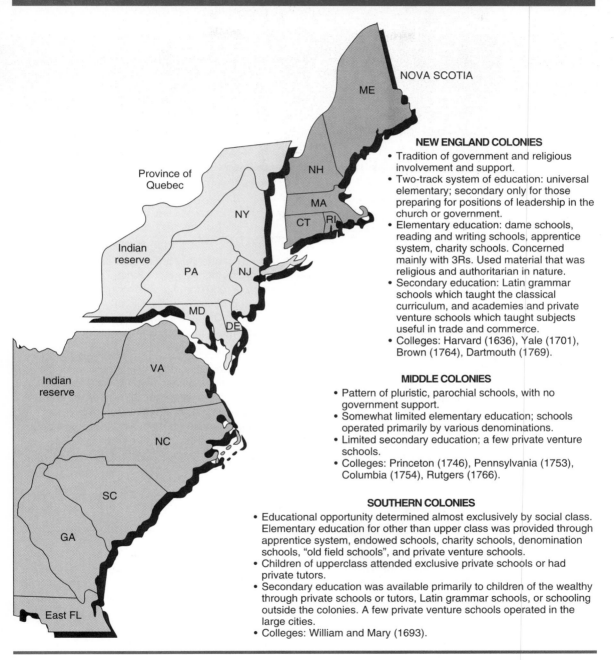

NEW ENGLAND COLONIES

- Tradition of government and religious involvement and support.
- Two-track system of education: universal elementary; secondary only for those preparing for positions of leadership in the church or government.
- Elementary education: dame schools, reading and writing schools, apprentice system, charity schools. Concerned mainly with 3Rs. Used material that was religious and authoritarian in nature.
- Secondary education: Latin grammar schools which taught the classical curriculum, and academies and private venture schools which taught subjects useful in trade and commerce.
- Colleges: Harvard (1636), Yale (1701), Brown (1764), Dartmouth (1769).

MIDDLE COLONIES

- Pattern of pluristic, parochial schools, with no government support.
- Somewhat limited elementary education; schools operated primarily by various denominations.
- Limited secondary education; a few private venture schools.
- Colleges: Princeton (1746), Pennsylvania (1753), Columbia (1754), Rutgers (1766).

SOUTHERN COLONIES

- Educational opportunity determined almost exclusively by social class. Elementary education for other than upper class was provided through apprentice system, endowed schools, charity schools, denomination schools, "old field schools", and private venture schools.
- Children of upperclass attended exclusive private schools or had private tutors.
- Secondary education was available primarily to children of the wealthy through private schools or tutors, Latin grammar schools, or schooling outside the colonies. A few private venture schools operated in the large cities.
- Colleges: William and Mary (1693).

Professional Reflections

"Teachers must realize that all students do not start at the same point or with the same agendas. Sometimes, just developing a classroom climate that is conducive to learning is a major obstacle."

Linda S. Bates, Teacher of the Year, New Mexico

"As teachers, we have a duty not only to see that our students' needs are met, but also to help them reach goals they might never dare set for themselves without our encouragement."

Marjorie West, Teacher of the Year, Colorado

Summary

The schools of the United States can trace their ancestry to those of ancient Greece and Rome. Educational idealism is based on the philosophy of Plato. The scientific method popularized in the twentieth century is rooted in the philosophy of realism espoused by Aristotle. A number of the more progressive educational positions of this century were advanced by the Roman educator Quintilian: opposition to corporal punishment, advancement of the concept of readiness learning, and support for the recognition of individual differences in learners.

The concept of universal public education that we enjoy today was a product of the Reformation. It was brought to New England by the Puritans who held the view that education was necessary for religious instruction and salvation, as well as for good citizenship. However, the earliest American educational systems were not free, were limited at the secondary levels, and, in ways that would be prohibited today, were dominated by the religious establishment. In the next chapter we will continue to trace the evolution of the American educational system from the revolution to the twentieth century.

Key Terms

Academy
Activity curriculum
Charity (pauper) school
Dame schools
Grammar school
Hornbook
Humanism
Naturalism

Object lesson
Paideia
Scholasticism
Sense realism
Seven liberal arts
Socratic method
Tabula rasa
Vernacular schools

Discussion Questions

1. How can a teacher learn more about students such as the student described in the incident at the beginning of the chapter without violating the student's or parent's right to privacy?

2. What impact did the Reformation have on the education of common people?

3. What ideas of Pestalozzi and Froebel are in practice in the schools of your community?

4. Describe the status of higher education in colonial America.

5. Contrast education in the New England, Middle Atlantic, and Southern colonies. Do any legacies of these differences remain today?

6. What was the contribution of the apprenticeship system to education in the colonies?

References

Adler, M. J. (1984). *The Paideia program: An educational syllabus.* New York: Macmillan Publishing Co.

Axtell, J. L. (Ed.). (1968). *The educational writings of John Locke.* Cambridge, England: Cambridge University Press.

Barrow, R. (1976). *Plato and education.* London: Routledge & Kegan Paul.

Beck, A. G. (1964). *Greek education 450–350 B.C.* London: Methuen & Co.

Bowen, J. (1972). *A history of Western education, 1.* London: Methuen & Co.

Carriedo, R. A., & Goren, P. D. (1979). Year round education through multitrack schools. *Policy Briefs,* No. 10. San Francisco, CA: Far West Laboratory.

Castle, E. B. (1967). *Ancient education and today.* Baltimore, MD: Penguin Books.

Cohen, S. S. (1974). *A history of colonial education, 1607–1776.* New York: John Wiley & Sons.

Cremin, L. A. (1970). *American education: The colonial experience, 1607–1783.* New York: Harper & Row.

Cubberley, E. P. (1934). *Readings in public education.* Cambridge, MA: Riverside Press.

Ford, P. L. (Ed.). (1962). *The New England primer.* New York: Columbia University Teachers College.

Gillett, M. (1966). *A history of education: Thought and practice.* Toronto: McGraw-Hill.

Gillett, M. (Ed.). (1969). *Readings in the history of education.* Toronto: McGraw-Hill.

Good, H. G., & Teller, J. D. (1969). *A history of Western education.* Toronto: Collier-Macmillan.

Gutek, G. L. (1991). *Education in the United States: An historical perspective.* Englewood Cliffs, NJ: Prentice-Hall.

Laurie, S. S. (1968). *Studies in the history of educational opinion from the Renaissance.* London: Frank Cass & Co.

Mayer, F. (1973). *A history of educational thought.* Columbus, OH: Merrill.

Meyer, A. E. (1972). *An educational history of the Western world.* New York: McGraw-Hill.

Monroe, P. (1939). *Source book of the history of education for the Greek and Roman period.* New York: Macmillan.

Rippa, S. A. (1988). *Education in a free society.* New York: Longman.

Wilkins, A. S. (1914). *Roman education.* Cambridge, England: Cambridge University Press.

Winn, C., and Jacks, M. (1967). *Aristotle.* London: Metheun & Co.

Woodward, W. H. (1906). *Studies in education during the age of the Renaissance, 1400–1600.* Cambridge, England: Cambridge University Press.

Chapter 4

American Education: From Revolution to the Twentieth Century

Those who cannot remember the past are condemned to repeat it.

Santayana

A Critical Incident in My Teaching Career . . .

> *As we sat talking in a conference, John's grandmother said to me, "You know John's mother doesn't want him anymore." We continued to talk and I suggested that John remain with me the next year in my blended 3–4 class.*
>
> *The next day John appeared and said, "My grandmother says you* want *me."*

> *I know that I make a difference; that my influence lasts more that one or two years. This knowledge dictates that I be the best model I can be for my students, every minute of every day.*
>
> Joanne E. Johnson
> Teacher of the Year, Oregon

Before the nation was 100 years old, it had already more than tripled in size and increased tenfold in population. Before the century was over, the population would double again. The educational system grew with the nation, sometimes responding to, sometimes leading social and economic changes.

As you study the history of American education from the birth of the nation to the beginning of the present century, think about the following objectives:

- Describe the impact of Thomas Jefferson and Noah Webster on American education in the early nineteenth century.
- Identify the contributions that monitorial schools, Sunday schools, infant schools, and free school societies made to the expansion of educational opportunities in the early national period.
- Compare the curriculum and purposes of the academy with that of the grammar school and the high school.
- Discuss the development of common schools in the United States and the roles that Horace Mann, Henry Barnard, Emma Willard, and Catherine Beecher played in that development.

- Outline the development of secondary education in the United States.
- Discuss the factors leading to the growth of higher education in nineteenth-century America.
- Compare the educational opportunities provided to Native Americans, Hispanic Americans, and black Americans in the nineteenth century.
- Trace the development of teacher education in the United States.

Education in the Revolutionary and Early National Period

On July 4, 1776, the 13 colonies declared their independence from England. Education was one of the casualties of the war that followed. Pulliam (1991) described the state of education during the war years:

> Illiteracy increased because rural schools had to close their doors and even the larger town Latin grammar schools were crippled. British occupation of New York caused schools to be abandoned there. New England schools continued to operate but they suffered from a lack of funds and teachers.
>
> Higher education was restricted in part because many talented teachers were Loyalists. Books were scarce since they came from England and colonial printers could not maintain their presses without outside supplies. Yale College was broken up into groups centered in different towns, while Harvard's buildings and those of the College of Rhode Island housed provincial troops. Dartmouth had neither money nor books, and classes had to be discontinued at the College of Philadelphia. The College of New Jersey and William and Mary also suffered but were not closed.
>
> British support, as in the case of the Anglican SPG, was cut off and never revived. Lack of money and the interruption of the normal economic process made the operation of educational institutions almost impossible. Teachers and scholars joined the fighting forces while school buildings were converted into barracks. Tory or Loyalist teachers were turned out of their schools. Sometimes the schools were burned and libraries scattered or destroyed. (pp. 46–47)

What would be the impact of a major war on colleges and universities today?

Articles of Confederation and the Constitution

After the war the leaders of the new nation set about the business of devising a government that would encompass the ideas for which they had fought. The first attempt at self-governance under the Articles of Confederation provided little authority to the central government and established no executive or judicial branches. When this government proved inadequate, delegates from each state met in the summer of 1787 and drafted the Constitution, which after ratification in 1789 launched the new republic. Perhaps because of the former colonists' suspicion of a strong central government, or perhaps because of the association of education with theology, neither the Articles of Confederation or the Constitution mentioned education.

Northwest Land Ordinances

Despite the fact that neither the Articles of Confederation or the U.S. Constitution mentioned education, there can be no doubt that the nation's founders recognized the importance of education to a country in which the quality of representation depended on citizens' ability to make informed choices at the ballot box. Their concern is made clear by both the legislation they enacted and congressional testimonies.

Even before the adoption of the Constitution, Congress enacted two ordinances that contained articles supportive of education. The Land Ordinance of 1785, which provided for a rectangular survey of the Northwest Territory, set aside the 16th section of land in each township for the support of education. Article Three of the Northwest Ordinance of 1787, which incorporated the Northwest Territory, proclaimed "Religion, morality, and knowledge being necessary to good government and the happiness of mankind, schools and the means of education shall be forever encouraged."

The Founding Fathers and Education

George Washington devoted a major portion of his first address to Congress to the importance of education: "There is nothing which can better deserve your patronage than the promotion of science and literature. Knowledge is in every country the surest basis of public happiness" (Madsen, 1974, p. 66).

The replies from the Senate and House expressed their agreement. From the Senate: "Literature and Science are essential to the preservation of a free constitution; the measures of government should therefore be calculated to strengthen the confidence that is due to that important truth." And from the House: "The promotion of science and literature will contribute to the security of free government" (Madsen, 1974, p. 66).

The Founding Fathers were aware that changing their form of government was only the beginning of the revolution. As Benjamin Rush, a proponent of a national university and universal education, remarked: "We have changed our form of government, but it remains to effect a revolution of our principles, opinions, and manners, so as to accommodate them to the forms of government we have adopted" (Cremin, 1982, p. 1). Rush and his compatriots worked untiringly at devising endless versions of political and educational arrangements. Although they differed on many details, there were at least four beliefs common to their discussions: (1) that the laws of education must be relative to the form of government, hence a republic needs an educational system that motivates citizens to choose public over private interest; (2) that what was needed was a truly American education purged of all vestiges of older, monarchical forms and dedicated to the creation of a cohesive and independent citizenry; (3) that education should be genuinely practical, aimed at the improvement of the human condition, with the new sciences at its heart; and (4) that American education should be exemplary and a means through which America could teach the world the glories of liberty and learning (Cremin, 1982).

Is there a place in today's educational system for a system of federally operated national universities as proposed by Dr. Rush?

Thomas Jefferson

While many of the Founding Fathers expressed their views on the importance of education, perhaps none is so well known for his educational views as Thomas Jefferson (1743–1826). Jefferson, who was strongly influenced by the philosophy of Locke, believed that government must be by the consent of the governed and that men were entitled to certain rights that could not be abridged by the government. Jefferson was one of the chief proponents of the addition of a Bill of

Rights to the Constitution. As Rippa (1988) noted, "Few statesmen in American history have so vigorously strived for an ideal (liberty); perhaps none has so consistently viewed education as the indispensable cornerstone of freedom" (p. 59).

Plan for a State Education System.   Jefferson's *Bill for the More General Diffusion of Knowledge,* introduced in the Virginia legislature in 1779, provided for the establishment of a system of public schools that would provide the masses with the basic education necessary to ensure good government, public safety, and happiness. Under the bill each county would be subdivided into parts called *hundreds;* each hundred was to provide an elementary school, supported by taxes. Attendance would be free for all white children, male and female, for three years. The curriculum would be reading, writing, arithmetic, and history. Jefferson believed that through the study of history students would learn to recognize tyranny and support democracy. The bill went on to propose that the state be divided into 20 districts and that a boarding grammar school be built at public expense in each district. Those attending would be not only those boys whose families could afford the tuition, but the brightest of the poorer students from the elementary schools whose tuition would be paid by the state. The curriculum of the grammar school was to include Latin, Greek, geography, English, grammar, and higher mathematics. Finally, upon completion of grammar school, ten of the scholarship students would receive three years' study at the College of William and Mary at state expense. The remaining scholarship students, according to Jefferson, would most likely become masters in the grammar schools.

Although this plan, viewed in today's light, appears strikingly elitist, in Jefferson's day it was considered excessively liberal and philanthropic. In fact, it was defeated by the Virginia legislature, no doubt in large part because of the unwillingness of the wealthy to pay for the education of the poor. Nonetheless, the plan is considered important because it removed the stigma of pauperism from elementary schooling (Rippa, 1988) and because it proposed a system of universal, free, public education, if only for three years.

Founding the University of Virginia.   Jefferson's interest in education also extended to establishing the University of Virginia. After leaving the presidency in 1809, he devoted much of his energies to that effort. Sometimes called "Mr. Jefferson's University," no college or university ever bore so completely the mark of one person. He created the project in every detail: he designed the buildings and landscape (even bought the bricks and picked out the trees to be used as lumber), chose the library books, designed the curriculum, and selected the students and faculty. The university opened in 1825, a year before Jefferson's death on July 4, 1826, exactly 50 years after the adoption of the immortal document he wrote—the Declaration of Independence (Rippa, 1988).

Noah Webster

It was a teacher, Noah Webster (1758–1843), who had the most influence on education in the new republic. Where the nation's founders had sought political independence from England, Webster sought cultural independence (Gutek, 1991). Like many of his contemporaries, Webster believed in the relationship between nationalistic aims and the educational process, that the primary purpose of education should be the inculcation of patriotism, and that what was needed was a truly American education rid of European influence (Madsen, 1974). These goals could best be accomplished, he believed, by creating a distinctive national language and curriculum. To this end Webster prepared a number of spelling, grammar, and reading books to replace the English texts then in use; an American version of the Bible; and what became the world-famous *American Dictionary of the English Language.*

Of his textbooks, the most important was the *Elementary Spelling Book,* published in 1783, often referred to as the "blue-back speller" because of the color of the binding. By 1875, 75 million copies of the speller had been sold (Spring, 1990), many of which were used again and again. The book included both a federal catechism with political and patriotic content, and a moral catechism whose content was related to respect for honest work and property rights, the value of money, the virtues of industry and thrift, the danger of drink, and contentment with one's economic status (Rippa, 1988; Spring, 1990). According to the noted historian Henry Steele Commager, "No other secular book had ever spread so wide, penetrated so deep, lasted so long" (cited in Rippa, 1988, p. 64).

Webster supported the concept of free schools in which all American children could learn the necessary patriotic and moral precepts. As a member of the Massachusetts legislature he worked for the establishment of a state system of education and is credited by some as initiating the common school movement, which culminated in Horace Mann's work in the 1830s (Spring, 1990). He also supported the education of women, as they would be the mothers of future citizens and the teachers of youth. However, he envisioned a rather limited and "female" education for them and counseled parents against sending their daughters to "demoralizing" boarding schools. A staunch patriot whose proposals sometimes bordered on the fanatic (e.g., the proposal that the first word a child learned should be "Washington"), Webster has been called the "Schoolmaster of the Republic."

What textbook in your elementary or secondary education had the greatest influence on you? Why?

Educational Innovations

Although Webster and others promoted the establishment of a uniquely American education, some of the major innovations in American education in the first quarter of the nineteenth century were of European origin. Among these were the monitorial school, the Sunday school, and the infant school. The period also witnessed the efforts of the free school societies and, more importantly, the rise of the academies. Each of these made a contribution, but the primary pattern of schooling that developed in the first half of the nineteenth century emerged from the common school movement, which is discussed in the next section. However, a review of these alternatives illustrates how the country, in the absence of established state systems, was searching for a suitable educational pattern for the new and developing nation (Gutek, 1991).

Monitorial Schools

Monitorial schools originated in England and were brought to America by a Quaker, Joseph Lancaster. In the Lancasterian monitorial system, one paid teacher instructed hundreds of pupils through the use of student teachers or monitors who were chosen for their academic abilities. Monitorial education was concerned with teaching only the basics of reading, writing, and arithmetic. The first monitorial school in the United States was opened in New York City in 1806 and the system spread rapidly throughout the states. One such school in Pennsylvania was designed to accommodate 450 students:

> The teacher sits at the head of the room on a raised platform. Beneath and in front of the teacher are three rows of monitors' desks placed directly in front of the pupils' desks. The pupils' desks are divided into three sections . . . and each section is in line with one of the rows of monitors' desks . . . a group of pupils would march to the front of the room and stand around the monitors' desks, where they would receive instruction from the monitors. When they finished, they would march to the rear part of their particular section and recite or receive further instruction from another monitor. While this group was marching to the rear, another group would be marching up to the front to take their places around the monitors. When finished, the pupils would march to the rear, and the group in the rear would move forward to the second part of their section to receive instruction from yet another monitor. Because each of the three sections had a group in front, one in the rear, and one in the middle working on different things, a total of nine different recitations could be carried on at one time. (Spring, 1990, pp. 56–57)

The monitorial system was attractive not only because it provided an inexpensive system for educating poor children, but because submission to the system was supposed to instill the virtues of orderliness, obedience, and industriousness. As already noted, the system gained wide appeal. Governor De Witt Clinton of New York declared the system "a blessing sent down from heaven to redeem the poor" (Spring, 1990, p. 56). However, in time the system declined. It appeared to be suited only for large cities with large numbers of students rather than small towns and rural areas. It was also criticized because it only afforded the most basic education. Yet, instead of being an educational dead end, as depicted by many educational historians, Lancasterian monitorialism may have been the model for the factorylike urban schools that emerged in the United States in the late nineteenth century (Gutek, 1991). And, the monitorial system epitomized an instructional strategy that has experienced a revival in recent years—peer tutoring.

Free School Societies: Charity Schools

What are the commonalities of the charity schools of the 1800s and public education today in relation to educating the poor?

The Lancasterian system was considered ideal for the schools operated by the various free school societies. These societies operated charity schools for the children of the poor in urban areas. In some instances, as in New York City, they received public support. Overall they were not a major factor in the history of education; nonetheless, for a period they did provide the only education some children received. For example, by 1820 the Free School Society of New York City (renamed the Public School Society in 1826 and placed under the city department of education in 1853) was teaching more than 2,000 children (Cremin, 1982).

Sunday Schools

Another educational plan introduced to America was the *Sunday school,* begun by Robert Raikes in 1780 in England. The first Sunday school in America opened in 1786 in Virginia. Its purpose was to offer the rudiments of reading and writing to children who worked during the week, primarily in the factories of the larger cities, and to provide them with an alternative to roaming the streets on Sunday. Although the Bible was commonly its textbook, originally the Sunday school was not seen as an adjunct of the church and was not intended to promote conversion. In 1815 these schools were still few in number and catered to a small number of children from lower-class homes. By 1830, however, their initial practical purpose had been superseded by religious interests and they had become primarily religious institutions operated by Sunday school societies with an evangelical mission. They grew in number, reaching out to the frontier and becoming available to children from homes of all sorts. In new communities they often paved the way for the common school (Cremin, 1982).

Infant Schools

The *infant school* was originated in England by Robert Owen, who also established one of the first infant schools in the United States at his would-be Utopia, a collective at New Harmony, Indiana. Established primarily in the eastern cities, these schools were taught by women and were designed for children aged four to seven who, because they would go to work in a factory at a very early age, probably would not receive any other schooling. The primary schools designed along this model did not survive long. However, in a few cities the primary schools had been designed as preparatory to entry into the elementary school and often became part of the town school system. In the 1850s the followers of Froebel revived the idea behind this form of infant school in the form of the kindergarten.

The Growth of the Academy

More significant in foreshadowing the coming changes in patterns of formal schooling was the growth of the academy. Although today the term *academy* brings to mind an exclusive private institution with a college-preparatory curriculum, or perhaps military training, in the late eighteenth and nineteenth centuries the term was more broadly applied. As we have seen, Franklin's academy and similar institutions were interested in providing an alternative to the traditional curriculum of the Latin grammar schools by providing a "practical" education.

The real growth of the academy occurred after the Revolutionary War and probably reached its height in the 1820s. The variations among academies were great. Some were indeed prestigious and exclusive. Others were nothing more than log cabins. Stimulated by the founding of the United States Military Academy at West Point in 1802 and the Naval Academy at Annapolis in 1848, many were established as military schools. Admission to some was open to all comers, others catered to special clients. Some were boarding schools, some were day schools. Some were teacher-owned, others were organized by groups of parents or individuals, and yet others by denominations or various societies.

Their curriculum usually depended, at least in part, on the students who were enrolled, but most offered an education beyond the three Rs. In the larger academies Latin and Greek were offered along with English grammar, geography, arithmetic, and other studies deemed "practical" or in demand. The academies are also noted for the importance placed on science in the curriculum. By the end of the early national period, some of the larger academies were also offering courses designed to provide preparation for teaching in the common schools (Cremin, 1982; Madsen, 1974).

Academies for Women

A number of the academies were established for women and are important for the role they played in extending educational opportunities to women. Some bore the name seminaries and were important in the training of female teachers, teaching being about the only profession open to women at the time. In 1821 the Troy Female Seminary in New York was opened by Emma Willard, a lifelong activist for women's rights. Opposed to the finishing school curriculum of the female boarding schools, Willard proposed a curriculum that was "solid and useful." Mount Holyoke Female Seminary, founded in 1837 by Mary Lyon, provided a demanding curriculum that included philosophy, mathematics, and science.

Catherine Beecher, the sister of Harriet Beecher Stowe, founded both the Hartford Female Seminary (1828) and the Western Institute for Women (1832). Beecher was a strong supporter of the common school and saw her task as focusing the attention of the nation on the need for a corps of female teachers to staff the common schools. She set forth a plan for a nationwide group of teacher training seminaries. Although the plan was not adopted, her efforts on behalf of

Do schools separated by gender have a place in today's world? What are the advantages and disadvantages of separate schools for women and men?

Mount Holyoke College, pictured here in an 1880s photograph, has remained a female-only institution.

the common school were a force in its acceptance, and her work on behalf of women pointed to a new American consensus concerning female roles (Cremin, 1982). Following the path forged by the female seminaries in New England, seminaries sprang up in other regions of the country, being especially popular in the South.

By the mid-nineteenth century there were more than 6,000 academies in the United States enrolling 263,000 students. The academy is considered by most educational historians as the forerunner of the American high school. Its broad range of curricular offerings responded to the demands of the growing middle class and demonstrated that there was an important place in the educational system for a secondary educational institution for non–college-bound as well as college-bound youth. The broadened curriculum combined with the more liberal entrance requirements allowed the entrance of people of various religious and social backgrounds and were major steps in the democratization of American secondary education (Rippa, 1988).

Figure 4.1 gives an overview of the nineteenth-century educational institutions we have discussed.

Figure 4.1: Nineteenth-Century Educational Innovations and Their Twentieth-Century Descendants

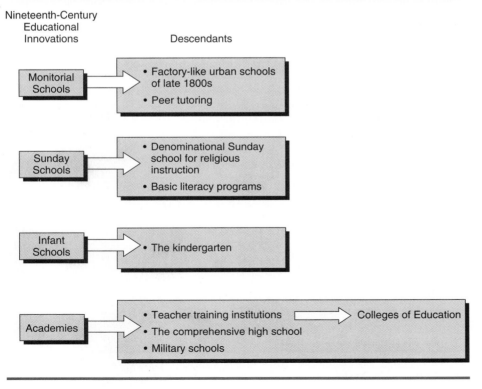

Education in the Nineteenth and Early Twentieth Centuries

The Common School Movement

The period 1830–1865 has been designated the age of the common school movement in American educational history. It is during this period that the American educational system as we know it today began to take form. Instead of sporadic state legislation and abdication of responsibility, state systems of education were established. State control as well as direct taxation for the support of the *common schools*—publicly supported schools attended *in common* by all children—became accepted practices.

Moving Forces

Demands of a Larger and More Urban Population.   The common school movement was the product of a variety of economic, social, and political factors. Between 1830 and 1860, 1,234,566 square miles of territory were added to the United States. During the same period the population exploded from 13 million to 32 million (see Table 4.1). Of this growth, 4 million came from immigration.

Not only was there an increase in immigration, but the national origins of the immigrants were different. Whereas before this era the majority of immigrants had come from Northern Europe and shared much the same cultural and religious backgrounds as the inhabitants of their new homeland, beginning in the 1830s and 1840s larger numbers came from Ireland, Germany, and Southern Europe and were often Roman Catholic. At the same time, the United States was rapidly changing from a predominantly rural nation to one that was scattered with cities. In 1820 there were only 12 cities in the then 23 states with a popula-

Table 4.1: Area and Population of the United States, 1790–1890

Year	Land Area (square miles)	Population
1790	864,746	3,929,214
1800	864,746	5,308,483
1810	1,681,824	7,239,881
1820	1,749,462	9,638,453
1830	1,749,462	12,865,020
1840	1,749,462	17,069,453
1850	2,940,042	23,191,876
1860	2,969,640	31,443,321
1870	2,969,640	39,818,449
1880	2,969,640	50,155,783
1890	2,969,640	62,947,714

Source: U.S. Bureau of the Census. (1975). *Historical statistics of the United States, colonial times to 1970* (p. 8). Washington, DC: U.S. Government Printing Office.

tion of over 10,000; by 1860 the number had increased to 101 and 8 had a population of over 100,000 (Binder, 1974).

The growth in the cities was a result of the growth in industrialization. For example, in 1807 only 15 cotton mills were in operation in the United States; by 1831 there were 801 mills employing 70,000 workers (Rippa, 1988). These changing economic and social patterns gave rise to an increasing urban population, which included concentrations of children who needed schooling, a more industrialized economy that required a trained workforce, and in certain areas a Roman Catholic population that challenged Protestant domination.

Demands of the Working Class.   In this context the common schools were seen by the working class, who could not afford to educate their children at private expense, as avenues for upward social and economic mobility. Critical of pauper or charity schools, the newly emerging workingmen's organizations were open in their support of tax-supported common schools. The common schools were seen as providing the education necessary for protection against the tyranny of the upper class and necessary for equal participation in a democratic form of government. The leaders of business and industry also supported common schools. They saw them as a means of ensuring a supply of literate and trained workers.

Social Control.   The dominant English-speaking, upper-class Protestants saw a different merit in the common schools. This group viewed the common schools as agencies of social control over the lower socioeconomic classes. According to Gutek (1991), social control in this context meant

> imposing by institutionalized education the language, beliefs, and values of the dominant group on outsiders, especially on the non-English speaking immigrants. Common schools were expected to create such conformity in American life by imposing the language and ideological outlook of the dominant group. For example, by using English as the medium of instruction, the common schools were expected to create an English-speaking citizenry; by cultivating a general value orientation based on Protestant Christianity, the schools were expected to create a general American ethic. (pp. 87–88)

Most social groups also saw the common schools as a means of controlling crime and social unrest. Knowledge was seen as "the great remedy for intemperance: for in proportion as we elevate men in the scale of existence . . . so do we reclaim them from all temptation of degrading vice and ruinous crimes" (Binder, 1974, p. 32).

Needs of the Frontier.   Interest in the establishment of common schools was not limited to the industrialized regions of the East. As the frontier moved steadily westward, the one-room schoolhouse, often the only public building in a community, became the symbol of civilization and the center of efforts to keep literacy, citizenship, and civilization alive in the wilderness (Gutek, 1991).

Extended Suffrage.   On the political front, the age of the common school coincided with the age of the common man. In the early years of the republic the right to vote in many states was limited to those who owned property. Gradually this began to change and many states, especially those on the frontier, extended suffrage to all white males. In 1828 the first "common man" was elected president—Andrew Jackson. The result of the extension of suffrage was not only increased office-holding by the common man, but an increased pressure for direct taxation to support common schools.

Education Journals and Organizations.   The movement for common schools began in the Northeast. To some extent the public had been introduced to the basic ideas of the common school movement through the writings of individuals like Webster and Rush, and through the arguments for social and moral reform made by the leaders of the charity school movement and the Lancasterian monitorial system. However, perhaps the two most important mechanisms for spreading the ideology of the common school were educational periodicals and educational organizations.

Do you subscribe to any educational journals? Which do you read regularly?

Between 1825 and 1850 more than 60 educational journals came into existence (Spring, 1990). Among the most important were the Massachusetts *Common School Journal,* founded and edited by Horace Mann; the *Connecticut Common School,* edited for several years by Henry Barnard; and the prestigious *American Journal of Education,* also edited from 1855 to 1881 by Henry Barnard. Among their other material, these journals printed part or all of several reports (e.g., the Cousin Report and the Stowe Report) describing and praising the Pestalozzian reforms of Prussian education (Rippa, 1988).

Of the educational organizations, the most noteworthy were the American Institute of Instruction, the Western Literary Institute and College of Professional Teachers, and on a more national scale, the American Lyceum. By 1839 there were 4,000–5,000 local lyceums in the United States actively presenting programs, mutual instruction, and informative lectures in favor of school reforms. Cremin (1982) credits the educational organizations with spearheading the common school movement, "articulating its ideals, publicizing its goals, and instructing one another in its political techniques; indeed, in the absence of a national ministry of education, it was their articulating, publicizing, and mutual instruction in politics that accounted for the spread of public education across the country" (p. 176).

Horace Mann

If any one person were to be given the title "Father of American Education," that person would be Horace Mann (1796–1859). Elected to the Massachusetts legislature in 1827, Mann, a brilliant orator, soon became the spokesperson for the common school movement. He led a campaign to organize the schools in Massachusetts into a state system and to establish a state board of education.

Upon the creation of the state board of education in 1837 Mann gave up his political career and a chance at the governorship to become the board's first secretary and the chief state school officer. He served in this position for 12 years and used it as a platform for proclaiming the ideology of the common school movement, as well as other educational ideals. In addition to his numerous lectures, editorships, and other writings, each year Mann wrote a report to the legislature reciting current educational practice and conditions and making recommendations for improvement. These reports were distributed in other states and abroad, and were significant in influencing educational legislation and practice throughout the country.

In his own state, Mann campaigned vigorously to increase public support for education and public awareness of the problems facing education in the form of dilapidated, unsanitary facilities and substandard materials, as well as the shortcomings of the local school committees. Mann was also critical of the status of the teaching profession and the training of teachers. As a result of his efforts, state appropriations to education were doubled, 50 new secondary schools were built, textbooks and equipment were improved, and teachers' salaries in Massachusetts were raised more than 50%. Mann also fought for the professional training of teachers and established three normal schools (teacher training institutions), the first such schools in America. The first of these normal schools was established in 1839 at Lexington, Massachusetts.

In his Tenth Annual Report (1846) Mann asserted that education was the right of every child and that it was the state's responsibility to ensure that every child was provided an education. Although Mann himself did not promote compulsory attendance but rather *regular* attendance, this report was instrumental in the adoption by the Massachusetts legislature of the nation's first compulsory attendance law in 1852.

Like several prominent educators of his time, Mann had visited the Prussian schools and observed the Pestalozzian methods. His Seventh Report (1843) gave a positive account of his observations. A humanitarian in all things (treatment of the mentally ill, abolition of slavery, etc.), he was particularly impressed with the love and rapport shared by the teachers and students involved in these schools. He also shared Pestalozzi's and Catherine Beecher's belief that women were the better teachers for the common schools.

The view Mann expounded on the role of the common school in promoting social harmony and ensuring the republic would be guided by an intelligent, moral citizenry was not original or unique. But at a time when the common school movement was spreading across the nation, when it came to defining its basic principles and articles of faith, he was unquestionably the chief spokesperson (Binder, 1974). The measure of his respect by contemporaries is reflected in a review of one of his annual reports by a Scottish newspaper not given to praising things American, the *Edinburgh Review:* "The volume is, indeed, a noble monument of civilized people; and, if America were sunk beneath the waves, would remain the fairest picture on record of that ideal commonwealth" (cited in Cremin, 1982, p. 142).

Henry Barnard

The other major leader of the common school movement was Henry Barnard (1811–1900). Like Mann he served in the state (Connecticut) legislature, worked to establish a state board of education, and then became the board's first secretary (1838–1842). He then served in a similar capacity in Rhode Island (1845–1849), as chancellor of the University of Wisconsin, president of St. John's College, and the first U.S. commissioner of education.

The American Journal of Education and Teachers' Institutes. Much of Barnard's influence on educational theory and practice came through his numerous lectures and writings, and more importantly, through his editorship of the *American Journal of Education,* the only educational journal of national significance at the time. The journal served not only to popularize education but to keep teachers informed of educational innovations and ideas from both home and abroad. Barnard is also credited with initiating the *teachers' institute* movement. These were meetings, lasting for a few days to several weeks, at which teachers met to be inspired by noted educators, instructed in new techniques, and informed of the most modern material (Binder, 1974).

Barnard's greatest successes lay in his democratic philosophy, "schools good enough for the best and cheap enough for the poorest," and as a disseminator of information about better schools. He is sometimes called the "Father of American School Administration" (Pulliam, 1991).

State Support

The idea of having universal common schools was one thing, but paying for them through direct taxation of the general public was another. Until the 1820s or 1830s, the only really free education was that provided by the charity schools, or in certain other schools if the parents were willing to declare themselves paupers. Often local or county taxes levied on specific activities, for example liquor licenses or marriage fees, provided partial support for the schools, but the remainder of the expenses were charged to the parents in the form of a *rate bill.* The rate bill was, in effect, a tuition fee based on the number of children. Even though the fee might be small, poor parents often could not afford it, so their children either did not attend school or took turns attending.

In some states, legislation provided for the establishment of school districts and allowed the districts to levy a school tax if the majority of the voters agreed. However, if the tax proceeds were insufficient to support the schools, the rate bill was used.

State support for the schools was very limited. One emphasis of the common school movement was greater state support. Beginning in the first quarter of the nineteenth century several states began to provide aid for public schools from either permanent school funds (derived largely from the sale of public lands), direct taxation, or appropriations from the general fund. Conditions were usually placed on the receipt of such funds; for example, that local support must equal or exceed state support or that the schools must be kept open a minimum length of time.

By 1865 systems of common schools had been established throughout the northern, midwestern, and western states, and more than 50% of the nation's children were enrolled in public schools. The lowest enrollments were in the South, where the common school movement had made little progress.

As the common school movement progressed, the pressure to make these schools completely tax supported increased. Massachusetts was the first state to do away with the rate bill, in 1827. Pennsylvania's Free School Act of 1834 was a model for eliminating the pauper school concept. Although other states soon followed these examples and by constitutional or legislative enactment adopted

How does the practice of some districts of charging fees for participation in extracurricular activities affect the participation of the children of the poor?

the concept of public support for public schools open to all children, it was not until 1871 that the last state (New Jersey) abolished the rate bill, making the schools truly free.

State Control

Creation of State Superintendents of Education. As is usually the case, increased support is accompanied by increased efforts to control. The effort to establish some control or supervision was marked by the creation of an office of state superintendent, or commissioner of education and a state board of education. In 1812 New York became the first state to appoint a state superintendent, Gideon Hawley. His tenure in office was filled with such controversy that in 1821 he was removed from office and the position was abolished and not recreated until 1854. Nonetheless, by the outbreak of the Civil War, 28 of the 34 states had established state boards of education and chief state school officers. By and large these officers and boards were vested with more supervisory power than real control. Initially their major responsibilities were involved with the distribution of the permanent school funds and the organization of a state system of common schools.

Creation of Local School Districts and Superintendents. The creation of a state system of common schools paralleled the establishment of school districts and the establishment of local and county superintendents. The New England states instituted the district system in the early years of the nineteenth century and it spread westward during the next three decades. Local supervision was provided by the district or county superintendent, whose primary duty was to supervise instruction. The development of the position of county superintendent of schools helped bring about some degree of standardization and uniformity in areas that had numerous small, rural school districts (Gutek, 1991). The evolution of the office of city school superintendent quickly followed that of the district and county office. The first city superintendent was appointed in Buffalo in 1837, and was quickly followed in Louisville, St. Louis, Providence, Springfield, Cleveland, Rochester, and New Orleans. One of the major responsibilities of the early city superintendents was to develop a uniform course of study. This development was concurrent with the establishment of graded schools (Spring, 1990).

Organization and Curriculum

The common schools varied in terms of size, organization, and curriculum, depending on their location. In rural areas the one- or two-room school was dominant; progress was not marked by movement from one grade to another, but by completing one text and beginning another. In larger cities and towns, grading had been introduced. On the frontier, where there remained some distrust for too much education, the curriculum was often limited to the three Rs; in larger cities it tended to be more broad. A great variety of textbooks appeared and their authors began to practice the more modern educational teachings. For example, the extremely popular *McGuffey Readers* continued to teach "the lessons of morality and patriotism, but the stern, direct preachments of earlier schoolbooks were replaced or supplemented by stories and essays designed to appeal to youthful

What would be the advantages of attending a one- or two-room rural school over a large, urban school? The disadvantages?

The one-room schoolhouse was the symbol of free, public education in rural and frontier America.

interest" (Cremin, 1982, p. 96). Rote learning, drill, and practice did not disappear from the classroom, but a more progressive approach that placed a value on the sensitivities and individuality of the child was making some inroads.

Secondary School Movement

Public *secondary schools* offering education beyond the elementary school did not become a firmly established part of the American educational scene until the last quarter of the nineteenth century. However, the beginnings of the movement occurred well before the Civil War. Perhaps not unexpectedly, the lead was taken by those states that had been first to establish systems of common schools. Boston inaugurated the high school movement in 1821 with the opening of the English Classical School, renamed the Boston English High School in 1824. Then, as now, the school was open to boys only. In calling for community support the Boston school committee made it clear that they wished to provide an alternative to the Latin grammar school and to provide locally "an education that shall fit him (the child) for active life, and shall serve as a foundation for eminence in his profession, whether Mercantile or Mechanical" (Binder, 1974, p. 107). Such an education, as we have seen, could otherwise be obtained only by sending the child to a private academy.

Ten years later, in 1831, the first American *comprehensive* (and coeducational) *high school*, offering both English and classical courses of study, was opened in Lowell, Massachusetts. In 1838 Philadelphia opened a coeducational high school with three tracks: a four-year classical curriculum, a four-year modern language curriculum, and a two-year English curriculum.

Slow Beginnings

In the years before the Civil War the high school movement expanded slowly. By 1860 there were only 300 high schools in the nation compared to more than 6,000 academies. Of the 300, more than 100 were located in Massachusetts. Massachusetts was unique in requiring communities of 50 families or more to provide secondary level education (Binder, 1974).

The slow growth of the high school can be partially explained by the fact that, unlike the common school, the high school was not being overwhelmingly demanded by the masses. It appeared to be more a reformer's response to urbanization and industrialization. Middle or upper class reformers, adopting the philosophy and rhetoric of the common school advocates, viewed their efforts as democratizing secondary education, providing a means of maintaining social values, and promoting economic progress. As a result, prior to the Civil War most high schools were located in urban areas; it was there that a sufficient number of students and tax support were most often found.

The Movement Grows as Industry and the Economy Grow

The years after the Civil War were marked by rapid industrial growth and technological change. These trends intensified the demand for skilled workers. A great tide of immigration brought people who needed not only skills but knowledge of American values and ideals. The mood of the masses changed, and a high school education was increasingly seen as necessary to the full realization of one's social and economic goals. Economic growth also created a larger tax base that could be used to support an expanded educational system. Consequently, the number of public high schools increased. During the 1880s the number of high schools surpassed the number of academies, and by 1890 there were 2,526 public high schools enrolling 202,063 students, compared to the 1,632 private academies with their 94,391 students (Gutek, 1991).

Herbert Spencer and the "Practical Curriculum"

The design of the curriculum of the high school was influenced by the English philosopher Herbert Spencer (1820–1903) who applied many of Darwin's concepts of evolution and the idea of the "survival of the fittest" to education. In his book *Education,* Spencer poses and answers the question, "What knowledge is of most worth?" He concluded that it was not the "ornamental" education predominant in English schools of the time, which emphasized a classical education. Rather, he maintained, it is one that is practical and emphasizes the study of science. The aim of education should be "to prepare us for complete living."

If you were designing a curriculum for "complete living" for today, what would be its essential features?

This can best be done by a curriculum that prepares the individual first for direct self-preservation (health), next for indirect self-preservation (earning a living), then parenthood, followed by citizenship, and last, use of leisure time. By placing the useful or practical first, and the arts last, such a curriculum was a reversal of the traditional curriculum of the grammar school.

Tax Support, Compulsory Attendance, and the Decline of Illiteracy

The public secondary school movement was given further impetus by the finding of the Michigan Supreme Court in the famous *Kalamazoo* case (1874). By its ruling that the legislature could tax for the support of both elementary and secondary schools the court provided the precedent for public support of secondary education. By the end of the century the publicly supported high school had replaced the academy in most communities and had become an established part of the common school system in every state.

The *Kalamazoo* decision having quashed the argument that public funds could not be used for secondary education, compulsory attendance laws soon followed. The passage of child labor laws and the increasing demand for an educated workforce were also instrumental in driving the adoption of compulsory attendance laws. By 1918 all states had enacted laws requiring full-time attendance until the child reached a certain age or completed a certain grade. One result of this increase in school attendance was the declining illiteracy rate from 20% of all persons over 10 years of age in 1870 to 7.7% in 1910 (Graham, 1974).

Illiteracy rates varied by segment of the population. As a result of the pre–Civil War prohibition on teaching blacks in most southern states and inadequate education after the war, blacks had the highest illiteracy rate, 30.4% in 1910. The illiteracy rate was also high among the older population, which had not been the beneficiary of universal, compulsory education. Whites who were the children of a foreign-born parent had the lowest illiteracy rate, 1.1%. Literacy rates also varied by region. The South, which not only had the most blacks but also had been the slowest in developing systems of common schools, had the highest illiteracy rate (Graham, 1974).

The Committee of Ten

As previously noted, in its origins the high school had been viewed as a provider of a more practical education. The need to assimilate the children of the new immigrants, and the more technical demands of industry, placed additional pressures on the schools to include a curriculum that could be immediately useful and that included vocational training (Graham, 1974). However, there were educators who did not share this esteem for the "practical curriculum." In 1892, in an effort to standardize the curriculum, the National Education Association established the Committee of Ten. The committee was chaired by Charles Eliot, the president of Harvard University, and was largely composed of representatives of higher education. The two major recommendations of the committee were (1) early introduction to the basic subjects, and (2) uniform subject matter and instruction for both college-bound and terminal students. While four curricula were recommended (classical, Latin-scientific, modern language, and English), the entire curriculum was dominated by college-preparatory courses. Using the psychology of mental discipline as a theoretical rationale, the Committee claimed that the recommended subjects would be used profitably by both college-bound and terminal students because they trained the powers of observation, memory, expression, and reasoning (Gutek, 1991).

The Seven Cardinal Principles of Secondary Education
The view of the Committee of Ten was immediately challenged by many educators; within 25 years there was little support for its position. In 1918 the National Education Association appointed another committee, the Commission on the Reorganization of Secondary Education, to review the curriculum and organization of secondary education in light of the many changes that had swept American society. The commission issued its seven *Cardinal Principles of Secondary Education*, which identified what should be the objectives of the high school curriculum:

- health

- command of fundamental processes

- worthy home membership

- vocational preparation

- citizenship

- worthwhile use of leisure time

- ethical character

As compared to the recommendations of the Committee of Ten, only one of these principles, command of fundamental processes, was concerned with college preparation. Instead, the commission viewed the high school as a much more comprehensive institution in terms of both integration of the various ethnic, religious, and socioeconomic groups, and accommodation of the various educational goals of students. Figure 4.2 shows the development of secondary schools in the United States.

Patterns of Curricular Organization
By the mid-1920s the essential shape of the American comprehensive high school was apparent. It was an institution that offered a range of curricula to students of differing abilities and interests. Four basic patterns of curricular organization were in evidence: (1) the college preparatory program, which included courses in English language and literature, foreign languages, mathematics, the natural and physical sciences, and history and social sciences; (2) the commercial or business program, which offered courses in bookkeeping, shorthand, and typing; (3) the industrial, vocational, home economics, and agricultural programs; and (4) a modified academic program for students who planned to terminate their formal education upon high school completion. The typical high school program was four years and was attended by students aged 14 to 18. Exceptions were the six-year combined junior-senior high schools (Gutek, 1991).

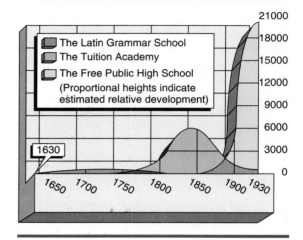

Figure 4.2: The Development of Secondary Schools in the United States, 1630–1930

The Latin Grammar School
The Tuition Academy
The Free Public High School
(Proportional heights indicate estimated relative development)

1630

Source: Cubberley, E. P. (1948). *The history of education* (p. 699). Cambridge, MA: Riverside Press.

The Junior High School

The two-year and three-year *junior high schools* offering grades six and seven, or six, seven, and eight, which also began to appear in some urban districts, were an outgrowth of the Committee of Ten's recommendation that academic work begin earlier and that elementary schooling be reduced from eight to six years. Their growth was also encouraged by the work of G. Stanley Hall, who wrote the first book on adolescent development and emphasized the developmental differences between childhood and preadolescence, which called for a reorganization of the eight–four system. Others felt greater opportunity for industrial and commercial training should be given before high school. As a result of these and other proposals, in 1909 junior high schools were established in Columbus, Ohio, and Berkeley, California. Other cities soon followed, and the junior high school became commonplace in the United States after 1930 (Pulliam, 1991).

Higher Education

As was discussed in the preceding chapter, nine colleges were founded during the colonial period. In the period after the Revolution and before the Civil War, the number increased dramatically. Although a large number did not survive, the net result was a twentyfold increase in the number of colleges that did survive, compared to a tenfold increase in the population during this period (Madsen, 1974). This increase was a result of both people moving westward who wanted colleges close at hand, and many denominations choosing to establish their own colleges rather than have their members educated at colleges

Did you attend a junior high school? If so, what educational experiences do you recall that reinforce the positive value of the junior high school over other organizational plans?

operated by other denominations. Thus, of the colleges founded before 1860, less than 10% were state institutions.

By and large the colleges were very small. For example, it was not until after the Civil War that Harvard had a graduating class of 100. During the late colonial and early national periods the curriculum of the colleges became more "liberal," but it retained its heavy classical overlay and its emphasis on religion.

In 1816 the New Hampshire legislature, dominated by the more liberal Jeffersonian Republicans and concerned by what appeared to be the antiliberal sentiments of the board of trustees, enacted legislation to convert Dartmouth College from a private to a state institution. In the *Dartmouth College* case (Trustees of Dartmouth College, 1819), the U.S. Supreme Court upheld the original contract from the king of England, which had given private status to the college. The effect of the case was not only to establish the principle that the state could not impair contracts, but to provide a secure foundation for the system of private colleges we have today.

Patterned after the English universities of Oxford and Cambridge, American colleges offered professional studies in theology, medicine, and eventually in law. Lecture and recitation remained the most common modes of instruction. Discipline was strict and the entire atmosphere authoritarian. As a result, student riots sometimes occurred: in 1807 over half the student body of Princeton was suspended; in 1830 Yale experienced the "bread and butter rebellion"; and on one occasion over half the senior class at Harvard was expelled. Intercollegiate athletics being unheard of, literary and debating societies provided some outlet for student enthusiasm (Madsen, 1974).

Growth of Public Institutions

The first state institutions of higher education were established in the South: the University of Georgia in 1785, the University of North Carolina in 1789, the University of Tennessee in 1794, and the University of South Carolina in 1801. In the second quarter of the nineteenth century the same nationalistic, democratic spirit that gave rise to the common school movement also produced an increase in public institutions of higher education. These appeared largely in the Midwest: Indiana University in 1820, the University of Michigan in 1837, and the University of Wisconsin in 1848.

State institutions, unlike denominational institutions, were publicly supported and controlled. In contrast to an emphasis on classical languages and philosophy, their curriculum tended to emphasize the sciences and modern languages. The growth of public institutions was also enhanced by the federal land-grant policy, which granted two townships of land to each state when it entered the union for the support of institutions of higher education.

The Morrill Acts and the Establishment of
Land-Grant Institutions

By the mid-nineteenth century there was growing recognition among farmers and laborers that equality of opportunity required an education that would contribute to an improved economic condition. Finding the majority of the existing colleges unresponsive and irrelevant to their needs, they urged the establishment of a new institution, the industrial college. In response, the first Morrill Act was passed by Congress and signed by President Lincoln in 1862. The act granted 30,000 acres of land to each state for each senator and representative it had in Congress based on the 1860 census. The income from the land was to be used to support at least one college that would "teach such branches of learning as are related to agriculture and mechanical arts, . . . in order to promote the liberal and practical education of the industrial classes in the several pursuits and professions of life."

The Second Morrill Act of 1890 provided for direct annual grants of $15,000 (increasing annually to $25,000) to each state to support land-grant colleges. The bill also provided that no grant would be given to any state that denied admission to its land-grant colleges because of race without providing "separate but equal" institutions.

As a result of the Morrill Acts, 65 new land-grant colleges were established. Among the first of the new institutions of higher education were the universities of Maine (1865), Illinois and West Virginia (1867), California (1868), Purdue and Nebraska (1869), Ohio State (1870), and Arkansas and Texas A & M (1871). Seventeen states, mostly in the South, also established separate land-grant colleges for blacks under the provisions of the Second Morrill Act. The Morrill Acts provided both the foundation for a new type of curriculum at government expense and powerful incentives for greatly expanded state systems of higher education (Rippa, 1988).

Higher Education for Women

Significant developments were also being made in the higher education of women during this period. As discussed earlier, a number of women's seminaries or colleges had been opened prior to the Civil War. A few coeducational colleges also existed before the Civil War (e.g., Oberlin, 1833; Antioch, 1853; and the State University of Iowa, 1858). However, it was not until after the Civil War that women's higher education really began to flourish. Several women's colleges (e.g., Vassar, 1865; Wellesley, 1875; Smith, 1875; Radcliffe, 1879; and Bryn Mawr, 1880) were established that offered programs comparable to those found in the colleges for men. In addition, an increasing number of formerly all-male institutions began admitting women, albeit selectively. By 1880 about half the colleges and universities admitted women (Pulliam, 1991). However, while a wide curriculum was open to them, teaching remained the most accessible and socially acceptable option.

The Emergence of the Modern University

In the last decades of the nineteenth century and the first decades of the twentieth century, two other institutions made their appearance on the higher educational scene in America: the university and the *junior college*. In contrast to the small, single-purpose, largely undergraduate colleges, the emerging universities were large and multipurpose. Influenced by the German universities where many of them had studied, American professors and college presidents worked to establish graduate programs and emphasize research. By the end of the nineteenth century, the American university had come to look much as we know it today with an undergraduate college of liberal arts and sciences, a graduate college, and various professional colleges.

Founding of Junior Colleges

The initiative for the establishment of junior colleges came in the late nineteenth century from a number of university presidents who viewed the first two years of higher education as more appropriate to secondary education. They wanted to free their faculty from what they considered secondary education responsibilities so that they could devote themselves more to research and graduate education. In 1901 the first public junior college was established, the Joliet (Illinois) Junior College. Although initially established to offer courses that would transfer to four-year institutions, it soon began to offer terminal and vocational programs as well (Gutek, 1991). In 1907 California passed a law permitting school boards to offer high school graduates courses similar to those required during the first two years of college (Rippa, 1988). By the early 1920s the concept of the junior college was well established. During the late 1920s, encouraged by the Smith-Hughes Act, which provided federal aid to vocational education, junior colleges developed more extensive vocational and technical education programs. In subsequent decades they not only expanded rapidly, but as their goal was expanded to include serving the broad-based needs of the community, they became transformed into today's community colleges (Gutek, 1991).

Table 4.2 lists some of the individuals we have been discussing who had an important effect on American education and the development of the elementary, secondary, and university school systems.

Have you ever attended a junior or community college? Would you support the movement toward having all lower division education take place at these institutions?

Education of Minorities

The progress of education in the United States has not been uniform across all regions, socioeconomic classes, or races. To many the schoolhouse door was closed and the promise of equal educational opportunity an unrealized dream. Native Americans, Hispanic Americans, and black Americans in particular have had to struggle to realize the promise of an equal education.

Education of Native Americans

The formal education of Native Americans was initiated by missionaries who equated education with Christianity and the virtues of civilized life. The Society for the Propagation of the Gospel and the Moravians were among the more active of the missionary groups. Just as education for the white colonists was primarily for the purpose of training for the ministry, so too it was hoped that education would equip Native Americans to become missionaries to their people. However, the efforts of missionary or philanthropic groups was limited, and the town and grammar schools enrolled few Native Americans. Efforts to provide any higher education were even more limited. In 1653 a college was founded at Harvard to instruct Native American students in the same classical education received by whites. Dartmouth College was originally established for the education of Native Americans, but was soon dominated by the children of the white colonists.

Table 4.2: They Made It Happen: Important Figures in Eighteenth- and Nineteenth-Century American Education History

Benjamin Franklin (1706–1790)	Established Franklin Academy in 1751 with a practical curriculum as an alternative to the Latin grammar school. Proposed first state school system.
Thomas Jefferson (1743–1826)	Proposed state system of free and universal elementary education and selected publicly supported secondary and higher education. Founded the University of Virginia (1825).
Noah Webster (1758–1843)	"Schoolmaster of the Republic." Sought to create a distinctive national language. Published a number of widely used spelling, grammar, and reading books, as well as a dictionary.
Joseph Lancaster (1778–1838)	Originated monitorial system of mass instruction in England in 1798; first monitorial school in U.S. in 1806. Concept widely promoted by Lancaster in U.S.
Robert Raikes (1735–1811)	Popularized Sunday schools in England to offer basic reading and writing to children who worked during the week. Practice brought to U.S. in late eighteenth century.
Robert Owen (1771–1858)	Originated infant schools in England for children of poor factory workers. Transplanted to the United States, infant schools evolved into primary schools. Founded community of New Harmony, Indiana.
Emma Willard (1787–1870)	Women's rights activist. Founded Troy Female Seminary in 1821, first U.S. institution of higher education for women, to train female teachers in the subject areas and pedagogy.
Mary Lyon (1797–1849)	Founded Mount Holyoke Female Seminary in 1837, the first permanent women's college in the U.S.
Catherine Beecher (1800–1878)	Founded Hartford Female Seminary. Supporter of common school movement. Advocated nationwide system of teacher training seminaries.
Horace Mann (1796–1859)	"Father of American Education." State superintendent of education in Massachusetts. Spokesperson for common school movement. Established first normal schools in U.S.
Henry Barnard (1811–1900)	Leader of common school movement. First U.S. commissioner of education. Editor of *American Journal of Education.* Initiated teachers' institutes.
Charles Eliot (1834–1926)	President of Harvard University (1869–1909). Chaired the Committee of Ten (1892), which recommended a classical curriculum for the secondary schools.

The initial response to the formal, traditional education offered by the colonists was distrust and rejection. Benjamin Franklin quoted one Native-American leader as saying:

> Several of our young people were formerly brought up at the colleges of the Northern Provinces; they were instructed in all your Sciences; but, when they came back to us, they were bad Runners, ignorant of every means of living in the Woods, unable to bear either Cold or Hunger, knew neither how to build a Cabin, take a Deer, or kill an Enemy, spoke our Language imperfectly, were therefore neither fit for Hunters, Warriors, nor Counsellors; they were totally good for nothing. (cited in Kidwell & Swift, 1976, p. 335)

Treaties and Mission Schools.   During the first century of the new republic much of the education of the Native Americans came about as a result of federal legislation or negotiated treaties. According to the terms of the treaties, 389 of which were signed with various tribes between 1778 and 1871, in return for relinquishing their land, the Native Americans were given money payments, guarantees of the integrity of the land they retained, and promises of educational services (Kidwell & Swift, 1976). The predominant means by which the federal government met its obligation to provide educational services was through support of mission schools operated on the reservation. These schools concentrated on the three Rs, some vocational and agricultural training, and, of course, religion. Instruction was given in the native tongue, as this was viewed as the best way to lead the Native Americans to conversion. In 1917 this arrangement, which in effect constituted government support of sectarian education, ended (Butts, 1978).

Boarding Schools.   The decline of the mission schools was accompanied by the establishment of three other forms of Native American education: the off-reservation boarding school, the reservation day school, and public schools. The off-reservation boarding school was a product of the *assimilation* approach that became popular in the post–Civil War decades. This approach advocated the incorporation of Native Americans into the predominant white culture, and was established on the belief that the most lasting and efficient way this assimilation could take place was to remove children from their tribal setting and subject them, in a strict disciplinary setting, to an infusion of American language and customs.

The first major boarding school was established in 1879 at Carlisle, Pennsylvania, by General Richard Pratt. Vocational and industrial training was emphasized at this and other off-reservation boarding schools. By the turn of the century, 25 off-reservation boarding schools had been established (Szasz, 1977). However, they were subject to much criticism. The physical and living conditions were often inadequate. The dropout rate was high. Students more often returned to the reservation rather than enter white society, and upon return to the reservation found they were either unable to apply the training they had received, or that it was irrelevant.

Reservation Day Schools and Public Schools.   The reservation day schools offered several advantages over the off-reservation boarding school; not only were they less expensive, they were more acceptable to parents. Consequently, day schools increased in number after the turn of the twentieth century.

Although Native Americans in the eastern United States who were not under the jurisdiction of the federal government had already been attending off-reservation public schools, a newer phenomenon was the public school located on the reservation. These schools initially had been built to accommodate the white people who rented land on some reservations. The on-reservation public schools tended to encourage not only assimilation, but learning. As one Indian agent wrote, "Indian children progress much faster when thrown in contact with white children than they do when they are all kept together with whites excluded" (Szasz, 1977, p. 11).

Class at Carlisle Indian boarding school, circa 1900.

The Meriam Report.   In the 1920s the appalling living conditions and reprehensible treatment of Native Americans were brought to public view by a number of reformers determined to improve their plight. In response the Bureau of Indian Affairs (BIA) commissioned the Brookings Institution for an independent study of Native American life in the United States. The report, called the Meriam Report, documented the intolerable conditions of Native American life and pointed out that much of their poverty was caused by their loss of land. It also criticized the BIA educational program, exposing the inadequate industrial training, overcrowded dormitories, inadequate diet, and physical punishment in the boarding schools. The report encouraged the construction of day schools that could also serve as community centers. The report accused the reservation system of creating isolation and concluded that the best way to improve the living standards of Native Americans was to educate them so they could be assimilated into white society (Kidwell & Swift, 1976).

The Meriam Report marked the beginning of a change in BIA policy. After 1928, BIA appropriations for education increased dramatically, efforts were made to deal with conditions in government schools, and curriculum reform was initiated. Soon a major share of the BIA's budget was allocated to education, with the goal of assimilating Native Americans into the mainstream society.

How successful have been efforts to assimilate Native Americans into mainstream society? Should these efforts continue?

Education of Hispanics

The story of the involvement of the United States in the education of Hispanics is largely to be told in relation to the Spanish-speaking peoples of the southwestern United States and begins with the acquisition of this territory from Mexico in 1848 at the end of the Mexican-American War. For the Mexicans who chose to remain in the territory after the U.S. takeover, or for those who fled across the border in the years that followed, life became marked by discrimination, prejudice, and segregation. Although segregation was not imposed by law (*de jure*) as it was for blacks in the South, it nonetheless existed by practice (*de facto*): separate schools and/or classes, poorer facilities, fewer well-trained teachers, and smaller budgets. English was used for instruction, whether understood or not, and the use of Spanish in the classroom or playground was often forbidden (Butts, 1978).

Any improvement in the educational condition of Mexican-American children was hampered by the attitudes of many of their parents who failed to see the value of an education that was aimed at undermining their traditional beliefs and culture. It was also hampered by the articulated views of the larger society, including many educators, that Mexican-Americans were mentally inferior. Many Mexican-American children also suffered the additional handicap of migrancy. Often those who traveled from place to place working in the fields did not attend school at all. Few attended beyond the primary years, and their failures were viewed as natural by educators and the Anglo society in general. Such schooling as they did receive emphasized learning English, vocational and manual arts training, health and hygiene, and the adoption of such American core values as cleanliness, thrift, and punctuality (Carter & Sequra, 1979).

During the Depression years many rural Mexican-Americans moved to the cities, bringing their problems to a wider consciousness. Also during the 1930s and 1940s greater attention was given to the concerns of Mexican Americans in some states, especially California and New Mexico (Carter & Sequra, 1979). However, it would not be until a quarter century later that any marked progress was made as the "consciousness and conscience of the nation began to stir under the proddings of a new generation of Anglo liberals and especially new Chicano leadership" (Butts, 1978, p. 251).

Education of Blacks

Although blacks came to America before the Puritans, 20 having been sold to the colonists at the Jamestown colony in 1619, their educational history was anything but similar. The vast majority of blacks living in the United States during the first 300 years of its history lived in the South and, until after the Civil War, as slaves. On the eve of the Civil War there were about 4 million black slaves and one-half million free blacks out of a total population of 31 million.

Education of Slaves.   For the slaves, education was virtually nonexistent. In the colonial period some missionary or philanthropic groups had provided limited and sporadic schooling, but by the third decade of the nineteenth century the rise of militant abolitionism and the fear of slave revolts had led to the enactment of the so-called "Black Codes" which, among other things, prohibited the education of slaves. As Pifer (1973) described the pre–Civil War status of education for the slave:

> Education was thought to give the slave too high an opinion of himself and access to such pernicious ideas as those expressed in our Declaration of Independence, namely, that all men are created equal and have certain inalienable rights. In short, education was dangerous. Nevertheless, some slaves and some whites, at great personal risk, defied these harsh laws and engaged in clandestine learning and teachings, but the sum total of education for slaves, all the same, was meager. (p. 8)

Education of Free Blacks Prior to the Civil War.   The education of free blacks in the South (some 10% of the free blacks did reside in the South) was also very limited. Before the institution of the Black Codes, black apprentices benefited from the requirement that apprentices be taught to read and write. But under the codes this requirement was repealed in some states as it applied to blacks. Outside the South, in some communities the children of free slaves did attend public schools or the private schools established by various religious, philanthropic, or abolitionist societies. The SPG was one of the most active groups in these efforts.

In the decades preceding the Civil War, as common school systems were developed in the North, blacks more often than not found themselves in segregated schools. An important legal support for this segregation (and also the legal basis for segregation for the remainder of the century) was provided by the Massachusetts Supreme Court decision in *Roberts v. City of Boston* (1850), which said that separate but equal schools did not violate the rights of the black child.

Despite the difficulties, some free blacks did obtain an education. The outbreak of the Civil War in 1861 found about 4,000 blacks in schools in the slave states and 23,000 in the free states (West, 1972). A few blacks even obtained a higher education. A small number went abroad to England or Scotland, a few attended the limited number of American colleges that admitted blacks, notably Oberlin in Ohio and Berea in Kentucky, and others attended the three black colleges established before 1860: Cheyney State College (1839) and Lincoln University (1854) in Pennsylvania and Wilberforce University (1856) in Ohio.

Many of the free blacks who gained a higher education prior to 1860 did so under the auspices of the American Colonization Society, which was established in 1817 to send free blacks to the colony of Liberia in Africa, founded by the society in 1822. The education of the free blacks was undertaken to provide the doctors, lawyers, teachers, clergy, and civil servants needed by the colony. Although not all those educated by the Society went to the colony, or if they went did not remain, enough did so to provide the colony and the Republic of Liberia, which it became in 1847, with its leadership elite (Pifer, 1973).

Reconstruction.   The period of Reconstruction (1865–1877) following the Civil War brought new factors to bear on education in the South in general and education of blacks in particular. One such force was the hundreds of teachers who, supported by various northern churches and missionary societies, moved to the South to educate those who had been liberated. Another factor was the emergence of charitable *educational foundations,* philanthropy in a new form. The first of these, established in 1867, was the Peabody Fund for the Advancement of Negro Education in the South. It later merged with the Slater Fund to support industrial education and teacher preparation. Among the others, the largest was the General Education Board set up by John D. Rockefeller in 1902 (Pifer, 1973; West, 1972).

Another major force affecting black education in the South during this period was the Freedmen's Bureau. The bureau was responsible for the establishment of some 3,000 schools, and by 1869 some 114,000 students were in attendance in bureau schools (the Historical Note on page 134 gives the account of one teacher in a freedmen's school). These schools followed the New England common school model in terms of their curriculum (reading, writing, grammar, geography, arithmetic, and music) and moral outlook (the importance of certain values and the responsibility of citizenship), but added a new dimension— industrial training. In the view of northern educators, industrial training would prepare blacks for the occupations they were most suited to perform in the South (Gutek, 1991).

Hampton and Tuskegee Institutes.   Industrial education was the basic mission of the Hampton Institute, founded in 1868 by a representative of the Freedmen's Bureau, General Samuel Chapman Armstrong. Booker T. Washington attended the institute and developed the educational ideas that led to the establishment of his Tuskegee Institute in 1880. Some, such as W. E. B. DuBois, who in 1907 co-founded the National Association for the Advancement of Colored People, argued against what they viewed as a position of accommodation or compromise and protested that it was wrong for blacks to be given only one educational direction (industrial) and whites several. However, to Washington and others who supported industrial education, this approach appeared the most immediate and practical way for blacks to improve their economic and social position.

Washington's efforts were successful: 10 years after its founding, Tuskegee had a faculty of 88 and a student body of 1,200, making it one of the largest institutions of higher education in the South. It is also significant to note that Tuskegee, and even more so the Hampton Institute, were important as centers for the training of black teachers. In fact, as one historian reminds us, the traditional attention given to Hampton as an agricultural and industrial school has obscured the fact that Hampton was founded and maintained primarily to train black teachers for the South. Indeed, between 1872 and 1890, 604 of Hampton's 723 graduates became teachers (Anderson, 1978).

Black Colleges and Universities.   In addition to Hampton and Tuskegee, several other distinguished black colleges and universities were established in the immediate post–Civil War years. These include Atlanta University, founded in 1865 by the American Baptist Mission Society; Howard University, chartered in 1868 by the Congregationalists; Fisk University, established in 1866 by the American Missionary Association; and Mehary Medical College, originally Walton College, founded in 1865 by the Methodist Episcopal Church. Somewhat later, as a result of the Second Morrill Act of 1890, black land-grant colleges were established in each of the southern and border states—17 in all (Pifer, 1973).

The topic of segregated universities is currently being revisited in discussions of the place of all-women colleges, Hispanic universities, etc. What is your position on voluntary segregated institutions of higher education?

Historical Note:
Zeal for Learning Among Freedmen, 1868

Dear Brethren and Sisters;

Since I last wrote I have commenced my school and have now been teaching just four weeks. Everything was finally arranged so that on Monday Nov. 30th I opened school with twenty-five scholars. Since then the number has been steadily increasing and now it numbers forty-two with a prospect of large additions after their great holiday Christmas week is past.

From all the accounts of Freedmen's schools which I had heard and read previous to coming here I expected to find them anxious to learn but after all, I confess I was unprepared for the amount of zeal manifested by most of them for an education. I can say as one did of old, "The half had not been told me." I am surprised each day by some new proof of their anxiety to learn.

Nearly all ages, colors, conditions and capacities are represented in my school. Ages ranging from five to sixty-five; Colors from jet-black with tight curling hair to pale brunette with waving brown hair.

Some, a few of them could read quite readily in a second reader and many more knew the alphabet and were trying patiently to spell out short easy words, while by far the greater number could not distinguish a letter. I have had as many as nineteen in my alphabet class at one time but it is now reduced to four.

One old woman over sixty, after spending three weeks on the alphabet and finally conquering it, said she wanted to learn to spell Jesus first before spelling easy words for said she, "Pears like I can learn the rest easier if I get that blessed name learned first." So now she looks through the Bible for that name and has learned to distinguish it at sight from other words. The older members of the school are as quiet and orderly as I could desire but the children are not so very different from other children. They love mischief and play and the prevailing vice among them is deceit. But education has all the charm of novelty to them and they learn with astonishing rapidity. They come to school as well provided with books as children usually do.

Your Sister in Christ,

Pamelia A. Hand

Source: Reprinted by permission of Macmillan Publishing Company from *The Black American and Education* (pp. 73–74) by Earle H. West. Copyright; © 1972 by Merrill Publishing Company.

Segregated Public Schools.   Yet another factor changing the face of education in the South during the Reconstruction period was legislation leading to the establishment of tax-supported public or common school systems. Many freedmen recently elected to state legislatures were a force in this movement. Many of these black legislators as well as some white legislators advocated integration in the newly established schools. In fact, many of the state statutes or constitutional provisions established the schools without making reference to either integration or segregation. However, none of the southern states actually instituted an integrated system, and what began as custom became law in all the southern states. Yet the efforts of the various groups and agencies did result in a dramatic reversal of the educational status of black Americans from a literacy rate estimated at 5% or 10% at the outbreak of the Civil War to one of 70% by 1910.

From the end of Reconstruction through the turn of the century a system of racial segregation was established in the South that remained in effect until the desegregation movement of the 1950s and 1960s. The practice of segregation was sanctioned by the 1896 U.S. Supreme Court decision in *Plessy v. Ferguson,* which said that separate railroad cars did not violate the Constitution. But the "separate but equal" doctrine, while always producing separate, rarely produced equal. After the 1870s the federal government effectively withdrew from the promotion of the civil and educational rights of blacks.

During this same period, ever-increasing numbers of white children from immigrant and lower socioeconomic families were entering the enlarged public school system; between 1880 and 1895 white enrollment in the public schools increased 106% compared to 59% for black enrollment (Frazer, cited in Hare & Swift, 1976). The "rise of the poor whites" placed increased financial demands on public revenues and often resulted in funds being diverted from black schools to improve other schools (Gutek, 1991). To this was added the disenfranchisement of blacks by many southern states and the delegation of authority to local school boards to divide state education funds as they saw fit. From the court approval of segregation, the loss of political power, and the decreased financial support emerged the "separate but inferior" system that marked so much of the South until after the middle of the twentieth century.

Teacher Education

The formal training of teachers in the United States did not begin until the nineteenth century. In colonial America teachers at the elementary level were often young men who taught for only a short time before studying for the ministry or law. Given the strong relationship between church and education, more often than not they were chosen more for their religious orthodoxy than their educational qualifications. In fact, they were often viewed as assistant pastors and in addition to their teaching they were expected to perform various duties related to the functioning of the church. In many small communities the minister himself was the schoolmaster.

Unfortunately, too often the "career teachers" were individuals who had been unsuccessful at other occupations or those whose personal character and civil conduct left something to be desired. It was also not uncommon in colonial America to find teachers who were indentured servants—persons who had sold their services for a period of years in exchange for passage to the New World. Perhaps the closest to any teacher preparation was that received by those individuals who entered teaching after serving as apprentices to schoolmasters. In fact, the educational historian Pulliam (1991) refers to the apprenticeship training received by Quaker teachers as the first teacher education in America.

A distinction was made between teachers at the elementary level and those at the secondary level, not in the teacher training they received, but in the higher status the secondary teachers held in society and the higher education they possessed. Teachers in the Latin grammar schools and academies were normally graduates of secondary schools, and, not uncommonly, had received some college education, while those at the elementary level very often had little more than an elementary education themselves.

Although most histories of education identify the Colombian School at Concord, Vermont, established by the Reverend Samuel Hall in 1823, as the first formal teacher training institution, a good argument can be made that the first such institution was actually the previously mentioned Troy Female Seminary opened by Emma Willard in 1821 (Spring, 1990). Willard established the seminary to train female teachers in both the subject areas and in pedagogy. Each graduate received a signed certificate confirming her qualifications to teach. Long before the first state-supported normal schools in Massachusetts were opened by Horace Mann, the Troy Seminary had prepared 200 teachers for the common schools (Rippa, 1988). In fact, this and other academies were responsible for not only expanding educational opportunities for women, but for preparing a large number of individuals for the teaching profession.

Establishment of Normal Schools

The greatest force, however, in increasing the professional training of teachers was the establishment of *normal schools*. As we have seen, Horace Mann, Henry Barnard, Catherine Beecher, and others who worked for the establishment of common school systems recognized that the success of such systems was dependent upon the preparation of a sufficient quantity of adequately trained teachers. This in turn demanded the establishment of institutions for the specific training of teachers, that is, normal schools. These educational leaders also believed that the teaching force for the common schools should be female, not only because women supposedly made better teachers at the elementary level, but because they were less expensive to hire. The fact that at least the latter was true is shown in Table 4.3, which compares the salaries of men and women teachers from the years 1841–1864, as well as the salaries of teachers in rural areas with those in cities.

The growing enrollments in the common schools also created a growing demand for teachers. The response in one state after another was the establishment of normal schools. The New York State Normal School at Albany, the next established (1844) after those in Massachusetts, was headed by David P. Page. His book, *Theory and Practice of Teaching or the Motives and Methods of Good School*

Table 4.3: Average Weekly Salaries of Teachers, 1841–1864

| Year | Rural | | City | |
	Men	Women	Men	Women
1841	$4.15	$2.51	$11.93	$4.44
1845	3.87	2.48	12.21	4.09
1850	4.25	2.89	13.37	4.71
1855	5.77	3.65	16.80	5.79
1860	6.28	4.12	18.56	6.99
1864	7.86	4.92	20.78	7.67

Source: From *The American School, 1642–1985: Varieties of Historical Interpretation of the Foundations and Development of American Education* by Joel Spring. Copyright © 1986 by Longman Publishing Group. Reprinted with permission from Longman Publishing Group.

Keeping, published in 1847, became the standard text in teacher education. By 1875 at least 70 normal schools were receiving some state support, and by 1900 there were a reported 345 normal schools in the United States (Pulliam, 1991).

Admission to the normal school required only an elementary education. The course of study lasted one or two years and included a review of material to be taught in the elementary school, instruction in methods of teaching, "mental philosophy" (i.e., educational psychology), and classroom management. Overriding the curriculum was a concern for the development of moral character. A prominent feature of these normal schools was the model school, the forerunner of the laboratory school, where the students could practice teaching.

Teacher Institutes

Despite the spread of normal schools, in some places, even reform-minded Massachusetts, as late as 1900 only a bare majority of teachers had attended normal schools. Before this time, and even into the twentieth century, the most important institution in the training of teachers was the teacher institute. A common practice of school districts was to hire individuals with no formal training, with the condition that their continued employment depended on attendance at a teacher institute. The typical institute met once or twice a year, from several days to four weeks, and usually in the summer months. In less populous areas the institutes were often conducted by the county superintendent of schools. Some were offered in connection with institutions of higher education. The primary purpose of the institute was to provide a brief course in the theory and practice of teaching. Great emphasis was placed on elevating the moral character of the teacher (Spring, 1990).

Normal School Curriculum and Standards Strengthened

Toward the end of the nineteenth century the character of the normal school began to change. Not only was the burgeoning population creating an increased demand for elementary or common school teachers, but the secondary school movement created a concomitant demand for secondary school teachers. To meet this demand, normal schools began to broaden their curriculum to include the training of secondary school teachers. At the same time, they began to require high school completion for admission. The passage of teacher certification statutes that specified the amount and type of training required of teachers contributed to the expansion of the normal school program from two to three years, and eventually, during the 1920s, to four years. By this time the normal schools were beginning to call themselves state teachers' colleges. In time, with the broadening of the curriculum to embrace many of the liberal arts, the "teacher" designation was dropped and most became simply "state colleges." Some of these former normal schools have become the largest and most respected universities in the United States.

Universities Enter Teacher Training

During the late nineteenth century the universities also became increasingly involved in teacher education. Teacher training at the college or university level

Are you attending or have you ever attended a college or university that began as a normal school? What influence has this history had on the institutional climate?

Professional Reflections

"The lessons we learn best we teach ourselves. Teachers should be the guides to students on a journey of self-discovery."

Cathy Pittman, Teacher of the Year, Georgia

"Always teach to the whole child; socially, physically, emotionally, and academically."

Sheba Brown, Teacher of the Year, Mississippi

had been offered at a limited number of institutions as early as the 1830s, but it was not until toward the end of the nineteenth century that universities entered the field of teacher preparation to any measurable extent (Pulliam, 1991). Their involvement stemmed in part from the increased demand for secondary school teachers. The universities had always been institutions for the education of those who taught in the grammar schools, academies, and high schools. However, they did not prepare these students as teachers *per se,* but as individuals who had advanced knowledge of certain subject matter. The increased demand for secondary school teachers, the late entrance of the normal schools into the training of secondary school teachers, and the growing recognition that the professionalization of teaching demanded study of its theory and practice led to the increased involvement of universities in teacher education. The University of Iowa established the first chair of education in 1873, other midwestern universities followed, and in 1892 the New York College for the Training of Teachers (Teachers College) became a part of Columbia University. After the turn of the century teacher training departments became commonplace in the universities.

Summary

The Founding Fathers recognized the importance of education to the development of the new nation. As the nation marched through the nineteenth century and became an industrial giant, the demand for skilled workers and the demand of the working class who saw education as a path to success combined to expand the offering of publicly supported education through the secondary school. The growth of higher education can also be attributed to these forces. Indeed, today it is the recognition of education's importance to our national prominence and its vital role in assuring our continued economic prosperity that has served as the motivation for much of the current activity to reform our nation's schools.

Unfortunately, while the educational opportunities afforded much of the population were greatly expanded in the nineteenth century, the history of the education of minorities was basically one of neglect and segregation. It would not be until the third quarter of the twentieth century that any marked progress would be made in improving the education of Native Americans, Mexican Americans, and blacks. In the next chapter many of these efforts will be detailed, as well as those designed to improve the professional training of teachers.

Key Terms

Assimilation	Junior college
Common school	Junior high school
Comprehensive high school	Normal school
De facto segregation	Rate bill
De jure segregation	Secondary school
Educational foundations	Sunday school
Infant school	Teachers' institute

Discussion Questions

1. The child described in the critical incident at the beginning of the chapter was made to feel wanted by Joanne Johnson. As a teacher, what can you do to make every child feel wanted? How can you know that you have really made a difference in the life of a child?

2. In what ways were Thomas Jefferson's plans for an educational system elitist? Egalitarian?

3. What was the significance of each of the following to expanding educational opportunities in the United States?

    a. monitorial schools
    b. Sunday schools
    c. infant schools
    d. free school societies

4. Describe the contributions of Horace Mann and Henry Barnard to the common school movement.

5. What influence did Prussian education have on American education in the early nineteenth century?

6. Describe the impact of the Second Morrill Act on the provision of education to minorities in the United States.

7. What impact has the historical neglect of the education of minorities had on their education and on the educational system today?

8. What was the contribution of Emma Willard to women's education? To teacher education?

9. Compare the role of the university with that of the normal school in the education of teachers.

References

Anderson, J. D. (1978). The Hampton model of normal school industrial education, 1868–1900. In V. P. Franklin & J. D. Anderson (Eds.), *New perspectives on black educational history.* Boston: G. K. Hall.

Binder, F. M. (1974). *The age of the common school, 1830–1865.* New York: John Wiley & Sons.

Butts, R. F. (1978). *Public education in the United States.* New York: Holt, Rinehart and Winston.

Carter, T. P., & Sequra, R. D. (1979). *Mexican Americans in school: A decade of change.* New York: College Entrance Examination Board.

Cremin, L. A. (1982). *American education: The national experience, 1783–1876.* New York: Harper and Row.

Frazer, D., Hare, N., & Swift, D. W. (1976). Black education. In D. W. Swift (Ed.), *American education: A sociological view.* Boston: Houghton Mifflin.

Graham, P. A. (1974). *Community & class in American education.* New York: John Wiley & Sons.

Gutek, G. L. (1991). *Education in the United States: An historical perspective* Englewood Cliffs, NJ: Prentice-Hall.

Kidwell, C. S., & Swift, D. W. (1976). Indian education. In D. W. Swift (Ed.), *American education: A sociological view.* Boston: Houghton Mifflin.

Madsen, D. L. (1974). *Early national education, 1776–1830.* New York: John Wiley & Sons.

Pifer, A. (1973). *The higher education of blacks in the United States.* New York: Carnegie Corporation.

Plessy v. Ferguson, 163 U.S. 537, 16 S. Ct. 1138 (1896).

Pulliam, J. D. (1991). *History of education in America* (5th ed.). New York: Merrill.

Rippa, S. A. (1988). *Education in a free society.* New York: Longman.

Roberts v. City of Boston, 59 Mass. (5 Cush.) 198 (1850).

Spring, J. (1990). *The American school 1642–1990,* 2d ed. New York: Longman.

Stuart et al. v. School District No. 1 of the Village of Kalamazoo, 30 Michigan 69 (1874).

Szasz, M. C. (1977). *Education and the American Indian.* Albuquerque, NM: University of New Mexico Press.

Trustees of Dartmouth College v. Woodward, 17 U.S. (4 Wheat) 518 (1819).

West, E. (1972). *The black American and education.* Columbus, OH: Merrill.

Chapter 5

Modern American Education: From the Progressive Movement to the Present

Human history becomes more and more a race between education and catastrophe.

H. G. Wells, The Outline of History *(1920)*

A Critical Incident in My Teaching Career . . .

In the beginning of the year I had a student tell me she hated to read. She found reading senseless and a waste of time, but her opinion of reading changed when we started to study the Holocaust. She became intrigued by the lives of the people in concentration camps and their ability to survive. She inquired as to what books she should read in order to learn more about this frightening period in history. I guided her to The Diary of Anne Frank *and other books on the subject I thought she would enjoy. I was delighted that one of my most reluctant students was becoming excited by history. We would spend hours talking about the contents of the books and our feelings about life and the choices it forces us to make. As I learned more about*

this student I understood why she was so attracted to these books on survival in the midst of chaos. She was facing the same situation in her home life. The books were her only refuge from the problems of the world. She fought for survival in her world of torment, confusion, and abandonment. School became a haven from the storms that consumed her fragmented and dysfunctional family life. The books on the Holocaust gave her hope that one day, through education and scholarships, she too could leave the world of abuse behind.

T. Tracey Fallon,
Teacher of the Year, New Jersey

In this chapter the history of American education begun in Chapters 3 and 4 is brought to the present. Although covering a relatively short period of time from a historical perspective, this period has witnessed the most rapid expansion of education in our nation's history and some of the most marked changes. So much has taken place that we could not focus in detail on every contributing personality or intervening variable. Consider the following objectives as you study this chapter:

- Identify the major economic, political, and social forces affecting education in the twentieth century.
- Describe the progressive education movement in the United States.
- Compare the impact of the Great Depression, World War II, and the Cold War on education.

- Evaluate the progress of the civil rights movement and the War on Poverty.
- Outline the developments in education during the 1970s and 1980s.
- Trace the fluctuation of federal support for education in the twentieth century.

The Twentieth Century Unfolds

The People and Nation Grow

The twentieth century brought marked changes in American social, economic, political, and educational life. Population growth continued at a staggering rate: from 50 million in 1880 to 76 million in 1900 and 106 million in 1920. Although birth rates declined, improvements in medicine and sanitation led to lower infant mortality and cut the overall death rate. A significant portion of the population growth was the result of immigration. In the two decades before the turn of the century, an average of almost 500,000 immigrants per year arrived in this country. The numbers grew to more than 1 million per year in 1905–07, 1910, and 1913–14 (U.S. Bureau of the Census, 1975).

At the same time that the population was experiencing rapid growth it was becoming increasingly urban. According to the 1920 census, for the first time in our nation's history, the number of those living in towns of 2,500 (54.2 million) exceeded those living in rural areas (51.6 million). Although the westward movement continued throughout the late nineteenth and early twentieth centuries, by 1890 the frontier was closed; that is, the Bureau of Census could not draw a line of demarcation beyond which the population was less than two persons per square mile.

America experienced growth not only at home, but on the international scene. In the last years of the nineteenth century and the beginning of the twentieth century the United States acquired Guam, the Philippines, Puerto Rico, the Hawaiian Islands, the Virgin Islands, and the Panama Canal Zone. The nation also engaged in a war with Spain; landed troops in Mexico, Nicaragua, and Haiti; helped put down a revolt in China; and in 1917 entered the fight to make the world safe for democracy.

Economic Growth

The economic growth of the United States during this period was even more profound than the population growth. Whereas the population increased less than fourfold in the post–Civil War to pre–World War I period, production increased tenfold (Gray & Peterson, 1974). This was a period of rapid growth for the railroads and other transportation and communication industries. The expansion of the railroads brought an end to the frontier and linked all parts of the nation, as did an ever-expanding network of telephone lines. At the same time, the transatlantic cable and transworld shipping linked this nation with others. The expansion in the transportation industry opened up new markets for the growing agricultural and manufacturing industries. By 1920 the United States had become the largest manufacturing nation in the world.

Paradoxically, this period of stellar economic growth is also regarded as a dark chapter in American history because of the abuses in industry (Gray & Peterson, 1974). The business leaders who helped bring about the growth and contributed to the abuses have been referred to as "robber barons," and the business and political corruption of the era touched every aspect of American life. The plight of workers (including children) in factories, the unsafe and unsanitary working conditions, the horrors of industrial accidents, and descriptions of life in the poverty-ridden slums filled the tabloids and stirred political and social reforms.

Politics and Reform

Antitrust legislation was enacted in an attempt to control monopolies and their unfair business practices. The progressive movement that emerged at the turn of the century was responsible for a flood of labor legislation addressed at regulating the labor of women and children, wages and hours, and health and safety conditions. Workers also sought to improve their plight through labor unions. Increased union activity met with harsh resistance and persecution; violence and loss of life were not uncommon. Yet by 1920 one-fifth of all nonagricultural workers in the nation were organized; in view of employer hostility, this was a considerable achievement (Kirkland, 1969).

In the political arena the progressive movement gained momentum in the years after 1900. Decrying the excesses of big business, the progressives challenged the cherished ideal of limited government and urged the government to protect consumers against unfair monopolistic practices, workers (particularly women and children) against exploitation, and the less fortunate against any form of social injustice. Reform became the "order of the day" on the local, state, and national levels as progressives sought to wrest control of government from the business community and use it to bring about social change. At the same time, progressives maintained a firm belief in representative democracy and individual freedom.

Forces in Education

Significant changes in the educational arena accompanied those in the social, economic, and political arenas. The urbanization of the population and the popularity of the automobile made possible the building of larger schools and contributed to the consolidation of rural school districts. The number of school districts in the United States continued to decrease gradually from over 130,000 at the turn of the century to approximately 15,500 in 1990. State control of education increased in a number of areas: certification of teachers, specification of requirements for teacher education programs, specification of curricular requirements for public elementary and secondary schools, establishment of minimal standards for school facilities, and provisions for financial support.

At the same time, the size of the school population increased more rapidly than the overall population. In the three decades between 1890 and 1920 the school-age population increased 49% and school enrollments 70%. The growth in the student population was accompanied by an 80% growth in the number of teachers and other nonsupervisory personnel. During the same period the average length of the school term increased by 27 days. More teachers and longer terms translated into significant increases in expenditures (see Table 5.1).

For a number of years the average length of the school term has been 180 days. Do you support current efforts to extend the school year? Why or why not?

Table 5.1: Historical Summary of U.S. Public Elementary and Secondary School Statistics, 1870–1930 (all dollars unadjusted)

	1870	1880	1890	1900	1910	1920	1930
Enrollments							
Total school age (5–17 yrs.) population (thous.)	12,055	15,066	18,543	21,573	24,009	27,556	31,417
Total enrollment in elementary and secondary schools (thous.)	6,872	9,867	12,723	15,503	17,814	21,578	25,678
Percent of population aged 5–17 enrolled in public schools	57.0	65.5	68.6	71.9	74.2	78.3	81.7
(in private schools)	(NA)	(NA)	(9.5)	(6.4)	(5.2)	(4.9)	(7.8)
Attendance							
Average daily attendance (thous.)	4,077	6,144	8,154	10,633	12,827	16,150	21,265
Average length of school terms (in days)	132.2	130.3	134.7	144.3	157.5	161.9	172.7
Average number of days attended per pupil enrolled	78.4	81.1	86.3	99.0	113.0	121.2	143.0
Instructional staff							
Total classroom teachers/nonsupervisory staff (thous.)	201	287	364	423	523	657	843
Men	78	123	126	127	110	93	140
Women	123	164	238	296	413	565	703
Average annual salary of instructional staff	$189	$195	$252	$325	$485	$871	$1,420
Finance							
Total revenue receipts (thous.)	(NA)	(NA)	$143,195	$219,766	$433,064	$970,120	$2,088,557
Percent of revenue receipts from:							
Federal government	(NA)	(NA)	(NA)	(NA)	(NA)	.3	.4
State government			18.2	17.3	15.0	16.5	16.9
Local government			67.8	67.7	72.1	83.5	82.7
Total expenditures per pupil in ADA	$16	$13	$17	$20	$33	$64	$108

Source: U.S. Department of Education, National Center for Education Statistics. (1982). *Digest of Education Statistics. 1982* (Table 27). Washington, DC: U.S. Government Printing Office

The Progressive Era in American Education

The Beginnings of Progressive Education

The progressive reform movement, which had such a widespread impact on political, social, and economic life, also found expression in education. Progressive education traces its intellectual roots to Rousseau and its beginnings in this country to Francis W. Parker, superintendent of schools in Quincy, Massachusetts, and later head of the Cook County Normal School in Chicago. Parker studied in Europe and became familiar with the work of Pestalozzi and Froebel. He shared their belief that learning should emanate from the interests and needs of the child and that the most appropriate curriculum was an activity-based one that encouraged children to express themselves freely and creatively.

The practice school of Cook County Normal School was organized as a model democratic community. Art was an integral part of the curriculum, as were nature studies, field trips, and social activities. Rather than deal with multiple, discrete subject matter, the curriculum attempted to integrate subjects in a way that made it more meaningful to the learner. In all things Parker's aim was to make the child the center of the educational process.

Dewey

Among the parents of children at Parker's school in Chicago was John Dewey, professor of philosophy and pedagogy at the University of Chicago. Dewey was impressed with the philosophy and methods of the school and in 1896 established his own laboratory school at the University of Chicago. The supervisor of instruction at Dewey's lab school, and later superintendent of schools in Chicago, was Ella Flagg Young, who is featured in the Historical Note on page 148. Through his many writings and articulation of his philosophy, Dewey provided the intellectual foundation for progressive education. In fact, Dewey was said to be "the real spokesman for intellectual America in the Progressive Era" (Bonner, 1963, p. 44).

First and foremost Dewey was a philosopher. He was one of the founders of the philosophy known as pragmatism, which holds that there are no absolutes: truth is that which results from the application of scientific thinking to experience. Scientific thinking, in turn, involves data gathering, hypothesis formulation, and testing.

Dewey's educational theories reflected his philosophy. He rejected the old, rigid, *subject-centered curriculum* in favor of the *child-centered curriculum* in which learning came through experience, not rote memorization. The classroom was a miniature of society, the problem-solving method was the preferred approach, and motivation was at the center of the learning process. The goal of education was to promote individual growth and to prepare the child for full participation in our democratic society.

Dewey maintained that the child should be viewed as a total organism and that education is most effective when it considers not only the intellectual but

Historical Note:
Ella Flagg Young, Pioneer School Administrator

Ella Flagg Young served as a teacher, principal, and area superintendent of schools before receiving her doctorate from the University of Chicago. From 1899 to 1904, she was a professor of pedagogy at the University of Chicago and a colleague of John Dewey with whom she collaborated on several published works. She also served as supervisor of instruction at Dewey's laboratory school at the university.

Dewey regarded Ella Flagg Young as the "wisest person on school matters" with whom he had ever come in contact. According to Dewey, he was "constantly getting ideas from her. . . . More times than I could well say I didn't see the meaning or force of some favorite conception of my own until Mrs. Young had given it back to me." Dewey further confessed that "it was from her that I learned that freedom and respect for freedom mean regard for the inquiring and reflective processes of individuals."

In 1905, Ella Flagg Young returned to the Chicago public schools, became principal of Chicago Normal School, and from 1907 to 1915 served as the superintendent of schools for Chicago,

the first woman to head a large city school system. In 1910, she was elected president of the National Education Association, the first woman to hold this office.

Throughout her career, Ella Flagg Young sought to improve the training and condition of teachers. She espoused democratic administration and organized teachers' councils to provide teachers with a greater voice in decision making. She worked for higher teachers' salaries and once resigned as a superintendent because of the Board of Education's policies regarding teachers' organizations and salaries. At the outbreak of World War I, she became chairman of the Women's Liberty Loan Committee and, although over 70 years old, traveled throughout the country in its behalf. While on one trip, she became ill and died on October 18, 1918.

Ella Flagg Young's capable administration of both the National Education Association and Chicago's schools was a victory for all women educators. She inspired many women to seek positions of leadership and led many men (and women) to reconsider the capabilities of women for administration.

the social, emotional, and physical needs of the child. He thought that education was a lifelong process and that the school should be an integral part of community life, a concept that gave support to the development of the community school. Dewey wrote some 500 articles and 40 books. His influence was felt not only in philosophy and education, but law, political theory, and social reform. He left an imprint on American education that has been unparalleled in this century. His classic *Democracy and Education* (1916) provided perhaps the strongest statement of his educational theories and provided the rationale for a generation of educators who were part of what was to be known as the progressive education movement.

Progressive Education Association

The formation of the Progressive Education Association (PEA) in 1919 gave what previously had been a "rather loosely joined revolt against pedagogical formalism" a vigorous organizational voice (Cremin, 1962). The association adopted seven guiding principles:

1. The child should be given the freedom to develop naturally.

2. Interest provides the motivation for all work.

3. The teacher should be a guide in the learning process, not the task-master.

4. The scientific study of pupil development should be promoted by the refocusing of information to be included on school records.

5. Greater attention should be given to everything that affects the child's physical development.

6. The school and home should cooperate to meet the natural interests and activities of the child.

7. The Progressive School should be a leader in educational movements. (*Progressive Education,* 1924, pp. 1–2)

The Progressive Education Association published a journal, *Progressive Education,* from 1924 to 1955. The journal became the forum for the educational opinions of its membership. In its early years *Progressive Education* devoted considerable space to the concept of "creative self-expression." According to Harold Rugg, professor at Teachers College, Columbia University and a leading spokesperson for the PEA, creative self-expression was the essence of the progressive education movement. In 1928, Rugg and Ann Schumaker published *The Child-Centered School,* an interpretive survey of progressive pedagogical innovations across the country (Cremin, 1962).

Another well-known spokesperson for progressive education, William H. Kilpatrick, was also on the faculty at Teachers College. Kilpatrick translated Dewey's philosophy into a practical methodology, the *project method.* The project method was an attempt to make education as "lifelike" as possible. At the heart of the educative process was to be "wholehearted purposeful activity," activity consistent with the child's own goals. Kilpatrick, while sharing Dewey's belief in the importance of problem-solving, went beyond Dewey in his child-centered emphasis and in his rejection of any organized subject matter (Cremin, 1962).

What activity in your educational experience was the best example of creative self-expression? Was it intended as such by the teacher, or did it take place by accident?

Higher Education

The influence of the progressive education movement was also felt in higher education. The great model of progressive higher education was the University of Wisconsin. The Wisconsin model was based on the idea that "the obligation of the university was to undertake leadership in the application of science to the improvement of the life of the citizenry in every domain" (Cremin, 1988, p. 246). This was accomplished through faculty research and service, the training of experts, and extended education.

College and university enrollments rose steadily during the pre–World War I years and then surged after the war, partly as a result of those who had come to higher education as part of the Student's Army Training Corps and then stayed after the war ended. Enrollments rose from almost 600,000 in 1919–20 to 1.1 million in 1929–30.

Most of these students were seeking a professional or technical education, primarily in education, business, and engineering, and enrolled not in the universities but in the growing number of junior colleges and the teacher education institutions. The number of junior colleges increased from 52 in 1920 to 277 in 1930, and to 456 in 1940 (U.S. Bureau of the Census, 1975); the number of colleges for teachers grew from 45 in 1920 to four times that number by 1940 (Pulliam, 1991). The normal schools across the country were as typical of the progressive service orientation in higher education as the state universities: "they presumed to prepare scientifically trained experts; they extended their learning to all comers; and they prided themselves on their sensitivity to popular need" (Cremin, 1988, p. 248).

The Child Study Movement

During the first two decades of the twentieth century, as the progressive movement was gaining momentum, two other related movements were also taking place that would have far-reaching consequences—the child study and measurement movements. The child study movement began with the pioneering work of G. Stanley Hall. Hall established a center for applied psychology at Johns Hopkins University in 1884, the year Dewey graduated from the same institution. Later, as president of Clark University, he brought together the first group of scholars interested in the scientific study of the child through the careful observation of children at school or at play and at various stages of development (Pulliam, 1991).

Hall and his colleagues recognized that emotional growth and personality development were just as important as cognitive development in understanding the child. They saw the child as an evolving organism and believed that once educators understood how the child developed they would be better able to foster that development (Perkinson, 1977). These early efforts were important in laying the foundation for educational psychology and for the recognition and inclusion of this discipline in teacher education. Child study, the stage theory of learning propounded by theorists such as Jean Piaget, the specialties of child and adolescent psychology, as well as developmental psychology and the study of exceptional children, all owe their beginnings to Hall's work (Pulliam, 1991).

The Measurement Movement

Another cornerstone of educational psychology was laid by Lewis M. Terman, Edward L. Thorndike, and other psychologists involved in the development of the measurement movement. Although intelligence and aptitude tests had been in use for some time, the real breakthrough came when the French psychologists Alfred Binet and Theodore Simon developed an instrument based on an intelligence scale that allowed comparison of individual intelligence to a norm. Of the many adaptations of the Binet-Simon scale the most important for education was the so-called Stanford revision by Lewis Terman of Stanford University. It was also Terman who developed the *intelligence quotient* (IQ), a number indicating the level of an individual's mental development. Meanwhile, Thorndike and his students at Columbia developed scales for measuring achievement in arithmetic, spelling, reading, language, and other areas (Cremin, 1962).

World War I was a major factor in the growth of the measuring movement. The military needed a massive mobilization of manpower. It also needed a way to determine which men were suited for service and for what type of service. Out of this need a number of group intelligence tests were developed and ultimately were administered to hundreds of thousands of recruits.

One unexpected result of this massive testing was the discovery of a large number of young men with educational (as well as physical) deficiencies: approximately one-quarter of all recruits were judged illiterate. Deficiencies were particularly high among rural youth.

Within a decade of the end of the war, the measurement movement had become a permanent part of American education. According to Heffernan (1968), the "apparent objectivity of the test results had a fascination for school administrators and teachers. Certainty seemed somehow to attach to these mathematically expressed comparisons of pupil achievement" (p. 229). Throughout the country students were classified, assigned, and compared on the basis of tests. Often the tests were used wisely to diagnose learning difficulties and assess individual differences. Unfortunately, they were also used to make comparisons without consideration of differences in school populations, to make judgments about the quality of teaching, and most distressing, to make subjective judgments about students' potential (Heffernan, 1968). Regrettably, these misuses of tests continue today.

Have you ever taken a test that you felt was biased in terms of race, ethnicity, or gender? What positive benefits have you gained from taking national standardized tests?

Education During the Great Depression

The crash of the stock market in October 1929 ushered in the greatest depression our nation has ever experienced. The period was marked by the failure of banks and businesses, the closing of factories, mass unemployment, bread lines, soup kitchens, and tent cities. Unemployment was particularly high among minorities and young people. As many as 6,000,000 young people were out of school and unemployed in 1933–1935. Many had no occupational training or experience. In a labor market overrun with experienced workers, they had few opportunities for employment (National Policies Commission, 1941).

The Depression also had a serious impact on the operation of schools. In many states, especially in the hard-pressed South and Southwest, schools were closed or the school year shortened. In school districts throughout the land local school boards were unable to pay their teachers and issued them promissory notes agreeing to pay them when revenues were collected. And in almost every school district the number of teachers was reduced, class size increased, and the number of courses in the high school curriculum cut (Gutek, 1991).

Until the Great Depression the relationship of the federal government to education was clear: Education was viewed as a function of the states and local school districts. These entities were responsible for operating educational programs. Beginning in 1933 with the creation of the Civilian Conservation Corps (CCC) and later the National Youth Administration (NYA), this established relationship changed markedly. The CCC and the NYA were two of the federal emergency agencies created under President Roosevelt's New Deal to provide "work relief" for the unemployed. The CCC provided temporary work for over 2 million people 18–25 years of age on various conservation projects, including reforestation, wildlife preservation, flood control, and forest fire prevention. The NYA administered two programs, a work relief and employment program for needy out of school youth aged 16–25, and a program that provided part-time employment to needy high school and college students to help them continue their education. At its peak in 1939–40 approximately 750,000 students in 1,750 colleges and 28,000 secondary schools participated in NYA programs.

When it became clear to officials of both the CCC and the NYA that many of the participants lacked not only vocational skills but basic skills in reading, writing, and arithmetic, they moved to meet those needs by means of educational activities operated and controlled by the agencies themselves. In time Congress changed the authorizing language of each agency to include an educational function. Although both these measures were terminated as the war economy stimulated employment, the fact that the federal government actually operated and controlled educational activities that could have been offered by state or local educational systems marked a departure from the past that was of concern to many educators, including the National Education Association (National Policies Commission, 1941).

Other New Deal programs provided relief to the financially depressed schools. The Public Works Administration (PWA) provided assistance for the building of numerous public buildings, including almost 13,000 schools. The Works Projects Administration (WPA) provided employment for teachers in adult education, art education, and nursery schools. Under a program that became the forerunner of the National School Lunch Program, the Department of Agriculture distributed surplus foods to the schools.

What effects do pronounced economic upswings and downswings have on the public schools and colleges and universities?

Indian New Deal

Several New Deal measures were directed at improving the plight of Native Americans and became known as the Indian New Deal. The Indian New Deal was an attempt to remedy the conditions described by the Meriam Report. Among the actions taken was the cessation of the sale of allotted Indian land, the organization of tribal councils as legal bodies, the investment of the Bureau of Indian Affairs with the right to contract with states for educational services, and the ending of the boarding school system (although because of distance constraints several off-reservation boarding schools still exist). The Johnson-O'Malley Act of 1934 provided supplemental funds to public schools to provide for the special needs of transportation, school lunches, or other expenses, such as those associated with graduation (Kidwell & Swift, 1976).

Native American education was also the beneficiary of other programs of Roosevelt's New Deal—the Works Projects Administration, the Public Works Administration, and the Civilian Conservation Corps—as they provided job training, income, and improvements on the reservations, including construction of schools and roads and conservation of land, water, and timber. The total result of the New Deal was "the most dynamic program of Indian education in the history of the Indian Service" with a "curriculum more suited to the needs of the

The Civilian Conservation Corps offered youth both employment and educational opportunities.

child; . . . community day schools and a decreased emphasis on boarding schools; and a better qualified faculty and staff" (Szasz, 1977, p. 48).

George C. Counts and the John Dewey Society

The experience of the Depression had a significant impact on many progressive educators who came to believe that the schools had a responsibility to redress social injustices. At the 1932 convention of the Progressive Education Association, in an address entitled "Dare Progressive Education Be Progressive," George C. Counts challenged the child-centered doctrine and urged educators to focus less on the child and more on society, to "face squarely and courageously every social issue, come to grips with life in all its stark reality . . . develop a realistic and comprehensive theory of welfare, fashion a compelling and challenging vision of human destiny . . ." (Perkinson, 1977). In effect, Counts asked the schools to take the lead in planning for an intelligent reconstruction of society. Although the *social reconstructionism* movement never gained much of a foothold in American education, it served to associate progressive education in the minds of many people with "an economic radicalism that smacked of socialism and communism" and ultimately contributed to its growing unpopularity in the post-war years (Spring, 1976).

Counts was joined in his deep concern about socioeconomic conditions in America and his belief that educators should do something to address them by liberal progressive educators such as William H. Kilpatrick and Harold Rugg. In 1935 these individuals joined with other social reformers to form the John Dewey Society for the Study of Education and Culture, and began publishing a journal, *The Social Frontier,* which became the focus of educational extremism during the 1930s. The position of Counts and his contemporaries was sharply criticized by many conservative progressives and was responsible for a deepening schism within the Progressive Education Association.

The Eight Year Study

During this same period a significant study was being conducted by the Progressive Education Association. The Eight Year Study (1932–1940) involved 30 high schools willing to experiment with their curriculum to discover the effectiveness of progressive educational approaches in preparing students for college. The results, published in 1942, showed that students from progressive high schools not only achieved higher than students from traditional high schools, but also were better adjusted socially.

Turning Tides

Although progressive education and innovations such as the community school and the project method were popular, protests against the child-centered ideal and its lack of emphasis on fundamentals gained momentum under another professor of education at Teachers College, William Bagley, and other educators associated with *essentialism* (Pulliam, 1991). The essentialists believed that the basic function of education should be to preserve and transmit those skills, arts, and sciences that have endured through time and are necessary for the continuation of civilization. Like Arthur Bestor in the 1950s and the reform reports in the 1980s, Bagley looked at American education and judged it weak, lacking in rigor, full of "frills," and inadequate in preparing youth for productive participation in society. The essentialists were also critical of the social reconstructionists and argued that instead of attempting to reconstruct society, educators would serve society better by preparing citizens who possessed the knowledge of the fundamental skills and subjects that provide a basis for understanding, and for the collective thought and judgment essential to the operation of our democratic institutions (Bagley, 1938).

The Influence of War

As the war with Nazi Germany spread in Europe and American factories increasingly were called on to supply the Allied war effort, the American economy began to recover from the Depression. Once this country entered the war, every institution, including the schools, was dominated by the war effort (see Figure 5.1). According to a statement made by the National Education Association shortly after the attack on Pearl Harbor:

> When the schools closed on Friday, December 5, they had many purposes, and they followed many roads to achieve those purposes. When the schools opened on

Monday, December 8, they had but one dominant purpose—complete, intelligent, and enthusiastic cooperation in the war effort. (Education Policies Commission, 1942, p. 3)

Impact on Schools

The war had a heavy impact on the schools. Not only did large numbers of teachers leave the classroom for the battlefield, but enrollment dropped significantly as youth chose not to return to school or to go to work. High school enrollments declined from 6.7 million in 1941 to 5.5 million in 1944 (Knight, 1952). In addition, financial support, already low because of the Depression, was further reduced as funds were diverted from education to other purposes. Some assistance was provided by the Lanham Act of 1941 to school districts overburdened by an influx of children from families employed in defense industries or on military bases. The so-called "impact aid" continues today under the provisions of Public Laws 815 and 874. Colleges and universities were also affected by the war. Enrollments declined sharply; the enrollment of civilian students was cut almost in half between 1940 and 1944. There was also a severe reduction in instructional staff and revenues. Institutional income in 1944 and 1945 was only 67% of what it had been in 1940 (Knight, 1952). Income would have been reduced even more dramatically had it not been for the large research projects commissioned by the federal government. These vast research enterprises transformed many

What is your position in the current debate about the appropriateness of ROTC on college and university campuses?

Figure 5.1: A War Policy for American Schools, A Statement of the Educational Policies Commission of the National Educational Association

The responsibilities of organized education for the successful outcome of the war involve at least the following activities:

- Training workers for war industries and services.
- Producing goods and services needed for the war.
- Conserving materials by prudent consumption and salvage.
- Helping to raise funds to finance the war.
- Increasing effective manpower by correcting educational deficiencies.
- Promoting health and physical efficiency.
- Protecting school children and property against attack.
- Protecting the ideals of democracy against war hazards.
- Teaching the issues, aims, and progress of war and the peace.
- Sustaining the morale of children and adults.
- Maintaining intelligent loyalty to American democracy.

Source: Educational Policies Commission. (1942). *A war policy for American schools.* Washington, DC: National Education Association.

universities into what Clark Kerr has termed "federal grant universities" (Kerr, 1963).

Colleges and universities also played a vital role in preparing men for military service, for war industries, and for essential civilian activities. By the end of 1943, 380,000 men were involved in specialized training in 489 colleges and universities, many as part of the Army Specialized Training Program or the Navy College Training Program (Knight, 1952).

The Postwar Years

Toward the end of the war, in an effort to assist veterans whose schooling had been interrupted by military service, the Servicemen's Readjustment Act of 1944 was passed. The G.I. Bill of Rights, as it became known, provided benefits to 7.8 million veterans of World War II to help them further their education. The benefits subsequently were extended to veterans of the Korean, "Cold," and Vietnam wars; eventually almost 15 million veterans were involved. The G.I. Bill also initiated a great postwar popularization of higher education. More men and women representing a greater age range and social, economic, cultural and racial groups attended colleges and universities than ever before (Cremin, 1988) (see Table 5.2).

In addition, while returning servicemen filled college and university classrooms after the war, within a decade the postwar "baby boom" hit the public schools. Between 1946 and 1956 kindergarten and elementary school enrollments increased 37%, from 17.7 million to 24.3 million (U.S. Bureau of the Census, 1975).

Life Adjustment Education

In the postwar years progressive education came under major criticism by those who held it responsible for the decline in educational standards in this country. By the 1950s it had become identified with an educational program known as *life adjustment education*. Life adjustment education was introduced in 1945 at a vocational education conference sponsored by the U.S. Office of Education. Fully supported by this office and spurred on by a series of conferences, state and national commissions, and numerous publications, it was seen by many as a nat-

Table 5.2: Institutions of Higher Education, Faculty, and Enrollments, 1919–20 to 1991–92

	1919–20	1929–30	1939–40	1949–50
Total institutions	1,041	1,409	1,708	1,851
Total faculty	48,615	82,386	146,929	245,722
Total enrollment	597,880	1,100,737	1,494,203	2,659,021

ural outgrowth of progressive education. Focusing on that majority of youth who do not attend college, life adjustment education stressed functional objectives such as vocation and health and rejected traditional academic studies. In many ways life adjustment education was indistinguishable from many other versions of progressive education already well established in schools across the country (Ravitch, 1983).

Critics of progressive education found in life adjustment education a perfect target: "it continued an abundance of slogans, jargon, and various anti-intellectualism; it carried the utilitarianism and group conformism of latter-day progressivism to its ultimate trivialization" (Ravitch, 1983, p. 70). The outpouring of criticism, coming at the same time as the teacher shortage and the onset of the baby boom, made it clear that the schools were in the middle of a crisis that could not be ignored. Throughout most of the 1950s the "crisis in education" and the debate over contemporary practices filled the pages of national journals (Ravitch, 1983).

The Critics and the Decline of Progressive Education

One of the foremost critics of progressive education at this time was Arthur Bestor. In his most famous critical study, *Educational Wastelands,* Bestor deplored the anti-intellectual quality of American schools, which he argued had been caused by progressive education. Bestor advocated a rigorous curriculum of well-defined subject matter disciplines and the development of the intellect as the primary goal of education. Bestor later became one of the founders of the Council on Basic Education, an organization dedicated to the promotion of a basic academic curriculum. Two other leading critics of the contemporary educational scene were former Harvard president James Conant and Admiral Hyman Rickover. Their criticisms foreshadowed the back to basics movement of the 1970s.

But in the end it was not its critics that killed progressive education. It died because it was no longer relevant to the time. The great debate about American education continued until 1957 when the Soviet Union launched Sputnik, the first space satellite. Then, in a nation suddenly concerned with intelligence and the need for increased science and mathematics skills, progressive education

1959–60	1969–70	1979–80	1989–90	1991–92
2,008	2,525	3,152	3,535	3,601
380,554	450,000	675,000	824,220	826,252
3,639,847	8,004,660	11,569,899	13,538,560	14,358,953

Source: U.S. Department of Education, National Center for Education Statistics. (1994). *Digest of Education Statistics 1994* (Table 168). Washington, DC: U.S. Government Printing Office.

seemed out of step. By the time it disappeared in the mid-1950s it had strayed far from the "humane, pragmatic, open-minded" approach proposed by Dewey,

> though surely the influence of its pioneers was present whenever projects, activities, and pupil experiences had been intelligently integrated into subject-matter teaching, wherever concern for health and vocation had gained a permanent place in the school program, and whenever awareness of individual differences among children had replaced lockstep institution and rote memorization. (Ravitch, 1983, p. 80)

Table 5.3 lists the contributions of major figures from the progressive era to American educational history.

Sputnik and After

Few times in history has a single event had such an impact on education as the launching of Sputnik in October 1957. The event seemed to confirm the growing fear that the United States was losing in the Cold War technological and military races with the Soviet Union because of a shortage of trained teachers, engineers, and students.

Curriculum Reforms

Reacting to public pressures, in 1958 the federal government passed the National Defense Education Act (NDEA). By directing significant federal funding to specific curricular areas, particularly mathematics, science, and modern foreign languages, the federal government for the first time attempted to influence the curriculum in general elementary and secondary education. The NDEA sponsored the efforts of academic specialists engaged in large-scale projects to revise the curriculum according to the latest theories and methods. Soon the "new math," "new chemistry," "new grammar," and other "new" revisions were being developed and introduced in the schools. Summer institutes were held for teachers to train them in the use of the new materials and methods. The NDEA also provided funding for science, mathematics, and foreign language laboratories; media and other instructional material; and improvement of guidance, counseling, and testing programs, especially those efforts directed at identification and encouragement of more capable students. Student loans and graduate fellowships were also funded under the NDEA.

The curriculum reforms initiated by the NDEA of 1958 and an expanded version of that act in 1964 were further stimulated by James Conant's widely publicized study of secondary education, *The American High School Today* (1959), which recommended increased rigor and an academic core of English, mathematics, science, and the social sciences. Underlying these curricular reforms was the learning theory of Jerome Bruner, which stressed the teaching of the structure of the disciplines (i.e., the major concepts and methods of inquiry of the discipline) and the stage concept of child development formulated by Jean Piaget. According to Bruner, some form of the structure of a discipline could be taught to students at each stage of their cognitive development. These theories

Table 5.3: They Made It Happen: Important Figures from the Progressive Era in American Educational History

Francis W. Parker (1837–1902)	Principal of Cook County Normal School in Chicago (1883–1896) and director of the University of Chicago School of Education (1901–1902). Began progressive education movement.
John Dewey (1859–1952)	Noted philosopher and educator. Advanced philosophy that became known as pragmatism or progressivism. Provided intellectual foundation and rationale for the progressive education movement.
Harold Rugg (1886–1960)	One of the founders and leading spokespersons of the Progressive Education Association. Leader in social reconstructionist movement.
William H. Kilpatrick (1871–1965)	Professor at Teachers College, Columbia University (1909–1938). Leader of progressive education movement and the Progressive Education Association. Originator of the project method.
G. Stanley Hall (1844–1924)	Psychologist, professor (taught Dewey) and president of Clark University (1889–1919). Founder of the child study movement. Important in providing foundation for the fields of child and adolescent psychology and the study of exceptional children.
Lewis M. Terman (1877–1956)	Pioneer in the measurement movement. Developed Stanford-Binet test using the intelligence quotient (IQ), a measure of mental development.
Edward L. Thorndike (1874–1949)	Experimental psychologist. Major early contributor to the measurement movement and educational psychology. Developed instruments to measure achievement in a number of academic areas.
George C. Counts (1889–1974)	President of the American Federation of Teachers (1934–1942). Professor at Teachers College, Columbia University (1927–1956). Critic of the child-centeredness of progressive education.
William Bagley (1874–1946)	Educator and theorist. Critic of progressive education. Founder and spokesperson for the essentialist movement.
Arthur Bestor (1879–1944)	Pioneer in adult education in United States. President of the Chautauqua Institution. Critic of progressive education. Cofounder of Council on Basic Education.

gave credence to the *spiral curriculum* sequencing pattern whereby subject matter is presented over a number of grades with increasing complexity and abstraction.

The NDEA set the stage for the federal government's increased involvement in education. In the decade that followed, the federal government waged another war in which it became, for perhaps the first time in our nation's history, a major force in the educational arena. This war was the War on Poverty.

Education and the War on Poverty

In the early 1960s large numbers of Americans became aware that at least one-quarter of the population had been bypassed by the postwar prosperity and lived in dire poverty. The results were rising crime rates, a decline in qualified manpower for military service, and a number of other social and economic prob-

If a major federal initiative such as the NDEA were being considered to fund programs to meet today's educational demands, what specific programs would you recommend be funded?

lems. Books, reports, and high-impact media coverage such as Edward R. Murrow's documentary on migrant farm workers, "Harvest of Shame," brought a flood of interest in the elimination of poverty. As a result, the Democratic administrations of John F. Kennedy in 1963 and Lyndon B. Johnson in 1964 declared a War on Poverty. In an effort to win the war, federal legislation was passed to subsidize low-income housing, improve health care, expand welfare services, provide job retraining, undertake regional planning in depressed areas such as Appalachia, and improve inner-city schools (Church & Sedlak, 1976).

Education was viewed as a major factor in the elimination of poverty. Poor children as well as those of certain minority groups, it was noted, consistently failed to achieve. In the optimistic view of many politicians, social scientists, and educators, the "cultural deprivation" (i.e., lack of middle-class attitudes and incomes) of the poor was attributable to a lack of education, and if the poor were provided the skills and education for employment they could achieve middle-class economic and social status and break the "cycle of poverty" (Zigler & Valentine, 1979).

Federal Education Legislation

The War on Poverty on the education front was waged by a number of initiatives. The Vocational Education Act of 1963 more than quadrupled federal funds for vocational education. The purpose of the act was to enhance occupational training opportunities for persons of all ages by providing financial assistance to vocational and technical programs in high schools and nonbaccalaureate postsecondary institutions. The Manpower Development and Training Act, enacted the same year, was directed at providing retraining for unemployed adults.

The Economic Opportunity Act (EOA) of 1964 established the Job Corps to train youth between 16 and 21 in basic literacy skills and for employment, and also established a type of domestic Peace Corps, Volunteers in Service to America (VISTA). Perhaps the most popular and controversial component of the EOA was Project Head Start, a program aimed at disadvantaged children three to five years old who would not normally attend preschool or kindergarten. President Johnson called Head Start a "landmark," not only in education but in "the maturity of our democracy." Head Start, he foretold, would "strike at the basic cause of poverty" by addressing it at its beginnings—the disadvantaged preschool child. As the name suggests, the intent of the program was to give disadvantaged children a head start in the educational race so that once in school they might be on equal terms with children from nondisadvantaged homes. The Head Start Program, while perhaps not living up to all of President Johnson's expectations, has proven since its initiation in 1965 to be the most successful of the compensatory education programs.

The major piece of educational legislation enacted as part of the War on Poverty was the Elementary and Secondary Education Act of 1965 (ESEA). The most far-reaching piece of federal education legislation to date, the ESEA provided over $1 billion in federal funds to education. Although it was directed at specific programs, populations, and purposes, it represented more general aid than previous federal aid programs.

Presidents Johnson and Kennedy declared a war on poverty, using education as a major weapon in the fight.

The ESEA included five major sections or titles. The largest, receiving about 80% of the funds, was Title I (now Chapter 1), which provided assistance to local school districts for the education of children from low-income families. The compensatory education programs funded through Title I were intended to maintain the educational progress begun in Head Start. Title I was to become the major education component of the War on Poverty (Spring, 1976). Other sections of the ESEA provided funds for library resources, textbooks, and instructional materials; supplemental education centers; educational research and training; and strengthening state departments of education. The act was expanded in 1966 and 1967 to include programs for Native American children, children of migrant workers, the handicapped (Title VI), and children with limited English-speaking ability (Title VII).

In the same year that the ESEA was passed, Congress passed the Higher Education Act, which provided direct assistance to institutes of higher education for facility construction and library and instructional improvement, as well as loans and scholarships to students. The year 1965 also saw the establishment of the National Foundation of the Arts and the Humanities to promote and encourage production, dissemination, and scholarship in the arts and humanities.

In 1967 the Educational Professions Development Act was signed into law by President Johnson. In 1968, the last year of Johnson's Great Society, the

Have you been a beneficiary of any federally sponsored educational program? What educational benefits did you receive from this participation?

Vocational Education Act was expanded and its funding authorization doubled. In addition, the Higher Education Act was amended to consolidate previous legislation involving higher education and a number of new program initiatives.

Between the years 1963 and 1969 Congress passed more than two dozen major pieces of legislation affecting education. These laws dramatically increased federal involvement in education and provided vast sums of money for elementary and secondary schools, vocational schools, colleges, and universities. In 1963–1964 federal funds for elementary and secondary schools totaled almost $900 million. By 1968–1969 this had rocketed to $3 billion, and the federal government's share of the financing of education had risen from 4.4% to 8.8%. Perhaps equally as important as the increased funding was the shift in emphasis from identifying the gifted, which had marked the 1950s, to a concern for the disadvantaged.

The Civil Rights Movement

The Brown Decision

The schools not only were given a major role in the War on Poverty, they became a stage for much of the drama of the civil rights movement. The *Brown v. Board of Education of Topeka* decision of 1954, which ordered an end to legalized segregation in education, stated that segregated educational facilities are inherently unequal and generate a feeling of inferiority that affects the child's motivation to learn. However, instead of being the climax of the struggle for racial equality in education, *Brown* marked the beginning of the civil rights revolution. Although the civil rights movement began with blacks, perhaps because the basic vision of what was wrong was most visible in the history of blacks in America, the general principles of the movement were later applied to advancing the rights of women, racial and ethnic groups, the aged, and the handicapped (Sowell, 1984).

The *Brown* decision met with massive nationwide resistance in the form of legal maneuvers and violence, resulting in countless confrontations between federal authorities who sought to enforce the law and local police or citizens who sought to obstruct it. The most dramatic physical confrontations occurred

> in 1957 when President Eisenhower sent federal troops to Little Rock to insure that black students were safely enrolled, over the objections of the state's governor, in Central High School; in 1962 when large numbers of federal marshals were required to force James Meredith's enrollment at the University of Mississippi over the objections of the state authorities, an incident in which two lives were lost; and in 1963 when President Kennedy nationalized the Alabama National Guard to enforce the integration at the state university. (Church & Sedlak, 1976, p. 446)

At the same time that school desegregation was making limited progress (see Chapter 9 for a discussion of desegregation), the civil rights movement was gaining momentum on other fronts. Freedom rides, sit-ins, boycotts, and other forms of nonviolent protest both appealed to the national conscience and focused national attention on a movement that would not be denied. President John F. Kennedy pressed for the passage of a federal civil rights statute that would end segregation in public facilities, attack discrimination in employment, and require nondiscriminatory practices in programs and institutions receiving federal funds. Five days after his assassination, his successor, Lyndon B. Johnson, appeared before Congress and sought its passage, declaring it the most fitting honor of his memory. The Civil Rights Act of 1964, when passed, became one of the most significant pieces of social legislation in the United States in this century (Spring, 1976).

The Civil Rights Act and Desegregation

The Civil Rights Act of 1964 further involved the federal government in the activities of the schools. Title VI of the Act prohibits discrimination against students on the basis of race, color, or national origin in all institutions receiving federal funds. Title VII forbids discrimination in employment based on race, religion, national origin, or—as of 1972—sex. The act authorized the withholding of federal funds from any institution or agency violating the law. It also authorized the U.S. attorney general to take legal action to achieve school desegregation and provided federal financial assistance to school districts attempting to desegregate.

The passage of the Civil Rights Act of 1964 and the education acts of 1965 combined with the growing intolerance of the Supreme Court to the resistance to the *Brown* decision to create a "carrot-and-stick" mechanism that dramatically increased the pace of school desegregation. Federal expenditures for education, including higher education, increased from $4.5 billion in 1966, to $8.8 billion in 1970, to $13.4 billion in 1974, to $19.5 billion in 1983—"thus the carrot; and the Supreme Court continued to strike down devices for evading school desegregation—thus the stick" (Cremin, 1988, p. 264). As detailed in Chapter 9, in a series of decisions between 1968 and 1972 the Supreme Court struck down *de jure* segregation in the South and *de facto* segregation in the North.

Further Advances

The civil rights movement in education also made advances on other fronts. Previously, instruction in most schools was given only in English. In the 1960s, however, attention was turned to the growing Hispanic population of the large cities and states outside the Southwest. In 1968 the Bilingual Education Act was passed, which gave federal funds to school districts to provide bilingual education to low-income students with limited English proficiency. Additional support for bilingual education was provided by the 1974 *Lau v. Nichols* decision by the Supreme Court, which said that schools must provide special language programs for non–English-speaking children. In response, Congress passed the Bilingual Education Act of 1974, which provided for bilingual education for *all* children with limited English ability as a means of promoting educational equity (Cremin, 1988). At the same time, the Indian Education Act of 1972 and the Indian Self-Determination and Education Assistance Act of 1975 expanded the rights of Native Americans in regard to the education of their youth, and sought to ensure increased educational opportunity for those youth.

Title IX of the 1972 Education Amendments, which prohibited discrimination against employees and students in educational programs receiving federal

To what do you attribute the increase in the number of incidences of racial violence in the schools and on college and university campuses?

funds, was a major victory in the extension of the civil rights movement to women. And in 1975, the landmark Education for All Handicapped Children Act established the right of all handicapped children to a free and appropriate education. Each of these topics is covered in greater detail in later chapters.

Social Unrest

The late 1960s and 1970s also saw a series of urban riots and the sometimes passive, sometimes violent student rights and anti-Vietnam War movements, which began with protests on college campuses but often spilled into the streets. Both movements tended to have a negative impact on the civil rights movement through a subliminal process of guilt by association. Many members of academia as well as the larger society became disenchanted with the civil rights movement, "not because they disagreed with or were unsympathetic to its legitimate claim, but because the Student Rights Movement, which they strongly opposed, got its impetus, simulation, and example from the Civil Rights Movement" (Tollett, 1983, p. 57). A campaign against demonstrations and riots and for the restoration of law and order helped put Richard Nixon in the White House in 1969 and reelect him in 1972.

During the 1980s the civil rights movement was slowed considerably by the actions of both the courts (see Chapters 9 and 12) and the Reagan administration. The budget of the Office of Civil Rights was cut, investigations were "cursory," and enforcement and compliance were loosened. The Department of Justice not only seemed uninterested in enforcing civil rights plans, it attempted to block efforts to broaden the scope of civil rights and to strengthen affirmative action. The current status of the various civil rights interests (e.g., desegregation, discrimination, education of minority and special populations) is discussed elsewhere in this text.

The 1970s: Retreat and Retrenchment

During the Nixon administration (1969–1974) support for many of the initiatives begun during the Kennedy and Johnson administrations was reduced. The hallmark of the Republican administrations of the 1970s and 1980s was transfer of responsibility for domestic programs from the federal government to state and local governments (see Table 5.4). However, the 1970s did witness increased attention to the needs of handicapped persons. The Vocational Rehabilitation Act of 1973 sought to increase the physical access of handicapped persons to educational institutions and vocational training and employment. And during the Ford administration (1974–1977) the Education for All Handicapped Children Act of 1975 (now the Individuals with Disabilities Education Act) was enacted (see Chapter 9).

Under the Carter administration (1977–1981) the federal education budget was increased, from 8.8% of the total elementary and secondary revenues in 1977 when Carter took office, to 9.8% in 1980, his last year in office (see Table 5.4). Under his administration a Department of Education was established. Keeping his campaign promise to the National Education Association, Carter was able to overcome congressional opposition and in 1979 legislation was

Table 5.4: Public Elementary and Secondary School Revenues, by Source, 1940–1992 (in thousands of dollars)

School Year Ending	Federal Amount	Federal Percent of Total	State Amount	State Percent of Total	Local Amount	Local Percent of Total	Total
1940	39,810	1.8	684,354	30.3	1,536,363	68.0	2,260,527
1950	155,848	2.9	2,165,689	39.8	3,115,507	57.3	5,437,044
1952	227,711	3.5	2,478,596	38.6	3,717,507	57.9	6,423,816
1954	355,237	4.5	2,944,103	37.4	4,567,512	58.1	7,866,852
1956	441,442	4.6	3,828,886	39.5	5,416,350	55.9	9,686,677
1958	486,484	4.0	4,800,368	39.4	6,894,661	58.6	12,181,513
1960	651,639	4.4	5,768,047	39.1	8,326,932	56.5	14,746,618
1962	760,975	4.3	6,789,190	38.7	9,977,542	56.9	17,527,707
1964	896,956	4.4	8,078,014	39.3	11,569,213	56.3	20,544,182
1966	1,996,954	7.9	9,920,219	39.1	13,439,886	53.0	25,356,858
1968	2,806,469	8.8	12,275,536	38.5	16,821,063	52.7	31,903,064
1970	3,219,557	8.0	16,062,776	39.9	20,984,589	52.1	40,266,923
1972	4,467,969	8.9	19,133,256	38.3	26,402,420	52.8	50,003,645
1974	4,930,351	8.5	24,113,409	41.4	29,187,132	50.1	58,230,892
1976	6,318,345	8.9	31,776,101	44.6	33,111,627	48.5	71,206,073
1978	7,694,194	9.4	35,013,266	43.0	38,735,700	47.6	81,443,160
1980	9,503,537	9.8	45,348,814	46.8	42,028,813	43.4	96,881,165
1982	8,186,466	7.4	52,436,435	49.7	49,568,346	45.0	110,191,257
1984	8,567,547	6.8	60,232,981	47.8	57,245,892	45.4	126,055,419
1985	9,105,569	6.6	67,168,684	48.9	61,020,425	44.4	137,294,678
1986	9,975,622	6.7	73,619,575	49.4	65,532,582	43.9	149,127,779
1987	10,146,013	6.4	78,830,437	49.7	69,547,243	43.9	158,523,693
1988	10,716,687	6.3	84,004,415	49.5	74,840,873	44.1	169,561,974
1989	11,902,001	6.2	91,768,911	47.8	88,345,462	46.0	192,016,374
1990	12,700,784	6.1	98,238,633	47.3	96,813,516	46.6	207,752,932
1991	13,776,066	6.2	105,324,533	47.2	104,239,939	46.7	223,340,537
1992	15,493,330	6.6	108,792,779	46.4	110,199,621	47.0	234,485,729

Source: U.S. Department of Education, National Center for Education Statistics. (1994). *Digest of Education Statistics,* (Table 157). Washington, DC: U.S. Government Printing Office.

passed to elevate the Office of Education to department status, making its secretary a member of the president's cabinet. Carter appointed Shirley Hufstadler, a federal appeals court judge, as the first secretary of education. The appointment of a federal judge was indicative of the Carter administration's commitment to enforcing legislation directed at protecting civil rights and promoting equality of educational opportunity (Ravitch, 1983).

The 1970s was a decade marked by economic uncertainty. Presidents Nixon, Ford, and Carter fought unsuccessfully to curb inflation, reduce unemployment, reduce the federal deficit, and reduce the imbalance of foreign trade. The impacts of rapid inflation and the energy crisis (resulting from the oil embargo of the United States by the Organization of Petroleum Exporting Countries in 1973) were sorely felt by the schools. At the same time that operating costs were spiraling and the salary demands of teachers hurt by inflation were becoming more strident, revenues were declining.

The decline in revenues was a result of two forces: (1) the "revolt" of taxpayers against rising taxes, especially property taxes, which are the major source of tax revenues for the schools, and (2) a decline in enrollments, which brought about a reduction in state revenues, since most states, to a large extent, base their aid to local school districts on enrollment. In 1971, for the first time since World War II, the total number of elementary and secondary students enrolled in the public schools declined (see Figure 5.2). This decline and its accompanying reduction in revenues led to various efforts to "trim the budget," including program cuts, teacher layoffs, and, in extreme cases, school closures.

The 1980s: A Decade of Reform

The election of Ronald Reagan in 1980 brought a resurgence of conservatism in both politics and education. The New Federalism called for reduced federal spending for social programs, including education, and encouraged a greater role for state and local governments. The Education Consolidation and Improvement Act of 1981 sought to consolidate the massive array of federal aid programs into several large block programs. However, Reagan's proposal for the entire block was

Figure 5.2: Enrollment in Public Elementary and Secondary Schools, by Grade Level, with Projections, Fall 1979–Fall 2004

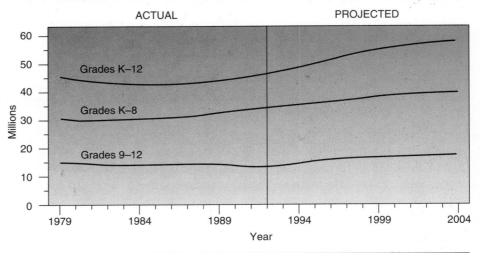

Source: U.S. Dept. of Education, National Center for Education Statistics. (1993). *Projections of education statistics to 2004.* Washington, DC: U.S. Government Printing Office.

less than what formerly had been spent for the ESEA alone. In fact, in every budget request made while he was in office, President Reagan proposed reductions in federal spending for education. Fortunately, Congress appropriated more than the president requested. Nonetheless, from fiscal years 1980 to 1989, federal funds for elementary and secondary education declined by 17%, and for higher education declined by 27% (U.S. Department of Education, 1989).

The 1980s also saw a renewal of public debate about the condition of American education. Where Sputnik and technological competition with the Russians had focused attention on the educational system in the 1950s, in the 1980s it was economic competition with the Japanese that brought the educational system into the forefront of public debate. In response to the growing belief that the decline in the quality of the educational system was a major factor in the nation's declining economic and intellectual competitiveness, President Reagan appointed a National Commission of Excellence in Education. Its report, *A Nation at Risk: The Imperative for Educational Reform,* in strong and stirring language described a "rising tide of mediocrity" and declared that it would have been seen as "an act of war" if any unfriendly power had imposed our educational system on us.

A Nation at Risk was followed throughout the 1980s by various other reports on the status of education. Collectively they are responsible for what has been referred to as "The Educational Reform Movement of the 1980s." This reform movement has been characterized as having two waves. The first wave responded to the recommendations of *A Nation at Risk* and similar reports and sought to bring about reform by state actions directed at improving achievement and accountability. States enacted higher graduation requirements, standardized curriculum mandates, increased the testing of both teachers and students, and raised certification requirements for teachers. In perhaps the most far reaching action, Kentucky replaced the state department of education with an agency that provides assistance to schools but has no regulatory power; gave school councils composed of parents, teachers, and principals the responsibility for hiring staff, deciding on curriculum, and setting disciplinary standards; and provided significant rewards or sanctions to schools based on student performance on state-imposed assessment measures. School districts throughout the nation increased their emphasis on computer literacy, homework, and basic skills; established minimum standards for participation in athletics; and lengthened the school day and the school year.

The second wave of reform, beginning in 1986, focused not at the state level, on state mandates and centralization of authority, but at the local level and at the structure and processes of the schools themselves. The second wave of reform also sought to balance the concern for excellence of the first wave with a concern for equity and the disadvantaged students who might become further disadvantaged by the "new standards of excellence." The recommendations from the second wave of reform dealt with such issues as decentralization, site-based management, teacher empowerment, parental involvement, and school choice. *Restructuring,* a buzzword of the second wave of reform, was associated with a number of prescriptions: year-round schools, longer school days and years, recast modes of governance, alternative funding patterns, all-out commitments to technology, and various combinations of these and other proposals (Kaplan, 1990). The reform of teacher education discussed in Chapter 1 to a significant degree also grew out of the second wave of reform. Other state and local responses to the second wave of reform continue into the 1990s and are discussed in the chapters that follow in this text.

The 1990s: National Goals and National Standards

The 1990s began with an unprecedented event—for the first time in our nation's history, state and national leaders joined in setting goals for the schools. The National Governors' Association and the Bush administration in early 1990 approved six national education goals to be accomplished by the year 2000:

- All children in America will start school ready to learn.

- The high school graduation rate will increase to at least 90%.

- American students will leave grades 4, 8, and 12 having demonstrated competency in challenging subject matter, including English, mathematics, science, history, and geography; and every school in America will ensure that all students learn to use their minds well, so they may be prepared for responsible citizenship, future learning, and productive employment in our modern economy.

- U.S. students will be first in the world in mathematics and science achievement.

- Every adult American will be literate and will possess the knowledge and skills necessary to compete in a global economy and exercise the rights and responsibilities of citizenship.

- Every school in America will be free of drugs and violence and will offer a disciplined environment conducive to learning.

President Bush was unable to gain Congressional support for his strategy for implementing the goals, a plan called America 2000, largely because of the controversy surrounding a key feature of the plan—vouchers to promote school choice.

The 1990s have also seen education assume a place of prominence on the political agenda that it has never before held. As observed by Terrel H. Bell, Secretary of Education under President Reagan:

> George Bush proclaimed himself to be the "Education President" during his successful 1988 campaign. President Bill Clinton brought the less-than-spectacular Bush record in education to the attention of the voters during the campaign of 1992 and promised to be a more effective "Education President." This has never happened in the nation's history. Education is now a major, high priority national concern, as well as a state and local responsibility.
>
> Gubernatorial attention has also flourished. . . . During the 1980s and into the 1990s candidates campaigning for governor have highlighted education and touted their plans to give their states better schools. (1993, p. 595)

President Clinton showed his commitment to education by signing the Goals 2000: Educate America Act.

The Clinton Administration did, in fact, attempt to keep its commitment to education. The Clinton plan to implement the national goals was called Goals 2000: Educate America Act. Goals 2000 adopted the six goals articulated by the National Governor's Association and added two new goals related to parent participation and teacher preparation. The act not only formalized the national education goals, it also formalized the development of national standards and new assessment systems, and established a "new federal partnership to reform the nation's educational system" (U.S. Department of Education, 1994). The Goals 2000 Act established an Education Standards and Improvement Council (NESIC) to develop model standards for all major academic areas. This included content standards, student performance standards, and "opportunity-to-learn" standards. The opportunity-to-learn standards are intended to establish a basis for giving all students the opportunity to achieve the content and performance standards. The opportunity-to-learn standards represent "the most contentious and ultimately the most far-reaching provision of the Goals 2000 legislation" because they shift the focus from equal *access* to "whether these services are actually delivered to all children" (Lewis, 1994, p. 601).

Professional Reflections

"To succeed as a teacher . . . make sure that students feel successful at learning. . . . Make them buy into the idea of learning . . . never make the assumption that all students come to class eager for academics. . . . Find a way to make students care, to make them want to learn. . . . See yourself as a salesman. . . . Ask, "If my lesson was a product I had to sell, how could I get my students to buy into it?" Making students feel like they can succeed at a task is a sure-fire way to get them involved."

Shawn Eric DeNight, Teacher of the Year, Florida

The NESIC will also provide voluntary national certification to content and performance standards submitted by state and local school districts. A major incentive for states and districts to develop such standards is $400 million in grants that is authorized under the act to those states that adopt reform plans. In the first six months after the passage of Goals 2000 almost three-fourths of the states had applied for funding to develop or expand reform efforts.

Another significant feature of the Goals 2000 Act was the creation of a National Skills Standards Board to develop entry-level standards (closely related to academic standards) for clusters of occupations. "Such standards have the potential to revolutionize vocational education and that vast area known as comprehensive education, which has been neither academic nor vocational" (Lewis, 1994, p. 660).

The first two years of the Clinton Administration have been said to be the most productive in terms of major education legislation since 1965–66. Goals 2000 was seen as providing the framework for relating and reinforcing other major education initiatives, which included:

- *The Student Loan Reform Act,* which allowed students to bypass banks and get loans directly from the educational institution and provided for a variety of repayment options, including income contingency. The act is expected to save billions of dollars by eliminating middlemen and reducing loan defaults.

- *The National Service Trust Act,* which established a Corporation for National Service and provided education grants of up to $4,725 per year for 2 years to people 17 or older before, during, or after post-secondary education for performing community service work.

- *The School to Work Opportunities Act,* which provided grants to states and communities to develop school-to-work-opportunity programs to train non–college-bound youth for careers in high skill occupations. Such programs must include school-based learning, work-based learning, and connecting activities that match students with employers who can provide work-based learning experiences and assist students who complete high school to find appropriate jobs or pursue future education or training.

Controversial Issues:
Parental Public School Choice

One of the most popular proposals of the emerging restructuring movement is the proposal to let parents choose the public school their children will attend. According to the Gallup Poll, 60% of Americans favor public school choice. However, a number of educational groups, as well as many in the lay public, oppose choice plans. The reasons stated by proponents of each side include the following:

Arguments For

1. Breaks the monopoly of the public schools and makes them more responsible to the forces of the marketplace.

2. Competition will promote efficiency and excellence in operation.

3. Encourages diversity in programs.

4. Students achieve better in schools they have chosen to attend.

5. Parents are more satisfied with and committed to the schools when they have a choice.

6. Teacher satisfaction and morale is higher in schools of choice.

Arguments Against

1. Will lead to ethnic, racial and socioeconomic segregation.

2. Conditions will worsen in poorest districts as students leave and take their per-pupil state aid with them.

3. Transportation costs will be dramatically increased.

4. Potential for fluctuations in enrollments make planning for staffing and budgeting difficult.

5. Most parents would not be able to make an informed choice among the alternative schools.

What, if any, support for parental choice is there in your state? How has it been evidenced? What is your position on parental public school choice?

- *The Safe Schools Act,* which funded violence prevention programs at schools and mandated a mandatory one-year suspension of students who bring guns to school.

- *The Head Start Reauthorization Act,* which expanded the Head Start Program, increasing by 90,000 the number of students served.

- *The Improving America's Schools Act,* which reauthorized the Elementary and Secondary Education Act for five years. A major provision of the act requires states (with the input of local school districts) to develop school improvement plans that establish high content and performance standards in order to become eligible to receive Chapter 1 grants, which account for over two-thirds of the total funds authorized by the act. This provision forces Chapter 1 schools to participate in the Goals 2000 Act.

A Look Ahead

The Republican takeover of the U.S. Congress and many state legislatures in the 1994 elections is likely to bring "more hospitable environments for ideas that have been identified with conservatives" (Harp, 1994, p. 17). At the federal level, the Republican majority is expected to "radically alter the prospects for education legislation and may curtail the federal role in setting education policy, which has taken on new importance under the Clinton Administration" (Pitsch, 1994, p. 1). Republicans are also likely to attempt to advance such controversial proposals as publicly supported vouchers for use at private schools, and school prayer (Pitsch, 1994).

At the state level, legislation to allow open enrollment and charter schools is expected to be pushed, along with strategies to reduce bureaucracy, increase accountability, and strengthen local control. Other predictions are that efforts to increase parental choice (see the Controversial Issue on page 171) will be expanded, along with additional receptivity to the various privitization initiatives (see Chapter 16), and that property tax limits may again be advanced. However, while conservative legislatures are not inclined to increase spending on education, the continued improvement of the economy may mitigate against any actual budget cuts, especially at the state level (Harp, 1994).

Summary

Much of the history of education in this century can be seen in terms of a swing from one view of education to another. The progressive education movement, which began at the turn of the century and continued to gain popularity through the 1930s, gave way in the post–World War II years to a more conservative view of the purpose of education, which was a response to a perceived decline in the nation's technological supremacy. In the 1960s the tide turned again in favor of a more liberal and child-centered approach and schools became a vital weapon in the War on Poverty.

The late 1970s and 1980s once again saw a renewed interest in basics and a national cry for reform of the entire educational system. The election of a Democratic president in 1992 brought with it a renewed federal commitment to education and the passage of legislation designed to make the federal government a partner in reform.

The Republican takeover of Congress just two years later has cast doubt on to what extent this partnership will continue, and has led many observers to predict renewed efforts at the federal level, as well as at the state level, to advance a conservative education agenda that includes support for deregulation, increased choice, vouchers, privatization, and school prayer. Other predictions about the future of education are found in Chapter 16. Before that, however, we will turn our attention to a number of topics, including an exploration of the major philosophies of education in Chapter 6.

Key Terms

Child-centered curriculum
Essentialism
Intelligence quotient
Life adjustment education
Project method

Restructuring
Social reconstructionism
Spiral curriculum
Subject-centered curriculum

Discussion Questions

 1. Like the student described in the incident at the beginning of the chapter, many students are struggling for survival amidst a dysfunctional family life. In addition to bibliotherapy, what are some other methods that can be used to reach these students?

2. Compare the high school curricula of 1930, 1960, and 1990.

3. Describe the impact of the two world wars on American higher education.

4. To what extent have the schools either changed society or adapted to changes in society in this century?

5. Trace the changing involvement of the federal government in education in the twentieth century. What has been the impact of declining federal financial support?

6. What have been the most significant positive and negative changes in education during your lifetime? What changes/reforms do you think need to be made?

References

Bagley, W. C. (1938). An essentialist platform for the advancement of American education. *Educational Administration and Supervision, 24,* 241–56.

Bell, T. H. (1993). Reflections one decade after *A Nation at Risk. Phi Delta Kappan, 74,* 592–597.

Bonner, T. N. (1963). *Our recent past: American civilization in the twentieth century.* Englewood Cliffs, NJ: Prentice-Hall.

Brown vs. Board of Education, 347 U.S. 463 (1954).

Church, R. L., & Sedlak, M. W. (1976). *Education in the United States.* New York: The Face Press.

Conant, J. B. (1959). *The American high school today.* New York: McGraw-Hill.

Cremin, L. A. (1962). *The transformation of the school.* New York: Alfred A. Knopf.

Cremin, L. A. (1988). *American education: The metropolitan experience, 1876–1980.* New York: Harper & Row.

Education Policies Commission. (1942). *A war policy for American schools.* Washington, DC: National Education Association.

Gray, R., & Peterson, J. M. (1974). *Economic development of the United States.* Homewood, IL: Richard D. Irwin.

Gutek, G. L. (1991). *Education in the United States: An historical perspective.* Englewood Cliffs, NJ: Prentice-Hall.

Harp, L. (1994, November 16). Educators predicted to feel 'staggering' legislative shifts. *Education Week,* 17, 23.

Heffernan, H. (1968). The school curriculum in American education. In *Education in the states: Nationwide development.* Washington, DC: Council of Chief State School Officials.

Kaplan, G. (1990). Pushing and shoving in videoland U.S.A.: TV's version of education (and what to do about it). *Phi Delta Kappan, 71,* K11–K12.

Kidwell, C. S., & Swift, D. W. (1976). Indian education. In D. W. Swift (Ed.), *American education: A sociological view.* Boston: Houghton Miffin.

Kirkland, E. C. (1969). *A history of American economic life* (4th ed.). New York: Appleton-Century-Crofts.

Knight, E. W. (1952). *Fifty years of American education.* New York: The Ronald Press.

Lewis, A. C. (1994). Goals 2000 is not more of the same. *Phi Delta Kappan, 75,* 660–601.

National Policies Commission. (1941). *The Civilian Conservation Corps, the National Youth Administration, and the public schools.* Washington, DC: National Education Association.

Perkinson, H. J. (1977). *The imperfect panacea: American faith in education, 1965–1976* (2d ed.). New York: Random House.

Pitsch, M. (1994, November 16). Congress likely to ponder federal role in education. *Education Week,* 1, 31.

Progressive Education. (1924). 1, 2.

Pulliam, J. D. (1991). *History of education in America* (4th ed.). Columbus, OH: Merrill.

Ravitch, D. (1983). *The troubled crusade—American education, 1945–1980.* New York: Basic Books.

Sowell, T. (1984). *Civil rights: Rhetoric or reality.* New York: William Morrow.

Spring, J. (1976). *The sorting machine: National educational policy 1945.* New York: David McKay.

Szasz, M. C. (1977). *Education and the American Indian.* Albuquerque, NM: University of New Mexico Press.

Tollett, K. S. (1983). *The right to education: Reaganism, Reaganomics, or human capital?* Washington, DC: Institute for the Study of Educational Policy, Howard University, 47.

U.S. Bureau of the Census. (1975). *Historical statistics of the United States, colonial times to 1970.* Washington, DC: U.S. Government Printing Office, Series H 316–326.

U.S. Department of Education, National Center for Education Statistics. (1994). *Condition of education 1994.* Washington, DC: U.S. Government Printing Office.

Zigler, E., & Valentine, J. (Eds.). (1979). *Project Head Start: A legacy of the War on Poverty.* New York: The Face Press.

PART THREE

Philosophy and Its Impact on the Schools

Chapter 6

The Major Philosophies

As Plato understood, there is really only one serious political topic. It is more serious than war, or even the New Federalism. It is the upbringing of children.

George F. Will, 1941

A Critical Incident in My Teaching Career . . .

    . . . I love to teach because I can reflect back on every year I have taught and see my growth as a human being. However, I have had one experience which I must consider pivotal because it reinforced all of the beliefs I profess.

    A student and her parents were leaving my room after a meeting in my laboratory. A drunk driver hit their car, and it took this wonderful child two days to die. I was forced into introspection at the essential purpose of teaching *and I very nearly quit. Finally, I came to realize that education only* reflects the larger successes and tragedies of the surrounding society. I realized that I will grow every year with new students, finding love again and again.

    I will never leave the classroom because although I will always have pain from failure, disappointment, or death, I believe teachers are a spark of optimism without which society simply cannot exist.

Richard R. Chapleau
Teacher of the Year, California

For many, philosophy connotes a certain type of abstract or theoretical thinking that seems far removed from the day-to-day life of the elementary or secondary classroom teacher. However, every teacher and every classroom reflects a set of assumptions about the world. Those principles or assumptions comprise one's personal philosophy as well as one's educational philosophy. In this chapter, we will outline some of the basic philosophic questions as well as review some of the major traditional (idealism, realism, and neo-Thomism) and contemporary (pragmatism and existentialism) philosophies. Lastly, the analytic approach to the study of philosophy will be described, along with its application to educational practice.

As you study the philosophies outlined in this chapter, you may begin to question your personal philosophy. To help you better understand the philosophies and where your personal philosophy fits within that framework, consider the following objectives:

- Explain the relationship between general philosophy and the philosophy of education.
- Discuss the three approaches to the study of philosophy.
- Describe the three branches of philosophy.
- Compare the metaphysics of idealism, realism, neo-Thomism, pragmatism, and existentialism.
- Compare the epistemology of idealism, realism, neo-Thomism, pragmatism, and existentialism.
- Compare the axiology of idealism, realism, neo-Thomism, pragmatism, and existentialism.
- Identify the philosophies that take an optimistic view of human nature and those that take a pessimistic view.
- Explain philosophic analysis in education.
- Contrast philosophic analysis with the descriptive study of philosophy.
- Discuss your philosophy of life and how it has changed over time.

What Is Philosophy?

One formal definition of philosophy as a discipline of inquiry states that philosophy is "the rational investigation of the truths and principles of being, knowledge, or conduct" (*Random House Dictionary*, 1986). Perhaps the most simple, yet comprehensive, definition is that philosophy is "love of wisdom and the search for it."

The formal study of philosophy enables us to better understand who we are, why we are here, and where we are going. Whereas our personal philosophy of life enables us to recognize the meaning of our personal existence, our *philosophy of education* enables us to recognize certain educational principles that define our views about the learner, the teacher, and the school. To teach without a firm understanding of one's personal philosophy and philosophy of education would be analogous to painting a portrait without the rudimentary knowledge and skills of basic design, perspective, or human anatomy. Although you may not have thought about your personal philosophy in a formal sense, you certainly have personal beliefs that have shaped your life. After you have studied and discussed this chapter, you should be able to better articulate your personal philosophy of life.

Approaches to the Study of Philosophy

According to Wingo (1974) there are three main approaches to the study of philosophy: (1) descriptive, (2) normative, and (3) analytic. The descriptive approach is concerned with learning about various schools of philosophic thought and how the philosophers associated with these schools created the thought or position. The normative approach is concerned with values. It is not interested in "what is" (which is the goal of descriptive philosophy) but rather, "what *ought* to be." Using this approach, the philosophic thought is explored and critiqued and determinations are made as to rightness and wrongness. The analytic approach is concerned with an analysis of language, concepts, and theories. The goal of analytic philosophy is to improve our understanding of education by clarifying our educational concepts, beliefs, arguments, and assumptions. For example, an analytic philosopher of education would attempt to understand questions such as these: What is experience? What is understanding? What is readiness? (See Figure 6.1 for further descriptions of these approaches to the study of philosophy.)

Jonas Soltis (1978), a noted philosopher of education, has suggested that the descriptive and normative approaches to the study of philosophy can be combined. To Soltis, these approaches represent the traditional view of philosophy as a discipline that seeks an understanding of human life, including the way the world is; the way it ought to be; and what is good, right, and suitable. Similar to Wingo, Soltis described the analytic approach to the study of philosophy as a more contemporary view that seeks a precise language by examining and questioning certain concepts. Also, according to Soltis, the various

Figure 6.1: Approaches to the Study of Philosophy

Approach	Definition	Example
Descriptive	Learning about various schools of philosophic thought.	Idealism stresses the world of the mind and ideas. Realism stresses the world of physical things.
Normative	Learning about values or "what ought to be."	Should birth control information be dispensed in health classes on high school campuses?
Analytic	Learning how to analyze language, concepts, and theories.	Explain the concept of discipline and its application to your philosophy of education.

approaches to philosophy are not mutually exclusive and can be incorporated. The analytic philosopher professes to be "doing" philosophy as opposed to "studying" about philosophy from a descriptive perspective.

In this chapter and the one that follows we incorporate all three approaches to the study of philosophy. The descriptive and normative approaches are utilized in the presentation of the major philosophies in this chapter and the major educational theories in Chapter 7. The analytic approach, with its analysis of selected educational concepts, is also described in the last section of this chapter.

Branches of Philosophy

Although there is much debate and little agreement about which of the schools of philosophy are most accurate, relevant, or even complete, there is general agreement concerning the basic components or branches of philosophy: metaphysics, epistemology, and axiology. These branches are concerned with the answers to the following three basic questions that are important in describing any philosophy:

- What is the nature of reality?

- What is the nature of knowledge?

- What is the nature of values?

The framework these questions provide enables us to study the major schools of philosophy from a descriptive approach. These branches and questions are elaborated upon in the following section and summarized in Figure 6.2.

Metaphysics: What Is the Nature of Reality?

Of the three basic questions, "What is the nature of reality?" is perhaps the most difficult to answer because its elements are vague, abstract, and not easily

Figure 6.2: Summary of Branches of Philosophy

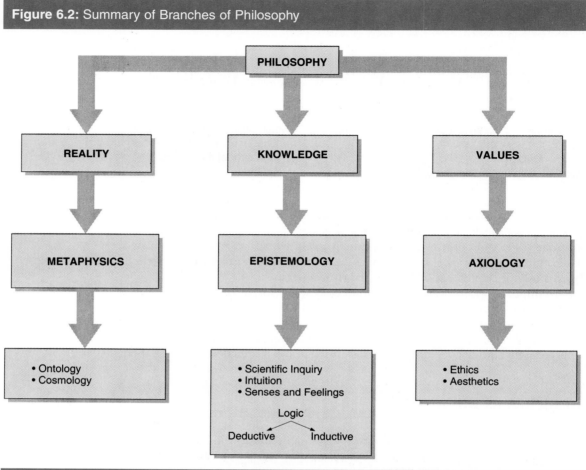

identifiable. According to two recognized educational philosophers, Van Cleve Morris and Young Pai (1976):

> Some individuals . . . consider reality a kind of "given" quality or "ground" of the human situation. We are unable to discuss the nature and character of this ground because we can never truly know it; there is nothing against which we can see it. It is . . . basically irrational or a-rational, possibly even transitional, or beyond the reach of human mentality, and hence not subject to intelligent study. (p. 28)

In spite of its abstraction and vagueness, most philosophers would agree that the study of the nature of reality (meaning of existence) is one of the key concepts in understanding any philosophy.

The branch of philosophy that is concerned with the nature of reality and existence is known as *metaphysics*. Metaphysics is concerned with the question of the nature of the person or self. It addresses such questions as whether human nature is basically good, evil, spiritual, mental, or physical. Metaphysics can be subdivided into the areas of ontology and cosmology.

Ontology raises some fundamental questions about what we mean by the nature of existence and what it means for anything "to be." *Cosmology* raises questions about the origin and organization of the universe, or cosmos.

Epistemology: What Is the Nature of Knowledge?

The branch of philosophy that is concerned with the investigation of the nature of knowledge is known as *epistemology*. To explore the nature of knowledge is to raise questions about the limits of knowledge, the sources of knowledge, the validity of knowledge, the cognitive processes, and how we know. There are several "ways of knowing," including scientific inquiry, intuition, insight, experience, the senses, feelings, trial and error, research, and logic (Eisner, 1985). Logic is a key dimension in the traditional philosophies. Logic is primarily concerned with making inferences, reasoning, or arguing in a rational manner, and includes the subdivisions of deduction and induction. *Deductive logic* involves deducing a concrete application from a general principle. *Inductive logic*, on the other hand, begins with a combination of facts or true examples and from these facts a general principle or rule is formulated. Figure 6.3 further describes these two types of logic.

Axiology: What Is the Nature of Values?

Where epistemology explores the question of knowledge, *axiology*, the study of the nature of values, seeks to determine what is of value. To evaluate, to make a judgment, to value, literally means applying a set of norms or standards to human conduct or beauty. Axiology is divided into two spheres: ethics and aesthetics. *Ethics* is concerned with the study of human conduct and examines moral values—right, wrong, good, or bad. *Aesthetics* is concerned with values in beauty, nature, and the "aesthetic experience." The creative production of beauty is usually associated with music, painting, literature, dance, or the so called "fine arts."

One of the current debates in education centers around the question of whether moral education, ethics, or values education should be a responsibility of the school. "Controversial Issues" on page 183 poses arguments for and against the place of moral education or values education in the classroom; "Ask Yourself" on page 184 lists a number of questions that are asked by the three branches of philosophy. The questions provide a framework for you to examine and perhaps articulate your own philosophy of life. Your answers to these questions also reflect some of the basic assumptions you hold, which will determine how you view your students and their capacity to learn; how you view the curriculum and its subject matter; how you view the evaluation process; and how you view the general classroom environment. Your philosophy of life and philosophy of education are interdependent and provide a basis for your view of life, as well as your view of teaching.

Should schools concern themselves with questions regarding the origin of the universe? Why or why not?

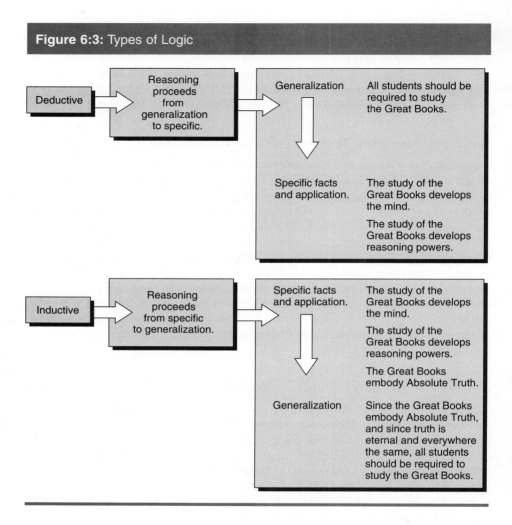

Figure 6:3: Types of Logic

Idealism

Idealism is considered the oldest philosophy of Western culture, dating back to ancient Greece and the time of Plato. For the idealist, the world of the mind, ideas, and reason is primary.

Metaphysics

If you were an idealist, what eternal ideas would you recommend be taught in the schools?

Idealism stresses mind over matter. For the idealist, nothing exists or is real except for an idea in the mind of the person or the mind of God, the Universal Mind. The universe can be explained as a creative and spiritual reality that includes the notions of permanence, order, and certainty. Morris and Pai (1976) suggest that there are two major divisions of reality in the world: apparent reality and real reality.

Controversial Issues:
Should Moral Education, Character Education, Ethics, or Values Education Be a Responsibility of the School?

Although axiology or the study of values is a major component or branch of all philosophies, the question of whether moral education, character education, ethics, or values education should be taught in the school remains a controversial issue. The history of American education confirms that the didactic teaching of moral values, including religious values, was once a central feature of the school. Today, some parents and educators are suggesting that ethical questions and moral dilemmas do indeed have a place in the educational enterprise. Others have expressed strong opinions against the school's role in moral or values education. The arguments, pro and con, concerning moral education or values education are:

Arguments For

1. The teaching of values is not a new phenomenon and follows the earlier works of Plato, Aristotle, Dewey, and Piaget who linked values to cognitive development, which has a place in the classroom.

2. Teachers can serve as an important value model for their students.

3. The discussion of moral dilemmas integrates critical thinking and ethics, which develops moral reasoning skills.

4. The school is the best place for assisting learners to understand their own attitudes, preferences, and values. The role of the school is to help students sort through value confusion so they can live by their values.

5. Students should become as adept in critical thinking principles of morality as we expect them to be in science and social studies.

Arguments Against

1. The teaching of values is not the purview of the school, but the family and church.

2. Too many teachers lecture their students about the importance of certain "appropriate" values without demonstrating those values by their own actions or behaviors.

3. No individual is "valueless," thus all teachers, by the nature of their position, have the potential of imposing their values on their students.

4. The function of the school is to educate, not proselytize or indoctrinate, therefore moral education and values education do not belong in the classroom.

What is your view of moral education or values education?

Apparent reality is made up of day-to-day experiences. "This is the region of change, of coming and going, of being born, growing, aging, and dying; it is the realm of imperfection, irregularity, and disorder; finally, it is the world of troubles and suffering, evil and sin" (Morris & Pai, 1976, p. 47). *Real reality*, on the other hand, is the realm of ideas and is therefore the realm of eternal truths, perfect order, and absolute values. For the idealist, real reality reigns above apparent reality, since real reality embodies perfection and eternal ideas that do not change (Morris & Pai, 1976).

Wingo (1974) summarized how the mind and spirit constitute reality and the perfect order for the idealist:

Ask Yourself:
What Is My Philosophy of Life?

Philosophic Questions	Branches of Philosophy
1. Are human beings basically good or is the essential nature of the human being evil?	What is the nature of reality? (Metaphysics–ontology)
2. What causes certain events in the universe to happen?	What is the nature of reality? (Metaphysics–cosmology)
3. What is your relationship to the universe?	What is the nature of reality? (Metaphysics–cosmology)
4. What is your relationship to a higher being (God)?	What is the nature of reality? (Metaphysics–ontology)
5. To what extent is your life basically free?	What is the nature of reality? (Metaphysics–ontology)
6. How is reality determined?	What is the nature of reality? (Metaphysics–ontology)
7. What is your basic purpose in life?	What is the nature of reality? (Metaphysics–ontology)
8. How is knowledge determined?	What is the nature of knowledge? (Epistemology)
9. What is truth?	What is the nature of knowledge? (Epistemology)
10. What are the limits of knowledge?	What is the nature of knowledge? (Epistemology)
11. What is the relationship between cognition and knowledge?	What is the nature of knowledge? (Epistemology)
12. Are there certain moral or ethical values that are universal?	What is the nature of values? (Axiology–ethics)
13. How is beauty determined?	What is the nature of values? (Axiology–aesthetics)
14. What constitutes aesthetic value?	What is the nature of values? (Axiology–aesthetics)
15. Who determines what is right, just, or good?	What is the nature of values? (Axiology–ethics)

One part of the basic thesis of all idealism is that mind is prior; that when we seek what is ultimate in the world, when we push back behind the veil of immediate sense experience, we shall find that what is ultimate in the whole universe is of the nature of mind or spirit (the two words are interchangeable in most discussions of idealism)—just as it is mind that is ultimate in the inner world of personal experience. (p. 95)

If the mind is prior, in the sense that it is ultimate, then material things either do not exist (i.e., are not real), or if they do exist, their existence depends in some fashion on the mind. For example, an idealist would contend that there is no such thing as a chair, there is only the idea of a chair.

The idealist's concept of reality considers the self as one in mind, soul, and spirit. Such a nature is capable of emulating the Absolute or Supreme Mind.

Epistemology

Since idealism accepts a primarily mental explanation for its metaphysics or reality, it is not surprising that idealists also accept the premise that all knowledge includes a mental grasp of ideas and concepts. Inductive and deductive logic are heavily emphasized by idealism. Since the mind is the primary reality, it is important to master the science of logic. Logic provides the framework for unifying our thoughts. While reason, logic, or revelation are primary ways "of knowing" by idealists, especially traditional idealists, modern idealists also accept intuition as a dimension of knowing.

One of the most important considerations of knowledge to the idealist is its relationship to truth. Idealists accept the following propositions concerning knowledge and truth:

1. The universe is rational and orderly and therefore intelligible.

2. There is an objective body of truth that has its origin and existence in the Absolute Mind and that can be known, at least in part, by the human mind.

3. The art of knowing is essentially an act of reconstructing the data of awareness into intelligible ideas and systems of ideas.

4. The criterion for the truth of an idea is coherence; that is, an idea is true when it is consistent with the existing and accepted body of truth. (Wingo, 1974, p. 103)

Some idealists believe that it is not necessarily truth that is important, but rather the search for truth that is the ultimate challenge. But they also believe that most of us resort to the lowest level (mere opinions about truth) and never reach what might be considered "Ultimate Truth." However, while we may never grasp all Truth, we have the potential to aspire to wisdom. We can improve on the quality of our ideas and move closer to the Ultimate Truth.

Axiology

Just as the idealists believe that order is an important element of reality, order is also considered a basic principle of values. Furthermore, values can be classified and ordered into a hierarchy or classification system. According to the educational philosopher Marler (1975), intuition is the means by which many idealists discover the presence of values and determine the hierarchy of those values.

Idealists believe that human behavior is intentional and not merely the response to external stimuli. Rather, within the human self is an inherent urge for self-realization, which provides the basic motivation for behavior. Since behavior is intentional, we cannot escape the need to value (or devalue) the things and events that we experience (Wingo, 1974).

To the idealist values are rooted in existence and are part of reality. "We enjoy values not only because our emotions and sentiments are appropriately aroused but because the things we value are realities that have existence themselves and are rooted in the very structure of the cosmos" (Butler, 1966, p. 74).

Values also are absolute. The good, the true, and the beautiful basically do not change from generation to generation, or from society to society. They are

Figure 6.4: Idealism at a Glance

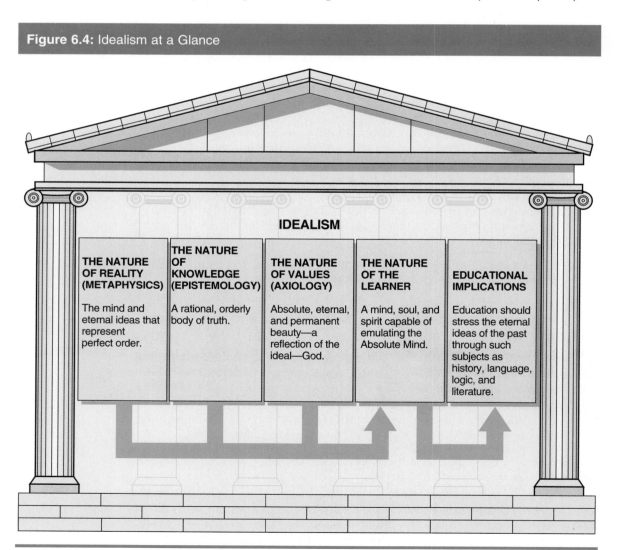

IDEALISM

THE NATURE OF REALITY (METAPHYSICS)	THE NATURE OF KNOWLEDGE (EPISTEMOLOGY)	THE NATURE OF VALUES (AXIOLOGY)	THE NATURE OF THE LEARNER	EDUCATIONAL IMPLICATIONS
The mind and eternal ideas that represent perfect order.	A rational, orderly body of truth.	Absolute, eternal, and permanent beauty—a reflection of the ideal—God.	A mind, soul, and spirit capable of emulating the Absolute Mind.	Education should stress the eternal ideas of the past through such subjects as history, language, logic, and literature.

not created by man but are part of the very nature and being of the universe (Kneller, 1971). They are, in fact, reflections of the Absolute Good, the Absolute Truth, and the Absolute Beauty-God. Figure 6.4 provides an overview of idealism.

Leading Proponents

As noted in Chapter 3, the Greek philosopher Plato, the disciple of Socrates, is considered the father of idealism. In his famous "Allegory of the Cave," found in *The Republic* (1958), Plato inferred that each of us lives in a cave of shadows, doubts, and distortions about reality. However, through education and enlightenment, the real world of pure ideas can be substituted for those distorted shadows and doubts.

Judaism and Christianity were both influenced by the philosophy of idealism in different ways. Judeo-Christian teaching suggested that ultimate reality could be found in God through the soul. A prominent theologian of the fourth and fifth centuries, and one who applied a number of Plato's assumptions to Christian thought, was St. Augustine (354–430). Plato's assumptions, as applied by St. Augustine, provided the rationale for the religious idealism that influenced Western thought for centuries (Ozmon & Craver, 1990).

Idealist thought influenced the writings of a number of major philosophers, including René Descartes, Immanuel Kant, and Georg Wilhelm Friedrich Hegel. The French philosopher Descartes (1596–1650), in his famous dictum, "*Cogito, ergo sum*—I think, therefore I am," declared that as humans we may doubt everything, but we cannot doubt our own existence. The concept of existence is further interpreted by Wingo (1974):

> I may succeed in doubting the existence of everything else, one thing is certain: every time I think, I exist. The primary and ultimate fact of my experience is mind and consciousness. It is not my physical body of members and organs that is necessarily real, for it is possible to believe that my body does not exist. The ultimate reality in my experience is my mind. It alone can be known to be real. (p. 95)

Descartes not only accepted the place of the finite mind and ideas as advanced by Plato, but determined that all ideas, save one, depend on other ideas. The only idea that does not depend on any idea other than itself is the idea of Perfect Being or God. The process used by Descartes, later known as the *Cartesian method*, involved the derivation of axioms upon which theories could be based by the purposeful and progressive elimination of all interpretations of experience except those that are absolutely certain. This method came to influence a number of fields of inquiry, including the sciences (Ozmon & Craver, 1990).

Immanuel Kant (1724–1804), recognized as one of the world's greatest philosophers, also incorporated the major tenets of idealism into his thinking. Kant believed there were certain universal moral laws known as *categorical imperatives* that guide our actions or behaviors. One of Kant's categorical imperatives was "above all things, obedience is an essential feature in the character of a child." This moral maxim has become a primary basis for moral training or character development in education (Ozmon & Craver, 1990).

Can you think of examples of categorical imperatives that might be espoused by idealists and that would be relevant to education?

The German philosopher Hegel (1770–1831) was an idealist who approached reality as a "contest of opposites" such as life and death, love and hate, individual and society. For Hegel, each idea (thesis) had its own opposite (antithesis). The confrontation of the thesis (e.g., man is an end in himself) and antithesis (e.g., man cannot be merely an end to himself—he must also live for others) produces a resolution or synthesis (e.g., man fulfills his true end by serving others). This synthesis becomes a new thesis, which when crossed with a new antithesis forms a new synthesis, and so on (Morris & Pai, 1976).

Other proponents of idealism include the philosophers Baruch Spinoza (1632–1677) and George Berkeley (1685–1753), as well as such leading literary figures as Samuel Coleridge (1772–1834), William Wordsworth (1770–1850), and Ralph Waldo Emerson (1803–1882).

Realism

Realism, like idealism, is one of the oldest philosophies of Western culture, dating back to ancient Greece and the time of Aristotle. Classical or Aristotelian realism is the antithesis of idealism. For the realist, the universe exists whether the human mind perceives it or not. Matter is primary and is considered an independent reality. The world of things is superior to the world of ideas.

Metaphysics

Realism stresses the world of nature or physical things and our experiences and perceptions of those things. Morris and Pai (1976) describe the role of human beings in relation to the world of nature:

> What are human beings, then, say the Realists, but tiny spectators of an enormous machine, the cosmos. They stand before it as fleas before an electronic computer, but with one advantage: intelligence. Gradually, piece by piece, they can come to a wider and fuller understanding of their world. And this is possible because this world, like any machine, is not a haphazard, fortuitous collection of atoms and molecules, but a structure built according to plan and endowed (as is the automobile engine) with predetermined and necessary movements. (p. 54)

For the realist, then, reality is composed of both matter (body) and form (mind). Matter can only "become" (be shaped or organized into being) by the mind. Moreover, the interaction of matter and form is governed not by God but by scientific, natural laws.

As to the nature of self, the realist considers the person a sensing and rational being capable of understanding the world of things. The person, like all matter and form, has evolved from and is subject to nature and its laws.

Epistemology

There are several methods of discovering knowledge that realists perceive to be important. For some realists, the objects of our knowledge are presented direct-

Consider yourself a realist. To what extent might you use the scientific method as a basis of inquiry in a beginning music class? In a class of preschoolers?

ly in consciousness with no intervening mental construct or mental state, and with none needed to account for our knowledge of the external world. That is, we know by direct sensing. For other realists, knowledge is established by the *scientific method*, that is, by the systematic reporting and analysis of what is observed, and the testing of hypotheses formulated from the observations. To these realists, the purpose of inquiry is to discover truth and follow the scientific laws that govern things and events (Wingo, 1974). In essence, a logical, systematic approach to the discovery of knowledge is fundamental to the realist.

Axiology

In the axiology of realism, values are derived from nature. In the area of ethics, natural law or moral law are the major determinants of what is good; that which is good is dependent on leading a virtuous life, one in keeping with these natural or moral laws.

Although realism does not adhere to any hard and fast set of rules, realists believe that deviating from moral truth will cause injury both to persons and to society. To protect the common good, certain codes of conduct or social laws have been written and must be followed (Power, 1982).

For the realist, aesthetics is the reflection of nature. What is valued is that which reflects the orderliness and rationality of nature. Figure 6.5 provides an overview of realism.

Today's students follow the precepts of Aristotle by formulating, testing, and discovering knowledge through the scientific method.

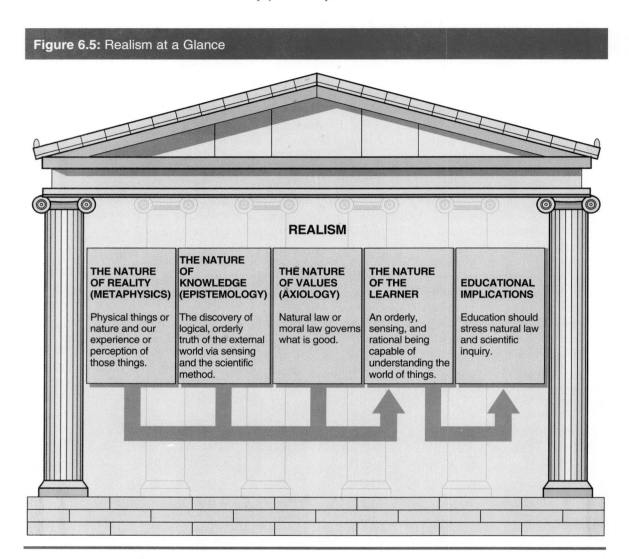

Figure 6.5: Realism at a Glance

REALISM

THE NATURE OF REALITY (METAPHYSICS)	THE NATURE OF KNOWLEDGE (EPISTEMOLOGY)	THE NATURE OF VALUES (AXIOLOGY)	THE NATURE OF THE LEARNER	EDUCATIONAL IMPLICATIONS
Physical things or nature and our experience or perception of those things.	The discovery of logical, orderly truth of the external world via sensing and the scientific method.	Natural law or moral law governs what is good.	An orderly, sensing, and rational being capable of understanding the world of things.	Education should stress natural law and scientific inquiry.

Leading Proponents

As discussed in Chapter 3, Aristotle, a pupil of Plato, is considered the father of realism. Aristotle disagreed with Plato's premise that only ideas are real. For Aristotle, reality, knowledge, and value exist independent of the mind and their existence is not predicated by our ideas. According to Aristotle, material things have existed since the beginning of time, prior to our knowledge of their existence, and they will continue to exist after we depart (Power, 1982).

Two other representatives of realism, also mentioned in Chapter 3, were Francis Bacon and John Locke. Bacon, both a philosopher and a politician, advanced a scientific form of realism that depended on the inductive method of inquiry. Following a similar path, Locke's advocacy of realism stemmed from his study of human knowledge. One of Locke's major notions, the *tabula rasa* concept, has gained wide acceptance. As explained in Chapter 3, according to this concept there are no such things as innate ideas. We come into the world with a mind like a blank sheet of paper. Knowledge is acquired from sources independent of the mind as a result of sensation and reflection (Ozmon & Craver, 1990).

Other major philosophers who contributed to realism as a scientific inquiry include the English mathematicians and philosophers Alfred North Whitehead (1861–1947) and Bertrand Russell (1872–1970).

Neo-Thomism

The third of the traditional philosophies is *neo-Thomism*. Neo-Thomism, or its antecedent, Thomism, dates to the time of St. Thomas Aquinas in the thirteenth century. As noted in Chapter 3, Aquinas attempted to bridge the dualism of idealism and realism that had separated philosophic thought up to his time. For the neo-Thomist, God exists and can be known by both faith and reason.

Metaphysics

Neo-Thomists believe that it is God who gives meaning and purpose to the universe. God is the Pure Being that represents the coming together of essence and existence. Things exist independently of ideas; however, both physical objects and human beings, including minds and ideas, are created by God. Thus, while both physical objects and God are real, God is preeminent. Neo-Thomists conceive of the essential nature of human beings as rational beings with souls, modeled after God, the Perfect Being.

Epistemology

Although some philosophers believe that one can come to know God only through faith or intuition, neo-Thomists believe that it is through both faith and our capacity to reason that we come to know God. Aquinas, like Aristotle, perceived that human beings were endowed with the powers of rationality and reason, which set them apart from other animals (Gutek, 1991).

To the neo-Thomist there is a hierarchy of knowing. At the lowest level is scientific or synthetic knowing. At the second level there is analytic or intuitive knowing. And at the highest level there is mystical or revelatory knowing (Morris & Pai, 1976).

Axiology

For the neo-Thomist, ethically speaking, goodness follows reason. That is, values are unchanging moral laws established by God, which can be discerned by reason. As a corollary, ignorance is the source of evil. If people do not know what is right, they cannot be expected to do what is right. If, on the other hand, people do know what is right, they can be held morally responsible for what they do. In

Have you ever attended or known anyone who attended a parochial school? How did that experience compare with attendance at a public institution?

terms of aesthetics, the reason, or intellect, is also the perceiver of beauty. That which is valued as beautiful is also found pleasing to the intellect (Morris & Pai, 1976). Figure 6.6 provides an overview of neo-Thomism.

Leading Proponents

Thomas Aquinas, a theologian of the thirteenth century from whom neo-Thomism takes its name, is credited with interfacing the secular ideas of Aristotle and the Christian teachings of St. Augustine. Neo-Thomism is also called "religious realism." Both Aristotle and Aquinas viewed reality via reason and sensation. Aquinas believed God created matter out of nothing and gave meaning and purpose to the universe. In his most noted work, *Summa Theologica,* he used the

Figure 6.6: Neo-Thomism at a Glance

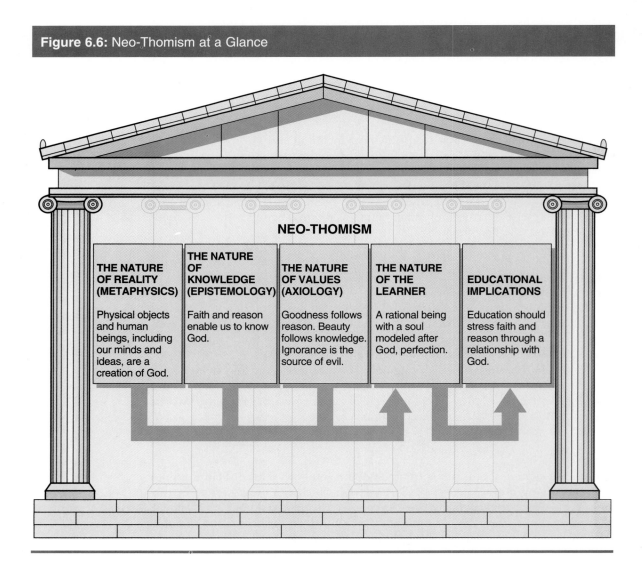

NEO-THOMISM

THE NATURE OF REALITY (METAPHYSICS)	THE NATURE OF KNOWLEDGE (EPISTEMOLOGY)	THE NATURE OF VALUES (AXIOLOGY)	THE NATURE OF THE LEARNER	EDUCATIONAL IMPLICATIONS
Physical objects and human beings, including our minds and ideas, are a creation of God.	Faith and reason enable us to know God.	Goodness follows reason. Beauty follows knowledge. Ignorance is the source of evil.	A rational being with a soul modeled after God, perfection.	Education should stress faith and reason through a relationship with God.

The teaching of Dewey is evident in classrooms where children actively participate in projects and social activities.

rational approach suggested by Aristotle to answer various questions regarding existence and Christianity. As a result, many of the supporting arguments of Christian beliefs rely on Thomas Aquinas, and Roman Catholicism considers Thomism its leading philosophy (Ozmon & Craver, 1990).

Pragmatism

Pragmatism, or *experimentalism,* as a philosophy, focuses on the things that work. Primarily viewed as a philosophy of the twentieth century developed by Americans such as John Dewey (see Chapter 5), pragmatism has its roots in British, European, and ancient Greek tradition (Ozmon & Craver, 1990). For the pragmatist, the world of experience is central.

Metaphysics

Unlike the classical or traditional philosophies, which view reality as a thing, metaphysics to the pragmatist is a process rather than a substantive "something." For the pragmatist, reality is an event, a process, a verb (Morris & Pai, 1976). As such, it is subject to constant change and lacks absolutes. Meaning is derived from experience, which is simply an interaction with one's environment (Garrison, 1994).

Epistemology

Since pragmatism's theory of knowledge accepts no truth as absolute, it advocates the idea that truth is determined by function or consequences. In fact, pragmatists shun the use of the word *truth* and at best speak of a "tentative truth" that will serve the purpose until experience evolves a new truth. Knowledge is arrived at by scientific inquiry, testing, questioning, and retesting—and is never conclusive.

Axiology

Where the traditional philosophers concentrated primarily on metaphysics and epistemology, the pragmatist has focused primarily on axiology or values. As with truths, values to the pragmatist are only tentative. They are constructed from experience and are subject to testing, questioning, and retesting. For the pragmatist, that which is ethically or morally good is that which works, that which leads to desirable consequences. The focus on consequences is not to imply that the pragmatist is only concerned with what works for the self. In fact, the pragmatist is concerned with social consequences. "What works" is what works for the larger community, not just the self.

Regarding aesthetic values, for pragmatists what is beautiful is not determined by some objective ideal but by what we experience when we see, feel, and touch. Art is a creative expression, and its function is to communicate. The goal of the artist is to arouse new dimensions, meanings, and feelings in the viewer. Figure 6.7 presents an overview of pragmatism.

Leading Proponents

An 80-year old woman who is dying of cancer has requested assistance from her son, husband, physician, and the Hemlock Society to aid her in the design of her own suicide. How might a pragmatist deal with this ethical dilemma?

Although there are a number of British and European philosophers who support the pragmatist philosophy, such as Jean-Jacques Rousseau (see Chapter 3), Auguste Comte (1798–1857), and Charles Darwin (1809–1882), pragmatism has received its major impetus from American philosophers such as Charles Sanders Peirce (1839–1914), William James (1842–1910), and John Dewey (1859–1952).

Peirce believed that true knowledge depends on verification of ideas through experience. Ideas are merely hypotheses until tested by experience. Although Peirce's philosophy was very complicated and included the concepts of the nature of God, immortality, and the self, his premise of verification by experience was the major influence on pragmatism (Ozmon & Craver, 1990). William James incorporated his views of pragmatism in both philosophy and psychology. James also emphasized the centrality of experience. To James there were no absolutes, no universals, only an ever-changing universe.

It was James's contemporary, John Dewey, who had the greatest influence on American pragmatism. For Dewey, experience, thought, and consequence were interrelated:

> Thought or reflection, as we have already seen virtually if not explicitly, is the discernment of the relation between what we try to do and what happens in consequence. No experience having a meaning is possible without some element of thought. But we may contrast two types of experience according to the proportion of reflection found in them. All our experiences have a phase of "cut and try" in

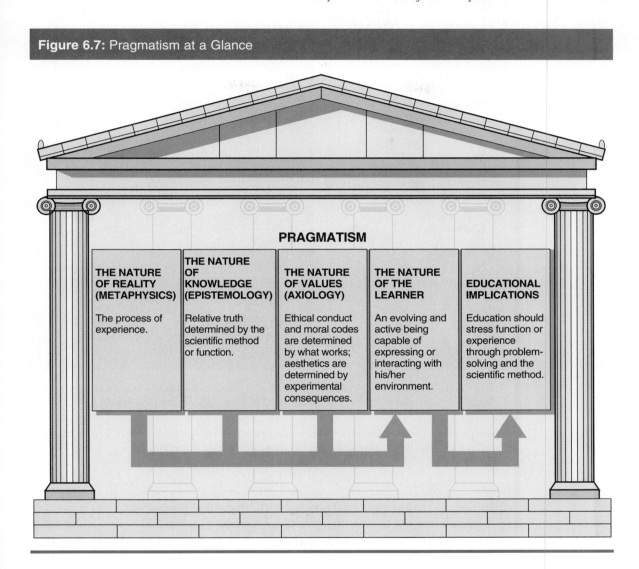

Figure 6.7: Pragmatism at a Glance

PRAGMATISM

THE NATURE OF REALITY (METAPHYSICS)

The process of experience.

THE NATURE OF KNOWLEDGE (EPISTEMOLOGY)

Relative truth determined by the scientific method or function.

THE NATURE OF VALUES (AXIOLOGY)

Ethical conduct and moral codes are determined by what works; aesthetics are determined by experimental consequences.

THE NATURE OF THE LEARNER

An evolving and active being capable of expressing or interacting with his/her environment.

EDUCATIONAL IMPLICATIONS

Education should stress function or experience through problem-solving and the scientific method.

them—what psychologists call the method of trial and error. We simply do something, and when it fails, we do something else, and keep on trying until we hit upon something which works, and then we adopt that method as a rule of thumb measure in subsequent procedures. (Dewey, 1916, pp. 169–170)

Existentialism

Existentialism appeared a century ago as a revolt against the mathematical, scientific, and objective philosophies that preceded it. Existentialism voiced disfavor with any effort toward social control or subjugation. Beginning with the work of the Danish philosopher Soren Kierkegaard (1813–1855), existentialism focused

The search for meaning, purpose in life, and individual existence continues to challenge contemporary youth as it challenged Kierkegaard in the nineteenth century.

on personal and subjective existence. For the existentialist, the world of existence, choice, and responsibility is primary.

Metaphysics

Unlike the realists and neo-Thomists who believe that essence precedes existence, the existentialists believe that existence precedes essence. For the existentialist there is neither meaning nor purpose to the physical universe. We are born into the universe by chance. Moreover, according to existentialism, since there is no world order or natural scheme of things into which we are born, we owe nothing to nature but our existence (Kneller, 1971). Existentialists believe that because we live in a world without purpose, we must create our own meaning (Gutek, 1988).

In addition to existence, the concept of choice is central to the metaphysics of existentialism. To decide who and what we are is to decide what reality is. Is it God? Reason? Nature? Science? By our choices we determine reality. According to a leading existentialist, Jean-Paul Sartre (1956), we cannot escape from the responsibility to choose, including the choice of how we view our past.

Epistemology

Similar to their position concerning reality, the existentialists believe that the way we come to know truth is by choice. The individual self must ultimately make the decision as to what is true and how we know. Whether we choose logic, intuition, scientific proof, or revelation is irrelevant; what matters is that we must eventually choose. The freedom to choose carries with it a tremendous burden of responsibility that we cannot escape. Because there are no absolutes, no authorities, and no single or correct way to the truth, the only authority is the authority of the self.

Axiology

For the existentialist, choice is imperative not only for determining reality and knowledge but also for determining value. Van Cleve Morris (1966) explains that concerning values, authenticity and choice are key:

> And who is the authentic? The individual whose example is perhaps beyond the reach of most of us; the individual who is free and who knows it, who knows that every deed and word is a choice and hence an act of value creation, and, finally and perhaps decisively, who knows that he is the author of his own life and must be held personally responsible for the values on behalf of which he has chosen to live it, and that these values can never be justified by referring to something or somebody outside himself. (p. 48)

Whether we are discussing ethics or aesthetics, we cannot escape our freedom to choose or our freedom to value. And here is the dilemma, say the existentialists. Since there are no norms, no standards, and no assurances that we have chosen correctly or rightly, choice is frustrating and exasperating at times. It is often much easier to be able to look to a standard or benchmark to determine what is right, just, or of value than to take responsibility for the choices we have made. Yet this is a very small price we pay for our free will. Figure 6.8 presents an overview of existentialism.

How would an existentialist respond to the schools' attempts to influence students' choice in matters such as birth control?

Leading Proponents

The leading proponent, indeed the "father of existentialism," was Soren Kierkegaard. Kierkegaard renounced scientific objectivity for subjectivity and personal choice. He was concerned with individual existence and attacked Hegelian philosophy on the grounds that it depersonalized the individual. He believed that we must understand our souls and destinies, and that we must take complete responsibility for the choices we make. He also believed in the reality of God (Ozmon & Craver, 1990).

Another nineteenth/twentieth-century expositor of existentialism was Martin Buber (1878–1965). Buber, a Jewish philosopher-theologian, advocated an "I-Thou" relationship whereby each individual recognizes the other's personal meaning and reality. Buber suggested that both the divine and human are related, and by one's personal relationship with the other, one can enhance one's spiritual life and relationship with God. Buber's humanistic existentialist views had a profound impact, not only on philosophy and theology but on psychology, psychiatry, literature, and education (Ozmon & Craver, 1990).

Influenced by the philosophy of Immanuel Kant and Edmund Husserl (1859–1938), who developed a philosophical method called *phenomenology*, or

Figure 6.8: Existenialism at a Glance

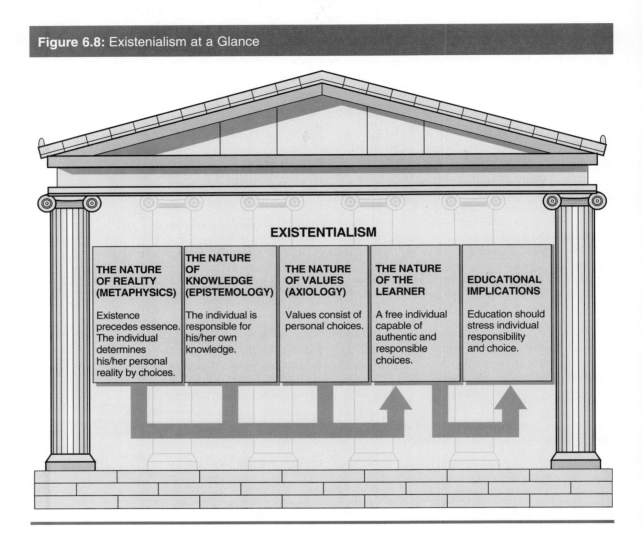

EXISTENTIALISM

THE NATURE OF REALITY (METAPHYSICS)

Existence precedes essence. The individual determines his/her personal reality by choices.

THE NATURE OF KNOWLEDGE (EPISTEMOLOGY)

The individual is responsible for his/her own knowledge.

THE NATURE OF VALUES (AXIOLOGY)

Values consist of personal choices.

THE NATURE OF THE LEARNER

A free individual capable of authentic and responsible choices.

EDUCATIONAL IMPLICATIONS

Education should stress individual responsibility and choice.

the study of phenomena, Martin Heidegger (1889–1976) expanded and revised phenomenology to another philosophical method known as *hermeneutics,* or the interpretation of lived experience (Ozmon & Craver, 1990). The major thesis of Heidegger's numerous writings was the search for meaning. For Heidegger, metaphysical reality had to include such emotional phenomena as dread, anguish, concern, and sensitivity.

Jean-Paul Sartre's (1905–1980) public appeal exceeded that of Kierkegaard and Heidegger, and many devotees of existentialism considered Sartre the spokesman for the human condition. Sartre claimed that free choice implies total responsibility for one's own existence. There are no antecedent principles or purposes that shape our destiny. Responsibility for our existence extends to situations of the gravest consequence, including the choice to commit suicide (Kneller, 1958). Sartre's major philosophic work, *Being and Nothingness* (1956), is considered one of the major philosophic treatises of the twentieth century. According to Sartre, since there is no God to give existence meaning, humanity exists without any meaning until we construct our own meaning and purpose.

Other proponents of existentialism include Friedrich Nietzsche, Karl Jaspers, and Franz Kafka. The French writers and philosophers Albert Camus (1913–1960), Gabriel Marcel (1889–1973), Maurice Merleau-Ponty (1908–1961); the philosopher-theologian Paul Tillich (1886–1965); as well as a number of playwrights who espouse the Theater of the Absurd (e.g., Eugene Ionesco, Samuel Beckett, and Edward Albee) are also considered spokespersons for the existentialist philosophy.

Analytic Philosophy

As we study the major philosophies and their corollary educational theories, it becomes evident that these descriptive schools of thought, or "isms" as they are often called, are very broad in their aims, are quite eclectic, and at times appear to lack clarity. Critics of the descriptive approach to philosophy point out that the philosophies of idealism, realism, neo-Thomism, and the like have major limitations in that they try to prescribe certain things and make normative judgements. Moreover, they render educational statements that are jargon-ridden and not verifiable. For these reasons a number of philosophers began to move away from traditional thinking about philosophy and theory as disciplines and began to focus their attention on analysis or clarification of the language, concepts, and methods that philosophers use (Ozmon & Craver, 1990; Partelli, 1987). The so-called "analytic movement" that resulted was less concerned with the underlying assumptions about reality, truth, and values addressed by descriptive philosophy than with clarification, definition, and the meaning of language.

One contemporary analytic philosopher is Jonas Soltis. Soltis (1978) pointed out the importance of philosophical analysis for teachers:

> We must be clear about its intent [language of education] and meaning and not be swayed by its imagery and poetry. The analytic temperament and techniques should prove very useful to all practicing educators in getting them to think through with care and precision just what it is they are buying from theorists, and more importantly, just what it is they're after and how best that might be achieved. (p. 88)

Analysis in philosophy began in the post–World War I era when a group of European natural scientists and social scientists formed what became known as the Vienna Circle. These scholars were particularly concerned about the alienation between philosophy and science that existed at that time. One of the major outcomes of the work of the Vienna Circle was that it clarified the joint roles of both science and philosophy. For example, it was determined that if the testing of hypotheses through experimentation and observation were to be the purview or charge of science, then the proper role of philosophy should be the analysis of the logical syntax of scientific language (Magee, 1971).

The concept of *logical positivism,* or *logical empiricism,* grew out of the thinking of the Vienna Circle. Logical positivism or logical empiricism suggests that

Professional Reflections

"Everything you learn in college is ideas. Take the risks to go beyond the boundaries of a book. Explore your own ideas or ideas inspired by someone. Find out what does and doesn't work for you. . . . "

Michael Soliday, Teacher of the Year, Nevada

the language of science consists of two types of expressions: logical and empirical. Eventually, the concept of logical positivism became associated with the "principle of verification." This principle asserts that no proposition should be accepted as meaningful unless it can be verified on formal grounds, logical or empirical (Magee, 1971).

One of the most important logical positivists was Ludwig Wittgenstein (1889–1951). Wittgenstein (1953) argued that the role of the sciences should be to discover true propositions and true facts while the role of philosophy should be to resolve confusion and clarify ideas.

The assumptions that were made by logical positivists became so rigid and restrictive that their popularity began to wane. Today, very few individuals identify themselves as logical positivists.

By the 1950s logical positivism shifted to linguistic analysis, or the analytic philosophy movement. A leading spokesperson for this paradigm shift was Israel Scheffler (b. 1923). In his first major work, *The Language of Education* (1960), Scheffler focused attention on how philosophical analysis can help teachers formulate their beliefs, arguments, and assumptions about topics that are particularly important to the teaching and learning process. Scheffler, and later Magee (1971), suggested that one of the best ways for teachers to do this is by answering the types of questions that analytic philosophers pose. Some of these questions might be:

How would you answer each of these questions?

1. What are teaching, learning, and education?

2. What is the meaning of authority in education?

3. What is the relationship between the concept of excellence and the concept of equality in a democratic educational system?

4. What is moral education? (Magee, 1971, p. 42)

Maxine Greene (1981), a leading contemporary existentialist philosopher, summarized the importance of subjecting one's ideas to the analytic process:

> To do philosophy in this fashion is to pose distinctive critical questions: questions that provoke reflection on the knowledge gathered in the several fields of inquiry, questions that lead to examination of underlying assumptions and disclosures of major premises. Equally important are questions that lead to the framing of conceptual frameworks, perspectives through which the field in its interrelationships can be seen. It is important to note that these are not questions susceptible of ordinary answers. (p. 34)

Each prospective teacher should learn the art or science of *philosophical analysis*. One of the first steps in learning this process is to raise questions about the assumptions we make, the values we hold, the theories we propose, the procedures we use, and the methods we trust. In short, philosophical analysis confronts the language of education and forces the educator to translate his or her professional expression into parsimonious and meaningful terms. This clarification is important in resolving educational controversies and in explaining educational policies (Gutek, 1988).

Summary

The study of philosophy enables us to better understand our philosophy of life. One of the most effective methods of developing a philosophy of life is to respond to three basic questions: What is the nature of reality? What is the nature of knowledge? What is the nature of values? These three questions and their accompanying responses comprise the branches of philosophy.

The philosophies of idealism, realism, and neo-Thomism are considered the classical or traditional philosophies, while pragmatism and existentialism represent the contemporary or modern philosophies. The traditional philosophies are more concerned with the past, truths, and absolutes, while the contemporary philosophies are more concerned with the present or future and do not subscribe to the idea of "absolute truths."

While the study of descriptive philosophy provides a mechanism for translating basic philosophic tenets into educational practice, it is quite restrictive. Most philosophies are too broad in scope and lack precise meaning and clarity. Today, many philosophers and educators believe that a more effective way to study philosophy is by philosophical analysis, which is concerned with clarifying the language we use to describe our educational concepts and assumptions.

In the next chapter, we will see how these basic philosophic views have led to a number of theories of education. We will also see the impact of these theories on educational programs and practices.

Key Terms

Aesthetics
Apparent reality
Axiology
Cartesian method
Categorical imperatives
Cosmology
Deductive logic
Epistemology
Ethics
Existentialism
Hermeneutics
Idealism

Inductive logic
Logical positivism (logical empiricism)
Metaphysics
Neo-Thomism
Ontology
Phenomenology
Philosophical analysis
Philosophy of education
Pragmatism
Real reality
Realism
Scientific method

Discussion Questions

 1. In the incident opening the chapter, Richard Chapleau states that "education only reflects the larger successes and tragedies of the surrounding society. What are some of society's successes and tragedies you see reflected in the schools? How can teachers serve as a "spark of optimism" for society?

2. Which of the philosophies discussed in this chapter is most like your own? In what ways? Which is the most unlike your own? In what ways?

3. List all the ways of knowing. Does what is to be known (i.e., the subject matter) dictate the approach to knowing? Explain.

4. How would representatives of each of the philosophies discussed in this chapter respond to the following statement? "Concepts such as understanding, insight, appreciation, and interest have no place in the curriculum since they cannot be observed."

5. Construct an argument using deductive reasoning to explain the following statement: "Teaching does not imply education and education does not imply learning."

6. Which of the major philosophies would be most apt to use the following fundamental principles: justice, freedom, truthfulness, should or "ought," and honesty?

7. The following metaphor, "learning is essentially growing," depicts which philosophy? Name three other metaphors that depict three other major philosophies.

8. Choose three basic educational concepts that are important to most educators. Describe the process you would go through in analyzing the language used to ensure that the meanings of the concepts were clear, concise, and verifiable.

References

Butler, J. D. (1966). *Idealism in education.* New York: Harper & Row.

Dewey, J. (1916). *Democracy and education: An introduction to the philosophy of education.* New York: Macmillan.

Eisner, E. (Ed.). (1985). *Learning and teaching the ways of knowing: The eighty-fourth yearbook of the National Society for the Study of Education.* Chicago: The University of Chicago Press.

Garrison, J. (1994). Realism, Deweyan, pragmatism, and educational research. *Educational Researcher, 23*(1), 5–14.

Greene, M. (1981). Contexts, corrections and consequences: The matter of philosophical and psychological foundations. *Journal of Teacher Education, 32*(4), 31–37.

Gutek, G. L. (1988). *Education and schooling in America.* Englewood Cliffs, NJ: Prentice-Hall.

Gutek, G. L. (1991). *Cultural foundations of education.* New York: Macmillan.

Kneller, G. F. (1958). *Existentialism and education.* New York: John Wiley & Sons.

Kneller, G. F. (1971). *Introduction to the philosophy of education.* New York: John Wiley & Sons.

Magee, J. B. (1971). *Philosophical analysis in education.* New York: Harper & Row.

Marler, C. D. (1975). *Philosophy and schooling.* Boston: Allyn & Bacon.

Morris, V. C. (1966). *Existentialism in education.* New York: Harper & Row.

Morris, V. C., & Pai, Y. (1976). *Philosophy and the American school.* Boston: Houghton Mifflin.

Ozmon, H. A., & Craver, S. M. (1990). *Philosophical foundations of education.* Columbus, OH: Merrill.

Partelli, J. P. (1987). Analytic philosophy of education: Development and misconceptions. *Journal of Educational Thought, 21*(1), 20–24.

Plato (1958). *The Republic.* (F. Carnford, Trans.). New York: Oxford University Press.

Power, E. J. (1982). *Philosophy of education: Studies in philosophies, schooling and educational policies.* Englewood Cliffs, NJ: Prentice-Hall.

Sartre, J. P. (1956). *Being and nothingness.* (H. Barnes, Trans.). New York: Philosophical Library.

Scheffler, I. (1960). *The language of education.* Springfield, IL: Charles C. Thomas.

Soltis, J. F. (1978). *An introduction to the analysis of educational concepts.* Reading, MA: Addison-Wesley.

Wingo, G. M. (1974). *Philosophies of education: An introduction.* Lexington, MA: D. C. Heath.

Wittgenstein, L. (1953). *Philosophical investigations.* New York: Macmillan.

Chapter 7

The Impact of Educational
Theories on Educational Practice

The roots of education are bitter, but the fruit is sweet.

Aristotle, 4th century B.C.

A Critical Incident in My Teaching Career . . .

Lydia was from a large family. She had been a student of mine for some time. One day she looked great and I told her so. "Lydia, wow, do you look beautiful. Your hair and makeup . . . wow." She ran from the room crying. What had I done?

I followed Lydia to the girl's bathroom. "Lydia, what's wrong," I asked. She told me no one had ever told her she was beautiful. No one.

Fifteen years is too long for any girl to wait to be told she is beautiful.

I remember now to constantly compliment my students.

Mary Wedding
Teacher of the Year, Wisconsin

Many students enrolled in preprofessional teacher education programs do not recognize the relationship between the study of philosophy and educational practice. One explanation for this is that much of the subject matter of teacher education is taught in a fragmented fashion with little or no connection to its philosophic roots. As a result, the student or novice teacher are unable to discern how important educational concepts such as curriculum, teaching methods, classroom management, evaluation, and the role of the teacher are related to educational theory or philosophy of education.

In this chapter you will be introduced to six major educational theories and their impact on educational practice. Based on these theories and their application to practice, you will be encouraged to formulate your own philosophy of education. Information regarding the impact of the six major educational theories on curriculum, teaching methods, classroom management, evaluation, and the role of the teacher will be presented. To help you study these important concepts, consider the following outcome objectives:

- Define an educational theory and explain its relationship to philosophy as a discipline.
- Identify the various underlying protests that led to the establishment of the theories of perennialism, progressivism, behaviorism, essentialism, existentialism, and social reconstructionism.
- Compare the curricula of perennialism, progressivism, behaviorism, essentialism, existentialism, and social reconstructionism, including neo-Marxism, critical theory, and post-modernism.
- Compare the teaching methods that characterize perennialism, progressivism, behaviorism, essentialism, existentialism, and social reconstructionism.
- Compare the preferred classroom management of perennialism, progressivism, behaviorism, essentialism, existentialism, and social reconstructionism.
- Compare the evaluation techniques of the perennialist, progressivist, behaviorist, essentialist, existentialist, and social reconstructionist.
- Describe the role of the teacher from a perennialist, progressivist, behaviorist, essentialist, existentialist, and social reconstructionist perspective.
- Formulate your philosophy of education.

205

Having examined the assumptions that underlie the major philosophies, it is now appropriate to examine how these basic assumptions translate to educational theories and practice. The major traditional and contemporary philosophies that were discussed in Chapter 6 each have a corollary educational theory. It is the combination of philosophy and theory that will enable us to frame our own philosophy of education.

Theories of Education

Theory may be defined in two ways. First, a theory is a hypothesis or set of hypotheses that have been verified by observation or experiment. Second, a theory is a general synonym for systematic thinking or a set of coherent thoughts. Thus a *theory of education* is a composite of systematic thinking or generalizations about schooling (Kneller, 1971).

A well–thought–out theory of education is important, for it helps to explain our orientation to teaching and allows us to defend our position with respect to how we manage learning. In short, a theory of education enables the teacher to explain what he or she is doing, and why. It provides academic accountability.

The major theories of education to be examined in this chapter include six schools of thought: perennialism, progressivism, behaviorism, essentialism, existentialism, and social reconstructionism. Each theory was developed as a protest against the prevailing social and educational climate of the time. For example, the protest culminating in perennialism was a protest against secularization and the excessive focus on science and technology, at the expense of reason, that dominated society and its educational institutions at the time.

As you review each educational theory, keep in mind the similarities and differences among the theories and the reason or rationale behind the protest that led to their development.

Perennialism

Eternal or perennial truths, permanence, order, certainty, rationality, and logic constitute the ideal for the perennialist. The philosophies of neo-Thomism and realism are embedded in the perennialist theory of education. Kneller (1971) described six basic principles of *perennialism:*

1. Despite differing environments, human nature remains the same everywhere; hence, education should be the same for everyone.

2. Since rationality is man's highest attribute, he must use it to direct his instinctual nature in accordance with deliberately chosen ends.

3. It is education's task to impart knowledge of eternal truth.

4. Education is not an imitation of life, but a preparation for it.

5. The student should be taught certain basic subjects that will acquaint him with the world's permanencies.

6. Students should study the great works of literature, philosophy, history, and science, in which men through the ages have revealed their greatest aspirations and achievements. (pp. 42–45)

The educational focus of perennialism is on the need to return to the past, namely, to universal truths and such absolutes as reason and faith. The views of Thomas Aquinas best personify this educational theory. (The Historical Note on page 208 gives a brief look at Aquinas' life.) Although perennialism has been associated historically with the teachings of the Roman Catholic Church, as a theory of education it has received widespread support from lay educators. Aristotle's views best represent this group of perennialists. Whether one is an ecclesiastical (Thomist) or a lay (neo-Thomist) perennialist, one would envision the purpose of schooling to be to cultivate the rational intellect and to search for the truth.

Curriculum

For the ecclesiastical perennialist, Christian doctrine is an important aspect of the curriculum. The holy scriptures, the catechism, and the teaching of Christian dogma play a significant role. Wherever possible, theistic works would take precedence over purely secular works (Morris & Pai, 1976).

The curriculum of the perennialist education emphasizes a concern for subject matter. The cognitive subjects of mathematics, especially algebra and geometry; history; languages; logic; literature (in particular, the *Great Books*); and science would occupy a central position in the perennialist curriculum. Mastery of these subjects is considered necessary for the training of the intellect. In addition, the perennialist would contend that character training and moral development have an appropriate place in the design of the curriculum.

More recently, perennialists such as Mortimer Adler (1984) have placed less emphasis on subject matter. Rather, they view it as the context for developing intellectual skills, including reading, writing, speaking, listening, observing, computing, measuring, estimating, and problem-solving.

Consider yourself a perennialist. Choose 10 Great Books that you believe best represent absolute truth. At what grade level would you introduce these Great Books?

Teaching Methods

Perennialists maintain that education involves confronting the problems and questions that have challenged people over the centuries. Adler (1984) suggests three specific methods of instruction:

1. Didactic teaching by lectures or through textbook assignments;

2. Coaching that forms the habits through which all skills are possessed; and

3. Socratic teaching by questioning and by conducting discussions of the answers elicited. (pp. 8–9)

Historical Note:
St. Thomas Aquinas

St. Thomas Aquinas was born of a noble family in Roccasecca, Italy, in 1224. From 1239 to 1244 he attended the University of Naples, where he came in contact with the Dominican order. Against the violent opposition of his parents, Thomas became a Dominican friar in 1244. During the years 1245 to 1252, he studied philosophy and theology under the tutelage of the German theologian St. Albertus Magnus. From 1252 to 1259 and again from 1269 to 1272 he taught at the University of Paris where he was known as "The Angelic Doctor." In between he taught at the Papal Curia in Italy.

Aquinas' two most influential works were the *Summa Contra Gentiles,* which expressed the doctrine of scholasticism or Christian philosophy, and his most important work, *Summa Theologica.* In the latter work Thomas attempted to explain the truth of Christian theology and advanced the proposition that conflict need not exist between reason and faith.

Thomas believed that the government had a moral responsibility to assist the individual to lead a virtuous life. He further postulated that governments must not violate human rights, including the right to life, education, religion, and reproduction. Laws passed by human beings must be in concert with divine laws. He died in 1274.

In 1323, Pope John XXII canonized Aquinas and since then his philosophy has become the official doctrine of the Roman Catholic Church. In 1567, Pope St. Pius V proclaimed him a doctor of the Church. He has also been proclaimed the patron saint of all Catholic schools, colleges, and universities.

Since the aim of the curriculum is to foster an intellectual and liberal approach to learning, any technique or strategy that would emphasize the laws of reasoning and the canons of induction would be chosen. In addition, teaching methods that promote memory, drill and practice, recitation, and computation would be stressed. Prior to studying the great works of literature, philosophy, history, and science, students would be taught methods of critical thinking and questioning strategies to prepare them to engage in "dialogue" with the classical writers.

For the ecclesiastical perennialists the highest goal of education is union with God. For these perennialists any type of teaching method that brings the learner into direct contact with the Supreme Being would be encouraged.

Classroom Management

In addition to training the intellect, perennialists believe that the teacher has the obligation to discipline in order to train the will. They would consider the most appropriate classroom environment for training the will to be one that is characterized as rigid and structured. A formal classroom that reinforces time on task, precision, and order best describes the learning environment of perennialism. In addition to orderliness and regularity, for the ecclesiastical perennialists the learning environment would also reflect an appreciation for prayer and contemplation.

Evaluation

The standardized, objective examination would be the favored evaluation tool of the perennialist. Because the study of the classical tradition of the Great Books promotes an exchange of ideas and insights, the essay examination would also be utilized.

The Perennialist Teacher

Perennialists view the teacher who is well educated in the liberal arts as the authority figure, the instrument that provides for the dissemination of truth. And if the teacher is the disseminator, then the student is the receptacle for learning. The metaphor "director of mental calisthenics" has been used to describe the perennialist teacher (Morris & Pai, 1976).

Another metaphor that describes the perennialist teacher is "the demonstrator or scientist." The perennialist teacher must be a model of intellectual and rational powers. He or she must be capable of logical analysis, comfortable with the scientific method, well versed in the classics, have a good memory, and be capable of the highest forms of mental reasoning. Kane (1950) describes the major qualifications of the perennialist teacher: "stability, that one may never deviate from the truth; clarity, that one may not teach with obscurity; and utility, that one may seek God's honor and glory and not his own" (p. 14).

Leading Educational Proponents

Jacques Maritain (1882–1973), a French Catholic philosopher who served as ambassador to the Holy See and who was a prominent figure in the United Nations Educational, Scientific and Cultural Organization (UNESCO), is perhaps the best spokesperson for the ecclesiastical perennialist position. According to Maritain (1941), intelligence alone is not sufficient to comprehend the universe fully. One's relationship to a Spiritual Being is necessary to understand the cosmos or universe. Robert M. Hutchins (1899-1977), former chancellor of the University of Chicago and founder of the Center on the Study of Democratic Institutions, was a noted spokesperson for the lay perennialist perspective. Hutchins (1936) argued that the ideal education is one that is designed to develop the mind. This can be done best by a curriculum that concentrates on the Great Books of Western civilization.

The work of Mortimer Adler in the 1980s represents a resurgence of perennialism. In *The Paideia Proposal: An Educational Manifesto* (1982), Adler advocated a curriculum that would be appropriate for all students. Adler, as well as Hutchins, opposed differential curricula (e.g., vocational vs. academic) and contended that all students in a democratic society should have access to the same high-quality education. This education is characterized by a curriculum that includes language, literature, mathematics, natural sciences, fine arts, history, geography, and social studies. Like Hutchins, Adler favored the Great Books tradition and maintained that by studying the great works of the past, one can learn enduring lessons about life that are relevant today.

Both Robert Hutchins (left) and Mortimer Adler (right) advocated the Great Books and the enduring lessons from the past.

As a response to Allan Bloom's perceived "crisis in our civilization," what suggestions would you make for revamping the general studies curriculum at the university level?

E. D. Hirsch, Jr., Diane Ravitch, and Chester Finn all speak from the perennialist position with their emphasis on preserving a defined body of knowledge. According to Hirsch, Kett, and Trefil (1993), this common knowledge or collective memory is not only shared by literate Americans but is characteristic of a national culture and is known as *cultural literacy*. Allan Bloom, another perennialist, has referred to the crisis of liberal education, particularly in the university, as an intellectual crisis. In his book *The Closing of the American Mind* (1987), Bloom refers to "cultural illiteracy" as the crisis of our civilization. Like Hutchins and Adler, Bloom advocates teaching and learning about the Great Books, as they provide knowledge and information that have lasting significance.

The curriculum of St. John's College at Annapolis, Maryland, and Santa Fe, New Mexico, which emphasizes the importance of studying the Great Books tradition, is an excellent example of the perennialist curriculum. Overall, there are few examples of perennialism in education today. Figure 7.1 presents an overview of perennialism.

Progressivism

There are a variety of opinions concerning whether it is most appropriate to describe the educational theory that follows as instrumentalism or *progressivism*.

Figure 7.1: Perennialism at a Glance

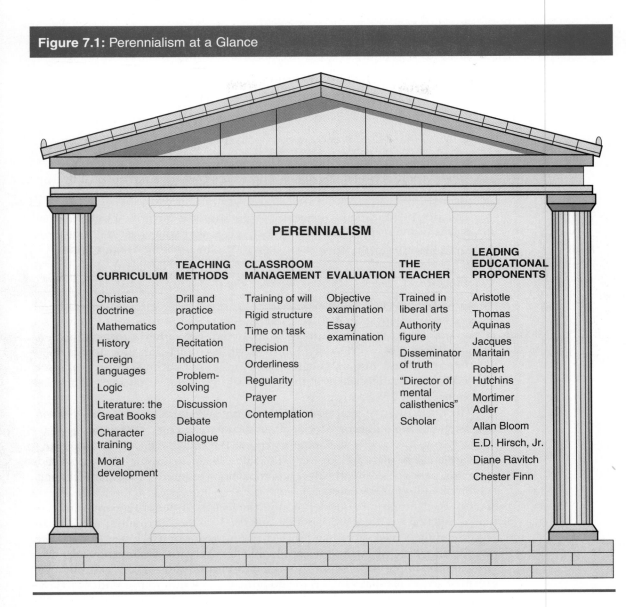

PERENNIALISM

CURRICULUM	TEACHING METHODS	CLASSROOM MANAGEMENT	EVALUATION	THE TEACHER	LEADING EDUCATIONAL PROPONENTS
Christian doctrine	Drill and practice	Training of will	Objective examination	Trained in liberal arts	Aristotle
Mathematics	Computation	Rigid structure	Essay examination	Authority figure	Thomas Aquinas
History	Recitation	Time on task		Disseminator of truth	Jacques Maritain
Foreign languages	Induction	Precision		"Director of mental calisthenics"	Robert Hutchins
Logic	Problem-solving	Orderliness			Mortimer Adler
Literature: the Great Books	Discussion	Regularity		Scholar	Allan Bloom
Character training	Debate	Prayer			E.D. Hirsch, Jr.
Moral development	Dialogue	Contemplation			Diane Ravitch
					Chester Finn

Regardless of the terminology used, what is common to any description of these terms is an educational theory that embraces the notion that the child is an experiencing organism who is capable of "learning by doing." The authors of this text believe that the term *progressivism* best describes this educational theory. The philosophy of pragmatism is embedded in the progressivist theory of education.

Kneller (1971) summarized six basic principles of the educational theory of progressivism:

1. Education should be life itself, not a preparation for living.

2. Learning should be directly related to the interests of the child.

3. Learning through problem-solving should take precedence over the inculcating of subject matter.

4. The teacher's role is not to direct but to advise.

5. The school should encourage cooperation rather than competition.

6. Only democracy permits—indeed encourages—the free interplay of ideas and personalities that is a necessary condition of true growth. (pp. 48–52)

This view of education is grounded in the scientific method of inductive reasoning. As an educational theory, it encourages the learner to seek out those processes that work, and to do those things that best achieve desirable ends.

Curriculum

The progressivist curriculum can be best described as experience-centered and focused on problem-solving. Such a curriculum would not consist of a given set of predetermined facts or truths to be mastered, but rather, a series of experiences to be gained. For Dewey (1963) "anything, which can be called a study, whether arithmetic, history, geography, or one of the natural sciences, must be derived from materials which at the onset fall within the scope of ordinary life-experiences" (p. 73).

The curriculum of progressivism would not reflect universal truths, a particular body of knowledge, or a set of prescribed core courses. Rather, it would be responsive to the needs and experiences of the individual, which would vary from situation to situation. Lerner (1962) described such a curriculum as child-centered, peer-centered, growth-centered, action-centered, process and change-centered, and equality-centered.

Another important consideration in the design of the progressivist curriculum is relevance. Any materials that are used in the curriculum are chosen because of their relevance. The progressivist is not interested in the study of the past, but is governed by the present. Unlike the perennialist or essentialist who advocate the importance of the cultural and historic roots of the past, the progressivist advocates that which is meaningful and relevant to the student today.

Teaching Methods

For the progressivist, since there is no rigid subject matter content and no absolute standard for what constitutes knowledge, the most appropriate teaching method is the project method. The experience-centered, problem-solving curriculum lends itself to cooperative group activities whereby students can learn to work together on units or projects that have relevance for their own lives. The indispensable instructional strategy that would be used along with the project method is the scientific method. However, unlike the perennialist or essentialist who view the scientific method as a means of verifying truth, the progressivist views scientific investigation as a means of verifying experience. What makes the outcome of certain hypotheses true for the progressivist is that they work and are related to the individual's experience.

Since the progressivist curriculum is not a static curriculum but rather an emerging one, any teaching method that would foster individual and group initiative, spontaneity of expression, and creative new ideas would be used. Classroom activities in critical thinking, problem-solving, decision-making, and cooperative learning are examples of some of the methods that would be incorporated in the curriculum. For the progressivist, "teaching is . . . exploratory rather than explanatory" (Bayles, 1966, p. 94).

Classroom Management

Progressivism views learning as educating "the whole child," including the physical, emotional, and social aspects of the individual. As a result of this holistic view of education, the environment is considered fundamental to the child's nature.

How can a subject-oriented secondary school teacher justify a holistic view of education?

The type of classroom management that would appeal to a progressivist would be an environment that stimulates or invites participation, involvement, and the democratic process. The atmosphere of the classroom would be active, experience-directed, and self-directed (Dewey, 1956). Such an environment would not only be child-centered or student-centered, but would also be community-centered. It would feature an open environment in which students would spend considerable time in direct contact with the community or cultural surroundings beyond the confines of the classroom or school. Students would experience the arts by frequenting museums and theaters. They would experience social studies by interacting with individuals from diverse social groups and social conditions. They would experience science by exploring their immediate physical world. All students would be involved in a "social" mode of learning (Westheimer & Kahne, 1993).

The progressivist teacher would foster a classroom environment that practices democracy. Students and parents would be encouraged to form their own councils and organizations within the school to address educational issues and advance social change. Teachers would advocate site-based management and democratic decision-making with regard to the administration of the school.

Since students would decide on appropriate rules and content to be studied, the teacher would manage groups of students engaged in a variety of simultaneous classroom tasks. Being able to distinguish between instructional and disruptive noise, to cope with a number of distractions, and to plan for the problems that emerge from a student-centered classroom are a few of the daily challenges that confront the progressivist teacher.

Evaluation

Because progressivism supports the group process, cooperative learning, and democratic participation, its approach to evaluation differs from the more traditional approaches. For example, the progressivist would engage in *formative evaluation,* which is process oriented and concerned with ongoing feedback about the activity underway, rather than the measurement of outcomes.

*What type of
process-oriented
evaluation would
you be most
comfortable
using in your
teaching?*

Monitoring what the students are doing, appraising what skills they still need to develop, and resolving unexpected problems as they occur would be typical of this type of evaluation used by the progressivist.

The Progressivist Teacher

The metaphor of the "teacher as facilitator" or "director of learning" might best describe the progressivist teacher. Such a teacher is not considered to be the authority, or disseminator of knowledge or truth, like the perennialist or essentialist teacher. Rather, he or she serves more as a guide or supervisor who facilitates learning by assisting the student to sample direct experience. The teacher's role is to help his or her pupils to acquire the values of the democratic system. Although the teacher is always interested in the individual development of each student, the progressivist instructor would envision his or her role as focusing beyond the individual. Progressivism by its very nature is socially oriented; thus the teacher would be a collaborative partner in making group decisions, keeping in mind their ultimate consequences for the students.

Leading Educational Proponents

Progressivism had its impetus in the first decades of the twentieth century at a time when many liberal thinkers alleged that American schools were out of touch with the advances that were being made in the physical and social sciences and technology (see Chapter 5). It is John Dewey who, perhaps more than any other American educator, is credited with having advanced progressivism. Dewey's approach to progressivism differed from earlier progressive educators in that rather than emphasize the individual learner, Dewey emphasized the importance of the teacher/student interaction and the importance of education as a social function.

One of the most important principles of Dewey's educational theory was the connection between education and personal experience. For Dewey (1938), experience was the basis of education. However, he cautioned that not all experiences are equal:

> The belief that all genuine education comes about through experience does not mean that all experiences are genuinely or equally educative. Experience and education cannot be directly equated to each other. For some experiences are mis-educative. Any experience is mis-education that has the effect of arresting or distorting the growth of further experience. (p. 25)

John Dewey's establishment of the University Laboratory School at the University of Chicago provided the clinical testing ground for his educational theory. His leadership at the University of Chicago and his subsequent work at Teachers College, Columbia, left a legacy to American education. Although some educators would argue that progressivism in education is no longer accepted as the leading philosophy of the 1990s, its profound impact on American education through the 1960s and 1970s is without debate. In fact, its critics contend that progressivism was the major cause of the decline in student performance in the 1960s and 1970s. Vestiges of progressivism can be found in *non-*

graded schools, alternative schools, the *whole-child movement, humanistic education,* bilingual education, and some of the "open" educational arrangements. Figure 7.2 presents an overview of progressivism.

Behaviorism

Behaviorism, or behavioral engineering is an educational theory that is predicated on the belief that human behavior can be explained in terms of responses to external stimuli. The basic principle of behaviorism is that education can best be achieved by modifying or changing student behaviors in a socially acceptable

What do you see as the advantages and disadvantages of a nongraded school?

Figure 7.2: Progressivism at a Glance

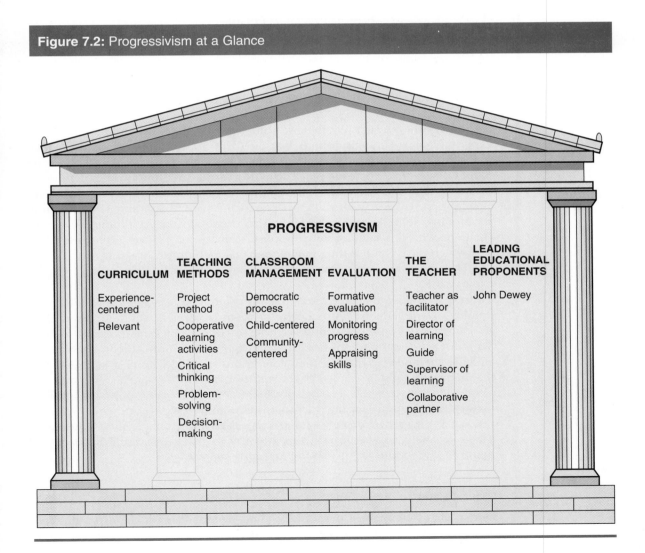

PROGRESSIVISM

CURRICULUM	TEACHING METHODS	CLASSROOM MANAGEMENT	EVALUATION	THE TEACHER	LEADING EDUCATIONAL PROPONENTS
Experience-centered	Project method	Democratic process	Formative evaluation	Teacher as facilitator	John Dewey
Relevant	Cooperative learning activities	Child-centered	Monitoring progress	Director of learning	
	Critical thinking	Community-centered	Appraising skills	Guide	
	Problem-solving			Supervisor of learning	
	Decision-making			Collaborative partner	

manner through the arrangement of the conditions for learning. For the behaviorist, the predictability and control of human behavior are paramount concepts. The control is obtained not by manipulating the individual, but by manipulating the environment.

The basic principles of the theory of behaviorism are as follows:

1. All behaviors are both objective and observable.

2. All behaviors are caused.

3. As natural organisms we seek positive reinforcement and avoid punishment.

4. The teacher should arrange conditions under which learning can occur.

5. Technology makes it possible for teachers to teach beyond their knowledge of content or subject matter.

6. Students will learn best by the use of carefully planned schedules of reinforcement.

There are two major types of behaviorism: (1) *classical conditioning*, or stimulus substitution behaviorism, and (2) *operant conditioning*, or response reinforcement behaviorism (Phillips & Soltis, 1991). Classical conditioning, based on the work of the Russian physiologist Ivan Pavlov (1849–1936) and the American experimental psychologist John B. Watson (1878–1958), demonstrates that a natural stimulus that produces a certain type of response can be replaced by a conditioned stimulus. For example, Pavlov found that in laboratory experiments with dogs a natural stimulus such as food will produce a natural response such as salivation. However, when Pavlov paired the natural stimulus (food) with a conditioned stimulus (bell), he found that eventually the conditioned stimulus (bell) produced a conditioned response (salivation). Watson eventually used Pavlov's classical conditioning model to explain all human learning.

The operant conditioning model can best be described by the work of psychologists E. L. Thorndike (1874–1949) and B. F. Skinner (1904–1990). Both Thorndike and Skinner suggested that any response to any stimulus can be conditioned by immediate reinforcement or reward. Skinner later determined that an action or response does not have to be rewarded each time it occurs. In fact, Skinner found that random reward, or intermittent reinforcement, was a more effective method for learning than continuous reward. Skinner also discovered that behavior could be shaped by the appropriate use of rewards.

As a theory of education, behaviorism was a protest against the importance placed on mental processes that could not be observed (e.g., thinking or motivation). Today, behaviorism has taken a more moderate stance, and has adopted a cognitive-behavioral approach that attempts to change the individual's cognitions, or perceptions, of the world and his or her self.

Curriculum

Unlike the curriculum of perennialism and essentialism, which advocate a prescribed subject matter, the behaviorist curriculum is not interested in subject matter *per se,* but is interested in environmental variables such as teaching materials, teaching methods, and teacher-classroom behaviors, since they directly influence the learner's behavior (Wittrock, 1987). The behaviorist curriculum includes cognitive problem-solving activities whereby students learn about their belief systems, recognize their power to influence their environment, and employ critical-thinking skills.

As a teacher, how could you help your students learn about their belief systems or values?

Teaching Methods

Behaviorist theory is primarily concerned with the process of providing contingencies of reinforcement as the basis for any strategy or method. If there are appropriate opportunities for the learner to respond, and appropriate reinforcers that are readily available, learning will take place, say the behaviorists. Skinner supported the use of the teaching machine, or *programmed instruction,* as an effective teaching method. Programmed instruction enables individual students to answer questions about a unit of study at their own rate, checking their own answers and advancing only after answering correctly. A chief advantage of the teaching machine, or programmed instruction, is the immediate reinforcement that it provides. Today, computers have replaced the teaching machine. A wide variety of computer-assisted instruction, including interactive multimedia, has become a favored teaching method of many educators, in particular the behaviorists.

Classroom Management

For the behaviorist, classroom management is an integral part of the process of learning. Emmer (1987) described two general principles that guide the behaviorist teacher in classroom management:

1. Identify expected student behavior. This implies that teachers must have a clear idea of what behaviors are appropriate and are not appropriate in advance of instruction.

2. Translate expectations into procedures and routines. Part of the process of translating expectations into procedures is to formulate some general rules governing conduct. (pp. 438–439)

Other components of good management include careful monitoring or observation of classroom events; prompt and appropriate handling of inappropriate behavior; using reward systems, penalties, and other consequences; establishing accountability for completion of assignments; and maintaining lesson or activity flow (Emmer, 1987). Behaviorism is widely used in special education and mainstream classroom environments.

Evaluation

Measurement and evaluation are central to the behaviorist. Specified *behavioral objectives* (e.g., the behaviors or knowledge that students are expected to demonstrate or learn) serve not only as guides to learning for the student, but as standards for evaluating the teaching-learning process. For the behaviorist, only those aspects of behavior that are observable, and preferably measurable, are of interest to the teacher. Advocates of behavioral objectives claim that if teachers know exactly what they want students to learn and how they want them to learn, using behavioral objectives can be an efficient method for gauging how much learning has occurred. Measurement and evaluation also provide a method for obtaining accountability from teachers since they are pivotal to the learning process. Two other types of evaluation used by the behaviorist teacher include performance contracting and teaching students to record their own progress.

The Behaviorist Teacher

Since education as behavioral engineering entails a variety of technical and observational skills, the behaviorist teacher must be skilled in a variety of these techniques. Moreover, since behavioral engineering depends on psychological principles, the teacher must be knowledgeable about psychology, in particular educational psychology that emphasizes learning. Also, since behaviorism focuses on empirical verification, the teacher must be well versed in the scientific method.

What type of reinforcer would be most apt to motivate you to learn?

The behaviorist teacher is very concerned about the consequences of classroom behavior. Therefore, the teacher must be able to recognize which reinforcers are most appropriate. In addition, the behaviorist teacher must be skilled in using a variety of schedules of reinforcement that are effective and efficient in shaping and maintaining desired responses.

To establish the behaviors that will be most beneficial to the learner, behaviorist teachers are most concerned with the student achieving specific objectives or competencies. For this reason the teacher must be capable of planning and using behavioral objectives, designing and using programmed instruction, using computers, and utilizing performance contracting. Two of the most appropriate metaphors for describing the behaviorist teacher are "the controller of behavior" and "the arranger of contingencies."

Leading Educational Proponents

As previously noted, classical conditioning had its beginnings with Pavlov and Watson. Both maintained that classical conditioning was the key mechanism underlying all human learning. The behaviorists Thorndike and Skinner are known for the concept of operant conditioning, which suggests that reinforcement of responses (operant behavior) underlies all types of learning. Another noted behaviorist, psychologist David Premack, determined that organisms often freely choose to engage in certain behaviors rather than other behaviors. Consequently, providing access to the preferred activities can serve as a reinforcement for not engaging in nonpreferred activities. To apply the *Premack principle* in the classroom, the teacher first must observe and carefully record the behavior that students more often freely choose to perform, and the relative frequency of competing behaviors (Bates, 1987). Figure 7.3 provides an overview of behaviorism.

Figure 7.3: Behaviorism at a Glance

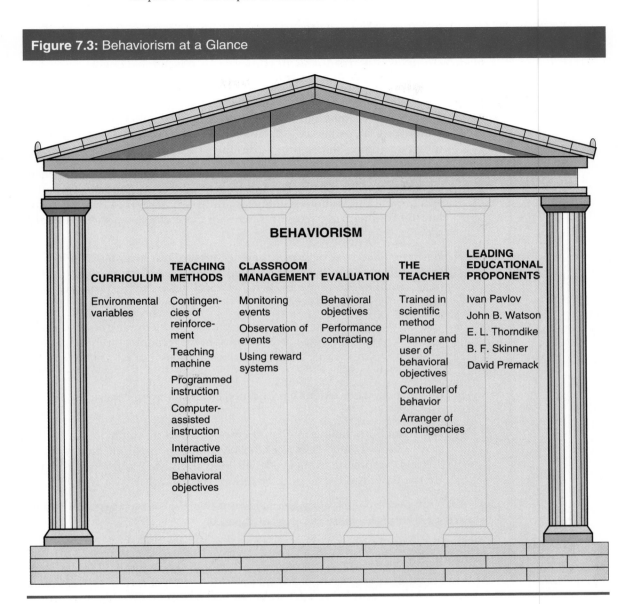

BEHAVIORISM

CURRICULUM	TEACHING METHODS	CLASSROOM MANAGEMENT	EVALUATION	THE TEACHER	LEADING EDUCATIONAL PROPONENTS
Environmental variables	Contingencies of reinforcement	Monitoring events	Behavioral objectives	Trained in scientific method	Ivan Pavlov
	Teaching machine	Observation of events	Performance contracting	Planner and user of behavioral objectives	John B. Watson
	Programmed instruction	Using reward systems		Controller of behavior	E. L. Thorndike
	Computer-assisted instruction			Arranger of contingencies	B. F. Skinner
	Interactive multimedia				David Premack
	Behavioral objectives				

Essentialism

Historically, there have been a variety of opinions concerning whether essentialism is a true educational theory. A number of scholars have suggested that essentialism is actually perennialism in disguise. If one were to choose an adjective that best describes essentialism, it would probably be "eclectic." The philosophies of idealism and realism are embedded in the essentialist theory of education.

Protesting against progressivism, essentialists believe that pragmatism, or progressivism, has had a negative impact on American education, and that there is a need to return to the traditional, or conservative, educational goals.

Wingo (1974) described six basic tenets of essentialism:

1. Americans largely have lost sight of the true purpose of education, which is intellectual training. We tend to confuse education with all kinds of social, psychological, and vocational services that often are lumped together under the rubric "life adjustment."

2. The rigor of our educational programs and teaching methods has been declining steadily for several decades. This is true in some measure of every level of the school system from the kindergarten to the university, but the condition is particularly acute in the elementary and secondary schools.

3. We have failed to provide for the education of our brightest children because instruction has been pitched at the level of the mediocre student, and the ablest have been systematically deprived in the name of "equality" and "democracy."

4. The curricula of our schools have been diluted by the introduction of courses consisting largely of "life adjustment" trivia, and these worthless substitutes have crowded out the historic disciplines that are the core of the true education.

5. Intellectual achievement has declined steadily among American students.

6. The schools are failing to meet their obligations to American youth and to American society. They are not only failing in the intellectual task, they also are failing in their responsibility to transmit those values that are the basis of the American tradition. (pp. 51–52)

Like the perennialists, essentialists believe that the best preparation for life is learning the culture and traditions of the past.

Curriculum

The curriculum of the essentialist school is a basic education that includes instruction in the "essentials," including reading, writing, and computing at the primary grades, and history, geography, natural sciences, and foreign languages at the upper elementary grades. At the secondary level, the curriculum would place a major emphasis on the common core that all students should complete. Such a core would normally include four years of English, three or four years of social studies, a course in American government, and a year of natural science and general mathematics or algebra (Conant, 1959). Such a common core represents the comprehensive high school that was most popular during the 1950s. Some essentialists believe that the educational curriculum should not be limited only to the academic disciplines. They suggest that the physical and emotional well-being of the child is important (Wingo, 1974). Overall, essentialists maintain that the educational program should not permit any "frivolous" subjects, but rather should adhere strictly to sound academic standards. Probably more than any other educational theory, essentialism deplores the lack of educational standards or the so-called "soft pedagogy."

What subjects might be construed as "frivolous" by an essentialist?

Teaching Methods

If the basic disciplines, or basic subjects, are at the heart of the school curriculum, then the methods of instruction that are to support such a curriculum include the more traditional instructional strategies such as lecture, recitation, discussion, and the Socratic dialogue. Written and oral communication occupy a prominent place in the instructional milieu of the essentialist school. Like perennialists, essentialists view books as an appropriate medium for instruction.

Generally, essentialist educators have found educational technology to be congruent with their educational theory. They prefer instructional materials that are paced and sequenced in such a way that students know what they are expected to master. Detailed syllabi, lesson plans, learning by objectives, competency-based instruction, computer-assisted instruction, and audio-tutorial laboratory methods are other examples of teaching strategies that would be acceptable to the modern-day essentialist.

Classroom Management

Like the perennialists, who advocate intellectual discipline as well as moral discipline, the essentialists maintain that character training deserves an important place in the school. William Bennett (1993), former Secretary of Education, has strongly endorsed essentialism since it advocates moral literacy. Bennett proposes the use of stories, poems, essays, and other works to help children achieve moral literacy and learn to possess the traits of character that society most admires. For the essentialist, students attend school to learn how to participate in society, not to manage the course of their own instruction. They prepare for life by being exposed to essential truths and values, as well as by exercising discipline. Thus, the essentialist teacher would take great pains in designing and controlling a classroom environment that creates an aura of certainty, an emphasis on regularity and uniformity, and a reverence for what is morally right.

Evaluation

Of all the theories of education, essentialism is perhaps most comfortable with testing. In fact, the entire essentialist curriculum reflects the influence of the testing movement. Extensive use of IQ tests, standardized achievement tests, diagnostic tests, and performance-based competency tests are examples of the widespread application of measurement techniques. Competency, accountability, mastery learning (see Chapter 15), and performance-based instruction have gained increasing acceptance by many educators as a result of the essentialists' influence on educational practice.

The Essentialist Teacher

The essentialist teacher, like the perennialist teacher, is an educator who has faith in the accumulated wisdom of the past. Rather than having majored in educational pedagogy, the essentialist teacher would have majored in a subject matter discipline, preferably in the liberal arts, science, or the humanities. The essentialist educator is viewed as either a link to the so-called "literary intellectual inheritance" (idealism), or as a demonstrator of the world model (realism). To be an essentialist teacher is to be well versed in the liberal arts and sciences, to be a respected member of the intellectual community, to be technically skilled in all forms of communication, and to be equipped with superior pedagogical skills to ensure competent instruction. One of the most important roles of the teacher is to set the character of the environment in which learning takes place (Butler, 1966).

Contemporary essentialists such as Delattre (1984) have been critical of the preprofessional training of teachers, since they believe that their training falls short of what is demanded of teachers today:

> Many have been subjected to too many textbooks and not enough original books: some have never read basic and profound works on learning, knowing, and teaching—have never been exposed to Deuteronomy, works by Plato, Aristotle, Loyola, Milton, Agassiz, Hadas, or Highet, not to mention Augustine and the intellectual predecessors of Dewey. That is, some cannot teach themselves in any systematic program of study because they do not know enough to design one, and their own teachers are not always qualified to do so for them. (p. 159)

Leading Educational Proponents

Although essentialism can be traced to Plato and Aristotle, its greatest popularity has emerged in the twentieth century. As noted in Chapter 5, in the 1930s and 1940s William C. Bagley, Arthur E. Bestor, and Herman H. Horne (1874–1946) led the essentialist criticism of the progressivism of Dewey and his followers. They formed the Essentialist Committee for the Advancement of American Education. In the 1950s, Admiral Hyman G. Rickover (1900–1986) became the spokesperson for the essentialists. According to Rickover (1963), the quality of American education declined considerably as a result of "watered-down" courses and "fads and frills." He called for a return to the basics, with particular emphasis on mathematics and science.

If you were an essentialist, would you raise the academic standards at the university? In what ways?

A major revival of essentialism has been evidenced by the *back-to-basics movement* that gained support in the 1970s and has been echoed in the education reform reports of the 1980s. For example, *A Nation at Risk* (National Commission on Excellence in Education, 1983), the premier of these reports, recommended a core of *new basics*: English, mathematics, science, social studies, and computer sciences, and for the college-bound a foreign language. Many of the other reports not only proposed similar cores, but called for improvement in their content and increased rigor in their standards (see Chapter 14). The success of the essentialist position is evidenced by the steps taken in a number of states to mandate curricula, strengthen graduation requirements, and increase student testing and evaluation. Essentialism is the dominant philosophy in our schools today. Figure 7.4 presents an overview of essentialism.

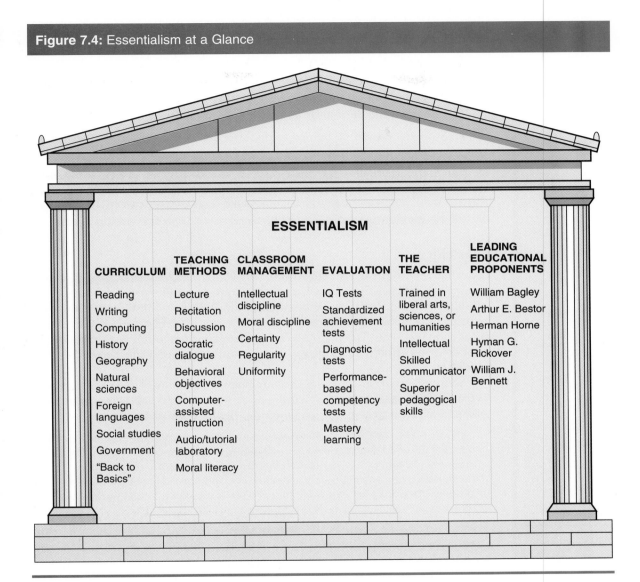

Figure 7.4: Essentialism at a Glance

ESSENTIALISM

CURRICULUM	TEACHING METHODS	CLASSROOM MANAGEMENT	EVALUATION	THE TEACHER	LEADING EDUCATIONAL PROPONENTS
Reading	Lecture	Intellectual discipline	IQ Tests	Trained in liberal arts, sciences, or humanities	William Bagley
Writing	Recitation	Moral discipline	Standardized achievement tests		Arthur E. Bestor
Computing	Discussion	Certainty		Intellectual	Herman Horne
History	Socratic dialogue	Regularity	Diagnostic tests	Skilled communicator	Hyman G. Rickover
Geography	Behavioral objectives	Uniformity	Performance-based competency tests	Superior pedagogical skills	William J. Bennett
Natural sciences	Computer-assisted instruction		Mastery learning		
Foreign languages	Audio/tutorial laboratory				
Social studies	Moral literacy				
Government					
"Back to Basics"					

Existentialism

Freedom, responsibility, choice, anxiety, authenticity, alienation, paradox, and human subjectivity are the hallmarks of existentialism. Existentialist philosophy represents a protest against the earlier efforts of Western philosophy to reduce the human being to an essence or universal—to an abstraction (Wingo, 1974). For the existentialist, to reduce human life to such an abstraction is to deny the individual his or her existence. The philosophy of existentialism is embedded in the existentialist theory of education. Kneller (1971) described some of the basic principles of the educational theory of existentialism:

1. Students should be urged to take responsibility for, and to deal with, the results of their actions.

2. Teachers should not simply impose discipline on their students but rather should demonstrate the value of discipline.

3. Students should be helped to discover that true freedom implies communion, not self-interest.

For the existentialist, the child or student has a "right to live the extreme choice, the right to change, and the right to spontaneous self-realization" (Barnes, 1968, p. 296). The purpose of education is to foster self-discovery and consciousness of the freedom of choice, as well as the responsibility for making choices.

Curriculum

Like that of progressivism, the curriculum of the existentialist school evolves around the student's needs and interests. However, unlike progressivism, which emphasizes group learning, existentialism emphasizes the individual and views learning as a private and personal matter. It is a student-centered curriculum of individual choice. The main objective of such a curriculum is to immerse the student in a variety of existential situations that authenticate his or her own exprience.

Although there are no universals in such a curriculum, there is a favored subject matter: the humanities. For the existentialist, the humanities offer visible evidence of the suffering that accompanies the human condition:

> Above all, it is the spiritual power of the humanities and the essential urge for affirmation inherent in all forms of art that attract the existentialist. To read and see how men in history have struggled with their conscience, labored with fate, rebelled against existing orders and absolutes, and poured life-blood into their creations becomes a source of inspiration for the existentialist in his approach to learning. (Kneller, 1958, p. 125)

Have you ever experienced "the existential moment"? Describe the experience.

The essence of the curriculum is to stress the awareness of "being" and the awareness of "nothingness." The assumption made by the existentialist is that by dwelling on the unpleasant idea of meaninglessness or nothingness and its accompanying anxiety and absurdity, we ultimately create an affirmation of self and find a purpose in life. The curriculum, then, awakens a fundamental awareness in the learner. Such a subjective awareness has been called "the existential moment" (Marler, 1975; Morris, 1966) which marks the beginning of taking responsibility for assigning meaning to one's own life. Unlike the curriculum of perennialism and essentialism, which seeks Absolute Truth, the existentialist seeks "personal truth."

Teaching Methods

Since existentialists view the greatest obstacles to authenticity to be fear and conformity (Kneller, 1984), the teaching methods they would use would not reinforce fear or conformity, but would value "existential anxiety," which is the anxiety associated with the freedom to choose. Existential anxiety is a prerequisite to growth, and as such is considered to be probably the most powerful experience that a student can have. It breaks down defenses, questions values and beliefs, and reveals the person as he or she really is. The best methods for encouraging and nourishing a certain amount of existential anxiety are those that teach decision-making, or choosing among alternatives.

The so-called "affective" approaches to values education, which engage students in cognitive discussions along with affective experiences, would be a favored teaching method of the existentialist teacher. In addition, the Socratic method, which includes asking questions, refining answers, and asking further questions until a conclusion is reached, would be another important instructional strategy because it produces self-knowledge. Nel Noddings (1993), a contemporary existential philosopher, describes some of the teaching strategies that are consistent with the existential pedagogy:

> In the discussion of religious, metaphysical, and existential questions, teachers and students are both seekers. Teachers tell stories, guide the logic of discussion, point to further readings, model both critical thinking and kindness, and show by their openness what it means to seek intelligent belief or unbelief. (p. 135)

Furthermore, the existentialist teacher would provide time for self-reflection and privacy because the questions of human existence are best addressed in the quietude of private time and space.

Describe how you might demonstrate the value of discipline rather than impose discipline in your classroom.

Classroom Management

The most appropriate metaphor for the classroom environment of an existential school is an *open classroom* (i.e., an open instructional space or "classroom without walls") where students enjoy the freedom to move about. Within such an environment, learning is dedicated to self-discovery and individual choice. Such a classroom invites participatory decision-making and does not view the teacher as the authority figure. Rather, the teacher is considered a mediator who permits students to exercise freedom within a nonpunitive, democratic community.

Evaluation

Because authenticity and authentic teaching reflect the uniqueness of the individual teacher, the existential teacher spurns the use of standardized tests, rejects the notion of accountability, and stresses a more subjective form of appraisal or evaluation. The school is viewed as a place for experiencing life and making meaning out of nonmeaning, a place where students come to grips with their own values. The source of those values is inconsequential. What matters most is that there is a personal endorsement for valuing and choosing. Within this paradigm of choice, the teacher is not viewed as an evaluator, monitor, or critic, but rather as a subjective or reflective artist who is committed to helping students fulfill their personal goals.

The Existentialist Teacher

With the overriding concern for the individual as the ultimate chooser, the existentialist teacher would model valuing, decision-making, and choosing. Such a teacher would pose moral and ethical, as well as intellectual, questions to his or her students. The teacher's job would be to awaken students to the ultimate responsibility that they must bear for the decisions that they make. The teacher who would be most comfortable with the tenets of existentialism is typically one who is flexible, nondirective, and impervious to the type of noise and disorder that often accompanies an informal, open class atmosphere (Kneller, 1984). The teacher's role is to help the individual achieve his or her potential and to strive for self-actualization (Greene, 1967).

The existentialist teacher attempts to become an excellent example of authenticity for students. By incorporating a humanistic approach to teaching, the existentialist educator would encourage a more personal and interactive teacher-student relationship. The whole child or student would be viewed as primary, and the existentialist would be concerned with the cognitive as well as affective components of the student's development. Furthermore, since the thrust of existentialism is the search for meaning and purpose, the teacher would be an individual who is comfortable with being introspective and reflective. Imagination and insight are important criteria for the existentialist teacher.

Lastly, the existentialist teacher is an advocate for self-education and academic freedom. The teacher would encourage students to take responsibility for their own learning and education. Teaching, says the existentialist, is neither a science nor a technology, but an art.

Leading Educational Proponents

Perhaps the most well-known educational existentialists are A. S. Neill (1883–1973), Carl Rogers (1902–1987), and John Holt (1923–1985), as well as contemporary writers Charles Silberman and Jonathan Kozol. Neill, who founded Summerhill School outside London shortly after World War I, offered an educational experience built on the principle of learning by discovery in an atmosphere of unrestrained freedom. He contended that learning will evolve from the student's interest. According to Neill (1960), regardless of their age or maturity level, students are capable of self-discipline and can be responsible for their own learning. A similar institution established in 1968 and still in operation today in Framingham, Massachusetts, is Sudbury Valley School, which operates on the existential principles that foster individual choice, democracy, and personal responsibility. Long and Ihle (1988) described the basic components of the school:

> Sudbury Valley operates on the principle that children's natural tendencies toward wanting to grow up, to be competent, to model older children and adults, and to fantasize, should be the foundation for education. Consequently, the school has set no curriculum and no activity takes place unless a student asks for it. Instead, the school offers a wide variety of educational options, including instruction in standard subjects in both group and tutorial formats; field trips to Boston, New York, and the nearby mountains, and seacoast; and facilities that include a labora-

Individual choice, democracy, and personal responsibility are key ingredients of Sudbury Valley School.

tory, a woodworking shop, a computer room, a kitchen, a darkroom, an art room, and a number of music rooms. (p. 449)

Carl Rogers (1969), in his *Freedom to Learn*, asserted that the only things that one person can teach another person are those that are relatively inconsequential and of little or no significance. Only learning that is self-discovered, self-appropriated through experience can significantly influence behavior.

John Holt (1981), Charles Silberman (1970), and Jonathan Kozol (1972; 1991) were supporters of the so-called open schools, free schools, or alternative schools that flourished during the mid-1960s. Similar to Summerhill or Sudbury Valley, these nontraditional schools emphasized a permissive, or humanistic education that abhorred any type of rigidity or structure. In spite of the appeal of the humanistic education movement, its heyday was very short-lived, and it was eventually replaced by the back-to-basics movement of the 1970s.

Two current spokespersons for the existentialist theory of education are Maxine Greene and Nel Noddings. Noddings, a former teacher of mathematics and currently a leading philosopher of education, suggests an alternative educational model that stresses the *challenge to care:*

> We must consider Heidegger's deepest sense of care. As human beings, we care what happens to us. We wonder whether there is a life after death, whether there is a deity who cares about us, whether we are loved by those we love, whether we belong anywhere; we wonder what we will become, who we are, how much control we have over our own fate. For adolescents these are among the most pressing questions: Who am I? Who will love me? How do others see me? Yet schools spend

If you had the opportunity to attend a school like Summerhill or Sudbury Valley, how different would your elementary education have been from the one you received?

more time on the quadratic formula than on any of these existential questions. (1992, p. 20)

Figure 7.5 presents an overview of existentialism.

Social Reconstructionism

Throughout history there have been social reconstructionists who have aspired to improve, change, or reform society, including its educational institutions. Certainly Plato, who advocated a design for a future state in the *Republic,* could be considered a social reconstructionist, as could the Christian philosopher Augustine, who sought to create an ideal Christian state. Likewise, Karl Marx

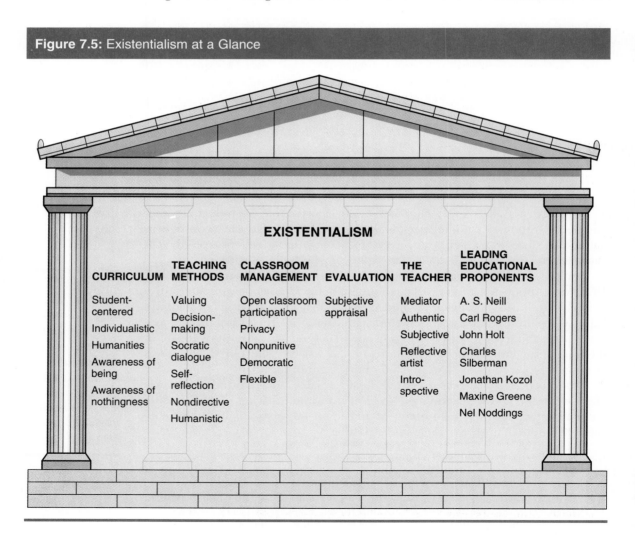

Figure 7.5: Existentialism at a Glance

EXISTENTIALISM

CURRICULUM	TEACHING METHODS	CLASSROOM MANAGEMENT	EVALUATION	THE TEACHER	LEADING EDUCATIONAL PROPONENTS
Student-centered	Valuing	Open classroom participation	Subjective appraisal	Mediator	A. S. Neill
Individualistic	Decision-making	Privacy		Authentic	Carl Rogers
Humanities	Socratic dialogue	Nonpunitive		Subjective	John Holt
Awareness of being	Self-reflection	Democratic		Reflective artist	Charles Silberman
Awareness of nothingness	Nondirective	Flexible		Intro-spective	Jonathan Kozol
	Humanistic				Maxine Greene
					Nel Noddings

(1818–1883), who envisioned a reconstructed world based on international communism, is considered a social reconstructionist (Ozmon & Craver, 1990). Each of these individuals advocated far-reaching changes that anticipated radical social and educational reforms.

The educational theory of social reconstructionism has two predominant themes: (1) society is in need of change or reconstruction, and (2) education must take the lead in the reconstruction of society. It was John Dewey who suggested the term "reconstructionism" by the title of his book, *Reconstruction in Philosophy* (1920). Shortly thereafter, in the early 1930s, a group known as the "Frontier Thinkers" looked to the schools for leadership in creating a "new" and "more equitable" society (Kneller, 1971). These educational reformers advocated changes beyond what Dewey envisioned in his theory of progressivism. His emphasis was on the democratic social experience, theirs was on social reform.

Modern social reconstructionism had its beginnings in Marxist philosophy. According to Marx, capitalism and its emphasis on competition and the control of property in the hands of a few led to an alienated workforce who found little meaning or purpose in their work. Marx's later writings recommended a total social revolution against the ruling class by the working class. Several major revolutionary figures were greatly influenced by the philosophy of Marx. Two such figures were Fredrich Engels (1820–1895) and Vladimir Ilich Lenin (1870–1924), both of whom proposed violent revolution by the working class.

Following the impact and influence of Marxism-Leninism in the East, Marxist thought spread to the West and became known as the "Frankfurt School." Eventually the term *critical theory* was applied to the Frankfurt School and included the melding of the philosophies and theories of Kant, Hegel, Freud, and Marx. At the heart of the Frankfurt School was analysis, scrutiny, and the critique of all ideologies. Some of the leading proponents of the Frankfurt School included Max Horkheimer (1895–1971), Theodor Adorno (1903–1969), and Herbert Marcuse (1898–1979) (Ozmon & Craver, 1990).

Today, critical theorists have moved beyond Marxism and have become spokespersons for liberation theology, feminism, racial equality, the ecology movement, and other forms of social reconstruction. One of the major contributions of critical theory has been to make known the political nature of education, including social control and power and its relationship to schooling. Stanley Aronowitz and Henry A. Giroux (1985), both leading contemporary proponents of critical theory and postmodern thought, look to the classroom teacher for a more activist role in bringing about change:

> If radical educators are going to take seriously the need to develop workable alternatives to the current forms of schooling, . . . they will . . . have to investigate how the teaching field has evolved under conditions where race, gender, and class-specific practices have become part and parcel of the teaching profession. This suggests that teachers be prepared not only to produce oppositional forms of knowledge and social practice, but that they also be prepared to struggle and to take risks in fighting against injustices . . . (p.161)

According to contemporary critical theorists, modern reconstructionists must help create communities of "responsible defiance and action," (Giroux,

Social reconstructionists aspire to improve, change, or reform society.

1988), a "language of critique," a "language of possibility," (McLaren, 1988), and a place for critical moral discourse. Modern reconstructionism has been called a "theory of vision," a "theory of education-as-politics," a "theory of transformation," and "a theory of social reform." For the social reconstructionist, the school should be an agency of social change, a participant in the construction of a society free of all forms of discrimination, and an institution that is concerned with issues of global welfare.

Curriculum

Since the majority of social reconstructionists believe in the importance of democracy and the proposition that the school is the fundamental institution in modern society, the curriculum of the social reconstructionist school would reflect those democratic ideals. The emphasis of the curriculum would be on literacy, not *cultural literacy*, but *critical literacy*. Such a curriculum would denounce any form of the politics of exclusion, including elevating Eurocentrism as the model for cultural literacy. Rather, it would challenge all unequal power relationships and focus on power as applied to class, gender, sexuality, race, and nationalism. Students would be challenged to think about the world in critical terms, to examine the hidden values of knowledge (Kincheloe, 1993), and to acquire and critically question moral beliefs (Liston & Zeichnar, 1988). Cultural pluralism, human relations, group dynamics, problem-detecting, problem-solving, and the politics of change would be highlighted. Rather than concentrate on separate subjects, societal problems such as the place of bio-medical ethics in improving the quality of life, the need to conserve our natural resources, and the issues of foreign policy and nationalism are a few examples of the curriculum of social reconstructionism.

Since the school should be viewed as an instrument for transformation and change, say the social reconstructionists, one of the most effective methods for initiating change would be by studying the future. Accordingly, the study of the thinking of various futurists would occupy a central place in the curriculum of the social reconstructionist school. In addition to the future, social reconstructionists believe that students should be engaged in learning about other cultures, other mores, and other languages. At the heart of the social reconstructionist curriculum would be activism and reform.

Teaching Methods

Teaching methods associated with social reconstructionism would encourage students to become involved in the social problems that confront the community and society. Rather than merely reading and studying about the problems of the poor or the disenfranchised, the students would spend time in the community becoming acquainted with and immersed in their problems and their possible solutions. They would interview community members to learn about the realities of their lives, including the constraints and obstacles they face in trying to change their situation; they would analyze, research, and link the underlying issues to institutions and structures in the community and larger society. Lastly, they would take some action or responsibility in planning for change.

The teaching strategies of computer simulation, role-playing, cooperative learning, internships, and work-study experiences would be compatible with social reconstruction. Students would work closely with older peers and adults on various aspects of problem-detection and problem-solving to enlarge their range of experience. Social reconstructionists, in particular, critical theorists, draw heavily on the use of the metaphor as a teaching method since it is essential to all scientific and creative thinking and involves the mix of different ideas in unforseen ways (Kincheloe, 1993).

Classroom Management

The classroom environment of the social reconstructionist would be a climate of inquiry that questions the assumptions of the status quo and examines societal issues and future trends. The social reconstructionist would strive to organize his or her classroom in a classless, nonsexist, and nonracist manner. Social reconstructionists have a penchant for utopian thinking and alternative solutions. Therefore, the environment of the classroom might take on a "think tank" or problem-solving atmosphere in which students would be encouraged to take on new roles and experiment with the ideal world. There would be less emphasis on management and control, and more focus on community building in the classroom. Individualized instruction based on the students' varied cultures, experiences, and needs would be important.

The teacher responsible for a reconstructionist classroom would model optimism and hope for the future. An atmosphere that promotes analysis, criticism, and action research would best describe this type of classroom environment. Conflict resolution and differences in world views would be encouraged and reinforced. The classroom in the school and life experience in the larger society would become the stage for experimentation and imaginative problem-solving. Individuals, groups, and teams of students would become engaged in a variety of creative problem-solving activities. The underlying goals of these activities would be to develop conceptual flexibility and the willingness to question assumptions. Such an environment would condone a new respect for "questioning the status quo."

Evaluation

For a social reconstructionist, the foundation for evaluation would evolve around the ability to think in critical terms and to expose underlying assumptions and practices. The type of evaluation that would be appropriate for both the student and the teacher in a social reconstructionist school would be formative evaluation that would entail a cooperative effort between student and teacher, student and student, teacher and administrator or supervisor, and community and teacher. The objectives of the evaluation would be developed in collaboration with all the parties concerned, and progress would be monitored according to an agreed-upon plan. Information would be shared regularly during periodic formal and informal conferences, and the student or teacher being evaluated would be an active participant in the process. Evaluation in an environment that promotes change would include ongoing feedback to students and teachers concerning their performances, strengths, deficiencies, and any corrective steps that should be taken to improve the situation. Although the social reconstructionist educator would consider the needs of the individual as well as the needs of the organization, conflict would not be viewed as failure, nor would the lack of consensus be considered problematic.

The Social Reconstructionist Teacher

The metaphors "shaper of a new society," "transformational leader," and "change agent" aptly describe the social reconstructionist teacher. George S. Counts (1933) described the teacher and his or her responsibilities for reform in the following way:

> To teach the ideal in its historic form, without the illumination that comes from an effort to apply it to contemporary society, is an extreme evidence of intellectual dishonesty. It constitutes an attempt to educate the youth for life in a world that does not exist. Teachers, therefore, cannot evade the responsibility of participating actively in the task of reconstituting the democratic tradition and of thus working positively toward a new society. (p. 19)

Social reconstructionist teachers must also be willing to engage in ongoing renewal of their personal and professional lives. They must be willing to critique and evaluate the conditions under which they work, and extend their educative role outside the domains of the classroom and school. They must have a high tolerance for ambiguity, must be comfortable with constant change, and be willing to think about their own thinking and the cultural and psycho-social forces that have shaped it. As an educational reformer, such a teacher detests the status quo and views the school as a particular culture in evolution. Moreover, he or she views the larger society as an experiment that will always be unfinished and in flux. Such a teacher must be willing to engage in, and form, alliances with community groups, neighborhood organizations, social movements, and parents to critique and question the practice of school democracy and school policy.

The social reconstructionist teacher should have excellent interpersonal communication skills and have command of languages. He or she should have a background in sociology of education, the politics of education, conflict management, organizational theory, and organizational development. The teacher must be open to diversity and view education from a global perspective. He or she must be widely read and be able to make available alternative materials and literature that reflect the amassed cultural experiences of marginal groups. According to Giroux (1993), the role of the teacher is: "to engage popular cul-

Can you name one or two so-called "Utopian thinkers"? How successful were they in achieving their ideal world?

Ivan Illich (left) and Paulo Freire (right) found new approaches to education that revolutionized schooling.

ture, to question and unlearn the benefits of privilege, and to allow those who have generally not been allowed to speak to narrate themselves, to speak from the specificity of their own voices" (p. 54).

Leading Educational Proponents

George S. Counts, Theodore Brameld (1904–1987), Harold Rugg, John Childs, and W. H. Kilpatrick were perhaps the best known of the American social reconstructionists who, in the early part of this century, attempted to bring about major educational reform. Each of these individuals advocated the transformation of society and envisioned an ideal and more equitable world. Two contemporary spokespersons for the social reconstructionist theory of education are Ivan Illich and Paulo Freire.

Illich (1974), in his *Deschooling Society,* maintained that since schools have corrupted society, one can create a better society only by abolishing schools altogether and finding new approaches to education. Illich called for a total political and educational revolution. Freire, who was born, educated, and taught in Latin America, proposed that education be drawn from the everyday life experiences of the learners. From his students, the illiterate and oppressed peasants of Brazil and Chile, he drew his theory of educational reconstructionism. In his *Pedagogy of the Oppressed* (1973), Freire maintained that students should not be manipulated or controlled but should be involved in their own learning. According to Freire, by exchanging and examining their experiences with peers and mentors, students who are socially, economically, and politically disadvantaged can plan, initiate, and take action for their own lives. As with any learners, the key to working with these disadvantaged individuals is a teacher who respects and cares about his or her students.

During the past two decades, several leading proponents of critical theory, or critical pedagogy, have gained prominence in the literature. They include Michael W. Apple, Stanley Aronowitz, Sam Bowles, Cleo Cherryholmes, Herbert Gintis, Henry A. Giroux, Joe L. Kincheloe, Colin Lankshear, Peter L. McLaren, Jane Roland Martin, William B. Stanley, and Robert E. Young.

More recently, some critical theorists have identified with a philosophical movement called *postmodernism,* or *poststructuralism.* Postmodernism is reflected in architecture, art, dance, music, and literature, in addition to philosophy. Similar to other social reconstructionists, postmodern theorists emphasize innovation, change, and diversity, but differ in their view of metaphysics or how reality is constructed and perceived. Some of the leading proponents of postmodernism include Jean-Francois Lyotard, Jacques Derrida, Michael Foucault, and Richard Rorty (Beck, 1994). Figure 7.6 on page 235 presents an overview of social reconstructionism.

Identifying Your Philosophy of Education

Educational philosophies and educational theories do not remain static, but constantly change depending on the social, economic, and political climate at

Figure 7.6: Reconstructionism at a Glance

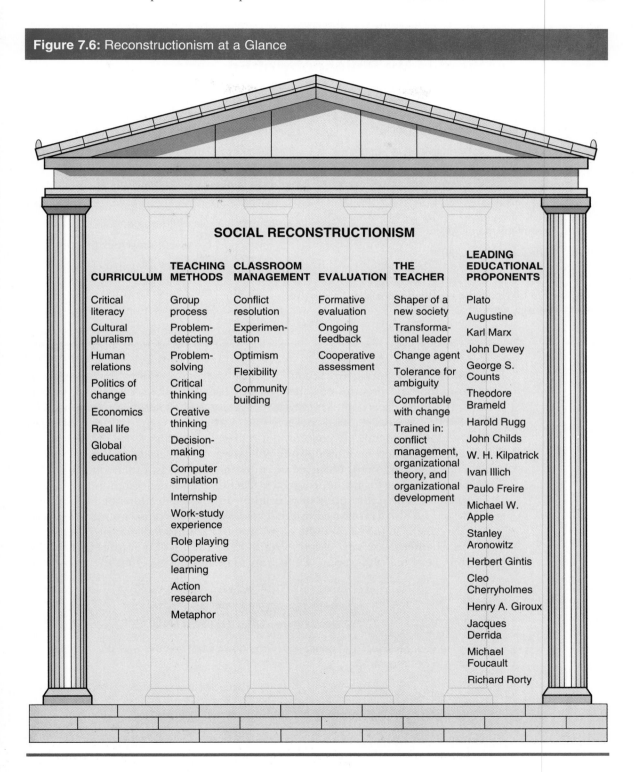

SOCIAL RECONSTRUCTIONISM

CURRICULUM	TEACHING METHODS	CLASSROOM MANAGEMENT	EVALUATION	THE TEACHER	LEADING EDUCATIONAL PROPONENTS
Critical literacy	Group process	Conflict resolution	Formative evaluation	Shaper of a new society	Plato
Cultural pluralism	Problem-detecting	Experimentation	Ongoing feedback	Transformational leader	Augustine
Human relations	Problem-solving	Optimism	Cooperative assessment	Change agent	Karl Marx
Politics of change	Critical thinking	Flexibility		Tolerance for ambiguity	John Dewey
Economics	Creative thinking	Community building		Comfortable with change	George S. Counts
Real life	Decision-making			Trained in: conflict management, organizational theory, and organizational development	Theodore Brameld
Global education	Computer simulation				Harold Rugg
	Internship				John Childs
	Work-study experience				W. H. Kilpatrick
	Role playing				Ivan Illich
	Cooperative learning				Paulo Freire
	Action research				Michael W. Apple
	Metaphor				Stanley Aronowitz
					Herbert Gintis
					Cleo Cherryholmes
					Henry A. Giroux
					Jacques Derrida
					Michael Foucault
					Richard Rorty

Ask Yourself:
What Is My Philosophy of Education?

To assess your preference for an educational philosophy, answer the following questions.

1. Are students intrinsically motivated to learn?

2. Should education be the same for everyone?

3. Are there certain universal truths that should be taught?

4. What determines morality?

5. What is the ideal curriculum?

6. What is the purpose of schooling?

7. If you were to choose one method or instructional strategy, what would it be?

＊ 8. What type of classroom environment is most conducive to learning?

9. How do you know when your students have learned?

＊10. What is the most important role of the teacher?

11. What is the role of the student?

12. How should prospective teachers be prepared?

---

the time. Upon visiting any school, it quickly becomes evident that a variety of philosophies and theories of education can coexist in the same school, or perhaps, the same classroom. Few teachers operate from a single philosophical or theoretical perspective. Most educators are eclectic and sample a variety of ideas, propositions, principles, or axioms that represent a smorgasbord of views.

Identifying and developing your philosophy of education may appear to be a formidable task. Yet, it is one of the most important tasks that you will probably be asked to perform as a prospective teacher. It is not uncommon to be asked to articulate your philosophy of education on job applications or in job interviews. School districts may require that you express your philosophical ideas and compare them to the philosophy or mission of the school district.

In Chapter 6 you were asked to respond to a series of questions that reflected your personal philosophy of life. You were also advised that the answers to

Professional Reflections

"Define your philosophy of education. Write down what you perceive it to be and then revisit it regularly."

Jacqueline Collier, Teacher of the Year, Ohio

"Never stop learning. Teaching and learning are synonymous."

Joyce G. Valenti, Teacher of the Year, New York

those questions represented some of the assumptions you hold about teaching and learning. The time has come to combine philosophy, theory, and practice in constructing your philosophy of education. Your responses to the basic theoretical questions listed on page 236 reflect your philosophy of education. As you ask yourself these questions, recall the importance of clarity and meaning in the language you choose. Your ideas about education may change before you enter the teaching profession, and may change one or more times during the course of your career. Nevertheless, it is vitally important that you begin to conceptualize those ideas at this stage of your professional development.

Summary

There are six major theories of education: perennialism, progressivism, behaviorism, essentialism, existentialism, and social reconstructionism. Educational theories influence educational practice by their impact on curriculum, teaching methods, classroom management, evaluation, and the role of the teacher. Each theory developed from a particular philosophy or philosophies. Most theories were formulated as a protest against the prevailing social and cultural forces at the time. The educational theories of perennialism and essentialism have much in common in that they underscore the importance of a liberal education and the wisdom of the past. Behaviorism differs from the other educational theories in that behaviorists believe all behaviors are both objective and observable, while the other theories do not.

Progressivism, existentialism, and social reconstructionism share a common theme in that each of them is more concerned with the study of the present and future than the past. Unlike the perennialist or essentialist who emphasize the important cultural and historic roots of the past, the progressivist, existentialist, and social reconstructionist stress that which is meaningful and relevant to the student today.

In the next chapter, we will leave the philosophies and theories of education and concentrate on the school and society, examining the school as a socializing agent.

Key Terms

Alternative schools
Back-to-basics movement
Behavioral objectives
Behaviorism
Classical conditioning
Critical literacy
Critical theory
Cultural literacy
Formative evaluation
Great Books
Humanistic education
New basics

Nongraded schools
Open classroom
Operant conditioning
Perennialism
Postmodernism
Premack principle
Programmed instruction
Progressivism
Theory
Theory of education
Whole-child movement

Discussion Questions

 1. Which educational theory best describes the teacher's response to Lydia in the incident described at the beginning of the chapter? Under what circumstances should a teacher not complement his/her students?

2. Describe the relationship among philosophy of life, educational theory, and philosophy of education.

3. Which of the theories of education presented in this chapter is most similar to your theory of education? In what ways is it similar?

4. B. F. Skinner and other advocates of operant conditioning have been criticized for their emphasis on control. Are freedom and control incompatible concepts in the classroom? Explain.

5. Of the six educational theories presented, which theory best exemplifies clarity and meaning in the language used? Why?

6. As a social reconstructionist, list five major changes that you would propose for education and schooling in the twenty-first century. Should teachers and students be involved in promoting these changes? Why? Why not?

7. Compare and contrast the teaching methods advocated by the essentialist and the existentialist.

8. Describe the classroom management strategies advocated by the perennialist. How do they differ from those of the behaviorist?

9. Choose a leading educational proponent of essentialism and, using his or her theory, construct a letter to the editor of a newspaper suggesting how the training of teachers today should be reformed.

References

Adler, M. (1982). *The Paideia proposal: An educational manifesto.* New York: Macmillan.

Adler, M. (1984). *The Paideia program.* New York: Macmillan.

Aronowitz, S. A., & Giroux, H. A. (1985). *Education under siege: The conservative, liberal and radical debate over schooling.* MA: Gergin & Garvey.

Barnes, H. E. (1968). *An existentialist ethics.* New York: Alfred A. Knopf.

Bates, J. A. (1987). Reinforcement. In M. J. Dunkin (Ed.), *The international encyclopedia of teaching and teacher education* (pp. 349–358). New York: Pergamon Books.

Bayles, E. E. (1966). *Pragmatism in education.* New York: Harper & Row.

Beck, C. (1994). Postmodernism, pedagogy, and philosophy of education. *Philosophy of education: Proceedings of the forty-ninth annual meeting of the philosophy of education society.* Urbana, IL: Philosophy of Education Society, University of Illinois.

Bennett, W. J. (1993). *The book of virtues: A treasury of great moral stories.* New York: Simon & Schuster.

Bloom, A. (1987). *The closing of the American mind.* New York: Simon and Schuster.

Butler, J. D. (1966). *Idealism in education.* New York: Harper & Row.

Conant, J. B. (1959). *The American high school today.* New York: McGraw-Hill.

Counts, G. S. (1933). *A call to the teachers of America.* New York: John Day Co.

Delattre, E. J. (1984). The intellectual lives of teachers. In C. E. Finn, D. Ravitch, & R. T. Fancher (Eds.), *Against mediocrity* (pp. 154–171). New York: Holmes & Meier.

Dewey, J. (1920). *Reconstruction in philosophy.* New York: H. Holt.

Dewey, J. (1938). *Experience and education.* New York: Macmillan.

Dewey, J. (1956). *The child and the curriculum and the school and society.* Chicago: The University of Chicago Press.

Dewey, J. (1963). *Experience and education.* New York: Collier.

Emmer, E. T. (1987). Classroom management. In M. J. Dunkin (Ed.), *The international encyclopedia of teaching and teacher education* (pp. 437–446). New York: Pergamon.

Freire, P. (1973). *Pedagogy of the oppressed.* New York: Seabury Press.

Giroux, H. A. (1988). *Schooling and the struggle for public life: Critical pedagogy in the modern age.* MN: University of Minnesota Press.

Giroux, H. A. (1993). *Living dangerously: Multiculturalism and the politics of difference.* New York: Peter Lang.

Greene, M. (1967). *Existential encounters for teachers.* New York: Random House.

Hirsch, E. D., Jr., Kett, J. F., & Trefil, J. (1993). *The dictionary of cultural literacy.* Boston: Houghton Mifflin.

Holt, J. (1981). *Teach your own.* New York: Delacorte/Seymour Laurence.

Hutchins, R. M. (1936). *The higher learning in America.* New Haven, CT: Yale University Press.

Illich, I. (1974). *Deschooling society.* New York: Harper & Row.

Kane, T. (1950). Noblest teacher of teachers. *Dominicans. 35,* 14.

Kincheloe, J. L. (1993). *Toward a critical politics of teacher thinking: Mapping the postmodern.* Westport, CT: Bergin & Garvey.

Kneller, G. F. (1958). *Existentialism and education.* New York: John Wiley & Sons.

Kneller, G. F. (1971). *Introduction to the philosophy of education.* New York: John Wiley & Sons.

Kneller, G. F. (1984). *Movements of thought in modern education.* New York: John Wiley & Sons.

Kozol, J. (1972). *Free schools.* Boston: Houghton Mifflin.

Kozol, J. (1991). *Savage inequalities.* New York: Crown.

Lerner, M. (1962). *Education and radical humanism.* Columbus, OH: Ohio State University Press.

Liston, D., & Zeichner, K. (1988). Critical. Paper presented to the American Educational Research Association, New Orleans, LA.

Long, L., & Ihle, E. (1988). Philosophy of education. In M. P. Sadker & D. M. Sadker, *Teachers, schools, and society* (pp. 422–459). New York: Random House.

McLaren, P. (1988). Broken dreams, false promises, and the decline of public schooling. *Journal of Education, 170* (1), 41–65.

Maritain, J. (1941). *Scholasticism and politics.* New York: Macmillan.

Marler, C. D. (1975). *Philosophy and schooling.* Boston: Gillyn & Bacon.

Morris, V. C. (1966). *Existentialism in education.* New York: Harper & Row.

Morris, V. C., & Pai, Y. (1976). *Philosophy in the American school.* Boston: Houghton Mifflin.

National Commission on Excellence in Education. (1983). *A nation at risk: The imperative for educational reform.* Washington, DC: U.S. Government Printing Office.

Neill, A. S. (1960). *Summerhill: A radical approach to child rearing.* New York: Hart.

Noddings, N. (1992). *The challenge to care in schools: An alternative approach to education.* New York: Teachers College Press.

Noddings, N. (1993). *Educating for intelligent belief or unbelief.* New York: Teachers College Press.

Ozmon, H. A., & Craver, S. M. (1990). *Philosophical foundations of education.* Columbus, OH: Merrill.

Phillips, D. C., & Soltis, J. F. (1991). *Perspectives on learning.* New York: Teachers College Press.

Rickover, H. G. (1963). *Education and freedom.* New York: New American Library.

Rogers, C. R. (1969). *Freedom to learn.* Columbus, OH: Merrill.

Silberman, C. (1970). *Crisis in the classroom.* New York: Random House.

Wingo, G. M. (1974). *Philosophies of education: An introduction.* Lexington, MA: D.C. Heath and Co.

Westheimer, J., & Kahne, J. (1993). Building school communities: An experience-based model. *Phi Delta Kappan, 75,* (4), 324–328.

Wittrock, M. C. (1987). Models of heuristic teaching. In M. J. Dunkin (Ed.), *The international encyclopedia of teaching and teacher education* (pp. 68–76). New York: Pergamon Books.

PART FOUR

The Schools and Society

Chapter 8

School and Society

In teaching there should be no class distinctions.

Confucius (551–478 B.C.)

A Critical Incident in My Teaching Career . . .

One memorable incident during my teaching career was "the day the kindergarten mommy cried" as her son left her arms on his first day of kindergarten. The moment my eyes met with hers, I *knew my task, responsibility, and commitment was not only to this little boy but also to his mother.*

Veronica Semien Harts
Teacher of the Year, Louisiana

In this chapter various dimensions of the relationship between the school and society are explored. First, the concepts of culture, subculture, society, socialization, and acculturation are examined. Then the purposes and expectations of schooling are described, and education and inequality are discussed. Lastly, educational achievement and attainment in relation to social class, ethnicity, race, and gender are examined. As you study this material, keep in mind the following objectives:

- Define the basic concepts of culture, subculture, society, socialization, and acculturation.
- Explain how the family, the peer group, and the mass media socialize children and youth.
- Describe the intellectual, political, economic, and social purposes of schooling.
- Compare the social selection and social mobility purposes of education.
- Identify the major issues related to the inequality of educational opportunity.

- Describe the social class system in the United States.
- Compare the educational attainment and achievement of social class groups, ethnic and racial groups, and males and females.
- Evaluate the causes of differences in educational achievement and attainment among social class groups, ethnic and racial groups, and between males and females.

Some Basic Concepts

Before we can fully comprehend the relationship between the school and society, it is important to understand the concepts of culture and subculture. *Culture* may be defined as the behavioral patterns, ideas, values, attitudes, religious and moral beliefs, customs, laws, language, institutions, art and all other material things and artifacts characteristic of a given people at a given period of time. Every culture passes on, or transmits, its patterns and products of learned behavior to the young, patterns that reflect its cultural values and norms, artifacts and symbols.

Complex societies such as the United States, in addition to having an overall culture, include a variety of subcultures. A *subculture* is a group of people distinguished by its ethnic, racial, religious, geographic, social, economic, or lifestyle traits. Most of us are members of a variety of subcultures.

In addition to understanding the concepts of culture and subculture, it is also important to understand the concept of society. A *society* refers to a group of persons who share a common culture, government, institutions, land, or a set of social relationships. A person may be a member of several societies at the same time: a religious society, a professional society, and a social society. Each of these societies also will have its own culture or subculture. *Socialization* is the process by which persons are conditioned to the customs or patterns of a particular culture. *Acculturation* is the adoption of the cultural patterns of the dominant group by the oppressed group (Gollnick & Chinn, 1994).

The concept of education is very similar to the concept of socialization, since both aim to preserve and transmit the intellectual, moral, and aesthetic values of the society. In addition, both socialization and education take place not only in school, but in a variety of institutions outside the school, such as the family, the peer group, and the mass media. These institutions, or agents of socialization, will be examined in the sections that follow.

Agents of Socialization

The Family

Describe the cultures, subcultures, and societies to which you currently belong.

Although the organization of the family varies from culture to culture and from one period of history to the next, there are certain basic functions that all families serve. One of those is its socialization function. Children are born into families and, for a significant period in their lives, in particular their early years, the family is the only world that the children know. Thus the family is the major socializing agent for the young. It is the family that first introduces the child to the world at large, and it is the family that transmits the culture's values to the young. Parents pass on their perceptions, values, beliefs, attitudes, experiences, and understandings to their children. These primary impressions are long-lasting and very difficult to modify or change. They also have significant impact on children's later educational development and success in school. The home and family environment, including parent/child interactions, the use of language in the home, child-rearing practices, and how sex roles are perceived in the home are a few of the many influences that are associated with the child's later educational attainment or achievement (Webb & Sherman, 1989).

Although traditionally the family has been the major instrument of socialization for the young, in the last quarter-century more and more of the responsibility for the socialization has been transferred to the school or other institutions. The major reason why the school and other institutions have taken on a greater role as a socializing agent is the change in the structure of the family.

The Changing Family

Since World War II, the family configuration has changed dramatically. In fact, change is the one constant that has been identified with the family (Wallis, 1992). Demographic, economic, and cultural changes have altered the very definition of "family" as we perceive it today. The "traditional" or nuclear family of two or more school-age children, with a father who works and a mother who stays home

Extended families in many cultures play a major role in the socialization of children.

What were the
child-rearing
practices in your
home during your
formative years?
How were sex
roles perceived?

to care for the children, is no longer the norm. Dual-career families, single-parent families, ethnically and linguistically different families, and blended families with previously divorced fathers and mothers living together with children from previous marriages and often children from the present marriage have become the norm rather than the exception. The percentage of "traditional family" households fell from 60% in 1955 to 26% in 1990 ("Traditional Families," 1986; Waldrop & Exter, 1991). Ward and Anthony (1992) suggest that over one half of all children in schools represent "nontraditional" families. However, they caution that one should not infer that "nontraditional" necessarily means unstable.

The following highlights describe the families and households of today:

- The average household size is 2.62 (U.S. Bureau of the Census, 1993b).

- Married-couple families constituted 55% of all households in 1992 compared to 71% in 1970 (U.S. Bureau of the Census, 1993b).

- Over half (54%) of the women age 18 to 44 years who had a child in 1991 were in the labor force in 1992, compared with 44% in 1982 and 31% in 1976 (U.S. Bureau of the Census, 1994).

- In 1991 approximately 20% of preschoolers (under age 5) whose mothers worked outside the home were cared for by their fathers, an increase from 15% in 1988 (U.S. Bureau of the Census, 1994).

- About 1 household in 10 is headed by a single parent. Over the past two decades, the number of children that are in families headed by single women increased by 40%. The incidence of poverty among such households is between seven and eight times higher than families headed by married couples ("More Families in Poverty," 1993).

- In 1993, of the 69.3 million children under 18 years old, 15.7 million, or 1 in 4, were living in households classified as below the poverty level (Usdansky & Edmonds, 1994).

- More than 3.3 million children younger than 18 are living in homes headed by a grandparent. In 44% of the cases, substance abuse by parents is the major reason (Helser, 1994).

How has your
family configura-
tion changed
over the past two
decades?

Socialization Responsibility Shifts

Today's families spend less time together than they did in the past. When they do spend time together, it is often spent watching television. Little interaction occurs and less time is given to teaching children acceptable values and behaviors. As a result, the school has taken on the function of teaching certain subjects that were once considered the purview of the family. For example, sex education and values education, domains that were traditionally considered the responsibility of the family and church, have been transferred to the school.

The schools also have become involved in other functions that historically were considered family responsibilities. For example, schools provide breakfast and lunch for needy children, offer counseling and mental health services, make referrals for medical and psychological needs, and offer parent education in after-school programs. These changes have left the family with fewer social roles and have diminished the family's socialization function.

The Peer Group

The peer group is one of the most significant institutions for socializing the child or adolescent. Each peer group has its own set of rules and regulations, its own social organization, its own customs, and in some cases, its own rituals and language. Children develop friendship patterns at a very early age. By the age of 11, these friendship groups are fairly well established. Although the peer group relationship may be transitory in nature, its influence can be profound. Unlike the family influence, which tends to lessen with time, the peer group becomes more influential with the advancing age of the child or adolescent (Levine & Havighurst, 1992).

As a socializing agency, the peer group reflects and reinforces the values of the adult society (e.g., competition, cooperation, honesty, and responsibility). The peer group communicates what constitutes appropriate sex roles and appropriate social behavior in the culture. It also legitimizes and prioritizes the value of information received from a variety of sources. The peer group serves as a reference group for the young. That is, the child or adolescent learns to judge himself or herself against the attitudes, values, and aspirations of his or her peers, and learns to act in accordance with those values (Levine & Havighurst, 1992).

In addition to peer groups within the school, peer groups outside the school serve as agents of socialization for children and adolescents. These peer groups consist of a variety of youth-serving agencies such as the Boy Scouts, Girl Scouts, YMCA, YWCA, and Little League, as well as male and female friendship cliques, and social and antisocial gangs. Like the peer groups within the school, these social groups offer opportunities for learning rules and rites of passage, as well as peer bonding.

Describe the peer groups in your early life that served as an agent of socialization for you.

The Mass Media

"The mass media" is a term commonly used to refer to the television, popular music, movie, music video, radio, newspaper, and magazine industries. Of these, the one that has perhaps the most influence on children and adolescents is television. In fact, increasingly it is acknowledged that the socialization effect of television is almost as strong as the home, school, and neighborhood in influencing children's development and behavior. Because of its strong impact, the mass media are often referred to as "the other curriculum" or "parallel school system" (Davies, 1993).

Time Watching Television

According to a recent report, while leisure reading has declined, television viewing has increased. For example, in 1992, 60% of 9-year-olds, 64% of 13-year-olds, and 47% of 17-year-olds reported watching television 3 or more hours per day. On the other hand, only 56% of the 9-year-olds, 37% of the 13-year-olds, and 27% of the 17-year-olds indicated that they read for enjoyment daily (U.S.

Department of Education, 1994). Of the 17-year-olds who watched 5 or more hours of television on weekdays, males and females were equally represented. However, blacks (21.3%), Hispanics (9.3%), and Native Americans (12.7%) are proportionately more represented than whites (6.4%) and Asian-Americans (6.4%) (U.S. Department of Education, 1994). Young minorities, those from the lower-socioeconomic class, and less educated families also tended to watch more television (Davies, 1993).

It has been estimated that by the time the average child graduates from high school, he or she will have spent more time being entertained by the media than any other activity except sleeping (Davies, 1993; Liebert & Sprafkin, 1988). Given that "observational learning and incorporation of social messages from television are a well-established phenomenon" (Anderson & Collins, 1988, p. 70), the potential effects of this much exposure to television are significant.

Effects of Television Viewing

Although the positive effects of television in broadening our experiences and shrinking our world have been tremendous, in recent years increasing concerns have been raised regarding the negative effects of:

- the transmission of violent and antisocial behavior.

- the transmission of inappropriate sexual values.

- the transmission of unrealistic attitudes toward drugs and alcohol.

- the promotion of irrational and superstitious beliefs.

- the devaluation of work.

- the underrepresentation of women and members of various races, ethnic backgrounds, and cultures.

- a neglect of reading. (Radeki, 1989)

Of these, perhaps the greatest concern is the effect of television (and film) violence on children. It is estimated that the average child is exposed to at least 13,000 violent deaths on television. While it is not possible to establish a direct cause and effect relationship, there is compelling evidence to link exposure to television acts of aggression with subsequent aggressive acts on the part of viewers (Feldman & Coats, 1993).

Also of concern is the message that the depiction of acts of violence communicates about the rules, power distribution, and conventional norms of the social order. While portraying the reality that our social system is one that includes aggressive acts, the pattern of television violence is one in which society's dominant groups consistently are depicted as triumphing over those of lesser status and power (Turiel, 1987).

Television and School Achievement

The relationship between television viewing and school achievement is also a matter of concern. Except for limited evidence that television viewing may increase vocabulary, most studies that have examined the relationship between television viewing and school achievement have found a negative correlation between the amount of viewing and the level of achievement, especially at the higher levels of viewing (Anderson & Collins, 1988; Beentjes & Van der Voort, 1988; Ritchie, Price, & Roberts, 1987). Many teachers also complain that increased television viewing shortens attention spans, interferes with homework, and creates in children an expectation that they must be entertained.

A recent National Assessment of Education Progress report indicated that, over all, as the number of hours of television increased, the average proficiency level in reading, mathematics, geography, and history decreased. Longitudinal data from the U. S. Department of Education also show that among high school seniors of various racial, ethnic, and socioeconomic groups, the groups with the highest percentages of seniors who watched five or more hours of television on weekdays were low socioeconomic status blacks and American Indians—the very same groups who scored among the lowest on the NAEP (U.S. Department of Education, 1994a).

Since television is here to stay and its impact on children is so profound, the challenge for parents and educators is to find ways to make it a positive educational tool and to mitigate against its negative influence. This can be done by reinforcing the positive messages and values communicated through television. Research has shown that the influence of television is greatest when its messages are confirmed by other social agents or when the influence of other institutions is declining. Thus, if the schools can combine the positive messages of television with other prosocial teachings, the television message may be kept in perspective. The reality is that it may be easier to develop media literacy (i.e., critical viewing skills) than to regulate television programming (Sleek, 1994; Webb & Sherman, 1989).

The Purposes and Expectations of Schooling

Just as there are a variety of theories of education that influence how we view the teaching and learning process, there are also a variety of theories or perspectives that influence what we perceive to be the primary purposes or functions of schooling. However, regardless of one's theoretical orientation, most would agree that schools serve an intellectual, political, economic, and social purpose (Bennett & LeCompte, 1990).

Intellectual Purpose: Acquisition of Knowledge and Skills

To acquire cognitive knowledge and skills has been lauded as one of the most desired goals and purposes of schooling. Although they may disagree on what body of knowledge and which skills are the most important, this purpose has been underscored by a number of philosophers and educational theorists as discussed in Chapters 6 and 7. The school has traditionally been viewed as the institution where students can acquire the necessary knowledge and skills to become responsible and productive citizens. That same theme has been reiterated down through the centuries all the way to the current spokespersons who support the national goals for education to be reached by the year 2000.

Political Purpose: Responding to Diversity

While most individuals would not dispute the most commonly recognized political purposes of schooling—the promotion of patriotism and law and order, selection of future political leaders, creation of a political consensus, and socialization of individuals for political systems (Spring, 1991)—some might question the means that the school has used to achieve its purposes. For example, challenges have been raised against such "patriotic" practices as mandatory flag salutes. However, there is one political purpose of schooling that has historically been the subject of considerable debate: the various efforts of the schools to "Americanize" racially and ethnically diverse groups.

Four distinct measures have been employed to accomplish this goal: (1) assimilation; (2) amalgamation; (3) cultural pluralism (Rose, 1964); and (4) separatism (Thomas, 1973). The first measure, *assimilation,* supports what Thomas (1973) refers to as the "Dick and Jane culture." According to Thomas, "assimilation requires conformity to a single model which was largely defined by traditional British political, social, cultural, and religious institutions" (p.50). The second approach, *amalgamation,* supports the "melting pot" notion that envisions American culture as emerging from the best elements of several cultures. In contrast, the *cultural pluralism* approach that followed supports "the maintenance of diversity, a respect for differences, and the right to participate actively in all aspects of society without having to give up one's unique identity" (Sletter & Grant, 1994, p. 170). Embedded in the cultural pluralism view is a commitment to *multicultural education.* More recently, the concept of pluralism has been extended beyond race and ethnicity to include gender, disability groups, and lifestyle differences.

Lastly, the *separatism* view suggests that by maintaining a separatist position one can maintain community control, self determination, and at least on a temporary basis, maintain identity and gain power. Some examples of the cultural separatist view include the Amish, Huterites, the Seventh Day Adventists, and the Black Muslims. Some of these groups maintain a separate system of schooling in addition to their separate social or ethnic identity (Levine & Havighurst, 1992).

Since the mid-1960s, the promotion of cultural pluralism, with its emphasis on multicultural education, has become the primary method used by the school to integrate its minority newcomers into American society. The social and educational goals of multicultural education are described in Chapter 9.

Economic Purpose: Contribution to Economic Growth and Development

One of the most important purposes of education is to advance economic growth and development. Education contributes to economic growth and development primarily through its effect on productivity, influencing productivity by upgrading the skills of the labor force. In addition, research has shown that more educated workers (1) are less likely to lose time because of unemployment and illness; (2) are more likely to innovate and be aware of, and receptive to, new ideas and knowledge; (3) produce better goods and render services with greater skill; and (4) produce more goods and services in a given period of time because of their skill, dexterity, and knowledge (Webb, McCarthy, & Thomas, 1988). In addition, schooling prepares children to support the economic system by enhancing the development of personal attributes compatible with the industrial workplace; it provides them with the credentials required for the practice of various occupations and careers. This purpose of schooling aimed at training students as future workers has also been referred to as its social efficiency goal (Labaree, 1994). Additionally, the school socializes the future worker for industry through the "hidden curriculum" (see Chapter 14), which emphasizes the need for planning, time on task, competition, individualism, independence, and obeying rules (Ogbu, 1986).

A recognition of the importance of education to the economic survival of our nation served as a major impetus for the reappraisal of education by the reform reports of the 1980s. The report makers asserted that the United States was losing in the competition with other industrialized nations, particularly Japan and West Germany. They praised the educational systems of these countries and attributed their economic success to the success of their schools.

Social Selection or Social Mobility

To acknowledge education's role in advancing economic growth and development is raising an important and controversial question. Should the schools promote social selection or social mobility in American education? One of the primary positions on this issue is the one shared by Marxists, neo-Marxists, and revisionists, which states that the schools serve a *social selection* purpose. According to this group, the schools essentially serve the wealthy and powerful at the expense of the poor. The schools, they contend, serve the upper classes by socializing the multitudes to conform to the values and beliefs that are necessary to maintain the existing social order. Revisionist scholars argue that the classroom, with its extrinsic reward system and hierarchical relationship between teacher and student, is like a miniature factory system. Through the hidden curriculum, students are taught the goals and ideology of the capitalist system. They further contend that the real purpose of schooling, which they point out is controlled by the elite, is to train the workers needed for business and industry, not to promote the movement of disadvantaged, lower-class youth into the upper classes (Apple, 1982; Bowles & Gintis, 1976; Giroux & Purpel, 1983; Illich, 1970; Spring, 1988).

An opposing point of view is that one of the purposes of the school is to advance *social mobility*. This position, often called the meritocratic position, recognizes that a class system does exist, but also recognizes that such a class system is not rigid; that school achievement and years of schooling attained, as well as other evidence of individual merit (ability and effort), significantly contribute to an improvement in social status. Those who espouse the meritocratic position

*Do you believe
that schools
promote social
selection or
social mobility?*

maintain that social class and a class society do not prevent individuals from improving their social status. Rather, they argue that individuals fail to improve their social class or social prestige because of numerous factors, including genetic inferiority, the organizational structure of the school, the attitudes and values of the educational staff, individual aspirations, and family environment (Selakovich, 1984).

Social Purpose: Cultural Socialization

One of the major purposes of schooling is to socialize the young in the norms and values of society. The school trains children for responsible citizenship and socializes them for their future adult roles. In short, the school trains the individual for life. Through the curriculum, classroom rules, and interactions with teachers and other adults, children learn the symbols and rituals of patriotism and the values of our democratic society. They also learn the behaviors that are supported and valued by the system. They come to understand that to be a "good boy" or a "good girl" means to obey and to succeed. To be bad is to disobey or to fail. Competition is valued, as is "working well together," "cooperating nicely," or "being a team player."

Within the culture of the school, teachers exercise significant control over how the culture is transmitted to the young. It is the teacher who ultimately determines what subject matter will be taught and the manner in which the subject matter will be conveyed. As a result of that control, teachers are one of the central figures in the socialization process. The teacher is the symbol of authority to the child. Within the social system and reward structure created by teachers in their classrooms, children learn the beliefs, values, and expectations of the larger society.

*Think back to
your elementary
school experi-
ence. Which
teachers had the
most impact on
you? Why?*

The schools also play an important role in promoting a sense of moral responsibility (Bennett & LeCompte, 1990). This was an explicit expectation of the schools throughout much of America's history. The textbooks and curriculum of the school were directed toward the development of character and moral behavior. Teachers were expected not only to exhibit high ethical and moral principles, but also to teach those principles to their students. Although the continued push for separation of church and state has greatly eliminated the religious involvement that was the vehicle for much of this training, the emphasis on moral development continues to be one of the important expectations of schooling. And, as the family has relinquished more and more of its role in transmitting moral responsibility, the school has, in part, taken on this function.

In fulfilling its socialization role, the school is constantly challenged to assume a major role in either (1) inculcating or reinforcing the past or present values of the social order or (2) encouraging the adoption of new and emerging values for the culture. Often, the school is called on to reinforce and transmit the common values of the past and, at the same time, to implement social change. However, despite challenges in fulfilling its socialization role

schools must ultimately take the responsibility for socializing our youth if their families fail to socialize them. It is better that schools take the responsibility for socializing children while they are still in their formative years than for our society to rehabilitate them after they have become destructive or dysfunctional. (Friedman, 1993, p. 178)

The Inequality of Educational Opportunity

Notwithstanding the popular rhetoric that schools advance economic growth, economic productivity, and social mobility, the goal of equal educational opportunity for all has never been fully achieved in the United States. One of the most widely published critics of the myth of equal educational opportunity has been James S. Coleman, noted researcher and professor of sociology and education. In his early writing, Coleman (1966) described some of the basic elements that traditionally have been considered in the concept of equal educational opportunity:

- Providing a free education up to the level that constitutes the principal entry point to the labor force.

- Providing a common curriculum for all children, regardless of background.

- Providing for children from diverse backgrounds to attend the same school.

- Providing equality of financial expenditures within a given locality.

However, Coleman asserted, providing the above elements, although meritorious, does not ensure equal educational opportunity. For example, providing a free education up to a certain level does not mean that children will stay in school to take advantage of it. Moreover, providing the education really only means exposure to a given curriculum; it does not ensure equality of achievement. Neither does a common curriculum assume equal educational opportunity. In fact, the change in the secondary school curriculum in the early twentieth century, from a classical curriculum appropriate for the college-bound to a nonclassical curriculum that supposedly was more fitting for the new majority, namely those adolescents seeking a terminal education, created a form of tracking that defined a certain expectation for the child's future. As the child is matched with the curriculum path (vocational vs. higher education), certain decisions and explicit assumptions are made about the child's future attainment and career goals.

The idea that equal educational opportunity will be accomplished if children from diverse backgrounds are allowed to attend the same school also was challenged by Coleman (1966; 1968). The fact that children of different races and backgrounds attend the same schools does not ensure equality of various intangibles (e.g., that they bring the same interest in learning, arouse the same expectations from teachers) nor equality of results.

Lastly, providing equality of expenditures within a given locality via local taxes does not lead automatically to equal educational opportunity. Here Coleman referred to his own research as well as to that of others, which demonstrated that expenditures had very little impact on educational attainment when compared to family characteristics and home environment.

The myth of equal educational opportunity is evident particularly when one examines certain subgroups in the society and their educational achievement and attainment. In the following section the educational achievement and attainment of the following subgroups will be examined: social class groups, ethnic groups, racial groups, and different genders.

Social Class Differences and School Achievement and Attainment

When asked to which social class they belong, the vast majority of Americans identify themselves as being middle class. Sociologists maintain that a number of social classes exist within most societies, distinguishable by great differences in wealth, prestige, and power. (See the Historical Note on page 255 for a review of the concept of social class.) One's social class or *socioeconomic status* (SES) is determined by a number of variables besides income, such as housing, organizational membership, occupation, formal education, race, ethnicity, and gender (Rich, 1992).

Social Classes in the United States

According to Levine and Havighurst (1992), not all sociologists agree that the *social class* system in the United States is still best represented by the traditional hierarchy of five classes or groups: upper class, upper middle class, lower middle class, working class, and lower class. They point out that to some extent, the differences between the classes have disappeared. For example, blue-collar workers of the working class have enjoyed greater gains in income during the past 30 years than lower middle class white-collar workers, thereby eliminating some of the earlier distinctions between the two groups. At the same time that some class distinctions are becoming more arbitrary, there is some indication that due to technological advancement and other economic reasons, the high income and high status upper class is growing at the same time that the low-income, low status lower class is also increasing (Levine & Havighurst, 1992).

While recognizing the changes occurring among the different classes, the five class structure still remains a viable and convenient method of differentiating one group from another. The *upper class,* which comprises only 1–3% of American society, includes those individuals who control great wealth, power, and influence. Members of the *upper middle class* do not have the family background of the upper class. They are generally leading professionals, high-level managers, or corporate executives who are well educated and financially well off. The *lower middle class* consists of middle-income business people, white-collar clerical and salespersons, skilled workers such as factory foremen, farm owners, and some semiprofessionals. The *working class* is made up largely of blue-collar workers in skilled, semiskilled, and unskilled jobs. Some white-collar workers also are considered upper working class. The *lower class* are often referred to as the *underclass* and are composed of individuals with incomes at or below the poverty level who are usually poorly educated and often unemployed. According to Rose (1992), underclass usually includes the hardcore unemployed who have lived in poverty

Historical Note:
The Concept of Social Class

The concept of social class and social stratification can be found as early as the time of Plato (427–347 B.C.) and Aristotle (384–322 B.C.). Although Plato and Aristotle did not attempt to advance any particular theory to explain the causes and consequences of such stratification, they did recognize the different classes that existed in their social structures. Both Plato and Aristotle discussed social class distinctions in the ideal society. Plato envisioned a utopian society that was divided into three social classes—guardians, auxiliaries, and workers. According to Plato, the guardians would be a disinterested ruling elite. Aristotle acknowledged three social classes including the very wealthy, the very poor, and the middle class. According to Aristotle, in the ideal political system the middle class would be the dominant or ruling class.

By the seventeenth and eighteenth centuries, the concept of social class was an important subject for discussion. During this period, John Locke (1632–1704) developed a theory of social class that identified two separate classes: property owners and laborers. In 1755 the French philosopher Jean-Jacques Rousseau recognized the existence of social classes by describing what he referred to as natural inequalities and those inequities that resulted from the social order.

Perhaps more than any other political philosopher, Karl Marx (1818–1883) was able to demonstrate the relationship between social class and the political economy. For Marx, what distinguishes one type of society from another is the mode of production (i.e., technology and the division of labor). Marx hypothesized that each mode of production creates a particular class system whereby one class controls the process of production and the other class or classes become the producers or service providers for the dominant/ruling class. Marx was primarily concerned with modern capitalist society. He envisioned a successful working class revolution and the birth of a new classless society.

---

for a lengthy period of time, such as 8 out of the last 10 years, and excludes those individuals who are temporarily poor due to loss of job or other unfortunate circumstances. An overview of these five classes in terms of income, occupation, wealth, status, family life, personal satisfaction, mental health, life expectancy, education, and political persuasion and participation is given in Table 8.1.

The socioeconomic distinctions among the social classes affect not only lifestyles, patterns of association, and friendships, but patterns of school attainment and achievement. In fact, the preponderance of evidence from all over the world suggests that socioeconomic status affects school attainment and achievement more than any other variable, including race (Brody, 1989).

Identify your current social class and indicate what impact your socioeconomic status has had on your educational achievement and attainment.

Social Class and School Achievement

One of the first and best known studies in the United States to address the relationship between achievement and socioeconomic variables was that conducted by James Coleman and his associates, who analyzed data from more than 645,000 students and about 4,000 schools (Coleman, 1966). Their report, *Equality of Educational Opportunity,* documented the relationship between test scores, ethnic and racial status, various socioeconomic characteristics of the student's family and peers, and various teacher and school characteristics (e.g., facilities, expenditures per pupil, number of library books, and class size). The findings showed

Table 8.1: The American Class System

Class (and approximate percentage of population)	Income	Occupation (responsibilities)	Wealth	Status
I Upper class (1 to 3%)	Very high income	Executives of big business, large scale banking (makers of large-scale, long-term policies; goal setters)	Great inherited wealth increased via investments and added earnings	High inherited status
				High earned status
II Upper-middle class (10 to 15%)	High income	Professionals, high-ranking business executives, military officers, civil servants (second-level decision makers, determiners of means, not ends)	Some inherited wealth (usually after death of parents), but largely accumulated wealth via savings and investments	
	Comfortable income			Middle status
III Lower-middle class, white-collar workers (30 to 35%)		Owners of small businesses, low-level professionals and semiprofessionals, sales workers (few decisions; narrow range of responsibilities), clerical workers	Little, if any, inherited wealth	
	Moderate income		Some savings	
IV Working class, blue-collar workers (40 to 45%)	Low income	Skilled workers, semiskilled and service workers, unskilled workers		Low status
			No savings	
V Lower class (10 to 20%)	Poverty income	High unemployment		Stigma of poverty status

Family Life	Personal Satisfaction Mental Health, Life Expectancy	Education	Political Persuasion and Participation
Stable	Good mental and physical health, high life expectancy, reported satisfaction with work and life	College Education liberal arts major, elite schools	High Participation, Republican, seldom run for office
Stable; some sex-role differentiation	Autonomous, good mental and physical health, long life expectancy, reported satisfaction with work and life	Graduate training, often at elite schools	High participation, conservative Republican (some "professional liberals"), may run for office
Higher incidence of women working; generally stable, but higher incidence of divorce; sharing of family duties	Higher stress, higher incidence of illness and job-related hazards, lower life expectancy, less reported satisfaction with life and work	College some college	Votes less frequently; Democrat, sometimes votes Republican
Unstable family life	Higher stress, higher incidence of illness and job-related hazards, lower life expectancy, less reported satisfaction with life and work	Junior college training, postsecondary vocational training, high school, some high school, grade school	Doesn't run for office, Democrat, conservative on some issues
Higher incidence of divorce, separation, and desertion	Poorer physical and mental health, lowest life expectancy, lowest reported satisfaction with life and work	Some high school, grade school, highest incidence of functional illiteracy	Seldom participates; Democrat

Source: Reprinted by permission of Macmillan Publishing Company from *Schooling and Society* (2nd Ed.) by Rodman B. Webb and Robert R. Sherman. Copyright © 1989 by Macmillan Publishing Company.

that the single most important variable accounting for differences in test scores was the educational and social class background of the family. The second most important variable was the educational and social class background of the other children in the school. The Coleman report generated considerable discussion regarding whether and to what extent schools do make a difference. Although the methodology was subject to criticism, reanalysis of this data by other researchers (Jencks et al., 1972; Mosteller & Moynihan, 1972) as well as numerous other studies since, have yielded the same result: Socioeconomic status is the major determinant of school success.

A number of indicators of school success have been linked to various indicators of *socioeconomic status*. The *National Assessment of Educational Progress (NAEP),* by congressional mandate, periodically tests a national representative sample of students in public and private schools in certain subject and skill areas such as mathematics and reading. The NAEP studies have revealed that achievement is related to parental education, an indicator of socioeconomic status. Proficiency scores at each age level consistently increase as level of parental education increases. Similar findings by the College Entrance Examination Board (see Table 8.2), indicate that students from families with the lowest parental education and income levels receive the lowest scores overall on the Scholastic Aptitude Test (SAT), the test most frequently taken by college-bound seniors (U.S. Department of Education, 1994a).

Table 8.2: Distribution of College-Bound Seniors and Average Verbal and Mathematics SAT Scores by Parents' Income and Educational Level (SES)

Characteristic	SAT mean score	
	Verbal	Mathematics
All students	**424**	**478**
Parents' Income		
Less than $10,000	352	416
$10,000–$20,000	379	434
$20,000–$30,000	404	453
$30,000–$40,000	418	469
$40,000–$50,000	431	483
$50,000–$60,000	440	493
$60,000–$70,000	449	504
$70,000 or more	472	533
Parents' highest education level		
No high school diploma	338	408
High school diploma	395	445
Associate's degree	408	457
Bachelor's degree	445	502
Graduate degree	478	534

Source: U.S. Department of Education, National Center for Education Statistics. (1994). *The condition of education 1994.* Washington, DC: U.S. Government Printing Office.

Additional documentation of the relationship between educational achievement and socioeconomic status comes from the National Longitudinal Studies of senior high school students. These studies revealed that students who represented the higher socioeconomic categories received better mean scores on tests that measured vocabulary, associative memory, reading, inductive reasoning, mathematical skills, and perceptual speed, while the lowest mean scores were achieved by those in the lowest socioeconomic class. Similarly, high school students from the highest socioeconomic groups achieved the highest grade point averages (g.p.a.). For example, high school seniors from the highest socioeconomic level had a mean g.p.a. of 3.07, as compared to 2.85 for seniors from the middle class and 2.68 for those from lower socioeconomic levels (Parelius & Parelius, 1987).

Social Class and Educational Attainment

The relationship between social class and educational attainment is evidenced by differences in dropout rates and continuation beyond high school. Regardless of race or ethnicity, students from low income or underclass families were more likely to repeat a grade and to drop out than those from middle or upper class families: the dropout rate for 16- to 24-year-olds from low income families was 25%, compared to 10% for those from middle income families, and 2% for those from high income families (U.S. Department of Education, 1994a). And, while 50% of the high school graduates from the highest socioeconomic strata continue their education at baccalaureate-granting institutions, less than 10% of those from the lowest strata matriculate at baccalaureate institutions (Levine & Havighurst, 1992).

Contributing Factors

The condition of poverty seems to be the major socioeconomic indicator affecting educational achievement and attainment. In 1993, nearly 40 million people, or 15% of the population, lived in families below the poverty level. In fact, more people live in poverty today than before the War on Poverty. An income of $14,763 in 1993 qualified for poverty level status. Among the poor, children represented the largest group (40%), even though they accounted for only 25% of the population. More than half (58%) of the children living in poverty live in a single parent home headed by a female (U.S. Bureau of the Census, 1994). These same children are often sick, hungry, and illiterate, and are deprived of safe and adequate housing.

The effects of poverty are seen early in the child's development and academic career. Poverty's adverse effects on achievement are visible as early as the first grade, and the differences appear to become greater as the child progresses through school. In addition, it is estimated that 11% of children end up in special education classes because of cognitive and developmental problems, many of which could have been prevented if even the most simple and inexpensive prenatal health care had been available to their mothers. And, the dehabilitation of young children in poverty carries over into adolescence in the form of high rates of suicide, drug abuse, and pregnancy (Haveman & Wolfe, 1994; Reed & Sautter, 1990).

Over 40 million people of all ages live in families with income below the poverty level.

The factors that seem to perpetuate poverty also seem to be related to education, and in the end a low education/poverty/low education cycle is created. That is, low educational attainment can lead to poverty, and poverty, in turn, has an impact on children's educational attainment and achievement.

The problem of low attainment among the children of the poor is made worse by the fact that the typical school serving these children faces a number of problems, including high rates of student mobility, high incidence of severe behavioral and emotional problems among students, large numbers of students with limited English proficiency, low staff morale, poor facilities, and inadequate resources (Knapp & Shields, 1990). In fact, after spending more than 20 years studying children in poverty, Haveman and Wolfe (1994) reached the grim conclusion that relative to the national average, these children "attend schools with low capacities to educate or inspire learning" (p. 3).

Perhaps the greatest challenge facing America today is to provide the programs and services necessary to ensure the educational success of these children and free them from the cycle of poverty. As the National Commission on Excellence in Education (1983) so succinctly pronounced over a decade ago in *A Nation at Risk:* "All, regardless of race, class or economic status are entitled to a fair chance" (p. 4).

Ethnic Differences and School Achievement and Attainment

Ethnic groups are subgroups of the population that are distinguished by having a common cultural heritage (language, customs, history, etc.). Significant differences in educational achievement and attainment are found among different ethnic groups in this country. The Hispanic population (24 million) is the largest and second-fastest-growing ethnic group in this country, representing 9% of the entire population. Hispanics are a diverse group made up of 56% Mexican-Americans, 11% Puerto Ricans, 4% Cubans, and 21% "Other," which includes persons from Spain, Central and South America, the Caribbean, and those who identify themselves as Latino, Hispano, Spanish-American, etc. It is anticipated that the growth of Hispanic-Americans will continue into the 21st century and could reach 31 million by the year 2000 and 81 million by the year 2050 (U.S. Bureau of the Census, 1993b).

Hispanics are geographically concentrated in a small number of states. One in three Hispanics resides in California. Texas is home for approximately one in every five Hispanics. Other large numbers of Hispanics reside in the Northeast in New York, New Jersey, and Massachusetts; Florida in the South; Illinois in the Midwest; and Arizona, New Mexico, and Colorado in the Southwest (U.S. Bureau of the Census, 1993a).

Hispanics and School Achievement

Hispanics continue to be one of the most undereducated groups in America. While they exhibit overall low academic achievement compared to their Anglo counterparts, they have made some gains. For example, while the most recent NAEP results (see Figure 8.1) indicate that Hispanic children's reading skills at ages 9, 13, and 17 continue to be substantially lower than their Anglo peers, since 1980 they improved at all age levels and are, in fact, higher than their African-American peers.

NAEP mathematics assessment results for the period 1978 to 1992 by race and ethnicity are depicted in Figure 8.2 (p. 263). Hispanic students demonstrated significant improvement in proficiency scores between 1978 and 1992, particularly the 13- and 17-year-old cohort. While Hispanics still trailed behind their non-Hispanic peers on mathematics proficiency, their proficiency scores exceeded those of blacks. Over the last two decades the mathematics scores of whites at ages 13 and 17 increased at a slower rate than those of either blacks or Hispanics, causing the gap to decrease between those groups.

In 1992, the average science proficiency scores of Hispanics continued to remain below those of whites but above those of blacks. Again, however, the scores have shown steady improvement, and between 1977 and 1992 the gap between whites and Hispanics decreased. The NAEP science assessment results for the period 1977 to 1992 by race and ethnicity are depicted in Figure 8.3 (p. 264).

The College Entrance Examination Board reported that in 1993, college bound Hispanic seniors showed steady improvement in their average SAT scores. Of all the Hispanic groups represented, the "Other Hispanic" group demon-

While the effects of poverty appear to be obvious, how do you explain why it has become increasingly difficult to convince legislators that we either pay now or will pay later for programs aimed at the disadvantaged?

What implications do the estimates regarding the increase in the Hispanic population have for you as an individual? For you as a prospective teacher?

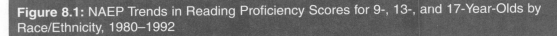

Figure 8.1: NAEP Trends in Reading Proficiency Scores for 9-, 13-, and 17-Year-Olds by Race/Ethnicity, 1980–1992

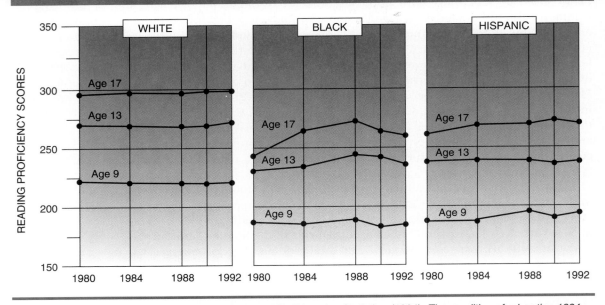

Source: U.S. Department of Education, National Center for Education Statistics. (1994). *The condition of education 1994.* Washington, DC: U.S. Government Printing Office.

strated the highest scores followed by the Mexican-American and Puerto Rican groups. Figure 8.4 (p. 265) shows the trends in verbal and mathematics SAT scores by race and ethnicity for the period 1976–1993.

Hispanics and Educational Attainment

Ethnic differences also have been shown to be related to educational attainment. Hispanics have the highest dropout rate of all major ethnic groups. By the time Hispanics reach high school age, approximately 25% are 2 or more years overage for their grade level, a condition that may place them at risk for dropping out. Nationally, approximately 28% of all Hispanics have dropped out of high school, compared to 14% of blacks and 8% of whites (U.S. Department of Education, 1994b). Most of the dropouts occur before the student reaches the tenth grade.

In 1993, 82% of whites 25 years of age and older had completed secondary school, compared to 53% of Hispanics. And, in the attainment of higher education, Hispanics also lag behind the non-Hispanic population: approximately 9% of the Hispanics 25 years old and older had attained 4 years or more of college compared to 23% of whites (see Figure 8.5, p. 266).

Contributing Factors

The low educational achievement and attainment of many Hispanic youth is no doubt associated with socioeconomic status. Approximately 29% of Hispanic

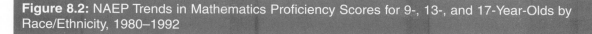

Figure 8.2: NAEP Trends in Mathematics Proficiency Scores for 9-, 13-, and 17-Year-Olds by Race/Ethnicity, 1980–1992

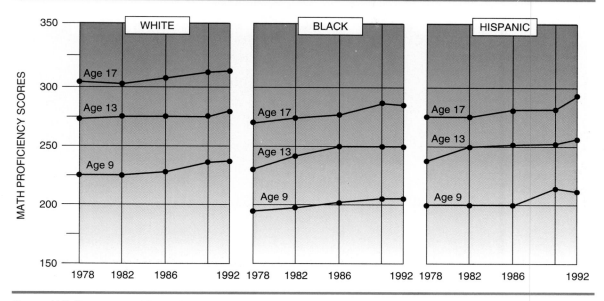

Source: U.S. Department of Education, National Center for Education Statistics. (1994). *The condition of education 1994.* Washington, DC: U.S. Government Printing Office.

families are below the poverty level, as compared to 12% for whites. In general, Hispanics experience higher unemployment and lower income than non-Hispanics. In 1992, the Hispanic unemployment rate was 11.3% compared to the unemployment rate of 7.5% for non-Hispanics, and the median Hispanic income in 1992 was $23,900 compared to $37,000 for non-Hispanic families (U.S. Bureau of the Census, 1993a). It is estimated that in 1993, 41% of Hispanic children were poor (Baumann, 1994).

A number of research studies have targeted the inferior and segregated schools that many Hispanic children attend, which are understaffed, poorly equipped, and poorly funded, as a primary factor in the underachievement of Hispanic children (Hyland, 1992; Orfield, 1987). Other factors cited that may account for the Hispanic low achievement and low attainment include inexperienced or indifferent teachers, low parental schooling levels, few Hispanics in the nation's teaching force, and the high English illiteracy among Hispanic adults (56%), which make it difficult for Hispanic parents to effectively participate in their children's education (Orum & Navarrete, 1991; Valdez, 1992).

Nationally, Hispanic children are also underrepresented in pre-primary education, which may explain their lack of readiness to participate in elementary school. The average pre-kindergarten enrollment rates of whites were 20 percentage points higher than those of Hispanics (U.S. Bureau of the Census, 1994).

Figure 8.3: NAEP Trends in Science Proficiency Scores for 9-, 13-, and 17-Year-Olds by Race/Ethnicity, 1977–1992

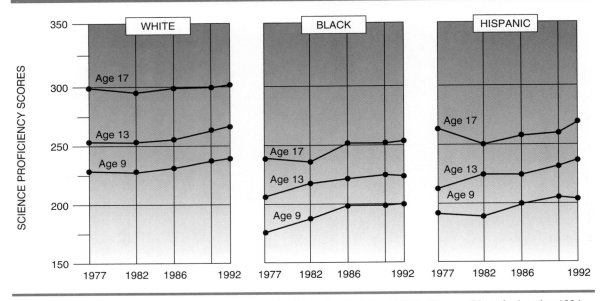

Source: U.S. Department of Education, National Center for Education Statistics. (1994). *The condition of education 1994.* Washington, DC: U.S. Government Printing Office.

A major explanation for the poorer performance of Hispanic children is their linguistic minority background. The term *linguistic minority* includes the growing population of nonnative English speakers, as well as other student populations who are native speakers of English but who have been exposed to some other language in the home since birth (O'Conner, 1989). Hispanic children whose primary language is not English have experienced many more academic difficulties than their English-speaking counterparts.

Racial Differences and School Achievement and Attainment

African-Americans

School Achievement.   The 31.4 million African-Americans (blacks) in the United States make up 12.5% of the population (Bennett, 1992). Like Hispanic students, black students have shown overall improvement in achievement during the past two or three decades, but still perform below the level of white students. For example, as was shown in Figure 8.1, for the ages of 9, 13, and 17, black students' performance was below that of white and Hispanic students in terms of the 1992 National Assessment for Educational Progress reading proficiency scores. With regard to the NAEP mathematics assessment (Figure 8.2), black students consistently scored below both white and Hispanic students at each age

Figure 8.4: Average Verbal and Mathematics SAT Scores by Race/Ethnicity, 1976–1993

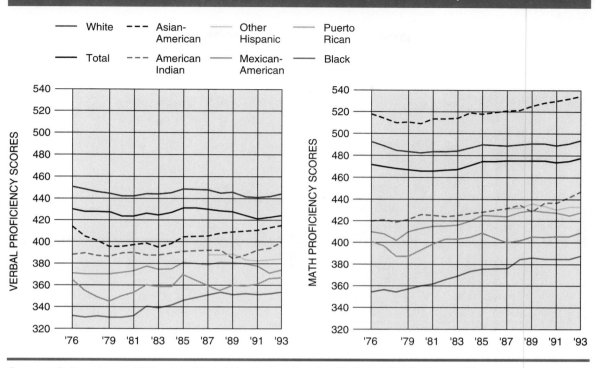

Source: U.S. Department of Education, National Center for Education Statistics. (1994). *The condition of education 1994.* Washington, DC: U.S. Government Printing Office.

level. The same is true for NAEP science proficiency scores (Figure 8.3), where the gap between blacks and whites, and blacks and Hispanics, is even greater. However, the overall improvement by black students, particularly at age 9, has narrowed the performance gap between white and black students.

Racial differences also are found in the results of other standardized tests. For example, while the mean SAT scores of black students have risen 21 points on the verbal section and 34 points on the mathematics section since 1976, the scores of black students continue to trail behind those of whites and Hispanics. As shown on Figure 8.4, the black college bound seniors who took the Scholastic Aptitude Test (SAT) in 1993 averaged 91 points lower than their white counterparts on the verbal section of the test, and 106 points lower on the mathematics section. Black students, like Hispanics, also are more likely to be enrolled in general and vocational programs and are less likely to be enrolled in academic or college preparatory programs.

Educational Attainment. Another indicator of racial differences can be found in high school completion rates. As shown in Figure 8.5, while the proportion of blacks 25 years of age or older who have completed high school has increased

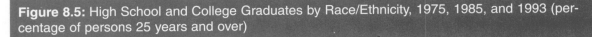

Figure 8.5: High School and College Graduates by Race/Ethnicity, 1975, 1985, and 1993 (percentage of persons 25 years and over)

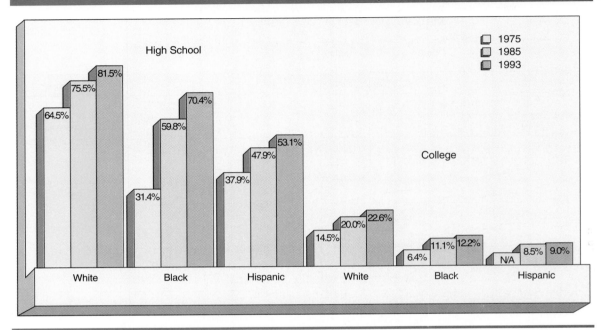

Source: U.S. Bureau of the Census. (1993). *U.S. Census of Population, U.S. Summary,* PC80-1-C1 and *Current Population Reports,* P20–455, P20–459, P20–462, P20–465RV, P20–475, and unpublished data.

considerably since 1975, the high school completion rate for blacks (70%) in 1993 was still significantly behind that of whites (82%). Blacks also tend to complete high school at an older age than whites, reflecting the fact that blacks are more likely than whites to fail and repeat one or more grades.

As also shown in Figure 8.5, the attainment of higher education also differs by race. In 1993, approximately 12% of blacks 25 years of age or older had attained a bachelors's degree or higher, compared to 23% of whites.

Contributing Factors. As in the case of Hispanics, explanations for achievement and attainment differences between blacks and whites are to be found in the lower socioeconomic status of blacks, and the social milieu of black families. For example, in 1992, 33% of black families lived below the poverty level, three times the rate for white families. Forty-six percent of black children lived in families who had an income below the poverty level, compared to 18% of white children. The black median family income was $18,660 in 1992 compared to $22,848 for Hispanics and $32,368 for whites (U.S. Bureau of the Census, 1994). Moreover, the unemployment rate for blacks in 1992 was more than twice that for whites (14% versus 6%) (Bennett, 1992).

Black children continue to be at an educational disadvantage relative to whites because of lower average levels of parental education and the greater likelihood of living in a single parent household that is living below the poverty level. They are also less likely to be enrolled in pre-primary education and are more likely to be below grade level for their respective age. Black adolescents are also more likely than whites to be either threatened or injured with a weapon in school (U.S. Department of Education, 1994a).

During the past decade it has become more apparent that one of the major reasons why black children do not achieve as well as white children is because the public schools are not meeting the needs of poor children in general. Also, it is suggested that many black children may bring to school skills, attitudes, and achievement orientations that differ from their white, middle-class peers. Too often, these differences are perceived as fixed deficits by teachers, counselors, and administrators who, rather than provide for these differences, often relegate black children to a permanently inferior position in the school and the self-fulfilling prophecy continues (Bock & Moore, 1986; Haskins, Walden, & Ramey, 1983).

Asian-Americans

Asian-Americans are defined as those Americans whose ancestry can be traced to such Asian countries as Cambodia, China, India, Japan, Korea, Laos, the Philippines, Thailand, and Vietnam. The Bureau of the Census combines Asian Americans with Pacific Islanders for reporting purposes. Pacific Islanders include such cultural groups as Polynesian, Micronesian, or Melanesian. It also includes Samoan, Guamanian, native Hawaiian, Tahitian, Northern Mariana Islander, Palauan, or Fijian groups. Approximately 60% of the total Asian-American and Pacific Islander population live in the western part of the United States (Parkay & Stanford, 1992). While these subgroups share different cultures, values, and customs, they also share a common goal, namely the respect for an education (Wong, 1992).

Although their percentage of the U.S. population is relatively small (3%), the 9 million Asian and Pacific Islanders in the United States are the fastest growing racial group in America. It is anticipated that by the year 2050, Asian-Americans may reach 41 million, or 11% of the total population (U.S. Bureau of the Census, 1993b).

School Achievement. Research on the achievement of Asian-Americans has been limited, a condition that has been justified by the fact that their achievement is generally greater than that of other racial and ethnic groups. For example, in 1993, the Asian-American college bound seniors outscored whites and all other racial/ethnic groups on the mathematics component of the Scholastic Aptitude Test (see Figure 8.4). Other examples of the high achievement of Asian-Americans can be found in the incidence of significant numbers of finalists and winners in the National Merit Scholarship Program, Presidential Scholars, and Westinghouse Science Talent Search Program (Sue & Okazaki, 1990).

Educational Attainment. Asian-Americans complete high school at a much higher rate than other racial and ethnic groups: Asian-Americans are also more likely to complete high school on time. For example, of those tenth-grade Asian-Americans who were part of a longitudinal study in 1980, approximately 90.8%

completed high school on time (1982) and 99.4% had completed high school by 1992. And, of Asian-American eighth-graders in 1989, only 7% had dropped out of school by 1992. This was the lowest percentage of dropouts among all racial and ethnic groups (U.S. Department of Education, 1994a). In 1993, 84% of Asian-Americans had completed high school, compared to the previously mentioned 82% for whites, 70% for blacks, and 53% for Hispanics (U.S. Bureau of the Census, 1994).

Regarding post-secondary education, in 1993, approximately 42% of Asian-Americans who were 25 years of age or older had completed 4 or more years of college compared to 23% of whites (U.S. Bureau of the Census, 1994).

Contributing Factors. Much of the research that has been done on Asian-American students' achievement has concentrated on the factors contributing to their success. Cultural factors have been found to be among the most important variables. Among the cultural variables noted are high expectations of parents and teachers, a supportive home learning environment that reinforces academic success, and a high value on education for self improvement and family honor (Baratz-Snowden, Rock, Pollack, & Wilder, 1988). Morrow (1991) explains that Southeast Asian children are taught from an early age to develop a sense of moral obligation and loyalty to the family that demands unquestioning loyalty and obedience to not only parents, but to all authority including teachers and other school personnel.

Another possible explanation for the academic success of Asian-Americans has been their advantaged socioeconomic standing: the median household income for Asian-Americans was $36,449 in 1993 compared to $31,569 for whites (U.S. Bureau of the Census, 1993b). As previously noted, a correlation does exist between socio-economic status and educational achievement and attainment.

To what do you attribute the proportional overrepresentation of Asian-Americans in the sciences as opposed to fields such as education or social work?

Native Americans

Native Americans are a diverse population of more than 500 different tribes, each with its own culture, and 200 surviving languages. The 1.2 million Native Americans make up only a little over one-half of 1% of the population (U.S. Bureau of the Census, 1991).

School Achievement. Even more limited than the research on the achievement of Asian-Americans is the research on the achievement and attainment of Native Americans. The third annual National Education Goals Report on reading achievement at grade 12 indicated that 24% of American Indian/Alaska Native students met the goals performance standard compared to 16% for blacks and 43% for whites (National Goals Panel, 1993).

Between 1992 and 1993, American Indians had the highest gains on both the verbal and mathematics sections of the Scholastic Aptitude Test (see Figure 8.4) and ranked above blacks and all Hispanic sub-groups on both verbal and mathematics scores.

Educational Attainment. The dropout rate for Native Americans is higher than that of any racial and ethnic group in the United States. For example, in the longitudinal study previously mentioned, of the Native Americans who were enrolled in the eighth-grade class of 1988, by 1992, 25.4% had dropped out of school. Similar findings were noted with regard to high school completion rates for the tenth-grade class of 1980. Approximately 65.4% of the Native Americans in the tenth-grade class of 1980 had completed high school on time and 81.7% had completed high school by 1992. This completion rate was the lowest of all racial and ethnic groups (U.S. Department of Education, 1994a).

Regarding higher education, of the Native Americans who were 25 years of age or older in 1992, approximately 9% had completed a bachelor's degree. While some improvement has been evidenced, Native Americans continue to lag behind Asians, whites, and blacks in the attainment of a bachelor's degree (U.S. Bureau of the Census, 1993b).

Contributing Factors.   There are a number of explanations for the lower levels of educational achievement and attainment of American Indian and Alaska Native students. Many Native American children come from disadvantaged homes in which parents have lower levels of educational attainment and lower socioeconomic status. The limited English proficiency of many Native American parents, coupled with the English only instruction in many schools, may also have exacerbated the problems of Native-American students and prevented their parents from becoming involved in their children's educational experience.

Other possible explanations for the academic deficiencies include the pronounced use of cultural referents that are foreign to the native cultures, language differences, the poor quality of prior education, and inadequate preparation for national testing (Tippeconnic & Swisher, 1992). Some studies have pointed out that the cultural values of Native American students promote a learning style that inhibits interaction with adults or in new situations, and creates a reluctance to volunteer to ask or answer questions (Baratz-Snowden et al., 1988).

Several recent studies have been conducted to determine the reasons for the high dropout rates of American Indian and Alaska Natives. The causes and reasons given for dropping out tend to differ based on the perceptions of students, educational staff, or parents. Students report that the major reasons for not staying in school are expulsions, lack of interest, pregnancy, inability to adjust to school, lack of parental support, problems at home, feelings of mistrust, alienation, and the importance of family responsibilities (Dehyle, 1992; Swisher & Hoisch, 1992). A recent BIA sponsored study of staff perceptions of why students drop out reported that staff believed the following to be the major reasons Native American students drop out: lack of parental skills to encourage and monitor school attendance, extra family responsibilities taken on by students that interfere with schooling, both student and parental substance abuse, poor study skills, and distrust of the BIA school system (Swisher & Hoisch, 1992).

Ledlow (1992) cautions educators to not conclude that there is a single cause or explanation for the disproportionate high rate of dropouts among Native American children and youth. According to Ledlow, the dropout rates vary from school to school, year to year, tribe to tribe, male to female, BIA to public school, etc. There is, however, overwhelming evidence that both economic and social issues are very significant in explaining the high dropout rate, and those same economic and social issues may also explain the lack of retention among other minority groups. Callahan and McIntire (1994) recommend that while it is important to recognize how the American Indian and Alaska Native student might differ from the dominant culture, it is equally as important to recognize the diversity among students within tribal groups. For example, the family's attitudes toward traditionalism, whether the student is from a multi-tribal home, the degree of monolingualism or bilingualism in the family, and the parents' educational background all impact educational outcomes.

Gender Differences and School Achievement and Attainment

Educational Achievement. Research over the past two decades has demonstrated that gender differences in educational attainment do not appear all at once, but rather develop gradually over a long period of time and are particularly evident by the seventh grade (Grossman & Grossman 1994; Schmuck & Schmuck, 1994). One consistent finding has also been that females outperform their male counterparts on most measures of verbal ability. For example, the average reading proficiency scores of females, as determined by the 1992 National Assessment of Educational Progress, were higher than males at all age groups (9, 13, and 17 years of age). This gender difference in reading proficiency has been consistent for the past 20 years (see Figure 8.6). Similar results can be found with the 1992 National Assessment of Educational Progress writing proficiency scores

Gender differences in mathematics continue to decline.

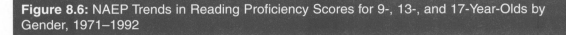

Figure 8.6: NAEP Trends in Reading Proficiency Scores for 9-, 13-, and 17-Year-Olds by Gender, 1971–1992

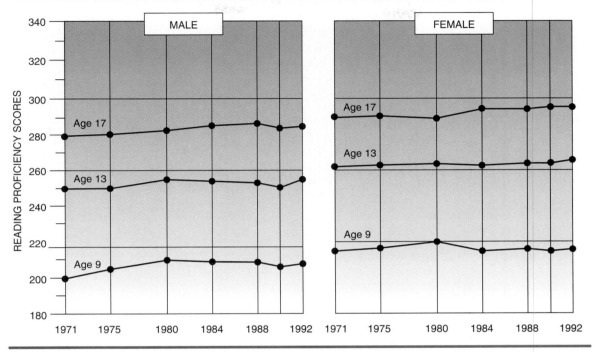

Source: U.S. Department of Education, National Center for Education Statistics. (1994). *The condition of education 1994.* Washington, DC: U.S. Government Printing Office.

for grades 4, 8, and 11. Females have outscored males in writing skills at all levels since 1984 (U. S. Department of Education, 1994a). Native American, black, and Hispanic-American girls, in particular, develop their verbal skills at an earlier age than boys, and consistently outperform boys on tests of verbal skills at both the elementary and secondary levels (Grossman & Grossman, 1994).

Despite the fact that females achieve higher course grades in most subjects, they still score lower than males on complex mathematics tests and are less willing to take risks in solving mathematics problems (Klein & Ortman, 1994). On the 1992 NAEP data on mathematics proficiency of 9-, 13-, and 17-year-olds, females scored lower than males at each grade level (see Figure 8.7, p. 272). While the gap between male and female science proficiency scores of 9-, 13-, and 17-year-olds has decreased over the past 10 years at ages 13 and 17, girls continue to lag behind their male peers (see Figure 8.8, p. 273).

Over the past decade there has been significant improvement by females on the mathematics section of the Scholastic Aptitude Test (SAT). While males continue to outscore females on the mathematics section by 41 points, this represents the smallest gap since 1971 (see Figure 8.9, p. 274). One explanation for the noticeable improvement is that more females are completing higher level

Figure 8.7: NAEP Trends in Mathematics Proficiency Scores for 9-, 13-, and 17-Year-Olds by Gender, 1973–1992

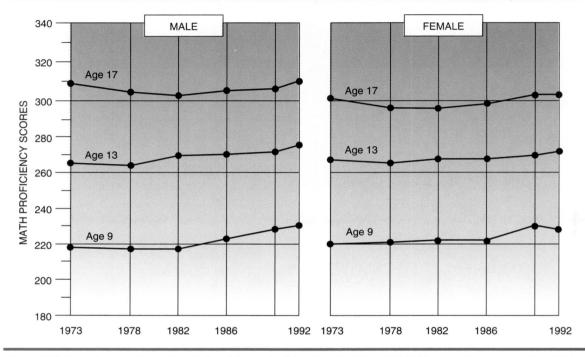

Source: U.S. Department of Education, National Center for Education Statistics. (1994). *The condition of education 1994.* Washington, DC: U.S. Government Printing Office.

mathematics courses like calculus and physics (Miller, 1994). Similar findings have been reported with the American College Testing (ACT) scores, where the women's average composite ACT score was 20.7 compared to 20.9 for men.

Educational Attainment. Sex differences are also evident in educational attainment. While in 1993 there were no differences in the high school completion rates by gender, there were differences found with college completion rates.

Professional Reflections

"Some of the responsibility of the future of this great nation rests upon the work you do in the classroom. Even though you will not wield a scalpel or command any army, your words, actions, and the very essence that makes you unique will leave a mark on each child whose life you touch."

Kay Brost, Teacher of the Year, Montana

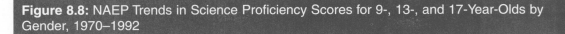

Figure 8.8: NAEP Trends in Science Proficiency Scores for 9-, 13-, and 17-Year-Olds by Gender, 1970–1992

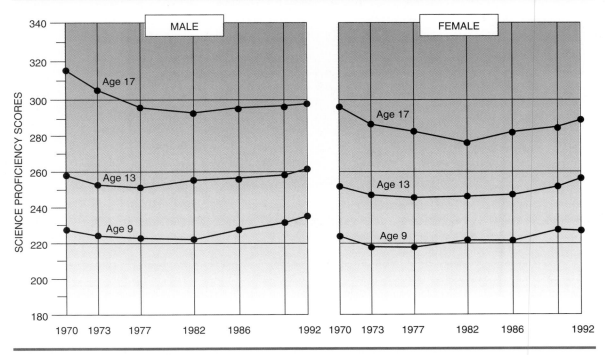

Source: U.S. Department of Education, National Center for Education Statistics. (1994). *The condition of education 1994.* Washington, DC: U.S. Government Printing Office.

Approximately 24.8% of males compared to 19.2% of females had completed college (U.S. Bureau of the Census, 1994). However, the completion rates did vary by age group. For individuals under 40 years of age, the completion rates between the sexes were relatively similar, but for those 40 years and older, a higher percentage of males than females completed a bachelor's degree (U.S. Department of Education, 1994a).

Contributing Factors.   A number of hypotheses have been offered to explain why males and females achieve differently. The most common explanation is that the differences can be largely attributed to the sex-role stereotyping and sex bias girls experience in the school and the larger society. The 1992 report of by the American Association of University Women (AAUW) discussed in the next chapter reported that girls from low income families and nonwhite females are most apt to face severe obstacles that mitigate against high academic performance or attainment. Some of these obstacles include low teacher expectations and inadequate nutrition and health care (AAUW, 1992).

Myra and David Sadker (1994), noted researchers on gender differences and sex roles, suggest the following ways that our school systems may cheat girls:

Have you ever taken either the ACT or the SAT? Do you feel your score was affected by your race, gender, or social class?

Figure 8.9: Average SAT Scores of College-Bound Seniors by Gender, 1972–1994.

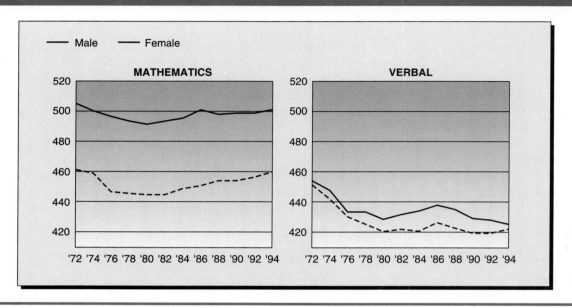

Source: U.S. Department of Education, National Center for Education Statistics. (1994). *The condition of education 1994.* Washington, DC: U.S. Government Printing Office.

> Girls and women learn to speak softly or not at all; to submerge honest feelings, withhold opinions, and defer to boys; to avoid math and science as male domains; to value neatness and quiet more than assertiveness and creativity; to emphasize appearance and hide intelligence. Through this curriculum in sexism they are turned into educational spectators instead of players. (p.13)

While important, gender is only a single contributing factor that affects the classroom interaction. Ability, race, ethnicity, and social class all play a significant role.

Summary

In this chapter the definitions of culture, subculture, society, socialization, and acculturation were presented. The family, the peer group, and the mass media were examined as agents of socialization. Of these institutions, the family has undergone the most significant changes since World War II. As a result of those changes, many of the earlier functions of the family have now been transferred to the school. At the same time, as children spend more time viewing television, its influence on children's behavior and school achievement has increased.

Schools have various purposes and serve an intellectual, political, economic, and social function. Of these, the debate as to whether the schools promote social selection or social mobility remains controversial in American education.

Many would agree that there are numerous opportunities for education, but most believe that equal educational opportunity is more a myth than a fact in the American educational system. The myth of equal educational opportunity is particularly evident as one examines differences in the educational achievement and attainment of social class groups, ethnic groups, racial groups, and the sexes. In the next chapter, we will look at some of the strategies that have been employed to increase equality of educational opportunity and ameliorate against the effects of economic and cultural deprivation and discrimination.

Key Terms

Acculturation
Amalgamation
Assimilation
Cultural pluralism
Culture
Ethnic group
Linguistic minority
National Assessment of Educational
    Progress (NAEP)

Separatism
Social class
Social mobility
Social selection
Socialization
Society
Socioeconomic status
Subculture

Discussion Questions

1. In the incident described at the beginning of the chapter Veronica Harts states that she knew that she had a commitment not only to the student but also to his mother. What are some of the ways that you as a teacher can demonstrate your care and commitment to not only your students but also to their parents or guardians?

2. How could you, as a teacher, attempt to mitigate against the negative influence of television on children's aggressive behavior? What suggestions would you make to parents?

3. Reflect on the high school from which you graduated. To what extent did it promote upward social mobility? In what ways did it resemble a miniature factory system?

4. Discuss what is meant by the cycle of poverty. What can the schools do to break this cycle?

5. Discuss the impact of differing cultural values on school achievement and attainment. Give specific examples.

6. Discuss the common factors contributing to the underachievement of Hispanics, blacks, and Native Americans.

7. What are the levels of educational attainment of the females in your family? The males? What factors account for any differences that may exist between the two groups? To what extent are the factors evident today?

References

American Association of University Women (AAUW). (1992). *How schools shortchange girls.* Wellesley, MA: Wellesley College, Center for Research on Women.

Anderson, D. R., & Collins, P. A. (1988). *The impact of children's education: Television's influence on cognitive development.* Washington, DC: U.S. Department of Education, Office of Educational Research and Improvement.

Apple, M. W. (1982). *Education and power.* New York: Routledge, Chapman, & Hall.

Baratz-Snowden, J., Rock, D., Pollack, J., & Wilder, G. (1988). *The educational progress of language minority children: Funding from the NAEP 1985–86 special study.* Princeton, NJ: National Assessment of Educational Progress/Educational Testing Service.

Baumann, M. (1994, November 14). Poverty has the face of a child. *USA Today,* 2A.

Beentjes, J. W., & Van der Voort, T. H. (1988). Television's impact on children's reading skills: A review of research. *Reading Research Quarterly, 23,* 389–413.

Bennett, C. E. (1992). *The black population in the United States.* U.S. Bureau of the Census. (Current Population Reports, Series P-20, No. 471), Washington, DC: U.S. Government Printing Office.

Bennett, K. P., & LeCompte, M. D. (1990). *How schools work: A sociological analysis of education.* New York: Longman.

Bock, R. D., & Moore, E. G. (1986). *Advantage and disadvantage: A profile of America's youth.* Hillsdale, NJ: Lawrence Erlbaum Associates.

Bowen, W. (1994, March 16). Media violence. *Education Week, 60,* 47.

Bowles, S., & Gintis, H. (1976). *Schooling in capitalist America.* New York: Basic Books.

Brody, J. (1989). Minority achievement. *Executive Educator, 11,* A9.

Callahan, C. M., & McIntire, J. A. (1994). *Identifying outstanding talent in American Indian and Alaska Native students.* Washington, DC: U.S. Department of Education, Office of Educational Research and Improvement.

Coleman, J. S. (1968). The concept of equality of educational opportunity. *Harvard Educational Review, 38,* 7–22.

Coleman, J. S., et al. (1966). *Equality of educational opportunity.* Washington, DC: U.S. Government Printing Office.

Davies, J. (1993). The impact of the mass media upon the health of early adolescents. *Journal of Health Education, 24,* 6, 528–535.

Dehyle, D. (1992). Constructing failure and maintaining cultural identity: Navajo and the school leavers. *Journal of American Indian Education, 31,* 24–47.

Feldman, R. S., & Coats, E. (1993). Socialization processes in encoding and decoding: Learning effective nonverbal behavior. A symposium paper presented at the annual meeting of the Society for Research in Child Development, New Orleans, LA.

Friedman, M. I. (1993). *Taking control: Vitalizing education.* Westport, CN: Praeger.

Giroux, H. A., & Purpel, D. (Eds.). (1983). *The hidden curriculum and moral education.* Berkeley, CA: McCutchan.

Gollnick, D. M., & Chinn, P. C. (1994). *Multicultural education in a pluralistic society.* New York: Merrill.

Grossman, H., & Grossman, S. (1994). *Gender issues in education.* Boston: Allyn & Bacon.

Haskins, R., Walden, T., & Ramey, C. T. (1983). Teacher and student behavior in high and low ability groups. *Journal of Educational Psychology, 75,* 865–876.

Haveman, R. H., & Wolfe, B. (1994). *Succeeding-generations: On the effects of investments in children.* NY: Russell Sage Foundation.

Helser, L. (1994, November 13). Grandparents raising grandkids: Trend widens to mainstream American households. *The Arizona Republic,* H1.

Hyland, C. R. (1989). What we know about the fast growing minority population: Hispanic Americans. *Educational Horizons, 67,* 131–135.

Illich, I. (1970). *Deschooling society.* New York: Harper & Row.

Jencks, C., Smith, M., Arland, H., Bane, M. J., Cohen, D., Gintis, H., Heyns, B., & Michelson, S. (1972). *Inequality: A reassessment of the effect of family and schooling in America.* New York: Basic Books.

Klein, S. S., & Ortman, P. E. (1994). Continuing the journey toward gender equity. *Educational Researcher, 23,* 13–21.

Knapp, M. S., & Shields, P. M. (1990). Reconceiving academic instruction for the children of poverty. *Phi Delta Kappan, 71,* 753–758.

Labaree, D. F. (1994). An unlovely legacy: The disabling impact of the market on American teacher education. *Phi Delta Kappan, 75,* 8, 591–595.

Ledlow, S. (1992). Is cultural discontinuity an adequate explanation for dropping out? *Journal of American Indian Education, 31,* 3, 21–36.

Levine, D. U., & Havighurst, R. J. (1992). *Society and education.* Boston, MA: Allyn & Bacon.

Liebert, R. M. & Sprafkin, J. (1988). *The early window: Effects of television on children and youth.* New York: Pergamon Press.

Miller, L. (1994, September 7). Women found to be making gains on college-entrance exam scores. *Education Week,* 10–11.

More families live in poverty. (1993). *Executive Educator, 15,* 9–10.

Morrow, R. D. (1991). The challenges of Southeast-Asian parental involvement. *Principal, 70,* 20–22.

Mosteller, F., & Moynihan, D. P. (Eds.) (1972). *On equality of educational opportunity: Papers deriving from the Harvard University faculty seminar on the Coleman Report.* New York: Random House.

National Commission on Excellence in Education. (1983). *A nation at risk: The imperative for education reform.* Washington, DC: U.S. Government Printing Office.

National Goals Panel. (1993). *The national education goals report.* Washington, DC: U.S. Government Printing Office.

O'Conner, M. C. (1989). Aspects of differential performance by minorities on standardized tests: Linguistic and sociocultural factors. In B. R. Gifford (Ed.), *Test policy and test performance: Education, language, and culture* (pp. 129–181). Boston, MA: Kleewer.

Ogbu, J. U. (1986). Structural constraints in school desegregation. In J. Prager, D. Longshore, & M. Seeman (Eds.), *School desegregation research: New directions in situational analysis* (pp. 21–45). New York: Plenum Press.

Orfield, G. (1987). *School segregation in the 1980s: Trends in the states and metropolitan areas.* Report to the Joint Center for Political Studies. Chicago, IL: National School Desegregation Project.

Orum, L., & Navarrete, L. (1991). Project EXCEL. *Community Education Journal, 18,* 4, 9–19.

Parelius, R. J., & Parelius, A. P. (1987). *The sociology of education.* Englewood Cliffs, NJ: Prentice-Hall.

Parkay, F. W., & Stanford, B. H. (1992). *Becoming a teacher: Accepting the challenge of a profession.* Boston: Allyn & Bacon.

Radeki, T. (1989). Television and film entertainment. *Mothering, 50,* 54.

Reed, S., & Sautter, R. C. (1990). Children of poverty: The status of 12 million young Americans. *Phi Delta Kappan, 71,* K1–K12.

Rich, J. M. (1992). *Foundations of education: Perspectives on American education.* New York: Merrill.

Ritchie, D., Price, V., & Roberts, D. F. (1987). Television, reading, and reading achievement. *Communications Research, 14,* 292–314.

Rose, S. J. (1992). *Social stratification in the United States.* New York: New Press.

Rose, P. (1964). *They and we.* New York: Random House.

Sadker, M., & Sadker, D. (1994). *Failing at fairness.* New York: Charles Scribner's Sons.

Schmuck, P. A., & Schmuck, R. A. (1994). Gender equity: A critical democratic component of America's high schools. *NASSP Bulletin, 78,* 22–31.

Selakovich, D. (1984). *Schooling in America: Social foundations of education.* New York: Longman.

Sleek, S. (1994, October). Captain Kangaroo gives a media lesson. The American *Psychological Association Monitor,* 26.

Sleeter, C. E., & Grant, C. A. (1994). *Making choices for multicultural education.* New York: Merrill.

Spring, J. (1988). *Conflicts of interests: The politics of American education.* New York: Longman.

Spring, J. (1991). *American education: An introduction to political and social aspects* (5th ed.). New York: Longman.

Sue, S., & Okazaki, S. (1990). Asian-American educational achievements: A phenomena in search of an explanation. *American Psychologist, 45,* 913–920.

Swisher, K., & Hoisch, M. (1992). Dropping out among American Indians and Alaska Natives: A review of studies. *Journal of American Indian Education, 31,* 2, 3–23.

Thomas, D. R. (1973). *The schools next time.* New York: McGraw-Hill.

Tippeconnic, J. W., III, & Swisher, K. (1992). American Indian education. In M. C. Alkin (Ed.), *Encyclopedia of Educational Research* (pp. 75–77). New York: Macmillan.

Traditional families: A dying breed. (1986, May 14). *Education Week,* 22.

Turiel, E. (1987). Potential relations between the development of social reasoning and childhood aggression. In D. H. Crowell, I. M. Evans, & C. R. O'Donnell (Eds.), *Childhood aggression and violence* (pp. 231–247). New York: Plenum Press.

U.S. Bureau of the Census. (1991). *1990 census of population: Population characteristics* (Current Population Reports, Series P–20). Washington, DC: U.S. Government Printing Office.

U.S. Bureau of the Census. (1993a). *Hispanic Americans today* (Current Population Reports, Series P–23, No. 183). Washington, DC: U.S. Government Printing Office.

U.S. Bureau of the Census. (1993b). *How we're changing: Demographic state of the nation* (Current Population Reports, Series P–23, No. 184). Washington, DC: U.S. Government Printing Office.

U.S. Bureau of the Census. (1994). *How we're changing: Demographic state of the nation* (Current Population Reports, Series P–23, No. 187). Washington, DC: U.S. Government Printing Office.

U.S. Department of Education, National Center for Education Statistics. (1994a). *The condition of education 1994.* Washington, DC: U.S. Government Printing Office.

U.S. Department of Education, National Center for Education Statistics. (1994b). *Dropout rates in the United States: 1993.* Washington, DC: U.S. Government Printing Office.

Usdansky, M. L., & Edmonds, P. (1994, November 14). In 1993, child poverty hit 30-year high. *USA Today.* 2A.

Valdez, C. (1992). Education of Hispanic-Americans. In M.C. Alkin (Ed.), *Encyclopedia of Educational Research* (pp. 592–597). New York: Macmillan.

Waldrop, J., & Exter, T. (1991). The legacy of the 1980s. *American Demographics. 13,* 3, 33–38.

Wallis, C. (1992). The nuclear family goes boom! *Time, 140,* 27, 42–44.

Ward, J. G., & Anthony, P. (1992). *Who pays for student diversity? Population changes and educational policy.* Newberry Park, CA: Corwin Press.

Webb, L. D., McCarthy, M. M., & Thomas, S. (1988). *Financing elementary and secondary education.* Columbus, OH: Merrill.

Webb, R. B., & Sherman, R. R. (1989). *Schooling and society.* New York: Macmillan.

Wong, L. Y. S. (1992). Education of Asian-Americans. In M. C. Alkin (Ed.), *Encyclopedia of Educational Research* (pp. 95–96). New York: Macmillan.

Chapter 9

Achieving Equity in Education

As the son of a tenant farmer, I know that education is the only valid passport from poverty. As a former teacher—and I hope a future one—I have great expectations of what this law will mean for all of our young people. . . . I believe deeply no law I have signed or will ever sign means more to the future of America.

President Lyndon Johnson upon signing the Elementary and Secondary Education Bill,
April 1, 1965

A Critical Incident in My Teaching Career . . .

Louis Garcia, a new student in my class, came in on his first day with a hard, mean look. He was an unhappy looking teenager, dressed in gang garb. The counselors informed me that he wasn't passing any of his classes. I soon found out why. He was tardy on a daily basis, never turned in any homework, and failed two exams in a row.

I decided to talk with Louis about his personal life, past and present. His family in Virginia gave up on him and sent him to his aunt here in Utah. She later threw him out of her house. Now, his foster parents had given him a final alternative, "pass a class or you're out."

Louis said that I seemed to be the only teacher with any interest or concern in him. Would I give him a D- on his take home progress report? I initially refused. After further thought (realizing he was a pretty good 'con' man) I did finally agree.

The next month proved very prosperous. Louis turned in every homework assignment and received a 61%, then a 72% on his next two chapter exams. I took a chance but now am glad I did. Daily doses of positive affirmation and a small pat on the back have given Louis hope.

Richard K. Bojak
Teacher of the Year, Utah

As we have seen in previous chapters of this text, a variety of circumstances have combined in society and the schools to restrict the educational opportunities of many students. This chapter presents a number of strategies for combating inequity and inequality in education. As you review these strategies, consider the following learning objectives:

- Differentiate the concepts of cultural pluralism, multicultural education, and bilingual education.
- Outline the principles inherent in the Individuals with Disabilities Education Act and their impact on American education.
- Describe the major compensatory education programs and their current status.
- Describe current issues in the education of Native Americans.
- List the major court decisions concerning segregation and their impact on local school districts.

- Discuss the possible effects of desegregation on the academic achievement and self-esteem of minority students and on community integration.
- Discuss the progress of gender equity in education and the process for its attainment.
- Evaluate the role of adult education in overcoming illiteracy.
- Outline the major secondary vocational education programs and comment on the reform movement's impact on them.

The burden of eliminating social inequality rests not with the schools but with social action programs and the enforcement of legal prohibitions against inequality; however, the schools do have a role in providing opportunities that foster social equality and in removing barriers that make it difficult for children and adults to take maximum advantage of educational opportunities (Cameron, 1987). Beginning in the 1960s with the civil rights movement and the federal government's War on Poverty, numerous federal programs were initiated to promote educational opportunity. In addition to the federal initiatives, state governments, professional organizations, and the private sector have introduced strategies to combat inequity in education. In this chapter the following strategies are discussed: multicultural and bilingual education, education of students with disabilities, compensatory education, Indian education, desegregation, promotion of gender equity, adult and continuing education, and vocational education.

Cultural Pluralism

The attention to cultural pluralism is a relatively new phenomenon in the United States, in spite of the fact that we have always been a pluralistic nation. *Cultural pluralism* is defined as "a state of equal co-existence in a mutually supportive relationship within the boundaries or framework of one nation of people of diverse cultures with significantly different patterns of belief, behavior, color, and in many cases with different languages" (Hazard & Stent, 1993, p. 14). It has been the growing acceptance of the cultural pluralism perspective over the past two decades that has helped to foster the development of multicultural and bilingual education programs discussed later in this section.

As briefly mentioned in the previous chapter, cultural pluralism is the latest in the progression of educational responses to diversity. The initial response, the assimilationist approach, dates from the colonial period and was particularly favored during the period from 1880 to 1945 when countless numbers of immigrants came to America from eastern and southern European nations. During this period, "military-style" assimilation was advocated, meaning the rapid assimilation of immigrant children, by force if necessary. Military-style assimilation encouraged English-only classrooms, the Anglicization of immigrants' names and of the school community, and no use of the native language, even outside the school environment. Since the Anglocentric curriculum was considered as standard, any other culture was viewed as substandard (Stein, 1986).

Did you or any of your ancestors come to America as immigrants? What was your or their assimilation experience?

From 1945 to 1968, assimilation continued; however, it was "missionary-style." This type of assimilation reflected the cultural deprivation theory, an environmentalist theory that blamed poor school achievement on deficiencies in the minority culture rather than on inheritance of low intelligence. It also reflected the amalgamation theory that contended that not to assimilate would be to preordain the immigrants to poverty and exclude them from the mainstream. The solution adopted by many school districts during this period was to attempt to replace parental and community values with the values of the Anglo middle class (Stein, 1986).

Programs were also initiated to overcome the so-called "language disability." *English as a second language (ESL)* programs flourished. ESL had been designed in the 1930s, primarily for instruction of foreign diplomats, business people, and government officials, but by 1950 ESL programs were introduced in many southwestern and eastern school districts to instruct poor Hispanic children. The ESL programs provided instruction in English-only classes. Students from a variety of language backgrounds participated in the same ESL class for the purpose of English language acquisition. The most common ESL program was a pullout program, which removed students from their regular classes daily or several times a week. These ESL programs were not particularly successful with Hispanic children and did not equip them with sufficient English to succeed in their content classes. The pullout method also exacerbated the problem by requiring the children to miss some of their content instruction, thereby causing them to fall behind and having to repeat a grade or grades (Stein, 1986).

Many believe that the cultural deprivation theory led to lowered expectations and a self-fulfilling prophecy of failure, particularly for Hispanics. Unfortunately, the concept of cultural deprivation became the operative theory behind the War on Poverty during the 1960s and eventually provided the theoretical basis for the use of bilingual education as a compensatory or remedial program (Stein, 1986).

In spite of the rhetoric concerning the importance of uniformity, patriotism, and the Anglo-Saxon tradition, by the 1960s it was quite clear that the assimilation approach had many shortcomings. Blacks, Hispanics, Native Americans, and other racial and ethnic groups continued to experience discrimination, and attempts to increase upward mobility of children from poor families were generally unsuccessful. Thus, during the 1960s, concurrent with the civil rights movement, the concept of cultural pluralism replaced the assimilation concept.

Explicit in the term *cultural pluralism* are references to race and ethnicity. More recently, advocates of multicultural education argue that because gender and social class are important determinants of "what happens, how it happens, and why it happens in society," these characteristics must also be considered in conceptualizing pluralism. Cultural pluralism related to class and gender means that males and females, as well as children from all social classes, should have gender-free and class-free repertoire of roles and styles to choose from and should be afforded equal educational opportunities, regardless of their gender or social class background (Sleeter & Grant, 1994).

Recognition of Cognitive Differences in Learning Styles

One way that school districts have endorsed cultural pluralism is by recognizing differences in learning or cognitive styles that stem from differences in socialization, and then accommodating these different styles by using different instructional approaches. For example, in terms of learning styles, some students respond better to learning environments that encourage cooperative learning activities; others may be more comfortable with an independent learning approach; and others may be more successful in an environment that stresses competitive learning.

How would you describe your learning and cognitive styles?

Differences in *cognitive styles* may be found between those who are characterized as field-independent analytic thinkers and those who are characterized as field-dependent descriptive thinkers. An individual with a field-independent style will tend to organize his or her environment and approach tasks on a step-by-step sequence, while an individual with a field-dependent style will be more likely to attend to global aspects of the curriculum and prefer multiple activites. Field-independent learners function well in competitive environments and prefer to work independently, while field-dependent learners prefer cooperative activities. Research has shown that differences in learning and cognitive styles are related to ethnic and racial differences. For example, there is some evidence that African-Americans, Native Americans, and Mexican-Americans are more field-dependent in their cognitive styles, approach tasks visually, and prefer discussion and oral communication (Shade, 1989; Swisher & Deyhle, 1994).

Multicultural Education

Students from varied backgrounds often find their school culture to be alien to their home environment. In recent years, research has suggested that when students' acculturation prepares them for a social context that differs from the social context of the school, alienation may result. *Multicultural education* is a strategy for addressing this alienation by recognizing, accepting, and affirming "human differences and similarities related to gender, race, ethnicity, disability, class, and (increasingly) sexual preference" (Sleeter & Grant, 1994). James Banks (1993), a leading proponent of multicultural education, describes multicultural education as having five dimensions:

- The *content integration dimension,* which deals with the extent to which teachers use examples, data, and other information from a variety of cultures and groups to illustrate the key concepts, principles, generalizations, and theories in the subject or discipline.

- The *knowledge construction dimension,* which includes discussion of the ways in which the implicit cultural assumptions, frames of reference, perspectives, and biases within a discipline influence the construction of knowledge.

- The *prejudice reduction dimension,* which focuses on the characteristics of children's racial attitudes and on strategies that can be used to help students develop more positive racial and ethnic attitudes.

- The *equity pedagogy dimension,* which exists when teachers use techniques and teaching methods that facilitate the academic achievement of students from diverse racial and ethnic groups and from all social classes.

- The *empowering school culture and social structure dimension,* which would require the restructuring of the culture and organization of the school so that students from diverse racial, ethnic, and social-class groups will experience equality and a sense of empowerment. (pp. 25, 27)

To accomplish the goals inherent in these dimensions, multicultural education employs a variety of curricular, instructional, and other educational practices, some of which are detailed in Table 9.1.

Multicultural education, while still on the margins rather than the center of the curriculum, has made significant progress in the last two decades. The integration of multicultural content is increasingly becoming a part of core courses at all levels of education, as well as textbooks. More and more of the teachers in today's classrooms have studied the concepts of multicultural education. Yet, misconception continues that multicultural education is an entitlement program and curriculum for "them" (Banks, 1993). And it will not be until its opponents realize that multicultural education is for *all of us* that it will assume a place of prominence in the life of the school.

Table 9.1: Multicultural Education

Societal goals:	Promote social structural equality and cultural pluralism (the United States as a "tossed salad")
School goals:	Promote equal opportunity in the school, cultural pluralism, and alternative life styles; respect for those who differ; and support for power equity among groups
Target students:	Everyone
Practices:	
Curriculum	Organized concepts around contributions and perspectives of several different groups; teach critical thinking, analysis of alternative viewpoints; make curriculum relevant to students' experiential backgrounds; promote use of more than one language
Instruction	Build on students' learning styles; adapt to students' skill levels; involve students actively in thinking and analyzing; use cooperative learning
Other aspects of classroom	Decorate classroom to reflect cultural pluralism, non-traditional sex roles, disabled people, and student interests
Support services	Help regular classroom adapt to as much diversity as possible
Other school-wide concerns	Involve lower-class and minority parents actively in the school; encourage staffing patterns to include diverse racial, gender, and disability groups in non-traditional roles; make use of decorations, special events, and school menus that reflect and include diverse groups; use library materials that portray diverse groups in diverse roles; include all student groups in extracurricular activities, and do not reinforce stereotypes; make sure discipline procedures do not penalize any group; make sure building is accessible to disabled people

Source: Sleeter, C. E. & Grant, C. A. (1994). *Making choices for multicultural education* (2nd ed.). New York: Macmillan.

Bilingual Education

In 1990, 14% of all children 5 to 17 years old in the United States spoke languages other than English at home. Over one-third of these had difficulty speaking English, an increase of 27% (from 1.9 million to 2.4 million) between 1980 and 1990 (U.S. Department of Education, 1994). *Bilingual education* is an instructional program designed to provide an effective education to students in their native language while they are learning English. Bilingual education, like multicultural education, is a vehicle for promoting cultural pluralism. In practice, bilingual education includes a broad range of programs and provides instruction for limited—English-proficient as well as non–English-proficient students.

Federal Involvement in Bilingual Education

Federal support for bilingual education programs began in 1968 through an amendment to the Elementary and Secondary Education Act of 1965 entitled the Title VII Bilingual Education Program, also referred to as the Bilingual Education Act (BEA). However, while the BEA prompted school districts to design and implement programs for language minority students, it was the Supreme Court decision in *Lau v. Nichols* (1974) that provided the major impetus for federal involvement in the education of children with English language deficiencies and raised public awareness of the need for bilingual education. In the *Lau* case, the court relied on Title VI of the Civil Rights Act of 1964 and concluded that school districts are obligated to provide assistance for all children with English language deficiencies. The Supreme Court ruled that:

> there is no equality of treatment merely by providing students with the same facilities, textbooks, teachers, and curriculum; for students who do not understand English are effectively foreclosed from any meaningful education. Basic English skills are at the very core of what these public schools teach. Imposition of a requirement that, before a child can effectively participate in the educational program, he must already have acquired those basic skills is to make a mockery of public education. We know that those who do not understand English are certain to find their classroom experiences wholly incomprehensible and in no way meaningful. (p. 566)

Although the court mandated that the schools provide assistance for children with English language deficiencies, it did not require a specific type of instructional model for language minority education. That is, the court did not specify whether Title VII requires bilingual education, English as a second language, or any nonbilingual educational approach. As a result, each state and territory has defined its own approach to the education of language minority students. State legislative provisions may also mandate the criteria for program eligibility and for the type of program to be offered. However, in most states school districts are allowed a great deal of latitude in determining the manner in which they incorporate the native language of the student. In the end, such local factors as languages spoken, resources available, and geographic dispersion will play major roles in defining the programs (Sevilla, 1992).

Support for bilingual education grew throughout the 1970s. However, in the 1980s bilingual education became a politically controversial issue when the Reagan administration opposed bilingual education and supported English immersion programs that had been used with earlier immigrant groups. Then Republican Senator S. I. Hayakawa headed an organization called U.S. English that sought to make English the official language of the nation, and in numerous states "English-only" promoters sought the passage of legislation to declare English to be the official language of the state and the only language to be used in conducting public affairs.

In 1988, major amendments to the Bilingual Education Act were made. These amendments provided additional funding for English-only instructional programs and decreased funding for bilingual programs. They also specified that a percentage of the funds be distributed for certain types of educational programs, special alternative instruction programs, developmental bilingual education programs, programs of academic excellence, family English literacy programs, and programs for special populations. The Act also limited student participation in bilingual programs to three years.

What position has your state government taken in regard to the English Only movement?

Bilingual Program Options

There is considerable controversy surrounding the most effective language minority program. Pai (1990) describes five possible program options:

- *Submersion.* By strict definition submersion programs would not be called bilingual because neither the student nor the teacher use a language other than English. Rather, students with limited English proficiency are placed in regular classrooms where English is the mode of instruction. Submersion programs are described as "sink or swim" programs.

- *English as a second language (ESL).* A combination of English instruction and submersion: non-English speaking and limited-English speaking students are assigned to all-English speaking classes and are also assigned to separate classes or tutors to learn English as a second language.

- *Immersion or sheltered English.* English is used in instruction and the native or home language is used in a limited way to enhance classroom communication. Students usually begin sheltered classes in less language-based classes such as mathematics, and then move to more language dependent courses such as social studies (Sevilla, 1992).

- *Transitional bilingual education.* The student's native language is used to make the transition to the total use of English as soon as possible. Gollnick and Chinn (1994) refer to this approach as an assimilationist approach because there is no attempt made to maintain the native language, which is phased out of use as rapidly as possible.

- *Bilingual maintenance.* Students are given instruction in both the native language and English. The goal is for students to become truly bilingual and to function effectively in both languages; neither language is given preeminence.

Whereas most bilingual educators favor the maintenance approach, the transitional approach is the approach used by most bilingual education programs in the United States (Gollnick & Chinn, 1994). The average length of stay in such programs is 3.5 years.

Regardless of the particular bilingual program approach, each assumes that the language and culture a child learns at home can foster normal and healthy psychological development and communication proficiency. Furthermore, research indicates that "children with well-developed first language skills acquire their second language with greater ease and success than children who are still learning their first language" (Sleeter & Grant, 1994, p. 56). For these reasons it is particularly important that bilingual education not be viewed as a threat to the "core" academic program, but as having a vital role to play in the reform of the educational system and in the attainment of equal educational opportunity for not only the growing number of language minority students, but all students.

Education of Children with Disabilities

Students with mental and physical disabilities make up approximately 12% of the student population in the United States (U.S. Department of Education, 1994). Special education for these children was not routinely provided by most state and local school systems until the third quarter of this century. In fact, prior to the 1970s most state laws allowed the expulsion or absolute exclusion from school of children who were deemed uneducable, untrainable, or otherwise unable to benefit from the regular education program. It was not until two important federal court decisions in the early 1970s (*Pennsylvania Association of Retarded Citizens v. Commonwealth of Pennsylvania,* 1972 and *Mills v. Board of Education,* 1972) that the right of children with disabilities to an education was recognized by most states and school districts.

Individuals with Disabilities Education Act

These decisions, combined with intense lobbying by special education professionals, interest groups, and parents of children with disabilities, led Congress in 1975 to pass the Education of the Handicapped Act (EHA) (Public Law 94–142). In 1990, the legislation reauthorizing the bill extended its outreach to include additional categories of disabilities and also renamed it, calling it the Individuals with Disabilities Education Act (IDEA). The changing of the term handicapped to "child/student/individual with a disability" was important because it reflected "the desire of individuals with disabilities for the law to indicate that a disability is one aspect of a person's total being" (First & Curcio, 1993, p. 8). The EHA, often referred to as the Bill of Rights for Handicapped Children, and its successors have served not only to guarantee the rights of children with disabilities but to define and expand the rights of all children.

The EHA introduced a number of principles that have had a great impact on American education. These principles, which have been expanded through the IDEA and subsequent legislation and litigation, are summarized below.

Right to an Education
Perhaps the most fundamental and important principle of the IDEA is that *all* children with disabilities have available to them a free appropriate education

and related services designed to meet their unique needs. This provision of the law means that *no* children, regardless of the nature or severity of their disability, can be denied a public education. While the EHA applied to children with disabilities aged 5 to 18, in 1986 it was amended (P. L. 99–457) to extend the right to an education to disabled children aged 3 through 5. In addition, P. L. 99–457 offers financial and technical assistance to school districts in developing preschool programs for disabled children from birth to age 3.

Nondiscriminatory Evaluation

This provision requires that each child must receive a comprehensive evaluation before being placed in any special education program. Placement cannot be made on the basis of a single test, but on multiple meaures and procedures. Additionally, whatever evaluation mechanisms are used must be nondiscriminatory in terms of culture, race, and language, and must be designed for assessment with specific handicaps (e.g., tests for non-English speakers or tests for the visually impaired).

Individualized Educational Program

The IDEA requires that an *individualized education program (IEP)* be prepared for each child who is to receive special education services. The IEP is "the backbone of the special education process . . . the formal mechanism by which the goal of an appropriate education is to be realized" (Shore, 1986, p. 6). Designed to meet the unique needs of the child for whom it is developed, the IEP is prepared by a team of educators, parents, and, if appropriate, the student. The IEP includes a description of present performance; a statement of annual goals, including short-term objectives; a statement of services to be provided and their duration; and evaluation criteria and procedures to determine if the objectives are being achieved. IEPs are reviewed annually and provide the means for ensuring parent involvement in the educational decisions affecting their children, the means for accountability for the delivery of services, and a record of progress.

The concept of the IEP has met with success for special education needs. How might the IEP be used with all students?

Least Restrictive Environment

The IDEA mandates that children with disabilities are to be educated in the *least restrictive environment* possible. This requirement has encouraged the practice of *mainstreaming* children with disabilities, to the maximum extent possible, into the regular classroom where they have contact with nondisabled children. The courts have interpreted this provision to mean that children with disabilities should not be removed from the regular educational setting unless the nature or severity of the disability is such that education in the regular classroom, even with the use of supplemental aids and services, cannot be achieved satisfactorily. In every case, a disabled child cannot be moved from the regular classroom without a due process hearing, and schools have been required to provide supplemental services in the regular classroom before moving the disabled child to a more restrictive environment.

The least restrictive environment principle does not require mainstreaming; in fact, the IDEA does not mention mainstreaming. What the principle does call for is the careful consideration of all possible placement alternatives for each disabled child before a final placement is made (Peterson, 1988). In the end it may be necessary to place the child in a segregated setting in order to provide him or her with the most appropriate education, or in order to prevent the disruption of the educational process for other students. Students may also be placed in private schools at public expense if the district is not able to provide an appropriate placement. See Figure 9.1 for the continuum of special education placements.

Due Process

The extensive procedural requirements of the IDEA are designed to ensure the rights of children with disabilities to receive a free appropriate education and to protect them from improper evaluation, classification, and placement. As shown in Figure 9.2, parents have the right to obtain an individual evaluation of their child in addition to that conducted by the school district, and to be involved in every stage of the evaluation, placement, and educational process. Parents must be informed of the IEP conference and encouraged to attend. In addition, the school district must inform parents in writing or in a format understandable by them before it initiates, changes, or refuses to initiate or change the identification, evaluation, or educational placement of the child. Parents also have the right to a due process hearing to challenge the district's decision on any of these matters and to examine all records pertaining to their children.

Current Enrollments

Since the EHA was implemented in 1978, the number of children enrolled in federally supported education programs has risen steadily (see Table 9.2). This is due primarily to the growth in the numbers of students classified as having a *learning disability*, that is, having a disorder or delayed development in one or more of the processes of thinking, speaking, reading, writing, listening, or doing arithmetic operations. The percentage of students classified as learning disabled rose from 22% to 45% between 1977 and 1992. According to officials at the U.S. Department of Education, the increase in the number of students classified as learning disabled "could be the result of an increasingly common tendency to label high functioning students with mental retardation and those with attention-deficit disorder as learning disabled" (Schnaiberg, 1994, p. 19). As shown in Table 9.2, in 1992 the second largest category of enrollment for students with disabilities was speech or language impairment, followed by mental retardation.

The "Appropriate" Services Debate

Over the years perhaps the most controversial and still unresolved issue in the implementation of the IDEA has been in regard to what is meant by an *appropriate* education. Because the act does not specify what programs and services must be provided to satisfy this guarantee, the provision of services has often been debated on a case-by-case basis. In *Board of Education v. Rowley* (1982) the U.S. Supreme Court stated that a free appropriate public education did not mean "an opportunity to achieve full potential commensurate with the opportunity provided to other children," but rather, "*access* to specialized instruction

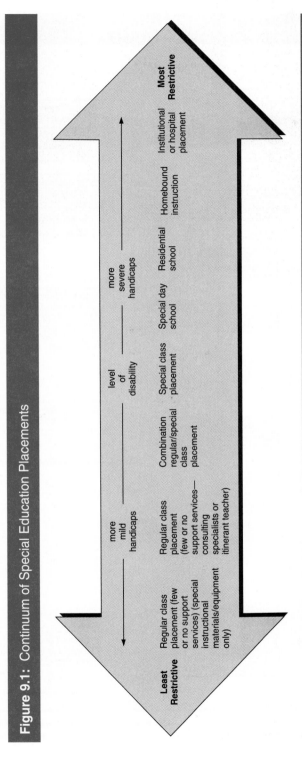

Figure 9.1: Continuum of Special Education Placements

Source: Peterson, N. L. (1988). *Early intervention for handicapped and at-risk children* (p. 337). Denver, CO: Love Publishing Company. Reprinted with permission.

Figure 9.2: The Special Education Process

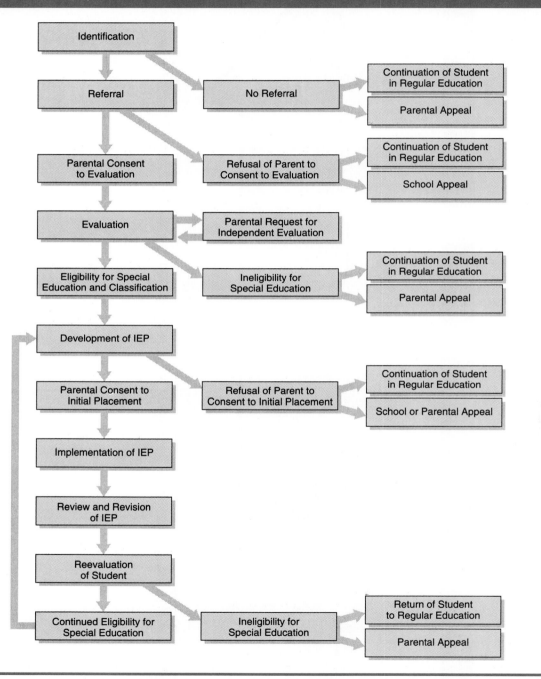

Table 9.2: Number of Elementary and Secondary Students Served in Federally Supported Education Programs for the Disabled and Number as a Percentage of Total K-12 Enrollment, by Type of Disability, School Year Ending 1978, 1988, 1992 (number served in thousands)

Type of Disability	1978 Number Served	1978 Percent of Total	1988 Number Served	1988 Percent of Total	1992 Number Served	1992 Percent of Total
Specific learning disabilities	964	2.21	1,928	4.82	2,234	5.31
Speech or language impairments	1,223	2.81	953	2.38	997	2.37
Mental retardation	933	2.14	582	1.45	538	1.28
Serious emotional disturbance	288	.66	373	.93	399	.95
Hearing impairments	85	.20	56	.14	60	.14
Orthopedic impairments	87	.20	47	.12	51	.12
Other health impairments	135	.31	45	.11	58	.14
Visual impairments	35	.08	22	.06	24	.06
Multiple disabilities	–	–	77	.19	97	.23
Deaf-blindness	–	–	1	<.005	1	<.005
Preschool disabled	–	–	363	.91	484	1.15
Autism and other	–	–	–	–	5	.01
Total	3,751	8.61	4,446	11.10	4,949	11.77

Source: U.S. Department of Education, National Center for Education Statistics. (1994). *Digest of education statistics* (Table 52). Washington, DC: U.S. Department of Education.

and related services which are designed to provide educational benefit to the handicapped child." This ruling left many educators and supporters of children with disabilities with the fear that the court had sacrificed the very heart of P. L. 94–142. Almost any program, no matter how ill conceived, might have *some* benefit. However, this fear has not been realized. In the hundreds of cases handed down by lower courts since *Rowley*, the courts have continued to support parents in their attempts to expand services to their disabled children, including year-round services, health services, and private residential placements (Gallegos, 1989). Nonetheless, cases are still determined on an individual basis and the courts do tend to accept the most *reasonable* program rather than require the *best* possible program.

The Least Restrictive Environment and Inclusion Debate

Just as the IDEA does not define what is meant by an appropriate education but leaves the issue to be decided on a case-by-case basis, so too it does not define what is meant by the "least restrictive environment" but leaves this to be decided one child at a time. The least restrictive environment issue has been central to recent and expanded efforts to increase the number of students with disabilities who are included into regular classroom settings. The *inclusion movement* is driven by a respect for diversity and by a strong commitment to the rights of stu-

How would you respond to having a student with a severe physical disability mainstreamed into your classroom?

dents with disabilities to be part of the schools and communities they share with nondisabled students (McLaughlin & Warren, 1994). To deny them this right would be discrimination (Lombardi, 1994). It has also been driven by a concern over the effectiveness of the current system from which only one in two actually graduate, and the fact that once a child is classified and placed on an IEP few actually leave special education. Those who support inclusion argue that inclusion not only contributes to the academic and social progress of children with disabilities, it creates greater tolerance on the part of students who are not disabled and better prepares them to live in an integrated society.

As a result of the inclusion movement, inclusion has become the norm, not the exception, for students with disabilities, and for the first time these students are spending more of their time in a regular classroom than in any other school setting. In 1992, 36% of disabled students spent 80% or more of their school day in regular classrooms. However, the inclusion movement has generated some concern over the extent to which students are being integrated without the support necessary to make the transition successful. Results of a longitudinal study reported by the U.S. Department of Education showed that students with disabilities who spend most of their time in regular classrooms are more likely to fail than those taught in alternative settings (Schnaiberg, 1994). There is also concern on the part of many educators and parents that inclusion is not only being used to save money at the expense of providing needed services to students with disabilities, but that it may have a detrimental effect on the learning of nondisabled students. Lastly, critics of inclusion warn against total inclusion for all children with disabilities and caution against abandoning the current continuum of placement that enables "responsible educators to make individualized decisions about the education of disabled students" (Lombardi, 1994, p. 8).

To assess your support for the concept of inclusion, complete the checklist on page 295.

Compensatory Education

Compensatory education programs designed to overcome the deficiencies associated with educational and socioeconomic disadvantages have been an important part of federal educational policy and funding since the Elementary and Secondary Education Act was passed in 1965. Title I of that act was the flagship of President Lyndon Johnson's Great Society education program (Elmore & McLaughlin, 1988). As a weapon in the War on Poverty, the intent of Title I was to "enhance the education of disadvantaged children, improve their achievement, and hence redistribute economic and social opportunities in society" (Durbin, 1989, p. 27). Federal funds were allocated to states to be reallocated to local school districts based on the number of low-income families, which was viewed as an indicator of student educational need. At the local level, services were provided to eligible students and to entire schools with high concentrations of disadvantaged students. Both disadvantaged public and nonpublic schools could receive services. The enactment of Title I stimulated a number of states to

Ask Yourself:
Inclusion Checklist

The following checklist for practicing (or prospective) teachers reflects an inclusion philosophy. The more "yes" answers, the more positive toward responsible inclusion is the respondent.

1. Are you (would you be) willing to have age-appropriate students with disabilities in your class?

2. Do (would) you modify your curriculum, instructional methods, and materials to meet the diverse needs of students in your class?

3. Are you (would you be) open to suggestions and modifications in your teaching and classroom management?

4. Are you (would you be) willing to share your teaching responsibilities with other professionals?

5. Do you expect disabled students to be as successful in meeting their own goals as nondisabled students are in meeting theirs?

6. Do (would) you call on students with disabilities as much as you call on other students in your class?

7. Do (would) you use heterogeneous grouping?

8. Do (would) you use peer tutoring?

9. Do (would) you use adaptive technology and customized software?

10. Have you attended training sessions about responsible inclusion?

Source: Lombardi, T. P. (1994). *Responsible inclusion of students with disabilities.* Bloomington, IN: Phi Delta Kappa Educational Foundation.

initiate their own compensatory education programs, not only because of the political popularity of social issues at the time, but because of the growing concern for issues of equity. By 1990, compensatory education programs were in place in over half the states (Thompson, Wood, & Honeyman, 1994).

Title I to Chapter 1 and Back

In 1981 Title I was converted into Chapter 1 of the Education Consolidation and Improvement Act. Chapter 1 retained essentially the same features as Title I, the major change being a reduction in federal regulations, placing greater responsibility for monitoring local programs on the states. In 1994, when Chapter 1 was reauthorized as part of the Elementary and Secondary Education Act, its label was changed back to Title I. More important than its name change, changes in the formula for distribution of funds favored those states with the most poor children. In addition, as pointed out in Chapter 5, in order to remain eligible for Title I funds states are required to develop school improvement plans that establish high content and performance standards, thereby linking Title I with the reform initiative laid out by the Goals 2000: Educate America Act. In 1995, approximately $7 billion in federal funds was appropriated for the Title I compensatory education program.

Types of Programs

Compensatory education programs encompass a variety of educational services delivered primarily in program-eligible schools during school hours. The most common types of programs are:

1. Early childhood readiness programs such as Head Start, which takes children between the ages of three and five and gets them ready for school. Head Start is a comprehensive program that combines educational programs, medical and nutritional benefits, parent involvement, and social services.

2. Enrichment programs in subject areas. Almost all (94%) Title I districts offer programs in reading, 64% offer math, and 25% offer programs in other language arts.

3. Programs for handicapped students. Almost three-fourths of the districts provide Title I services to mentally handicapped students. In most districts, these students must be eligible for Title I to receive services.

4. English as a second language (ESL). ESL instruction is offered to students with limited English proficiency in 8% of the districts. Again, normally the students must be eligible for Title I to receive services.

5. Programs for migrant students. Most commonly found in larger districts, these programs are offered by 14% of Title I districts. (Williams, Thorne, Michie, & Hamar, 1987)

6. Programs for primary students such as Transition Head Start, which continues Head Start services into the second grade.

7. Programs for secondary education students. Programs such as Upward Bound are directed at increasing the preparation and participation of disadvantaged youth for post-secondary education.

Most Title I instruction is provided through the "pullout" method, in which eligible students are removed from the regular classroom to receive additional instruction. Instruction is delivered in smaller classes by separately hired "Title I teachers," often with the assistance of aides and often with more equipment and materials than are available in the regular classroom. Even though there is some criticism of pullout models, they are popular with school districts because they are the safest way of meeting the requirement that Title I funds be spent only on students eligible for Title 1.

What are the disadvantages of pulling students out of the regular class to receive compensatory instruction?

Program Effectiveness

The effectiveness of compensatory education has been the subject of some controversy, especially in the early years. Studies from the late 1960s did not show Title I to be very effective in achieving lasting or long-term improvement in student achievement. More recent longitudinal studies indicate that compensatory education programs do have a positive effect on the cognitive development that is mostly observable in the primary grades and is strongest in mathematics (Ralph,

1989). These studies also show compensatory education programs to be a factor in reducing special education placements and in success in later life (Frazier, 1990). However, one troubling finding is that Title I programs are most effective with marginal students, who often make rapid improvements and are then transferred out of the program, rather than with the weakest students, who remain in the program year after year (Ralph, 1989). Another troubling result is that the positive gains observed in the early grades often are not sustained through the middle grades, when most compensatory education services end. This pattern is particularly obvious in the case of students enrolled in urban schools with a high concentration of students in poverty (Levine & Havighurst, 1992).

Meeting the Needs

To address these and other perceived shortcomings of current compensatory education policies, the suggestion has been made that Title I services be extended into the high school and be expanded to include all eligible students. Currently only 20–30% of districts operating Title I programs serve grades 10, 11, and 12. Head Start, one of the programs that appears to have the most positive results, currently serves only about one in four of all eligible 3- to 5-year-olds. Overall, Title I serves only about half of those eligible to receive remedial help (William T. Grant Foundation, 1988). Although it would require at least a doubling of current Title I funding to extend and expand the program, thoughtful

What types of compensatory education programs should be operated at the secondary level?

Teachers need to recognize the variety of learning styles related to ethnic and social differences.

policy makers and educators realize that this is what is required if President Johnson's dream of breaking the cycle of poverty is to be realized. It is also required if the very first National Education Goal, "All children in America will start school ready to learn," is to be met.

Indian Education

Indian education is the term used by most states and the federal government to refer to educational programs specifically directed at Native American children and adults. The education of Native Americans has a unique history in this country because the federal government was obligated by various treaties to provide for the education of Native American children. The course of this federal involvement, which was detailed in earlier chapters, was largely one of dictating educational policy and practice. It was not until the self-determination movement gained strength in the late 1960s that a serious commitment was made in federal policy to increase the involvement of Native Americans in the management of their own affairs, including education.

The Self-Determination Movement

The commitment to increase participation was actualized in the Indian Education Act of 1972 and its successor, the Indian Self-Determination and Education Assistance Act of 1975, and the Indian Education Amendments of 1988, all of which mandate increased participation and decision making by Native Americans. While "relearning the hard lessons of self-rule" has brought its challenges (Garcia & Ahler, 1994), the results have been significant. A number of tribes have opted to operate schools under contract with the federal government, rather than leave their operation to the Bureau of Indian Affairs (BIA). Funding is provided by the BIA, but the schools have elected Indian school boards. More Native American parents than ever before are involved actively in the education of their children, serve on school boards or special committees, or are otherwise involved in providing direction to the schools serving Native American children.

There has been a recent revival of interest in Indian education matching that shown in the late 1960s and 1970s. This has been evidenced in the Native American Languages Act of 1990 directed at the survival of Native American languages, the activities of the Indian Nations At-Risk Task Force, and the White House Conference on Indian Education (1992), whose stated purpose was to develop recommendations for the improvement of educational programs for Indians and make them more relevant to the needs of Indians. One major difference marks the current interest in Indian Education from those in the past: today Native Americans, rather than non-Indian missionaries and government officials are serving on committees and task-forces and are taking the lead in working for new legislation affecting the education of Native American children (Reyhner, 1994).

Many Native Americans have looked to the Indian Nations At-Risk Task Force to start the process of change in Indian education. The task force commissioned papers from experts in Indian education, conducted site visits and interviews, and held hearings throughout 1990 and 1991. Based on their findings the task force issued a final report and recommendations in 1991, part of which included a set of 10 educational goals for all federal, tribal, private, and public schools that educate Native American children. These goals, patterned after the National Education Goals, are presented in Figure 9.3.

Enrollments

More than 87% of Native American school children (about 300,000) attend public schools, 10% (40,000 students) attend BIA schools, and the remaining 3% (10,000 students) attend private schools (Reyhner, 1994). The combination of a growing population and limited jobs has forced many Native Americans to leave the reservation to find work (Chavers, 1994). As a result, about one-half of the Native American children attending public schools attend urban and inner city schools. There, they are likely to encounter "the same kinds of pressures and problems faced by black and Hispanic students—with the additional burden of a sometimes fierce battle of cultures" (Reeves, 1989, p. 4).

Federal Support

Public schools enrolling Native American students receive federal assistance under several programs. Public school districts that include federal, nontaxable Indian reservations receive federal impact aid as a substitute for lost tax revenues. Funds are provided under the Johnson O'Malley Act for supplemental programs in public schools that benefit Indian children and have been approved by an Indian education committee. Examples include home-school coordinators, remedial tutoring, field trips, and cultural programs (Mueller & Mueller, 1992). Funds are also provided under the Indian Education Act for supplemental instructional activities for Native American students in public schools. To ensure that Indians have a voice in the development and delivery of these programs, parental and community participation is required.

The federal government also supports the construction, operation, and maintenance of BIA schools, of which there are approximately 180, located primarily in Arizona, New Mexico, North Dakota, and South Dakota. BIA schools include day schools, boarding schools, schools operated under contract with tribal governments, and schools operated cooperatively with public schools (Mueller & Mueller, 1992). In addition, Native American students in both BIA-supported and public schools receive special services if they are disadvantaged, have no or limited English proficiency, have a disability, or are enrolled in vocational education.

The School Experience

Despite the many changes and improvements in Indian education, the hearings, conferences, individual meetings held by the Indian Nations At-Risk Task Force

Figure 9.3: National Education Goals for American Indians and Alaska Natives

Goal 1: Readiness for School

By the year 2000 all Native children will have access to early childhood education programs that provide the language, social, physical, spiritual, and cultural foundations they need to succeed in school and to reach their full potential as adults.

Goal 2: Maintain Native Languages and Cultures

By the year 2000 all schools will offer Native students the opportunity to maintain and develop their tribal languages and will create a multicultural environment that enhances the many cultures represented in the school.

Goal 3: Literacy

By the year 2000 all Native children in school will be literate in the language skills appropriate for their individual levels of development. They will be competent in their English oral, reading, listening, and writing skills.

Goal 4: Student Academic Achievement

By the year 2000 every Native student will demonstrate mastery of English, mathematics, science, history, geography, and other challenging academic skills necessary for an educated citizenry.

Goal 5: High School Graduation

By the year 2000 all Native students capable of completing high school will graduate. They will demonstrate civic, social, creative, and critical thinking skills necessary for ethical, moral, and responsible citizenship and important in modern tribal, national, and world societies.

Goal 6: High-Quality Native and non-Native School Personnel

By the year 2000 the numbers of Native educators will double, and the colleges and universities that train the nation's teachers will develop a curriculum that prepares teachers to work effectively with the variety of cultures, including the Native cultures, that are served by schools.

Goal 7: Safe and Alcohol-Free and Drug-Free Schools

By the year 2000 every school responsible for educating Native students will be free of alcohol and drugs and will provide safe facilities and an environment conductive to learning.

Goal 8: Adult Education and Lifelong Learning

By the year 2000 every Native adult will have the opportunity to be literate and to obtain the necessary academic, vocational and technical skills and knowledge needed to gain meaningful employment and to exercise the rights and responsibilities of tribal and national citizenship.

Goal 9: Restructuring Schools

By the year 2000 schools serving Native children will be restructured to effectively meet the academic, cultural, spiritual, and social needs of students for developing strong, healthy, self-sufficient communities.

Goal 10: Parental, Community, and Tribal Partnerships

By the year 2000 every school responsible for educating Native students will provide opportunities for Native parents and tribal leaders to help plan and evaluate the governance, operation, and performance of their educational programs.

Source: U.S. Department of Education (1991). *Indian Nations at Risk: An Educational Strategy for Action, Final Report of the Indian Nations at Risk Task Force.* Washington, DC: U.S. Department of Education.

(INATF) in preparation for its report, and the preparation for the White House Conference on Indian Education revealed that many Native American children attend schools with an unfriendly climate "that fails to promote appropriate academic, social, cultural, and spiritual development," and where the curriculum is presented "from a purely Western (European) perspective, ignoring all that the historical perspective of American Indians and Alaskan Natives has to contribute," by teachers "with inadequate skills and training to teach Native children effectively," and "with few Native educators as role models." In such an environment, Native students tend to lose their native language abilities and find themselves relegated to lower ability tracks (INATF, 1991). And, in far too many public schools, "perfunctory parent committees funded by meagerly funded federal projects" is the only involvement Native Americans have in the administration of the education of their children (Charleston, 1994).

While there are many excellent schools serving Native American/Alaskan Native children, the above description would not be an uncommon one. Some of the disastrous results have been described elsewhere in this text: the highest dropout rate of any racial or ethnic group, lower levels of educational attainment, and the lowest rate of postsecondary participation of any group. Absenteeism also runs high among Native American students: from 15% to 25% per year, compared to the national averages of 7% (Chavers, 1991). And, tragically, a suicide rate for adolescents that is 10 times that of their Anglo peers.

The Response

To address these conditions, the Indian Nations At-Risk Task Force declared four national priorities for American Indian/Alaskan Native education:

- Developing parent-based and culturally, linguistically, and developmentally appropriate early childhood education;

- Making the promotion of students' tribal language and culture a responsibility of the school;

- training more Native teachers; and

- strengthening tribal and Bureau of Indian Affairs colleges. (Reyhner, 1994, p. 35)

Recommendations of the White House Conference on Indian Education were similar. In particular, heavy emphasis was placed on tribal involvement and control of education at all levels as a necessary step to reforming Indian education. According to the Final Report of the White House Conference (1992b): "Local control and determination of needs is a demand and goal of all segments of society. Indian country is not different in this respect, but there is additional weight behind this demand given the inability of society to accurately perceive the cultural aspects integral to the values and goals of Indian communities" (p. 47).

Many of the problems of Indian education are a result of problems in the larger society, including racism and poverty, and until these problems are solved Indian education will continue to reflect them (White House Conference on Indian Education, 1992a). Nonetheless, there is much that can be done, and is being done, to improve Indian education. Native American/Alaskan Native communities have become increasingly aware of the fact that they must take responsibility for the educational systems to whom they entrust their youth. Fortunately, these communities are willing and anxious to assume this responsibility. As was affirmed at the White House Conference:

> Tribal people want the highest quality education possible for all people of all ages in their population. . . . We firmly believe education is the key to finding solutions to the problems confronting us. . . . We must establish education systems that contribute productively to the growth and development of all American societies. (Charleston, 1994, pp. 18–19)

Desegregation

School *desegregation* is a complex and controversial issue. It is multidimensional in that it has personal, political, social, legal, and educational aspects. Historically, children and youth in the United States generally have attended socially segregated schools, a reflection of a segregated society. They also have attended socioeconomically segregated schools. This is particularly true for black children, but it is also true for other social and ethnic minority groups. School segregation also extends to teachers. Black teachers typically are concentrated in schools that primarily serve black students, while white teachers tend to be concentrated in schools that primarily serve white students.

The First Phase

Desegregation is a strategy for realizing constitutional protection and equality of educational opportunity. Desegregation became a major issue in American education with the landmark Supreme Court case of *Brown v. Board of Education* (1954). This case involved elementary school students in Topeka, Kansas, who filed suit challenging a Kansas law that sanctioned racially separate schools. The Court ruled that segregation has a detrimental effect and concluded that the doctrine of "separate but equal" has no place in public education. Recognizing the importance of any order they might make and the uniqueness of each community, the Court ordered that schools must desegregate "with all deliberate speed." Local school districts were charged with the responsibility of creating desegregation plans under the supervision of the closest federal district court.

Desegregation Techniques

The design of any specific desegregation plan is determined by the extent of the segregation, geographic considerations, demographic trends, community support and, of course, the law. Desegregation plans employ a variety of techniques that may be classified as voluntary or involuntary, depending on whether students are allowed to choose the school they attend. Specific desegregation plans may include predominantly mandatory techniques, voluntary techniques, or a combination of the two (Fife, 1992). Figure 9.4 presents a summary of the most common desegregation techniques.

Figure 9.4: Desegregation Plans

Voluntary

1. *Open enrollment plans* (freedom of choice) allow students to attend any school in the district and are rarely used anymore because they also serve the interests of those attempting to escape desegregation.
2. *Magnet plans* may involve an entire school focusing on a particular curriculum or teaching style (dedicated magnets) or only part of the school curriculum having a special focus (minimagnets).
3. *Majority-to-minority transfers* allow students to transfer from a school where they are in the majority to a school where they are in the minority, or in some cases to schools where they are less in the majority. Participation is greater if transportation is provided.

Involuntary

1. *Pairing and clustering,* which involves exchanging students of two or more schools (one white, one black) by sending half the students to one school and half to the other, or sending certain grades to one school and the other grades to the other.
2. *Rezoning* involves changing attendance zones to improve the racial balance between two or more schools.
3. *Magnet schools* under involuntary plans also have a special curriculum or teaching style and are intended to reduce "white flight."

Source: Fife, B. L. (1992). *Desegregation in American schools: Comparative intervention strategies.* New York: Praeger.

In the early years of school desegregation, attention was focused on the *de jure* segregated districts in the southern states. Initially, districts attempted to accomplish desegregation by adopting freedom of choice plans. In most instances, these plans had little impact on the level of segregation, and a decade after *Brown* little progress toward integration had been made. In *Green v. County School Board of New Kent County* (1968), the Supreme Court ruled that if freedom of choice plans were not working, other means *must* be used. These means could include forced busing, as established in *Swann v. Charlotte-Mecklenburg Board of Education* (1971), when the Court endorsed the use of reasonable student busing as well as pairing schools, consolidating schools, rezoning, reassigning teachers, and racial quotas. Following *Swann,* the courts exercised broad powers in ordering remedies, and substantial desegregation was attained in southern school districts (McCarthy & McCabe, 1992). Table 9.3 lists some important Supreme Court desegregation cases related to public schools.

The Second Phase

The second phase of desegregation moved beyond the *de jure* segregation in the South to the *de facto* segregation that existed in many communities outside the South. In these communities, state law did not explicitly mandate segregation, but local zoning ordinances, housing restrictions, attendance zones, gerrymandering, or other deliberate official actions were designed to segregate blacks. In 1972, 46% of all black students in the South attended schools where whites were in the majority, as compared to only 28% in the North and the West (Webb & Sherman, 1989). The next year, in a case involving Denver, Colorado, *Keyes v. School District No. 1* (1973), the Supreme Court held that when official actions

Table 9.3: Selected U.S. Supreme Court Desegregation Cases Related to the Public Schools

Case	Decision
Brown v. Board of Education of Topeka (1954)	The doctrine of separate but equal in education is a violation of the Fourteenth Amendment.
Green v. County School Board of New Kent County (1968)	Local school boards should immediately take whatever steps are necessary to achieve a unitary system.
Swann v. Charlotte-Mecklenburg Board of Education (1971)	Transportation of students to opposite-race school is permissible to achieve desegregation.
Keyes v. School District No. 1 (Denver) (1973)	Proof of intent to segregate in one part of a district is sufficient to find the district to be segregated and to warrant a districtwide remedy. For purposes of defining a segregated school, blacks and Hispanics may be considered together.
Milliken v. Bradley (1974)	In devising judicial remedies for desegregation, the scope of the desegregation remedy cannot exceed the scope of the violation.
Dayton Board of Education v. Brinkman (1977)	Judicially mandated desegregation plans cannot exceed the impact of the segregatory practices.
Board of Education of Oklahoma City Public Schools v. Dowell (1991)	Desegregation decrees are not intended to operate in perpetuity, and can be dissolved when a district has made good faith effort to comply and to the extent practical has eliminated the vestiges of past discrimination.
Freeman v. Pitts (1992)	Lower courts can relinquish supervision of a school district under desegregation decree in incremental stages before full compliance has been achieved in every area of school operations.

had a segregative intent, they were just as illegal as *de jure* segregation. In subsequent cases, the Court clarified that the mere existence of segregation was not sufficient evidence to warrant court action (*Washington v. Davis*, 1976) and that the scope of the remedy could not exceed the scope of the violation (*Milliken v. Bradley*, 1974) or the impact of the segregatory practices (*Dayton Board of Education v. Brinkman*, 1977). Any concern that the Court might be retreating from the desegregation arena was satisfied by two 1979 decisions involving Detroit, and Columbus, Ohio, where the Court reasoned that:

if school officials are unable to refute that intentional school segregation existed when *Brown I* was rendered, their post-1954 acts must be assessed in light of their *continuing affirmative duty* to eliminate the effects of such segregation. . . . Racially neutral actions cannot satisfy this duty; school officials must take affirmative steps to eradicate school segregation until all vestiges of discrimination are eliminated. (McCarthy & McCabe, 1992, pp. 487–88)

During the 1980s, although the Reagan administration did little to pursue desegregation cases, numerous school districts continued to be involved in desegregation struggles. And, magnet schools became a popular strategy to achieve desegregation and to reduce *white flight. Magnet school plans* were one of the favored strategies of the Reagan administration in out-of-court settlements of desegregation cases, and by the 1990s were incorporated into the concept of *choice* in education (Spring, 1991). Magnet school plans are also a response to the substantial opposition to transferring pupils for desegregation purposes and the growing minority population in urban areas that works against achieving desired levels of integration.

What types of magnet schools have proven to be most success-ful in achieving integration? What made them attractive?

New Directions in School Desegregation

In the decades after *Brown* numerous districts across the country came under court decree to end segregation. Many of these tried in good faith for years to implement the court's decree but were frustrated in their efforts by changing community demographics. When taken back to court, school officials argued that these changes were beyond their control and asked that the decrees be lifted or that the remedies be amended, especially those that depended on such remedies as wide-scale busing (Vacca & Hudgins, 1992). Direction was finally given by the Supreme Court in 1991 in *Board of Education of Oklahoma City Public Schools v. Dowell.* The court ruled that a court order desegregation decree can be terminated or dissolved when the school board has *in good faith* made efforts to comply with the decree and has *to the extent practical,* given past history and current conditions, eliminated the vestiges of past discrimination. According to the court, school desegregation decrees "are not intended to operate in perpetuity." In effect, the court told the lower courts overseeing desegregation decrees that "old issues must be laid to rest after a reasonable period of years, and today's business must move into the future as necessitated by changing internal and external needs" (Vacca & Hudgins, 1992, p. 443).

The next year, in *Freeman v. Pitts,* the Supreme Court continued down the course charted by *Dowell* and ruled that federal judges can exercise "incremental withdrawal" of their supervision of desegregation orders and suggested that a specific time limit should be placed on a district's efforts to desegregate, especially if the district is one experiencing rapid demographic changes. The effect of these two decisions has been to not only bring an end to the judicial oversight of desegregation plans for a number of school districts, but to provide these districts the opportunity to fashion new remedies that appear more likely to be successful given the current circumstances of the district.

While on the one hand the courts have agreed that changing demographics may warrant the disolution of desegregation decrees, on the other hand, other courts have recently ruled that mere implementation of the desegregation plan is not sufficient to warrant lifting of the decree if there has been no improvement in student outcomes. For example, in cases involving Yonkers, New York, and Kansas City, the courts have looked at the lagging achievement outcomes of minority students and said that equality of access was not enough, that some level of improvement had to be reached before the desegregation decree could be lifted. At the time of this writing the Kansas City case (*Missouri v. Jenkins*) has been accepted for review by the Supreme Court. The outcome could not only signal a whole new standard for desegregation cases, but for the entire educational system.

Effects of School Desegregation

Of the numerous possible effects of desegregation, the most attention has been focused on three: the effect on the academic achievement of minority students, the effect on self-esteem and racial/ethnic identity of minority students, and the effect on interracial contact and community integration.

Effect on Academic Achievement

The voluminous body of research regarding the effects of desegregation on academic achievement has yielded mixed results. However, the evidence seems to suggest some small though positive effect on the achievement of minority students (Schofield, 1989), and no effect on the achievement of majority students. Where desegregation has resulted in positive gains in achievement, the most likely explanation seems to be that the desegregation brought about changes in context and opportunities that increase: (1) the expectations of students to achieve, (2) the competence and motivation of teachers, and (3) the facilities, learning materials, and other resources to which minority students have access (Hawley, 1992). The level of integration also appears to be an important variable in how much positive gain is realized. The research suggests that desegregation is most effective when minority enrollment reaches 20% to 30%. At very small numbers, minority children are likely to feel isolated or stereotyped. At large percentages of minority student enrollments, majority withdrawals increase, resulting in resegregation (Yinger, 1986).

Effect on Self-Esteem of and Racial Identity of Minority Students

A common concern among minority parents is the extent to which integration will negatively effect their children's self-esteem and racial identity. In fact, a number of studies have shown that minority children's self-esteem is lowered by desegregation, at least in the short run. However, the majority of the studies show either no effect (Dawkins, 1994), or that the longer the minority student remains in the integrated school, the higher his or her self-esteem becomes (Webb & Sherman, 1989).

Effect on Interracial Contact and Community Integration

There is a growing body of evidence that desegregation in education promotes integration in the community, in higher education, and in the workplace. The

Busing as a strategy to achieve school desegregation has met with mixed results.

research shows that blacks who have been educated in desegregated schools are more likely than blacks educated in segregated schools: (1) to attend and succeed in predominantly white colleges and universities, (2) to work in desegregated job settings, (3) to have white social contacts and live in integrated neighborhoods, and (4) to have higher levels of educational attainment (Dawkins, 1994).

The Current Struggle

While many districts across the nation have successfully achieved desegregation, on a national level segregation is actually on the rise. A recent study by the Harvard Project on School Resegregation found that two out of every three black children attended schools in which blacks are the majority of the student population. This is the highest rate of segregation since 1968 when 77% of black

Were you involved in any school desegregation programs? What were the advantages? Disadvantages?

students attended predominantly black schools. Hispanic students are even more likely to experience segregation: 73% attend minority-dominated schools ("Segregation is on the Rise," 1994). Large urban districts in particular have become more segregated as poor black and Hispanic students are segregated by housing patterns into neighborhoods and schools with other poor students. However, while the segregation efforts of the last quarter century have not brought about the changes in the schools or in the communities they serve that many envisioned, there is no question that desegregated schools are a condition of a desegregated society. In the past, the courts have been a major instrument for achieving desegregation. Their retreat from the foreground places responsibility on our political leaders. Unless a commitment to the desegregation of our schools is made by the political leadership of the nation, the states, and local communities, equality of educational opportunity for children of every race will remain a dream.

Promotion of Gender Equity

In education, the term *gender equity* refers to "the elimination of sex-role stereotyping and sex bias from the educational process, thus providing the opportunity and environment to validate and empower individuals as they make appropriate career and life choices" (Hilke & Conway-Gerhardt, 1994, p. 8). In the 1970s, national attention was focused on gender equity in education, which it was hoped would be achieved with the passage of Title IX in 1972 (and its implementing regulations in 1975) prohibiting sex discrimination in access to courses, extracurricular programs, instructional materials, counseling and counseling materials, employment, and any other policies and regulations governing the treatment of students and employees. And, indeed, Title IX did result in some significant changes.

The Persistence of Gender Inequity

Yet more than two decades after the passage of Title IX, gender equity in education is far from being achieved. According to the much debated 1992 report of the American Association of University Women (AAUW), *How Schools Shortchange Girls:* "Whether one looks at achievement scores, curriculum design, self-esteem levels, or staffing patterns, it is clear that sex and gender make a difference in the nation's . . . schools. There is clear evidence that the educational system is not meeting girls' needs" (p. 2). The 1992 AAUW was one of three reports issued in a three-year period in a stated attempt to include concern for gender equity in the ongoing debates on education reform. The concerns highlighted by these reports, which mirror those of a large body of previous research, are discussed below.

The first AAUW report, *Shortchanging Girls, Shortchanging America* (1991), documented the results of a survey of 3,000 school children and reported a "dramatic and disproportionate loss of self-esteem among adolescent girls and linked it to the way they were treated by schools" (Schmidt, 1994, p. 16). This decline in self-esteem becomes greater as girls progress through school (Sadker & Sadker, 1994). The AAUW report found that:

- Teachers initiate more communication with males than females in the classroom, strengthening boy's sense of importance.

- Boys are praised more often than girls for the intellectual content and quality of their work, while girls are praised more often for neatness and form.

- When teachers criticize boys, they often tell them that their failings are due to lack of effort. Girls are not given this message, suggesting that effort would not improve their results. (pp. 19–20)

Not surprisingly, since self-esteem affects aspirations, the study also found that as girls grow older they become less confident in their academic abilities, and express more limited career aspirations.

Have you experienced sex bias in your education? Sex discrimination?

The second AAUW report, *How Schools Shortchange Girls* (1992), represented a comprehensive compilation of more than 1,300 research studies on the experience of girls in schools. The research reviewed documented the differential treatment of girls across a number of dimensions in the classroom and the curriculum, and that this differential treatment is consistent across grades, subjects, districts, and the sex or experience of the teacher. Among the findings from the review were that boys receive more teacher attention of all kinds, that girls remain underrepresented in curriculum materials, and that the instructional activities that are used appeal more to boys' interests than girls and are presented in formats in which boys excel.

More importantly, the report found that the results of this differential treatment are evidenced in the lower academic performance of girls documented in the previous chapter, and in lower levels of self-confidence, which affects their choice of classes and careers. The study found that girls and boys begin their school experience equal in measured ability, but by the time they reach high school girls have fallen behind. Girls are also less likely to take advanced placement courses, and even when their math scores are the same as boys, they are likely to be placed in a lower ability group (Scott & McCollum, 1993).

The third AAUW report, *Hostile Hallways,* dealt with the problem of sexual harassment in school. The results of this national survey are discussed in the following chapter.

Obviously the schools are not solely responsible for the decline in girls' self-esteem, achievement, or career choices. Society still holds different expectations for girls than boys, and sex-role stereotypes and sex bias abound. However, the schools do contribute to the way society shortchanges girls and can therefore make an important contribution toward correcting gender equity (Scollay, 1994).

In Search of Gender Equity

The reform movement has focused attention on many of the problems and issues facing the schools with one notable exception. The issue of gender and the problem of gender bias were conspicuously absent from the reports, and subsequently from reform efforts (Scollay, 1994). Yet, if gender equity is to become a reality in our schools, and not rhetoric, more must be done than ensuring that boys and girls are taught in the same classroom or have the same right to enroll in courses or participate in extracurricular activities (Fennema, 1987). The attainment of gender equity requires the elimination of three forms of limitations by sex: sex role stereotyping, sex bias, and sex discrimination. *Sex role stereotyping* is the attribution of specific behaviors, abilities, personality characteristics, and interests to one sex. *Sex bias* is the biased behavior that results from believing in the sex role stereotypes. *Sex discrimination* is any action that denies opportunities, privileges, or rewards to a person or persons because of their sex, in violation of the law (Carelli, 1988).

The promotion of gender equity in education is a cyclical process (see Figure 9.5) that involves four major steps:

- *Awareness* involves sharing with staff, students, families, and the community ways that students are treated differently in school, the home, and the community. This can be done as part of activities involved in the development of a board-approved plan to promote gender equity.

- *Analysis* involves having all stakeholders evaluate their particular setting—classroom, home, worksite—to determine how and where gender disequity exists. This can be done through the use of such methods as gender equity checklists, videotaping for analysis, and peer interaction.

- *Action* involves just that—taking positive steps toward achieving gender equity in the school, home, or worksite.

Figure 9.5: A Model for Eliminating Gender Inequity

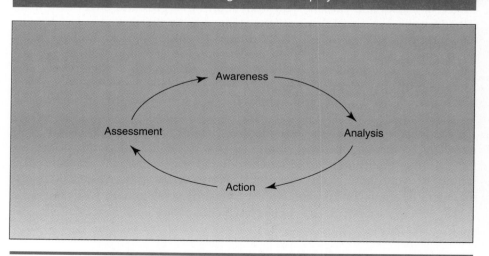

Source: Hilke, E. V., & Conway-Gerhardt, C. (1994). *Gender equity in education* (p. 18). Bloomington, IN: Phi Delta Kappa Educational Foundation.

Assessment involves assessing the effectiveness of the actions taken to direct future awareness activities, needs analysis, and action plans (Hilke & Conway-Gerhardt, 1994).

One positive indication that the recent attention given to gender equity is having positive results is the inclusion of gender equity provisions in a number of programs authorized by the 1994 reauthorization of the Elementary and Secondary Education Act. Yet more is needed. The attainment of gender equity should be a primary goal of all educational institutions. As we strive to prepare our citizens for the twenty-first century and to remain competitive in the world markets, Plato's words of 2,500 years ago seem remarkably relevant: "Nothing can be more absurd than the practice . . . of men and women not following the same pursuits with all their strength and with one mind, for thus the state . . . is reduced to a half" (Laws, VII, 805).

Adult and Continuing Education

Adult education is instruction provided to individuals beyond the age of compulsory attendance who have either completed or interrupted their formal education. Each year billions of dollars are spent on adult education. Millions of adults commit even more millions of hours to adult education activities. This monetary and time expenditure represents a significant involvement in education that is not part of the formal educational system, but is part of a changing concept of education, one in which education does not end with high school or college graduation but is a lifelong process (U.S. Department of Education, 1987). In 1991, a staggering 57.4 million adults were enrolled in some type of adult education. Of these, 30% said their reason for taking the course was personal/social, 60% said the reason was to advance on the job, for 9% the reason was to train for a new job, and for 13% the reason was to complete a degree or diploma (U.S. Bureau of the Census, 1994).

Adult and Continuing Education Defined

The terms *adult education* and *continuing education* are often used interchangeably, although some educators limit discussion of adult education to the so-called entitlement programs for disadvantaged adults funded under Title I of the Education Amendments of 1984: adult basic education (ABE), high school equivalency (general education diploma or GED), and English as a second language (ESL). Continuing education is considered to be a much broader concept, including not only compensatory education programs for adults but career development programs, degree programs, and vocational offerings.

Adult Education Providers

Adult education providers include (1) *tax supported agencies and institutions*—colleges and universities, community and technical colleges, cooperative extension services, the armed forces, correctional institutions, and libraries and museums; (2) *nonprofit, self-supporting agencies and institutions*—religious institutions, health institutions, community-based agencies, service clubs, voluntary organizations, professional organizations, worker education programs, and national adult education organizations; (3) *for-profit providers*—correspondence schools, proprietary schools, private tutors and teachers, degree-granting colleges and universities, consultant and workshop providers, publishers of how-to books, videotapes, and audio tapes, and business and industry human resource development programs; and (4) *non organized learning opportunities* (Apps, 1992).

Influence of Technology

How might distance education be used to provide professional development for teachers?

Adult education is offered in a variety of formats, including formal courses, television courses, workshops, seminars, lectures, institutes, correspondence courses, audio and video tapes, interactive technologies, and distance education. *Distance education* is characterized by a separation in space and time for the majority of teaching and learning activities. Teaching takes place to a large extent through audio, video, computer, and print technologies, and learning generally is on an individual basis through independent study in the student's home or workplace (Kaye, 1989). Correspondence courses are perhaps the oldest form of distance education. More recently, distance education has concentrated on the use of technology to provide greater learning opportunities for adults. For example:

> using teleconferencing, students and the instructor can be scattered over great distances. The instructor can use satellite television to provide information, video clips, still photographs, and graphics. In most situations, students can get an instructor's immediate response to their questions via an 800-number telephone system. (Apps, 1992, p. 32)

Multimedia technology is also having a positive impact on adult education. Multimedia programs often make it possible for previously illiterate adults to become literate faster than through traditional forms of instruction. And, in business and industry, a number of large corporations have created multimedia environments that facilitate self-directed learning through interactive training programs, often accessible at the workstation (Dickinson, 1991).

Adult Education, Illiteracy, and Economic Development

In recent years, adult education has been viewed as a major weapon in the battle against illiteracy and as a means of economic development. An estimated 25 million Americans—nearly 1 in every 7—are functionally illiterate and another 20 to 30 million function at the fifth to eighth grade level.

Recognizing the magnitude of the illiteracy problem and its impact on economic development, President Reagan announced a National Adult Education Initiative in 1983. In the years immediately following, a number of major initiatives were launched, including B. Dalton Bookseller's National Literacy Initiative and Project Literacy U.S. (PLUS), a federally sponsored program that has as its

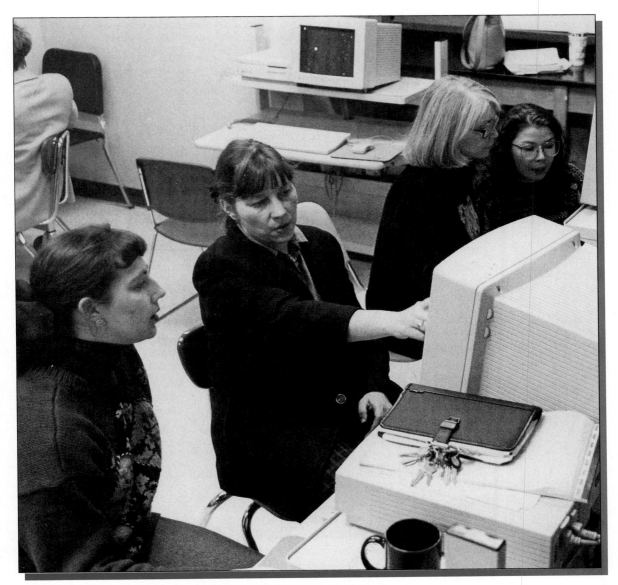

Adult learners comprise a growing segment of today's population.

goal the complete elimination of illiteracy in the United States. As a result of these campaigns, millions of calls have been received at local and national hotlines from students and potential volunteers. In fact, many of the literacy programs in the United States are sponsored by organizations made up of volunteer tutors. Two such volunteer organizations, Literacy Volunteers of America and Laubach Literacy Action, serve more than 200,000 adults. The primary target of these two groups are adults with little or no literacy skills (Farris, 1992).

As discussed in the preceding chapter, higher levels of education are associated with higher earnings, higher socioeconomic status, and reduced unemployment. Higher levels of educational attainment are also associated with higher levels of worker productivity and the ability of workers to adapt to changes in technology, better health, increased participation in the democratic process, and a host of other benefits to the individual receiving the education, his or her family, and the community where he or she resides. Adult education is one of the best investments society can make, and without it the National Education Goal, "By the year 2000 every adult American will be literate and will possess the knowledge and skills necessary to compete in a global economy and exercise the rights and responsibilities of citizenship," will surely not be met.

Vocational-Technical Education

One-half of high school graduates do not go on to college; they enter the world of work. *Vocational-technical education* is designed to provide an alternative to college preparation and to prepare students for employment in all occupations except those requiring at least a baccalaureate degree. Most vocational-technical education offered at the secondary level occurs in comprehensive high schools, though vocational technical high schools are also common. While almost all high school students take at least one vocational education course before they graduate (vocational education is the major provider of computer training in secondary schools), less than one in four graduate as a vocational student, defined as having earned at least 3 credits within one vocational program area ("National Report Card for Vo-tech," 1994). Enrollments in vocational education have been declining steadily over the last decade or longer. This decline has been attributed to the increased academic graduation requirements that have been enacted by a number of states. To provide for the required increase in academic courses within their budgetary limits, some high schools have had to reduce their vocational educational offerings.

The historic goal of vocational education has been to address the needs of the student as well as the labor market. However, in the last decade, high youth unemployment, the large numbers of youth who have graduated from vocational programs but are unemployed or employed outside their field of training, increased international competition, and a series of reports that have raised serious concerns about the current status and future supply of skilled workers have brought into question the extent to which vocational education is meeting these goals. At the same time, reports such as *America's Choice: Higher Skills or Lower Wages* (NCEE, 1990) have emphasized the serious national imperative in terms of educating a highly qualified, technologically competent workforce. Reports such as these, and the attention given them, has "lifted vocational-technical education from relative obscurity to a place of prominence in the ongoing debate surrounding school reform" (National Center for Research on Vocational Education, 1993, p. 11).

Have you participated in any vocational education program? How has it benefited you in your college career?

The Transformation of Vocational-Technical Education

Although the financial support and the delivery of vocational-technical education is primarily the responsibility of the local school district, and although local programs are determined to a great extent by the needs of the local community, the federal government has also played a key role in shaping the face of vocational-technical education by the leadership and policy direction that it has provided on a national level. The federal government has traditionally viewed vocational-technical education as vital both to our national defense and to our continued economic development. Federal support for vocational-technical education began with the Smith Hughes Act of 1917. Unfortunately, the key provisions of the Smith Hughes Act, and subsequent reauthorizations and amendments, contributed to a separation of vocational education from other parts of the curriculum. For example, in order to receive funds, each state was required to have a state board for vocational education. This requirement often led to the creation of a board separate from the state board of education, and in some states two distinct and separate governance structures were created (National Center for Research in Vocational Education, 1993). The impact of this separation has been evidenced through the years not only in such obvious ways as the development of separate teacher education programs, but in less obvious ways such as the ascribing of a lower status to vocational education, its teachers, and students.

The Perkins Act

A dramatic change in the direction of federal policy relative to vocational-technical education came with the passage of the Carl D. Perkins Vocational and Applied Technology Education Act of 1990. Of major importance, the act calls for the *integration* of academic and vocational education. In so ordering, for the first time federal vocational legislation shifted its focus "from the traditional jobs-skills orientation toward the broader purposes of using vocational education as a vehicle for learning academic and other kinds of thinking skills and for linking thought with action" (Wirt, 1991, p. 426).

The Perkins Act also sought to encourage articulation between two parts of the educational system involved in vocational-education by providing funding for *"Tech Prep"* programs—cooperative arrangements that combine two years of technology-oriented preparation in high school with two years of advanced preparation at the community college. Tech prep represents a shift of emphasis for secondary vocational-technical education from preparation for work to preparation for post-secondary education. Many educators view tech-prep programs as one of the most effective strategies to produce the technological workforce needed to assure the nation's international competitiveness (Wilcox, 1991). If tech-prep programs are successful in attracting minorities and women, they could play a significant role in increasing the educational and professional attainments of these groups (Petrina, Craven, & Powell, 1993).

Two other important features of the Perkins Act were the targeting of 75% of the Act's funds to programs that serve large concentrations of poor, handicapped, and English language deficient students, and grants to encourage cooperative arrangements between business and education to prepare students for transition from school to the world of work. As noted by Rep. Perkins at the House hearings on the bill, "every other major industrial nation has a structured system to assist young people make the transition from school to work; in the United States, high school graduates must rely on an ad hoc network of parents, relatives, school counselors, and the want-ads to find a job" (Black, 1993, p. 25).

In the few years since the passage of the Perkins Act, school districts across the country have increased their efforts to establish school-to-work programs, and several states have adopted mandates requiring school districts to provide work transition programs (Black, 1993). A brief description of these programs follows.

School-to-Work Transition Programs

As the pace of adoption of school-to-work transition programs has quickened, a number of program models have emerged: the previously described tech-prep; career academies (schools-within-schools where students explore careers while continuing with their rigorous academic program [Black, 1993]); school-to-apprenticeship programs, cooperative education, youth apprenticeships, and business-education compacts (Hudelson, 1994). The biggest impetus for school-to-work transition programs has come from the 1994 School-to-Work Opportunities Act. As described in Chapter 5, this act provides funds to states and school districts to develop school-to-work programs that include a school-based learning component, a work-based learning component, and connecting activities such as guidance and counseling, mentoring, technical assistance to employers, and coordinating with employers. In order to qualify for funding, in addition to these components a program must:

- integrate work-based and school-based learning and academic and vocational learning,
- build effective linkages between secondary and postsecondary education,
- provide all students opportunities to complete a career major,
- give students a clear understanding of the industry they are preparing to enter (including appropriate work experience),
- provide all students with equal access to the full range of program offerings. (Hudelson, 1994, p. 23)

While most school-to-work programs are too new to have undergone any evaluation using longitudinal data, preliminary data do indicate that students involved in these programs are more likely to stay in school than drop out. For many, the opportunities these programs provide to work closely with an interested adult and to receive more career counseling may be what is making the difference (Black, 1993). Results also indicate that the integration of academic and vocational programs is having positive results in terms of meeting the goal of the Perkins Act "to make the U.S. more competitive in the world economy by developing more fully the academic and occupational skills of all segments of the population."

Professional Reflections

"We must strive to help our children develop confidence in their abilities to learn and to realize there is no limit to their potential. Teachers must establish positive, high expectations for all students and provide the support that it takes to live up to those expectations . . .

Sharon Johnson, Teacher of the Year, Arkansas

"Value every student and believe that each one can be successful. Be friendly to them all, but don't be their pal. They need a mentor. Treat them as well as you would treat an adult guest in your home, and never take personally negative comments they may make. You must be the role model for how you wish for them to behave."

Sarah Pratt, Teacher of the Year, North Carolina

National Skills Standards

A part of the concern about the current status of vocational-technical education has focused on whether students are gaining the skills that are expected of entry-level workers by industry, and whether they are and will receive the skills needed for the workforce of tomorrow. One attempt to establish standards came from the Labor Department's Secretary's Commission on Achieving Necessary Skills (SCANS), which has developed generic skills standards that are said to be needed of all workers. While this effort is of some value, it provides no insight as to what level of skill is needed for any particular job. To more directly address this issue, the Goals 2000 Act established a National Skills Standards Board to develop entry-level standards for clusters of occupations.

The establishment of standards is seen as a way to promote clearer goals and direction for the curriculum and students, greater accountability for programs and students, higher wages and greater mobility, and higher public confidence and satisfaction (Hoachlander & Rahn, 1994). Establishing an effective system of national standards involves resolving a host of issues ranging from how and by whom standards will be determined, to how they will be measured. While tough challenges, the benefits justify the effort. As noted in Chapter 5, these standards have the potential to revolutionize vocational education.

Future Prospects

The future of vocational-technical education will undoubtedly be shaped by the development of national skills standards and the establishment of a system of school-to-work transition programs in this country similar to that found in other industrialized nations. The increased emphasis on readiness and the integration of the academic and vocational programs serves to not only strengthen the vocational-technical program, but to enrich the general and college-preparatory programs as well. The growth of collaborative ventures between vocational-technical education and business make the corporate sector a more active partner in the preparation of students. And, the rapid advances in technology, while placing increased demands on vocational-technical education, also promise to raise its status (Silberman, 1991).

We are now in a period during which vocational-technical education has the potential to regain the position of importance in the educational system it held in earlier periods of our nation's history. Perhaps now more than ever there is a growing recognition that a strong vocational-technical system is a necessary ingredient in the reform of the educational system of this country, the achievement of the national educational goals, and the effective preparation of the workforce of the future.

Summary

Desegregation is one of many strategies for realizing equality of educational opportunity. It is also a strategy based on constitutionally guaranteed protections. Educating children with disabilities and language minority students, and ensuring sex equity, are other strategies similarly based. Although the financial support afforded these programs is not guaranteed, unless the Supreme Court reverses current law and decisions, their existence is. Other strategies—compensatory education, Indian education, adult education, and vocational education—are solely creations of statute and rely entirely on state and federal statutes for their existence.

The presence of each of these strategies in the American educational system has served to expand not only the educational opportunities of the targeted populations, but of all students. It is largely through the efforts of those asserting their rights under the constitutionally based programs that the rights of all students have been expanded. The success of our educational system and, indeed, our economic and social structure depends on the full participation of all children. This chapter focused attention on strategies for increasing equality of educational opportunity. The next chapter turns to strategies directed at specific populations of "at-risk" youth.

Key Terms

Adult education
Bilingual education
Cognitive styles
Compensatory education
Continuing education
Desegregation
Distance education
English as a Second Language (ESL)
Gender Equity
Indian Education
Individualized Education Program (IEP)

Learning disability
Least restrictive environment
Magnet school
Mainstreaming
Multicultural education
Sex bias
Sex discrimination
Sex role stereotyping
Vocational-technical education
White flight

Discussion Questions

 1. Today, like Louis Garcia, many youth feel alienated from the school and find little identification and meaning in the educational process. As a teacher, what can you do to reach these students?

2. What do you see as the major obstacles to racial and ethnic integration in the schools?

3. Discuss ways in which the Individuals with Disabilities Education Act has benefited all children.

4. What economic benefits can the nation hope to gain from significantly increased funding of compensatory education?

5. Describe the bilingual education program in a school district with which you are familiar. What evidence exists that it has improved the academic performance of its participants? Is it viewed as helping or hindering progress toward racial or ethnic integration?

6. Compare the treatment of males and females in the schools with their treatment in other institutions.

7. How do the missions of adult education, bilingual education, special education, vocational education, and sex equity in education complement each other?

References

American Association of University Women (AAUW). (1990). *Shortchanging girls, shortchanging America.* Washington, DC: The AAUW Educational Foundation.

American Association of University Women (AAUW). (1992). *How schools shortchange girls: A study of major findings on girls and education.* Washington, DC: AAUW Educational Foundation and the National Education Association.

American Association of University Women (AAUW). (1993). *Hostile hallways: The AAUW survey on sexual harassment in America's schools.* Washington, DC: The AAUW Educational Foundation.

Apps, J. W. (1992). *Adult education: The way to lifelong learning.* Bloomington, IN: Phi Delta Kappa Foundation.

Banks, J. A. (1993). Multicultural education: Development, dimensions, and challenges. *Phi Delta Kappan, 1,* 22–28.

Black, S. (1993). Real life 101. *Executive Educator, 15*(12), 24–27.

Board of Education of Oklahoma City Schools v. Dowell, 111 S.Ct. 630 (1991).

Board of Education v. Rowley, 458 U.S. 175 (1982).

Brown v. Board of Education, 347 U.S. 483 (1954).

Cameron, C. E. (1987). Adult education as a force toward social equity. *Adult Education Quarterly, 37,* 173–177.

Carelli, A. O. (Ed.) (1988). *Sex equity in education: Reading and strategies.* Springfield, IL: Charles C. Thomas.

Charleston, G. M. (1994). Toward true native education: A treaty of 1992. *Journal of American Indian Education, 33*(2), pp. 12–56.

Chavers, D. (1991). Indian education: Dealing with a disaster. *Principal, 70*(1), 28–29.

Dawkins, M. P. (1994). Long-term effects of school desegregation of African-Americans: Evidence from the national survey of black Americans. *The Negro Educational Review, 45,* 4–15.

Dayton Board of Education v. Brinkman, 433 U.S. 406 (1977).

Dickinson, D. (1991). *Positive trends in learning: Meeting the needs of a rapidly changing world.* Atlanta, GA: IBM Corp.

Durbin, J. (1989). *Assessment of the vertical equity of state supported compensatory education programs in Arizona.* Unpublished doctoral dissertation, Arizona State University, Tempe.

Elmore, R. F., & McLaughlin, M. W. (1988). *Steady work: Policy, practice, and the reform of American education.* Santa Monica, CA: The Rand Corporation.

Farris, P. J. (1992). *Achieving adult literacy.* Bloomington, IN: Phi Delta Kappa Foundation.

Fennema, E. (1987). Sex-related differences in education: Myths, realities, and interventions. In V. Richardson-Koehler (Ed.), *Educator's handbook: A research perspective* (pp. 329–347). New York: Longman.

Fife, B. L. (1992). *Desegregation in American Schools.* New York: Praeger.

First, P. F., & Curcio, J. L. (1993). *Implementing the disabilities acts: Implications for educators.* Bloomington, IN: Phi Delta Kappa Foundation.

Freeman v. Pitts, 112 S.Ct. 1430 (1992).

Gallegos, E. M. (1989). Beyond Board of Education v. Rowley: Education benefit for the handicapped. *American Journal of Education, 97,* 258–288.

Garcia, R. L., & Ahler, J. G. (1994). Indian education: Assumptions, ideologies, strategies. In J. Reyhner (Ed.), *Teaching American Indian Students.* Norman, OK: University of Oklahoma Press.

Gollnick, D. M., & Chinn, P. C. (1994). *Multicultural education in a pluralistic society* (4th ed.). New York: Merrill.

Green v. County School Board of New Kent County, 391 U.S. 430 (1968).

Hawley, W. D. (1992). School desegregation. In M. C. Alkin (Ed.), *Encyclopedia of Educational Research* (pp. 1132–1139). New York: Macmillan.

Hazard, W. R., & Stent, M. D. (1973). Cultural pluralism and schooling: Some preliminary observations. In W. R. Hazard, M. D. Stent, & H. N. Rivling (Eds.), *Cultural pluralism in education: A mandate for change* (pp. 13–25). Englewood Cliffs, NJ: Prentice-Hall.

Hilke, E. V., & Conway-Gerhardt, C. (1994). *Gender equity in education.* Bloomington, IN: Phi Delta Educational Foundation.

Hoachlander, G.,& Rahn, M. L. (1994). National skills standards. *Vocational Education Journal, 66*(1), 30–31.

Hudelson, D. (1994). Getting off the tracks. *Vocational Education Journal, 67*(7), 22–23, 68.

Indian Nations At-Risk Task Force. (1991). *Indian nations at-risk: An educational strategy for action.* Final report. Washington, DC: U.S. Department of Education.

Kaye, A. (1989). Computer-mediated communication and distance education. In R. Mason & A. Kaye (Eds.), *Mindweave: Communications, computers, and distance education* (pp. 3–21). New York: Pergamon Press.

Keyes v. School District No. 1, 413 U.S. 189 (1973).

Lau v. Nichols, 414 U.S. 563 (1974).

Levine, D. U., & Havighurst, R. J. (1991). *Society and education* (8th ed.). Boston: Allyn & Bacon.

Lombardi, T. P. (1994). *Responsible inclusion of students with disabilities.* Bloomington, IN: Phi Delta Kappa Foundation.

McCarthy, M. M., & McCabe, N. H. (1992). *Public school law* (3rd ed.). Boston: Allyn & Bacon.

McLaughlin, M. J., & Warren, S. H. (1994). The costs of inclusion. *The School Administrator, 51*(10), 8–19.

Milliken v. Bradley, 418 U.S. 717 (1974).

Mills v. Board of Education of the District of Columbia, 348 F. Supp. 866 D.D.C. (1972).

Mueller, M. I. K., & Mueller, V. D. (1992). Federal legislation effecting American Indian students. In P. Anthony & S. L. Jacobson (Eds.), *Helping at-risk students: What are the educational and financial costs?* (pp. 38–63). Newbury Park, CA: Corwin Press.

National Center for Research in Vocational Education. (1993). The changing role of vocational-technical education in the United States. *Centerwork, 4*(2), 1,3.

National Center on Education and the Economy (NCEE). (1990). *America's choice: Higher skills or lower wages.* Rochester, NY: NCEE.

A national report card for vo-tech. (1994). *Vocational Education Journal, 69*(8), 43–44, 46–47.

Pai, Y. (1990). *Cultural foundations of education.* Columbus, OH: Merrill.

Pennsylvania Association of Retarded Citizens v. Commonwealth of Pennsylvania, 343 R. Supp. 279 (E. D. Pa. 1972).

Peterson, N. L. (1988). *Early intervention for handicapped and at-risk children.* Denver, CO: Love Publishing Company.

Petrina, S., Craven, H., & Powell, A. (1993). The United States economic transition and vocational education reform. *Journal of Industrial Teacher Education, 31,* 105–111.

Ralph, J. (1989). Improving education for the disadvantaged: Do we know whom to help? *Phi Delta Kappan, 70,* 395–401.

Reeves, M. S. (August 2, 1989). The high cost of endurance. *Education Week,* 2–4.

Reyhner, J. (1994). *American Indian/Alaskan Native Education.* Bloomington, IN: Phi Delta Kappa Foundation.

Sadker, M., & Sadker, D. (1994). *Failing at fairness: How America's schools cheat girls.* New York: Charles Scribner's Sons.

Schmidt, P. (1994, September 28). Idea of 'gender gap' in schools under attack. *Education Week, 1,* 18.

Schnaiberg, L. (1994, October 19). E. D. report documents 'full inclusion' trend. *Education Week, 17,* 19.

Schofield, J. W. (1989). *Review of research on school desegregation's impact on elementary and secondary school students.* Hartford CN: Connecticut State Department of Education.

Scollay, S. (1994). The forgotten half: Are U.S. schools shortchanging girls? *American School Board Journal, 181*(4), 46, 48.

Scott, E., & McCollum, H. (1993). Making it happen: Gender equitable classrooms. In S. K. Bilken & D. Pollard (Eds.), *Gender and education: Ninety second yearbook of the National Society for the Study of Education* (pp. 174–190). Chicago: University of Chicago Press.

Segregation is on the rise. (1994). *American School Board Journal, 181*(1), 14–15.

Sevilla, J. (1992). Bilingual education: The last 25 years. In P. Anthony & S. L. Jacobson (Eds.), *Helping at-risk students: What are the educational and financial costs?* (pp. 38–63). Newbury Park, CA: Corwin Press.

Shade, B. J. R. (1989). *Culture, style and the educative process.* Springfield, IL: Charles C. Thomas.

Shore, K. (1986). *The special education handbook.* New York: Teachers College Press, Columbia University.

Silberman, H. F. (1991). Improvements coming, but problems remain. *Vocational Education Journal, 66*(1), 30–31.

Sleeter, C. E., & Grant, C. A. (1994). *Making choices for multicultural education* (2nd ed.). New York: Merrill.

Spring, J. (1991). *American education: An introduction to political and social aspects* (5th ed.). New York: Longman.

Stein, C. B., Jr. (1986). *Sink or swim: The politics of bilingual education.* New York: Praeger.

Swann v. Charlotte-Mecklenburg Board of Education, 402 U.S. 1 (1971).

Swisher, K., & Deyhle, D. (1994). Adapting instruction to culture. In J. Reyhner (Ed.), *Teaching American Indian Students.* Norman, OK: University of Oklahoma Press.

Thompson, D. C., Wood, R. C., & Honeyman, D. S. (1994). *Fiscal leadership for schools: Concepts and practices.* New York: Longman.

U.S. Bureau of the Census. (1994). *Statistical Abstract of the United States 1994.* Washington, DC: U.S. Government Printing Office.

U.S. Department of Education, National Center for Education Statistics. (1987). *Trends in adult education 1969–1984.* Washington, DC: U.S. Government Printing Office.

U.S. Department of Education, National Center for Education Statistics. (1994). *Condition of education 1994.* Washington, DC: U.S. Government Printing Office.

U. S. General Accounting Office (USGAO). (1990). *The urban underclass: Disturbing problems demanding attention.* Washington, DC: U.S. Government Printing Office.

Vacca, R. S., & Hudgins, H. C. (1992). The Supreme Court charts a new course for school desegregation in the 1990s: Dowell's pivotal position. *West's Education Law Quarterly, 1,* 430–448.

Washington v. Davis, 426 U.S. 229 (1976).

Webb, R. B., & Sherman, R. R. (1989). *Schooling and society.* New York: Macmillan.

White House Conference on Indian Education. (1992a). *The final report of the White House Conference on Indian Education: Executive Summary.* Washington, DC: White House Conference on Indian Education.

White House Conference on Indian Education. (1992b). *The final report of the White House Conference on Indian Education.* Washington, DC: White House Conference on Indian Education.

Wilcox, J. (1991). The Perkins Act at a glance. *Vocational Education Journal, 6*(2), 16–17.

The William T. Grant Foundation Commission on Work, Family and Citizenship. (1988). The forgotten half: Non–college-bound youth in America. *Phi Delta Kappan, 69,* 409–414.

Williams, B. I., Thorne, J. M., Michie, J. S., & Hamar, R. (1987). *The district survey: A study of local implementation of ECIA Chapter I.* Chapel Hill, NC: Research and Evaluation.

Wirt, J. G. (1991). A new federal law on vocational education: Will reform follow? *Phi Delta Kappan, 72,* 425–433.

Wirt, J. G., Muraskin, L. D., Goodwin, D. A., & Meyer, R. H. (1989). *Final report volume I: Summary of findings and recommendations.* Washington, DC: U.S. Department of Education, National Assessment of Vocational Education.

Yinger, J. M. (1986). The research agenda: New directions for desegregation studies. In J. Prager, D. Longshore, & M. Seeman (Eds.), *School desegregation research* (pp. 229–254). New York: Plenum Press.

Chapter 10

Students at Risk

Child abuse casts a shadow the length of a lifetime.

Herbert Ward, 1985

A Critical Incident in My Teaching Career . . .

Several years ago I had a child in my class who was severely troubled. He was, in fact, suicidal. He came in on a transfer and though extremely bright, had a rough time in school. Because he was so volatile, he spent all day with me, all preps, all activities, and I bonded to him. I was overwhelmed by how much emotional pain he had to endure and how he still wanted to please me and be liked. It made me aware of how unprepared teachers are for the "real world" their children live in and how important just loving these children is.

Anita Skep
Teacher of the Year, New York

There are millions of youth in and out of our schools whose life experiences and situations place them at risk for educational, emotional, mental, and physical problems. In this chapter at-risk children and youth are described. In addition, methods of identifying a number of at-risk conditions and behaviors are suggested, and prevention and intervention strategies that are used successfully in the schools are presented. The following objectives should guide you in your study of at-risk populations:

- Identify the predictors of being at risk.
- Describe the conditions or behaviors associated with substance abuse.
- Discuss prevention and intervention strategies aimed at reducing the occurrence of substance use and abuse in children and adolescents.
- Identify the suicidal child or adolescent.
- Review strategies for suicide prevention and intervention.
- Explain the incidence and consequence of dropping out of school.
- Describe successful pregnancy prevention and intervention programs.
- Suggest reasons why certain adolescents are at high risk for AIDS.
- Name the common signs or indicators of sexual abuse.
- Discuss the problem of homeless and runaway youth.
- Review the extent of the problem of crime, violence, and gangs in the schools.
- Explain why gay and lesbian youth are at risk for a variety of self-destructive behaviors.

At-Risk Children and Youth

A variety of terms have been used to describe children and adolescents who are in need of special treatment or special services. We are not referring here to the special education student, but to that group of students described as *at risk:* children and adolescents who are already achieving below grade level or are likely to experience educational problems in the future. The term also is used to describe children and adolescents who are already or are likely to experience physical and mental health problems.

Frymier and Gansneder (1989) describe the severity of being at risk as a function of the negative experiences or events that happen to a child or youth, the severity and frequency of these experiences or events, and other intervening variables in the child's or adolescent's immediate environment that either help or hinder the youngster's ability to cope. They offer the following example:

> A pregnant 14-year-old is at risk. But a pregnant 14-year-old who uses drugs is even more at risk. And a pregnant 14-year-old who uses drugs, has been retained in grade, has missed 30 days of school, and has a low sense of self-esteem is still more seriously at risk. (p. 142)

To be at risk is not solely a phenomenon of adolescence. Children at any age who are victims of abuse—sexual, physical, or emotional—are at risk. Children as young as five or six can be at risk. For example, a child whose parents are in the process of finalizing a divorce and who is failing in school is definitely at risk. So is a seven-year-old whose older sister just committed suicide, or a preschooler whose mother is an alcoholic and whose father has been cited for sexually abusing his teenage daughter. All of these youngsters are at risk not only for academic underachievement but also for mental health problems.

The state of adolescent health in America has reached crisis proportions, and the numbers of at-risk adolescents are staggering. According to the Carnegie Council on Adolescent Development and their report, *Fateful Choices:*

> By age fifteen, about a quarter of all young adolescents are engaged in behaviors that are harmful or dangerous to themselves and others. Of 28 million adolescents between the ages of ten and eighteen, approximately 7 million are at-risk of being harmed by health and even life-threatening activity, as well as by school failure. (Hechinger, 1992, pp. 21–22)

Identifying the At-Risk Student

Early identification is the key to developing and implementing effective educational programs for at-risk students. Among the most prominent behaviors or factors that identify the at-risk student are underachievement; retention in grade; discipline problems; dropping out of school; low parental support; physical problems; using and abusing drugs or alcohol; engaging in premature, unprotected sexual activity; being a victim or perpetrator of violence; and contemplating or attempting suicide. Other researchers have reported additional risk factors: being born to, or raised by, a mentally ill parent; suffering from the loss of a significant other; having experienced prenatal trauma or poor health status at birth; having been born to a teenage mother; having been abused or physically or emotionally neglected; being from a poor family; and living in an abject environment such as being homeless (Gersten & Shamis, 1988).

The research also indicates that a disproportionate number of ethnic/minority children, in particular black, Hispanic, and Native American children, non–English-speaking children, children of single-parent families, and gay and lesbian youth, are represented among the at-risk population. Certain individuals in these groups have a high incidence of at-risk behavior, including low achievement, dropping out of school, teen pregnancy, and suicide.

The following sections of this chapter describe a number of at-risk conditions or behaviors and discuss how they might be identified. In addition, for each at-risk condition or behavior, prevention and intervention strategies are discussed. The conditions or behaviors to be discussed include drug and alcohol use and abuse; suicide; dropping out of school; teenage pregnancy; AIDS; child abuse, including sexual abuse; homelessness, and running away; and teen violence. The conditions that place gay and lesbian youth at risk for a variety of self-destructive behaviors will also be presented.

Are you familiar with the term "at risk"? Could you, a member of your family, or a close friend be classified as at risk? On what basis?

Drug and Alcohol Use and Abuse

The use and abuse of chemical substances and alcohol by children and adolescents is one of the most challenging problems facing schools today. Children and teenagers use alcohol, cigarettes, and a wide assortment of illicit chemical substances including marijuana; stimulants (e.g., amphetamines, cocaine, "crack," "rock," and "uppers"); inhalants (e.g., solvents, aerosols, and nitrites); dissociative anesthetics (e.g., PCP [Phencyclidine] or "angel dust"); anabolic steroids; depressants (e.g., barbiturates, "ludes," tranquilizers or "downers"); hallucinogens (e.g., LSD, mescaline, and STP); and narcotics (e.g., opium, morphine, heroin, codeine, and methadone).

The Effects of Abuse

The abuse of these and other substances often is associated with harmful and deleterious effects on both the individual and society. On an individual level, drug and alcohol abuse interferes with cognitive development and academic achievement. On a societal level, neighborhoods near schools often become the target of drug dealers, many of whom are students themselves. Additionally, crimes of violence often are associated with substance abuse, particularly among teenage gang members. Research also suggests that teenage drug abuse is a contributing factor to personal, social, and occupational maladjustment in later young adulthood. For example, it has been found that habitual use of marijuana and hard drugs as a teen are predictive of later job instability, emotional turmoil, and early divorce. It has also been found that use of hard drugs (hypnotics, stimulants, cocaine, inhalants, and narcotics) as a teenager appears to contribute to deterioration in social relationships, increased loneliness, and suicidal ideation as an adult (Guy, Smith, & Bentler, 1994).

Trends in Use

Has the increase in the use of drugs and alcohol among high school students also been evidenced among college students? Among your age cohort?

While tobacco use among individuals 18 years of age and older is decreasing, U.S. teens today are smoking as much as they did a decade ago in spite of the efforts to warn them of the negative effects of smoking on their health. Approximately 19% of high school seniors reported smoking in 1993, up from 17% in 1992 ("U.S. Teens," 1994).

Although the level of drug and alcohol use among teens remains alarmingly high, statistics do show some decline in alcohol use. For example, in 1993 approximately 76% of 12th-graders reported that they used alcohol in the past 12 months compared to 86% in 1987 (National Institute on Drug Abuse, 1994). However, while the use of illicit drugs such as marijuana, hallucinogens, heroin or other opiates, stimulants, barbiturates, and tranquilizers has also decreased since 1980, recently it has shown a slight increase. A recent study of 52,000 students from 420 public and private secondary schools in the United States indicated that approximately 46% of 12th-graders had used an "illicit" drug at least once in their life, an increase from 43% in 1993. And, approximately one out of every five or six students in the three grade levels surveyed (8th, 10th, and 12th) reported using inhalants. The highest use was at the 8th-grade level (Zielinski, 1994).

Cocaine and marijuana use has also increased after declining for a number of years. While 12.3% of the 12th-graders surveyed in 1980 reported that they had used cocaine in the last 12 months, 3.1% reported its use in 1992, and 3.3% in 1993. Similar trends are found related to marijuana use: in 1980, approximately 49% of the 12th-graders reported marijuana use in the previous year compared to 22% in 1992 and 26% in 1993 (National Institute on Drug Abuse, 1994) (see Figure 10.1).

There are age and racial/ethnic differences with regard to alcohol and drug use. For example, alcohol and marijuana use seem to be more prevalent among older students, and black students report the lowest rates of alcohol and drug use at each grade level. On the other hand, an increasing use of both alcohol and marijuana is reported for Hispanic youth (Johnson, O'Malley, & Bachman, 1993).

In 1992, one in ten 8th-graders, nearly one in five 10th-graders, and almost one in four 12th-graders reported that they were approached at school by someone who attempted to sell or give them drugs during the prior year (U.S. Department of Education, 1993). Students from low-income public high schools were more likely to be approached than students from higher-income private schools. Hispanic and Native American students were more apt to be approached than white, black, or Asian youth (U.S. Department of Education, 1994a). More than one fourth of all students report that beer or wine, liquor, and marijuana are easy to obtain at school or on school grounds (U.S. Department of Education, 1993). And, during 1993, one third of all students

Figure 10.1: Trends in the Use of Drugs and Alcohol by High School Seniors, 1980–1993 (percentage of seniors using in past 12 months)

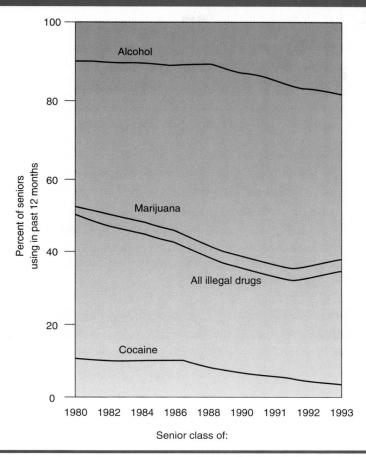

Source: National Institute on Drug Abuse (NIDA). (1994). *Monitoring the future study, 1975–1993: National high school senior drug abuse survey.* Rockville, MD: NIDA

reported that they had witnessed other students high on drugs or intoxicated at school (National Education Goals Panel, 1993).

Most of the research that has been completed on youth substance use has been limited to students who remain in school. If dropouts were included in those studies, more than likely the magnitude of the problem of substance use would far exceed the current estimates (Eggert & Herting, 1993).

The younger children are when they begin using tobacco, alcohol, and marijuana, the more likely they will progress from casual to regular use, and eventually may go on to use hard drugs (U.S. Department of Education, 1993). Tobacco, alcohol, and marijuana are truly *gateway drugs* for the very young child (Horton, 1992).

Identifying Alcohol and Drug Use

Parents, teachers, counselors, and administrators are better prepared to provide early intervention when they recognize the difference between normal childhood and adolescent behavior and behavior that may indicate substance use or abuse. Figure 10.2 identifies some of the behaviors that have been found to be associated with substance abuse.

Psychological and interpersonal factors that place certain adolescents at risk for alcohol and drug use include low self-esteem, unassertive behavior, antisocial and aggressive behavior, lack of commitment to the school, and poor school achievement. The strongest risk predictors are attitudes toward drug use and association with peers. Family factors such as substance abuse by parents or siblings coupled with environmental factors such as poverty and violence make certain youngsters more vulnerable than others (U.S. Department of Education, 1993). Family victimization such as sexual molestation is also believed to be a contributing factor to drug and alcohol abuse (Watts & Ellis, 1993).

The differences between so-called normal behavior and behavior that may reflect substance use or abuse often are a matter of degree. For example, it is normal for a child or adolescent to desire to spend time alone, but it may not be normal to exhibit sudden, almost complete withdrawal from family or friends. A pattern of changes, not any single behavior, best predicts possible substance abuse (Dorman, Geldof, & Scarborough, 1982).

Figure 10.2: Behavioral Characteristics Associated with Substance Abuse

- Abrupt changes in work or school attendance, quality of work, work output, grades, discipline

- General attitude changes and/or irritability

- Withdrawal from responsibility

- Deterioration of physical appearance and grooming

- Impaired performance on the job or in the classroom

- Wearing of sunglasses at inappropriate times (to hide dilated or constricted pupils)

- Continual wearing of long-sleeved garments (to hide injection marks), particularly in hot weather, or reluctance to wear short-sleeved attire when appropriate

- Association with known substance abusers

- Unusual borrowing of money from friends, co-workers, or parents

- Stealing small items from employer, home, or school

- Secretive behavior regarding actions and possessions; poorly concealed attempts to avoid attention and suspicions such as frequent trips to storage rooms, closets, restrooms, basements (to use drugs)

Source: Pharmaceutical Manufacturers Association. (1987). *Substance abuse: Signs and symptoms.* Washington, DC: Author. Reprinted with the permission of: The Pharmaceutical Manufacturers Association, 1100 Fifteenth Street, NW, Washington, DC 20005

Early prevention efforts are a key to combating this serious problem that affects adolescents of all cultures and socioeconomic classes.

Prevention Strategies

Prevention strategies include those programs, activities, and services that help reduce the occurrence of substance use and abuse in children and adolescents. The Drug Free Schools and Communities Act (as amended) assists states in establishing new drug prevention programs or supplementing existing programs. With the assistance provided by federal funds under this act, a number of states have developed substance-abuse prevention programs and have provided training for educators. In a number of locales, mental health agencies have collaborated with school districts to develop and implement substance-abuse prevention curricula that emphasize problem-solving, life skills training, assertion training, peer resistance training, decision-making, affective education, self-esteem building, and health-wellness. Research has demonstrated that successful substance-abuse prevention programs teach resistance skills while correcting erroneous perceptions about the prevalence and acceptability of drug use among peers (U.S. Department of Education, 1993).

Although the developmental level of the child will determine the specific design of the drug and alcohol prevention curriculum, certain themes should be present at all grade levels. The U.S. Department of Education (1988) recommends the following themes:

- A clear and consistent message that the use of alcohol, tobacco, and other illicit drugs is unhealthy and harmful.

- Knowledge of all types of drugs, including what medicines are, why they are used, and who should (or should not) administer them.

- The social consequences of substance abuse.

- Respect for the laws and values of society.

- Promotion of healthy, safe, and responsible attitudes and behaviors by correcting mistaken beliefs and assumptions, disarming the sense of personal invulnerability, and building resistance to influences that encourage substance abuse.

- Strategies to involve parents, family members, and the community in the effort to prevent use of illicit substances.

- Appropriate information on intervention and referral services, plus similar information on contacting responsible adults when help is needed in emergencies.

- Sensitivity to the specific needs of the local school and community in terms of cultural appropriateness and local substance abuse problems. (p. 10)

Drug use prevention has shifted from a single and simplistic approach to a more comprehensive approach that takes into consideration the multitude of factors that make children vulnerable to drug use. Regardless of the thrust of the prevention program, it is important that parental involvement be a component of the substance-abuse prevention curriculum.

Community-based organizations also have become increasingly involved in alcohol- and drug-abuse prevention activities. Examples of these community efforts include Mothers Against Drunk Driving (MADD), which has influenced the drunk-driving laws; the "Chemical People" campaign on public television, which spearheaded local drug-abuse prevention task forces in at least 10,000 communities; and Project DARE (Drug Abuse Resistance Education), offered in the schools by law enforcement agencies. Similarly, a number of major community organizations such as the Lions Club, Junior Leagues, and Parent-Teacher Associations have become actively involved in the fight against youth alcohol and drug use.

What programs are available in your community to discourage drug and alcohol abuse among young children?

Intervention Strategies

School-sponsored *intervention programs* are aimed at providing assistance to those children and adolescents who are already using or abusing drugs or alcohol.

Among the more widely used intervention strategies are referral to mental health agencies and psychiatric hospitals for treatment; peer counseling programs aimed at teens helping teens; school-based individual and group counseling; mental health consultation whereby community health agencies offer psychological services to school districts; and community practitioners, educators, and former substance abusers who monitor and treat children and teens who have drug and alcohol problems (Salzman & Salzman, 1989).

Chemical dependency has serious implications for the schools. Practically every teacher at all grade levels from middle school on will be confronted by a sizable number of students who are engaging in regular use of drugs and/or alcohol. Beginning teachers need to become familiar with the educational prevention programs offered by their district and their school. They also need to become acquainted with the treatment programs available in the community for children and adolescents. The school counselor, social worker, or psychologist will be an invaluable resource to the beginning teacher who may feel unprepared to deal with this particular type of problem.

One of the six National Education Goals states "By the year 2000, every school in America will be free of drugs and violence and will offer a disciplined environment conducive to learning." Much work is yet to be done if we are to realize this ambitious goal.

Suicide

Extent of the Problem

Suicide is the third leading cause of death among youth 15 to 24 years of age; only accidents and homicides rank higher (NIMH, 1992). It is estimated that suicide accounts for more than 5,000 deaths each year for this age group. The Centers for Disease Control and Prevention (1992) reported that 8% of high school students attempted suicide, 27% seriously contemplated it, and 16% had planned to commit suicide. Other research has suggested that between 6% and 13% of adolescents have attempted suicide (Gallup Organization, 1991; Meehan, Lamb, Saltzman, & O'Carroll, 1991) and 11 in 100,000 actually complete suicide (Haveman & Wolfe, 1994). For each completed suicide, it is estimated there are 300 attempts (Lawton, 1991). Yet, since many suicides and suicide attempts go undetected or unreported, these data probably do not reflect the true magnitude of the problem. It has been predicted that in the average high school approximately 35 to 60 students will attempt suicide every year and that at least one student will commit suicide every five years (Phi Delta Kappa, 1988).

Although suicide is considered rare in children under the age of 12, thoughts of suicide or *suicide ideation,* suicidal threats and gestures, and suicide attempts are common even among young children (Strother, 1986). A strong association has been found between depression and severe suicidal behaviors in these children (Pfeffer, 1986).

Group Differences

Gender, race/ethnicity, geographic locale, and sexual preference have influenced the suicide rates among teens. For example, boys are more apt to *complete* or commit suicide while girls are more likely to *attempt* suicide. The difference in rate may be explained by the methods used. Boys use violent means such as firearms to commit suicide; girls tend to use less lethal means such as injecting drugs or slashing wrists. The rate of suicide for black youth is approximately one-fifth that of whites. Native Americans are 10 times more likely to commit suicide than their white peers. Rural youth tend to resort to self-destructive behavior more than do urban youth (Frymier, 1988). And, according to some research, gay and lesbian youth account for approximately 30% of all teen suicides (Walling, 1993).

Identifying the Suicidal Child or Adolescent

What suicide messages are there in rock music? To what extent do they influence children and adolescents?

Many of the symptoms of suicidal thoughts or actions are similar to the symptoms of depression. Parents, teachers, and counselors should be aware of the warning signs or indications that a child or adolescent may be suicidal. Table 10.1 presents the major indicators of possible childhood or adolescent suicidal behavior. Of these indicators, a previous suicide attempt, a family history of suicide, *clinical depression,* substance abuse, stressful life events, gender identity issues, and accessibility to firearms deserve mention because of their particular importance in predicting self-destructive behavior. In addition, those children who tend to be preoccupied with death or who know a teenager who has attempted suicide have also been found to be at risk for self-destructive behavior.

The research suggests that substance abuse is linked closely to suicide and that drugs or alcohol may temper the fear of death (Garrison, McKeown, Valois, & Vincent, 1993). Similarly, the child or adolescent who experiences a significant number of stressful life events such as death of a parent, separation or divorce of parents, family turmoil or conflict, school failure, sexual or physical assault, or interpersonal conflict with boyfriend or girlfriend may also be at risk particularly if those stressors occur in combination with alcohol and drug use and the availability of firearms (Keitner, Ryan, Miller, Epstein, Bishop, & Norman, 1990; Pfeffer, 1991).

Signs of Depression

The clinically depressed child or youth is likely to exhibit signs of hopelessness, a change in eating and sleeping habits, withdrawal from family and friends, substance abuse, persistent boredom, loss of interest in pleasurable activities, neglect of personal appearance, violent or rebellious behavior, and frequent complaints about physical symptoms. In early adolescence, the depression is often masked by acting out or delinquent behavior. Older adolescents are more apt to resort to drugs, alcohol, and sex rather than face their pain (Greuling & DeBlassie, 1980).

All children and youth may experience some depression with its highs and lows, but the clinically depressed youngster experiences a more serious depression, with persistent symptoms that typically last for at least two or more weeks.

Table 10.1: Indicators of Childhood or Adolescent Suicide

Psychosocial	Familial	Psychiatric	Situational
1. Poor self-esteem and feelings of inadequacy.	1. Disintegrating family relationships.	1. Prior suicide attempt.	1. Stressful life events.
2. Hypersensitivity and suggestibility.	2. Economic difficulties and family stresses.	2. Verbalization of suicide or talk of self-harm	
3. Perfectionism.	3. Child and adolescent abuse.	3. Preoccupation with death.	
4. Sudden change in social behavior.	4. Ambivalence concerning dependence v. independence.	4. Repeated suicide ideation.	
5. Academic deterioration.	5. running away.	5. Daredevil or self-abusive behavior.	
6. Underachievement and learning disabilities.	6. Family history of suicide.	6. Mental illness such as delusions or hallucinations in schizophrenia.	
		7. Overwhelming sense of guilt.	
		8. Obsessional self-doubt.	
		9. Phobic anxiety.	
		10. Clinical depression.	
		11. Substance abuse.	

Source: Adapted from Metha, A., & Dunham, H.J. (1988). Behavioral indicators. In Capuzzi, D., & Golden., L. *Preventing adolescent suicide* (pp. 49–86). Muncie, IN: Accelerated Development Inc. Reprinted with permission.

It is the clinically depressed child who is most at risk for suicide (Frazier, 1985). The period when the depression appears to subside is the most vulnerable time, for that is when the child has the psychic energy to become acutely suicidal (Hipple & Cimbolic, 1979).

Although most children and youth will exhibit a number of verbal and non-verbal warning signs and clues of possible suicidal behavior, the majority will not be suicidal. However, it behooves every parent and educator to be sensitive to any one of the signs or clues, since it may be the youngster's last desperate plea for understanding and help. If one or more of these signs is observed, the parent or educator should talk to the child about his or her concerns and seek professional help if those concerns or problems continue to persist. If we fail to recognize the child's pain, fear, doubt, and confusion, we may have missed an opportunity to save a life.

Prevention Strategies

The focus of suicide prevention programs is on identification or detection. The majority of prevention programs in the schools emphasize strategies that focus on building self-esteem, decision-making, coping skills, and problem-solving. Many of the prevention programs include information about recognizing the signs and symptoms of suicidal behavior and how to access help from the school and community (Kalafat & Elias, 1994). The first wave of research on school-based suicide prevention programs reported that such programs may have a negative effect on certain students who are already at risk, in particular, students who had made an earlier suicide attempt (Shaffer, Garland, Underwood, & Whittle, 1987). However, there is no evidence in the research literature that exposure to such a curriculum has caused a suicide or suicide attempt.

Some states have passed legislation requiring the department of public instruction to develop a suicide prevention curriculum. In most cases, such a curriculum has been incorporated in the regular health curriculum of the school. The impetus for developing suicide prevention programs in the schools has also come from the courts. A decision of the Ninth Circuit Court of Appeals in *Kelson v. The City of Springfield* (1985) held that the parents of a deceased child may bring action against the school if the death allegedly resulted because of the lack of a suicide prevention program. On page 337 are arguments for and against the schools taking a role in suicide prevention.

What is your position on the enactment of gun control laws as a suicide prevention measure?

Intervention Strategies

The most common suicide intervention program is the *crisis intervention team* approach. The typical crisis intervention team is composed of volunteer teachers, counselors, administrators, social workers, school nurses, and school psychologists. The members of the crisis team meet regularly and participate in training workshops conducted by local community mental health agencies. The role of crisis team members is to network with each other and identify the youngster who appears to be overwhelmed by stress or displays a *suicide gesture* or *suicide threat*. Problems often are solved at the team level; however, the crisis team may refer a student to a community mental health agency or hospital for emergency care. Other intervention strategies include individual and group counseling, peer counseling, and referral to a suicide hotline for students who are in crisis when school is not in session. School personnel must notify parents if they suspect that a child or adolescent is suicidal.

Postvention Strategies

In addition to prevention and intervention strategies, a *postvention program* also is important for the school. The purpose of a postvention program is to help the school return to normal in the aftermath of a suicide and to prevent *cluster suicides*. Grief counseling, support groups, interacting with the media, and follow-up care are examples of postvention strategies facilitated by the crisis intervention team.

Controversial Issues:
The School's Role in Suicide Prevention

The school's role in suicide prevention was a controversial issue of the 1980s and probably will continue to be debated during the 1990s. The extent to which the schools should assume this role is debated by educators, school boards, and parents. The reasons often given in favor or against suicide prevention in the school are:

Arguments For

1. Suicide prevention programs can help students cope with the various stresses they experience in their school and personal lives

2. The suicide prevention programs usually include a curricula that teaches coping, problem solving and survival skills which are valuable life skills for all students.

3. Suicide prevention programs help teachers and students recognize the warning signs of the suicidal child or adolescent, enabling them to make a timely referral if necessary.

4. Suicide prevention programs offer training in peer counseling, which has been an invaluable strategy for identifying the suicidal child or adolescent.

5. The alarming statistics concerning suicide among children and adolescents require that schools take a proactive step in addressing the problem.

Arguments Against

1. School counselors, teachers, and other professional staff do not have the time or training to deal effectively with the suicidal youngster.

2. There is little research evidence that confirms that suicide prevention programs lessen suicidal behavior.

3. The liability of the school is unclear concerning suicide prevention programming.

4. Recent research on imitative and modeling behavior raises serious questions about offering suicide prevention programs in the schools, i.e., teaching about suicide will trigger a suicide, since children and youth are so suggestible.

What is your view of suicide prevention in the school? What types of program(s) exist in a school with which you are familiar?

Schools are in a better position to respond to suicidal concerns if they have prevention, intervention, and postvention policies and procedures in place (Malley & Kush, 1994). The worst time to plan for a crisis such as a suicide or attempted suicide is during the crisis.

Today, no school is immune to the loss of a child or adolescent by suicide. Parents and teachers are often the last to recognize that the child or adolescent is at risk for taking his or her own life. The peer group will probably be the first to know that the child is in need of immediate help. Teachers need to be able to establish a trust relationship with students so that the students will come forward to seek the help they need to respond to a suicidal friend. Many beginning teachers feel very inadequate and fearful of handling a suicidal student for fear that their actions may precipitate an actual suicide or suicide attempt. The truth is that talking about suicidal tendencies will not exacerbate a suicide or suicide attempt. Most youngsters at risk for suicide are relieved to be able to articulate their fears and concerns to an adult who will listen. The worst response is no response.

Dropping Out of School

The majority of states and school districts define the *dropout* as a student who leaves school for any reason before graduation or completion of a program of study without transferring to another school or institution. Although the dropout rate has declined steadily for all racial and ethnic groups over the last two decades, the dropout rate in the United States continues to be a major problem. The latest available data show that for the year 1993, approximately 4.5%, or 381,000, of 10th- through 12th-graders dropped out of school. The data also show that 3.4 million, or 11%, of the 16- to 24-year-olds in 1993 were high school dropouts (U.S. Department of Education, 1994b).

The dropout rate is highest for students from low-income families and from those living in the South or West. And, while low-income students are often minority and are most at risk of dropping out, the vast majority of dropouts 16 to 24 years of age are white and represent middle-income families from urban neighborhoods. The dropout rates for males and females 16 to 24 years old are similar: 11.2% for males and 10.9% for females. However, there are racial and ethnic differences. The dropout rate is highest among Hispanics, in particular, non-English speaking Hispanics. Hispanics made up 29% of all dropouts in the 16-to 24-year-old age group, even though they represented only 12% of that population (U.S. Department of Education, 1994b). (See Chapter 8 for a more detailed comparison of high school attainment among various racial and ethnic groups.) Figure 10.3 depicts the trend in the percentage of dropouts ages 16 to 24 by race, ethnicity, and gender for the period 1972 through 1993.

Poor attendance is a common characteristic of students who are at risk for dropping out of school, and the loss of attendance has had a significant impact on schools. For example, a large high school in Los Angeles County reported that the loss of state funding can reach as high as $200,000 in a given year (Mayer, Mitchell, Clementi, Clement-Robertson, Myatt, & Bullara, 1993).

Economic Consequences

The dropout problem has significant economic consequences for this nation. The projected lifetime earnings of a high school graduate is $200,000 more than a dropout (National Goals Panel, 1993). It has been estimated that billions of dollars in local, state, and federal tax revenues are lost each year from the reduced earnings of dropouts. If the costs associated with unemployment, welfare, and other social services provided to dropouts and their families are considered, the combined economic costs to society are significant.

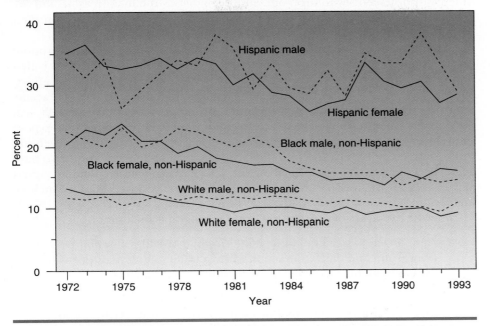

Figure 10.3: Percentage of High School Dropouts Among Persons Age 16–24 by Race, Ethnicity, and Gender 1972–1993

Source: U.S. Department of Education, National Center for Education Statistics. (1994). *Dropout rates in the United States:* 1993 Washington, DC: U.S. Government Printing Office.

Identifying the Potential Dropout

Although not every student who leaves school prior to graduation will possess these characteristics, Grossnickle (1986) lists the following as the most common signs of a potential dropout: poor attendance; absenteeism; tardiness; underachievement; lack of basic skills, in particular, reading; problems at home; poor communication between home and school; poorly developed organizational skills; a history of school transfers and family moves; poor social adjustment; failure to foresee the importance of an education; inability to relate to authority figures; having a parent or older sibling who is a dropout; and low self-esteem. Other research has found that dropouts often are overage students who have been retained at earlier grade levels, those who have a lengthy history of law violations, those who are drug or alcohol abusers, or those who are pregnant (Bialo & Sivin, 1989; Feldman, 1994).

Prevention Strategies

Students drop out of school for a variety of reasons: family background, in particular, low socioeconomic status; limited English proficiency; and lack of parental involvement with the school. They also leave school because of employ-

Why would dropping out of school have a more deleterious effect on females than on males?

ment responsibilities as well as the influence of the peer group. The most common reason given by students is that they dislike school and perceive the school climate to be negative and punitive (Lawton, 1994). In addition, more than 25% of female adolescents who drop out cite pregnancy as the main reason, and 8% of male dropouts indicate that their decision to leave school was based on their added responsibilities of parenthood (Feldman, 1994).

As with other at-risk behaviors, timely identification of the potential dropout is very important. The earlier the student is identified, the more likely it is that prevention efforts will be successful. And since research indicates that the effects of dropping out are more devastating for females than males in terms of academic and economic implications, prevention programs should be especially sensitive to the needs of females. Mentoring programs and programs that expose students to nontraditional occupations are two examples of positive prevention strategies (Hayes, 1987). Since punitive school and classroom environments have been cited as an important contributor to a lack of attendance, schools should make every effort to make the school climate more positive (Mayer, Mitchell, Clementi, Clement-Robertson, Myatt, & Bullara, 1993).

Specific examples of dropout prevention programs include:

- An intermediate school in Reston, Virginia, provides a weekly peer support group and daily interaction with volunteer adult mentors who serve as role models and caring advisors (Blum & Jones, 1994).

- A Los Angeles County high school offers tutoring and career development activities for potential dropouts throughout the year. It also includes an intensive summer school program as well as community-based activities to expose students to such resources as museums outside of their immediate neighborhood (Mayer et al., 1994).

- The San Fernando, California, Middle School's prevention program entitled "Achievement for Latinos through Academic Success" (ALAS) provides tutoring, counselor-advocates, daily evaluation of classroom behavior, and compliance with homework and other assignments that are shared with parents. The program is geared to improve the student's sense of belonging and identification with the school (Lawton, 1994).

- A ninth grade program, implemented in all high schools of the Pasco County School District in Florida, focuses on positive peer relationships through the use of a buddy system, class meetings, open houses, and cookouts. Teachers and administrators participate in each activity to improve their relationships with students (Pearson & Banerji, 1993).

Intervention Strategies

Of all intervention strategies, mandatory suspension of a driver's license is probably the most controversial. Known as the "dropouts don't drive law," this strategy is intended to keep teens in school by revoking their driver's license if they drop out of school. Florida and West Virginia have passed such legislation (McGarrahan & Brecher, 1989).

All teachers have an obligation to try to prevent students from dropping out of school. School districts must improve their efforts at identifying the potential dropout and must find effective methods of working with the families of students who are at risk, in particular, non-English speaking families.

Do you advocate the "dropouts don't drive law" as an intervention strategy? Why or why not?

Teenage Pregnancy

Of all the at-risk behaviors described in this chapter, the sobering statistics of the number of births to unmarried teenagers has probably attracted the most attention. The children of teen mothers are very much at risk for a number of reasons. They are more likely to grow up in a poor and single-parent family. They will probably live in a poor or underclass neighborhood. And, they will no doubt be vulnerable to a host of health problems as well as for school failure (Haveman & Wolfe, 1994).

While the number of teens giving birth continues to be a social, economic, and educational problem in the United States, in 1992 the birth rates for girls 15 to 17 years of age actually declined for the first time in nearly a decade. Specifically, following a 27% increase between 1986 and 1991, the birth rates for this age group dropped by 2% from 1991 to 1992 (Portner, 1994). Approximately 7 in 10 births to teen mothers are unplanned (Haveman & Wolfe, 1994).

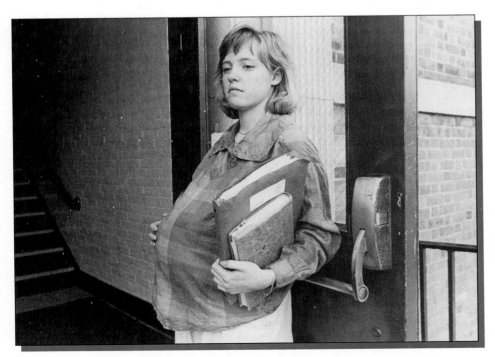

Pregnant teens are at high risk for dropping out of school.

The United States has the highest adolescent birth rate of all Western industrialized countries (Scott-Jones, 1993). Canada and the United Kingdom have birth rates less than one-half of the U.S. rate, while northern European countries report a birth rate one-third of that in the United States (Haveman & Wolfe, 1994). There are a variety of possible explanations that have been advanced to explain these differences. One reason may be that sex education, contraceptives, and abortion services are more widely available in the comparison countries (Jones, 1986). Another explanation may be that while the rate of sexual activity among U.S. youth is not necessarily greater than the comparison countries, perhaps teenagers in other industrialized nations may be more responsible when they become sexually active (Scott-Jones, 1993).

There are several myths surrounding the teenage pregnancy problem. One myth is that teen pregnancy affects primarily minority teens. In reality, teen pregnancy affects all racial/ethnic and socioeconomic groups. In fact, the majority of teenage births are to whites (66%) (Haveman & Wolfe, 1994).

A second myth is that teen pregnancy is an adolescent problem. According to a detailed two-year study of American teens by the Alan Guttmacher Institute (1981), only 25% of the fathers of babies born to mothers age 17 and younger are also in their teens. In nearly one-third of births to 15-year-olds, the father was at least 6 years older than the mother (Vobejda, 1994). The average age of teen mothers is 18.5 years, which has remained stable, while the average age of their male partner has declined but still remains in the twenties (Males, 1993).

A third myth is that American adolescents who have had sexual intercourse have done so voluntarily. In truth, the majority have reported that they had done so involuntarily. Nearly 75% of young women who had sexual intercourse before the age of 14 report that at some point they had been forced to have sex against their will (Vobejda, 1994). And it has been suggested that at least 5% of all births to teenage mothers are the result of rape (Boyer & Fine, 1992).

Regardless of race or ethnicity, the typical adolescent who becomes pregnant usually performs below average in school subjects and on academic achievement tests prior to her pregnancy (Upchurch & McCarthy, 1990). She tends to demonstrate a lack of identification with the school, and displays a lack of motivation for an education, vocation, or a career (Scott-Jones, 1993).

Consequences of Adolescent Pregnancy

Adolescent parenthood has profound implications for health care and social services, for poverty and crime, for family relationships, and for the institution of the school. Since so many teenage parents often lack sufficient health care insurance and the necessary funds for the delivery, they must resort to outside subsidies to meet their financial commitments. In addition, they often lack proper prenatal care, one of the major prerequisites of a healthy delivery. This, coupled with inadequate diet, has resulted in a significant number of premature deliveries with accompanying low birth weight. Unfortunately, premature infants often are at risk for a host of serious health problems at a later date. The mortality rate for teenage mothers also is higher than for any age group. Because teen mothers experience so many health problems before and after the birth, they place heavy demands on the accompanying social service agencies, which accentuates the costs for the teen, her family, and society.

Economic Consequences

Teenage pregnancy has several major economic consequences. While it is true that significant numbers of pregnant adolescents fail to complete the eighth grade or do not graduate from high school, pregnant girls are three times more likely to graduate from high school today than in 1959 (Males, 1993). However, for those who do drop out, their earning potential is seriously hampered and many become caught in the web of being poor, on welfare, and out of the labor force (Haveman & Wolfe, 1994). And, there is strong evidence that the transfer of poverty from the mother to her offspring may create a continued cycle of poverty for generations to come (Caldas, 1994). The most important cause of the rising social costs of teen childbearing is the increasing failure of fathers, most of whom are adult, to pay child support (Males, 1994; Whitehead, 1993), a situation that recent welfare reform proposals aim to address.

Prevention Strategies

The major aim of pregnancy prevention programs is to keep teens from conceiving. School district policies and practices vary widely on this and other controversial issues, so it is important that teachers be aware of the policies of their district. Some prevention programs in the schools encourage adolescents to abstain from sexual activity, others provide birth control information, and a few provide contraceptive devices. The majority limit their prevention strategies to critical thinking and communication skills, family life planning, or some form of reproductive health curriculum.

Of all prevention strategies, in-school health clinics appear to be the most successful. These clinics offer a wide range of services, including counseling, physical examinations, and immunization. A decade ago such school affiliated health clinics were rare. Today they number approximately 500 or more across the country and serve as the principal source of health care for many students, in particular, students from impoverished families (Sleek, 1994). School-based clinics are designed to provide contraceptive counseling and related health services to adolescents, and to provide referrals to other community agencies.

Intervention Strategies

The major goals of most intervention strategies are to provide prenatal care, parenting skills, and vocational and personal counseling to adolescent mothers in an effort to reduce the cycle of repeated pregnancies, welfare dependency, and potential child abuse (The Flinn Foundation, 1989). Parent resource centers, which are usually coordinated with school health clinics, have proven to be a promising intervention strategy. Typically, such parent resource centers provide pregnant and parenting students with a wide range of health, educational, and social services. A case management team that includes a social worker, teacher,

To what extent should the school bear the cost and responsibility for providing a pregnancy prevention and intervention program?

and nurse interacts with the students' parents and closely monitors the academic progress, attendance, and health of each girl.

Since there is a strong correlation between teenage pregnancy and dropping out of school, the school has an added challenge to find ways to help teen mothers to continue with their education. The school's problems are not over if the teen mother chooses to drop out. Unfortunately, many of the children of teen mothers become at risk educationally and psychologically and often are overrepresented in classes for the learning disabled and emotionally disturbed (Bonjean & Rittenmeyer, 1987). These "children of children" very often become adolescent parents themselves, repeating the cycle and worsening the problem.

AIDS

Acquired immune deficiency syndrome (AIDS) is a serious disease caused by *human immunodeficiency virus* (HIV), which destroys the immune system and leaves the body susceptible to infection. Two diseases identified in AIDS patients are *Pneumocystis carinii* pneumonia, an infection of the lungs, and a rare form of cancer, *Kaposi's sarcoma,* both of which can cause death.

About 1.5 million Americans have been infected with the AIDS virus (U.S. Bureau of the Census, 1994). Since a cure has not yet been found for AIDS, it is estimated that 99% of all individuals with HIV will develop AIDS and die within 5 to 10 years following diagnosis. Using the most conservative estimates, it is projected that more people will die from AIDS than were killed in the Vietnam War, Korean War, World War II, World War I, and the Civil War, conflicts that led to the deaths of 560,000 U.S. military personnel (Popham, 1993). The AIDS virus is the fastest growing cause of death, exceeding both death by motor vehicle accidents and death by illicit use of drugs. Between 1993 and 1994, the number of AIDS related deaths increased by 20% ("Lethal Combination," 1994).

Vulnerability of Teens and Youth

There is growing evidence that children and adolescents are increasingly at risk for contracting AIDS. In the period 1988–1993, as many as 3,917 children under the age of 13 were diagnosed with AIDS, more than triple the number between 1982 and 1987. During the same period, 1,239 adolescents between the ages of 13 and 19 had also been diagnosed with AIDS, most of them male (see Figure 10.4). Although the number of AIDS cases reported for the 13- to 19-year-olds is small compared to the total number of AIDS cases, many more of them are infected with HIV. And, since 20% of all reported AIDS cases are diagnosed in young adults 20 to 29 years of age, and the average incubation period between HIV infection and AIDS diagnosis is 10 years, it is certain that many of these young adults became infected when they were teenagers ("Preventing Risk Behaviors Among Students," 1992).

There are several reasons why adolescents are at high risk for AIDS:

- A significant number of adolescents are sexually active, which increases their risk of exposure to the AIDS virus and other sexually transmitted diseases (STDs). Research indicates that by age 19, approximately 50% to 70% of teenagers report being sexually active. Of this age group, only 47% of males and 25% of females indicate that they use condoms as a protective measure (Stevens-Smith & Remley, 1994).

- Approximately 5 million teenagers are intravenous drug users (Yarber, 1987), and sharing of needles by drug users greatly increases the risk of infection of the AIDS virus.

- As many as 80% of teenage runaways eventually become involved in prostitution, which places them at high risk for AIDS ("AIDS and Teens," 1987).

Identifying AIDS

The following are some of the more common symptoms of AIDS or a less severe condition known as AIDS-Related Complex (ARC): (1) low energy, easy fatigue, or generalized weakness; (2) fevers or night sweats; (3) weight loss; (4) persistent cough; (5) persistent diarrhea; (6) depression or anxiety; (7) lack of concentration or forgetfulness; and (8) headache, nausea, and vomiting (Social Security Administration, 1989).

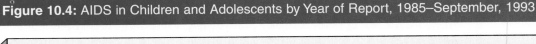

Figure 10.4: AIDS in Children and Adolescents by Year of Report, 1985–September, 1993

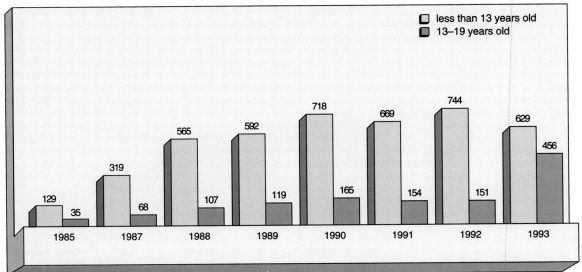

Source: National Center for Health Statistics. (1994). *Health of the United States, 1993.* Hyattsville, MD: Public Health Service.

Prevention Strategies

What type of AIDS educational curriculum would be best suited for the elementary school?

Since AIDS is a serious public health problem that has far-reaching implications for our society, the schools have an obligation to offer prevention or educational strategies that address this problem. However, there is considerable controversy among school officials, health educators, and governmental officials regarding the most effective approach to AIDS education. While a number of vocal community and religious groups have argued that sexual abstinence and marital fidelity should be the only prevention method emphasized in the AIDS educational program, a number of school and health officials concerned about the spread of AIDS among youth have suggested that the educational curricula should also include information on such topics as condom use and restricting sex to monogamous relationships.

Popham (1993) recommends that the following elements be included in all AIDS prevention curriculum: "(1) basic knowledge about how HIV is transmitted and how to reduce the risk of becoming infected; (2) interpersonal skills to be able to avoid, refuse, escape, or protect oneself in an HIV risk situation, such as a situation where there is the likelihood of unprotected sexual intercourse or needle sharing by intravenous drug users; and (3) suggestions for motivation to use the HIV relevant knowledge and skills" (p. 561).

Most communities do support AIDS education in the schools. However, a number of communities have requested that parental consent should be obtained before any student participates in such an education program.

Intervention Strategies

In 1985, the Centers for Disease Control and Prevention issued guidelines to assist schools in developing policies and procedures for individuals with AIDS in the school environment. These guidelines recommend that students who have developed AIDS or are infected with the AIDS virus should not be excluded from school attendance except under certain circumstances (see discussion in Chapter 12). It behooves each school district to develop an AIDS education curriculum and establish policies and procedures concerning how the institution will respond to those who already have AIDS or are carrying the AIDS virus. To do less would be negligent.

Today's teacher cannot ignore the reality of AIDS or ARC. With the increasing number of adolescents who are sexually active, are intravenous drug users, or are runaways who become involved in prostitution, most teachers will probably encounter a student with the AIDS virus at some time in their career.

Child Abuse

Child abuse is an injury or pattern of injuries to a child that includes physical abuse, sexual molestation or sexual abuse, emotional abuse, or neglect ("Child Abuse," 1994). More than 2 million cases of child abuse are reported to local child protective service agencies each year.

Physical Abuse

According to the National Committee for the Prevention of Child Abuse, *physical abuse* encompasses approximately 27% of the child abuse cases each year and includes intermittent abuse, chronic abuse over an extended period of time, physical restraint, or torture ("Child Abuse," 1994). A recent study of child abuse reported that one out of four children and youth between the ages of 10 and 16 is a victim of physical abuse or physical assault each year. Of those who have been physically abused, 1 out of 8 report having sustained an injury. In 1 out of 100 cases, the injury was severe enough to warrant medical attention. According to the same study, more girls are abused than boys, and most of the assaults are committed by acquaintances (72%) and juveniles (42%) ("Youths Report Cases of Abuse," 1994).

Sexual Abuse

It is estimated that at least 15% of the child abuse cases are the result of *sexual molestation* or *sexual abuse*. Sexual molestation includes sexual contact, intercourse, or prostitution with a minor who is under the age of 16, or between a child and an adult whereby the child is exploited for sexual stimulation or financial gain by the adult ("Child Abuse," 1994). Approximately 27% of girls and 16% of boys are sexually abused prior to their 18th birthday (Calderone & Johnson, 1989). One-half of all rape victims are also children and adolescents who are between the ages of 10 and 19, with 50% of those under the age of 16 (Greydanus & Shearing, 1990). Adolescent girls are especially vulnerable to date rape or acquaintance rape (American Psychological Association, 1993). Children and adolescents with disabilities are also at risk for both physical and sexual abuse (American Psychological Association, 1993). As was previously noted, many pregnant teens also have histories of rape, sexual abuse, and physical abuse.

Another form of sexual abuse that has been increasing is *peer-to-peer sexual harassment*. During the past few years significant numbers of cases of sexual harassment have been reported in middle schools and high schools. For example, a recent survey of 1,632 students in grades 8 through 11 in 79 schools across the country reported that four out of five students acknowledge having been sexually harassed in school. Seventy-five percent of the girls and 56% of boys reported that they had been touched, pinched, or grabbed in a sexual gesture. In addition, 13% of the girls and 9% of the boys reported that they had been forced to engage in activities of a sexual nature in school other than kissing. Of those who reported having been sexually harassed, the majority indicated that a current or former student was to blame. The report also noted that black girls (33%) are more likely to be sexually harassed by an adult in school than are white (25%) or Hispanic (17%) girls ("Sexual Harassment Widespread," 1993).

Emotional Abuse

Emotional abuse includes such nonphysical abusive behaviors as blaming, disparaging, or rejecting the child; treating siblings unequally; deliberately enforcing isolation; and continually withholding security and affection. It is estimated that approximately 13% of the child abuse cases are caused by emotional abuse ("Child Abuse," 1994).

Neglect

Neglect, one of the most severe forms of child abuse, occurs when the parent, guardian, or caretaker is unwilling to provide for the basic needs of the child, such as food, clothing, shelter, medical care, or supervision. Neglect accounts for most of the reported cases of child abuse (46%) ("Child Abuse," 1994).

Identifying Child Abuse

What are the procedures for reporting child abuse in your state?

Some of the common signs or indicators of child abuse include repeated physical injuries such as bruises, cuts, burns, missing hair, etc. The abused child will often exhibit a variety of behavior changes including aggressive or withdrawn behavior, neglected appearance, anxiety or fear, attention seeking behavior, fatigue, and frequent tardiness or absence from school. The adult abuser may appear super-critical, seem unconcerned about the child's welfare, and become defensive when questioned about the child's health or safety (Bete, 1990). Some of the indicators of sexual abuse you should be on the alert for as a teacher are listed in Table 10.2. While these indicators may or may not point to sexual molestation, if two or more of them appear the matter should be investigated and, if warranted, reported to the appropriate authority.

As discussed in Chapter 12, state child abuse statutes require that child abuse, including child molestation, be reported by school counselors, school psychologists, social workers, teachers, nurses, or administrators to the local child protective agency, department of welfare, or law enforcement agency. It is important that prospective and practicing teachers be familiar with the applicable statutes in their state. It is also important that teachers become familiar with the school district's policies prohibiting sexual harassment by employees and students.

Prevention Strategies

Since 1980, a number of child abuse and, in particular, sexual abuse, prevention programs have been introduced. The majority of these programs serve the following objectives: (1) to increase the child's and teen's knowledge about sexual abuse; (2) to enhance the child's and teen's awareness of the risk of sexual molestation; and (3) to identify children and adolescents who are in abusive situations (Graham & Harris-Hart, 1988). Many school districts have incorporated the prevention program content into the health education curriculum in order to keep it outside the controversial sex education domain. The use of humor and entertainment also have been used with all grade levels to transmit information about sexual abuse through theater performances, art, role playing, play therapy, puppets, coloring books, *bibliotherapy,* and so forth. Bibliotherapy includes the use of selected reading materials as a therapeutic prevention technique.

Table 10.2: Indicators of Sexual Abuse

The following are some behavioral indicators of sexual abuse that you are in a position to observe as a teacher:

- personality change

- change from being outgoing to clingy

- regression in toilet-training habits

- signs of being uncomfortable with someone formerly trusted

- withdrawal into self

- sophisticated sexual knowledge, beyond what is expected for age group

- moodiness, excessive crying

- changes in eating, sleeping habits

- increased activity

- behavior problems

- unusual shyness

- sudden, unfounded fears

- unusual need for reassurance, needing to be told "you're okay"

- unnatural interest in own or other's genitals

- poor peer relations or absence of friends

- Gender role confusion

- consistently leaving early for school and arriving late

- inappropriate sexual self-consciousness

Source: Herman, P. (1985). Educating children about sexual abuse. *Childhood Education, 61,* 174. Reprinted by permission of the Association for Childhood Education International, 11501 Georgia Avenue, Suite 315, Wheaton, MD. Copyright © 1985 by the Association.

The key elements of a prevention program designed to educate children about sexual abuse include (1) an awareness of body parts and how to distinguish between "good touch," "bad touch," and "confusing touch;" (2) the development of decision-making skills; (3) the development of assertiveness or refusal skills; and (4) a discussion of how and where to obtain help (Minard, 1993).

Intervention Strategies

The most important intervention strategy, particularly for the child or teen who suffers from physical injury, malnutrition, or neglect, is immediate treatment. Support services and counseling also are important interventions for the victim. Crisis intervention centers, self-help groups, crisis hotlines, and law enforcement agencies all have contributed to intervention efforts for the abused child or adolescent and his or her family. Of all the prevention and early intervention efforts, strengthening the family is probably the best hope for preventing any future child abuse, sexual molestation, or neglect.

Since child abuse and sexual abuse are prevalent in all socioeconomic classes and ethnic and racial groups, it is possible that you will be confronted with this problem during your teaching career. When this happens, it is important to remember not only your legal obligations but your obligations to your students. Although these are normally delicate and emotionally charged situations, avoidance is not the appropriate response. If you are in error, better that it be on the side of the child's welfare. Remember, you are protected from civil or criminal liability for reporting the alleged abuse.

Homelessness

The Problem of Homelessness in America

It is estimated that approximately 450,000 children of all ages are homeless in the United States ("Serving Homeless Children," 1992). Most social service providers and policymakers are convinced that those estimates are low and that the real problem is of greater magnitude. One of the greatest challenges to communities is to meet the physical, social, emotional, and educational needs of these youngsters. For example, in San Francisco, the Office of Mayor projects that at least 5,000 homeless youth are in need of social services. Even though a network of social service agencies serves over 1,600 of the homeless and runaway teens in that community, only 750 homeless students are enrolled in the San Francisco Unified School District (Gracenin, 1993).

Homeless children and youth have several characteristics in common:

What type of shelters are available in your community for runaway and homeless youth? Has there been community resistance to the location of these shelters?

- Inadequate medical care coupled with lack of proper nutrition is the leading cause of health problems for homeless children and adolescents. In addition, since homeless shelters are often overcrowded, many of their inhabitants are at risk for a series of medical problems, including diarrhea, gastroenteritis, and upper-respiratory infections ("Serving Homeless Children," 1992).

- Because homeless families are in constant upheaval with having to encounter persistent migration, these children and youth are frustrated, insecure, and have great difficulty enduring the discomfort of uncertainty and multiple transitions ("Serving Homeless Children," 1992).

- Many homeless children and adolescents come from unstable family environments where they have been subjected to early deprivation and abuse. As a result, they are likely to distrust authority, including school personnel, and may display outward hostility in their interaction with adult figures. They may also commit such self-defeating behaviors as petty criminal activity and other delinquent acts (Gracenin, 1993).

Prevention Strategies

The two major barriers to educating homeless children and adolescents are getting them into school and keeping them in school (Gracenin, 1993). Since homeless youth are especially at risk for dropping out of school, it is imperative that the school make every effort to assist the homeless student to remain in school and succeed. The following are some effective prevention strategies to prevent homeless students from dropping out:

- Flexible admissions criteria, including developing procedures for locating or preparing affidavits if student records are missing.

- Flexible attendance policies that do not penalize students since they lack control over their environment.

- Flexible course offerings, including miniclasses and courses divided into segments or modules for partial credit.

- Special education services for those who experience developmental problems or emotional problems due to the cumulative effect of being homeless.

- Transportation services, such as a voucher system for the use of buses or taxis.

- Community partnerships with the school to ensure that each student is provided the basic necessities for survival ("Serving Homeless Children," 1992; Vissing, Schroepfer, & Bloise, 1994).

The Steward B. McKinney Homeless Assistance Act has been reauthorized to ensure that all children and youth have the right to receive high quality educational and social services in a safe and caring environment. As a result of this federal legislation, state and local education agencies have received some assistance in providing support services needed to help homeless children and youth remain and succeed in school.

Intervention Strategies

One of the most effective intervention strategies that the school can use is to collaborate with other community agencies to provide the needed services for its homeless population. The following are two examples of how schools can intervene in a collaborative partnership with the community:

- The New York City Board of Education's Students Living in Temporary Housing Program has assigned family assistants at each participating homeless shelter who visit the shelter daily and work with the homeless parents and children to ensure that their educational and physical needs are being met ("Serving Homeless Children," 1992).

- The Oakland, California, Salvation Army Shelter and the Oakland Unified School District have formed a partnership to provide needed services and support for homeless children and youth ("Serving Homeless Children," 1992).

Runaway Youth

Runaway youth are adolescents who are under the age of 18 and who leave their home for more than eight hours without parental permission with the clear intent to run away. The major reasons cited for running away include physical abuse, neglect or rejection by parents, sexual exploitation, unreasonable restriction, dysfunctional families with drug abusing or alcoholic parents, parental separation or divorce, illness, death of a loved one, and school related problems. Most runaways wish to escape what is perceived as an intolerable situation (Hersch, 1988; Post & McCoard, 1994; Rohr & James, 1994).

Many runaway youth experience severe emotional problems such as depression, antisocial behavior, suicide ideation, suicide attempts, substance abuse and addiction, and gender-identity issues (Rohr & James, 1994). A large number of female runaways have had one or more pregnancies (Landers, 1989). Similar to homeless children and adolescents, runaway youth exhibit a wide range of health problems, including infectious diseases such as tuberculosis and whooping cough (Reed & Sautter, 1990). Many others are in extraordinary danger of contracting AIDS since they often resort to prostitution for income.

Identifying Potential Runaway Youth

As with other conditions for which youth are at risk, experience and research have revealed certain warning signs that may be used in identification and prevention efforts. Among these are the following:

- discipline problems at school
- alcohol and other substance abuse
- increased sleeping or a desire to be alone
- poor school performance or an unusual drop in grades
- repeated truancy
- abrupt mood swings
- increased breaking of rules (Bete, 1989, p. 6)

The majority of youth who exhibit some of the above symptoms will probably never run away. However, these signs may help identify a potential runaway youngster who is in need of professional help.

Prevention Strategies

Parents and teachers are in a key position in regard to preventing their children and students from running away. Some recommended prevention efforts include providing accurate information about drugs, alcohol, and sex; encouraging responsible decision-making; building self-esteem; making learning a positive experience; getting professional help where necessary; setting up rules and regulations that are fair and appropriate for youth; being honest with one's feelings; and being a good listener (Bete, 1989). Since most runaways are attempting to escape from what they perceive to be a major family conflict, the school should seek ways to encourage both the potential runaway and members of his or her family to participate in appropriate family counseling referral activities.

Intervention Strategies

Intervention strategies are normally outside the domain of the schools. Runaway shelters, runaway hotlines, and a host of other outreach projects designed to provide emergency help in the form of counseling, temporary housing, and medical care are the major intervention strategies used with runaway and homeless youth.

Any teacher who is employed by a public school in an urban setting is bound to come in contact with both homeless and runaway students. One of the important first steps in providing assistance for these youngsters is to become familiar with the extent of the problem in your community and the types of programs that are available.

Teen Violence

Each month approximately 420 children die from a gunshot injury, and each year approximately $64 billion dollars are spent as a result of violence (Prothrow-Stith, 1994). Each year over 3 million crimes, 11% of all crimes, occur in the public schools. Of these, 35 deaths and 92 injuries are the result of guns in schools. Moreover, the National Education Association estimates that 160,000 students stay home from school on any given day because of their fear of violence on the way to, from, or in school (Sautter, 1995).

The intensity of the violence against children and youth has risen dramatically, particularly toward certain populations: females, gay and lesbian youth, children and adolescents with disabilities, and ethnic/minorities (American Psychological Association, 1993). For example, homicide is the leading cause of death for young African-American males and females. African-American males are 11 times more likely to die by homicide than their non–African-American peers. Similarly, African-American females are four times more likely to die by homicide (American Psychological Association, 1993).

The incidence of serious acts of violence, including gang-related violence, is not limited to the urban inner-city communities. Violence has spilled over to all communities as well as public, private, and nonsectarian schools throughout the country.

Youth Gangs

Much of the violence involving youth is prompted by gangs. Gang activity in the United States is increasing at a very rapid rate. The majority of gangs are made up of males and racial/ethnic minorities, and encompass a wide range of ages, from as young as age 9 to age 30. Approximately 90% of gang members are either African-American (55%) or Hispanic (33%). While non-Hispanic gangs such as *Skinheads,* or neo-Nazi groups, are increasing, so are Asian- and Pacific Island-American gangs (American Psychological Association, 1993).

What gangs are active in your community? To what extent have they been associated with youth violence?

Some youth gang activities are limited to the wearing of so called "gang attire," "gang colors," the appearance of "gang graffiti," minor fights, or acts of intimidation. However, a sizeable number of other gang activities are associated with more serious violent crimes. These crimes include *gangbanging,* or drive-by shootings, aggravated assaults, and homicides. It is estimated that 80% to 90% of gang members have access to illegal weapons or firearms (Kwok & Hermann, 1994).

Prevention Strategies

At the present time there are more than 300 violence-prevention programs and more than 100 conflict-resolution curricula available for middle and high school students. Like many other prevention programs, very few of these programs have been evaluated, so it is difficult to determine their effectiveness (Lawton, 1994). The data that do exist suggest that an effective, ideal school-based violence prevention program will include the following elements: teaching pro-social skills and problem-solving with a companion course for parents, peer-mentoring program, teaching conflict-resolution skills, after-school activities, a gang and drug prevention program component, and teaching peer leadership and peer mediation skills (Prothrow-Stith, 1994).

Another important prevention activity includes having in place a crisis response plan for managing a school crisis or emergency. Policies and proce-

Skinheads tend to identify with hate movements and are a growing subculture.

Professional Reflections

"Children (students, learners) will not succeed unless they are safe. Safe from the physical dangers of the world. Safe from the worries of care and hunger. Safe enough to trust the one responsible for guiding them through the learning process. Create this safety for your students so that they can, and will, learn. The physical safety is usually easy to create. It is the emotional safety that is sometimes over-looked, yet equally essential. Let your students know that they can make a mistake, whether learning the ABCs or choosing an issue in a debate. Only when they feel safe will they dare to take the risk so necessary for learning!"

Ralph Marston Perry, Teacher of the Year, Rhode Island

dures should clearly delineate who in the school will respond to a given crisis situation. In addition to a carefully developed plan of action, in-service training for school personnel and continuous crisis drills are important prevention activities (Poland, 1994).

The schools are in a critical position to prevent violence or gang activity before it occurs by identifying the potential youth offender or troublemaker. Once these troublemakers are identified, supervision plans can be implemented and an appropriate referral can be made to prevent these youngsters from further violence and victimization (Stephens, 1994).

Intervention Strategies

One of the most effective intervention strategies used by schools is the trained crisis intervention team. As was previously discussed with regard to suicide intervention, the purpose of such a team is to minimize the effects of a crisis and prevent it from escalating. For example, members of a crisis team might be responsible for evacuating students to a safe area in the case of a violent act on campus, a bomb threat, or a natural disaster such as an earthquake; debriefing and leading a discussion or support group following the death or loss of one of the members of the school; and monitoring and supporting friends of a suicide or homicide victim (Poland, 1994). Most crisis teams are comprised of volunteer school personnel and are encouraged to work closely with their local community mental health agencies, local law enforcement representatives, probation officers, and other youth-serving professionals. School crisis intervention teams are in a strategic position to prevent and reduce school violence and trauma (Poland, 1994).

Gay and Lesbian Youth

Gay and lesbian adolescents are at risk for a variety of major problems that have been discussed in this chapter: alienation from family and peer group, violence, sexual abuse, school failure, running away or being truant, sexually transmitted diseases including HIV infection, substance use and abuse, depression, and suicide. Estimates regarding the number of teens who are gay or lesbian range from 5% to 15% (Walling, 1993).

One of the most difficult struggles that many gay and lesbian youth must face is the rejection, alienation, and isolation they often feel as a result of their homosexuality. To be cast out of one's home, to be expelled from one's peer group, or to question one's sexual identity are traumatic experiences for any individual. Yet, many of these students must resort to confronting these issues alone. The seriousness of their feelings of isolation can be illustrated by the high incidence of suicide attempts and completions among gay and lesbian teens.

Violence, sexual abuse, and harassment directed at homosexuals is commonplace and often is projected by the family, peer group, or the school. According to the National Gay and Lesbian Task Force, an education and advocacy group for homosexual rights, 49% of gay high school students and 20% of lesbian students have been verbally or physically assaulted in school because of their sexual orientation (Portner, 1994). Many teens endure intense physical and emotional suffering from such acts of violence. The guilt, self-contempt, and hopelessness that they often feel as a result of such acts of violence put them at risk for self-destructive behaviors.

Improving the School Climate

In spite of the fact that numerous professional organizations, including the American Psychiatric Association, the American Medical Association, The American Psychological Association, The American Nurses's Association, The National Education Association, and the American Federation of Teachers, have all made public declarations that homosexuality or bisexuality should not be viewed as abnormal, deviant, shameful, or the manifestation of a "disease," too many gay and lesbian students are still being subjected to *homophobic harassment* and intimidation in the classroom and in the school (Anderson, 1994). If schools are to provide for the social, psychological, and educational welfare of *all* students—including gay, lesbian, and bisexual teens—then schools must examine their attitudes and policies regarding these students. A small number of states have ensured the rights and protection of gay students through legislation. And, since the late 1980s, school districts in such cities as Los Angeles, Philadelphia, and Madison, Wisconsin have passed broad antiharassment measures to protect gay and lesbian students' rights (Portner, 1994).

The following strategies have been recommended to improve the school climate for gay and lesbian students:

- School personnel, in particular teachers and counselors, should use inclusive language that indicates an awareness of sexual diversity and does not make the assumption that all adolescents are heterosexual (Krueger, 1993; Walling, 1993).

  Nondiscrimination policies that protect gay and lesbian employees and students from harassment, violence, and discrimination should be developed by the school district. In addition, teachers, counselors, and administrators should challenge antigay epithets and should speak out against harassment (Anderson, 1994; Walling, 1993).

- Teachers should be encouraged to include gay and lesbian issues in their curriculum and lesson plans where appropriate. Resources and materials on homosexuality should be visible and accessible to students (Anderson, 1994).

- Professional development activities for school personnel should include accurate information about gay and lesbian issues, should encourage them to examine their beliefs and attitudes toward homosexuals, and should familiarize them with the resources in the community that can provide support services for teens who are struggling with their emerging sexual orientation (Anderson, 1994; Portner, 1994; Walling, 1993).

Intervention Strategies

School counselors are in a unique position to assist gay and lesbian students to cope with the psychological, social, and educational barriers that they often face. They can provide help for adolescents who are struggling with the confusion and fear associated with issues of adolescent sexuality (Robinson, 1994). Counselors should be aware of the resources that are available in both the gay and the general communities. Among the resources that can be helpful to gay and lesbian youth are gay community centers, telephone hotlines, and especially such organizations as Planned Parenthood, SIECUS (Sexuality Information and Education Council of the United States), and Parents and Friends of Lesbians and Gays (PLAG). If a counselor has several self-identified homosexual students, he or she may wish to consider providing a special support group for these youngsters as part of the school counseling services (Robinson, 1994).

Summary

At-risk children and youth are a particular challenge for school personnel and mental health professionals. There are, however, a number of predictors for identifying the at-risk student. Because of their association with students, teachers play a vital role in identifying at-risk students.

Prevention and intervention programs for a variety of at-risk behaviors have become the combined responsibility of schools, social service agencies, religious organizations, parent groups, and law enforcement agencies. Although for each at-risk behavior a number of prevention and intervention strategies and programs have been devised, growing evidence supports the primacy of early identification and treatment, reinforcing both the opportunity and the responsibility of teachers and other educators in the success of prevention and intervention efforts.

In Chapter 12 we will expand our discussion of the responsibilities of teachers. We will also consider their legal rights, as well as those of their students. But first we will explore the legal basis for public education and the legal issues surrounding the church-state relationship in education in Chapter 11.

Key Terms

Acquired immune deficiency syndrome (AIDS)
At-risk
Bibliotherapy
Child abuse
Clinical depression
Cluster suicides
Crisis intervention team
Dropout
Emotional abuse
Gateway drugs
Human immunodeficiency virus

Homophobic harassment
Intervention programs
Neglect
Peer-to-peer sexual harassment
Postvention programs
Prevention strategies
Sexual abuse
Skinheads
Suicide gesture
Suicide ideation
Suicide threat

Discussion Questions

1. If, like Anita Skep, you were confronted with a suicidal child in your classroom, what steps might you take to ensure his or her safety? What type of information and experiences do prospective teachers need to better prepare them to work effectively with children who are at risk for suicidal behavior?

2. How can the school help in combating teen pregnancy? AIDS? How comfortable would you be in discussing "safe sex" with students in the middle grades?

3. How does peer pressure contribute to adolescent substance abuse and youth violence? How can teachers use the power of peer influence to combat these same problems?

4. Compare the behavioral indicators of substance abuse with those of child abuse and sexual abuse.

5. A popular television advertisement states that society will either "pay now, or pay later." Discuss this message in relation to investments in educational programs to combat the dropout problem.

6. What is the relationship between being at risk for becoming a runaway and other at-risk conditions? What are the common identifying characteristics?

References

AIDS, and teens and sex and drugs. (July/August, 1987). *Chemical People Newsletter.*
Alan Guttmacher Institute (1981). *Teenage pregnancy: The problem that hasn't gone away.* New York: Author.
American Psychological Association. (1993). *Violence & youth.* Washington, DC.
Anderson, J. (1994). School climate for gay and lesbian students and staff members. *Phi Delta Kappan, 76,* 151–154.
Bete, C. L. (1989). *About youth runaways.* South Deerfield, MA: Channing L. Bete Co.

Bete, C. L. (1990). *About child abuse.* South Deerfield, MA: Channing L. Bete Co.

Bialo, E. R., & Sivin, J. P. (1989). Computers and at-risk youth: A partial solution to a complex problem. *Classroom Computer Learning, 9*(5), 48–52.

Bonjean, L. M., & Rittenmeyer, D. C. (1987). *Teenage parenthood: The school's response.* Bloomington, IN: Phi Delta Kappa Educational Foundation.

Blum, D. J., & Jones, L. A. (1993). Academic growth group and mentoring program for potential dropouts. *The School Counselor, 40,* 207–212.

Boyer, D., & Fine, D. (1992). Sexual abuse as a factor in adolescent childbearing and child maltreatment. *Family Planning Perspectives, 24,* 4–11, 19.

Caldas, S. (1994). Teen pregnancy: Why it remains a social, economic, and educational problem in the U.S. *Phi Delta Kappan, 75,* 402–406.

Calderone, M. S., & Johnson, E. W. (1985). *Family book about sexuality.* New York: Harper & Row.

Centers for Disease Control & Prevention. (1992). *Youth suicide prevention programs: A resource guide.* Atlanta, GA: U.S. Department of Health & Human Services.

Child abuse. (1994). *The schools and the courts, 20*(1), 1027–1028.

Dorman, G., Geldof, D., & Scarborough, B. (1982). *Living with 10-to-15-year-olds: A parent education curriculum.* Carrboro, NC: Center for Early Adolescence, University of North Carolina-Chapel Hill.

Eggert, L. L. , & Herting, J. R. (1993). Drug involvement among potential dropouts and "typical" youth. *Journal of Drug Education, 23,* 31–55.

Feldman, C. (1994, September 14). Parenthood linked to dropouts. *The Phoenix Gazette,* A16.

The Flinn Foundation. (1989). *An occasional report about the ongoing work of grantees of the Flinn Foundation.* Phoenix, AZ: Author.

Frazier, S. H. (June, 1985). *Task force on youth suicide.* Paper presented at the meeting of the National Conference on Youth Suicide, Washington, DC.

Frymier, J. (1988). Understanding and preventing teen suicide: An interview with Barry Garfinkle. *Phi Delta Kappan, 70,* 290–293.

Frymier, J., & Gansneder, B. (1989). The Phi Delta Kappa study of students at risk. *Phi Delta Kappan, 71,* 142–146.

Gallup Organization. (1991). *Teenage suicide study: Executive summary.* Princeton, NJ.

Garrison, C. Z., McKeown, R. E., Valois, R. F., & Vincent, M. L. (1993). Aggression, substance use, and suicidal behaviors in high school students. *American Journal of Public Health, 82,* 179–184.

Gersten, J. C., & Shamis, S. (1988). Review of risk factors for children's mental health problems. *Children at risk.* Tempe, AZ: Arizona State University, 1–96.

Graham, L., & Harris-Hart, M. (1988). Meeting the challenge of child sexual abuse. *Journal of School Health, 58,* 292–294.

Gracenin, D. (1993). On their own terms. *The Executive Educator, 15*(10), 31–34.

Greydanus, D. E., & Shearin, R. B. (1990). *Adolescent sexuality and gynecology.* Philadelphia: Lea & Febiger.

Greuling, J. W., & DeBlassie, R. R. (1980). Adolescent suicide. *Adolescence, 15,* 589–601.

Grossnickle, D. R. (1986). High school dropouts: Causes, consequences, and cure. Bloomington, IN: *Phi Delta Kappa Educational Foundation,* 1–26.

Guy, S. M., Smith, G. M., & Bentler, P. M. (1994). Consequences of adolescent drug use and personality factors on adult drug use. *Journal of Drug Education, 24,* 109–132.

Haveman, P., & Wolfe, B. (1994). *Succeeding generations: On the effects of investments in children.* New York: Russell Sage Foundation.

Hayes, L. (September 24, 1987). Dropout problem attracts widespread attention. *Guidepost.* Washington, DC: American Association for Counseling and Development, 10.

Hechinger, F. M. (1992). *Fateful choices: Healthy youth for the 21st century.* New York: Carnegie Corporation.

Hersch, P. (1988). Coming of age on city streets. *Psychology Today, 22,* 28–37.

Hipple, J., & Cimbolic, P. (1979). *The counselor and suicidal crisis.* Springfield, IL: Charles C. Thomas.

Horton, L. (1992). *Developing effective drug education programs.* Bloomington, IN: Phi Delta Kappa Education Foundation.

Johnston, L. D., O'Malley, P. M., & Bachman, J. G. (1993). *Selected 1992 outcome measures from the monitoring the future study for goal 6 of the National Education Goals: A special report.* Ann Arbor, MI: University of Michigan.

Jones, E. (1986). *Teenage pregnancy in industrialized countries.* New Haven, CN: Yale University Press.

Jones, E. et al. (1986). *Teenage pregnancy in industrialized countries.* New Haven, CN: Yale University Press.

Kalafat, J., & Elias, M. (1994). An evaluation of a school-based suicide awareness intervention. *Suicide and Life-Threatening Behavior, 24,* 224–233.

Keitner, G. I., Ryan, C. E., Miller, I. W., Epstein, N. B., Bishop, D. S., & Norman, W. H. (1990). Family functioning, social adjustment, and recurrence of suicidality. *Psychiatry, 53,* 17–30.

Kelson v. The City of Springfield, 767 F 2d. 651 (1985), *aff'd.*823F 2d. 554.

Krueger, M. (1993). Everyone is an exception: Assumptions to avoid in the sex education classroom. *Phi Delta Kappan, 74,* 569–572.

Kwok, A., & Hermann, W. (1993, May 23). Gangs' killing fields. *The Arizona Republic,* A1.

Landers, S. (1989). For runaway youth, a homeless existence. *The APA Monitor, 20,* 27.

Lawton, M. (1994, June 8). Against all odds. *Education Week,* 21–24.

Lawton, M. (1994, November 9). Violence-prevention curricula: What works best? *Education Week,* 12–13.

Lawton, M. (1991, April 10). More than a third of teens surveyed say they have contemplated suicide. *Education Week,* 5.

Lethal combination: Sex and death often mix in U.S. (1994, January/February). *Family Planning World, 4,* 1.

Males, M. (1994). Poverty, rape, adult/teen sex: Why "pregnancy prevention" programs don't work. *Phi Delta Kappan, 75,* 407–410.

Males, M. (1993). Schools, society, and "teen" pregnancy. *Phi Delta Kappan, 74,* 566–568.

Malley, P. B., & Kush, F. (1994). Comprehensive and systematic school-based suicide prevention programs: A checklist for counselors. *The School Counselor, 41,* 191–195.

Mayer, G. R., Mitchell, L. K., Clementi, T., Clement-Robertson, E., Myatt, R., & Bullara, D. T. (1993). A dropout prevention program for at-risk high school students: Emphasizing consulting to promote positive classroom climates. *Education and Treatment of Children, 16,* 135–146.

McGarrahan, E., & Brecher, E. J. (December 19, 1989). Pulling driving rights of dropouts triggers an outburst of yawns. *The Arizona Republic,* A6.

Meehan, P. J., Lamb, J. A., Saltzman, L. E., & O'Carroll, P. W. (1991). Attempted suicide among young adults: Progress toward a meaningful estimate of prevalence. *American Journal of Psychiatry, 149,* 41–44.

Minard, S. (1993). The school counselor's role in confronting child sexual abuse. *The School Counselor, 41,* 9–15.

National Education Goals Panel. (1993). *The National Education Goals Report.* Washington, DC: U.S. Government Printing Office.

National Institute of Mental Health (NIMH). (1992). *Suicide fact sheet.* Washington, DC: U.S. Government Printing Office.

National Institute of Drug Abuse (NIDA). (1994). *Monitoring the Future Study, 1975–1993: National high school drug abuse survey.* Rockville, MD: NIDA.

Pearson, L. C., & Banerji, M. (1993). Effects of a ninth-grade dropout prevention program on student academic achievement, school attendance, and dropout rate. *Journal of Experimental Education, 61,* 247–256.

Pfeffer, C. (1991). Family characteristics and support systems as risk factors for youthful suicidal behavior. In L. Davidson, & M. Linnoila (Eds). *Risk factors for youth suicide* (pp. 55–71). New York: Hemisphere.

Pfeffer, C. (1986). *The suicidal child.* New York: Guilford Press.

Phi Delta Kappa. (September, 1988). Current issues memo: Responding to student suicide—The first 48 hours. Bloomington, IN: Author.

Poland, S. (1994). The role of school crisis intervention teams to prevent and reduce school violence and trauma. *School Psychology Review, 23,* 175–189.

Popham, W. J. (1993). Wanted: AIDS education that works. *Phi Delta Kappan, 74,* 559–562.

Portner, J. (1994, October 5). Districts adopting policies to protect gay students' rights. *Education Week,* 8.

Portner, J. (1994, November 2). Teenage birthrates decline for the 1st time since '86: New federal study reports. *Education Week,* 9.

Preventing risk behaviors among students. (1992). *CDC HIV/AIDS Prevention Newsletter, 3*(3), 1.

Prothrow-Stith, D. (1994). Building violence prevention into the curriculum. *The School Administrator, 51,* 8–12.

Reed, S., & Sautter, R. C. (1990). Children of poverty: The status report of 12 million young Americans. *Phi Delta Kappan, 71,* K1–K12.

Robinson, K. E. (1994). Addressing the needs of gay and lesbian students: The school counselor's role. *The School Counselor, 41,* 326–332.

Rohr, M. E., & James. R. (1994). Runaways: Some suggestions for prevention, coordinating services, and expediting the reentry process. *The School Counselor, 42,* 40–47.

Salzman, K. P., & Salzman, S. A. (1989). *Characteristics of adolescents at risk for psychological dysfunction and school failure.* Paper presented at the Annual Convention of the American Educational Research Association, San Francisco, CA.

Sautter, R. C. (1995). Standing up to violence. *Phi Delta Kappan, 76,* K1–K12.

Scott-Jones, D. (1993). Adolescent childbearing: Whose problem? What can we do? *Kappan Special Report, 75,* K1–K12.

Serving homeless children: The responsibilities of educators.(1992). Washington, DC: Policy Studies Associates.

Sexual harassment widespread, report says. (1993). *The Executive Educator, 15,* (7), 8.

Shaffer, D., Garland, A., Underwood, M., & Whittle, B. (1987). *An evaluation of three youth prevention programs in New Jersey.* Report prepared for the New Jersey State Department of Health & Human Services.

Sleek, S. (1994, September). Psychology is finding a home in school-based health clinics. *American Psychological Association Monitor, 1,* 34.

Social Security Administration. (April, 1989). *Providing medical evidence for individuals with AIDS and ARC: A guide for health professionals.* Washington, DC: U.S. Government Printing Office.

Stevens-Smith, P., & Remley, T., Jr. (1994). Drugs, AIDS, and teens: Intervention and the school counselor. *The School Counselor, 41,* 180–183.

Strother, D. B. (1986). Practical applications of research: Suicide among the young. *Phi Delta Kappan, 67,* 756–759.

Upchurch, D. M. & McCarthy, J. (1990). The timing of a first birth and high school completion. *American Sociological Review, 55,* 224–234.

U.S. Bureau of the Census. (1994). *Statistical abstract of the United States 1994.* Washington, DC: U.S. Government Printing Office.

U.S. Department of Education, National Center for Education Statistics. (1994a). *Condition of education 1994.* Washington, DC: U.S. Government Printing Office.

U.S. Department of Education, National Center for Education Statistics. (1994b). *Dropout rate in the United States: 1993.* Washington, DC: U.S. Government Printing Office.

U.S. Department of Education, National Center for Education Statistics. (1993). *Reaching the goals: Safe, disciplined, and drug-free schools.* Washington, DC: U.S Government Printing Office.

U.S. Department of Education, Office of Educational Research and Improvement. (1988). *Drug prevention curricula: A guide to selection and implementation.* Washington, DC: U.S. Government Printing Office.

U.S. teens smoking as much now as in '84, despite caveats (1994, November 17), *The Arizona Republic,* A13.

Vissing, Y. M., Schroepfer, D., & Bloise, F. (1994). Homeless students, heroic students. *Phi Delta Kappan, 75,* 535–539.

Vobejda, B. (1994, June 7). Teens' use of birth control up, study says. *The Arizona Republic,* A1.

Walling, S. R. (1993). *Gay teens at risk.* Bloomington, IN: Phi Delta Kappa Educational Foundation.

Watts, W. D., & Ellis, A. M. (1993). Sexual abuse and drinking and drug use: Implications for prevention. *Journal of Drug Education, 23,* 183–200.

Whitehead, B. D. (1993). Dan Qualye was right. *Atlantic, 271,* 47–84.

Yarber, W. L. (1987). *AIDS education: Curriculum and health policy.* Bloomington, IN: Phi Delta Kappa Educational Foundation.

Youths report cases of abuse, assault in survey. (1994, October 26). *Education Week,* 10.

Zielinski, G. (1994, December 13). Students' use of pot on rise. *The Arizona Republic,* A1, A10.

PART FIVE

Legal and Political Control and Financial Support

Chapter 11

Legal Framework for the Public Schools

The Law is the true embodiment
Of everything that's excellent.

W. S. Gilbert (1836–1911)

A Critical Incident in My Teaching Career . . .

Paul was a nonreader, a social outcast, and every teacher's nightmare. The early months were a test for survival as he yelled, kicked, and stole his way through every day. We persevered, but sometimes at a great price. Then one day this troubled, insecure little boy requested to speak to the class. With his body touching mine for strength and in a halting voice he asked forgiveness for being so mean and thanked everyone for trying to be nice to him. That day, as Paul's world began to change slowly, I knew mine had changed forever.

Lynn Rylander Kaufman
Teacher of the Year, Nebraska

The *law* may be defined as "a body of rules of action or conduct prescribed by controlling authority, and having binding legal force" (Black, 1990, p. 457). It is within the rules of action or conduct provided by federal and state constitutional provisions, federal and state statutory law, regulations and decisions of administrative agencies, court decisions, and attorney general opinions that the framework is established for the operation of the public schools. Before going into the specifics of the law as they affect students' and teachers' rights, this chapter provides a brief overview of the major sources of school law, the federal and state court systems, and their interrelationship in forming the legal basis for public education. After reading this chapter you should be able to:

- Identify federal constitutional provisions affecting education.
- Discuss the importance of state constitutional provisions affecting education.
- Compare statutory law, common law, and administrative law.
- Describe the levels of the federal court system and those of a typical state court system.
- Explain how challenges under the establishment clause are evaluated.
- Give the current posture of the courts in regard to prayer and Bible reading, student devotional activities, compulsory attendance, and private and home schooling.
- Distinguish between permissible and impermissible state aid to nonpublic education.

Federal Constitutional Provisions Affecting Education

Written contracts for the establishment of governments, known as *constitutions,* are uniquely American (Collins, 1969). Constitutions are the highest level of law. They are the fundamental laws of the people of a state or nation, establishing the very character and concept of their government, its organization and officers, its sovereign powers, and the limitations of its power. Constitutions are written broadly so as to endure changing times and circumstances. While constitutions can be changed by amendment, the process is normally difficult and is seldom utilized. The Constitution of the United States, written over 200 years ago, has served the needs of a fledgling nation and a world power, with only 26 amendments.

Education, though, is not mentioned in the U.S. Constitution. It is therefore considered to be one of the powers reserved to the States by the Tenth Amendment, which states, "The powers not delegated to the United States by the Constitution, nor prohibited by it to the States, are reserved to the States respectively, or to the people." Although the provision of education is considered one of the powers of the state, the supremacy clause of the Constitution (Article VI, Section 2) declares that the Constitution and the laws enacted by the U.S. Congress are the supreme law of the land. Thus the states, in exercising their authority, may not enact any laws that violate any provisions of the federal Constitution.

Several important sections of the federal Constitution have an impact on the schools (see Figure 11.1). Among these are Article I, Section 8; Article I, Section 10; and the First, Fourth, Fifth, Eighth, Ninth, Tenth, and Fourteenth Amendments. These constitutional provisions serve as the basis for education-related cases being brought to federal courts.

General Welfare Clause

In what ways does federal support of education contribute to the "common defense" of the United States?

Article I, Section 8, known as the general welfare clause, gives Congress the power to tax and to "provide for the common defense and general welfare of the United States." Over the years, the Supreme Court has interpreted the general welfare clause as authorizing Congress to tax and spend money for a variety of activities, education among them, that were construed as being in the general welfare. However, the general welfare clause does not give Congress the authority to do anything it pleases to provide for the general welfare, only to tax for that purpose. In regard to education, this means that while Congress may levy taxes to provide support for education, it may not legislate control of education. However, in recent years the Supreme Court has ruled that the federal government can attach conditions to the use of federal funds which, if not complied with, may result in the denial or withdrawal of the funds.

Exercising its authority under the general welfare clause, Congress has enacted a massive body of legislation that has provided direct federal support for a variety of instructional programs (e.g., foreign language education, math education, science education, adult education, career education, and vocational and technical education), as well as providing services and programs for identified

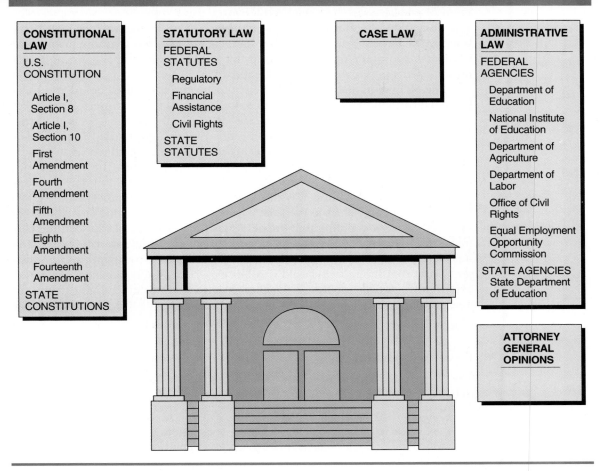

Figure 11.1: Laws Affecting the Schools

CONSTITUTIONAL LAW

U.S. CONSTITUTION

Article I, Section 8

Article I, Section 10

First Amendment

Fourth Amendment

Fifth Amendment

Eighth Amendment

Fourteenth Amendment

STATE CONSTITUTIONS

STATUTORY LAW

FEDERAL STATUTES

Regulatory

Financial Assistance

Civil Rights

STATE STATUTES

CASE LAW

ADMINISTRATIVE LAW

FEDERAL AGENCIES

Department of Education

National Institute of Education

Department of Agriculture

Department of Labor

Office of Civil Rights

Equal Employment Opportunity Commission

STATE AGENCIES
State Department of Education

ATTORNEY GENERAL OPINIONS

special need students (e.g., free and reduced-cost food programs, special education, bilingual education) and financial assistance to prospective teachers. Article I, Section 8 has also served as the authority for the federal government to establish the U.S. military academies (Air Force, Army, Coast Guard, and Navy); operate overseas schools for dependents of military and civilian personnel; and establish schools on Indian reservations, in the U.S. territories, and in the District of Columbia. In addition, Congress may operate libraries, such as the Library of Congress, and conduct a variety of other activities and operations deemed educational in nature.

Obligations of Contracts Clause

Article I, Section 10, the obligation of contracts clause, declares: "No state shall . . . pass any Bill of Attainder, *ex post facto* law, or law impairing the obligation of

Contracts." This provision of the Constitution prohibits a state legislature from passing a law relative to teacher tenure or retirement that would be to the detriment of teachers who had acquired a contractive status under existing statutes. The obligation of contracts clause also protects school personnel who have contracts from arbitrary dismissals. That is, a teacher who has a contract cannot be dismissed during the term of that contract without a showing of cause and without due process (see discussion in Chapter 12).

The obligation of contracts clause protects both the school board and those businesses and individuals with whom it does business from nonperformance relative to the terms of the contract. For example, a Louisiana school district entered into a contract for the building of a junior high school to replace one that had burned down. The contract provided that the building was to be substantially completed by August 1. According to the contract, the school board was to be paid $200 for every day after August 1 that the building was not completed. When the building was not completed until September 4 the school board withheld $6,600 from the final payment to the contractor. The contractor sued for recovery, claiming that the delay was excused under a clause in the contract that allowed for extensions caused by adverse weather conditions. The school board's action was upheld on appeal because the contractor did not present proof that the rain and cold weather experienced was in excess of what an experienced contractor should have taken into account in estimating time for weather losses when bidding on contracts that have a term for performance (*S. J. Lemoine v. St. Landry Parrish School,* 1988).

First Amendment

The First Amendment addresses several basic personal freedoms. It provides that:

> Congress shall make no law respecting an establishment of religion, or prohibiting the free exercise thereof; or abridging the freedom of speech or of the press; or of the right of the people peaceably to assemble, and to petition the Government for a redress of grievances.

Increasingly, the first clause of the First Amendment, the establishment and free exercise of religion clause, has become the focus of litigation in education. The schools have become a battleground for some of the most volatile disputes over the appropriate governmental relationship vis-a-vis religion (McCarthy & Cambron-McCabe, 1992). As discussed later in this chapter, these cases have dealt with numerous issues surrounding (1) school practices objected to on the basis of promoting or inhibiting religion (e.g., released time, prayer, and Bible reading), (2) curriculum content, and (3) public funds used to provide support to nonpublic schools or to students or parents of students attending nonpublic schools.

The second clause of the First Amendment, that dealing with the freedom of speech and press, has also been the subject of a growing number of education cases in recent years. Both teachers and students have increasingly protested abridgements of their rights to express themselves—from wearing of long hair to publicly criticizing school board practices. Teachers have also become more concerned with what they consider attempts to infringe upon their academic freedom to select textbooks and other teaching materials and to practice certain teaching methodologies.

The third clause of the First Amendment, which deals with the rights of citizens to assemble, has also been called into question in a number of education cases concerning the freedom of association. Both students and teachers have become more assertive of their right to belong to various organizations, including those that may have goals contrary to that of the school system. The question of freedom of association has also been at issue in a number of cases dealing with teachers' associations or unions. Questions of non–school-sponsored student assemblies are usually not addressed under this clause but under the freedom of religion (if that is their purpose) or freedom of expression clauses.

Fourth Amendment

The Fourth Amendment provides that the right of the people to be "secure in their persons, houses, papers, and effects, against unreasonable searches and seizures, shall not be violated and no warrants shall issue, but upon probable cause." The growing problem of student possession of drugs and other contraband has led to an increasing number of student searches. As we will see in the next chapter, the Fourth Amendment has served as the basis for a number of student challenges to warrantless searches of their automobiles, lockers, or persons by school officials and others. A few cases involving searches of teachers' desks or other personal belongings have also been heard.

Fifth Amendment

According to the provisions of the Fifth Amendment, no person shall be "compelled in any criminal case to be a witness against himself, nor be deprived of life, liberty, or property, without due process of law; nor shall private property be taken for public use, without just compensation." The first clause of the Fifth Amendment, the self-incrimination clause, permits individuals to refuse to answer questions, the answers to which might be used against them or might subject them to prosecution by the state. In education cases, this clause has been invoked by teachers in refusing to answer questions about their affiliations and activities outside the school. However, the courts have ruled that teachers may not use the Fifth Amendment to avoid answering questions about their activities outside the classroom that relate to their qualifications or fitness to teach (*Beilan v. Board of Public Education*, 1958).

The due process protection of the Fifth Amendment is not usually involved in education cases. Rather, the due process clause of the Fourteenth Amendment is used because it relates directly to the states.

The last clause of the Fifth Amendment is relevant in those few cases where the state or school system is seeking to obtain private property for school purposes in the exercise of the government's right of *eminent domain*, the right to take private property for public use. Thus a school district attempting to gain property to enlarge a school may find it necessary to exercise its power of emi-

The use of drug-sniffing dogs is one of the most controversial issues regarding student searches.

nent domain (if such power has been given it by the state) if it has not been able to negotiate a voluntary purchase of the needed property. Whenever the power of eminent domain is exercised, just compensation must be given to the owners of the property that is taken.

Eighth Amendment

How have society's views regarding corporal punishment in the schools changed since you began school?

The Eighth Amendment, in part, provides protection against "cruel and unusual punishments." This amendment on occasion has been involved in challenging the practice or use of corporal punishment in schools. The Supreme Court has held, however, that disciplinary corporal punishment *per se* is not cruel and unusual punishment as anticipated by the Eighth Amendment (*Ingraham v. Wright,* 1977). This does not mean, however, that corporal punishment may not be prohibited by state or school district regulations or that punishment can be excessive. In fact, if the punishment causes physical harm it may be grounds for a civil action for assault and battery.

Fourteenth Amendment

The Fourteenth Amendment is the federal constitutional provision most often involved in education-related cases because it pertains specifically to state actions and, as previously stated, education is a state function. The Fourteenth Amendment states:

No State shall make or enforce any law which shall abridge the privileges or immunities of citizens of the United States; nor shall any State deprive any person of life, liberty, or property, without due process of law; nor deny to any person within its jurisdiction the equal protection of the laws.

The due process clause of the Fourteenth Amendment has proved to be of great importance to students in disciplinary actions and to teachers in negative personnel actions, and has been invoked in a wide array of issues involving student and teacher rights. As discussed in the next chapter, the equal protection clause has served as the basis for numerous cases involving discrimination on the basis of race, sex, handicapping condition, or other classifications used in the schools.

State Constitutional Provisions Affecting Education

Like the federal Constitution, state constitutions have provided the foundation for the enactment of subsequent innumerable statutes that govern the activities of the state and its citizens. However, unlike the federal Constitution, which contains no reference to education, every state constitution includes a provision for education, and all but one expressly provides for the establishment of a system of public schools. These provisions range from very general to very specific, but their overall intent is to ensure that schools and education be encouraged and that a uniform system of schools be established. For example, Article X, Section 3 (as amended, April 1972) of the Wisconsin constitution provides:

> The Legislature shall provide by law for the establishment of district schools, which shall be as nearly uniform as practical; and such schools shall be free and without charge for tuition to all children between the ages of 4 and 20 years.

The constitutions of 45 states provide for the establishment of "common schools" (see Chapter 4 for history of common schools), and 35 states establish specific methods for financial support (Collins, 1969). The constitutions of 30 states expressly prohibit the use of public funds for the use of religious schools, and the constitution of every state except Maine and North Carolina contains a provision prohibiting religious instruction in the public schools. In addition, some state constitutions also specifically prohibit both religious and political requirements for admission. For example, Article XI, Section 7 of the Arizona constitution provides:

> No sectarian instruction shall be imparted in any school or State educational institution and no religious or political test or qualification shall ever be required as a condition of admission into any public educational institution of the State, as teacher, student, or pupil.

The wording of the state constitutional provision for education has proven to be very important to the courts in determining whether particular legislative enactments were constitutionally permissible or required. For example, a Court of Appeals ruled that the constitutional requirements that the state legislature provide for a system of free common schools did not require that free textbooks be provided to high school students (*Carpio v. Tucson High School District No. 1,* 1974). The basis for the court's decision was its interpretation of common schools as consisting only of grades one through eight.

Regardless of the particular provisions related to education contained in a state's constitution, the state constitution does not grant unlimited power to the state legislature in providing for the public schools. Rather, it establishes the boundaries within which the legislature may operate. The legislature may not then enact legislation exceeding these parameters or violate any provisions of the federal Constitution, which is the supreme law of the land.

Statutory Law

Statutory law is that body of law consisting of the written enactments of a legislative body. These written enactments, called statutes, constitute the second highest level of law, following constitutions. Where constitutions provide broad statements of policy, statutes establish the specifics of operation. Both the U.S. Congress and state legislatures have enacted innumerable statutes affecting the provision of education in this country. These statutes are continually reviewed and often revised or supplemented by successive legislatures. They are also subject to review by the courts to determine their intent and to determine if they are in violation of the constitution. If they do not violate constitutional limitations, they are binding on all citizens and governmental agencies (Valente, 1994).

Federal Statutes

Despite the federal constitutional silence on education, during each session the U.S. Congress enacts or renews numerous statutes that affect the public schools. Some of these, such as the Occupational Safety and Health Act (OSHA), which requires employers to furnish a safe working environment, although not directed specifically at school districts, do affect their operation. Many of the statutes enacted by Congress are related to the provision of financial assistance to the schools for a variety of special instructional programs, research, or programs for needy children. Yet another finance bill, the Servicemen's Readjustment Act, popularly known as the G.I. Bill, provides aid to veterans to complete their education, including those who want to complete a regular high school program.

In addition to federal statutes providing financial assistance, federal civil rights statutes also have had a considerable impact on educational programs and personnel. An overview of the major civil rights statutes affecting schools is provided in Table 11.1. They are discussed in more detail in relevant sections of this text.

State Statutes

Most of the statutory laws affecting the public schools are enacted by state legislatures. The power of the state legislature is *plenary,* or absolute; it may enact any legislation that is not contrary to federal and state constitutions. Although the

Table 11.1: Summary of Major Civil Rights Statutes Affecting Education

Statute	Major Provision
Civil Rights Act of 1866, 1870 42 U.S.C. §1981	Provides all citizens equal rights under the law regardless of race
Civil Rights Act of 1871 42 U.S.C. §1983	Any person who deprives another of his/her rights may be held liable to the injured party
Civil Rights Act of 1871 42 U.S.C. §1985 and 1986	Persons conspiring to deprive another of his/her rights, or any person having knowledge of any such conspiracy, are subject to any action to recover damages
Civil Rights Act of 1866, 1870 (as amended) 42 U.S.C. §1988	Courts may award reasonable attorney fees to the prevailing party in any action arising out of the above acts and Title VI of the Civil Rights of 1964
Civil Rights Act of 1964, Title VI 42 U.S.C. § 2000(d)	Prohibits discrimination on the basis of race, color, or national origin
Civil Rights Act of 1964, Title VII 42 U.S.C. § 2000(e)	Prohibits discrimination in employment on the basis of race, color, religion, sex, or national origin
Education Amendments of 1972, Title IX 20 U.S.C. §1681	Prohibits sex discrimination in any education program or activity receiving federal financial assistance
Equal Pay Act of 1964 29 U.S.C. § 206(D)	Prohibits sex discrimination in pay
Age Discrimination in Employment Act of 1967 29 U.S.C. § 621	Prohibits discrimination against any individual with respect to employment unless age is a bona fide occupational qualification
Equal Educational Opportunities Act of 1974 20 U.S.C. §1703	Prohibits any state from denying equal educational opportunities to any individual based on his/her race, color, sex, or national origin
Rehabilitation Act of 1973 (as amended) 29 U.S.C. § 791	Prohibits discrimination against any "otherwise qualified handicapped individual"
Americans with Disabilities Act of 1990 42 U.S.C. §12112	Prohibits discrimination against persons with disabilities
Individuals with Disabilities Education Act of 1990 20 U.S.C. §1400–1485	Individuals with disabilities must be guaranteed a free appropriate education by programs receiving federal financial assistance
Civil Rights Restoration Act of 1991 42 U.S.C. §1981 et seq.	Amends the Civil Rights Act of 1964, the Age Discrimination in Employment Act of 1967, and the Americans with Disabilities Act of 1990 with regard to employment discrimination

What laws or statutes have recently been passed in your state that affect certification?

principle is challenged every year by local school districts, the courts have clearly established that education is a function of the state, not an inherent function of the local school district, and that the local district has only those powers delegated to it by the state legislature. The courts have also affirmed the authority of the state to regulate such matters as certification, powers of school boards, accreditation, curriculum, the school calendar, graduation requirements, facilities construction and operation, and raising and spending of monies. In fact, the courts have made it clear that school districts have no inherent right to exist; they exist only at the will of the legislature and can be created, reorganized, or abolished by legislative prerogative.

Although the state legislature has in fact delegated the actual operation of the majority of the schools to the local school districts (state governments often retain operation of certain types of specialized schools, such as schools for the deaf and blind), the legislature still must pass legislation to administer the system as a whole and to provide for its financing and operation. Consequently, numerous education statutes exist in every state, and in every legislative session new statutes will be enacted that affect education.

Case Law

Distinct from statutes, regulations, or other sources of law is that body of law originating with historical usages and customs, including court decisions. This body of law is referred to as case law, or common law. Case law is based on the doctrine of *stare decisis,* which means "let the decision stand." The doctrine requires that once a court has laid down a principle of law as applicable to a certain set of facts, it will apply it to all future cases where the facts are substantially the same, and other courts of equal or lesser rank will similarly apply the principle (Black, 1990). However, adherence to the doctrine of *stare decisis* does not mean that all previous decisions may never be challenged or overturned. On numerous occasions a higher or subsequent court, has rejected the reasoning of a lower or earlier court, or constitutional or statutory changes, in effect, have overturned the previous decision.

Administrative Law

Administrative law consists of the formal regulations and decisions of those state or federal agencies that are authorized by law to regulate public functions. These regulations carry the force of law, are subject to judicial review, and will stand as law unless found to be in conflict with federal or state constitutional provisions, statutes, or court decisions.

The U.S. Department of Education and the National Institute of Education are the federal agencies most directly concerned with education. The secretary of education and the director of the National Institute of Education are both appointed by the president. The regulations issued by the Office of Civil Rights of the Department of Education in regard to the implementation of Title IX are a prime example of the profound impact that administrative law can have on the operations of the schools.

Among the other federal agencies that have significant interaction with schools are the Department of Agriculture, which administers the National School Lunch Act; the Department of the Interior, Bureau of Indian Affairs, which administers numerous programs aimed at improving the education of Native Americans; and the Department of Labor, which administers the Occupational Safety and Health Act. In addition, both the Office of Civil Rights of the Department of Education and another federal agency, the Equal Employment Opportunity Commission, are charged with enforcement of civil rights and nondiscrimination legislation.

The state agency that has the most direct control and responsibility over education is the state department of education. A large body of administrative law is generated by this agency as a result of the promulgation of numerous rules and regulations relating to such areas as certification of teachers, accreditation of schools, adoption of textbooks, courses of study, minimum standards for specified areas, and distribution of state funds.

Attorney General Opinions

Yet another source of education law is the opinions of the state attorney general. The *attorney general* is the chief legal officer of the state and acts as legal advisor to state agencies. The attorney general is normally required to furnish written opinions concerning an interpretation of law to the governor and other state and local officials (i.e., not to private citizens or school personnel such as teachers or even principals, but to officials such as the chairperson of the school board). State attorney generals are often called on to interpret state constitutional or statutory provisions (existing or proposed), school board policies, or questionable administrative actions. While such opinions are only advisory, they are helpful in clarification and interpretation of the law (LaMorte, 1993). For example, in a 1988 opinion to the executive secretary-treasurer of the Georgia Teachers' Retirement System, the Georgia attorney general concluded that the same period of military service could not be counted for credit for both military retirement and state retirement. To do so would constitute "double dipping" (Ga. Op. Atty. Gen., 1988).

Powers and Organization of the Courts

According to our system of government a separation of power exists between the executive, legislative, and judicial branches of the government. In school-related matters, the courts have generally taken the position that they will not intervene in a dispute unless all internal appeals have been exhausted. For example, where school board policy provides teachers with the right of direct appeal to the board in cases involving involuntary teacher transfers, this avenue of appeal must be exhausted before the courts will hear the appeal. The exceptions to this provision are those cases involving an alleged violation of a constitutionally protected right.

Courts cannot become involved in education cases of their own initiative. A case must be brought to the court for resolution. The most common type of school case brought to the court is one that requires the court to interpret laws within its jurisdiction. Another common type of school case requires the court to determine the constitutionality of legislative or administrative enactments.

Federal courts generally are involved in only two kinds of issues: those involving questions of interpretations of the federal Constitution or federal statutes, and those involving parties of different states. Sometimes a case will involve questions of both federal and state law. When this occurs, the federal court can decide on the state issue, but it must do so according to the rules governing the courts of that state. Most education cases that come to federal courts involve alleged violations of constitutionally protected rights or interpretations of federal statutes.

The Federal Court System

The federal court system consists of three levels of courts of general jurisdiction: a supreme court, district courts, and courts of appeals. In addition, the federal court system includes courts of special jurisdiction, such as the Customs Court or the Tax Court. These courts would normally not be involved in education cases (see Figure 11.2).

District Courts

How many district courts are in your state? What is the name of the district court in the area in which you reside?

The lowest level federal courts are district courts. There are more than 90 district courts: at least one in each state, and in the more populated states, such as California, New York, and Texas, as many as four. Federal district courts are given names reflective of the geographic area they serve; for example, S.D. Ohio indicates the Southern District of Ohio. District courts are the courts of initiation or original jurisdiction for most cases filed in the federal court system, including most education cases. They are trial courts, meaning a jury hears the case. The decisions of federal district courts have an automatic right of appeal to the next level of federal courts—U.S. Circuit Courts of Appeals.

Circuit Courts

There are 13 circuit courts of appeals in the federal system. Like the district courts, each court of appeals has jurisdiction over a specific geographic area (see Figure 11.3). The circuit court carries the name of the geographic circuit it serves (e.g., the Sixth Circuit, abbreviated as 6th Cir.). A circuit court hears appeals from the decisions of district courts and certain federal administrative agencies. It hears arguments from attorneys, but it does not retry the case. There is no jury. A panel of judges, usually three, hears the case and can affirm, reverse, or modify the decision of the lower court, or remand the case back to the lower court for modifications or retrial.

The decision of a federal circuit court is binding only on federal district courts within its geographic jurisdiction. Circuit courts have no power over state

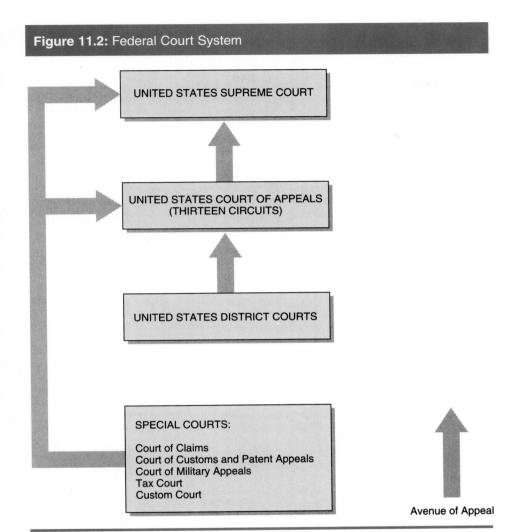

Figure 11.2: Federal Court System

UNITED STATES SUPREME COURT

UNITED STATES COURT OF APPEALS
(THIRTEEN CIRCUITS)

UNITED STATES DISTRICT COURTS

SPECIAL COURTS:

Court of Claims
Court of Customs and Patent Appeals
Court of Military Appeals
Tax Court
Custom Court

Avenue of Appeal

courts and do not hear appeals from them, nor does the decision of one circuit court bind other circuit courts or the district courts in other circuits. Thus it is possible, and indeed it happens quite often, that one circuit court will rule one way, for example, that the wearing of long hair is constitutionally protected, while another circuit court will rule in the reverse.

U.S. Supreme Court

The highest federal appeals court, indeed the highest court in the land, is the U.S. Supreme Court. Decisions of the Supreme Court are absolute: there is no appeal. If Congress or citizens do not agree with a decision of the Supreme Court, the only ways they can mediate against the effect of the decision are to pass a law or to get the court to reconsider the issue in a later case. Both of these

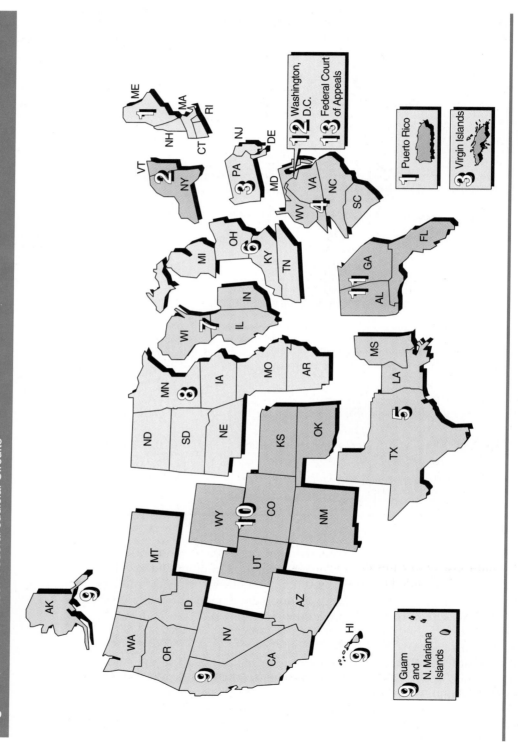

Figure 11.3: The Thirteen Federal Judicial Circuits

Historical Note:
U.S. Supreme Court Justices

John Marshall served longer than any other justice, over 34 years. Four other justices also served over 30 years. William J. Brennan (33 years), Stephen J. Field (34 years), John McLean (32 years), and Joseph Story (34 years).

While a number of justices were said to be able sportsmen, perhaps the one who demonstrated this most visibly was Byron R. White, who played three seasons in the National Football League.

Several justices resigned to assume other public offices. James F. Brynes left in 1942 to become director of the Office of War Mobilization. Arthur Goldburg became U.S. ambassador to the United Nations, and John Rutledge became chief justice of the South Carolina Supreme Court. Rutledge later returned to the Court and served as chief justice *pro tem* for one year, but his apparent insanity led the Senate to reject his nomination. Charles Evans Hughes resigned to run unsuccessfully as the Republican candidate for the presidency in 1916. In 1930, upon nomination by President Herbert Hoover, he returned to the Court as its chief justice.

Some justices have done double duty. While serving as chief justice, John Jay also served as ambassador to Great Britain; and while serving on the Court, Robert Jackson became chief counsel to the United States at the Nuremburg war crimes trials.

---

events happen with some regularity. A notable example in education of the Supreme Court reversing itself on reconsideration is the case of *Brown v. Board of Education of Topeka* (1954). In *Plessey v. Ferguson* (1896), the Supreme Court had said "separate but equal" public facilities for blacks and whites were constitutionally permissible. But in 1954 in the *Brown* decision, the court reversed this position and ruled that separate educational facilities for blacks and whites were inherently unequal.

The Supreme Court hears cases on appeal from lower federal courts or from state supreme courts if the state case involves questions of federal law. While thousands of cases are appealed to the Supreme Court each year, only a small number are heard. However, in recent years the number of education cases being appealed to the Supreme Court and heard by it has increased.

The State Court Systems

Since most education cases do not involve the federal Constitution or federal statutes, they are handled by state courts rather than federal courts. Like the federal court system, the state court system is created by the state constitution and subsequent legislative enactments. Although the specific structure of the court system and the names given to courts vary from state to state, there are sufficient commonalities to permit a description of the general structure for state courts as shown in Figure 11.4.

Most states have courts that are designated as courts of limited or special jurisdiction. The limitation may be related to the types of cases they may handle (e.g., probate courts or juvenile courts) or the amount in controversy (e.g., small claims courts or traffic courts). Generally, state court systems do not permit appeal of the decisions of courts of limited jurisdiction.

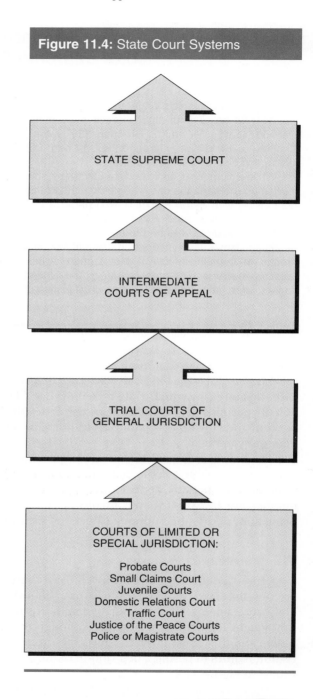

Figure 11.4: State Court Systems

STATE SUPREME COURT

INTERMEDIATE
COURTS OF APPEAL

TRIAL COURTS OF
GENERAL JURISDICTION

COURTS OF LIMITED OR
SPECIAL JURISDICTION:

Probate Courts
Small Claims Court
Juvenile Courts
Domestic Relations Court
Traffic Court
Justice of the Peace Courts
Police or Magistrate Courts

All states have courts of general jurisdiction. Courts of general jurisdiction are generally trial courts, and as such hear witnesses, admit evidence, and, when appropriate, conduct jury trials. Depending on the state, courts of general jurisdiction may be referred to as district courts, county courts, circuit courts, superior courts, or supreme courts (in New York State). Appeals from the decisions of courts of general jurisdiction are made to state appellate courts, often referred to as courts of appeals. Appellate courts are found in all state court systems. Normally they are organized by geographic area. Like the federal appellate courts, state appellate courts do not retry cases but sit as a panel of judges (usually three) to review the record of the trial court and hear attorneys' arguments.

The final appeal in state court systems is to the state supreme court, the final authority on questions related to the state constitution or state law. If the case involves federal issues, however, appeal may be taken from the state supreme court to the U.S. Supreme Court.

Church-State Relations

The issue of the appropriate relationship between religion and the state has been one of the most controversial in American legal history. The "establishment and free exercise" clauses of the First Amendment state that "Congress shall make no law respecting an establishment of religion or prohibiting the free exercise thereof." The experience of the nation's founders with state control of education prompted a desire to erect what Jefferson called "a wall of separation between Church and State." Although the clause makes reference only to actions of the federal government (Congress), it is made applicable to the states by the Fourteenth Amendment, which prohibits state actions that violate the constitutional rights of citizens.

Maintaining the wall of separation without being "hostile to religion" has been the challenge faced by policy makers at every level of government, as well as by public school teachers and administrators. Often they find their actions challenged in the courts, and a few cases have reached the U.S. Supreme Court (see Table 11.2). The issues most often contested can be categorized into three broad areas: religious activities, curriculum bias, and public support. Other areas of importance, if not as litigious, involve compulsory attendance and private and home schooling.

Religious Activities

Released Time

Traditionally, a not uncommon practice in American public schools was the releasing of children during the school day for religious instruction. The first case to reach the Supreme Court, *McCollum v. Board of Education* (1948), resulted in a ruling that the released time program violated the establishment clause of the First Amendment. In this case, students were excused from regular classes to attend private religious instruction in another part of the building. Four years later the court upheld a program in which, by parental request, children were permitted to leave the public school to receive religious instruction (*Zorach v. Clauson*, 1952). As in *McCollum*, the instructors were not paid by the school. The distinction made by the court between *Zorach* and *McCollum* was that public school facilities were not involved in *Zorach*.

Table 11.2 Overview of Selected U.S. Supreme Court Cases Affecting Church-School Relations

Case	Decision
Pierce v. Society of Sisters (1925)	Parents have the right to educate their children in private schools.
Cochran v. Louisiana State Board of Education (1930)	States may provide secular textbooks to children attending sectarian schools.
West Virginia State Board of Education v. Varnette (1943)	Public schools may not require the salute to the flag.
Everson v. Board of Education (1947)	States may use public funds to provide for transportation of children to and from private, sectarian schools where state constitution permits it.
Illinois ex rel. McCollum v. Board of Education (1948)	Released time program whereby instruction is provided during school hours on school grounds is unconstitutional.
Zorach v. Clauson (1952)	Released time program whereby students are released to go off campus to receive instruction and where no state support is provided is constitutional.
Engel v. Vitale (1962)	Public schools may not require the recitation of prayers.
School District of Abington Township v. Schempp (19653)	State may not promote Bible readings and prayers, even when participation is not compulsory.
Epperson v. Arkansas (1968)	State law forbidding the teaching of evolution is unconstitutional.
Lemon v. Kurtzman (1971)	State support to nonpublic schools, their personnel, and their students is unconstitutional if it (1) has a primarily religious purpose, (2) either advances or inhibits religion, or (3) creates an excessive entanglement between church and state.
Muller v. Allen (1983)	State may provide income tax deduction for educational expenses of nonpublic school parents if also available to public school parents.
Wallace v. Jaffree (1985)	State laws authorizing classroom periods of silent meditation or prayer are unconstitutional.
Edwards v. Aguillard (1987)	Public schools may not be required to teach creationism.
Board of Education of Westside Community Schools v. Mergens (1990)	Schools must provide access to student-sponsored religious groups if access is provided to other student groups not directly related to the school's curriculum.
Lee v. Weisman (1992)	School-sponsored prayers at graduation exercises are unconstitutional.
Zobrest v. Catalina Foothills School District (1993)	School district provision of the services of a sign language interpreter to a student attending a sectarian school is constitutional.

Almost two decades after *Zorach,* the court adopted a tripartite test to evaluate claims under the establishment clause, including those related to released time. The test, often called the *Lemon test* (from the case in which it was developed, *Lemon v. Kurtzman,* 1971), asks three questions, all of which must be answered in the negative if the policy or action is to be judged constitutional (1) Does the policy or action have a primarily religious purpose? (2) Does the policy or action have the primary effect of advancing or inhibiting religion? (3) Does the policy or action foster an excessive entanglement between the state and religion?

In applying the test to a case in Utah that involved instruction of high school students at a Mormon seminary, the Tenth Circuit Court of Appeals found the program unconstitutional in two areas that created "excessive entanglements." The first involved sending a public school student to the school to gather attendance slips (as opposed to *Zorach* where attendance was sent to the public school by the religious school); second was the awarding of credit toward graduation for successful completion of courses in the Old and New Testament. The court maintained that the assessment and monitoring of the course content to assess whether the course content was mainly denominational would necessitate the state being too involved with the church (*Lanner v. Wimmer,* 1981).

Flag Salute, Prayer, and Bible Reading

Two of the most controversial rulings ever made by the U.S. Supreme Court involved compulsory flag salute and prayer in the public schools. In *West Virginia State Board of Education v. Barnette* (1943), the Court ruled that the compulsory flag salute violated the religious freedom of Jehovah's Witnesses. Following *Barnette,* the position of the courts has been that schools may lead the Pledge of Allegiance so long as students are free to not participate. In *Engel v. Vitale* (1962), parents challenged the use of a prayer composed by the New York Board of Regents as part of morning exercises. The denominationally neutral prayer read: "Almighty God, we acknowledge our dependence upon thee, and we beg thy blessings upon us, our parents, our teachers, and our country." The Court held that "it is no part of the business of government to impose official prayers for any group of American people" and to do so constituted a violation of the establishment clause.

The following year, the Supreme Court rendered another significant decision affecting school prayer. In *School District of Abington Township v. Schempp* (1963), the Court declared unconstitutional Pennsylvania and Maryland statutes that required daily Bible reading and recitation of the Lord's Prayer (optional in Pennsylvania). Although children could be exempted from participation in the Maryland case upon request by their parents, the Court held that such activities, held in public school buildings under the supervision of public school personnel, served to advance religion in violation of the establishment clause of the First Amendment. While prohibiting Bible readings as a religious exercise, the Court in *Schempp* did specifically note that its opinion did not prevent studying the Bible as literature and studying *about* religion. A Supreme Court decision 20 years later overturned a Kentucky statute that required every public school classroom to have one portion of the Bible—the Ten Commandments—posted on the wall (*Stone v. Graham,* 1980).

Do you recall being involved in any religious activities in a public school situation? If you attended a private school, was religion an important part of your day?

Not only are state-imposed prayers and Bible readings constitutionally impermissible, so too are voluntary prayers and Bible readings in the classroom, whether given by teachers or students, or even if requested by students. The courts have found little to distinguish these from state-imposed prayers in that both are sanctioned by the school (*Jaffree v. Wallace,* 1985). Likewise, the courts have in recent years shown a reluctance to accept the stated nonsectarian purpose of periods of silent meditation (or silent prayer). In the lead U.S. Supreme Court decision, *Wallace v. Jaffree* (1985), the Court concluded that the intent of a 1981 Alabama statute providing for a period of silent meditation or prayer was clearly to encourage and/or accommodate prayer and thus violated the establishment clause. However, the Court did indicate that statutes providing for periods of silence that did not demonstrate legislative intent to encourage prayers would probably be upheld. Currently, "moment of silence" laws are in effect in about half the states, and the legality of each is subject to determination on a state-by-state basis.

Prayers held outside the classroom but at school-sponsored activities are also the subject of some controversy. Overall, the courts have been rather consistent in their disapproval of organized prayers at activities such as band practice and athletic events. For example, the Supreme Court let stand an Eleventh Circuit Court of Appeals ruling that banned organized prayers before high school football games (*Jager v. Douglas County School District,* 1989). The circuit court rejected the school district's contention that the purpose of such prayers was not religious but was to provide "inspirational speeches about sportsmanship, safety, and the values of teamwork and competition." The court ruled that these purposes could be accomplished by secular inspirational speeches, and that the prayers constituted a public endorsement of Christianity in violation of the establishment clause.

One of the most frequently litigated areas relative to prayers has been prayers at graduation ceremonies. In the years following *Engel* and *Schempp* some courts ruled against such practices, while others found no establishment clause violation, judging them to be more ceremonial in nature with no intent to indoctrinate. The issue was at last addressed by the U.S. Supreme Court in 1992 in *Lee v. Weisman.* The case involved the practice of the Providence, Rhode Island, school system of allowing principals to select clergy to deliver prayers at graduation ceremonies. Because of the negative experience one parent had when he attended the middle school graduation of an older daughter and a Baptist minister asked the audience to stand for a moment of silence and give thanks to Jesus Christ, the parent, who was Jewish, asked that prayers be excluded from the graduation ceremony of another daughter. The principal refused, but did advise the rabbi who had been selected to deliver the prayers that they were to be nonsectarian and gave the rabbi a copy of "Guidelines for Civic Occasions" prepared by the National Conference of Christians and Jews. After failing to secure a restraining order to stop the prayers, the parent attended the ceremony, but filed suit to prohibit the inclusion of prayers at future ceremonies.

The Supreme Court, in a 5 to 4 decision, ruled that the school's policy violated the establishment clause. The Court focused on the fact that the school selected the clergy to deliver the prayers and gave directions to him. The Court

The issue of prayer in the public schools has become the subject of increasing legal and political debate.

did not apply the *Lemon* test, but employed what has since been referred to as the "coercion test." In the opinion of the Court, the "psychological coercion" placed on student dissenters to attend graduation ceremonies had the effect of government coercion of students to attend religious exercises. In the words of the Court:

> high school graduation is one of life's most significant occasions . . . a student is not free to absent herself from the graduation exercise in any real sense of the term, "voluntary," for absence would require forfeiture of those intangible benefits which have motivated the student through youth and all her high school years . . . (t)he Constitution forbids the State to exact religious conformity from a student as the price of attending her own high school graduation. (pp. 2659–2660)

Lee v. Weisman left unanswered the question of the constitutionality of graduation prayers that are delivered by students. However, soon after *Lee*, the Fifth Circuit addressed this question in *Jones v. Clear Creek Independent School District* (1992). Here the court applied *Lee's* coercion test for the first time in review of a school district policy that allowed prayers offered by student volunteers selected by the graduating seniors. The court ruled that the practice was not an unconstitutional endorsement of religion because it was the decision of the seniors whether or not to have the prayer, not school officials. It also found that the practice did not coerce participation by objectors. According to the court, since the graduating class selected the presenter, students knew that the prayers "represent the will of their peers who are less able to coerce participation than an authority figure from the state or clergy" (p. 971).

Following the Supreme Court's refusal to review the decision in *Jones*, a number of states, as well as the U.S. Congress, have introduced legislation to introduce voluntary or student-led prayer into the public schools. Various amendments to the Constitution to authorize prayers or Bible reading in the schools have also been proposed. While such efforts have not yet succeeded at the national level, prayer supporters have been successful in including a school prayer provision into the Goals 2000: Educate America Act (P. L. 103–227) that prohibits state and local education agencies from using funds appropriated under the Act to adopt policies that prevent voluntary school prayer.

In spite of the U.S. Supreme Court's rulings on prayers and Bible readings, these practices continue in schools across the nation in open defiance of the Court. However, teachers and administrators should remember that at the present time both school sanctioned prayers and Bible reading are considered unconstitutional under the establishment clause, and school personnel who encourage or permit such practices are subject to liability for the violation of students' constitutionally protected rights (see, e.g., *Steele v. Van Buren Public School District*, 1988).

Equal Access for Student Devotional Meetings

Partially in response to public sentiment that prayer and other devotional activities should not be banned from the school grounds, in 1984 Congress passed the Equal Access Act (20 U.S.C., sections 4071–73). The Act specified that if a federally assisted public secondary school provides a *limited open forum* to noncurriculum student groups to meet on school premises during noninstructional time, "equal access" to that forum cannot be denied because of the "religious, political, philosophical, or other content of the speech at such meetings."

In the years after its adoption, there were judicial contradictions as to the application of the law and as to whether the Equal Access Act (EAA) violated the establishment clause. Several circuit courts and district courts ruled that student devotional meetings held at a time closely associated with the school day and under the supervision of public school personnel implied recognition of the religious activities and served to advance religion, in violation of the establishment clause. Then, in 1990, the U.S. Supreme Court ruled on the constitutional question and asserted that secondary students are mature enough to understand that a school does not endorse or support a particular speech just because it permits it on a nondiscriminatory basis (*Board of Education of Westside Community Schools v. Mergens*, 1990). In this case, the Court also attempted to clarify the meaning and scope of "curriculum related" under the EAA. According to the Court, a noncurriculum related student group is:

> any student group that does not *directly* relate to the body of courses offered by the school . . . (and) a student group directly relates to a school's curriculum if the subject matter of the group is actually taught, or will soon be taught, in a regularly offered course; if the subject matter of the group concerns the body of courses as a

whole; if participation in the group is required for a particular course; or if participation in the group results in academic credit. (pp. 4723–24)

While the Court acknowledged that whether a specific group is "noncurriculum related" would depend on a particular school's curriculum, if even one noncurriculum-related student club is allowed, the school has opened a limited open forum and cannot discriminate against students based on the content of the students' speech at the club's meetings. Central to the Court's decision upholding the request by students to form a Christian Bible Study Club in *Mergens* was the finding that the school's existing student clubs included one or more other noncurriculum-related clubs (e.g., a chess club).

As a result of *Mergens,* schools have two options in regard to granting access to school facilities to student religious clubs. One option is to restructure student clubs so that all are curriculum related. This would mean that no limited open forum has been created; thus the EAA would not be triggered and student religious clubs could be denied access to school facilities. The other option is to specifically create a limited open forum by allowing noncurriculum related clubs and, in compliance with the EAA, grant them access to school facilities. However, a problem with exercising the second option is that some states have constitutional provisions that prohibit the use of school facilities by religious oriented groups. And, one district court has already held that Congress did not intend the EAA to preempt such state constitutional provisions (*Garnett v. Renton School District,* 1991). With almost 20 other states having constitutional provisions similar to Washington, continuing litigation over the implementation of the EAA is probable (Bjorklun, 1992).

In light of the Supreme Court decision in Mergens, *should school districts attempt to eliminate all noncurriculum-related student clubs or seek to accommodate a plethora of such clubs?*

Use of school facilities by community groups, where there is no school sponsorship or supervision, while very different from use by student-initiated groups under the EAA, has also been the subject of ongoing controversy. Following *Mergens,* access to school facilities was expanded even further by the U.S. Supreme Court in *Lamb's Chapel v. Center Moriches School District* (1993), which said that school districts that allow community groups to use school facilities for civic or social purposes have created a limited open forum and cannot, therefore, bar religious groups from using the facilities on the same terms. According to the Court: "the First Amendment forbids the government to regulate speech in ways that favor some viewpoints or ideas at the expense of others" (p. 2142). Later that same year, the Religious Freedom Restoration Act, which President Clinton signed into law, stipulates that no governmental entity can restrict the free exercise of religion without a compelling interest and unless there is no less restrictive alternative means to achieve that interest.

Challenges to the Curriculum

Challenges to the curriculum traditionally have been brought by parents attempting to eliminate specific courses, activities, or materials thought to be advancing religion. Recent challenges brought with this same goal have raised the complex question as to what constitutes "religion." Increasingly, fundamentalist parents contend that certain courses, materials, and practices in the curriculum promote the "religion" of *secular humanism,* allegedly a faith that denies

God, deifies man, and glorifies reason. The fundamentalists demand that the influences of secular humanism be removed from the curriculum or that Christian doctrine be inserted in the curriculum to bring balance.

In the majority of cases thus far, the courts have rejected the secular humanism argument and reaffirmed the position of the Supreme Court in *Epperson v. Arkansas* (1968), in which the Court struck down an Arkansas law forbidding instruction in evolution. The Court said: "The state has no legitimate interest in protecting any or all religions from views distasteful to them." For example, the courts have not been convinced that the teaching of sex education promotes an antitheistic faith. The courts consistently have found that sex education courses present public health information that promotes legitimate educational objectives, and that the establishment clause prevents the state from barring such instruction simply to conform to the religious beliefs of some parents (McCarthy & Cambron-McCabe, 1992).

The courts generally are satisfied in these and other areas where parents or students challenge religiously objectionable curricular content if statutes or policies allow the student to be exempted from the course or exposure to the content. However, there are numerous instances in which schools have refused the exemption and have been upheld by the courts. For example, in *Ware v. Valley Stream High School District* (1989), the Court ruled that a New York regulation that required all primary and secondary students receive instruction regarding AIDS prevention and alcohol and drug abuse did not violate the First Amendment rights of parents who believed that such education was "evil." The Court held that the state had a compelling interest in educating children regarding the danger of drug and alcohol abuse and AIDS transmission.

The teaching of evolution is another area that has been targeted as advancing secular humanism. Following the ruling in *Epperson* that evolution is a science, not a secular religion, and that states cannot restrict student access to such information to satisfy religious preferences, attempts were made in several states to secure "balanced treatment" or "equal time" for the teaching of creationism. However, these statutes also have been invalidated (*Edwards v. Aguillard,* 1987).

In addition to challenges to curricular programs, another set of challenges have focused on the use of specific curriculum materials. A group of fundamentalist parents in Tennessee brought suit against the school district claiming that the required use of the 1983 Holt, Rinehart, and Winston basic reading series violated their rights by exposing their children to beliefs that were offensive to their religious beliefs. The parents maintained that after reading the series, a child might adopt the views of "a feminist, a humanist, a pacifist, an anti-Christian, a vegetarian, or an advocate of the 'one-world government.'" On appeal, the Sixth Circuit Court of Appeals concluded that exposure to concepts does not constitute promotion of the concepts, and that no evidence existed that students were asked to affirm or deny any religious beliefs, to engage in activity forbidden by their religious beliefs, or to refrain from engaging in any action required by their religious beliefs. Accordingly, no constitutional violations were found (*Mozert v. Hawkins County Public Schools,* 1987).

Secular humanism was acknowledged as a religion by a district court in an Alabama case challenging 44 various books on the state-approved textbook list.

However, the Fifth Circuit Court reversed the ruling and spoke directly to the demand of many fundamentalists that religion be given equal time with secular humanism in the curriculum. According to the appellate court, what the establishment clause requires is not the comprehensive identification of the state with religion, but the separation of the state from religion. Separation requires that there be no fusing of government functions and religious sects, not merely that the state treat them all equally. The court also found that the materials in question did not promote secular humanism or any religion, rather, they attempted to instill in Alabama public school children such values as "independent thought, tolerance of diverse views, self-respect, matur-ity, self-reliance, and logical decision-making" (*Smith v. Board of School Commissioners*, 1987, p. 692).

While there are few areas of the curriculum that have not been challenged as advancing secular humanism, or more recently, "New Age theology," in the past several years certain programs have become focal points. One popular target is the *Quest* drug prevention curriculum. Another that has received considerable media attention is outcome-based education. Yet another, multicultural education, is faulted for threatening traditional values and cultural heritage. Global education, psychology, sociology, and instruction pertaining to values clarification and self-esteem are also vulnerable to attack (McCarthy, 1994). This vast body of litigation has not resulted in a concrete list of what can be included and what must be excluded from the school curriculum. However, some conclusions can be drawn:

> The judiciary's interpretation of the religion clauses of the Constitution bars both some aspects of religious belief and some aspects of secular humanism from the schools. On the one hand, schools may not tailor their programs in accordance with religious beliefs, offer religious instruction or theistic moral training, or endorse the Bible as the only true source of knowledge. On the other hand, schools may not systematically purge the curriculum of all mention of religion or ideas that are consistent with religious belief, endorse atheism, or declare that science is the only real source of knowledge or that the Bible is not true . . .
>
> Schools are free to teach the importance of critical thinking, reasoning, and the need for personal inquiry and choice. They may teach tolerance, open-mindedness, and receptivity to different cultures and values. Thus, there is much of the secular humanist agenda that may be taught. But schools are also free to teach much of the agenda of many traditional religious groups such as patriotism, family values, and the duty to obey the law. (Imber & Van Geel, 1993, pp. 125–126)

Many of the curricular materials being objected to have been used for 20 years or more with limited objection (e.g., Huckleberry Finn, Catcher in the Rye, Of Mice and Men). To what do you attribute the recent objections to such material?

Public Support of Nonpublic Schools

As noted in Chapter 13, nonpublic schools educate a significant number of children in the United States. In recognition of the role that they play in the educational system, and of the financial burden placed on parents who pay property taxes to support the public schools as well as tuition at nonpublic schools, legislatures have regularly attempted to provide some type of public support to these schools or their clients. The legal issue involved in these attempts is whether the assistance violates the First Amendment prohibition against governmental actions that promote the establishment of religion.

Student Support

The courts have recognized that direct subsidies to nonpublic schools violate the establishment clause. Most state constitutions also forbid state aid to religious schools. However, the courts have relied on the *child benefit theory* to provide several types of assistance that primarily benefit the private school child rather than the private school itself. This theory was first articulated by the U.S. Supreme Court in *Cochran v. Louisiana State Board of Education* (1930). The Court upheld a Louisiana law that provided textbooks directly to children attending nonpublic schools.

The same rationale was applied in another Supreme Court decision, *Everson v. Board of Education* (1947), which supported a New Jersey law reimbursing parents for the cost of bus transportation for children attending both public and nonpublic schools. However, the fact that the U.S. Supreme Court has said that transportation, textbooks, or the provision of other services is permissible under the federal Constitution does not mean that states *must* provide this assistance, or that such assistance may not be prohibited by state laws or constitutions.

Since 1970, the courts have applied the *Lemon* test in determining the constitutionality of various state aid programs. The result has been a patchwork of inconsistent rulings (Imber & Van Geel, 1993). In *Wolman v. Walter* (1977), the Court ruled on an Ohio statute that sought to provide broad support for nonpublic schools. The court found the following aid to be constitutional:

1. the purchase or loan of secular textbooks

2. the provision and scoring of such standardized tests as are available in the public schools of the state

3. speech, hearing, and psychological diagnostic services provided at the nonpublic schools by employees of the public schools

4. therapeutic and remedial services provided by employees of the public schools so long as they are off the premises of the nonpublic school

Ruled unconstitutional were:

1. the purchase or loan of instructional materials and audiovisual equipment (science kits, maps, globes, and charts)

2. providing funds for field trips

In other decisions, the Court has approved support for the cost of testing and record-keeping required by the state (*Committee for Public Education and Religious Liberty v. Regan,* 1980), but disallowed support for teacher-prepared tests (*Levitt v. Committee for Public Education and Religious Liberty,* 1973), the maintenance and repair of school facilities (*Committee for Public Education and Religious Liberty v. Nyquist,* 1973), salary reimbursement or supplements for parochial school teachers (*Lemon v. Kurtzman,* 1971), and the offering of remedial and enrichment courses at parochial schools during the day, as well as community education programs after school hours (*School District of City of Grand Rapids v. Ball,* 1985).

In recent years, the courts have shown a greater receptivity to various types of aid directed at providing services to students. For example, in *Zobrest v.*

The courts have shown increasing favor toward state aid programs directed to parochial school students, as opposed to the schools they attend.

Catalina Foothills School District (1993), using not the *Lemon* test but more the "child benefit theory" or neutrality principle, the Supreme Court ruled in favor of a deaf student's request that the school district provide him with a sign language interpreter in the Catholic school he attended. The Court stated that:

> When the government offers a neutral service on the premises of a sectarian school as part of a general program that is in no way skewed towards religion, it follows . . . that provision of service does not offend the Establishment Clause. (p. 2462)

Although finding no Establishment Clause violation, the court did not hold that the Individuals With Disabilities Act requires public school districts provide such services in parochial schools.

While upholding the provision of services in the *Catalina Foothills* case, in other cases the courts have found that the very monitoring of the services to ensure that they are not advancing religion can create an excessive entanglement. For example, in *Aguilar v. Felton* (1985), the Supreme Court invalidated the use of Chapter 1 funds to pay public school teachers to provide remedial ser-

**Professional Reflections**

". . . it is especially important for a teacher to be involved in the community. . . . Service clubs, community clubs, and church groups offer the teacher an opportunity to learn about their community, meet interesting citizens, and even work directly with students' parents. As the community gets to know the teacher, the teacher will find the community not only interested in what is happening in our schools, but also willing to get more involved."

Keith Robinson, Teacher of the Year, Iowa

vices to children at parochial schools on the grounds that the administration of the services fostered excessive entanglement. However, the Court has subsequently upheld the provision of such services when delivered off school grounds or when rendered in a mobile or portable unit on school grounds but away from the parochial school building (_Pulido v. Cavazos,_ 1991).

The body of law on public support of nonpublic school students has not provided clear judicial guidance distinguishing permissible from impermissible aid. As a result, states will undoubtedly continue to attempt to provide various forms of aid, and challenges to these attempts will be resolved on a case-by-case basis.

Vouchers

Vouchers are seen as a means to provide all parents greater choice in the school their child attends. The last decade saw increasing support for the voucher concept, and this will undoubtedly continue given the government's current support of parental choice in education. However, to date, all attempts to provide vouchers for students to attend parochial schools have been overturned by the courts. There appears to be no doubt however, that efforts to fashion voucher plans that will pass judicial muster will continue unabated.

Tax Benefits

What effect might the reduction in income tax collections resulting from tax benefit proposals have on the financing of public schools? How should replacement tax revenues be generated?

Various tax deduction and tax credit proposals have been introduced in the U.S. Congress, as well as in almost every state legislature. They have invariably invoked challenges on establishment clause grounds. Two have reached the U.S. Supreme Court. In _Committee for Public Education and Religious Liberty v. Nyquist_ (1973), the Court overturned a New York statute that allowed state income tax credits for parents of nonpublic school students. Although the plan aided parents rather than the schools, the court said it was nonetheless an aid to religion in violation of the establishment clause.

In the decade after _Nyquist,_ various other tax relief measures were struck down by the courts. Then, in _Mueller v. Allen_ (1983), the Supreme Court upheld a Minnesota statute that permitted a state income tax deduction to parents of both public and nonpublic school students for expenses for tuition, books, and transportation. The Court distinguished this case from _Nyquist_ in that the New York statute provided the tax benefits only to parents of nonpublic school students. Here, the Court said, a secular purpose was served in providing financial assistance to a "broad spectrum" of the state's citizens. Following *Mueller,* a number of states considered similar tax benefit packages, but only Iowa passed legislation. However, advocates undoubtedly will continue to lobby for their passage.

Compulsory Attendance

Each of the 50 states has legislation requiring school attendance—at a public, private, or parochial school—by children of a certain age range residing within the state. The age range is normally from 6 or 7 to 16 or 18. Although attendance is compulsory, attendance in a particular school district normally requires that the parents or legal guardian be a resident of the district. Additionally, attendance at a specific school within the district may legally be restricted to those residing within a certain attendance zone or may be determined by voluntary or court-ordered desegregation remedies.

The residency requirement is not the same as a citizenship requirement. The U.S. Supreme Court, in *Plyler v. Doe* (1982), upheld the right of children of illegal aliens to attend school in the district of their residence. According to the Court, the state's interest in deterring illegal entry was insufficient to justify the creation and perpetuation of a subclass of illiterates within our borders. On a similar note, the courts have ruled that school districts also must educate homeless youth who have no address but are living within their boundaries.

Although it is clearly established that compulsory attendance laws are not unconstitutional, the courts have placed some limits on the right of the state to compel school attendance. In 1972, in *Wisconsin v. Yoder,* the U.S. Supreme Court recognized the interests of the Amish people in preserving their 200-year-old established way of life from the teaching of the values and worldly knowledge found in the public high schools. While these values and knowledge are deemed necessary for success outside the Amish community, the Court recognized that they were inconsistent with Amish religious beliefs. The Amish are a traditional, pacifist religious group that has rejected modern dress, modern conveniences, and other aspects of modern life. Within the Amish community, children are given continued education beyond elementary education through vocational training. The U.S. Supreme Court, examining the successful existence of the Amish way of life, found it to be, in effect, an alternative to formal secondary education that did fulfill the state's stated goals in compelling school attendance— to prepare children to be productive and contributing members of society.

The exception given to the Amish is not likely to be extended to other religious groups. The Court emphasized that the long history of the Amish way of life was important to its decision and that other groups "claiming to have recently discovered some other 'progressive' or more enlightened process for rearing children for modern life" would not qualify for similar exemptions.

Private and Home Schooling

The states' right to mandate school attendance does not extend to requiring that schooling takes place in the public schools. In 1925, in *Pierce v. Society of Sisters,* the Supreme Court recognized the right of parents to educate their children in

What are the statutory provisions related to home schooling in your state?

private schools. However, the decision also recognized the right of the state to regulate private schools, including requiring that their teachers be certified and that their curricula comply with established state guidelines.

Home schooling as a form of private schooling is another alternative to attendance in the public schools. The interest in home schooling has increased in the last decade as many parents, primarily members of fundamentalist religious sects, have objected to the instruction provided in the public schools. The U.S. Department of Education estimated that in 1990–91, 250,000–300,000 school age children were being educated at home. The Home School Legal Defense Association estimates are even higher: 750,000–1,000,000 for 1993–94, up from 15,000 in the early 1980s (Thomas, 1994). There are now a number of state and national organizations that support the efforts of home schoolers, and a vast array of commercial curriculum materials are directed at the home schooling market.

Thirty-two states have adopted home school statutes or regulations (Richardson, 1989). They range from those that are very strict to those that require no more than that the parents notify the local school board that they are educating their child at home (Lufler, 1994). More commonly, state statutes or regulations will require that (1) instruction be essentially equivalent to that taught in the public schools and include the subjects required by state law, (2) the parent or other adult providing the instruction be qualified (not necessarily certified) to teach, (3) some systematic reporting be made to local school authorities, and (4) a minimum number of hours of instruction per day be provided. In 15 states and the District of Columbia, home schools must be approved by the local school board (Richardson, 1989). And in about two-thirds of the states, students in home schools must be tested to ensure that they are mastering basic skills.

Summary

The legal foundation of education derives from state and federal constitutional provisions, the laws of state and federal legislatures, the enactments of state and federal agencies, court decisions, and state attorney general opinions. Every state constitution includes a provision for education, and the wording of the provision has proved important in determining the obligation of the state in providing for education and the constitutionality of legislative action. Although the federal Constitution does not mention education, a number of its provisions affect education and afford protection to school personnel, pupils, and patrons.

The interaction of the institutions of religion and education has become the source of increasing legal controversy in recent years. A tension exists between the efforts of the schools to accommodate religion and yet maintain the wall of separation between church and state required by the First Amendment. Thus far the courts generally have been consistent in their decisions keeping religious practices and proselytizing efforts out of the schools. However, the decisions of the U.S. Supreme Court in *Mergens* and *Zobrest* represent not only a potential crack in the wall of separation between church and state, but the growing conservative thrust of the Court. In the next chapter other constitutional rights of teachers and students are explored. Generally the courts have tended to constrain expressions of religion in the schools, but, as we will see, these same courts have expanded the rights of teachers and students in a number of other areas.

Key Terms

Administrative law	*Lemon* test
Attorney general	Limited open forum
Child benefit theory	Plenary
Constitution	Secular humanism
Eminent domain	*Stare decisis*
Ex post facto law	Statutory law
Home schooling	Tax benefits
Law	Voucher

Discussion Questions

1. How might being a nonreader have contributed to Paul's antisocial behavior in the critical incident at the beginning of the chapter? Speculate on what might have brought about the change in Paul.

2. What are the provisions of your state constitution regarding education?

3. Describe the levels and types of state courts in your state.

4. What is your school (or school system) policy on silent meditation? Is there support for prayer or Bible reading? On what grounds?

5. What is meant by the *Lemon* test? How effective has it been in distinguishing permissible and impermissible aid to nonpublic school students?

6. How does the child benefit theory serve to justify educational vouchers? How does it operate in the school systems in your area? Are textbooks provided? Is bus transportation provided?

7. What First Amendment issues are currently being debated in the schools in your area?

References

Aguilar v. Felton, 105 S. Ct. 3232 (1985).

Beilan v. Board of Public Education of Philadelphia, 357 U.S. 399 (1958).

Bjorklun, E. C. (1992). Implementing the Equal Access Act and state constitutional provisions. *West's Education Law Quarterly, 1,* 309–316.

Black, H. C. (1990). *Black's law dictionary.* St. Paul, MN: West Publishing Co.

Board of Education of Westside Community Schools v. Mergens, 58 L.W. 4720 (1990).

Brown v. Board of Education of Topeka, 347 U.S. 483 (1954).

Carpio v. Tucson High School District No. 1 of Pima County, 517 P. 2d 1288 (1974).

Cochran v. Louisiana State Board of Education, 281 U.S. 370 (1930).

Collins, G. J. (1969). Constitutional and legal basis for state action. In E. Fuller & J. B. Pearon (Eds.), *Education in the states: Nationwide development since 1900.* Washington, D.C.: National Education Association.

Committee for Public Education and Religious Liberty v. Nyquist, 413 U.S. 756 (1973).

Committee for Public Education and Religious Liberty v. Regan, 444 U.S. 646 (1980).

Edwards v. Aguillard, 107 S. Ct. 2573 (1987).

Engel v. Vitale, 370 U.S. 421 (1962).

Epperson v. Arkansas, 393 U.S. 97 (1968).

Everson v. Board of Education, 330 U.S. 1 (1947).

Ga. Op. Atty. Gen. 1988, No. 18, p. 52.

Garnett v. Renton School District, 772 F. Supp. 531 (W.D. Wash. 1991)

Imber, M., & Van Geel, T. (1993). *Education law.* New York: McGraw-Hill, Inc.

Ingraham v. Wright, 430 U.S. 651 (1977).

Jaffree v. Wallace, 472 U.S. 38 (1985).

Jager v. Douglas County School District, 862 F. 2d 824 (11th Cir. 1989), *cert. denied* (1989).

Jones v. Clear Creek Independent School District, 977 F. 2d 963 (5th Cir. 1992).

Lamb's Chapel v. Center Moriches School District, 959 F. 2d 381 (2d Cir. 1992), *rev'd,* 113 S. Ct. 2141 (1993).

LaMorte, M. W. (1993). *School law: Cases and concepts* (4th ed.). Boston: Allyn and Bacon.

Lanner v. Wimmer, 662 F. 2d 1349 (10th Cir. 1981).

Lemon v. Kurtzman, 93 S. Ct. 1463 (1971).

Levitt v. Committee for Public Education and Religious Liberty, 413 U.S. 472 (1973).

Lufler, H. S., Jr. (1994). Pupils. In S. B. Thomas (Ed.), *The yearbook of education law 1994* (pp. 59–87). Topeka, KN: National Organization on Legal Problems of Education.

McCarthy, M. M. (1994). External challenges to public education: Values in conflict. Paper presented at the annual meeting of the American Educational Research Association, New Orleans, April, 1994.

McCarthy, M., & Cambron-McCabe, N. (1992). *Public school law: Teachers and students rights* (3rd ed.). Boston: Allyn and Bacon.

McCollum v. Board of Education of School District No. 71, 68 S. Ct. 461 (1948).

Mozert v. Hawkins County Public Schools, 827 F. 2d 1058 (6th Cir. 1987).

Mueller v. Allen, 103 S. Ct. 3062 (1983).

Pierce v. Society of Sisters, 268 U.S. 510 (1925).

Plessey v. Ferguson, 16 S. Ct. 1138 (1896).

Plyler v. Doe, 457 U.S. 202 (1982).

Pulido v. Cavazos, 934 F. 2d 912 (8th Cir. 1991).

Richardson, S. N. (1989). Home schooling. *NOLPE Notes, 24*(6), 6.

School District of Abington Township v. Schempp, 374 U.S. 203 (1963).

School District of City of Grand Rapids v. Ball, 718 F. 2d 1389 (6th Cir. 1983), *aff'd,* 473 U. S. 373 (1985).

S. J. Lemoine v. St. Landry Parish School, 527 So. 2d 1150 (La. App. 3d Cir. 1988).

Smith v. Board of School Commissioners of Mobile County, 655 F. Supp. 939 (S. D. Ala. 1987, *rev'd,* 827 F. 2d 684 (11th Cir. 1987).

Stone v. Graham, 449 U.S. 39 (1980).

Steele v. Van Buren Public School District, 845 F. 2d 1492 (8th Cir. 1988).

Thomas, K. (1944, April 6). Learning at home: Education outside school gains respect. *USA Today,* 5D.

Valente, W. D. (1994). *Law in the schools* (3rd ed.). New York: Macmillian.

Wallace v. Jaffree, 105 S. Ct. 2479 (1985).

Ware v. Valley Stream High School District, 545 N.Y.S. 2d 316 (N. Y. App. Div.), appeal denied, 545 N.Y.S. 2d 539 (N.Y. 1989).

West Virginia State Board of Education v. Barnette, 319 U.S. 624 (1943).

Wisconsin v. Yoder, 406 U.S. 205 (1972).

Wolman v. Walter, 433 U.S. 229 (1977).

Zorach v. Clauson, 72 S. Ct. 679 (1952).

Zobrest v. Catalina Foothills School District, 113 S. Ct. 2462 (1993).

Chapter 12

Teachers, Students, and the Law

If there is any principle of the Constitution that more imperatively calls for attachment than any other it is the principle of free thought—not free thought for those who agree with us, but freedom for the thought that we hate.

Justice Oliver Wendell Holmes, Jr.
(1841–1935)

A Critical Incident in My Teaching Career . . .

At the end of the first semester, I ask my students to evaluate me. One of the questions I ask is, "Do you think I like you?" As I thumbed through a stack of positive responses, two years ago, one response leapt out at me: "No! You've pushed me away all year!"

I recognized the scrawled handwriting—Ashley. Ashley was chronically tardy, whined continually, and alternated between jumping up out of her seat and keeping her head on her desk. Her response was like a punch in the stomach. It was true.

I began making a special effort with Ashley. I greeted her with a smile, gave her an occasional hug, a pat, a compliment, or sometimes just a wink. Ashley started dropping by after school. One day she shared some problems with me—problems that will always haunt me—but finally she began to blossom, to enjoy class, and to wink back at me.

Ashley couldn't learn when she didn't feel that I cared. She taught me what a teacher is—a caring instructor who finds value in each child.

Anne Jolly
Teacher of the Year, Alabama

Every day teachers must make decisions that affect the rights of students, their own rights, and their professional lives. Therefore, it is imperative that teachers be knowledgeable about applicable state and federal legislation, school board policies, and court decisions. After completing this chapter, you will be able to:

- Identify the personal and professional requirements for employment of prospective teachers.
- Describe teachers' employment rights as derived from the employment contract and tenure status.
- Discuss the teacher's responsibility in reporting child abuse and using copyrighted materials.
- Outline the legal requirements for dismissing a teacher.
- Provide an overview of teachers' rights, inside and outside the classroom.
- Define the elements of negligence.
- Compare discrimination, equal opportunity, and affirmative action.

- Contrast the procedural requirements for suspension, expulsion, and corporal punishment.
- Trace the development of student rights in the area of search and seizure.
- Explain the restraints that may be placed on student expression and personal appearance.
- Discuss how the Buckley Amendment has expanded parental and student rights in regard to student records.
- Summarize the response of the courts and school districts to school attendance by AIDS victims.

Teacher Rights and Responsibilities

Although school personnel are not expected to be legal experts, it is imperative that they understand their rights and obligations under the law and that these rights and obligations be translated into everyday practices in the schools. In this chapter the basic concepts of law are presented as they relate to terms and conditions of employment; teacher dismissal; teacher rights outside the classroom; tort liability; and discrimination, equal opportunity, and affirmative action. Although there is some variation in the application of these legal concepts from one state or locality to another, certain topics and issues are of sufficient importance and similarity to warrant consideration. Some of these topics are also discussed in other chapters of this text. Here, attention is given to the legal considerations of these topics.

Terms and Conditions of Employment

As emphasized in the previous chapter, within the framework provided by state and federal constitutional and statutory protections, the state has complete power to conduct and regulate public education. Through its legislature, state board of education, state department of education, and local school boards, the state promulgates the rules and regulations for the operation of the schools. Among these rules and regulations are those establishing the terms and conditions of employment. The areas most often covered by state statutory and regulatory provisions are those dealing with certification, teacher competency testing, loyalty oaths, citizenship and residency requirements, health and physical requirements, contracts, and tenure.

Certification

As noted in Chapter 1, to qualify for most professional teaching, administrative, and other positions in the public schools, an individual must acquire a valid certificate or license. The certificate does not constitute a contract or guarantee of employment; it only makes the holder eligible for employment.

All states have established certification requirements for prospective teachers. These requirements may include a college degree with minimum credit hours in specific curricular areas, evidence of specific job experience, "good moral character," a specified age, U.S. citizenship, the signing of a loyalty oath, good health, and a minimum score on a job-related exam. Where specified certification requirements exist, failure to meet the requirements can result in dismissal of the employee.

Competency Testing

The growing use of competency tests as either a prerequisite to certification or in the evaluation of practicing educators has generated substantial controversy. The legal question is not whether tests can be used; in fact, the Civil Rights Act of 1964, as amended, sanctions the use of "professionally developed" tests, and the U.S. Supreme Court has specifically approved teacher testing. Rather, the primary issues involve questions of discrimination in violation of Title VII, as well

Does certification ensure a quality teaching force? How have certification standards changed in the state in which you plan to teach since the education reform movement began in the mid-1980s?

as unreasonableness in violation of the equal protection clause of the Fourteenth Amendment.

The concern arises as a result of the fact that in most instances where tests have been used in employment decisions, their use has disqualified proportionately more minorities than whites. In these instances the courts have disallowed the tests if the state or school district cannot show the tests are significantly related to successful job performance, but has upheld their use if it is shown that the tests have been validated for job relatedness and serve a legitimate state purpose. In the lead case in education, *United States v. South Carolina* (1978), the state conducted content validation studies, pilot tested the test, and submitted test items to a panel of expert reviewers. When the test was administered, a disproportionate number of blacks fell short of the minimum score. The U.S. Supreme Court ruled that the validation procedure was sufficient and that the test was rationally related to a legitimate state purpose: that of ensuring that certified teachers possess the minimum level of knowledge necessary for effective teaching.

The most recent focus of litigation about teacher testing is on the testing of practicing educators. This testing has been challenged in Arkansas and Texas, two of the three states that have such programs. The Texas testing program required that both teachers and administrators pass an examination as a condition of recertification. The Supreme Court of Texas upheld the requirements, finding that (1) because the teaching certificate is a license, not a contract, the constitutional prohibition against impairment of contracts is not violated, (2) due process was not violated because teachers were given the right to appeal and the right to take the test more than once, and (3) teacher testing is a rational means of achieving a legitimate state purpose, namely, maintaining competent teachers in the public schools (*State of Texas v. Project Principle, Inc.,* 1987). A later decision by the Fifth Circuit Court of Appeals found no discrimination against teachers who were dismissed after failing the test (*Fields v. Hallsville Independent School District,* 1991).

Loyalty Oaths

Although there has been increased opposition to loyalty oaths in the last quarter century, they still are required by most states and many school districts as a requirement for certification or as a condition of employment. The courts have said that school employees can be required to sign an oath pledging faithful performance of duties and support for the U.S. Constitution or an individual state constitution (*Ohlson v. Phillips,* 1970). However, oaths that require employees to disavow *membership* in an allegedly subversive organization are not allowed (*Keyishian v. Board of Regents,* 1967). The courts have held such oaths to be unconstitutionally vague and an infringement on the First Amendment right of association.

Citizenship and Residency Requirements

The courts have upheld both citizenship and residency requirements for certification and/or as a condition of employment. With regard to the citizenship requirement, the U.S. Supreme Court has held that education is among those governmental functions that is "so bound up with the operation of the state as a

Does your state require a competency test for certification? Do you feel this type of test is necessary for those who have graduated from a state-approved teacher preparation program?

governmental entity as to permit the exclusion from those functions of all persons who have not become part of the process of self-government" (*Ambach v. Norwick,* 1979, pp. 73–74).

Requirements that teachers reside within the district where they are employed have been upheld if it can be shown that there is a rational basis for the requirements. For example, the Arkansas Supreme Court determined that a school district requirement that teachers reside within the district or within 10 miles of town was "rationally related to community involvement and district identity as it related to tax base in support of district tax levies, and (the) 10 mile limit was reasonable commuting distance and was not arbitrary" (*McClelland v. Paris Public Schools,* 1988, p. 908).

Health and Physical Requirements

Most states and school boards have adopted health and physical requirements for teachers. The courts have recognized that such requirements are necessary to protect the health and welfare of students and other employees. Accordingly, the courts have upheld the release or reassignment of employees whose failed eyesight or hearing made it impossible for them to meet their contractual duties as well as the mandatory psychiatric examination of a principal (as a condition of continued employment) who had become involved in physical altercations with other administrators as well as a child, and who admitted he was under stress and needed tranquilizers (*Daury v. Smith,* 1988).

While the courts have upheld school districts' imposition of health and physical requirements, they are concerned that such requirements not be arbitrarily applied or violate state and federal laws intended to protect the rights of the handicapped (McCarthy & Cambron-McCabe, 1992). For example, Section 504 of the Rehabilitation Act of 1973, which protects otherwise qualified handicapped individuals from discrimination, served as the basis for a 1987 U.S. Supreme Court ruling that overturned the dismissal of an Arkansas teacher with tuberculosis (*School Board of Nassau County v. Arline,* 1987). The court concluded that persons suffering from the contagious disease of tuberculosis had a physical impairment that justified their being considered handicapped persons within the meaning of the Rehabilitation Act. Accordingly, discrimination based solely on fear of contamination is to be considered discrimination against the handicapped. Thus, the district could not dismiss the teacher without proof that the teacher was otherwise not qualified to teach.

How would you respond to being assigned to team teach with a colleague who has a contagious disease?

The decision in *Arline* has been relied on by plaintiff teachers in cases involving AIDS. In the lead case, Vincent Chalk, a California teacher of hearing-impaired children, was excluded from the classroom and given an administrative assignment after having been diagnosed as having AIDS. Chalk sought an injunction ordering the school district to restore him to his classroom duties (*Chalk v. U.S. District Court Cent. Dist. of California,* 1988). The U.S. District Court, in granting the injunction, relied heavily on the standard articulated in *Arline* for determining when a contagious disease would prevent an individual from being "otherwise qualified"—that a person who poses a significant risk of communicating an infectious disease to others will not be considered "otherwise qualified" if reasonable accommodation will not eliminate that risk. In applying the "significant

Most states now require that prospective teachers pass a specified test prior to certification.

risk of communicating" standard in this instance the court found that the over-whelming consensus of medical and scientific opinion regarding the nature and transmission of AIDS did not support a conclusion that Chalk posed a "signifi-cant" risk of communicating the disease to children or others through casual social contact.

A more recent federal statute impacting on health and physical require-ments for school district employees is the Americans With Disabilities Act of 1990, which prohibits employment discrimination against "qualified individuals with a disability." Such a person is defined as one who "satisfies the requisite skill, experience, education, and other job-related requirements of the (position). . . and who, with or without reasonable accommodation, can perform the essential functions" of the position. While the law does not require the hiring or retention of unqualified persons, it does prohibit specific actions of employers that adversely affect the employment opportunities of disabled persons, and it does require employers to make "reasonable accommodation" for a known mental or physical disability.

An area of current dispute in regard to health and physical requirements for school employees involves mandatory testing for AIDS infection and alcohol or drug use. To date the courts have held that *mandatory* urine and blood tests that are not part of a routine medical examination required by law or agreed to by the employee violate the Fourth Amendment prohibition against unreasonable searches unless there is an "individualized reasonable suspicion" of a condition that imperils the proper functioning of the teacher or the well-being of others. However, where an employee's history or job duties implicate student safety, he or she may be required to undergo testing without violating the Fourth Amendment (Valente, 1994).

The Employment Contract

The general principles of contract law apply to the teacher employment contract. That is, in order for the contract to be valid, it must contain the basic elements of (1) offer and acceptance, (2) legally competent parties, (3) consideration (compensation), (4) legal subject matter, and (5) agreement in form required by law. In addition, the employment contract must meet the specific requirements of applicable state law.

The authority to contract lies exclusively with the school board. Although the superintendent or other officials may screen candidates and recommend employment, only the school board is authorized to enter into contracts, and only when it is a legally constituted body. That is, contracts issued when a quorum of the board is not present, or at an illegally called meeting of the board (e.g., adequate notice is not given), are not valid.

In order to be enforceable, a contract must pertain to a legal subject matter (i.e., a contract for the purchase of illegal substances or the performance of illegal services is not enforceable). Also, the contract must be in the proper form required by law.

The employee's rights and obligations of employment are derived from the contract. The courts have held that all valid rules and regulations of the school board, as well as all applicable state statutes, are part of the contract, even if not specifically included. Accordingly, employees may be required to perform certain tasks incidental to classroom activities, regardless of whether the contract specifically mentions them. These have included such activities as field trips, playground and cafeteria duty, supervision of extracurricular activities, and club sponsorship. Teachers cannot, however, be required to drive a bus, perform janitorial duties, or perform duties unrelated to the school program.

Tenure

Tenure is "the status conferred upon teachers who have served a period . . . which then guarantees them continual employment, until retirement, subject to the requirements of good behavior and financial necessity" (Gee & Sperry, 1978, p. T–7). Tenure is a creation of statute designed to maintain permanent and qualified instructional personnel. Most state statutes specify the requirements and procedures for obtaining tenure, which normally include the satisfactory completion of a probationary period of three years. During the probationary period the teacher is usually issued a one-year contract that, subject to satisfactory service and district finances, is renewable at the end of each of the probationary years prior to tenure. However, satisfactory completion of the probationary period does not guarantee tenure. While in some states tenure is automatically awarded at the end of the probationary period unless the school board notifies the teacher that he or she will not be rehired, in others states official action of the school board is necessary for the awarding of tenure.

Tenure statutes also normally specify the grounds for dismissal of a tenured teacher and the procedures that must be followed in the dismissal. The dismissal protection afforded tenured teachers is perhaps the major benefit of obtaining tenure. Tenure status gives teachers the security of practicing their profession without threat of removal for arbitrary, capricious, or political motivations. In fact, the courts have said that the granting of tenure in effect awards the teacher with a *property right* to continued employment that cannot be taken away without due process of law.

However, the awarding of tenure does not guarantee permanent employment. The teacher may be dismissed for disciplinary reasons or because of declining enrollments or financial exigencies. Nor does the granting of tenure guarantee the right to teach in a particular school, grade, or subject area. Subject to due process requirements, teachers may be reassigned to any position for which they are certified.

Does a tenure system protect incompetent teachers? What is your response to proposals that the tenure system be abolished?

Other Employment Requirements

In addition to the terms and conditions of employment disclosed in the preceding section, other requirements may be made as a condition of teacher employment as long as they do not violate teacher rights or state or federal law. Some requirements, such as those related to providing reasonable care and maintaining discipline, are discussed later in this chapter. Requirements related to two topics, reporting child abuse and use of copyrighted materials, are discussed here. These topics have become increasingly important to educators in the last decade.

Reporting Child Abuse and Neglect

As discussed in Chapter 10, teachers are among those professionals named in state statutes as being required to report suspected child abuse and neglect. Under most such statutes, failure to report abuse may result in the teacher being found criminally liable, with penalties as high as a year in jail and a fine of $1,000 (Fischer, Schimmel, & Kelly, 1995). A civil suit claiming negligence also may be brought against the teacher for failure to report child abuse. Because of the serious consequences of failure to report child abuse, both to the child and to the teacher (and possibly the district), most school boards also have adopted policies affirming the responsibility of district employees to report child abuse and detailing the procedures to be followed when abuse is suspected.

State statutes that require teachers to report suspected child abuse do not demand that reporters be absolutely sure that the child has been abused, only that there be "reasonable cause to believe" that the child is subject to abuse or neglect. Under all state statutes, school employees who report suspected child abuse or neglect are immune from civil and criminal prosecution if the report was made in good faith, and in many states good faith is presumed and the person challenging the reporter would have to prove he or she acted in bad faith (Fischer, Schimmel, & Kelly, 1995).

Use of Copyrighted Materials

Copyright laws are designed to protect the author or originator of an original work from unauthorized reproduction or use of the work. Because of their widespread use of print and nonprint material in the classroom, it is important that teachers be knowledgeable about, and comply with, federal copyright laws. The *fair use doctrine* allows the nonprofit reproduction and use of certain materials for classroom use without permission of the copyright owner if each copy bears the copyright notice and meets the tests of brevity, spontaneity, and cumulative effect outlined in the Guidelines for Classroom Copying presented on page 409.

The increasing use of instructional technology has brought to light a number of issues related to use of copyrighted nonprint materials, namely, television programs, videotapes, and computer software. In 1981 Congress issued Guidelines for Off-the-Air Recording of Broadcast Programming for Educational Purposes. The guidelines provide that a nonprofit educational institution may tape television programs for classroom use if requested by an individual teacher. Programs also may be taped at home by the teacher. All copies must include the copyright notice on the program. During the first 10 days after taping, the material may be shown once by the individual teacher and may be repeated only once for purposes of instructional reinforcement. Additional use is limited to viewing for evaluating the program. After 45 days the tape must be erased or destroyed. All other off-the-air recording (except for the purpose of time shifting for personal use) is illegal unless the program is recorded from educational television. These recordings may be shown for a period of seven days after the broadcast, but must then be erased or destroyed. Tapes rented by the teacher from a video store may be shown to the class in a face-to-face classroom situation (i.e., not over a closed circuit system) without violating copyright law (Murray, 1994).

The copying of computer software has become a major area of copyright infringement. The high cost of software, combined with limited school budgets, has resulted in numerous cases of unauthorized copying of software. The 1980 amendments to the copyright law permit one archival or backup copy to be made of the master program; making multiple copies, even for educational purposes, would be a violation of the fair use principle. In the use of copyrighted software, as in the use of any copyrighted material, teachers are required to obey both the letter and the spirit of copyright laws and adhere to any relevant school board policies or guidelines.

Teacher Dismissal

Teacher dismissal actions take several forms. Among them are dismissal for cause, reduction in force, and nonrenewal of contract. The legal requirements for dismissal vary not only among the states but with the form of dismissal and the status (tenured or nontenured) of the teacher. In this section, broad legal concepts applicable to these three forms are discussed.

Dismissal for Cause

All states have some statutory provisions regarding teacher dismissal for cause. The reasons most frequently cited in statutes are immorality, incompetency, and insubordination. Among the other commonly mentioned reasons are neglect of duty, unprofessional conduct, unfitness to teach, and the catch-all, "other good and just cause." Most challenges to dismissals center around two primary issues: did the conduct in question fit the statutory grounds for dismissal, and, if so, did the school board present the facts necessary to sustain the charge. The burden of proof lies with the school board and must be supported by substantial evidence (Valente, 1994).

Figure 12.1: Guidelines for Classroom Copying

1. A single copy may be made of any of the following for your own scholarly research or use in teaching:

    A. A chapter from a book;

    B. An article from a periodical or newspaper;

    C. A short story, short essay, or short poem;

    D. A chart, graph, diagram, drawing, cartoon or picture from a book, periodical, or newspaper.

2. Multiple copies (not to exceed in any event more than one copy per pupil in a course) may be made for classroom use or discussion, provided that each copy includes a notice of copyright and that the following tests are met:

    A. Brevity Test

       (i) Poetry: (a) a complete poem if less than 250 words and if printed on not more than two pages, or (b) from a longer poem, an excerpt of not more than 250 words.
       (ii) Prose: (a) Either a complete article, story, or essay of less than 2,500 words, or (b) an excerpt from any prose work of not more than 1,000 words or 10 percent of the work, whichever is less, but in any event a minimum of 500 words.
       (iii) Illustration: One chart, graph, diagram, drawing, cartoon or picture per book or per periodical issue.
       (iv) "Special" works in poetry, prose, or in "poetic prose" that combine language with illustrations and are less than 2,500 words in their entirety may not be reproduced in their entirety; however, an excerpt of not more than two of the published pages of such special work and containing not more than 10 percent of the words may be reproduced.

    B. Spontaneity Test

       (i) The copying is at your instance and inspiration, and
       (ii) The inspiration and decision to use the work and the moment of its use for maximum teaching effectiveness are so close in time that it would be unreasonable to expect you would receive a timely reply to a request for permission.

    C. Cumulative Effect Test

       (i) The coping of the material is for only one course in the school in which the copies are made.
       (ii) Not more than one short poem, article, story, essay or two excerpts may be copied from the same author, nor more than three from the same collective work or periodical volume during one class term.
       (iii) There cannot be more than nine instances of multiple copying for one course during one class term.

    [These limitations do not apply to current news periodicals and newspapers and current news sections of other periodicals.]

3. Copying cannot be used to create or to replace or substitute for anthologies, compilations, or collective works.

4. There can be no copying of, or from, "consumable" works (e.g., workbooks, exercises, standardized tests and test booklets and answer sheets).

5. Copying cannot substitute for the purchase of books, publishers' reprints, or periodicals.

6. Copying cannot be directed by a higher authority.

7. You cannot copy the same item from term to term.

8. No charge can be made to the student beyond the actual cost of the photocopying.

Source: Excerpt from Report of the House Committee on the Judiciary (House Report No. 94–1476).

Teachers are responsible for prohibiting unauthorized use of copyrighted computer software in their classes.

Immorality.   Although immorality is the most frequently cited ground for dismissal in state statutes, they normally do not define the term or discuss its application to specific conduct. As a consequence, these tasks have been left to the courts. A review of cases challenging dismissals related to immorality shows that they generally have been based on one or more of the following categories of conduct: (1) sexual conduct with students; (2) sexual conduct with nonstudents; (3) homosexuality; (4) making sexually explicit remarks or talking about sex unrelated to the curriculum; (5) distribution of sexually explicit materials to classes; (6) use of obscene, profane, or abusive language; (7) possession and use of controlled substances; (8) other criminal misconduct; and (9) dishonesty.

While acknowledging that the concept of immorality "is subject to ranging interpretations based on shifting social attitudes (and therefore) must be resolved on the facts and circumstances of each case" (*Ficus v. Board of School Trustees of Central School District,* 1987, p. 1,140), some standards have evolved from the cases in this area and are often applied to other cases involving dismissal for immorality. The first is the exemplar standard. While not as universally accepted today as in the past, the courts do recognize that there are "legitimate standards to be expected of those who teach in the public schools" (*Reitmeyer v. Unemployment Compensation Board of Review,* 1992, p. 508—teacher dismissed for distribution of racist "joke sheet" to coworkers). Second, there must be a connection between the out-of-school conduct of the teacher and the teacher's ability to teach, or the conduct must have an adverse effect on the school or be the subject of notoriety.

Should teachers be held to a higher standard of conduct than other professionals? Why or why not?

Since the facts of no two cases are exactly the same, the connection may exist in one case involving a particular conduct but not in another. Cases involving alleged immorality must be decided on a case-by-case basis, balancing the teacher's personal freedom against the school board's interest in maintaining a proper educational environment and taking into consideration the size of the community, its values, and when and where the conduct took place. Thus, while there is no definitive list of impermissible or immoral behaviors in case law, the courts have provided guidance on some issues. For example, most courts have not supported the dismissal of pregnant, unwed teachers or the dismissal of teachers for consenting sexual relationships out of wedlock, unless it can be shown that the teacher's effectiveness has been impaired by his or her action.

The courts also have held that conviction of a felony or misdemeanor, including possession of illegal drugs, does not necessarily, in and of itself, serve as grounds for dismissal. Again, the circumstances of each case are important, especially the effect on the school, students, and co-workers. For example, courts might not uphold the dismissal of a teacher solely because he or she once was indicted for possession of a small amount of marijuana. But they probably would support a firing based on evidence of a widely publicized conviction, combined with testimony that the teacher's criminal behavior would undermine his or her effectiveness as a teacher (Fischer, Schimmel, & Kelly, 1995).

The exceptions to the principle that to sustain a dismissal the behavior must affect teaching performance or become the subject of notoriety have been made most often in regard to notoriously illegal or immoral behavior, including sexual conduct with minors and homosexual conduct. In some states, engaging in certain homosexual activity is a violation of state sodomy laws, and a conviction of such a violation could serve as the basis for dismissal. In states other than California the courts have upheld the dismissal of homosexual and bisexual teachers based only on their private conduct, when no conviction of law had taken place. In Washington, a high school teacher was dismissed after admitting to his assistant principal that he was a homosexual. Although it was not the teacher but school officials who then publicized his homosexual status, the court accepted the officials' testimony that his continued presence would interfere with the orderly operation of the school (*Gaylord v. Tacoma School District No. 10,* 1977).

Incompetency.   Those conditions or behaviors that have been sustained most successfully as constituting *incompetence* fall into four general categories: (1) inadequate teaching, (2) poor discipline, (3) physical or mental incapacity, and (4) counterproductive personality traits. As with dismissals for alleged immorality, in dismissals for incompetence the courts require that there be an established relationship between the employee's conduct and the operation of the school. Additionally, the standard against which the teacher is measured must be one used for other teachers in a similar position, not some hypothetical standard of perfection, and the conduct must not be an isolated incident but a demonstrated *pattern* of incompetence. Most jurisdictions also require that before termination a determination be made whether the behavior in question is remedial and that, in jurisdictions where remediation is required, a reasonable period for remediation be provided (Landauer, Spanfer, & Van Horn, 1983).

Insubordination.   Regardless of whether or not it is specified in statute, *insubordination* is an acceptable cause for dismissal in all states. Insubordination involves the *persistent* and *willful* violation of a reasonable rule or direct order from a recognized authority. The rule must not only be reasonable, but it must be clearly communicated and cannot be an infringement upon the teacher's constitutional rights. For example, rules that limit what teachers can say or write may in some cases violate their First Amendment right to free speech. Normally, unless the insubordinate act is severe, a single action is insufficient grounds for dismissal.

In cases involving insubordination it is not necessary to establish a relationship between the insubordinate action(s) and teaching effectiveness. Among the actions that have been held to constitute insubordination are unauthorized absence from duty, abuse of sick leave, refusal to follow established policies and procedures, inappropriate use of corporal punishment, refusal to meet with superiors, encouraging students to disobey school authority, refusal to perform assigned nonteaching duties, failure to acquire required approval for use of instructional materials, and refusal to cease extemporaneous prayer and the reading of Bible stories.

Reduction in Force (RIF)

Declining enrollments, school consolidations, financial shortfalls, curriculum changes, and other occurrences often result in a *reduction in force* (RIF), i.e., reduction of the total number of employees needed by the district. Normally, neither tenured nor nontenured teachers released because of position abolition are entitled to a hearing unless it is required by statute. The courts consider these dismissals to be impersonal, in no way impugning the teacher and therefore outside the scope of teacher termination statutes. However, the reasons articulated by the district must be real, reasonable, and supported by substantial evidence and limited to the grounds listed in the RIF statutes (Valente, 1994).

The majority of litigation related to RIF has been concerned with two issues: whether the abolition of the position was *bona fide* and whether the release of a particular employee was justified. While the burden of proof is on the RIFed employee, teachers who can prove that the specified statutory condition for RIFing (e.g., enrollment decline or fiscal shortfall) did not exist, or that the purported abolition of the position was an illusion (e.g., another person was given the same position but with a different title), are almost always successful in obtaining reinstatement without having to prove fraud or bad faith (Valente, 1994).

The second issue, who should be released, involves the question of preference. State statutes and school board policies often specify the order of release in terms of tenure, seniority, or other criteria. When statutes or policies are silent or ambiguous about order of release, the courts have tended to give qualified tenured teachers priority over nontenured teachers in similar positions. Certification has been the major, but not the exclusive, criterion considered by the courts in determining "qualifiedness." Among tenured teachers holding similar positions, seniority has been the primary, but not the exclusive, factor in determining order of release. Seniority rights may be qualified by other factors such as performance evaluations, areas of need, affirmative action goals, or collective bargaining agreements.

The order of recall of RIF employees, should vacancies arise for which they are qualified, is roughly the inverse of the order of release. That is, qualified tenured teachers would be called back before nontenured teachers and in the order of seniority within each group.

Nonrenewal of Contract

The contracts of tenured teachers are renewed automatically unless they are dismissed for cause or declared excess. The renewal of nontenured teachers' contracts, however, requires the formal approval of the school board. And, unless required by state statute or negotiated contract, school boards may terminate nontenured teachers without any due process and without giving any statement of reasons or providing a hearing on the decision not to renew. However, in most states school boards are required to provide the nontenured teacher with a timely notification of intent to nonrenew. And, if the nontenured teacher is dismissed before the expiration of the contract, the teacher is entitled to due process.

Procedural Due Process

In keeping with the Fourteenth Amendment, if the dismissal of a teacher involves a liberty or property right, procedural *due process* must be provided. As previously noted, tenured teachers have a property right to continued employment. Nontenured teachers do not have a property right claim to due process unless they are dismissed during the contract year or unless the dismissal action impairs a fundamental constitutional right, creates a stigma, or damages the employee's reputation to the extent that it forecloses other employment opportunities. Nontenured teachers may also establish a liberty interest claim if the nonrenewal decision was made to retaliate for the teacher's exercise of one of his or her fundamental liberties.

Once it has been established that a school district action requires procedural due process, the central issue becomes *what process is due*. In arriving at its decision the court will look to the procedural due process requirements in state statutes, state agency or school board regulations, or employment contracts to determine both their propriety and the extent to which they were followed.

What do the statutes say in the state in which you plan to teach regarding the nonrenewal of contracts of nontenured teachers? What, if any, due process is required?

Generally the courts have held that an employee facing a severe loss such as termination of employment must be ensured the following procedural elements:

1. notice of charges

2. the opportunity for a hearing

3. adequate time to prepare a rebuttal to the charges

4. the names of witnesses and access to evidence

5. a hearing before an impartial tribunal

6. the right to representation by legal counsel

7. the opportunity to introduce evidence and cross-examine witnesses

8. a decision based solely on the evidence presented and the findings of the hearing

9. a transcript or record of the hearing

10. the opportunity to appeal (McCarthy & Cambron-McCabe, 1992)

Notice must not merely be given, it must be timely (on or before an established date) and in sufficient specificity to enable the employee to attempt to remediate or to prepare an adequate defense. A formal hearing as practiced in courts is not required, but the hearing must provide the employee a full and fair opportunity to rebut all charges. Table 12.1 lists some Supreme Court cases affecting teachers' rights in matters of employment and in matters inside and outside the classroom.

Teacher Rights Outside the Classroom

School boards in this country have historically considered it their right, indeed their responsibility, to control the personal as well as the professional conduct of teachers. School boards have sought to regulate teachers' dress, speech, religion, and association. As the twentieth century has progressed, teacher activism, court decisions, and enlightened legislators and school boards have greatly expanded the rights of teachers.

Freedom of Expression

In the landmark U.S. Supreme Court decision regarding freedom of expression in the public schools, *Tinker v. Des Moines* (1969), the Court ruled that neither teachers nor students shed their constitutional rights to freedom of speech or expression when they enter the schoolhouse gate. However, this does not mean that teachers or students are free to say or write anything they wish. Rather, in reviewing cases involving expression, the courts attempt to balance the rights of the individual against the harm caused to the schools.

In the lead case involving teachers' freedom of expression, Marvin Pickering, a high school teacher in Illinois, was terminated after writing a letter to the newspaper severely criticizing the superintendent and school board for

Table 12.1: Selected U.S. Supreme Court Cases Affecting Teachers' Rights

Case	Decision
Indiana *ex rel.* Anderson v. Brand (1938)	Tenure statutes provide qualifying teachers with contractual rights that cannot be altered by the state without good cause.
Keyishian v. Board of Regents (1967)	Loyalty oaths that make mere membership in a subversive organization grounds for dismissal are unconstitutionally overbroad.
Pickering v. Board of Education (1968)	Absent proof of false statements knowingly or recklessly made, teachers may not be dismissed for exercising the freedom to speak on matters of public interest.
Board of Regents v. Roth (1972)	A nontenured teacher does not have a property right to continued employment and can be dismissed without a statement of cause or a hearing as long as the employee's reputation or future employment have not been impaired.
Perry v. Sindermann (1972)	Teachers may not be dismissed for public criticism of superiors on matters of public concern.
Hortonville Joint School District No. 1 v. Hortonville Education Association (1976)	A school board may serve as the impartial hearing body in a due process hearing.
Washington v. Davis (1976)	To sustain a claim of discrimination an employee must show that the employer's action was a deliberate attempt to discriminate, not just that the action resulted in a disproportionate impact.
Mount Healthy City School District v. Doyle (1977)	To prevail in a First Amendment dismissal case school district employees must show that the conduct was protected and was a substantial and motivating decision not to renew the contract and the school board must prove that it would have reached the same decision in the absence of the protected conduct.
United States v. South Carolina (1978)	Use of the National Teachers Examinations both as a requirement for certification and as a factor in salary determination serves a legitimate state purpose and is not unconstitutional despite its disparate racial impact.
Connick v. Myers (1983)	The First Amendment guarantee of freedom of expression does not extend to teachers' public comments on matters of personal interest (as opposed to matters of public concern).
Cleveland Board of Education v. Laudermill (1985)	A teacher who can be dismissed only for cause is entitled to an oral or written notice of charges, a statement of the evidence against him or her, and the opportunity to present his or her side prior to termination.
Garland Independent School District v. Texas State Teachers Association (1986)	Teachers can use the interschool mail system and school mailboxes to distribute union material.
Wygant v. Jackson Board of Education (1986)	Absent evidence that the school board has engaged in discrimination or that the preferred employees have been victims of discrimination, school board policies may not give preferential treatment based on race or ethnicity in layoff decisions.
School Board of Nassau County v. Arline (1987)	Persons suffering from contagious diseases are considered handicapped persons, and discrimination against them based solely on fear of contamination is considered unconstitutional discrimination against the handicapped.

their handling of school funds. On appeal the U.S. Supreme Court (*Pickering v. Board of Education,* 1968) overturned his dismissal and ruled that teachers, as citizens, do have the right to make critical public comments on matters of public concern. The Court further held that unless the expression undermines (1) the effectiveness of the working relationship between the teacher and the immediate superior, (2) harmony among co-workers, (3) the proper performance of the teacher's duties in the classroom, or (4) the orderly operation of the schools, such expression may not furnish grounds for reprisal. Finding that the issue of school board spending is an issue of legitimate public concern and that Pickering's statements were not directed at people he normally worked with, nor that there was any undermining of the operation of the schools (in fact, the letter had been greeted with apathy by everyone but the board), the Supreme Court overturned Pickering's dismissal.

If, however, the public comment is not related to matters of public concern, it is not protected. The U.S. Supreme Court ruled in *Connick v. Myers* (1983) that free expression is not protected when a public employee "speaks not as a citizen upon matters of public concern, but instead as an employee upon matters only of personal interest" (p. 138). Thus, comments related to political advocacy and policies governing the welfare of students or the school district have been found to be matters of public concern, while comments or complaints about individual work assignments, conditions of employment, or relations with superiors generally have not been found to be matters of public concern (McCarthy & Cambron-McCabe, 1992).

Even if expression does involve a public issue, it still is not protected if the impact of the expression undermines the effectiveness of working relationships or the normal operation of the schools. For example, the Fourth Circuit upheld the dismissal of a teacher who wrote and circulated a letter to fellow teachers objecting to a delay in receiving summer pay, complaining about budgetary management, and encouraging teachers to stage a "sick-out" during final examination week. The court ruled that any First Amendment interest inherent in the letter was outweighed by the *public interest* in having public education provided by teachers loyal to that service (i. e., not causing a disruption of exams by a sick-out that was in violation of district policy and the teachers contract and professionally questionable behavior), and by the *employer interest* "in having its employees abide by reasonable policies adopted to control sick leave and maintain morale and effective operation of the schools" (*Stroman v. Colleton County School District,* 1992, p. 159).

Right to Organize, Bargain Collectively, and Strike

The associational rights of teachers have been greatly expanded in the last quarter century. The courts have ruled that teachers have the right of free association, and unjustified interference with this right by school boards violates the Fourteenth Amendment. In fact, the Supreme Court has sanctioned the use of the school mail for dissemination of union literature, as well as the right to engage in discussion of union activities during nonclass time (*Texas State Teachers' Association v. Garland Independent School District,* 1986).

Although teachers have a right to form or join a union or professional association, whether they have a right to engage in collective bargaining depends on state law. About 40 states have passed laws permitting school boards to engage in collective bargaining with teacher groups. The collective bargaining laws vary widely. Some states require school boards only to "meet and confer" with the teacher organization. Other statutes are much more detailed, specifying the topics to be negotiated (typically, salary, leaves of absence, job benefits, and transfers) and the procedures to be followed if an impasse occurs in negotiations (Fischer, Schimmel, & Kelly, 1995).

Despite the recognition of the right of teachers to organize, the right to strike has not been recognized by the courts and is denied by about half the states. In those states where strikes are allowed, they usually are allowed only after the requirements for impasse resolution have been met and only after the school board has been notified of the intent to strike. When teachers strike in violation of state law or without having met the requirements of the law, the school board may seek an injunction to prohibit the strike. Violation of a court order or an injunction ordering strikers back to work may result in a contempt of court decree and fine or imprisonment. Moreover, those who engage in illegal strikes may be subject to economic sanctions (e.g., withholding of raises or fines) or disciplinary actions, including dismissal (*Hortonville Joint School District No. 1 v. Hortonville Education Association,* 1979).

Political Activity

Teachers have the right to engage in political activities and hold public office; however, restrictions may be placed on the exercise of this right. For example, teachers may discuss political issues and candidates in a nonpartisan manner in the classroom and even wear political buttons, badges, or armbands to class. However, they may not make campaign speeches in the classroom or otherwise take advantage of their position of authority over a captive audience to promote their own political views. Political activity in the schools that would cause divisiveness among the faculty or otherwise be disruptive also may be restricted if the school can demonstrate it is necessary to meet a compelling public need to protect efficiency and integrity in the school.

The authority of the school board to restrict teachers' political activities outside the school setting is far less than their authority to restrict activities in the schools. The courts have upheld teachers' rights to support candidates of their choice, display political buttons and stickers, and participate in demonstrations. In addition, the courts generally have upheld the right of teachers to run for and hold public office. However, the courts also have indicated that if the time and activities associated with running for or holding office interfere with the performance of teaching duties, the teacher may be required to take a leave of absence or even resign. Also, the courts in some states have found the holding of certain political offices (e.g., school board member or member of a board that has supervisory powers over the employing school district) to present a conflict of interest with employment in the schools and therefore forbid the joint occupancy of both positions.

Should teachers be denied the right to strike? What would you do if your professional association called for a strike when state law forbids teachers to strike?

If you felt strongly that a particular candidate would be in the best interest of education in your community or state, how would you work for his or her election? Would you consider running for public office as an "education candidate" in order to improve education?

Academic Freedom

Academic freedom refers to the teacher's freedom to discuss the subject matter discipline and to determine the most appropriate instructional materials and teaching strategies without unwarranted restrictions. Academic freedom is not without limits. For example, teachers do not have the ultimate right to determine course content or select textbooks; that authority belongs to the school board. The school board may also require that teachers receive prior approval for the use of supplementary materials. Teachers also do not have the right to ignore prescribed content or to refuse to follow the designated scope and sequence of content or materials, even if the refusal is for religious reasons.

Although teachers have limited freedom in determining the content of the curriculum, they have greater freedom in choosing the particular strategies to teach the prescribed content. In reviewing school board attempts to restrict teachers' methodologies, the courts consider a number of factors, including

> the adequacy of notice that use of specific teaching methodologies will result in disciplinary action, the relevance of the method to the course of study, the support for the strategy or materials by the teaching profession, and the threat of disruption posed by the method. The judiciary also has considered community standards in assessing challenges to various teaching methods. However, if a particular strategy is instructionally relevant and supported by the profession, it will probably survive judicial review even though it might offend some parents. (McCarthy, 1989, p. 260)

In a case in point, a Texas teacher was discharged for failure to obey a school board warning that she refrain from using a role-playing simulation to teach about post–Civil War American history (*Kingsville Independent School District v. Cooper*, 1980). Parents had complained that the simulation aroused strong feelings about racial issues. When the teacher refused to obey the district's directive "not to discuss Blacks in American history," her contract was not renewed. The Fifth Circuit Court of Appeals reinstated the teacher and awarded back pay and attorney's fees, finding that the district violated her constitutional rights by basing the nonrenewal on classroom discussions that were protected by the First Amendment.

If, however, the teacher is discussing or distributing material that is not relevant, or using a teaching method that is not supported by the profession, the teacher may be sanctioned. This was the case when a teacher was dismissed for refusing to stop using a classroom management technique he had developed called "Learnball," which included a sports format, dividing the class into teams, and a system of rewards that included radio playing and shooting foam basketballs in class. The teacher not only continued to use the technique, but advocated its use by others, and in connection with his advocacy publicly criticized the school system. While acknowledging the teacher's First Amendment right to advocate Learnball and to criticize school officials, the court ruled that the teacher had "no constitutional right to use Learnball in the classroom" (*Bradley v. Pittsburgh Board of Education*, 1990).

Book Banning.   Currently, perhaps the most contested academic freedom issue involves attempts to censor the curriculum by excluding certain offerings (e.g., evolution, sex education, and values clarification) or materials deemed vulgar, offensive, or that promote secular humanism. The courts typically have supported the school board in the face of parental attempts to censor the curriculum or ban certain books from the school library. However, when it is the school board itself that advocates censorship, judicial support is not as easily won. This is because the courts traditionally have recognized the authority of the school board to determine the curriculum, select texts, purchase books for the library, approve the use of supplementary materials, and perform a host of other curriculum-related activities. Nonetheless, in a number of instances the courts have found that specific censorship activities violated the teacher's right to academic freedom or students' First Amendment rights to have access to information. While acknowledging that the banning of books and materials on the basis of obscenity or educational unsuitability is permissible, the courts in these cases have held that censorship motivated primarily by the preferences of school board members or to suppress particular viewpoints or controversial ideas contained in the book, or by their desire to impose on students a particular religious or political orthodoxy, is not permissible (*McCarthy v. Fletcher,* 1989).

The controversy regarding who controls instructional and curricular matters, teachers or the school board, is likely to continue, as are parental attempts to exert greater control over the curriculum. Until definitive guidance is provided by the Supreme Court, resolution will continue on a case-by-case basis, attempting to balance the teacher's interest in academic freedom against the school board's interest in promoting an appropriate educational environment.

Tort Liability of Teachers

A *tort* is defined as a civil wrong that leads to injury to another (criminal wrongs are not torts) and for which a court will provide a remedy in the form of an action for damages. Historically, school districts were protected from acts of tort liability by the doctrine of *sovereign immunity,* which prevents potential litigants from suing the government unless the government consents to the suit. Over the years, the doctrine has been weakened as over half the states have abandoned this protection. Even when the district has immunity, teachers and others do not. To protect both school district employees and school board members against financial loss resulting from a tort suit, many school districts purchase liability insurance. Many educators also participate in liability insurance programs through their professional organizations.

The most common category of torts in education is *negligence.* Basically, negligence can be defined as a failure to do (or not do) what a reasonable and prudent person would have done under the same or similar circumstances, resulting in injury to another. Before an educator can be found guilty of negligence, four elements must be proved:

1. The educator had a duty to provide an appropriate standard of care to another individual (student, coworker, the public).

2. The educator failed in his or her duty to provide the reasonable standard of care.

3. There is a causal relationship between the negligent action and the resultant injury (i.e., the action was the *proximate cause* of the injury).

4. There is a physical or mental injury resulting in actual loss.

Standard of Care and Duty

Although teachers have the responsibility of providing an appropriate standard of care for their students, the standard of care expected is not the same for all teachers and all students. Teachers of younger children are held to a higher standard of care than teachers of more mature students. A higher standard of care also is required of teachers of the physically or mentally handicapped, as well as of physical education and vocational and industrial arts teachers because of the inherent dangers in the activities involved.

Reasonableness Doctrine.   In determining whether the educator failed to provide the appropriate standard of care, the courts compare the teacher's actions with those of the hypothetical "reasonable and prudent" teacher—one with average intelligence and physical attributes, normal perception and memory, and possessing the same special knowledge and skills as others with his or her training and experience—not some "ideal" or "super" teacher.

Foreseeable Doctrine.   A related element is whether the hypothetical reasonable teacher could have foreseen, and thus prevented, the injury. The actions of the teacher are compared with those of the reasonable teacher to determine negligence.

Proximate Cause

Even in situations in which the teacher has failed in his or her recognized duty to provide a reasonable standard of care, liability will not be assessed unless it can be shown that the teacher's action was the *proximate cause* of the injury, that is, that the injury would not have occurred had it not been for the teacher's conduct. In some cases an intervening event, such as the negligent act of a third party, may relieve the teacher of liability. Because each case brings with it a set of circumstances distinct from all others, the determination of proximate cause must be made on a case-by-case basis.

Educational Malpractice

What impact does the potential for negligence suits have on educational practice?

Historically, most educational liability litigation has involved pupil injuries. In the last two decades, however, a new topic of negligence litigation called *educational malpractice* has emerged and become the focus of concerned discussion in both the educational and legal communities. As in medical malpractice, the term is concerned with some negligence on the part of the professional. In general, there are three kinds of educational malpractice suits: (1) instructional malpractice suits concerned with students who have received certificates or diplomas and do not possess basic academic skills, (2) suits involving misdiagnosis or improper educational placement, and (3) suits involving the failure of school personnel to protect students known to be at risk for suicide or harm to another.

Some activities, such as physical education, require that teachers exercise a higher standard of care.

In regard to the first kind of suit, the courts have continued to reject student claims that they have a right to a predetermined level of achievement in return for compulsory school attendance. In the seminal case in this area, *Peter W. v. San Francisco Unified School District* (1976), Peter W. was awarded a high school diploma even though he was functionally illiterate. Peter W. sued the district for negligence in allowing him to graduate. The courts dismissed the case, finding no certainty that a causal relationship existed between the defendants' conduct and Peter W.'s injuries. In *Peter W.* and a similar action in New York, *Donohue v. Copiague Union Free Schools* (1979), the courts noted that allowing such suits would require the courts to intervene in matters of educational policy and to become entangled in educational questions—actions judged inappropriate for the courts and likely to flood the courts with similar suits.

In the lead case concerned with placement malpractice, *Hoffman v. Board of Education of the City of New York* (1979), plaintiff Hoffman was examined by a school psychologist upon entry to kindergarten using the Stanford-Binet intelligence test, which, in part, requires verbal responses. Hoffman had a severe speech defect. The psychologist recommended that he be placed in a class for the mentally retarded, but also that he be reexamined in two years. No reexamination took place for 13 years, and then only at his mother's request. This examination showed him to be of normal intelligence. Hoffman sued and was awarded $750,000 in damages by the jury. A New York Court of Appeals later overturned the award, stating that it was unwilling to

> substitute its judgment for the professional judgment of the board of education as to the type of psychometric devices to be used and the frequency with which such

tests are to be given. . . . To do so would open the door to an examination of the propriety of each of the procedures used in the education of every student in our school system. (p. 320)

Although other cases involving alleged negligence in diagnosis and placement have been equally unsuccessful, the courts have recognized that there might be cases in which defendants knowingly violated statutes related to special education placements or intentionally misplaced students that would be actionable under tort law (see, e.g., *B. M. by Berger v. State of Montana*, 1982; *Hunter v. Board of Education of Montgomery County*, 1982).

The third category of educational malpractice is based on the case law related to the medical profession, which says that despite patient or client confidentiality, these professionals have a duty to warn and attempt to protect those at risk for harm. In the first case of this kind, *Eisel v. Board of Education of Montgomery* (1991), two school counselors were found negligent in failing to communicate to a parent a student's suicidal statements made to other students and told to them. The counselors had questioned the student about the statements, but when she denied them they did nothing further. The court ruled that "school counselors have a duty to use reasonable means to prevent a suicide when they are on notice of a child or adolescent student's suicidal intent" (p. 456).

Discrimination, Equal Opportunity, and Affirmative Action

Discrimination

School districts and their employees are prohibited by the Fourteenth Amendment and numerous state and federal statutes from engaging in practices that intentionally discriminate against employees or students on the basis of race, sex, age, religion, national origin, or handicapping condition. To be successful in a claim of *discrimination* under the Fourteenth Amendment, the employee must prove that the district's action constituted a deliberate intent to discriminate, not just that the action resulted in a disproportionate impact (*Washington v. Davis*, 1976). Because of the difficulty in proving intentional discrimination, most cases alleging discrimination are brought under Title VII or one of the other civil rights statutes detailed in Table 11.1.

Two types of discrimination claims are typically brought under Title VII: *discriminatory treatment,* which requires that the plaintiff prove that he or she was treated less favorably than others by some employment practice or policy, and *disparate impact,* which requires that the plaintiff show that an employment practice or policy results in a disparate impact on a protected class. If the employer answers the challenge by claiming the policy or practice is job-related and consistent with a business necessity, the employee can still prevail by showing that the district could have accomplished its goal by less discriminatory means. For example, a female applicant for a high school biology teaching position was successful in a sex discrimination suit on the basis that the district's requirement that applicants also have the ability to coach varsity softball had a disparate impact on women (*Civil Rights Division v. Amphitheater Unified School District*, 1983). The court rejected the district's business necessity defense because the district was unable to demonstrate that less discriminatory alternatives had been attempted.

Equal Opportunity

The legal principle of *equal opportunity,* whether equal employment opportunity or equal educational opportunity, is founded in antidiscrimination legislation. Equal opportunity requires that school districts and other agencies develop policies and procedures to ensure that the rights of employees and students are protected, and that they are given equal treatment in employment practices, access to programs, or other educational opportunities.

Affirmative Action

Affirmative action goes beyond equal opportunity. The principle of affirmative action holds that ensuring nondiscrimination is not enough; what is needed are affirmative steps to recruit, hire, and retain individuals who are underrepresented in the workplace or the classroom. Many school districts have adopted affirmative action plans that set forth their intended goals in these areas and their intended actions to achieve these goals.

What should school districts do to increase the number of women in school administration?

The U.S. Supreme Court, in *Regents of the University of California v. Alan Bakke* (1978), ruled against the establishment of firm quotas that designate a predetermined number of "slots" only for minorities, resulting in so-called *reverse discrimination.* However, the court has upheld the voluntary adoption of goals and race-conscious remedies in hiring practices that are designed to bring balance to the composition of the workforce or student body. Nonetheless, as the U.S. Supreme Court ruled in *Wygant v. Jackson Board of Education* (1986), which overturned a Michigan school district's collective bargaining agreement that released white employees with greater seniority than black employees in order to preserve the percentage of minority teachers employed prior to the layoffs, affirmative action plans must be designed to remedy location-specific past discrimination, not general societal discrimination. That is, there must be evidence that remedial action is necessary and, second, the plan must be "narrowly tailored" to remedy the past discrimination.

Student Rights and Responsibilities

Traditionally, it was accepted that school officials had considerable authority in controlling student conduct. Operating under the doctrine of *in loco parentis* (in place of a parent), school authorities exercised almost unlimited and usually unchallenged discretion in restricting the rights of students and in disciplining students. However, beginning in the late 1960s students increasingly challenged the authority and actions of school officials. Subsequent court decisions have broadened the scope of student rights and, at the same time, have attempted to maintain a balance between the rights of students and the responsibilities of school officials (see Figure 12.2 and the discussion of "no pass, no play" on p. 424).

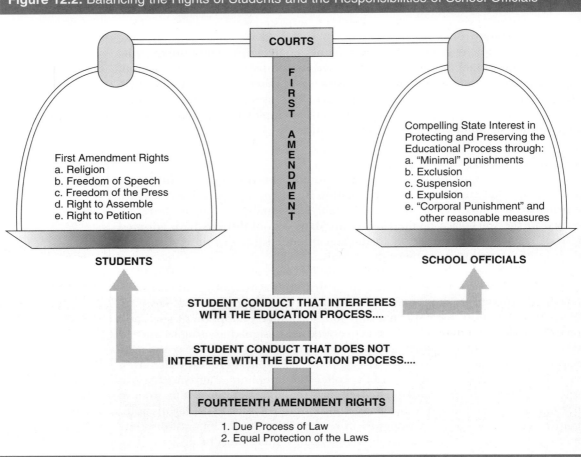

Figure 12.2: Balancing the Rights of Students and the Responsibilities of School Officials

COURTS

FIRST AMENDMENT

First Amendment Rights
a. Religion
b. Freedom of Speech
c. Freedom of the Press
d. Right to Assemble
e. Right to Petition

Compelling State Interest in
Protecting and Preserving the
Educational Process through:
a. "Minimal" punishments
b. Exclusion
c. Suspension
d. Expulsion
e. "Corporal Punishment" and
   other reasonable measures

STUDENTS

SCHOOL OFFICIALS

**STUDENT CONDUCT THAT INTERFERES
WITH THE EDUCATION PROCESS....**

**STUDENT CONDUCT THAT DOES NOT
INTERFERE WITH THE EDUCATION PROCESS....**

FOURTEENTH AMENDMENT RIGHTS

1. Due Process of Law
2. Equal Protection of the Laws

Source: From *The Schools, the Courts, and the Public Interest* by J. C. Hogan. Copyright © 1974, 1985 by Lexington Books, an imprint of Macmillan, Inc.

Student Discipline

Although the *in loco parentis* doctrine has been weakened in recent years, school officials do have the authority—and in fact the duty—to establish reasonable rules of student conduct designed to protect students and employees, as well as rules necessary to establish and maintain a climate conducive to learning. The authority and responsibility to establish rules of conduct carries with it the authority to discipline students for violations of these rules. The severity of the violation will determine the nature of the discipline and the due process required. Because state compulsory attendance laws give students a property right to attend school, if disciplinary action involves exclusion from school or the removal of the student from the classroom for even a minimal period of time, some due process is required, even if in the latter instance it is only informally providing the student the opportunity to give his or her side of the story.

Suspensions and Expulsions

Short-term *suspensions* usually are defined as exclusions from school for periods of time of 10 days or less; *expulsions* (i.e., long-term suspensions) are for periods of time in excess of 10 days. While a teacher or administrator may initiate an expulsion proceeding, normally only the school board can expel the student. Because of the severity of expulsions, state statutes and school board regulations detail the procedures that must be followed. Such procedures usually include the right to:

1. a written notice specifying the charges, the time and place of the hearing, and the procedures to be followed at the hearing

2. a hearing before an impartial tribunal

3. cross-examine witnesses and present witnesses and evidence to refute adverse evidence

4. representation by counsel (usually only in the more serious disciplinary actions)

5. a written statement of the findings/recommendations of the hearing body

6. a written or taped record of the hearing if appeal is to be made

7. a clear statement of the right to appeal

In contrast to the detailed statutory guidelines pertaining to expulsions, state laws and school board policies traditionally did not address short-term suspensions; therefore, practices have varied across the country. In 1975, however, in *Goss v. Lopez,* the U.S. Supreme Court established the basic procedures that must be followed in short-term suspensions. The Court held that for suspensions of less than 10 days the student must be given oral or written notice of the charges, and if the student denies the charges, he or she must be given a hearing with the opportunity to rebut the charges before an objective decision maker and be given an explanation of the evidence against him or her. The Court in *Goss* also recognized that there might be situations that would require more detailed procedures, such as situations in which the facts are disputed and not easily resolved, as well as emergency situations in which the safety of persons or property is threatened and no due process is required prior to disciplinary action. However, even in these situations due process must be followed as soon as possible after the danger of harm has passed. While *Goss* specified only the basics of due process that must be followed for short-term suspensions, state laws may, and often do, require additional procedures.

One month after *Goss,* the Supreme Court handed down another decision that had further impact on student exclusion cases. In *Wood v. Strickland* (1975), the Court held that students may sue school board members for monetary damages under the Civil Rights Act of 1871 if their constitutional rights are violated. In this case, two girls were suspended from school without a hearing for spiking the punch at a school party. The Supreme Court clarified its *Wood* decision in *Carey v. Piphus* (1978). The Court said that in order to collect damages when

What effect does the expansion of due process rights of students have on the willingness of educators to discipline disobedient or disruptive students?

Controversial Issues:
No Pass, No Play

In the search to find ways to curb declining academic achievement and failing grades, "no pass, no play" rules are being adopted by school districts across the country. Such rules require students to pass a minimum number of courses to be eligible to participate in school-sponsored cocurricular activities.

Arguments For	Arguments Against
1. Students who do not perform in the classroom should not be allowed to perform on the athletic field, stage, etc.	1. Students who might have stayed in school to participate in cocurricular activities drop out.
2. Such rules are needed to ensure that students place the appropriate priority on academic achievement—the primary purpose of attending school.	2. Such rules do nothing for students who do not participate in cocurricular activities—the students most at risk for dropping out.
3. Students enrolled in cocurricular activities fail fewer courses and are more likely to complete high school.	3. Discourages students from participating in activities.
4. No pass, no play rules provide the impetus for students to improve their study skills, manage their time more wisely, and exercise self-discipline.	4. Participation in cocurricular activities should not be made subject to academic achievement. The implication is that the development of the intellect is more important than the development of other domains (social, physical, emotional).
5. Maintaining only a passing grade is a minimum, not maximum, requirement.	5. Students are discouraged from taking more challenging courses for fear of losing their eligibility.
6. Fosters success in later life.	6. Such rules discriminate against learning disabled and minority students.

Should participation in cocurricular activities be made contingent upon academic achievement?

their rights have been violated, students must show that they have sustained an actual injury. Otherwise, they are entitled to recover only the nominal damage amount of $1.

In a more recent decision, the Supreme Court has held that disruptive handicapped students can be suspended for up to 10 days, but that they cannot be summarily expelled for disciplinary reasons (*Honig v. Doe,* 1988). Expulsions or long-term suspension would be a change in placement and cannot take place until the necessary procedural requirements under P.L. 94–142 have been satisfied and an alternative placement has been agreed upon.

Corporal Punishment
Although the U.S. Supreme Court has said that corporal punishment is not prohibited by the Eighth Amendment, as noted in the previous chapter, if the punishment is excessive, the student may have an assault and battery claim, and the

administrator or teacher administering the punishment may be found liable for the injuries sustained. In addition, five circuit courts have acknowledged that grossly excessive corporal punishment might be a violation of the substantive due process right to be "free of state intrusions into realms of personal privacy and bodily security" (see, e.g., *Garcia v. Miera,* 1987).

Half the states prohibit corporal punishment (Dayton, 1994). In a number of others, corporal punishment is prohibited by school board policy. In the states and school districts where corporal punishment is permitted, school board policies will normally dictate the conditions under which corporal punishment can be administered. In any instance, a teacher administering corporal punishment would be wise "(a) to have another adult present when administering corporal punishment, (b) to be sure that its use is reasonable in light of the student's age and circumstances necessitating the punishment, and (c) to administer the punishment without malice" (McCarthy, 1989).

Search and Seizure

The issues surrounding search and seizure of students have increased in recent years, along with the concern about drug use among school-age children. The Fourth Amendment protection against unreasonable search and seizure has been interpreted as requiring law enforcement officials to have probable cause that a crime has been committed and to obtain a search warrant before conducting a search. Prior to 1985, some courts held school officials to the same standard. However, in *New Jersey v. T.L.O.* (1985), the Supreme Court ruled that school officials' interest in maintaining discipline in the schools was sufficient to justify their being held to a lesser standard than probable cause. Rather, school officials may conduct searches based on a "reasonable suspicion" provided that: (1) there is "individualized" reasonable cause or suspicion that the search will reveal evidence of a violation of the law or school rules, and (2) the scope of the search is reasonably related to the objective of the search and is not "excessively intrusive" in light of the age and sex of the child and the nature of the alleged infraction.

What would be some examples of student conduct that would constitute "reasonable suspicion" for you to institute a search for drugs?

In determining whether a particular search is reasonable, the courts have distinguished between school property, such as lockers, and personal property. The courts have held that while a student may have exclusive use of a locker in regard to other students, the possession is not exclusive in regard to school officials who retain control of the lockers. In fact, the courts have said that it is not only the right but the duty of school officials to search a locker if suspicion arises that something of an illegal nature may be concealed there (*People v. Overton,* 1969).

The use of drug-sniffing dogs is currently one of the most unsettled issues in the area of student searches. In *Doe v. Renfrow* (1980), the Seventh Circuit Court viewed the use of dogs as preliminary to the search itself and legal, provided the dogs were used to sniff particular students, not all students or random groups. An opposing conclusion was reached by the Fifth Circuit in *Horton v. Goose Creek Independent School District* (1982), which ruled the use of drug-detecting dogs to sniff students to be an unconstitutional invasion of the student's privacy.

However, the *Horton* court did say that the use of dogs in sniffing lockers and cars is permissible.

Strip searches, because of their intrusive nature, are carefully scrutinized and most often disallowed by the courts. However, they will be allowed if they meet the *T.L.O.* standards, particularly in regard to the scope of the search. In a case in point, the Court upheld the strip search of a student suspected by a teacher of "crotching" drugs. The student, previously reported by his school bus driver and fellow students as a drug user, was taken to the gym and told to take off his clothes and put on a gym uniform. Although a visual inspection of his body and a search of his cloths revealed no drugs, the Court concluded that the students's previous suspected drug use, combined with the teacher's report, gave school authorities reasonable suspicion to conduct the specific search undertaken (*Cornfield v. Consolidated School District No. 230,* 1993).

Perhaps the most controversial current issue in the area of student searches is drug testing of students. Thus far, the courts have invalidated blanket drug testing of the general student population on the basis of the individualized suspicion standard (*Anable v. Ford,* 1985; *Odenheim v. Carlstadt-East Rutherford School District,* 1985). However, the question of "suspicionless" random drug testing of students who wish to participate in extracurricular activities has yielded opposing decisions from the circuit courts. In the Seventh Circuit the random testing of interscholastic athletes and cheerleaders as a condition of participation was upheld (*Schaill v. Tippecanoe Country School Corp.,* 1988). Those testing positive were not excluded from school, only from participation in the sport, and any evidence obtained was not used for criminal prosecution but for prevention and rehabilitation. According to the court, suspicionless searches are more likely to be permissible in circumstances in which a student has a diminished expectation of privacy, particularly in regard to urine testing. And, student athletes who have a urinalysis as part of the general physical required for participation are among those who would have a diminished expectation of privacy in regard to urine testing.

Five years later, the Ninth Circuit, relying on two Supreme Court decisions handed down since *Schaill,* found that the school district's interest in drug testing did not outweigh the privacy rights of students (*Acton v. Vernonia School District,* 1994). However, the Court did give some guidance to school districts who wish to establish a drug testing program by noting that a truly voluntary program might pass constitutional muster. For the time being, however, "(I)t appears as though the drug problem in our nation's schools must get worse before a mandatory suspicionless drug testing program can be used as a universal solution" (Rossow & Parkinson, 1994, p. 2). Table 12.2 lists some Supreme Court decisions affecting students' rights.

Freedom of Expression

In 1965, several students in Des Moines, Iowa, were suspended after wearing black armbands to school to demonstrate their opposition to the Vietnam War. The wearing of armbands was prohibited by a school district policy, which had been adopted by Des Moines principals to prevent possible disturbances after

Table 12.2: Selected U.S. Supreme Court Cases Affecting Students' Rights	

Case	Decision
Tinker v. Des Moines (1969)	School officials cannot limit students' rights to free expression unless there is evidence of a material disruption or substantial disorder.
Goss v. Lopez (1975)	For suspensions of less than 10 days, the student must be given an oral or written notice of charges, an explanation of the evidence against him or her, and the opportunity to rebut the charges before an objective decision maker.
Wood v. Strickland (1975)	Students may sue school board members for monetary damages under the Civil Rights Act of 1871.
Ingraham v. Wright (1977)	Corporal punishment does not constitute cruel and unusual punishment under the Eighth Amendment and does not require due process prior to administration.
Board of Education, Island Trees Union Free School District v. Pico (1982)	Censorship by the school board acting in narrowly partisan or political manner violates the First Amendment rights of students.
Pyler v. Doe (1982)	The denial of a free public education to undocumented alien children violates the equal protection guarantees of the Fourteenth Amendment.
Bethel School District v. Fraser (1985)	School boards have the authority to determine what speech is inappropriate in the school and need not tolerate speech that is lewd or offensive.
New Jersey v. T.L.O. (1986)	School officials are not required to obtain a search warrant or show probable cause to search a student, only reasonable suspicion that the search will turn up evidence of a violation of the law or school rules.
Hazelwood School District v. Kuhlmier (1988)	School officials may limit school-sponsored student speech as long as their actions are related to a legitimate pedagogical concern.

they learned of the students' plan to wear the armbands. The suspended students filed suit, and the decision by the Supreme Court (*Tinker v. Des Moines*, 1969) has become a landmark case not only in student expression, but in the broader area of student rights. In finding for the students, the Court said that students have the freedom to express their views by speech or other forms of expression so long as the exercise of this freedom does not cause "material disruption," "substantial disorder," or invade the rights of others. According to the Court:

> In order for the State in the person of school officials to justify prohibition of a particular expression of opinion, it must be able to show that its action was caused by something more than a mere desire to avoid the discomfort and unpleasantness that always accompany an unpopular viewpoint. . . . undifferentiated fear or apprehension of disturbance is not enough to overcome the right to freedom of expression. (pp. 508–509)

The "material and substantive disruption" standard articulated in *Tinker* has been applied to numerous student expression cases in the more than quarter-century following the decision. Subsequent rulings have clarified that while the fear of disruption must be based on fact, not intuition (*Butts v. Dallas Independent*

School District, 1971), school officials need not wait until a disruption has occurred to take action. If school officials possess sufficient evidence on which to base a "reasonable forecast" of disruption, action to restrict student expression is justified (*Dodd v. Rambis,* 1981).

Disruptive Speech

Freedom of expression does not include the right to use lewd and offensive speech, even if it does not cause disruption. At a high school assembly in Washington, Matthew Fraser nominated a classmate for a student council office using what the court described as "an elaborate, graphic, and explicit sexual metaphor." Fraser was suspended for two days. Both the district court and the circuit court held his suspension to be a violation of his rights to free speech and stated that his speech was not disruptive under the *Tinker* guidelines. The U.S. Supreme Court, however, went beyond *Tinker's* concern with the *effect* of the students's speech to the *content* of the speech, and concluded that the school board has the authority to determine what speech in the classroom or in school assembly is inappropriate, and that "lewd, indecent, or offensive speech or conduct" need not be tolerated (*Bethel School District No. 403 v. Fraser,* 1986).

Student Publications

Although students have the right to publish and distribute literature published both on and off campus, school officials can enact reasonable rules as to the time, place, and manner of distribution. In addition, the courts have said school officials can interfere with the publication and distribution of material that is libelous, obscene, disruptive of school activities, or psychologically harmful. However, until recently, the courts have been careful to emphasize that in cases in which school policies require faculty or administrative approval before publication, censorship is only justified if the material is libelous, obscene, or likely to cause material and substantial disruption. In addition, the procedures and standards for review must be clearly articulated. Unpopular or controversial content, or content critical of school officials, was considered insufficient justification for restricting student expression. This standard was applied to school-sponsored as well as to nonsponsored publications.

In a 1988 case, however, the Supreme Court awarded significant discretion to school authorities in censoring school-sponsored publications. In this case, *Hazelwood School District v. Kuhlmeier,* a school principal deleted two articles from a school newspaper, one dealing with pregnant students and their sexual histories and use or nonuse of birth control, and the other on the impact of divorce on students, which included quotes from a student condemning her father. According to the principal, he was not concerned with the content of the articles, but felt that they were not well written by journalistic standards (e.g., did not maintain student anonymity or give the father a chance to defend himself). Believing that there was not enough time before the publication deadline to make the needed changes in the articles, he deleted the two articles.

The Supreme Court decision said that school officials "do not offend the First Amendment by exercising editorial control over the style and content of student speech in school-sponsored expressive activities so long as their actions are reasonably related to legitimate pedagogical concerns." Such concerns were described as "speech that is ungrammatical, poorly written, inadequately researched, biased or prejudiced, vulgar or profane, or unsuitable for immature audiences."

In making its decision, the Court made a distinction between personal expressions by students and those activities that students, parents, and the public might reasonably assume bear the "imprimatur of the school." In the latter category, the Court included not only school-sponsored publications but "theatrical productions and other expressive activities."

The effect of the *Hazelwood* decision has been to allow school officials greater discretion in determining what is inappropriate student speech and expression. School officials can limit student speech or expression that is vulgar or otherwise offensive, intrudes on the rights of others, or is inconsistent with the overall curriculum mission of the school. A recent case also emphasized the age of the children involved as a factor that can be considered by school officials. In *Baxter v. Vigo County School Corp.* (1994), the action of a principal in prohibiting an elementary school student from wearing T-shirts proclaiming "I hate Lost Creek" (the name of the school), "Racism," and "Unfair Grades" was upheld. The Court noted that most free speech cases have involved older students, and that in the absence of any definition of the free speech rights of elementary students, the principal could not have knowingly violated these rights. The Court further concluded, based on a review of case law, that "age is a relevant factor in assessing the extent of a student's free speech rights in school."

Students' Appearance

Although attempts by school officials to regulate students' appearance have become less stringent over the years, students have become more assertive in expressing themselves through their appearance. The U.S. Supreme Court has not provided any guidance in the area of student appearance, but the majority of lower courts have recognized that students have either a liberty right or a right of expression that can be violated by appearance regulations that are unduly vague or restrictive. As a general rule the courts will not uphold appearance regulations unless the district can show a compelling interest in having such a regulation, such as the disruptive effects of the appearance on the educational process or for health and safety reasons. However, schools have been successful in prohibiting dirty, scant, or revealing clothing; excessively tight skirts or pants; clothing displaying obscene pictures, sexually provocative slogans, or vulgar and offensive language; clothing caricaturing school administrators as being drunk; loose clothing in shop areas; attending the school prom dressed in clothing of the opposite sex; or other dress deemed likely to cause a material or substantial disruption to school operations.

An area of recent concern regarding student dress is the wearing of clothing, jewelry, or other symbols of gang membership. Schools have responded to the increased gang activity on campus by enacting stricter dress codes. The courts have held that schools may prohibit students from wearing specific clothing or other symbols of gang membership if it can be shown that in fact a rela-

Did the elementary and secondary schools you attended have dress codes or regulations regulating student appearance? How did you respond to them at the time? Do you now feel they served any educational purpose?

tionship exits between the particular item(s) prohibited and the public policy goal of curbing gang activity on campus (e.g., *Olesen v. Board of Education,* 1987). However, if the relationship cannot be established, the school district policy will not be upheld. The dress code of a California school district for elementary, middle, and secondary students prohibited the wearing of clothing identifying any college or professional sports teams. However, testimony showed that gang members were, in fact, wearing Pendleton shirts; Nike shoes; white T-shirts; baggy, dickie, or black pants; and that there was negligible gang activity at the middle school and no gang activity at the elementary level. Absent a rational relationship between the dress code and the activity it deemed to curtail, the Court found the code as it related to elementary and middle school students, and as it related to the wearing of clothing with insignia of professional and college sports teams, to be in violation of students' First Amendment rights to free expression (*Jeglin v. San Jacinto Unified School District,* 1993).

Student Records

What kind of information would you record in your personal notes that you would not record in a student's official record?

For every student who attends the public schools, a permanent record is kept by school authorities. Questions about the contents of this record, and who has access to it, have been the source of serious contention over the years. Until the passage of the Family Educational Rights and Privacy Act, also known as the Buckley Amendment, in 1974, parents often were denied access to these records, while they were open to various nonschool personnel (e.g., employers). The Buckley Amendment sought to redress this situation by:

1. Requiring school districts to establish procedures for accessing student records and informing parents, guardians, and eligible students (over 18 years old) of their rights under the law.

2. Requiring written permission from parents or eligible students before sharing the records with anyone other than educators in the same school who have a legitimate educational interest; officials of a school to which the student is transferring; persons who have obtained a court order; persons for whom the information is necessary "to protect the health or safety of the student or other individuals"; or in connection with financial aid for which the student has applied.

3. Providing a complaint and investigation mechanism for alleged violations.

4. Providing for the loss of federal funds to districts found not in compliance with the law.

When students become 18 years old or enroll in a postsecondary institution, they must be allowed to see the record if they so desire.

Although the Buckley Amendment guarantees parents and eligible students access to records, this does not mean that records must be produced anytime or anywhere on demand. School officials can adopt rules that specify reasonable time, place, and notice requirements for reviewing. Neither does this law give

---

Professional Reflections

". . . When you become a teacher you become so much more. You become a child psychologist, a child advocate, activist, social worker, guidance counselor, advisor, confessor, builder of dreams, molder of futures, inventor, cheerleader, and educator."

T. Tracey Fallon, Teacher of the Year, New Jersey

---

parents the right to review the personal notes of teachers and administrators if these records are in their sole possession and not shared with anyone except a substitute teacher.

Parental rights under the Buckley Amendment are not limited to custodial parents. Unless prohibited by court order, a separated parent who is not the custodial parent or guardian has the same right of access to the student's record as does the custodial parent.

After reviewing the record, if the parents (or the eligible student) believe that information contained in the record is inaccurate, misleading, or in violation of the rights of the student, they can request that the information be amended. If school officials refuse, the parents or eligible student must be advised of their right to a hearing. If the hearing officer also agrees that the record should not be amended, the parents or student are entitled to place a statement of explanation or objection in the record.

Students with AIDS

The initial response by school districts to AIDS-infected children was to exclude them from the school setting and provide home instruction or separate facilities for their instruction. More recently, in part as a result of more information and education on how the disease is transmitted, there appears to be a growing belief that children with AIDS should be educated in the school environment if their health permits their attendance. A number of court decisions also have been instrumental in increasing access for AIDS victims. The courts have held that children infected with the AIDS virus are protected from discrimination by section 504 of the Rehabilitation Act and by the Individuals with Disabilities Act. The courts have been unanimous in rejecting exclusion as the automatic answer to dealing with AIDS-infected students (e.g., *Doe v. Donton Elementary School District*, 1988; *Phipps v. Saddleback Valley Unified School District*, 1988). Rather, the courts now must consider the "significant risk of communicating standard" spelled out by the Supreme Court in *Arline*. Another important factor that the courts have looked at, when weighing the interests of the child against those of protecting the health and safety of other students, has been the potential effect of the exclusion or isolation on the social and emotional well-being of the child.

The widespread public concern over the spread of AIDS has prompted most states and school districts to adopt policies regarding the admission and instruc-

Figure 12.3

tion of infected children. These policies often are modeled after guidelines issued by the National Centers for Disease Control (CDC), which recommends that children with AIDS be allowed to attend public schools unless they have open lesions, cannot control their bodily functions, or display behavior practices such as biting, in which case they might still be allowed to attend school, but in a more restrictive environment. The CDC also recommends that the determination of whether individual students pose a "significant risk" should be made on a case-by-case basis by a team composed of health and educational personnel. State policies also provide guidelines for handling body fluids and other procedures designed to protect fellow students and personnel in the school, as well as steps to protect the privacy of victims and to educate both school district personnel and parents.

Summary

The educational process takes place in an environment in which the rights of teachers and students are constantly being balanced against the rights and responsibilities of school officials to maintain a safe and orderly environment conducive to learning. Although the rights of both teachers and students have been greatly expanded in the last quarter-century, they do not include the right to say, publish, or teach whatever one feels or believes. The courts continue to uphold the rights and responsibilities of school districts to limit teacher conduct that has a negative impact on performance in the classroom, that is unrelated to the course of study, or that is materially or substantially disruptive. Teachers also have the responsibility to comply with various statutory requirements related to terms of employment, copyright, and so on, and to provide a reasonable standard of care for their students. When they do not comply with these statutory requirements or when they breach the standard of care, they can be subjected to a variety of disciplinary actions both within and outside the school system. While every situation is unique, certain legal principles have been established that can provide direction in many situations. It is imperative that teachers not only be knowledgeable about these principles, many of which are broadly discussed in this chapter, but that they become familiar with applicable law and school board policy in their state and district.

In the next chapter, we will discuss a topic that sometimes is not given sufficient attention in teacher preparation programs—the governance structure of the public schools. Yet, as you will see, the way schools are organized, administered, and financed has a vital impact on the teacher and the educational program.

Key Terms

Academic freedom
Affirmative action
Discrimination
Disparate impact
Due process
Educational malpractice
Equal opportunity
Expulsion
Fair use doctrine
In loco parentis
Incompetence

Insubordination
Negligence
Property right
Proximate cause
Reduction in force (RIF)
Reverse discrimination
Sovereign immunity
Suspension
Tenure
Tort

Discussion Questions

⟨✕⟩ 1. The teacher in the incident described at the beginning of the chapter talks of giving the student a hug and a pat. Under what circumstances is it appropriate for a teacher to give children hugs or pats? How can teachers who use hugs or pats as reinforcers protect themselves against allegations of child abuse?

2. What limits can be placed on teachers expressing themselves on political issues in the classroom? Outside the classroom?

3. Describe the "reasonable teacher" guideline as it relates to tort liability.

4. What should be the role of the schools in confronting the AIDS epidemic?

5. To what extent should teachers, administrators, and school board members be held liable for the education, or lack of education, received by the students under their control?

6. What are the statutory requirements in your state regarding student expulsions? Student suspensions?

7. How does the doctrine of *in loco parentis* serve to give students expectations about the care given them in the schools? How does the doctrine serve to define the teacher's right to control and supervise students?

References

Acton v. Vernonia School District, 23 F. 3rd 1514 (9th Cir. 1994).

Ambach v. Norwick, 441 U.S. 68 (1979).

Anable v. Ford, 653 F. Supp. 22 (W. D. Ark, 1985), *modified,* 663 F. Supp. 149 (W. D. Ark. 1985).

B. M. by Berger v. State of Montana, 649 P. 2d 425 (Mont. 1982).

Baxter v. Vigo County School Corp., 1994 WL 259703 (7th Cir. 1994).

Bethel School District No. 403 v. Fraser, 106 St. Ct. 3159 (1986).

Bradley v. Pittsburgh Board of Education, 913 F. 2d 1064 (3d Cir. 1990)

Butts v. Dallas Independent School District, 436 F. 2d 728 (5th Cir. 1971).

Carey v. Piphus, 435 U.S. 247 (1978).

Chalk v. U.S. District Court Cent. Dist. of California, 840 F. 2d 701 (9th Cir. 1988).

Civil Rights Division of the Arizona Department of Law v. Amphitheater Unified School District No. 10, 680 P. 2d 517 (Ariz. 1983).

Connick v. Myers, 461 U.S. 138 (1983).

Cornfield by Lewis v. Consolidated School District No. 230, 991 F. 2d 1316 (7th Cir. 1993).

Daury v. Smith, 842 F. 2d 9 (1st Cir. 1988).

Dayton, J. (1994). Corporal punishment in public schools: The legal and political battle continues. *West's Education Law Quarterly, 3,* 448–459.

Dodd v. Rambis, 535 F. Supp. 23 (S.D. Ind. 1981).

Doe v. Donton Elementary School District, 694 F. Supp. 440 (N.D. Ill. 1988).

Doe v. Renfrow, 631 F. 2d 91 (7th Cir. 1980), *cert. denied,* 451 U.S. 1022 (1981).

Donohue v. Copiague Union Free Schools, 407 N.Y.S. 2d 874 (App. Div. 1978), *aff'd,* 391 N.E. 1352 (N.Y. 1979).

Eisel V. Board of Education of Montgomery County, 597 A. 2d 447 (Md. 1991).

Ficus v. Board of School Trustees of Central School District of Green County, 509 N.E. 2d 1137 (Ind. App.1 Dist. 1987).

Fields v. Hallsville Independent School District, 906 F. 2d 1017 (5th Cir. 1990), *cert. denied,* 111 S. Ct. 676 (1991).

Fischer, L., Schimmel, D., & Kelly, C. (1995). *Teachers and the law* (3rd ed.). New York: Longman.

Garcia v. Miera, 817 F. 2d 650 (10th Cir. 1987).

Gaylord v. Tacoma School District No. 10, 559 P. 2d 1340 (Wash. 1977).

Gee, E. G., & Sperry, D. J. (1978). *Education law and the public schools: A compendium.* Boston: Allyn and Bacon.

Goss v. Lopez, 419 U.S. 565 (1975).

Hazelwood School District v. Kuhlmeier, 108 S. Ct. 562 (1988).

Hoffman v. Board of Education of the City of New York, 400 N.E. 2d 317 (1979).

Honig v. Doe, 198 S. Ct. 592 (1988).

Horton v. Goose Creek Independent School District, 677 F. 2d 471 (5th Cir. 1982).

Hortonville Joint School District No. 1 v. Hortonville Education Association, 225 N.W. 2d 658 (Wis. 1975), rev'd on other grounds and remained, 426 U.S. 482 (1976), *aff'd,* 274 N.W. 2d 697 (Wis. 1979).

Ingraham v. Wright, 430 U.S. 651 (1977).

Jeglin v. San Jacinto Unified School District, 827 F.Supp. 1459 (C.D.Cal. 1993).

Keyishian v. Board of Regents of University of State of New York, 385 U.S. 589 (1967).

Kingsville Independent School District v. Cooper, 611 F. 2d 1109 (5th Cir. 1980).

Landauer, W. L., Spanfer, J. H., & Van Horn, Jr., B. F. (1983). Good cause dismissal of education employees. In J. Beckham & P. A. Zirkel (Eds.), *Legal issues in public school employment* (pp. 154–169). Bloomington, IN: Phi Delta Kappa.

McCarthy, M. (1989). Legal rights and responsibilities of public school teachers. In M. C. Reynolds (Ed.), *Knowledge base for the beginning teacher* (pp. 255-266). New York: Pergamon Press.

McCarthy, M. M., & Cambron-McCabe, N. H. (1992). *Public school law: Teachers' and students' rights* (3rd ed.). Boston: Allyn and Bacon.

McCarthy v. Fletcher, 254 Cal.Rptr. 714 (Cal. App. 1989).

McClelland v. Paris Public Schools, 742 S.W. 2d 907 (Ark. 1988).

Murray, K.T. (1994). Copyright and the educator. *Phi Delta Kappan, 75,* 552–555.

New Jersey, Petitioner v. T.L.O., 105 S. Ct. 733 (1985).

Odenheim v. Carlstadt-East Rutherford School District, 510 A. 2d 709 (N.J. Super. 1985).

Ohlson v. Phillips, 397 U.S. 317 (1970).

Olesen v. Board of Education of School District No. 228, 676 F. Supp. 820 (N.D.Ill. 1987).

People v. Overton, 249 N.E. 2d 366 (N.Y. 1969).

Peter W. v. San Francisco Unified School District, 131 Cal. Rptr. 854 (Cal. App. 1976).

Phipps v. Saddleback Valley Unified School District, 251 Cal. Rptr. 720 (Cal. Ct. App. 1988).

Pickering v. Board of Education, 391 U.S. 563 (1968).

Regents of the University of California v. Alan Bakke, 438 U.S. 265 (1978).

Reitmeyer v. Unemployment Compensation Board of Review, 602 A. 2d 505 (Pa.Comwlth. 1992).

Rossow, L. F., Parkinson, J. R. (1994). Third circuit invalidates *Schaill* type high school athletic drug testing program: Acton v. Vernonia School District. *School Law Reporter, 36* (9), 1–2.

Schaill v. Tippecanoe County School Corp., 864 F. 2d 1309 (7th Cir. 1988).

School Board of Nassau County v. Arline 107 S. Ct. 1129 (1987).

State of Texas v. Project Principle, Inc., 724 S.W. 2d 387 (Tex. 1987).

Stroman v. Colleton County School District, 981 F. 2d 152 (4th Cir. 1992).

Texas State Teachers' Association v. Garland Independent School District, 777 F. 2d 1046 (5th Cir. 1985), *aff'd,* 107 S. Ct. 41 (1986).

Tinker v. Des Moines Independent Community School District, 393 U.S. 503 (1969).

United States v. South Carolina, 445 F. Supp. 1094 (D.S.C. 1977), *aff'd* 434 U.S. 1026 (1978).

Valente, W. D. (1994). *Law in the schools* (3rd ed.). New York: Merrill.

Washington v. Davis, 426 U.S. 229 (1976).

Wood v. Strickland, 420 U.S. 308 (1975).

Wygant v. Jackson Board of Education, 106 S. Ct. 1842 (1986).

Chapter 13

Governance and Financing of Elementary and Secondary Schools

We may have reached the time when the public will not grant us more money for public instruction unless we can show greater efficiency in spending the dollars which have already been voted for school use.

NASSP Fifth Yearbook, 1921

A Critical Incident in My Teaching Career . . .

As a first-year teacher in 1973, I was eager for every child to succeed. I had one precious little boy who fell asleep almost every day, no matter how interesting the activities were. I was admonishing him one day after school when big tears appeared in his eyes. He told me that he babysat each night for his five brothers and sisters; two were infants. His mom worked all night as a barmaid.

I came to realize that for me to be an effective teacher, I must be concerned with the whole child and also learn as much as possible about a child's environment.

Shaba Brown
Teacher of the Year, Mississippi

The purpose of this chapter is to increase your understanding of how schools are financed and governed and related issues. Teachers will be more effective in their daily work if they understand the organization, administration, and financing of public education; issues surrounding the governance of education; and ways in which the structure affects the work of teachers. Throughout your career as an educator you will be asked to explain how schools are governed, to justify educational funding, and to explain how funds are expended. Since education is the nation's largest industry with the largest public expenditure except for defense, a high level of public interest is to be expected and justified. As you read and discuss this chapter and undertake the related activities, consider the following objectives and their impact upon you in your future role as a teacher. After reading the chapter, you should be able to:

- Discuss the impact that school-site decision making might have on the roles and responsibilities of the classroom teacher.
- Determine the number and different types of local school districts in your state.
- Describe the roles of the local school board and the superintendent of schools.
- Differentiate between the roles of the local school superintendent and the chief state school officer.
- Discuss the role of the federal government in elementary and secondary education.
- Identify the effect of federal programs on local school district decisions about educational programs.
- Discuss the perception of education as an investment.
- Describe the three goals of school finance programs.
- Compare the goals of the various state school finance programs.
- Identify the criteria used to evaluate a tax structure.
- Identify the major local, state, and federal revenue sources.
- Discuss the role of private education in America.

Consistent with the checks and balances inherent in the American governmental system, the governance system for public elementary and secondary education also has its checks and balances. Among the nations of the world, the United States is unique in the emphasis placed on decentralization and local participation in the conduct of public elementary and secondary education. Each state establishes the governance system for its schools, provides for the funding of the schools, and establishes various minimum standards for school operation. The primary concerns of the federal government are funding for the educational needs of special populations, national research priorities, and data gathering and reporting.

In the following overview of the governance and financing structure for public elementary and secondary education in the United States, initial attention is given to the overall governance structure of public education. Following this overview of governance, the discussion focuses on state school finance programs and revenues for schools. The chapter concludes with a brief discussion of private education.

The Context of the Public Schools

Public elementary and secondary education has been referred to as a state responsibility, a local function, and a federal concern. These principles are illustrated in both the governance structure and the financial structure of the public schools. Even though education is not referred to in the Federal Constitution, an education clause can be found in each state's constitution. In many ways the provisions are similar; however, none of them are identical. Each state has chosen to express its function in somewhat different ways. References are made to an efficient system of schools, a common system of schools, a general and uniform system of schools, or a thorough and efficient system of schools. The technical wording of these provisions has become critical during the past 25 years when state systems for financing schools have been challenged in the courts.

Among the states, there are great similarities in the organization and financing of schools. For example, the grade structure of kindergarten through grade 12 is found in all states. Statutes and regulations for teacher licenses do not vary greatly among the states; usually, only limited additional study is required to receive a license in another state. Textbooks are published for a national market. All states except Hawaii have local school districts to operate schools and rely on state and local tax sources to fund schools.

Organization for Education

Public interest in education is high; major concerns are school violence, student discipline, and the level of funding to be provided for the schools (Elam, Rose, & Gallup, 1994). Other concerns include national standards; the ability of graduates to do their jobs or succeed in post-secondary education; and the competition for public funds from other public services such as health care, mental health, and law enforcement.

The complexity of the educational enterprise is awesome. For example, one person in five either attends or is employed in the nation's public elementary and secondary schools. Rather than a single monolithic system of schools like a large corporation, the American educational delivery system operates through 50 separate state educational agencies with instruction being provided by 16,000 local school districts in about 80,000 schools. Operational policies are set by governors, state legislatures, and state and local school boards. Governors and legislators not only face the public policy challenge of determining the funding system for the schools, but also are expected to provide adequate and equitable financing for this system of schools. The organizational structure is illustrated in Figure 13.1.

Support for elementary and secondary education is the largest single item in the budgets of many state and local governments. Expenditures for public elementary and secondary schools likely will exceed $300 billion annually by the turn of the century. While funds come from a combination of local, state, and federal sources, the great majority of the money will be from state and local taxes. Federal funds are targeted for special programs or conditions rather than designed to provide a significant portion of the general funding. Figure 13.2 shows the national average sources of funding for education from each of the three levels of government.

Figure 13.1: Education Governance

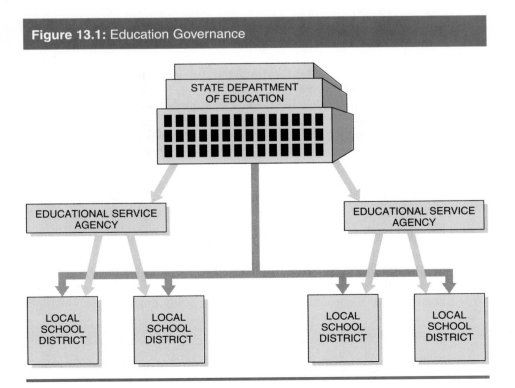

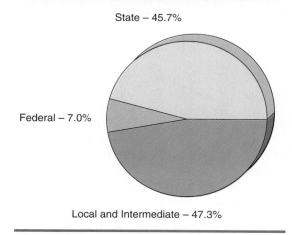

Figure 13.2: Sources of Funds for Public Elementary and Secondary Schools, 1993–94

State – 45.7%

Federal – 7.0%

Local and Intermediate – 47.3%

Source: Education vital signs. (1994). *American School Board Journal,* (December), A24–A31.

Unlike governmental functions such as national defense, interstate commerce, and international relations, which have a heavy federal orientation, the governmental structure for the public schools has evolved as a combination of state and local powers and responsibilities. Rather than being the source of centralized educational *policies* and decisions about the operation of public elementary and secondary schools, the federal government has a very limited role. This structure has been reinforced by the various recommendations and actions associated with educational reform in the 1980s and 1990s. In the quest for educational improvement, state legislative actions have resulted in increased duties, responsibilities, and expectations being placed on local school districts.

Education at the Local Level

Public education in the United States is a highly decentralized endeavor. States have provided for the creation of local school districts that are responsible for the actual operation of schools. Their sole purpose is to operate elementary and secondary schools. Even though there are state requirements and national goals, local school districts and individual schools have great freedom in organizing their programs and the teaching/learning environment. These freedoms are being expanded with the emphasis on decentralization and site-based decision making. The primary functions of local school districts are to:

- Adopt policies and regulations for the operation of schools.

- Within the context of state guidelines, adopt the curriculum for the schools.

- Serve as linkages between community patrons and the schools and provide periodic reports about the schools.

- Provide the human and material resources needed to operate schools.

- Take the necessary steps to provide and maintain adequate facilities for instruction.

- Provide the state department of education and other agencies with required information about the schools.

Local school districts and their governing bodies, local *school boards,* are often the targets of criticism, but they appear to be permanent features in the structure of American government. Citizens place a high value on this opportunity to participate in educational decision making. In a variety of ways, these citizens determine the direction that the schools will take.

What should be the qualifications for local school board members?

The Myth of Local Control

Since their origin in colonial days, local school districts always have been subject to the control of state legislatures. Local school districts have two kinds of powers, stated and implied. Stated powers are explicit in actions of the state legislature or provisions of the state constitution. Implied powers are implicit, but are required to carry out the stated powers or the assigned functions. An example of these implied powers is the authority of the school district to purchase chalk and custodial cleaning materials. The likelihood of these items being mentioned specifically in state statutes is slim, but they fall under the category of implied powers because they are necessary for the effective operation of schools.

To illustrate the various ways in which the states have retained control over public education, local school districts only have the taxing powers that have been granted by the state. In some states, school districts do not have the authority to adopt budgets and set tax rates; they must submit their budgets to municipal or county governments for review and final approval before finalizing their fiscal plans for the school year. On the other hand, state legislatures have granted to state boards of education such powers as setting minimum standards for teacher licensing or certification, minimum graduation requirements, minimum length of school day, and minimum number of school days in a year.

The recent interest in education reform has resulted in state legislatures and state boards of education imposing a variety of additional requirements on local school districts (Stedman & Jordan, 1986). Examples include graduation requirements and "no pass, no play" requirements for participants in high school interscholastic activities. However, these requirements typically are imposed as minimums; local schools have the authority to exceed the imposed minimums.

Local School Boards

State statutes provide for the selection of lay citizens to serve on school boards that govern the operation of school districts. Each district has a chief administrator, typically referred to as the superintendent; this person usually has been a teacher and has professional training to prepare for the job. The delivery point for the

What powers
should local
school boards
have in making
decisions about
school operation?

education of youth is the individual classroom. The primary reasons for the existence of schools, school districts, state education agencies, and federal education activities are (1) to support the process of instruction in the classroom and (2) to ensure that the public's goals are being observed in the educational process.

The legal power of lay citizens to control public education through a system of local school boards is a unique feature of the American educational system. In principle, school boards represent all the people; members are chosen as stewards with a public trust. There is no time or place for personal agendas. Through the schools, these lay citizens help build the future of the nation (American Association of School Administrators, 1946).

Local school boards are either appointed or elected. In most cases, there are no educational requirements for school board membership. Members come from all walks of life. People seek appointment or election to school boards for a variety of reasons. The only prerequisite may be that the board member be a resident of the school district.

The primary function of the local school board is to set the policies under which the schools will operate. Before making decisions, the board has a responsibility to consider the beliefs, values, and traditions of the community. However, boards typically rely on the counsel and recommendations of the superintendent. As they serve, board members must function as a group, for they only have power and authority when the board is in session (Orlosky, McCleary, Shapiro, & Webb, 1984).

Other functions of the school board include budget adoption, approval of expenditures, approval of the school's organizational pattern, employment of personnel, and issuance of contracts. These legal functions are in addition to the role of the school board in informing the community. Community support is especially critical because of the role of the local property tax in financing schools in many states and the importance of maintaining a strong base of citizen support for the public schools.

Local school boards have been a part of the governance system for America's schools longer than superintendents of schools. In rural areas, many local school districts consisted of a one-room school staffed by one teacher and governed by a three- to five-member school board. Thus, at one time, there were more school board members than teachers in some localities. In other instances, the school principal also functioned as the superintendent of schools or may have been a teaching principal. As enrollments increased and as school districts became more complex organizations, the need for full-time professional leadership and management became evident, and the position of superintendent of schools became a full-time position. The typical administrative organization in many school districts is illustrated in Figure 13.3.

Local School District Planning and Budgeting
Public elementary and secondary schools are labor-intensive endeavors. Personnel costs represent the majority of expenditures in local school budgets. About 70% of the typical school district's expenditures are for instructional services, with 50% being for teachers' salaries. Funds for administrator salaries at both the central office and the building level account for less than 10% of the

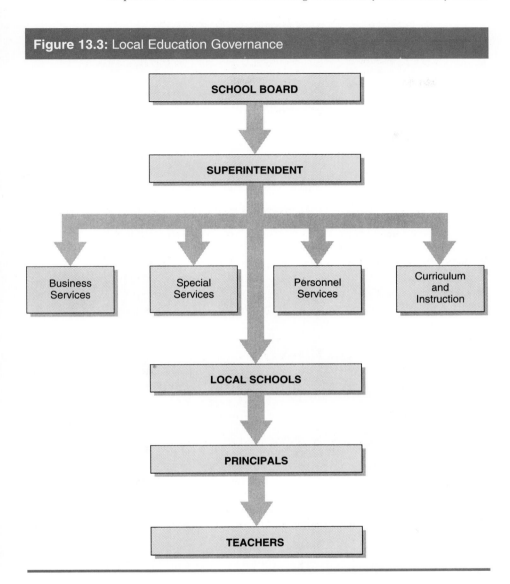

Figure 13.3: Local Education Governance

total. Figure 13.4 shows the percentage of the budget allocated for the various major functions in the typical local school district (Robinson & Protheroe, 1994).

The concept of *strategic planning* has become an important component in the program planning and funding decisions of local school districts. Starting with the school district's or the school's mission statement supported by goals and objectives, funding priorities are linked to resource allocations to ensure that budgetary decisions are compatible with program priorities. However, strategic planning by a school district does not automatically result in participative decision making. If the planning process is to be from the bottom up, teach-

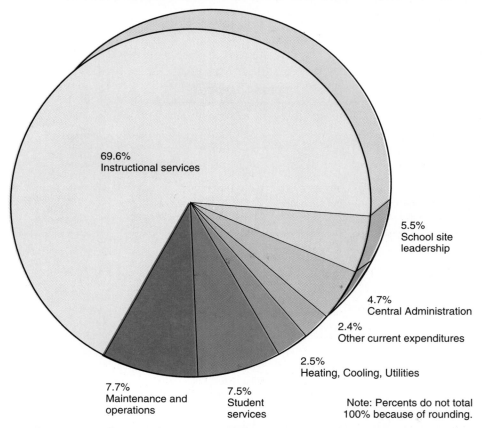

Figure 13.4: Average Allocation of 1993–94 School District Operating Budgets

69.6%
Instructional services

5.5%
School site
leadership

4.7%
Central Administration

2.4%
Other current expenditures

2.5%
Heating, Cooling, Utilities

7.7%
Maintenance and
operations

7.5%
Student
services

Note: Percents do not total
100% because of rounding.

Source: Robinson, G. & Protheroe, N. (1994). Local school budget profiles study. *School Business Affairs, 60*(9), 31–40.

ers will be active participants. They will be members of the school working committee and possibly also of various subcommittees. However, if the planning process is to be top down, opportunities for broad-based teacher participation will be limited.

As the smallest management unit of the school district, the local school is the most critical unit in the educational delivery system. One focus of the education reform movement in the 1980s was the emphasis on decentralized or school-site decision making as a way to increase teacher morale, improve the management of schools, and raise student performance. This concept was endorsed by the Committee for Economic Development (1994) in its report entitled *Putting Learning First: Governing and Managing the Schools for High Achievement.* A key element was perceived to be greater control of resources at the school site level. To achieve this new pattern of operation, the report called for greater flexibility in

How many school districts are in your state? What is their range in enrollment?

Controversial Issues:
Site- or School-Based Management

The one-room schoolhouse was the ultimate in site-based management. In addition to teaching, the teacher often served as the custodian, principal, bookkeeper, and clerk for the school board. As schools were consolidated, management became more centralized and often detached from the classroom. This centralization trend continued through the mid-1960s when interest in citizen involvement in schools began to develop. About two decades later, the school reform reports made multiple references to the potential benefits of increasing the authority of personnel at the school level. The concept of site-based management can have a significant impact on how individual schools are organized and how decisions are made.

Arguments For

1. Level of decision making is closer to the client, i.e., students.

2. Involvement of teachers and school patrons increases commitment to the goals of the school.

3. Resources are allocated according to the goals of the school.

4. Schools can adapt programs and allocate resources to meet local needs.

Arguments Against

1. Joint decision making takes teacher time away from instruction and increases the administrative paperwork burden on the principal.

2. Central office loses control over the curriculum and fiscal affairs.

3. Building level personnel do not have the expertise to develop and manage budgets.

4. Decentralized decision making can contribute to schools making decisions contrary to school district goals.

How would the role of the teacher in a school with site-based management be different from the role of a teacher in a school with centralized management? In which system would you prefer to teach?

---

school decision making and increased involvement of school faculties, parents, and community leaders.

Models for involvement and decision making include school-site budgeting as well as school-level decision making. One potential problem with this management technique is the lack of open communication between the central office and the school site. Steps should be taken to ensure that school-level personnel do not invest major amounts of time and energy and then find that their proposals have been ignored or rejected. The principal concepts related to *site-based management* are outlined above.

Calls for greater teacher participation in school level decisions have been operationalized as school-site decision making. Complete decentralization in decision making is not possible because local schools, as part of a school district within a state educational agency, are subject to statutes, policies, and regulations from the school district and the state. However, there seems to be a consensus that schools are more successful when teachers have a voice in decisions about their working conditions and the operation of the local school.

Decentralization does not ensure parental and staff participation in decision making. A principal can still make decisions without staff or community participation; however, this latter management style is not consistent with the principles of decentralized decision making. An underlying assumption is that teachers should be heavily involved in planning, discussing, and making the final decisions. This process also is viewed as an opportunity to increase parental participation in schools by involving parents in critical aspects of school-site decision making.

Building Principal

The key participant with the primary responsibility for the success or failure of the educational program in each local school is the *building principal*. Successful administration of a school requires that the principal exercise leadership as well as management and planning skills. The person may serve as an assistant principal before becoming a principal. Historically, some have viewed the principalship as a career and others have considered the job to be a stepping stone to a position such as assistant superintendent or superintendent. Recently, a new career pattern has emerged. The principalship has come to be viewed as a career opportunity with a unique set of skills and professional opportunities. One reason for this change in perception is that decentralized decision making will require that the principal develop an expanded set of human relations as well as technical and planning skills. The principal will spend much more time planning and working with, rather than directing, faculty members and community patrons.

Should it be a requirement that school administrators have been successful teachers before becoming school administrators?

Superintendent of Schools

As the role and responsibilities of the *superintendent of schools* have evolved, the job has become chief executive officer of the local school district. Typically, educational program and related responsibilities of the superintendent include planning, staffing, coordinating, budgeting, administering, evaluating, and reporting. The superintendent's primary responsibility is to work with the local school board to improve educational programs in the district.

When compared with private business, in many ways the local school board functions like the board of directors of a corporation. The superintendent of schools, the counterpart of the chief executive officer of the corporation, is responsible for the day-to-day operation of the enterprise, the schools (Campbell, Cunningham, Nystrand, & Usdan, 1985).

In contrast to an earlier time when the superintendent on occasion was a part-time teacher, today's superintendent has a full-time position and may view the job as a career. School superintendents typically come from the ranks of teachers. Today, specialized training in educational administration beyond the master's degree is typically required for licensing or certification. Many states require the equivalent of two years of graduate work, and the trend is toward requiring the doctorate in educational administration for permanent certification (Report of the National Policy Board, 1989). However, among the states there appears to be some interest in nontraditional certification for persons with leadership potential who have demonstrated in other fields that they possess the management and leadership skills required to be a successful superintendent of schools.

Pattern of School Districts in the States

Among the states, the number of school districts varies greatly and is associated with differences in educational opportunity for students. The number of school districts in each state is shown in Table 13.1. As indicated in the table, excluding Hawaii and the District of Columbia, the number of school districts in a state ranges from 17 in Nevada, 19 in Delaware, and 24 in Maryland to about 1,000 in California, Illinois, and Texas. Other states with relatively few school districts include Florida, Louisiana, New Mexico, Utah, and West Virginia.

Data in the table indicate that the number of school districts in a state is not related to either the total enrollment or geographic size of the state. For example, California, Illinois, Nebraska, New York, and Texas all have large numbers of school districts, but Nebraska has a much lower total enrollment than the other states. Another example is that Montana has 539 districts and Wyoming has 49 districts.

Southeastern states tend to have the fewest school districts. In several states, school districts are organized on a county unit basis where the county and school

Table 13.1: Number of School Districts by State, 1992–93

50 States and D.C.	15,025	Missouri	538
Alabama	129	Montana	539
Alaska	56	Nebraska	729
Arizona	229	Nevada	17
Arkansas	319	New Hampshire	178
California	1,002	New Jersey	608
Colorado	176	New Mexico	88
Connecticut	166	New York	716
Delaware	19	North Carolina	133
District of Columbia	1	North Dakota	270
Florida	67	Ohio	612
Georgia	183	Oklahoma	568
Hawaii	1	Oregon	295
Idaho	114	Pennsylvania	501
Illinois	930	Rhode Island	36
Indiana	296	South Carolina	95
Iowa	437	South Dakota	178
Kansas	304	Tennessee	140
Kentucky	176	Texas	1,048
Louisiana	66	Utah	40
Maine	283	Vermont	285
Maryland	24	Virginia	141
Massachusetts	345	Washington	296
Michigan	558	West Virginia	55
Minnesota	413	Wisconsin	427
Mississippi	149	Wyoming	49

Source: U. S. Department of Education, National Center for Education Statistics. (1994). *Digest of education statistics.* Washington, DC: U.S. Department of Education, p. 97.

district have the same boundary. States in the Midwest and Great Plains tend to have more districts because the civil township was a beginning point for their school districts. However, in the 1950s and 1960s, several states took action to consolidate small school districts so that educational opportunities for students would be enhanced. Since 1950, the number of school districts in the nation has been reduced from 100,000 to 15,000. For the past two decades, the number has remained constant at slightly more than 15,000. The number of school districts has little relationship to the number of schools in a state. For the nation, the number of public schools totals about 80,000. The number of schools in a school district may be the result of enrollment changes, population shifts, topographical conditions, or tradition.

As they organized their school districts, states created different types of school districts. The typical pattern of school district organization is the unit school district that provides educational programs for students in kindergarten through grade 12. However, a few states (Arizona, Illinois, and Montana) permit the operation of separate high school districts serving grades 9 through 12 and elementary districts serving students in kindergarten through grade 8. Only a few states have three types of school districts: K–8, 9–12, and K–12. The original rationale for separate high school and elementary districts may have been that this arrangement would increase the high school offerings available to students, but the benefits of the K-12 unified school districts seem to outweigh the disadvantages. Educational program planning and sequencing can be handled more efficiently, and students can be assisted in making the transition from elementary to high school.

A major problem with the multiple types of districts is that neither the elementary nor the high school district is held accountable for the educational outcomes of students as they attempt to make the transition into high school. A critical consideration is the lack of articulation or coordination between the elementary schools and the high schools. Courses and programs may not be coordinated between elementary and high school districts, and students may experience difficulty in making the transition from grade 8 to grade 9.

Intermediate Educational Service Agencies

The concept of the *intermediate educational service agency* (IESA) has been part of the organizational structure of public education in America for more than 150 years. About 40 states have some form of intermediate unit (Campbell, Cunningham, Nystrand, & Usdan, 1985). Without some type of outside assistance, many small, isolated local school districts, with their varied enrollments and separate elementary and high school districts, cannot provide a full range of programs and services for the education of the handicapped and specialized vocational education programs. When only a small percentage of the students need a particular program or service, IESAs can be a source of increased efficiency and better programs.

IESAs typically fall into three groups—the county superintendent, special districts, or cooperative education service agencies. The groups differ in their legal basis, programs and services, governance, and financing. The *county superintendent* usually provides service and oversight for local school districts.

Typically, the *special district* is established by the state legislature and provides various services to the state education agency (SEA) and a defined group of local school districts. These agencies deliver specific services to local school districts or conduct certain activities for the SEA. Some provide only administrative services, others provide specific educational programs or services, and still others provide both administrative services and educational programs or services. In contrast to the top-down orientation of IESAs that are linked to SEAs, the functions and activities of the *cooperative education service agency* are determined by the local school districts in the cooperative. These agencies may be multipurpose or single purpose, but their orientation is to serve their constituent school districts.

Education at the State Level

The legal principle of education being a state responsibility contributes to state educational agencies playing a key role in the development of the structure and delivery system for public elementary and secondary education. Each state has a state-level administrative agency whose primary functions include:

- Setting broad policies for the operation of the state's public elementary and secondary schools.

- Monitoring the schools in accordance with legislative mandates.

- Providing the state legislature and citizens with information about the schools.

- Providing technical assistance to the schools.

- Collecting data about the schools.

- Disbursing state funds for the operation of local school districts.

This state-level governance structure typically includes a *state board of education* as the policy-making body, a state administrative agency typically referred to as the *state department of education,* and a *chief state school officer* who serves as executive officer of the state board of education and as administrator of the state department of education. Figure 13.5 reflects the state-level administrative organization in many states.

State Boards of Education

State boards of education have various responsibilities. These boards usually are charged with adopting regulations and monitoring local school districts to ensure implementation of the constitutional and statutory mandates related to the operation of the state system of schools. Their directives and mandates are related to policy formulation and enforcement within the context of the state's statutory provisions. Examples include graduation requirements for high school students and mandated curricular offerings in schools. Advisory functions are related to leadership, encouragement, and interactions with local school districts. Among the important state board functions are providing the state legislature with timely reports about the schools, proposing changes in statutes, serving as advocates for new initiatives and programs, and presenting and serving as

What should be the qualifications for members of the state board of education?

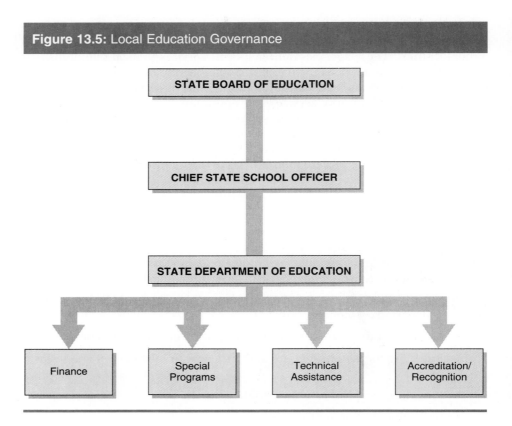

Figure 13.5: Local Education Governance

an advocate for the budget for state support of schools. Most state boards are not responsible for the direct operation of educational institutions or schools; rather, their concern is with the overall direction of the state's schools.

Virtually all states have a state board of education, but they differ in composition, method of selection, relationship with the chief state school officer, and functions. For example, in Florida, the cabinet consisting of the state's elected officials also serves as the state board of education. The state superintendent of public instruction is elected and is a member of the cabinet. This is in contrast to Texas, where members of the state board are elected on a population-based district basis. In other states, members of the state board of education are appointed by the governor, sometimes with the consent of the state legislature.

Chief State School Officer

Each state has either constitutional or statutory provisions for a chief state school officer; the person often is referred to as the superintendent of public instruction or the commissioner of education. In most instances, responsibilities are limited to elementary and secondary education, but in a few states the person also has responsibilities for higher education.

The professional status of the position is improving, but in several states required qualifications are either unstated or very broad. This is especially true

What should be the qualifications for the chief state school officer?

Public elementary and secondary education is a responsibility and function of state government. State constitutional provisions and legislative actions prescribe how schools will be governed and financed. Most states utilize a system of local school districts to operate schools.

in those states where the chief state school officer is elected. In states where the chief state school officer is appointed, the tendency is to select a person with professional training and experience in educational administration. Over 30 of the 50 chief state school officers are appointed either by the governor or the state board of education. The others are elected on a popular basis statewide (Campbell, Cunningham, Nystrand, & Usdan, 1985).

State Secretaries of Education

Recently, several states have adopted the federal cabinet system with a secretary of education who is responsible to the governor. Usually, the statutory provisions related to the chief state school officer and the state board of education have not been greatly altered by the creation of this cabinet position, and the state department of education has remained in place. The primary duties of the secretary of education have been related to long-range planning and budgeting rather than to administering the state department of education or monitoring schools.

The Federal Government and Public Education

As noted in Chapter 4, the absence of mention of education in the Federal Constitution and the reservation of this function to the states should not be

What effect will changes in the Congress and the Presidency likely have on new federal initiatives and the level of federal funding?

interpreted as indicating a lack of interest in education by the nation's founders. When the Constitution was being written, several states already had provided for education in their state constitutions and leaders in those states did not want the federal government to interfere with those provisions. In addition, private and church-related schools were numerous in some states and some persons may have supported this option for providing education. Questions also may have been raised about the relative merits of educating the masses (Grieder, Pierce, & Jordan, 1969).

Federal Role and Involvement

The federal interest in education has been influenced by the national and economic interests prevalent at the time of federal actions. For example, the Northwest Ordinances in the 1780s and the Morrill Act in 1862 can be perceived as responses to the interest in promoting the westward expansion of the nation (see Chapter 4). The Morrill Act was the enabling legislation for the land grant college system. The enactment of federal funding for vocational education in 1917 was related to the need for trained workers on the assembly lines of the growing manufacturing establishment. Surplus agricultural commodities provided some of the impetus for the development of the federal school lunch program in the 1940s.

These patterns also can be observed in recent federal education programs. As discussed in Chapter 5, the launch of Sputnik in the Soviet space program was an incentive for the enactment of the National Defense Education Act in 1958. National concerns about the economic effects of poverty and disadvantaged youth were major reasons for the enactment of the Elementary and Secondary Education Act in 1965. Programs for education of the handicapped in the 1970s came in response to court cases and concerns about the national neglect of handicapped youth. The 1981 consolidation of categorical educational programs under President Reagan reflected a desire to diminish the federal role in determining educational priorities.

Should federal funds be limited to special purposes, or should the funds be for general operation?

The emphases of current federal education programs are threefold. First, the major portions of the funds are for programs and services for special populations; these include funding for programs to serve students with disabilities, educationally disadvantaged youth, financially needy college students, and vocational education students. Recent amendments to federal education legislation have granted local school districts greater flexibility in administering these programs.

The second emphasis area is educational statistics and research. Since the creation of the first Department of Education in 1867, the one continuing role of the federal education agency has been data gathering. Even though education is a state function, there is an interest in national information about the educational enterprise. Rather than each individual state gathering and reporting data in the state's format, it has been more cost-effective for the function to be performed by a federal education agency, the National Center for Education Statistics. Reporting of consistent and comparable data can be enhanced and information can be provided for international comparisons.

A third emphasis has been research and demonstration projects. Since the creation of the Cooperative Research Program in 1957, the federal government has funded educational demonstration and research projects. Responsibility for these functions now is assigned to an assistant secretary of education in charge of the Office of Educational Research and Information in the Department of Education. The rationales for federal support of educational research and demonstration projects are similar to those for data gathering and reporting. Cost-effectiveness will be improved by central funding of national research priorities and disseminating this information for better informed educational decision making. These programs often are funded through competitive grants; demonstration projects also are conducted by local school districts or state educational agencies.

As a part of the research activities, federal funding is provided for the administration of the National Assessment of Educational Progress (NAEP). NAEP consists of a series of tests that are given to a sample of students throughout the nation. The purpose is to provide information about the general level of performance of elementary and secondary school students. State-by-state comparisons and comparisons by race, ethnicity, and gender are available (see Chapter 8). However, the tests are not designed to provide detailed information about the performance of each student. The intent is to provide national or state summary information rather than give direction to efforts to revise a school district's or a school's curriculum. State and national educational leaders have been concerned about NAEP because of the potential pressures for a national curriculum to ensure that students perform well on the NAEP tests. This latter issue has become more critical with the current interest in national goals and standards.

Department of Education

For more than 120 years, some type of federal agency for education has been in existence. Starting in 1867 with the creation of a Department of Education without cabinet status, various federal agencies have had responsibility for education. The chronology suggests an uncertainty in the federal commitment to education. For example, in 1869 the title was changed to Office of Education, in 1870 to Bureau of Education, and in 1929 back to Office of Education (Grieder, Pierce, & Jordan, 1969). That designation was retained until the creation of the Department of Education in 1980, when education was given cabinet status. Until the creation of the Department of Education with a *secretary of education,* the federal education agency had been administered by a commissioner of education.

Secretary of Education

The first secretary of education, Shirley Hufsteder, was a federal judge at the time of appointment. The second, Terrel Bell, was a former U.S. commissioner of education, chief state school officer in Utah, local superintendent, and college professor. Next was William Bennett, a former college professor appointed to the position from another federal position; after him, Lauro Cavazos, a university president at the time of appointment. In 1991, President Bush nominated Lamar Alexander, former governor of Tennessee, to succeed Cavazos as secretary of education. President Clinton's appointment as secretary of education was William Riley, former education reform governor of South Carolina.

Some secretaries of education have viewed the position as an opportunity to ensure that all students have access to educational programs and services. Others have tried to maintain and expand federal educational programs and services. Some have viewed the position as a "bully pulpit" from which to improve education by promoting different education reforms.

Financing of Education

In addition to establishing the governance structure for education, state legislatures also establish the basic structure for financing public elementary and secondary schools. The state enacts the funding system for schools and sets the taxing and spending powers of local school districts. This includes the state's method for funding schools, the types of taxes that may be used, and the tax rate that may be levied.

Methods of financing public elementary and secondary schools and funding levels per pupil differ in a variety of ways both within and among states. However, two basic legal principles guide the financing of the public schools in the United States. First, education is a responsibility of the state level of government. Second, in the design and implementation of the state school finance program, the state has an equal responsibility to each pupil (Jordan & Lyons, 1992). Adhering to these principles has been difficult because the states have chosen to let the local school districts, with their wide differences in enrollment, taxable wealth, and citizen aspirations, administer and deliver education.

Education—An Expense or an Investment?

A continuing question about funding for education is whether the activity should be viewed as a public expense or a societal investment. The consensus is that funding for a quality education should not be viewed as an expense, but as an investment in the future of the nation. The failure of a nation to educate its populace results in an expense for both society and individuals. The Committee for Economic Development (1987) has estimated that each year's class of dropouts will cost the nation $240 billion in lost earnings and unpaid taxes over their lifetime. This projection does not include the billions more for crime control, welfare, health care, and other social services that this undereducated group will cost the nation. Increasing attention is being given to ways in which states can fund programs and services for at-risk youth. (See Chapter 10 for a discussion of the costs associated with at-risk youth.)

Potential problems resulting from inadequate funding for schools are especially severe in those states with projections of above-average growth in the number of youth who are likely to be educationally disadvantaged because of English language deficiencies and economic poverty (see Chapter 8). Educational interventions to address these problems not only can increase the productivity of the state's youth, but they also can reduce the long-term social burden associated with poverty, welfare, and crime. Providing these youth with a quality education requires lower pupil-teacher ratios and special instructional materials. Rather

Many communities whose students have complex educational needs do not have sufficient funds for their schools because of the heavy reliance on the local property tax as a major source of funds for schools.

than assuming that these problems can be addressed by reallocation and more efficient use of current resources, the Committee for Economic Development (1987) stated that any plan for improving the education of disadvantaged youth is doomed to failure if it does not recognize the need for additional resources over a sustained period. Businesses have become especially interested in the quality of America's educational system because of the important role that a well-educated and well-qualified workforce has in maintaining and improving the nation's, or a state's, competitive economic position.

The contributions of education to the economy occur in different ways. As discussed in Chapter 8, well-educated workers increase productivity and are needed to help industry compete internationally. The assumption is that these workers will have the income required to purchase consumer goods and thus will support the economy.

Public Policy Goals in School Finance

State systems for financing schools are imperfect and full of educational and political compromises. Public policy decisions about how schools should be financed are made with three goals in mind: equity, choice, and adequacy (Jordan & Lyons, 1992). Of these goals, equity is the most important. The problem with equity is that the majority may not be able to agree that equity has been attained, but they can agree that equity has *not* been attained as long as large disparities in per-pupil expenditures exist.

Equity

The concept of *equity* refers to the equal treatment of persons in equal circumstances. For students, this means an equal opportunity for education. For taxpayers, this means equal tax rates on similar property in districts with different levels of taxable wealth per pupil. The problem is that equity may not result in sufficient funds for schools; it may only result in equal treatment.

Horizontal equity assumes that students who are alike should be treated the same way. *Vertical equity* assumes that groups of students with different educational and service needs should be treated differently and also that those with similar needs in different districts should have similar access to educational programs and services.

Choice

In the 1990s, the term *choice* is being used to refer to two different goals. One is local control of funding decisions. Traditionally, local school boards have been permitted to choose the level of funding for the schools. In some cases, equity and choice have come into conflict because a district's freedom to choose the level of funding has resulted in inequitable treatment of taxpayers and students. Currently, choice also is being used to refer to the power of parents to select the school that their child will attend. There have not been enough experiences with this type of choice to indicate the impact on equity to either students or taxpayers.

Adequacy

Adequacy refers to the extent to which funding for programs and learning opportunities is sufficient to provide the programs and services needed by students. Factors affecting adequacy include staff, materials, and skill levels of teachers.

State School Finance Programs

What kind of state school finance program is used to fund schools in your state?

The history of state school finance programs can be traced to about 1900, when Ellwood Cubberley contended that the state had a responsibility to address the unfairness of a school finance system that relied almost exclusively on the local property tax to finance schools. As a result of his efforts, state school finance equalization models were developed in the early decades of the twentieth century; prior to that time, state funds were limited and typically were distributed on a flat-grant basis irrespective of differences in local wealth or educational need. The forerunner of today's commonly used state school finance programs can be traced to that period.

Of the five major models or funding approaches, three are equalization models: equalized foundation grants, equalized reward for tax effort, and full state funding. The other two models are flat grants and categorical funding.

To equalize access to funds for education, states have enacted statutes designed to compensate for the differences in taxable wealth among local school districts. These equalization models generally have been modified by state legislators to accommodate specific state needs. The most frequently used approach is equalized foundation grants. About two-thirds of the states use a school finance formula that can be classified as a foundation program (Gold, Smith, Lawton, & Hyary, 1992).

Although state school finance laws originally were developed to assist schools in the poorer rural areas, it is the urban school districts that now require additional help. They have two types of additional burdens. One is *educational overburden,* which refers to the relatively larger number of pupils in city schools who require high-cost educational programs and the higher costs of instructional goods and services in urban areas. A related problem is *municipal overburden,* which refers to the need for a greater range of social services in urban areas that must be paid for by the same taxpayers who support the schools.

Foundation Programs

The major state school finance programs are illustrated in Figure 13.6. The Strayer-Haig model, typically referred to as the *foundation plan,* provides the difference between a fixed amount per pupil and the amount the district can collect locally through a uniform tax rate (Strayer & Haig, 1923). For example, if the foundation plan provides for $4,000 per pupil and the yield from a prescribed local tax rate for a school district raises $2,500 per pupil, the state payment would be $1,500 per pupil. If the prescribed local tax rate raises $1,000 per pupil, the state payment would be $3,000 per pupil. However, if the prescribed local tax rate raises $5,000 per pupil, the state would make no payment to the local school district. The different amounts of state payments illustrate the ways in which equalization can be operationalized so that state and local revenues provide a foundation of funds. In terms of the previously discussed school finance goals, equity and adequacy can be achieved if the foundation amount per pupil is sufficiently high.

This program has been criticized because funding may be at a minimum level and not be sufficient to support an adequate educational program. This inability to meet the adequacy criterion has a stifling effect because the state typically does not provide funds beyond the minimum level. In terms of other school finance goals, student and taxpayer equity can be attained, but choice will be dependent upon the discretion granted to local school districts.

Power Equalization Programs

Under *power equalization* formulas, local school officials choose the level of funding they desire for their schools. Revenues raised by taxes in the district are "equalized" by state allocations (Updegraff, 1922). This differs from the foundation plan in which the state sets the target amount per pupil or per teacher. In the early 1990s, eight states were using the power equalization concept as the primary funding method. (Gold, Smith, Lawton, & Hyary, 1992).

In states using power equalization funding programs, the local school board sets a tax rate and the state then guarantees a specified amount per unit of tax rate (Coons, Clune, & Sugarman, 1970). For example, if the state guarantees $50 per pupil per penny of tax rate and a penny in district A raises $30 per pupil, the state would provide $20 per pupil per penny of tax rate. If a one-penny tax rate raises $10 in district B, the state would provide $40 per pupil per penny of tax rate. Under this option, the state does not provide a foundation funding level, but allocates funds in relation to the tax rates selected in local school districts.

In terms of the previously discussed school finance goals, taxpayer equity and local district choice can be achieved, but there is no assurance that the level of funding will be adequate or sufficient. In addition, this option may not treat students equitably in their access to a quality education.

What is the range in per-pupil expenditures among school districts in your state?

Figure 13.6: Current Funding Approaches

Description	Who Uses It?	Problems
Strayer-Haig Equalization Funding Model (foundation plan)		
Developed in 1920s by George D. Strayer and Robert M. Haig at Columbia University.	Used in some form in over half the states.	Keeps funding at a minimum level; insufficient to support an adequate educational program.
Provides difference between district's need and amount collectible locally.		State does not participate in efforts to provide funds beyond minimum.
Uniform tax rate applied to assessed value of property in school district.		
Entitlement based on funds required to ensure a minimum per pupil or per teacher; minimum determined by legislature.		
Adjusted to recognize additional funds needed for concentration of pupils with special needs.		
Power Equalization (effort oriented)		
Developed in 1922 by Harlan Updegraff at University of Pennsylvania.	About one-third of states use it in some form in the late 1980s.	No state was recapturing all "excess" funds in late 1980s.
Local school officials choose level of funding		No assurance of funding at an adequate level.
Tax revenues in district "equalized" by state allocations.		
Any excess raised in a district sent to state treasury.		
Full State Funding		
No local taxes collected.	Used only in Hawaii.	No local choice permitted.
Flat grants		
State provides uniform amount per student; funds available for any legal educational purpose.	Original most common form of state support.	Funds do not generally go to area of greatest need.
	May be used with an equalization program to ensure that wealthy school districts receive some funds.	
Categorical Funding		
State funds are allocated for specific purpose (e.g., bilingual education, in-service programs for teachers, instructional materials, etc.).	Often used to encourage specific programs that are not mandated by state law.	Typically allocated irrespective of district's wealth.

Full State Funding

Full state funding for public schools occurs when no local tax revenues are collected for support of schools. All funds for schools come from state-level taxes (Morrison, 1930). This model is used only in Hawaii, which has just one school district for administrative management of all state schools (Gold, Smith, Lawton, & Hyary, 1992). A single teacher's salary schedule is in effect for all schools on the islands.

Under full state funding, students and taxpayers are treated equally, but attainment of adequacy will be dependent upon the funding level. No opportunity for local district choice is available.

Flat Grants

Originally the most common form of state payment to school districts, *flat grants* have now been replaced by foundation or equalization programs. Under the flat grant program, states provide a uniform amount per student and the funds may be used for any legal educational purpose (Cubberley, 1905). Several states still include a low-level flat grant program when enacting an equalization program to provide some state funds to high-wealth schools that might not receive funds under the equalization program. In the early 1990s, only two states were using the flat grant as the primary funding method (Gold, Smith, Lawton, & Hyary, 1992).

Under the flat grant, students and taxpayers are treated equitably, but attainment of adequacy will be dependent upon the funding level. Choice is sacrificed unless the flat grant can be supplemented.

Categorical Funding

Categorical funding means that state funds are allocated for a specific educational purpose, (e.g., bilingual education, education of handicapped pupils, pupil transportation, in-service programs for teachers, or instructional materials). Most states have some type of categorical funding for special programs, but this is not the principal method for funding schools.

In categorical programs, students and taxpayers are treated equally, but attainment of adequacy will be dependent upon the funding level. Students not in the program will not be treated equitably. Choice will be sacrificed unless other funding is available.

State Spending and Enrollment Differences

In 1994–95, among the 50 states and the District of Columbia, per-pupil expenditures for current operation (excluding school construction and retirement of debt) ranged from $9,429 in New Jersey to $3,158 in Utah. The 1994–95 national average was $5,314 per pupil (National Center for Education Statistics, 1994). Data for each state are presented in Table 13.2.

Among the 50 states, the estimated number of pupils in 1994–95 ranged from 5,285,000 in California and 3,616,547 in Texas to 101,899 in Wyoming and 100,000 in Vermont. The 10 states with more than 1 million pupils accounted for over 55% of the slightly more than 43 million pupils (National Center for Education Statistics, 1994).

Table 13.2: Estimated Membership and Current Expenditures per Pupil by State, 1993–1994		
	Membership	**Current Expenditures**
50 States and D.C.	43,353,428	$5,314
Alabama	730,509	3,757
Alaska	125,564	7,721
Arizona	669,459	4,182
Arkansas	450,672	3,556
California	5,285,000	4,623
Colorado	625,062	4,584
Connecticut	493,500	7,558
Delaware	105,547	5,779
District of Columbia	80,678	8,057
Florida	2,039,385	4,893
Georgia	1,235,304	4,174
Hawaii	179,876	5,620
Idaho	236,774	3,540
Illinois	1,886,947	5,299
Indiana	961,534	5,096
Iowa	497,912	5,217
Kansas	458,538	5,087
Kentucky	639,200	4,650
Louisiana	799,917	4,402
Maine	212,245	5,439
Maryland	772,638	6,117
Massachusetts	878,734	6,361
Michigan	1,613,700	5,989
Minnesota	807,760	5,610
Mississippi	503,374	3,231

Sources of Tax Revenue for Schools

The principal sources of funds for public elementary and secondary schools are the various types of taxes levied by local, state, and federal governments. As indicated previously, the proportion of revenues from each source varies both among and within states. This section discusses the criteria for evaluating a tax system and analyzes the major tax sources in terms of these criteria.

Criteria for Evaluating Taxes

Taxation systems have effects beyond the raising of revenues. They must be evaluated in terms of their impact on overall social, political, and economic conditions. The criteria of economic distortions, equity, compliance, and revenue elasticity are used to evaluate the tax structure of a governmental unit (Due, 1970).

A tax should not cause *economic distortions*. That is, a tax should not alter consumer spending patterns; create business preferences for particular geographic areas; or affect the willingness of a person or a business to be part of the local, state, or national economy.

Table 13.2: *Continued*

	Membership	Current Expenditures
Missouri	870,086	4,391
Montana	162,891	4,788
Nebraska	284,458	5,410
Nevada	235,800	4,547
New Hampshire	182,835	6,426
New Jersey	1,152,205	9,429
New Mexico	321,164	4,150
New York	2,746,200	7,642
North Carolina	1,123,636	4,388
North Dakota	118,500	4,497
Ohio	1,812,300	5,570
Oklahoma	598,000	3,390
Oregon	516,610	5,246
Pennsylvania	1,745,230	6,804
Rhode Island	145,676	6,409
South Carolina	636,297	4,083
South Dakota	151,073	3,874
Tennessee	857,051	4,053
Texas	3,616,547	4,926
Utah	488,675	3,158
Vermont	100,000	6,867
Virginia	1,045,472	5,169
Washington	916,928	5,537
West Virginia	313,750	5,782
Wisconsin	841,856	5,779
Wyoming	100,899	5,550

Source: U. S. Department of Education, National Center for Education Statistics. (1994). *Public Elementary and Secondary Statistics: School Year 1993–94.* Washington, DC: U.S. Department of Education, p. 9.

A tax should be equitable. Persons in the same relative circumstances should share the tax burden equally. A tax is progressive when those with greater incomes pay a higher tax rate. A tax is called regressive if persons with greater incomes pay a smaller proportion in taxes.

For a tax to be effective, the rate of compliance should be high. This means there will be a minimum cost for enforcement, a reasonable cost for collection, and no loopholes to allow persons to evade the tax.

Revenue elasticity is an important criterion for a tax program. The revenues from the taxing system should respond to the economy. *Revenue elasticity* occurs when the tax yield increases during inflation and declines during a recession.

Sources of Tax Revenues

Funds for schools come from a limited number of revenue sources, and the relative merits of each can be evaluated in terms of the four general criteria discussed above.

The principal source of local revenue for schools is the *ad valorem* tax on real property or, in common terminology, the *local property tax*. This tax is levied on the value of land, residences, apartment buildings, commercial buildings, railroads, and utilities. On average, over 90% of all local tax revenues for schools come from taxes on real property.

The property tax fails to meet some of the criteria used in evaluating a taxation system. Variations in property wealth and resulting differences in tax rates among taxing jurisdictions tend to create economic distortions. Businesses may choose to locate in areas with lower property taxes, resulting in citizens who reside in one area having easier access to the business than those who live in others. Residences in a low-tax area may sell more easily than those in a high-tax area. However, the property tax is considered a desirable tax because it discourages the hoarding of property and the concentration of wealth in the hands of a few citizens.

The equity of the property tax has been criticized from several different perspectives:

What kind of state taxes are levied in your state?

1. The tax impacts heaviest on fixed-income taxpayers whose residences are increasing in value at a rate greater than their income from which taxes must be paid. In such cases, the property tax is considered to be regressive.

2. Various types of property often are assessed at different rates for taxpaying purposes. The rates are set by the state legislature, and certain types of property or taxpayers may be favored.

3. The property tax has a potential punitive effect because failure to pay can result in forfeit of the property. This action may be taken even if the property is not generating income and the person is unable to pay the taxes.

4. The costs of administering and collecting the property tax are much higher than for sales or income taxes. An extensive administrative bureaucracy is required for the maintenance of records related to the ownership of property, assessment of property, and tax collection.

5. Assessment is a major administrative cost. Therefore, assessors must be trained and their assessments have to be verified to ensure accuracy. In addition, provisions must be made for taxpayers to appeal the assessment decision.

The property tax does not fare well on the criterion related to a minimum cost for enforcement and a reasonable cost for collection. But it has the advantage of being more stable than other taxes, such as sales and income. Property tax receipts can be projected with reasonable accuracy for a budget year. In contrast, sales tax receipts are immediately responsive to economic shifts, and income taxes are only slightly more stable.

State sales and income taxes are the principal sources of state revenues for schools. The taxes are levied on retail sales and on personal and business income. In 1991–92, sales and gross receipts tax revenues accounted for 50% of

Equity in school finance is achieved through a balanced system of state and local taxes and a state funding program that recognizes differences in educational needs among students and school districts.

state revenues. Statewide individual income tax revenues accounted for 32% of total state revenues (Government Finances: 1991–92, 1994). As shown in the following discussion, both sales and income taxes fail to meet several criteria used in evaluating a taxation system.

All states have either sales or income taxes, and many have both. The resulting choices of where to live and to purchase goods and services tend to create economic distortions. Individuals may choose to locate in states without personal income taxes. For example, people may work in Boston and live in New Hampshire, a state without a personal income tax. Oregon has an income tax but no sales tax, and Washington has a sales tax but no income tax. Similarly, different levels of sales taxes or the absence of a sales tax may result in persons electing to make their purchases across the state boundary to escape some or all of the sales tax payments.

The sales tax is considered to be inequitable unless exemptions are granted for such necessities as groceries, essential basic clothing, and medical prescriptions. This type of tax is considered to be regressive, or less equitable, because it has the strongest impact on those least able to pay. For example, a low-income person will pay a larger percentage of actual income in the form of sales taxes than a high-income person.

Compliance with the sales tax can be more easily monitored because payments are made at the point of purchase and retail establishments can be identified and policed. Even though both sales and income taxes require an administrative bureaucracy, the costs of administering and collecting either tax are much less than for the property tax. Enforcement problems may be encountered, but both taxes fare well on the criteria related to a minimum cost for enforcement and a reasonable cost for collection.

The scenario for the state income tax is quite different. Most state income taxes include a rate structure in which the rate increases with income. Thus, the person with the highest income pays a higher rate. In these instances, the income tax is considered to be more equitable because the tax is progressive.

Compliance rates for payment of state income taxes are subject to interpretation. State income tax systems often utilize some parts of the federal income tax system. When significant changes are made in the federal income tax structure, states often find it necessary to adjust their systems because of the linkages between exemptions and rates in state and federal income taxes.

Both sales and income taxes respond quickly to changes in the economy. Thus, they may not have the level of stability desired to permit sound fiscal planning because revenue receipts can shift within a tax year if economic predictions are not correct. This is different from the property tax, which is a more stable source of revenue. The combination of sales and income with property taxes has considerable merit; the joint system has a mix of the desired qualities of stability and responsiveness.

A majority of the states raise some amount of revenue through lotteries. The proceeds typically become a part of the state's general fund, but education often benefits. (See the Historical Note on page 467.)

The principal source of federal revenue for education is the federal income tax, but federal funding for elementary and secondary education has been limited. In 1991–92, about 85% of the revenues of the federal government came from corporate and personal income taxes (Government Finances: 1991–92, 1994).

A major advantage of the federal income tax is that it relies on the entire nation as the taxpaying base. Because the tax is collected throughout the nation, the possibility of creating economic distortions through taxation is minimized. However, economic distortions can be created through the tax's exemption rate structure. Exemptions can be used to discourage or encourage certain economic behavior by taxpayers (e.g., deductions for interest charges associated with home mortgages). The federal income tax is considered to be equitable because of its progressive rate structure.

Compliance rates for payment of the federal income tax are matters of concern, but the Internal Revenue Service has established a complex system of reporting to increase collections and ease enforcement. Even though the federal income tax has a large administrative bureaucracy, the costs of administering and collecting this tax have been estimated to be much less than for any other tax. The federal income tax fares well on the compliance criterion because of its relatively low cost for enforcement and collection.

The federal income tax is more stable than state sales and income taxes because of the national economic base. However, revenues from this tax respond to changes in the economy. The federal income tax ranks second to the property tax as a stable source of revenue, but it has greater elasticity.

This discussion illustrates that no single tax is the perfect solution to providing funds for schools. The optimal taxation system consists of a balance between stability and responsiveness with a progressive effect. In addition, the taxing system should not place an unfair or confiscatory burden on any group of taxpayers or encourage undesirable economic behavior.

Differences Among States in Sources of Revenue

In school year 1993–94, excluding Hawaii and the District of Columbia, the percentage of the total revenues for schools that came from local tax sources ranged

Historical Note:
The Lotteries and Education

The use of lotteries, both for settling disputes and as games of chance, has been traced to 3500 B.C. When the English colonists came to the New World, they brought with them a tradition of private and public lotteries. Colonial churches and governments made use of the lottery. Benjamin Franklin and other leading citizens of Philadelphia sponsored a lottery to raise money to buy a battery of cannons for the city. The Continental Congress used a lottery to generate funds to support the troops. In the 1790s, lotteries were used to help finance the construction and improvement of Washington, D.C.

Lotteries were also used by various educational institutions. Dartmouth, Harvard, Kings College (Columbia University), Pennsylvania, Princeton, and William and Mary are among the colonial colleges that benefited from lotteries. From the signing of the Constitution to the Civil War, some 300 elementary and secondary schools and 47 colleges were beneficiaries of lotteries (Ezell, 1960).

Unfortunately, as the use of lotteries grew, so did the abuses and irregularities associated with them. In the second and third quarters of the nineteenth century, state after state passed antilottery bills, and by 1878 all states except Louisiana prohibited lotteries. Louisiana's "Golden Octopus" lotteries, so called because they reached into every state and large city in the nation, had also died by the end of the century.

The first modern government-operated lottery in the United States was instituted in 1964 by the state of New Hampshire as a means of generating revenues for education. In 1967, New York started a lottery. Within the next decade, a dozen other states joined the list of those operating lotteries. Today, 30 states operate lotteries and in about 20 states, education is beneficiary of part or all of the lottery proceeds.

---

from 88.9% in New Hampshire to 11.9% in New Mexico. The percentage from state tax sources ranged from 75.3% in New Mexico to 8.3% in New Hampshire. The percentage from the federal government ranged from 17.7% in Mississippi to 2.8% in New Hampshire. The national average was 47.3% from local sources, 45.7% from state sources, and 7.0% from federal sources. Data for each state are presented in Table 13.3.

Sources for Nontax Revenues

An effect of the recent court cases seeking greater equity in school funding has been the development of greater reliance on nontax sources of funding for schools. The pressures for greater equity have been countered by local citizens' creativity in finding other sources of funding for schools, including participation or user fees for school activities, formation of nonprofit educational foundations at the school or school district level, and local profit-making activities.

Participation fees are becoming a significant source of revenues in many school districts. Increased reliance on fees to participate in school activities conflicts with the court cases that are seeking greater equity in funding and equality of access to educational programs and services. For example, athletes are being required to purchase their equipment. In some instances, local school officials provide waivers for those students unable to pay the fees, but the effect is

Table 13.3: Percentage Distribution of Total Revenues for Public Elementary and Secondary Schools, by Source and State: School Year 1993–94

	Local	State	Federal
50 States and D.C.	47.30	45.70	7.0
Alabama	21.60	65.70	12.70
Alaska	23.80	63.60	12.60
Arizona	48.90	43.20	8.90
Arkansas	27.90	62.70	9.40
California	36.90	54.30	8.80
Colorado	52.30	42.80	5.0
Connecticut	55.30	40.10	4.60
Delaware	25.30	66.40	8.30
District of Columbia	87.10	0.0	12.90
Florida	41.90	48.70	9.40
Georgia	44.30	47.90	7.80
Hawaii	1.80	90.30	7.90
Idaho	29.40	62.40	8.30
Illinois	59.10	32.80	8.20
Indiana	43.60	51.20	5.20
Iowa	42.90	51.60	5.50
Kansas	44.80	49.80	5.50
Kentucky	21.70	68.30	9.90
Louisiana	32.90	55.40	11.70
Maine	44.10	48.30	7.60
Maryland	55.40	39.0	5.60
Massachusetts	62.90	31.0	6.10
Michigan	62.20	32.10	5.70
Minnesota	45.10	50.60	4.30
Mississippi	30.50	51.80	17.70

that poor children will have less opportunity to participate in many school activities. The basic question may be whether the activity is considered a necessary part of the school program or a truly extracurricular activity being provided under the sponsorship of the school. If the activity is a basic part of the school program, charging a participation fee might be considered discriminatory because a poor student is denied access to the program.

Another source of nontax revenues for schools is found in educational foundations. Some school districts have created nonprofit educational foundations to provide funds for programs and services that cannot be supported from tax funds. As a result of state restrictions on local school spending and court actions seeking greater equity in funding for public education, schools have been forced to curtail programs and services. In an effort to find alternative ways to fund and maintain programs, some local schools have formed educational foundations that can receive tax-deductible gifts from parents, interested citizens, and businesses.

As funds from traditional public taxation sources have failed to keep pace with the need for additional revenues, some schools have become involved in *for-*

Table 13.3: *Continued*

	Local	State	Federal
Missouri	56.20	37.40	6.40
Montana	53.90	36.70	9.40
Nebraska	47.60	46.30	6.10
Nevada	59.30	36.0	4.60
New Hampshire	88.90	8.30	2.80
New Jersey	53.60	42.90	3.40
New Mexico	11.90	75.30	12.80
New York	54.70	39.50	5.90
North Carolina	28.20	64.30	7.50
North Dakota	45.70	42.60	11.80
Ohio	53.90	40.10	6.0
Oklahoma	29.40	63.30	7.40
Oregon	51.70	41.0	7.30
Pennsylvania	53.20	42.10	4.60
Rhode Island	58.30	36.50	5.20
South Carolina	43.30	47.40	9.30
South Dakota	60.90	27.10	12.0
Tennessee	41.80	48.60	9.60
Texas	49.50	43.20	7.30
Utah	37.50	55.60	6.80
Vermont	63.40	31.70	4.90
Virginia	60.70	34.40	4.80
Washington	22.60	71.50	5.80
West Virginia	25.0	67.10	7.90
Wisconsin	58.30	37.10	4.60
Wyoming	43.20	50.90	5.90

Source: State of the states. (1994). *American School Board Journal,* 180, A24–A31.

profit enterprise activities. The concept of school districts initiating profit-making activities is somewhat different from the previous two examples of efforts to secure more funds for school operation. An enterprise activity refers to the involvement of the schools in some type of profit-making venture to enhance funding. Enterprise ventures might include development of a catering service that uses the school's bulk food preparation facilities. Some schools are selling advertising space in the school buildings and on school buses; others are marketing products bearing school logos (Lindsay, 1994). Public resistance to such ventures might develop, and the involvement of the school in a profit-making activity in direct competition with local businesses might be challenged.

The Courts and School Finance

Since 1970, state programs for financing the public schools have been challenged in over 40 states (McCarthy, 1994). Litigation has been initiated in both federal and state courts. The issues are related to contentions that the state is failing to provide "equal protection" for students because the state system for financing education has resulted in unequal levels of spending among school districts, and the differences in spending are related to differences in wealth among districts. In this context, wealth refers to assessed value of taxable real property per student.

In *San Antonio v. Rodriguez* (1973), the U.S. Supreme Court rejected the argument that education is a constitutionally protected right and that equal treatment is required in providing education under the U.S. Constitution. Then, some observers thought that the amount of legal actions would diminish, but the number of cases in state courts suggests a continuing interest in challenging state school finance programs. The effect of *Rodriguez* was to base challenges of existing state school finance programs on the technical provisions of the state constitutions rather than provisions in the U.S. Constitution.

These legal challenges have been initiated because of the interaction of two conditions—the use of the local property tax as a major source of revenue for schools and the wide differences in taxable wealth per pupil among local school districts. As a result of these conditions, tax rates to provide an equal level of funding for education and per-pupil spending vary among school districts. This condition is viewed as being unfair to both taxpayers and students; depending on the district, taxpayers must be taxed at different rates to provide the same level of support. The result is that students in poor districts are at a disadvantage relative to students in other districts with greater wealth or higher tax rates.

Trends in the court decisions are difficult to determine. Of the decisions that have been issued by state supreme courts, recently, a slight majority of the decisions have held the state system to be unconstitutional. In the decisions that have upheld the existing funding systems, education has been viewed as an important government service, but not a fundamental right under which each student in the state would be guaranteed equal treatment. In most instances, the courts have been critical of the financing systems but have indicated that the problem should be resolved by legislative actions rather than judicial decisions (McCarthy, 1994).

In the decisions that have thrown out state school finance programs, the courts have held that the current system was unconstitutional on the grounds of unfairness to both taxpayers and students. Unequal tax burdens were considered to be in violation of the equal protection provisions of the state constitutions, and differences in expenditures per pupil were found to be in violation of the equal protection provisions of the state constitutions or the technical provisions of the state constitution pertaining to education (McCarthy, 1994).

The 1989 actions of the highest state court in Kentucky illustrate how the courts can affect the schools. The state's entire system of education was found to be in violation of the state constitution because of unequal spending per pupil and low student achievement in low spending/low wealth districts. In 1990, the Kentucky General Assembly responded to the court decision by enacting legislation to meet the requirements of the court decision. If the legislature had not acted, Kentucky's entire system of education would have been dissolved. The legislative reform covers school governance, curriculum, and accountability, as well as the state financing system (Walker, 1989). This is the most dramatic court decision that has been issued, and the resulting reforms in the schools will be interesting to observe.

Litigation has been active in California and New Jersey for most of the past 25 years. In the 1990s, courts in Alabama, Arizona, Missouri, and Texas ruled that the states' school finance systems were in violation of the state constitutions' equal protection and/or education clause. After revisions by the Texas legislature and repeated appeals, the Texas school finance system was declared to be constitutional. The concerns were related to different levels of spending and differences in the access that students had to educational programs, materials, equipment, facilities, and related opportunities. The state's responsibility to provide each child with equal access to an education has been upheld.

Federal Aid for Elementary and Secondary Schools

Consistent with the concept that education is a state responsibility and a local function, the federal government has played a limited role in the financing of elementary and secondary education. Less than 10% of the total expenditures for elementary and secondary education comes from federal revenue sources. Even though its role has been limited, the federal government's involvement in education has consisted of a series of recurring controversies.

Education of Special Needs Youth

Of the federally funded elementary and secondary education programs, the largest is for the Title I programs for the education of disadvantaged pupils. The funding level for this program was about $6.7 billion annually in 1995 for programs in local school districts (Schnaiberg, 1994). As discussed in Chapter 9, the intent of the program is to improve educational programs for disadvantaged pupils from low-income homes. These programs are funded completely by the federal government and would not be continued if the federal funds were terminated.

Federal funds and regulations for education of children with disabilities under Public Law 94–142, as amended by the Americans with Disabilities Act, represent a different type of major federal initiative. Under the statute and resulting regulations, local school districts have to provide eligible pupils who have disabilities with a free and appropriate education irrespective of the level of federal funds. About 7% of the total school-age population has been classified as disabled and in need of special education programs and services. Funds for this federal program reached about $3.3 billion in 1995 (Schnaiberg, 1994). While this seems to be a significant amount, this funding level, as well as the $6.7 billion in federal funds for the education of disadvantaged pupils, should be placed in the context of the more than $230 billion in annual funding from all revenue sources for public elementary and secondary education. (See Chapter 9 for a more detailed discussion of P.L. 94–142.)

The federally funded Head Start program for low-income preschool children typically is not operated by public school districts, but is an important program. Funding for this program in 1995 was $3.5 billion. This was a slight increase from 1994 but not as great as sought by the advocates for the program (Schnaiberg, 1994). Obviously, this program is important in efforts to attain the national goal of readiness for school.

Through careful analysis of local conditions and adaptation of research findings to local schools, teachers and administrators can work together to attain school improvement goals.

Federal funds have been provided for vocational education since the enactment of the Smith Hughes Act in 1917. This program was started in response to the need for trained workers following World War I. Since that time, the emphasis of vocational education has shifted as the nation's economy and job needs have changed. In 1994 the federal government provided about $1.2 billion to support vocational education, representing about 10% of the total spending for public school vocational education programs (Schnaiberg, 1994).

Another long-standing federal program is impact aid for school districts that educate youth residing with parents who live and/or work on federal property or are active duty uniformed military personnel. Funding for this program in 1995 was $728 million, a $70 million reduction from 1994 (Schnaiberg, 1994).

Educational Research and Assessment

As the federal government has provided more funds for elementary and secondary education programs, interest in federal funds for a national research program has increased. Currently, federal research funds for education are administered through the Office for Educational Research and Improvement in the Department of Education. In 1990, the Department of Education was projected to spend over $167 million on educational research and statistics (Schnaiberg, 1994). The actual level of federal funding for educational research efforts is difficult to determine because research programs are funded by a variety of federal agencies, including the National Science Foundation, Department of Energy, and Department of Defense.

Funding for school reform has been limited to relatively small amounts for limited purposes, but $403 million was appropriated in 1995 for the *Goals 2000:*

Educate America Act. Funds under this program are to be used for grants to state and local school reform efforts (Schnaiberg, 1994).

Private Education

In contrast to public education being provided through a range of school districts with multiple schools, private education typically is provided through a system of independent schools. As individually controlled schools, they have been created for a variety of reasons including college-prep programs, religious instruction, and family values.

With the rising level of concern about a variety of educational issues, interest in the private school alternative is being expressed by a wide spectrum of parents. The private school option is not new; it has provided an alternative to public education in the United States since the colonial period. However, these schools take different forms in response to parents who want their children to have broader educational opportunities, who seek a more rigorous or more restrictive environment for their children, or who desire a more permissive environment than the public schools can provide. This pattern of diverse aspirations has contributed to the development of private schools noted more for their differences than their similarities. They include traditional church-related schools, schools associated with evangelical groups, private traditional day schools, and "free" schools in which students can pursue individual interests.

Private School Enrollments

In 1992–93, about 5 million students were enrolled in private schools, or about 12% of the total number of students enrolled in elementary and secondary schools; data for the past several years indicate a slight increase in private school enrollments. The vast majority (80%) of private schools are church-related, or *parochial schools,* and over 60% of those that are church-related are Roman Catholic (National Center for Education Statistics, 1993). Overall enrollments in private elementary and secondary schools have remained relatively stable over the past 20 years. Declining enrollments in Roman Catholic-affiliated schools appear to have been reversed; enrollments in these schools have increased slightly in the past two years to over 2.5 million students (Lawton, 1994). Non-Catholic enrollment increases have been largely in schools operated by evangelical and fundamentalist Christian denominations.

During the past two decades, minority enrollments in private schools have increased, particularly in Catholic-affiliated schools in urban areas. The percentage of minority enrollments in Catholic-affiliated schools more than doubled from 1970–71 to 1993–94, from 10.8% to 24.7% (Lawton, 1994). This trend takes on special significance, considering that achievement differences between white students and minority students are less in private schools than in public schools. Smaller differences in student achievement between white and minority students at all socioeconomic levels in type of program enrollments (e.g., col-

Why should states exercise controls over private schools?

lege preparatory, vocational, and general education) have been found in the Catholic-affiliated schools. In addition, more than 85% of private school students graduate from high school as compared to 73% of public school students (Orstein, 1989). These observations suggest the need for a careful study of the differences between public and private schools and their student bodies to identify ways in which the success rates of all students might be improved (Hispanic Policy Development Project, 1987).

Proprietary Schools

Schools operated for profit make up a growing sector of the private school market. *Proprietary schools* have been an educational option since the colonization of America, but recently their numbers have been increasing. Their popularity has been attributed to parents being attracted to the high standards that many espouse, the extras (e.g., before and after school remediation and counseling and a wide variety of extracurricular activities), in-depth education, and smaller class size. Although proprietary schools represent only 1% of all elementary and secondary schools, the National Education Association (NEA) considers privatization to be a threat to America's public schools. The NEA has expressed concern about the lack of accountability (i.e., many do not have governing boards) and the equity implications of an educational option that essentially is available only to upper-income families. Other concerns are related to the need for regulations. The attention of educators and policy makers to these issues likely will increase if the number of proprietary schools continues to grow (Bridgman, 1988).

In spite of the recent private school enrollment growth in some sectors, projections suggest that the overall percentage of American students enrolled in private elementary and secondary schools will remain stable for the next several years. However, if states and/or the federal government provide public funds for the general operation of nonpublic schools, the percentage of students enrolled in these schools might increase dramatically.

Current Issues in the Organization and Financing of Education

Concerns about the role of education in the development of youth and the importance of an educated populace in a democracy are being expressed in a variety of ways. The challenge confronting public school advocates is to generate and maintain citizen support for the funds required to provide quality education in the 1990s. Maintaining public support for public elementary and secondary schools is becoming more difficult because of a series of interactive social and economic developments.

Changes in the Population

The American population is becoming younger and older at the same time; that is, both the proportion of the population that is of school age and the proportion that is elderly or retired are increasing. Further, youth who comprise the increases in the school-age population tend to be educationally disadvantaged because they often live in urban areas, are poor, and come to school with limited English-speaking ability. Consequently, providing these youth with an adequate education requires more funds.

Special Needs Students

Special needs students often are as diverse as other students. In addition to children with disabilities, special needs youth also include those who are at risk of not completing school. Policy makers are involved in different but interrelated issues concerning the education of special needs youth. One is the extent to which children with disabilities should be included in the regular classroom. Issues include the benefits or disservice to regular children and children with disabilities, and the ability of the classroom teacher to provide all students with sufficient attention (Polansky, 1994). A second issue is the challenge to secure adequate funding for specialized programs and services that will increase the likelihood that at-risk youth will remain in, and profit from, school. A third issue is that state funding for the full range of special needs youth often is not sufficient, and local districts with fiscal constraints must reduce programs for regular students to provide programs and services for special needs students.

Competition for Funds

In addition to the need for more funds to support education, competition for scarce public funds will come from the elderly population that is in need of a variety of services, including better health care and other social services. Many of the elderly are on fixed incomes and must have some type of public assistance for medical and other essential social services. Reconciling these two social pressures will be a formidable challenge to public policy makers.

Equity in State Funding Systems

A continuing issue is the extent to which a state's school funding system should reduce the disparities in educational opportunity for pupils among districts and move the state toward providing an adequate program for all pupils. Local school officials seek predictable and relatively stable levels of funding for schools to facilitate orderly budgetary and educational planning. Taxpayers seek stability in their tax rates so that they can plan their businesses.

From a different perspective, local school officials seek a state system for financing schools that will respond to changing economic and demographic conditions. As the number of pupils increases and as costs for services and materials increase, pressures for equity in state school finance systems likely will increase.

Accountability

Concerns also are being expressed about *accountability* in terms of the performance and responsiveness of schools. Some have advocated that funding for schools be based on pupil performance. However, local school officials seek a level of stability in funding that might be threatened if performance fluctuates. Caution has been advocated because reducing state aid to an underachieving school district would mean that the district would have less to spend on programs even though its need would be greater.

Education Reform

As noted elsewhere in this text, the 1980s were characterized by broad-based calls for reform of public elementary and secondary education. The principal justification for the various school reform reports has been the need to improve America's competitive position in the world economy. Many of the early reform recommendations were additive (i.e., they call for increased requirements for graduation, longer school days and years, and higher teacher salaries), and they will require additional funds. Additional state and federal funds for the implementation of reforms have been limited. With the passage of the *Goals 2000: Educate America Act,* the education reform appears to be entering a new phase, with the adoption of national goals for education and the development of curricular standards for subject matter areas.

Private Contractors for School Operation

In isolated but highly publicized instances, public school districts are contracting with private firms for the operation of one or more schools. The most comprehensive effort has been in Hartford, Connecticut, where a private firm has been awarded a contract to operate all of the city's schools. Private firms have contracts to operate individual schools in Miami and Baltimore; in Minneapolis, the school board has contracted with a private firm under a performance-based contract to provide the superintendent of schools. A more extensive effort has been the Edison Project, which seeks to manage individual schools for profit (Schmidt, 1994).

The two main rationales for private contracting to provide social services are that cost reduction is achieved through competition and private delivery of services, and that schools can benefit by the introduction of private management techniques (Brodinskey, 1993; Nelson, 1992). Some of the critical questions about private contracting relate to the curricular content, recognition of students' rights, the role and job security for teachers in these schools, and the extent to which these privately-operated public schools provide programs and serve students in the same manner as traditionally operated public schools. Additional discussion of this issue may be found in Chapter 16.

Summary

State governmental and organizational structures for schools differ in some ways, but the general pattern is consistent. Greater differences can be found in the patterns of school finance and the range in the proportion of funds that comes from state and local revenue sources. The organizational structure of American education is constantly undergoing changes. The balance between school-site decision making and uniform state standards for school performance likely will be one of the focal points for discussion in the 1990s. As pressures for accountability increase, reporting and monitoring requirements likely will increase.

The annual cost of public elementary and secondary education, the largest item in some state and local budgets, will approach $300 billion by the turn of the century. This outlay is viewed as an investment because education contributes trained workers who support the economy through the purchase of consumer goods. The challenge is to find the funds needed and to distribute them in an equitable manner.

In terms of state provision for education, one challenge will be to develop school finance programs that provide for an acceptable balance between the conflicting goals of equity, adequacy, and choice. A second challenge will be to raise the revenues for the programs in a fair and equitable manner.

Providing adequate funds for education will become more difficult. More older citizens and an increased number of educationally disadvantaged students will be competing for scarce public funds. While state programs look for stability in funding, local school officials seek a system that will respond to changes. The responses will depend on whether policy makers view funds for education as an expenditure or an investment.

With this background on school organization, administration, and finance, you have a context in which to place the discussion of school curriculum in the following chapter.

Key Terms

Accountability
Adequacy
Building principal
Categorical funding
Chief state school officer
Choice
Cooperative education service agency
County superintendent
Economic distortions
Educational overburden
Equity
Flat grants
For-profit enterprise activities
Foundation plan
Full state funding
Horizontal equity
Intermediate education service agency (IESA)

Local property tax
Municipal overburden
Parochial school
Policies
Power equalization
Proprietary school
Revenue elasticity
School board
Secretary of education
Site-based management
Special district
State board of education
State department of education
Strategic planning
Superintendent of schools
Vertical equity

Discussion Questions

1. What does it mean to be concerned about the whole child? How does a teacher integrate information about the child's out-of-school environment into classroom planning? What teaching strategies might you adopt to address the individual needs of children?

2. How does education being a state function affect the powers of citizens to determine programs in local schools?

3. What qualifications should a person have to hold membership on a local school board, to be a principal, or to be a superintendent?

4. What kinds of responsibilities should teachers have in the administration of an individual school?

5. In what ways are private schools and their students different from public schools and their students?

6. How does the per-pupil funding level for schools in your state compare with the level in other states?

7. In what ways does education represent an investment in the future of the nation rather than an expenditure?

8. What are the implications of relying on various types of taxes for the support of schools?

9. What programs should the federal government finance?

10. Given the reduced rate of economic growth, shortage of funds for public services, and increased demand for public services, what should be the priority—funding for education or health care, funding for children with special needs, funding for regular children, or funding for all children?

References

American Association of School Administrators. (1946). *School boards in action,* 24th yearbook. Arlington, VA: American Association of School Administrators.

Bridgman, A. (1988). Private, for-profit schools: Where they stand. *Education Digest, 23*(6), 10–13.

Brodinsky, B. (1993). How "new" will the "new" Whittle American School be: A case study in privatization. *Phi Delta Kappan, 74*(7), 540–547.

Campbell, R. F., Cunningham, L. L., Nystrand, R. O., & Usdan, M. D. (1985). *The organization and control of American schools* (5th ed.) Columbus, OH: Merrill.

Committee for Economic Development. (1987). *Children in need: Investment strategies for the educationally disadvantaged.* New York: Committee for Economic Development.

Committee for Economic Development. (1994). *Putting learning first: Governing and managing the schools for high achievement.* New York: Committee for Economic Development.

Coons, J. E., Clune, W. H., III, & Sugarman, S. D. (1970). *Private wealth and public education.* Cambridge, MA: Belknap Press.

Cubberley, E. P. (1905). *School funds and their apportionment.* New York: Teachers College, Columbia University.

Due, J. F. (1970). Alternative tax sources for education. In R. L. Johns, I. J. Goffman, K. Alexander, & D. H. Stollar (Eds.), *Economic factors affecting the financing of education* (pp. 291–328). Gainesville, FL: National Educational Finance Project.

Education vital signs. (1994). *American School Board Journal,* (December), A24–A31.

Elam, S., Rose, L., & Gallup, A. (1994). The 26th annual Gallup Poll of the public's attitudes toward the public schools. *Phi Delta Kappan, 76*(1), 41–56.

Ezell, J. S. (1960). *Fortune's merry wheel, the lottery in America.* Cambridge, MA: Harvard University Press.

Gold, S., Smith, D., Lawton, S., & Hyary, A. (1992). *Public school finance programs of the United States and Canada, 1990–91.* Albany, NY: American Educational Finance Association, Center for the Study of the States, State University of New York.

Government Finances: 1991–92. (1994). GF/92–5P. Washington: Bureau of the Census, U.S. Department of Commerce.

Grieder, C., Pierce, T. M., & Jordan, K. F. (1969). *Public school administration.* New York: Ronald Press.

Hispanic Policy Development Project. (1987). Policy remedies. *The Research Bulletin, 1*(2), 9.

Jordan, K. F., & Lyons, T. S. (1992). *Financing public education in an era of change.* Bloomington, IN: Phi Delta Kappa Educational Foundation.

Lawton, M. (1994). Catholic schools record increase in enrollment for 2nd straight year. *Education Week, 13,* April 13, 5.

Lindsay, D. (1994). Schools look beyond budgets for outside income. *Education Week, 14*(14), 3.

Mahar, M. (Ed.) (1989). *Catholic schools in America: 1989* (17th ed.). Montrose, CO: Fisher Publishing Co.

McCarthy, M. (1994). The courts and school finance reform. *Theory into Practice, 33*(2): 89–97.

Morrison, H. C. (1930). *School revenue.* Chicago: University of Chicago Press.

Mort, P. R. (1933). *State support for public education.* Washington, DC: American Council on Education.

National Center for Education Statistics (1994a). *Digest of Education Statistics, 1994.* NCES 94–115. Washington, DC: U.S. Department of Education p. 97.

National Center for Education Statistics (1994b). *Public elementary and secondary statistics: School year 1993–94.* NCES 94–428. Washington, DC: U.S. Department of Education.

National Center for Education Statistics (1993a). *Digest of education statistics, 1993.* NCES 93–292. Washington, DC: U.S. Department of Education.

National Center for Education Statistics (1993b). *Public elementary and secondary aggregate data, by state for school years 1991–92 and 1990–91.* NCES 93–327. Washington, DC: U.S. Department of Education.

Nelson, J. (1992). Social welfare and the market economy. *Social Science Quarterly, 73,* 4, 815–828.

Orlosky, D. E., McCleary, L. E., Shapiro, A., & Webb, L. D. (1984). *Educational administration today.* Columbus, OH: Merrill.

Orstein, A. C. (1989). The growing non-public school movement. *Educational Horizons, 67*(71), 74.

Polansky, H. (1994). The meaning of inclusion: Is it an option or a mandate? *School Business Affairs*. July, 1994, 27–29.

Report of the National Policy Board. (1989). Charlottesville, VA: Curry School of Education, University of Virginia.

Robinson, G. E., & Protheroe N. (1994). Local school budget profiles study. *School Business Affairs, 60*(9):31–40.

San Antonio Independent School District v. Rodriguez (1973). 411 U.S. 1.

Schmidt, P. (1994). Hartford hires E.A.I. to run entire district. *Education Week, 14*(6), 1, 14.

Schnaiberg, L. (1994), '95 budget accord increases education aid slightly. *Education Week, 14*(4)23.

Stedman, J. B., & Jordan, K. F. (1986). *Education reform reports: Content and impact* (86–56 EPW). Washington, DC: Congressional Research Service, Library of Congress.

Strayer, G. D., & Haig, R. M. (1923). *The financing of education in the state of New York*. Report of the Educational Finance Commission 1. New York: Macmillan.

Updegraff, H. (1922). *Rural school survey in New York state: Financial support*. Ithaca, NY: Author.

Walker, R. (1989). Lawmakers floating "radical" ideas to shift control of Kentucky schools. *Education Week, 9*(1):1–20.

PART SIX

Curriculum and Instruction

Chapter 14

The School Curriculum: Development and Design

The young man taught all he knew and more;
The middle-aged man taught all he knew;
The old man taught all that his students could understand.

Arnold Ross

A Critical Incident in My Teaching Career . . .

During my first year of teaching, a brilliant young man entered my junior English class in a wrinkled shirt and worn pants. Later I discovered that he came from an extremely dysfunctional family who had always lived in poverty. Nonetheless, he was determined to finish high school, a first for his family, and to help keep the family afloat (financially) in the mean time. He did well in school in spite of it all and we maintained a close mentor/student relationship through his senior year. As graduation drew near, I noticed that he had not ordered his supplies. Knowing that he would never ask for help, I rallied the faculty and we began our joy of getting him ready for the big day. He had no appropriate clothing. I took him after school to purchase a pair of dress shoes to replace his worn tennis shoes. We had great fun picking them out. When he got out of the car to go into his home, he started to cry. I was distressed! "What's wrong?" I asked.

He stuttered, "This is the first pair of new shoes I've ever had. Thank you."

This young man taught me the meaning of courage and commitment, that I can learn as much from my students as they learn from me, that every child is valuable, and that I don't teach subject matter, I teach human beings. . .

Sarah Pratt
Teacher of the Year, North Carolina

The nation's elementary and secondary schools have become involved in a period of widespread public debate over what should be taught in the schools and who should control the curriculum. Curriculum issues have increasingly become issues of class, race, ethnicity, gender, and religion. In this chapter the concept of curriculum is explored from its many perspectives, ranging from curriculum as content to curriculum as experiences. This chapter provides information to help you to:

- Review the sociopolitical forces that influence curriculum policy making and design.
- Contrast the technical production process of curriculum development with the critical theorist process of curriculum development.
- Compare the subject-centered and student-centered patterns of curriculum organization.
- Describe the hidden curriculum and its effects on schooling.

The term *curriculum* is a complex and evasive notion. Curriculum theorists do not agree on any one definition. Broadly defined, curriculum is said to be all the educational experiences of students that take place in the school. A 1973 study identified 119 different definitions of curriculum (Rule, cited in Portelli, 1987). Another two or three dozen could probably be added today. Yet how we conceive of curriculum is important because our conception of curriculum reflects and shapes how we think about, study, and act on the education provided to students (Cornbleth, 1988).

In this chapter, various concepts of the curriculum will be examined. First, the influence of a number of sociopolitical forces on curriculum policy making and design will be reviewed. Specific attention will be given to the potential impact of the national goals for education and public support for a national curriculum. Next, the curriculum development process will be summarized. Last, the major patterns of intended curricular organization or design will be described, followed by a discussion of the unintended, or hidden, curriculum.

Forces Influencing the Curriculum

Should parents have the ultimate decision as to what their children are taught? Why or why not?

Decisions about the curriculum are not made in a vacuum by teachers, administrators, and curriculum specialists. They take place in the context of a particular community, state, and nation at a particular time. At different times various professional, political, social, economic, and religious forces have attempted to influence the curriculum. Their motives, methods, strengths, and successes have varied. As noted in the following discussion, concerns about student performance and international competitiveness have contributed to a much more active national interest in education. These interests may contribute to greater uniformity in curricular content and student assessment. In this section, the influence of the following forces on curriculum are briefly discussed: parent and community groups, local school boards, state governments, the federal government, professional organizations, national committees and reports, national goals and standards, national testing, and textbooks.

Parent and Community Groups

Because of their vested interest in the local school and their proximity to local decision makers, parents and community groups have the potential for exercising tremendous influence on the curriculum. For example, in recent years parent groups active in the areas of special education and gifted education have had great success in encouraging educational programs for these groups. Parents often serve on textbook adoption committees or education committees at the local, state, or national level. Parent Teacher Associations, band boosters, and other special interest groups are often active in supporting special programs or influencing legislation and the outcome of tax or spending referenda. Still other groups have brought pressure on school boards and school officials to include or not include curriculum material on sex education, substance abuse, suicide, ethnic or women's studies, and religion. Currently, fundamentalist groups of the new right are bringing unrelenting pressure on local school boards, state boards of education, political decision makers, and the textbook industry to rid our schools of all material and teaching that promotes secular humanism and ignores religion (see Chapter 11).

Local School Boards

Local school boards make a host of curriculum decisions about the content and learning opportunities that are provided for children. Within the limits of state authority, local boards decide what electives will be offered, which textbooks and other instructional materials will be purchased, which curriculum guides are to be followed, what teachers will be hired, how the budget will be spent, and how to respond to innumerable other issues that directly or indirectly influence the curriculum. It is the local school board that most often feels the pressure of parents and special interest groups, for it is the local school board that decides such matters as whether a new program will be piloted, whether such courses as sex education will be offered, or whether a program for the hearing-impaired will be offered by the district.

In recent years, increasing concern has been expressed regarding the extent to which the local school board represents all constituencies in the community. One concern is that local boards are influenced too much by small but vocal groups of parents or concerned citizens. Another concern is the elitist composition of boards of education. Except for rural school boards, most school boards tend to be composed of a disproportionate number of upper-income males who are college educated and have high-status occupations (Spring, 1991).

What are the backgrounds and occupations of the members of the school board in your community? How representative are they of the members of the local community?

State Governments

As the level of government with legal responsibility for education, the state obviously has an interest in curricular matters. The state's influence over the curriculum is exercised in several ways. First, state statutes often mandate that certain subjects be included in the curriculum. Some states also specify what cannot be taught (e.g., communism). The state's impact on the curriculum has been particularly evident in the aftermath of the reform reports of the 1980s. The reports have called for more state requirements as well as for the decentralization of decision making. In response, the states have taken a more active role in prescribing the curriculum for local schools (Elmore & Fuhrman, 1994).

A major recommendation of many of the reform reports was that students be required to take an increased number of basic courses in English, social studies, mathematics, and science (see Table 14.1, pp. 486–487). In response, 40 states increased minimum high school graduation requirements during the period 1980 to 1990. Mathematics requirements were increased in 41 states, science requirements in 34 states, English/language arts in 19 states, and social studies in 26 states (Medrick, Brown, & Henke, 1992). Figure 14.1 on page 488 provides a comparison of the number of states with specific subject area requirements for graduation and the average number of units required in 1980 and 1990. Despite the increase in graduation requirements, the majority of the states still do not require as many credits as recommended by the first, and perhaps the foremost,

What are the subject requirements for high school graduation in the state in which you plan to teach?

Table 14.1: Curriculum Recommendations from Selected Education Reform Reports

Reform Report	Recommendations
A Nation at Risk (The National Commission on Excellence in Education)	• Significantly more time should be devoted to learning the "new basics"—English, mathematics, science, social studies, computer science, and, for the college-bound, a foreign language. • Elementary schools should provide a sound base in English language development and writing, computational and problem-solving skills, science, social studies, foreign language, and the arts. • Foreign languages should be started in the elementary grades. • All students seeking a diploma should be required to complete four years of English; three years each of mathematics, science, and social studies; and one-half year of computer science.
Making the Grade (Twentieth Century Fund Task Force)	• The federal government should clearly state that the most important objective of elementary and secondary education in the United States is the development of literacy in the English language. • A common core should include the basic skills of reading, writing, and calculating; technical capability in computers; training in science and foreign languages; and knowledge of civics.
Action for Excellence (Education Commission of the States Task Force on Education for Economic Growth)	• The academic experience should be more intense and more productive. Courses in all disciplines must be enlivened and improved. The goal should be both richer substance and greater motivational power—elimination of "soft," nonessential courses, more enthusiastic involvement of students in learning, encouragement of mastery of skills beyond the basics, e.g., problem-solving, analysis, interpretation, and persuasive writing. • Educators, business and labor leaders, and other interested parties should clearly identify the skills that the schools are expected to impart to students for effective employment and citizenship.

reform report, *A Nation at Risk,* which recommended a minimum of four credits of English and three credits each of social studies, mathematics, and science.

Accompanying the movement to increase graduation requirements, 21 states have imposed a minimum competency test that must be passed before a diploma will be awarded. In two additional states, assessment is required, but local districts select the method (Coley & Goertz, 1990). This latter development may be more consistent with projected trends for the next century; the prediction is that the high school diploma will be replaced by achievement goals (Lemonick, 1992).

In addition to statutory requirements, the state influences the curriculum through the state board of education which, in many states, is authorized to decide upon curriculum requirements, review curriculum proposals, promulgate curricular guidelines, and establish teacher certification requirements. Yet another state entity, the state department of education, also influences the curriculum through leadership, instructional resources and support, and publication of curriculum guides that are provided to local school districts. State curriculum guides

Table 14.1: Continued	
Reform Report	**Recommendations**
American High School Study (Ernest L. Boyer, Carnegie Foundation)	• In elementary schools, the focus should be on communication skills. All high school students should complete a basic English course with an emphasis on writing. The high school core should stress the spoken word. • Required courses in the student's core should be increased from one-half to two-thirds of the total required for graduation. The core would include three units of English; two and a half units of history; two units each of science, mathematics, and foreign language; one unit of civics; one-half unit each of technology and health; a seminar on work; and a senior independent social issues project. • In the last two years of high school, students should enroll in a cluster of electives and explore career options. • A service requirement involving school or community volunteer work should be added.
A Place Called School (John Goodlad)	• There should be a better balance in the curriculum of the school and the student. The individual curriculum should be devoted to up to 18% language and literature, up to 18% mathematics and science, up to 15% each to society and social studies, the arts, and the vocations, and the remaining 10% to guided individual choice.
The Paideia Proposal (Mortimer Adler)	• There should be a common curriculum for all students involving: (a) acquisition of knowledge through didactic instruction in three subject areas: language, literature, and fine arts; mathematics and natural sciences; history, geography, and social sciences; (b) the development of intellectual skills in linguistics, mathematics, and science through coaching, exercise, and practice; and (c) the enlargement of understanding, insight, and aesthetic appreciation through the Socratic discussion of books and other works of art and participation in artistic activities such as music, drama, and the visual arts. • The only elective in the 12 years of school should be for a second language.

often detail the goals and objectives, competencies, and instructional activities for every subject at every grade level. (See Chapter 13 for a discussion of the roles and responsibilities of state boards and departments of education.)

Another important way in which the state influences the curriculum is through the textbook adoption and selection process. Books are adopted on the basis of state-mandated criteria. In many states, local school districts cannot purchase textbooks unless they are on a state adoption list. In some states, such as California, the state adoption committee determines the approach and perspective a text must have in order to be approved.

The Federal Government

The federal government's influence over the curriculum does not come from mandating that certain courses or programs of study be taught, but from providing support for specific initiatives and drawing attention to certain perceived national problems and issues. For example, as noted in previous chapters, when

Figure 14.1: Minimum High School Graduation Requirements, 1980 and 1990

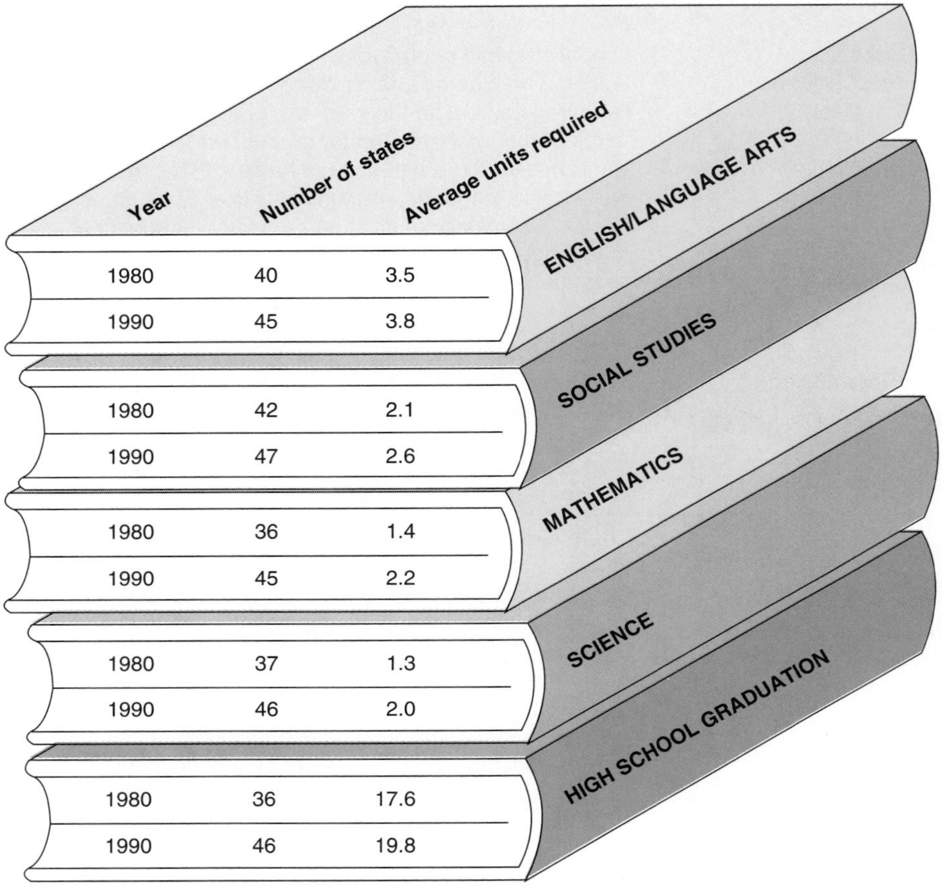

Year	Number of states	Average units required
ENGLISH/LANGUAGE ARTS		
1980	40	3.5
1990	45	3.8
SOCIAL STUDIES		
1980	42	2.1
1990	47	2.6
MATHEMATICS		
1980	36	1.4
1990	45	2.2
SCIENCE		
1980	37	1.3
1990	46	2.0
HIGH SCHOOL GRADUATION		
1980	36	17.6
1990	46	19.8

Source: Medrick, E. A., Brown, C. L., & Henke, R. R. (1992). *Overview and inventory of state requirements for school coursework and attendance.* NCES 92–663. Washington, DC: National Center for Education Statistics, U.S. Department of Education, table A-1, 72–77. Figure style reprinted with permission, from *The American School Board Journal,* October. Copyright, 1989, The National School Boards Association. All rights reserved.

the launching of the Sputnik spacecraft by the Soviet Union in 1957 caused fear that we were falling behind in the space race, the federal government did not respond by mandating more mathematics or science offerings, or higher graduation requirements, but by passing the National Defense Education Act. This act provided financial encouragement to schools to upgrade their mathematics, science, and foreign language offerings. In later years, the National Science Foundation became instrumental in curricular revision in mathematics.

Vocational education is an area that has been heavily influenced by federal legislation. In fact, it was federal legislation that often set the course for, or at

least stimulated, state action, and state programs often paralleled federal programs in vocational education. Federal legislation in other areas, including compensatory education, bilingual education, sex equity, career education, and
adult education has also tended to direct attention in the curriculum
deemed important at the federal level. The federal government also in
curriculum development by virtue of the support given to research in
areas, which has the effect of promoting curriculum reform in these ar

Recent developments suggest that the federal government likely wil
a more influential role in decisions about curricular content in the
schools. Currently, efforts are under way in a venture that can lead to tl
opment of a *national curriculum* for the nation's schools. The provision
Goals 2000: Educate America Act and earlier federal legislation provide
appointment of two national bodies to develop and oversee the nation
and national standards. They are the National Goals Panel and the
Education Standards and Improvement Council.

With funding from the U.S. Department of Education, various pro
organizations are developing curricular standards for their discipline a
the *National Goals for Education* effort (Smith, Fuhrman, & O'Day, 1994). '
dards are being developed by the relevant professional organization, a
are being made for wide distribution of the standards (Diegmueller, 199

The function of the National Goals Panel is to review and certify education
standards and assessments. The work of this oversight group is being coordinated with the National Education Standards and Improvement Council, whose
mission is to provide support and quality control for the several standards setting
efforts that have been funded by the U.S. Department of Education (Olson,
1994a). Even though these two bodies and the standards from the professional
organizations do not have the legal status of requirements on the schools, they
represent a much more active role of the federal government in education than
has existed previously. These standards likely will be reflected in curriculum
development and revision efforts and also in textbook revisions. The standards
have a special status and high credibility as a result of their having been developed by the appropriate national professional organization with federal funding.

With the shift from democratic to republican control of the U.S. Congress
in 1994, the future of the federal interest in promotion of national goals for education and financial support for development of national standards is somewhat
unclear. Two conditions suggest a change in federal direction. The sentiment of
the new congressional majority not only appears to favor a reduction in the federal role in education, but also is seeking to reduce federal expenditures. This
latter interest may result in a decline in funding for some current federal education activities. With the passage of time, the effect of this new sentiment on the
full range of federal education initiatives will provide interesting opportunities
for study.

National Committees and Reports

As was discussed in several other sections of this text, it has been a practice in this
country throughout this century for select national committees to be formed to

study and make recommendations regarding some aspect of education. The curriculum impact of some of these committees has been profound. For example, the *Cardinal Principles of Secondary Education,* issued by the NEA Commission on the Reorganization of Secondary Education in 1918, played a major role in the establishment of the comprehensive high school.

The most recent series of national committees and reports contain a number of observations and recommendations directed at the curriculum. The first wave of these reports tended to look at a number of things that were alleged to be "wrong" with the nation's schools, the curriculum being one of them. Required courses, their number and content, and minimum skills and competencies are all addressed by the reports. A second wave of reports, appearing at the end of the 1980s, focused more directly on specific academic components of the curriculum and are noted in the next section. The curriculum recommendations of the major reports in the first wave are summarized in Table 14.1.

The various reports appear to be having a significant impact on education policy. For example, the effect of their support for the "new basics" is evident. They can also be credited with the increased attention given to homework, mastery learning, and competency testing. Some of the recommendations, such as merit pay, the extended day, and the extended year have not been widely adopted. It is safe to say, however, that these reports have received more publicity and have been the subject of more discussion by professional educators, educational decision makers, and lay citizens than any educational event in the past quarter century. They have provided the impetus for the National Goals for Education, federal funding for the development of national standards, and expansion of the National Assessment of Educational Progress. One of the interesting dimensions of these recent reform reports has been the level of interest and participation from the business community; such groups as the Committee for Economic Development (1994) have been very active and supportive of the school reform movement.

Professional Organizations

In addition to their individual influence, educators historically had influence over the curriculum through their collective association in professional organizations. Both the National Education Association and the American Federation of Teachers, the two largest organizations, attempt to influence public policy about curriculum through full-time lobbying efforts directed at the state and national legislatures. These and other influential professional organizations, such as the National Council of Social Studies, National Council for Teachers of Mathematics, National Science Teachers Association, International Reading Association, Association for Supervision and Curriculum Development, and American Association of School Administrators influence the profile and direction of the school curriculum as they set national agendas and goals and raise their collective voices.

The second wave of school reform reports, concerned with curriculum and emanating primarily from these professional organizations, is the most recent example of their involvement and attempt to provide direction for the school

Various interest groups are concerned about the content of textbooks and instructional materials. Schools need to respect this public interest while retaining an appropriate level of professional autonomy.

curriculum. Directed at the core subjects of mathematics, science, language arts, and social studies, these reports have focused on essential knowledge and skills, called for more rigorous content, and encouraged the development of critical thinking skills (Lewis, 1990). Among the more widely publicized of these curriculum reports are:

- National Council of Teachers of Mathematics—*Curriculum and Evaluation Standards for School Mathematics* (1989)

- National Science Teachers Association—*Essential Changes in Secondary Science: Scope, Sequence, and Coordination* (1989)

- American Association for the Advancement of Science—*Science for All Americans* (1989)

- National Research Council—*Everybody Counts: A Report to the Nation on the Future of Mathematics Education* (1989)

- National Council of Teachers of English—*The English Coalition Conference: Democracy Through Language* (1989)

- National Commission on Social Studies in the Schools—*Charting a Course: Social Studies for the 21st Century* (1989)

As an extension of these efforts, several professional organizations have received federal and foundation grants to develop model standards for their particular disciplines. The National Council of Teachers of Mathematics

(Diegmueller, 1994c), National Council for the Social Studies (Diegmueller, 1994b), and a few other professional groups have completed their efforts, and the materials are being disseminated. However, the U.S. Department of Education did not renew the contract for standards development in English with the International Reading Association and the National Council of Teachers of English. Reportedly, the reasons were a lack of progress and deficiencies; these groups are proceeding to develop standards without federal funds. News reports indicate that the Department of Education is contacting other groups to determine their interest in developing these standards (Diegmueller, 1994a).

Another organizational model for the development of national standards is illustrated in the 18 standards for teaching geography that were developed by the National Geographic Society (*Geography for Life,* 1994). The major goals of the standards development effort are that standards would be available for each discipline and that they would be used in determining what is taught and assessed.

National Testing

The impact of national standardized tests on the entire educational enterprise in the last two decades has been nothing short of overwhelming. Students, schools, and school districts are praised or prodded based on test results. Students are admitted to postsecondary institutions, private elementary and secondary schools, and specialized programs in the public schools based on their test results. Many scholarships are based all or in part on test results. Teachers, programs, and schools are considered more or less effective based on test results. The admission of prospective teachers and administrators into degree or certification programs, or their later certification, is determined by test results. Practicing teachers and administrators are tested in some states. Many accountability or merit pay plans include test results as output indicators.

To a large extent, these tests function as "gatekeepers of knowledge" (Spring, 1989). The knowledge tested is that which is considered the most worthy by test developers. Although within any discipline there is usually considerable debate as to what knowledge is of most worth, in the end it is often the viewpoint of the test makers that gives direction to the curriculum. While not necessarily advocating "teaching to the test," school boards, administrators, and teachers themselves seek to ensure that the schools' curriculum "prepare[s] students to do well on the test." If test scores are down in a certain curriculum area, district resources and instruction may be redirected to that area. Increasingly, individual students and their families invest in tutorial books, computer software, and seminars in an attempt to raise test scores.

Standardized tests can play an important role in providing standards and data needed for curriculum assessment, but their limits must be recognized. Educators, policy makers, and parents should keep in mind that the only thing that most of the tests measure is *achievement;* they do not measure other desired outputs of the learning experience. Nor do they measure whether individual teachers or schools are achieving their own instructional goals. Thus, to allow the concern about national standardized tests to dictate the curriculum would be a serious error.

This is particularly true in light of the concerns expressed by many educators and psychologists that some tests are biased against females, minorities, and those from lower socioeconomic strata. Although the testing industry has taken steps to rid tests of their blatant white, male, middle-class bias, test analyses continue to reveal content that discriminates against certain populations. An overreliance on items that assume experiences or knowledge not common to certain gender, racial, and ethnic groups illustrates the type of content that causes test bias. Rather than being a measure of student performance, a recent analysis found that much of the variability in state scores can be accounted for by such demographic variables as number of parents in the home, level of parental education, type of community, and poverty rates for ages 5–17. The test data may be more an index of educational challenge than a measure of educational performance (Robinson & Brandon, 1994). Although the decision to administer most tests is not within the authority of teachers, they can play a role in examining tests for bias and in ensuring that results are properly interpreted, communicated, and utilized.

In addition to the previously discussed concerns about national testing, this issue also has been raised in reference to assessment of the national goals for education. The national goals and standards movement has emphasized the importance of focusing student assessment efforts on observable behaviors and levels of student performance. Many public policy figures appear to have great confidence in the ability of tests to measure the desired outcomes. The Committee for Economic Development (1994) has supported the concept of national assessment to determine whether students are attaining the national standards. However, reservations have been expressed about the capacity of available tests, the potential misuse of testing information, and the ability of a test to determine the extent to which an individual is capable of applying knowledge in addressing problems outside the classroom (Resnick & Klopfer, 1989; Nickerson, 1989). From a somewhat different perspective, the Educational Excellence Network, composed of several persons active in the Reagan and Bush administrations, has advocated that states be required to develop a system of standards and assessments (Olson, 1994b). These comments, in the context of the two federal panels and the efforts to develop national standards, suggest an expanded and more active role for the federal government in *influencing* school curricular content and state and local assessment practices and policies.

Textbooks

In the course of his or her educational career a student may be exposed to hundreds of textbooks. In the classroom, students spend at least two-thirds of their time using textbooks. Teachers rely heavily on textbooks for instructional content, organization, and evaluation. Without question, textbooks and other published instructional materials influence what is taught and learned in the classroom. By virtue of their influence in determining *what content* is included and how it is portrayed, textbooks, textbook publishers, and state adoption policies have an impact on not only the knowledge base of students, but also their attitudes and beliefs (Apple, 1993). It is because they recognize the powerful influence of textbooks that religious and other special interest groups have been so vocal and persistent in their attempts to influence not only textbook adoption decisions but the textbook industry itself.

What is the text-book adoption process used in your state?

In addition to the previously discussed concerns about content expressed by some religious groups, textbooks have also been criticized for being too "soft" on communism, being too "hard" on American institutions and activities, and presenting an inadequate portrayal of women, minorities, and other groups. That is, women and minorities are often portrayed in traditional and lower status roles or are given limited coverage. The elderly and handicapped often are excluded from narrative discussion or pictures and illustrations.

Given the potential influence of textbooks and the unresolved concerns about their content, it is important that teachers be sensitive to cultural diversity, gender differences, and special populations. Teachers should actively participate in the textbook selection process. Unfortunately, far too often teachers have not received training in the evaluation of instructional material or are not given sufficient time to thoroughly review the textbooks under consideration. Ultimately, the influence that textbooks have on the curriculum is determined by the care taken in their selection and how they are used in the classroom.

National Goals and Standards

As a result of the adoption of the National Goals for Education by the National Governor's Association (1990) and the enactment of the *Goals 2000: Educate America Act,* increased attention is being given to national goals and standards for education. The adoption of national education goals by the president and the nation's governors is the first time that political leaders have made a comprehensive formal statement about goals for the public schools. Further evidence of the commitment of political figures to school reform is shown in the Clinton Administration's support of the federal legislation to develop national standards, even when the legislation was originally proposed by President Bush.

As listed in Chapter 5, the goals originally focused on readiness for school, retention of students in school, student performance, good citizenship, adult literacy, and a safe, drug-free environment for teaching and learning. Lacking the authority to take formal action, the National Governors Association adopted a resolution calling for state-by-state discussion of these goals (National Governors Association, 1990). The original six goals have been expanded to eight with the enactment of the *Goals 2000: Educate America Act;* the new goals are related to parent participation and teacher preparation.

In most of the discussions, goals are generally aspirational statements; the unknown element is the public response when the goals have or have not been attained. In contrast to goals, the standards being developed by various subject matter professional organizations provide the measures that can be used to determine the extent to which the schools have attained the goals. This interaction of goals and standards provides the framework for designing curriculum experiences.

Much of the criticism toward the national goals has been focused on the absence of the additional fiscal and material resources that schools need if they are to attain the national goals. This discussion has contributed to suggestions that attention should be given to the opportunity to learn standards before expecting students to make the level of improvements sought in the national goals. These preconditions have been identified as critical if schools and students are to attain the national goals; they draw attention to the resources and materials that should be made available if students are to attain the national goals. As noted in Chapter 5, the *Goals 2000: Educate America Act* federal legislation linked the national goals to opportunities to learn standards, and limited federal funds were made available in the form of grants to states for the development of these and related standards. The dilemma is that states typically have not provided full funding for the new initiatives. Responsibility for identifying solutions and sources of funding resides with state and local school officials, and the task of implementation resides with the 16,000 local school districts (Murphy, 1990).

Questions are being raised about the extent to which national goals and standards for public elementary and secondary education threaten state and local control of education (Pitsch, 1994). The concept of national goals and standards appears to conflict with the traditional position that education is a local function, state responsibility, and national concern. However, various writers have emphasized that the goals and standards are "national" in terms of being important to the nation's citizens rather than "federal" in terms of being mandates from the federal government.

A different perspective has been presented in a recent critique of the efforts to reform education; Astuto, Clark, Read, McGree, & Fernandez (1994) contend that many of the efforts to reform American education have been misplaced. These authors do not accept the assumption that schools will improve by raising standards and imposing various requirements. Rather, they contend that schools will be improved by teachers and students, not legislative and regulatory bodies. Thus, the current energies should be used to help and support individual schools and teachers in the classrooms. The assumption is that this relatively isolated environment is the critical component in the success or failure of American education.

Support for a National Curriculum

The desire to improve the schools because of declining student performance, increased international competition, and low overall quality of the schools has become so great that less importance is being given to traditional anxieties about the emergence of a national curriculum and the potential loss of local control over schools. Evidence of public support for a national curriculum and national assessment for public schools was found in the 1994 Phi Delta Kappa poll of the public's attitudes toward education. Of the respondents, 83% favored a standardized national curriculum and 73% favored a standardized national testing program for promotion and high school graduation. Over 60% of the respondents favored more effort to reach agreement on academic achievement goals (Elam, Rose, & Gallup, 1994).

Persons with both conservative and liberal positions appear to be supportive of a national curriculum. This impetus for the development of a national curriculum and national goals and standards could have a significant impact on public education. However, there are reservations about the nature of the impact. They include the concern about the capacity of the curriculum to accommodate the diversity in student aspirations, cultural heritages, and conditions that affect learning, and the additional funds that will be needed to provide all students with equal access to the learning opportunities (Chira, 1989).

Additional evidence of the merits of this concern was noted in the 1994 yearbook of the Association for Supervision and Curriculum Development. Elmore and Fuhrman (1994) identified trends that represented new directions in curriculum and school governance—an increasing state and national influence on school requirements and curricular content, linking of student assessment with curricular content, and increased emphasis on improving student performance. This movement likely will impact on the daily life of each teacher and reduce some of the flexibility that has been a characteristic of the American public schools. To counter this force, Elmore and Fuhrman have contended that teachers should become better informed, focus their attention on the important issues, form networks to influence policy, emphasize best practice, and push the limits of policy to maintain their professional status.

Curriculum Development

The curriculum development and planning literature is replete with models, paradigms, and "steps," which all can be categorized according to two perspectives: the technical production perspective and the critical perspective. The technical production perspective has dominated thought on curriculum planning for 40 years. The newer critical perspective takes issue with the very assumptions underlying the technical production perspective and advocates critical reflection on all assumptions in discussions about the curriculum (Posner, 1992).

Technical Production Perspective

The technical production perspective views curriculum planning as a rational and technical process that can be accomplished by objective decision making. Further, curriculum planning is presumed to be a production-oriented enterprise in which the planner objectively and, if possible, scientifically establishes the means to obtain the desired educational outcomes. The technical production model has been popular for so long because it is congruent with the prevailing assumption that education is a production process in which individual learning is the primary product (Posner, 1992).

The technical production perspective is best represented by the work of Ralph Tyler (1949). Tyler's rationale for curriculum planning is organized around four steps. First, the planners must determine what educational purposes (aims and objectives) the school(s) should pursue. As discussed in Chapters 6 and 7, there are widely varying schools of thought about the purpose of education, and these are translated into curriculum and instructional practice.

After deciding on the educational objectives, as a second step planners must decide what learning experiences can be provided that are likely to attain these purposes. Once developed, possible experiences must be checked to see if they give students the opportunity to acquire the behavior stated in the objectives and if they lead to the effect intended (Walker & Soltis, 1986).

In the third step, planners must decide how the learning experiences can be organized effectively. Here, attention must be given to the *continuity* and *sequence* of experiences. Consistent with Piaget's theory that cognitive development is gradual (progressing through four levels) and that any subject can be taught in some form to any child at any stage of development, continuity is concerned with the reiteration of major curriculum elements so that skills can be practiced and developed. Sequencing aims at ensuring that successive experiences build on preceding ones. The concepts of continuity and sequence, which Tyler refers to as vertical organizational dimensions, also correspond to Bruner's concept of the spiral curriculum, which, as explained in Chapter 5, proposes that concepts and topics be treated at progressive grade levels in increasing complexity and detail.

The effective organization of experiences also involves the *integration* of skills and knowledge across disciplines. Tyler refers to integration as the horizontal dimension of curriculum organization. As the fourth step in the Tyler model, the planner must develop a means of evaluating whether the stated purposes are being attained by the selected learning experiences.

Tyler (1949) viewed curriculum planning as a continuous process whereby:

> as materials and procedures are developed, they are tried out, their results appraised, their inadequacies identified, suggested improvements indicated; there is replanning, redevelopment and then reappraisal; and in this kind of continuing cycle, it is possible for the curriculum and instructional program to be continuously improved over the years. (p. 123)

Figure 14.2 provides a graphic depiction of Tyler's curriculum planning cycle.

Critical Perspective

In sharp contrast to the technical production perspective is the critical perspective, which rejects the notion that curriculum planning can be an objective, value-free process. Rather, this perspective argues that curriculum decisions are essentially ideological and sociopolitical. As some critical theorists point out, the very decisions about what the objectives should be, what knowledge is of most value, how the curriculum will be organized and delivered, to whom it will be delivered, and how it will be evaluated involve assumptions and values that reinforce the existing power and social structure. For example, because of the relationship between evaluators and employers, if it were known to an evaluator that the administration of a district had been active in initiating a particular curriculum and had fought hard to secure financial support for the program, the evaluator would probably feel great pressure to discover results not unfavorable to the program.

Figure 14.2: The Tyler Planning Cycle

1. Determine Educational Purposes
   (aims and objectives)

2. Select
   Learning
   Experiences
   to Achieve
   the Stated
   Objectives

THE
TYLER
PLANNING
CYCLE

4. Evaluate the
   Effectiveness
   of the
   Learning
   Experience in
   Achieving the
   Objectives

3. Organize Learning Experiences
   for Effective Instruction
   • Continuity
   • Sequence
   • Integration

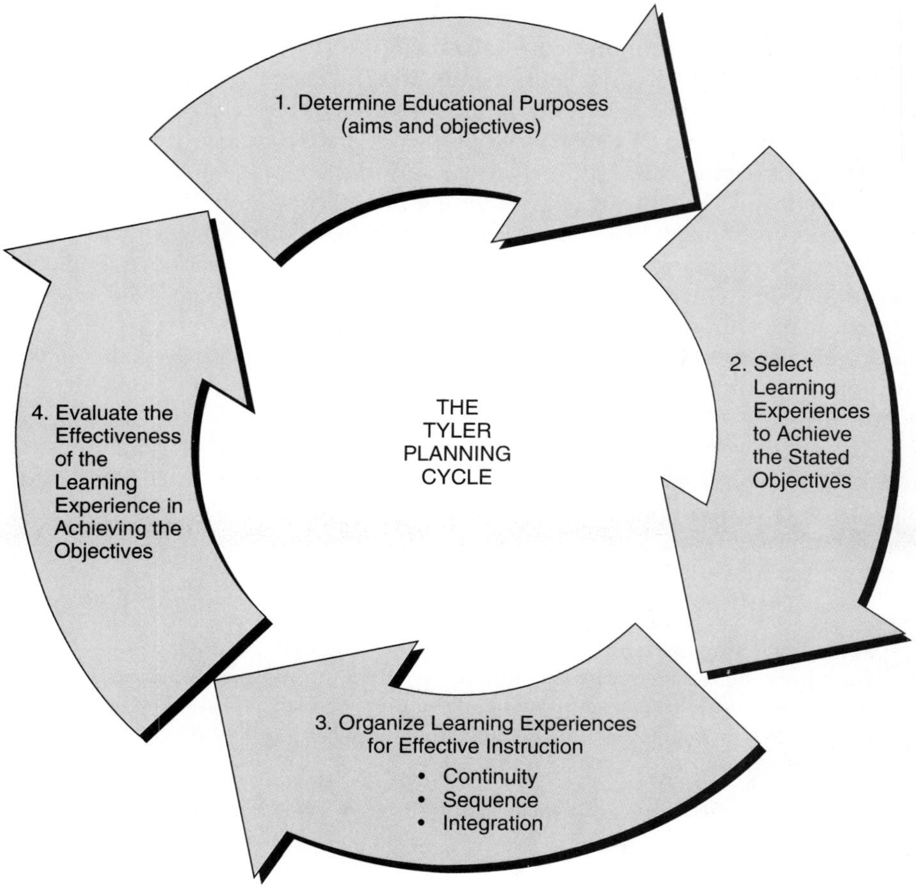

Each of these perspectives is important in curriculum development. Knowing how to develop a curriculum involves technique. Being able to identify the assumptions underlying curriculum discussions requires a curriculum conscience. Curriculum planning without technique is incompetent, and without curriculum conscience, is ungrounded (Posner, 1992).

Patterns of Curriculum Organization

Decisions about how the curriculum should be organized involve choices about what subjects to study and how these subjects will be presented to the students.

Although there are many different structures that reflect alternative perspectives about the nature of the curriculum, these alternatives can be classified as being either subject-centered or student-centered. The subject-centered perspective is the older, more traditional, and most common. It views the curriculum as a program of studies or collection of courses that represents what students should know. The second perspective focuses on the needs and interests of the child and the process by which learning takes place.

The subject-centered and student-centered perspectives are the two ends of a continuum of curricular design. In this section six alternative curriculum designs along this continuum are examined: subject-area design, integrated design, core curriculum design, child-centered design, social reconstruction design, and deschooling design.

The Subject-Area Design

The *subject-area curriculum* design is the oldest and most common organization plan for the curriculum. This design views the curriculum as a group of subjects or body of subject matter. The subject matter to be included in the curriculum is that which has survived the test of time. It is also that which is perceived to be of most value in the development of the intellect—said by supporters to be the primary purpose of education. The subject-area curriculum is consistent with the essentialist philosophy of education.

The subject area design has its roots in classical Greece. In this country William T. Harris, superintendent of schools in St. Louis, Missouri, in the 1870s and U.S. commissioner of education from 1886 to 1906, is credited with establishing this design, which has been the dominant curriculum organization for over a century. Harris viewed the curriculum as the means by which the child is introduced to the essential knowledge and values of society and transformed into a reasoning and responsible citizen. The curriculum of the elementary school was to include the fundamentals, which Harris called the "five windows of the soul": mathematics, geography, literature and art, grammar, and history. In the high school, concentration was on the classics, languages, and mathematics (Cremin, 1962). Electives in languages, fine arts, and industrial arts were to be used to develop specific skills or meet special interests (Ellis, Mackey, & Glenn, 1988).

Modern spokespersons for the subject-area curriculum include Arthur Bestor, Mortimer Adler, and Robert Hutchins. They have been joined in their call for a return to fundamentals and a curriculum of basic studies by supporters of the back-to-basics movement and ultraconservative groups. The back-to-basics movement grew out of parents' and educators' disappointment with the level of knowledge and skills learned by students and declining student test scores. The same concerns have been used by ultraconservative groups such as the *new right* to justify the elimination of *nonessential* subjects that they dislike; specific examples include sex education and environmental studies (Pulliam, 1991).

Those who criticize the subject-area curriculum claim that it ignores the needs, interests, and experiences of students and discourages creativity on the part of both students and teachers. Another major criticism of the subject-area curriculum is that it is fragmented and compartmentalized. The subject-area curriculum is also faulted for failing to adequately consider both individual differences and contemporary social issues. The primary teaching methods of the subject-area curriculum are lecture and discussion. Rote memorization and recitation are required of students.

The subject-area curriculum has remained the most popular and dominant curriculum design for four basic reasons. First, most teachers, especially secondary school teachers, are trained in the subject areas. Secondary school teachers usually think of themselves as American history teachers, biology teachers, English teachers, or whatever. Second, organizing the school by subject matter makes it easy for parents and other adults to understand children's education since most adults attended schools that were organized by subject matter. Third, the subject-area organization makes it easy for teachers to develop curriculum and goals: the content provides the organization and focus needed in planning. Finally, textbooks and other instructional materials are usually developed for subject-area use (Ellis, Mackey, & Glenn, 1988). Because the subject-area design has been so dominant in this country, it is possible to go into schools from Seattle to Key West and find much the same curriculum.

The Integrated Design

The *integrated curriculum* design emerged as a response to the multiplication of courses resulting from the subject-centered design. In this design emphasis remains on subjects, but in place of separate courses in history, geography, economics, political science, anthropology, and sociology, for example, an integrated course in social studies might be offered. By this approach, it is claimed, knowledge is integrated in a way that makes it more meaningful to the learner. The integrated design also provides greater flexibility to the teacher in choosing subject matter.

Among the more common integrated courses are language arts, which has taken the place of separate courses in reading, writing, spelling, speaking, grammar, drama, and literature; mathematics, which integrates arithmetic, geometry, and algebra; general science, which includes botany, biology, chemistry, and geology or earth science; and the previously mentioned social studies. Although the integrated design usually combines separate subjects within the same discipline, in some instances content from two or more branches of study have been integrated into a new field of study. Futuristics, which integrates knowledge from mathematics, sociology, statistics, political science, economics, education, and a number of other fields, is one such new field of study. Multicultural education, which integrates knowledge from sociology, psychology, history, and anthropology, is another relatively new area (Ornstein & Hunkins, 1988).

The integrated curriculum has been widely accepted at the elementary level. Where once a number of separate subjects were taught for shorter periods of time, the typical elementary curriculum is now more likely to integrate these subjects into "subject areas" that are taught in longer blocks of time. At the secondary level, the integrated curriculum has experienced limited success. A few integrated courses can be found (e.g., Problems of American Democracy), but as previously noted, the subject-area design dominates secondary school curricula. However, recent efforts in reading and writing across the curriculum are an attempt to respond to reform recommendations that the curriculum not be presented in such discrete, independent blocks and that students be provided greater opportunity to synthesize and integrate knowledge and skills. A major criticism of the integrated curriculum is that in providing breadth, it provides only a cursory knowledge of any subject. While depth may not be considered necessary at the elementary level, the bias towards discipline mastery remains at the secondary level.

The Core Curriculum Design

The definition of a *core curriculum* has changed significantly since it was first advanced in the 1930s. Originally, the core curriculum was proposed as an interdisciplinary approach of relating one subject to another in the study of everyday situations of interest and value to students. The content of the core was taught in an extended block of time centered around defining and solving problems of concern to all students. Attention was directed to the study of culture and fundamental social values. Typical core courses dealt with how to earn a living, social relations, or life adjustment. As described at the time, the core curriculum was said to be:

> made up of those educational experiences which are thought to be important for each citizen in our democracy. Students and teachers do not consider subject matter to be important in itself. It becomes meaningful only as it helps the group to solve the problems which have been selected for study. (MacConnell et al., cited in Goodlad, 1987, p. 10)

Different interpretations of the core concept have emerged in the last decade, primarily as a result of the national reports of the early 1980s. Alternately, the concept of a core curriculum is used to refer to the required minimum "subjects and topics within subjects that all students in a given system are required to or expected to learn" (Skilbeck, 1989, p. 198) or, more broadly, "the comprehensive body of common learnings deemed necessary for all" (Goodlad, 1987, p. 11).

The support for the "new core" came from the same disillusionment with American education that fed the back-to-basics movement that began in the 1970s. The curriculum was said to be lacking in rigor, to contain too many "frills" and soft courses, and to inadequately prepare students to effectively participate and contribute to our increasingly technological and global society. Serious deficits in mathematics, science, and languages also were noted.

The response of some of the national studies was to recommend a core of subjects to be taken by all students. As seen in Table 14.1, the National Commission on Excellence recommended 13.5 units in "the Five New Basics," Boyer proposed a "core of common learning" consisting of 14.5 units, and others wanted less specific, but still identifiable, cores. To others the concept of a core is more reminiscent of the core curriculum espoused by the progressive educators of the 1930s, 1940s, and early 1950s. For example, although Goodlad

Parents, policymakers, and educators are calling for increased attention to the "basics" in the schools. The challenge will be to provide students with the opportunity to develop their individual talents and interests.

What impact have the back-to-basics movement and other interest groups had on your discipline?

in *A Place Called School* "deliberately and reluctantly" defined a core in conventional terms, he subsequently has joined that body of educators who recognize that increasingly the expectations of schooling are broad and transcend mere academic outcomes. What is needed is not a core of subjects to be taken by all students but a core curriculum consisting of the domains of human experience and thought that should be encountered by all students. The American Association for Supervision and Curriculum Development (ASCD), like Boyer, refers to a core of common learning to help ensure that "all students are provided the curriculum content and learning experiences most appropriate to their future lives" (Cawelti, 1989, p. 33). The ASCD also makes the broad proposal that the core curriculum should center around "fundamental concerns such as global interdependence, civic responsibility, ecology, economic productivity, and world peace" (Cawelti, 1989, p. 33).

Yet many educators are concerned that it is not possible to have a core curriculum for all students and still maintain quality. Others are concerned about the impact of a universal core requirement on the schools' ability to meet the needs of different populations, including those interested in vocational preparation. Probably all agree that the task of defining the proper core will be among the most challenging professional tasks facing educators.

The Child-Centered Design

The concept of the child-centered curriculum has its roots in the efforts of Rousseau, Pestalozzi, and Froebel (see Chapter 4). In the United States, the concept was revived by the progressive education movement. There are a number of variations of the child-centered curriculum, including the experience- and activity-centered curriculum and the humanistic curriculum. The emphasis of all child-centered curricula is on the child's freedom to learn and on activities and creative self-expression.

Where the traditional curriculum is organized around the teaching of discrete subject matter, in the child-centered curriculum children come to the subject matter out of their own needs and interests. The child-centered curriculum focuses on the individual learner and the development of the whole child. The scope of the child-centered curriculum is as broad as all of human life and society. The goal of the curriculum is to motivate and interest the child in the learning process. To achieve this goal, the curriculum encompasses a wide range of activities, including field geography, nature study, number concepts, games, drama, storytelling, music, art, handicrafts, other creative and expressive activities, physical education, and community involvement projects.

Child-centered designs are often criticized for being too broad and for being so inclusive as to be nonfunctional (Portelli, 1987). They are also criticized for being too permissive and for their lack of attention to subject matter mastery. Modern proponents (e.g., John Holt, Herbert Kohl, and Elliot Eisner) counter that the child-centered curriculum enhances learning because it is based on the needs and interests of the learner. Child-centered curricula have operated in numerous districts and schools throughout this century, primarily at the elementary level. However, they have never been seriously considered at the secondary level.

The Social Reconstruction Design

The *social reconstruction curriculum* design is based on the belief that through the curriculum the school can and should effect social change and create a more equitable society. As discussed in Chapter 5, the social reconstruction movement in education emerged in the 1930s and had its origin in the progressive education movement. In 1932, in his book *Dare the Schools Build a New Social Order?*, George Counts (1969) proposed that the schools involve students in a curriculum designed to reconstruct society. Modern reconstructionists such as Theodore Brameld continue to advocate that the schools become the agents of social change and improvement.

The major assumption underlying the social reconstruction curriculum is that the future is not fixed, but is amenable to modification and improvement. Accordingly, the social reconstruction curriculum seeks "to equip students with tools (skills) for dealing with changes about them. So equipped, the student can meet an unknown future with attitudes and habits of action" (Wiles & Bondi, 1993, p. 353). The primary goal of the curriculum according to the social reconstructionist view is to engage students in a critical analysis of society at every level so that they can improve it.

The social reconstruction design combines classroom learning with application outside the school. Teachers and students join in inquiry. Instruction is often carried on in a problem-solving or inquiry format (Wiles & Bondi, 1993).

What kinds of instructional materials would be used in a social reconstruction curriculum? How difficult would it be to obtain the materials?

The Deschooling Design

Supporters of the *deschooling curriculum* design seek to disestablish formal schooling because they believe that the values promoted by formal educational institutions are unhealthy and harmful. Unlike the school reconstructionists, who are willing to attempt a reformation of the present structure, the deschooling critics do not believe reformation is possible and call for an end to the public school system. According to this view's chief spokesperson, Ivan Illich (1973), compulsory attendance in government-sponsored schools, along with the requirements for academic certificates, actually inhibits the learner's "private initiative to decide what he will learn and his inalienable right to learn what he likes rather than what is useful to somebody else" (p. 2). Schools, say Illich, operate for the benefit of a few and function as a screening device for the gifted few or "to justify the existence of high schools and colleges for the children of the wealthy and powerful." According to Illich, the disadvantaged are hurt by the formal system of schooling because they not only do not receive an education of value, but are further discriminated against by a system that makes them dependent upon its credentials for the opportunity to advance. In fact, government-sponsored schools, by their very nature, are incapable of meeting the needs of the disadvantaged and compensating for racial and ethnic differences.

The best examples of deschooling design are to be found in the private *free schools* and, to a lesser extent, the private and public alternative schools, which received national attention in the late 1960s and early 1970s. Although not representing a complete deschooling of education, they did "lend support to the fast growing assumption that out-of-school activities were equal in educational value, and perhaps actually superior, to in-school activities" (Ravitch, 1983, p. 238). The free schools and alternative schools sought to release students from the institutional oppression of the traditional school by providing travel-learn programs, work and apprenticeship programs, and affective experiences, as well as the opportunity for volunteer service and informal study in the community (Glatthorn, 1975). In the free schools emphasis was placed on children discovering for themselves what they want to learn and on the abolishment of the authority relationship between the teacher and the student.

Although the free school movement has declined and the disestablishment of the formal educational system in this country does not seem likely, efforts to break the monopoly of the formal educational system continue. The charter school and privatization movements discussed in Chapter 16 are clear evidence of these efforts.

Curriculum Contrasts

In practice, most schools do not adopt a strictly subject-centered or student-centered design, but use variations of both in their curriculum organization. Historically, elementary schools have tended to be more student-centered in their orientation and secondary schools more subject-centered. Ultimately, the choice of curriculum design reflects philosophical orientation. The major arguments in support of the subject-centered and student-centered curricula are summarized on page 507.

The Hidden Curriculum

Perhaps even more important than the formal curriculum is the *hidden curriculum*. This concept was briefly mentioned in Chapter 8 in regard to the socialization role of the school. In contrast to the formal curriculum, which is designed to produce intended effects, the hidden curriculum involves the unintended effects of schooling, or what Apple (1979) terms "incidental learning."

Figure 14.3: Patterns of Curriculum Organization

Curriculum Design	Philosophical Orientation	Curriculum Focus	Proponents
Subject-centered	Essentialism	A group of subjects or subject matter that represent the essential knowledge and values of society that have survived the test of time.	Bestor Adler Hutchins
Integrated	Experimentalism	The integration of two or more subjects, both within and across disciplines, into an integrated course.	Broudy Silberman Sarason
Core curriculum	Perennialism	A common body of curriculum content and learning experience that should be encountered by all students; the Great Books.	Goodlad Boyer
Child-centered	Progressivism	Learning activities centered around the interests and needs of the child, designed to motivate and interest the child in the learning process.	Dewey Holt Kohl Eisner
Social reconstructionist	Social reconstructionism	Critical analysis of the political, social, and economic problems facing society; future trends; social action projects designed to bring about social change.	Counts Rugg Bramald Shane
Deschooling	Social reconstructionism	In-school experiences, primarily in the social sciences, designed to develop the child's sense of freedom from the domination of the political, social, and economic systems; out-of-school experiences of equal value.	Illich Goodman Friedenberg Friere

Professional Reflections

"Remember that at the core of education is children. Children are each unique, and so the purpose of education is to meet the needs of those individual children in any way we can. Curriculum is a vehicle, not an end."

Jacqueline Collier, Teacher of the Year, Ohio

According to Apple (1988), the hidden curriculum includes three areas. One is the hidden social messages present in textbooks and other curriculum materials. A second includes the norms and values taught by the rules, regulations, rituals, school structure, and interactions that are part of the everyday life of the school. Through the hidden curriculum students learn how to cope with power, praise, reward, and authority in the classroom (Apple, 1979); how to move through both social and physical spaces (Bowers, 1984); and the value of competition, obedience, the proper use of time, and seriousness of purpose.

The third area Apple included in the hidden curriculum is the knowledge or information that is not included in the overt curriculum, or what Eisner (1994) has termed the *null curriculum*. The null curriculum, which is potentially infinite, refers to those things that are consciously excluded because of their controversial nature, because they represent different values, because of a lack of time, or that cannot be included because of a lack of resources. It also includes those things that are unintentionally excluded because educators are uninformed or because relevant materials are nonexistent. The null curriculum also may include such practical topics as study skills, critical thinking skills, time management, and mediation (Pratt, 1994).

The null curriculum, like all areas of the hidden curriculum, does not have the same impact on all students. That is, not only are different values and norms stressed with different social classes or different sexes, but differences are also found even within the same school or classroom in what students have the opportunity to learn. Historically, what is now called the hidden curriculum was not hidden because the schools explicitly served a social control function in unifying a diverse population, advancing a common culture, and preparing individuals economically for their place in society. In fact, the hidden curriculum did not become hidden until the end of the nineteenth century "when the education system shifted from one that provided uniform experience for the good of society to a system that was concerned with individual and personal advancement" (King, 1988, p. 86).

In recent years increasing attention has been focused on the hidden curriculum as more has been learned about the strength of its influence. Particular concern exists about its negative influence. For example, the lessons of the hidden curriculum tend to promote conformity and in the process may stifle creativity and independent thinking. The hidden curriculum also teaches children to avoid conflict and change and to support the dominant orientation at all costs (Apple, 1979). Through the hidden curriculum, bias and stereotyping of race, gender, and class are reproduced and reinforced.

Controversial Issues:
The Subject-Centered and Student-Centered Curricula

The debate between the essentialists and others who support the subject-centered curriculum and the progressives and others who support a child-centered curriculum has continued unabated for almost a decade and appears likely to continue into the next century. Among the arguments the proponents of each orientation give are the following:

Arguments for the Subject-Centered Curricula

1. Introduces learners to the cultural heritage.

2. Gives teachers a sense of security by specifying what their responsibilities are for developing given skills and knowledge.

3. Reduces repetition or overlap between grade levels or different sections of the same class.

4. Increases the likelihood that learners will be exposed to knowledge and develop skills in an orderly manner.

5. Permits methodical assessment of pupil progress; assumes that knowledge is the only measurable outcome of learning experiences.

6. Facilitates cooperative group planning by educators in allocating the scope and sequence of learning experiences.

Arguments for the Student-Centered Curricula

1. Releases the teacher from the pressure to follow a prescribed scope and sequence that invariably does not meet all learners' needs.

2. Has a positive influence on learners as they find that instruction is varied to meet individual needs and purposes.

3. Encourages teacher judgment in selecting the content deemed most suitable for a group of learners.

4. Increases the likelihood that content has relevance to learners.

5. Modifies instruction to accommodate developmental changes and behavioral tasks as individual differences are identified and monitored.

6. Allows much more latitude for creative planning by the individual teacher.

What other arguments can you think of for the subject-centered or student-centered curriculum?

Source: Shane, H. G., & Tabler, M. B. (1981). *Educating for a new millennium* (pp. 79–80). Bloomington, IN: Phi Delta Kappa. Reprinted with permission.

Teachers affect the hidden curriculum through their own personalities, values, interests, strengths, and weaknesses, which they communicate as they teach the overt curriculum, establish and maintain order and discipline, and attend to their other responsibilities (McCutcheon, 1988). For this reason it is important that teachers understand their own philosophy of education (see Chapter 7). The important role of teachers in relation to the hidden curriculum is to become more conscious of it, to examine the social and political assumptions within the materials and practices they employ (Apple, 1988), and to find ways to take advantage of this important opportunity for learning. By doing this, teachers can reinforce the positive lessons of the hidden curriculum, ameliorate the negative lessons, and make the hidden curriculum more visible.

What impact might the hidden curriculum have on your role as a beginning teacher?

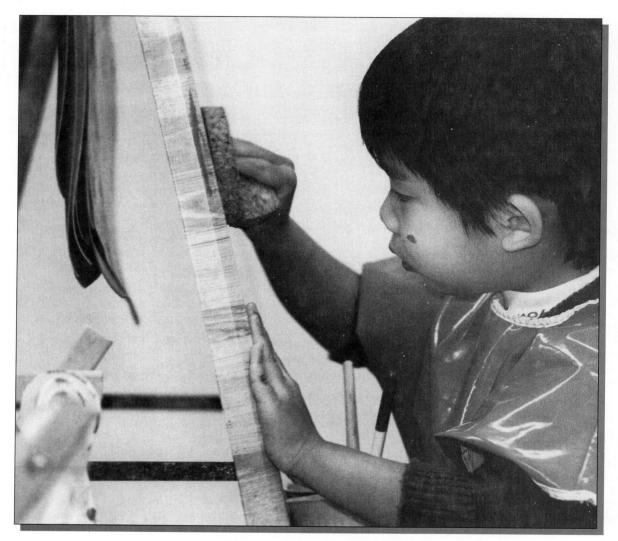

Students learn more in a responsible and stimulating learning environment.

The Curriculum Cycle

Throughout the twentieth century, the curriculum in America's schools has shifted between a subject-centered orientation and a student-centered orientation. The first two decades of the century were dominated by the progressive movement and its child-centeredness. In the wake of World War I came a more conservative political posture and a renewal of interest in a more orderly academic curriculum. Out of the social upheaval of the Great Depression emerged a more liberal voice that championed concern for the individual. In the 1950s, Conant's study of secondary schools, which underscored the need for greater attention to academic studies, was reinforced by the Soviet launching of Sputnik, and a curriculum reform movement was initiated aimed at strengthening mathematics, science, and foreign language offerings and providing greater rigor in all disciplines. The Great Society of the 1960s drove the cycle in the opposite direction. The open school and alternative school movements were the most visible reflections of the increased attention being focused on students. By the late 1970s many of the curricular innovations of the previous decade had disappeared, and again a call was heard for a return to the basic academic subjects and an elimination of the frills. This mood dominated the 1980s and has continued into the 1990s.

In the 1990s, the curricular reform cycle appears to be responding to the interest in national goals and performance standards. The unknown is the degree of attention that will be given to values education, decision making and critical thinking skills, development of self-esteem, and the individuality of students. For those who are concerned about the direction of the curriculum cycle, the consolation is that the cycle is short and directions change (McDaniel, 1989).

Summary

The decade of the 1990s has seen the school reform movement focus its attention on the curriculum in an effort to achieve what increasing core requirements and expenditures had not been able to do—increase student performance. The increased attention on the curriculum has served not only to highlight the controversy about various curriculum orientations, but to emphasize the sociopolitical context within which curriculum decisions are made.

The 1990s have brought a shift in the dominant curriculum orientation. The conservative, subject-centered approach that was emphasized by the first wave of reform reports is giving way to a more balanced approach that incorporates greater concern for national goals and performance standards. The involvement of various professional educational associations and the nation's governors in the reform arena should bring new force to curriculum change.

A curriculum standing alone is of little value. Not until it is implemented does it take on meaning. The process by which it is implemented, termed instruction, is discussed in the following chapter, along with the emerging issues and trends in curriculum and instruction.

Key Terms

Continuity	Integration
Core curriculum	National curriculum
Curriculum	National Goals for Education
Deschooling curriculum	Null curriculum
Free schools	Sequence
Hidden curriculum	Social reconstruction curriculum
Integrated curriculum	Subject-area curriculum

Discussion Questions

◇✕◇ 1. How can you as a teacher help children identify and reach their individual life goals? How does family dysfunction impact on school success? How can you provide your students with assistance while respecting their dignity and independence?

2. How would you define the terms *curriculum* and *hidden curriculum?* Should the lessons of the hidden curriculum be incorporated into the formal curriculum? If not, how can they be dealt with by the teacher? Should they be dealt with?

3. Which of the agencies or groups discussed in this chapter has had the most influence on the curriculum in your district in the last five years?

4. How will the national goals and standards movement impact on the professional life of the individual teacher?

5. Who should have the most input on textbook content? The author? The publisher? The user?

6. Which of the curricular designs discussed in this chapter is most consistent with your philosophy of education as identified in Chapters 6 and 7?

7. Describe the curriculum that would best prepare students for the twenty-first century.

References

Apple, M. W. (1979). *Ideology and curriculum.* Boston, MA: Routledge & Kegan Paul.

Apple, M. W. (1988). Hidden curriculum. In R. A. Gorton, G. T. Schneider, & J. C. Fisher (Eds.), *Encyclopedia of school administration* (p. 137). Phoenix, AZ: The Oryx Press.

Apple, M. W. (1993). *Official knowledge: Democratic education in a conservative age.* New York: Routledge.

Astuto, T., Clark, D., Read, A., McGree, K., & Fernandez, L. (1994). *Roots of reform: Challenging the assumptions that control change in education.* Bloomington, IN: Phi Delta Kappa Educational Foundation.

Bowers, C. A. (1984). *The promise of theory: Education and the politics of cultural change.* New York: Longman.

Cawelti, G. (1989). Designing high schools for the future. *Educational Leadership, 47*(1), 33.

Chira, S. (December 26, 1989). National standards for schools gain. *The New York Times National,* 10.

Committee for Economic Development. (1994). *Putting learning first: Governing and managing the schools for high achievement.* New York: Committee for Economic Development.

Cornbleth, C. (1988). Curriculum in and out of context. *Journal of Curriculum and Supervision, 3,* 85–96.

Counts, G. S. (1969). *Dare the schools build a new social order?* New York: John Dey.

Coley, R., & Goertz, M. (1990). *Educational standards in the 50 states: 1990.* Princeton, NJ: Educational Testing Service Policy Information Center.

Cremin, L. A. (1962). *The transformation of the school.* New York: Alfred A. Knopf.

Diegmueller, K. (1994a, September 7). Flap over English standards sparks strong words. *Education Week, 14,* 9.

Diegmueller, K. (1994b, September 28). Social studies council issues model standards for K–12 curriculum. *Education Week, 14,* 14.

Diegmueller, K. (1994c, September 28). Standards-setters hope to publish best sellers. *Education Week, 14,* 1, 15.

Eisner, E. (1994). *The educational imagination* (3rd ed.). New York: Macmillan.

Elam, S., Rose, L., & Gallup, A. (1994). The 26th annual Gallup Poll of the public's attitudes toward the public schools. *Phi Delta Kappan, 76,* 41–56.

Ellis, A. K., Mackey, J. A., & Glenn, A. D. (1988). *The school curriculum.* Boston, MA: Allyn and Bacon.

Elmore, R., & Fuhrman, S. (1994). Educational professionals and curriculum governance in R. Elmore & S. Fuhrman, (Eds.), *The governance of curriculum.* Alexandria, VA: Association for Supervision and Curriculum Development.

Finn, C. (1989). National standards for American education: A symposium. *Teachers College Record, 91*(1), 3–29.

Geography for life (1994). Washington: National Geographic Society.

Glatthorn, A. (1975). *Alternatives in education: Schools and programs.* New York: Dodd, Mead.

Goodlad, J. I. (1987). A new look at an old idea: Core curriculum. *Educational Leadership, 44*(4), 10.

Illich, I. (1973). After deschooling, what? In A. Gartner, C. Greer, & F. Riessman (Eds.), *After deschooling, what?* New York: Perennial Library.

King, S. E. (1988). Inquiring into the hidden curriculum. *Journal of Curriculum and Supervision, 2,* 86.

Lewis, A. C. (1990). Getting unstuck: Curriculum as a tool of reform. *Phi Delta Kappan, 71,* 534–538.

Lemonick, M. D. (1992). Tomorrow's lesson: Learn or perish. *Time.* special edition, fall, 59–60.

McCutcheon, G. (1988). Curriculum and the work of teachers. In L. E. Beyer & M. W. Apple (Eds.), *The Curriculum: Problems, politics, and possibilities* (pp. 191–203). Albany, NY: State University of New York.

McDaniel, T. R. (1989). Demilitarizing public education: School reform in the era of George Bush. *Phi Delta Kappan, 71,* 15–18.

Medrick, E., Brown, C., & Henke, R. (1992). *Overview and inventory of state requirements for course work and attendance.* NCES 92–663. Washington: National Center for Education Statistics, U.S. Department of Education.

Murphy, J. (1990). *The educational reform movement of the 1980s: Perspectives and cases.* Berkeley, CA: McCutchan.

National Governors Association. (1990). *National education goals.* Washington, DC: National Governors Association.

Olson, L. (1994a, August 3). Clinton expected to name standards board this month. *Education Week, 13,* 28.

Olson, L. (1994b, September 17). 'Fuzzy' talk on standards imperils reform. *Education Week, 14,* 12.

Ornstein, A. C., & Hunkins, F. P. (1988). *Curriculum: Foundations, principles, and issues.* Englewood Cliffs, NY: Prentice Hall.

Pitsch, M. (1994). Critics target Goals 2000 in schools "war." *Education Week, 14,*(7), 1, 21.

Portelli, J. P. (1987). On defining curriculum. *Journal of Curriculum and Supervision, 2,* 354–367.

Posner, G. (1992). *Analyzing the curriculum.* New York: McGraw-Hill.

Pratt, D. C. (1994). *Curriculum planning: A handbook for professionals.* Fort Worth, TX: Harcourt Brace.

Pulliam, J. D. (1991). *History of education in America* (5th ed.). Columbus, OH: Merrill.

Ravitch, D. (1983). *The troubled crusade.* New York: Basic Books.

Robinson, G., & Brandon, D. (1994). *NAEP test scores: Should they be used to compare and rank state educational quality?* Arlington, VA: Educational Research Service.

Skilbeck, M. (1989). Revitalizing the core curriculum. *Journal of Curriculum and Supervision, 4,* 198.

Smith, M., Fuhrman, S., & O'Day, J. (1994). Governors and education policy in the 1990s in R. Elmore & S. Fuhrman (Eds.), *The governance of curriculum.* Alexandria, VA: Association for Supervision and Curriculum Development.

Spring, J. (1991). *American education: An introduction to social and political aspects,* (5th ed.). New York: Longman.

Spring, J. (1989). *American education: An introduction to social and political aspects,* (4th ed.). New York: Longman.

Tyler, R. W. (1949). *Basic principles of curriculum and instruction.* Chicago: University of Chicago Press.

Walker, D. E., & Soltis, J. F. (1986). *Curriculum and aims.* New York: Teachers College Press, Columbia University.

Wiles, J., & Bondi, J. (1993). *Curriculum development* (4th ed.). New York: Merrill.

Chapter 15

Instructional Practices in Effective Schools

All education is a continuous dialogue —questions and answers that pursue every problem to the horizon.

William O. Douglas
Wisdom, *October 1956*

A Critical Incident in My Teaching Career . . .

During the second and third years of my teaching career, I taught a young man for two years in a row. I was teaching in middle school and taught social studies and reading. During my second year, I taught 7th grade and Jimmy was a nice, quiet student who sat in the front row and made a B. Still trying to develop my teaching skills I paid very little attention to Jimmy. The saying "The broken wheel gets the grease" applied to this situation. I was so busy with the bad students, I ignored the good ones and counted them among my blessings.

The next year I moved to the 8th grade and Jimmy was once again in my classroom. At the conclusion of that school year, all I still knew about Jimmy was that he was nice, quiet, sat in the front row and made a B. I taught this student 35 weeks and never made the effort to get to know him. This was inexcusable.

Four years later, when Jimmy was a senior, I had transferred to the same high school. I waved to Jimmy as he walked down the hall, but again I did not try to get to know his personality. The week after Jimmy graduated and on the eve of his wedding, he was killed in a car accident.

I now make every student on the first day of each semester write down something I should know about them. I then go on to build a relationship with each one of them. Jimmy taught me a valuable lesson.

Cathy Pittman
Teacher of the Year, Georgia

Instructional practices differ among schools, and exciting discussions are under way about the goals and objectives of education and the ways in which teachers and students interact. Increasing attention is being given to discussions about the characteristics of effective schools. As you study, observe, and analyze the practices found in today's classrooms and schools, this chapter should provide you with information that will help you to:

- Describe the difference between educational goals and instructional objectives.
- Relate the ways in which district goals, objectives, and outcomes will affect how a teacher organizes instruction and works with students.
- Discuss methods of organizing for instruction.
- Identify the components of mastery learning.

- Compare and contrast four different teaching strategies.
- Discuss the effect of technology on instruction.
- Discuss the characteristics of effective schools.
- Describe the current issues in curriculum and instruction.

Schools for All

The organization of America's schools and the ways that teachers work with students in the classroom are extensions of the overarching goals of American education. The schools and the classrooms are the arena in which the goal of free public instruction for all citizens is achieved.

This chapter reviews various instructional practices associated with good teaching and the characteristics of effective schools. Rather than advocating a particular approach, the focus is on different techniques and approaches that teachers may use for different purposes with different groups of students. First, attention is given to the importance of instructional goals and objectives in schools. The second section contains a discussion of how schools may be organized for instruction. Teaching strategies are discussed in the third section, followed by an overview of the concept of mastery learning. Next, we focus on some of the implications of technological developments on the instructional process. This section is followed by a discussion of the characteristics of effective schools.

Instructional Goals and Objectives

An overarching goal of American public education, and thus of states, school districts, and individual schools, has been to provide free public instruction for all citizens. This goal, together with more specific educational and instructional goals, should guide school districts and schools as they select educational and instructional objectives. The interaction between educational goals and objectives is discussed in the following paragraphs.

Educational Goals

In making decisions about education, the first issue is to decide what to teach. To make that decision, educators and policy makers need clearly defined goals and objectives for instruction and information about the roles and responsibilities of learners in relation to the specific goals and objectives.

Educational goals are broad general statements of desired learning outcomes (Kourilsky & Quaranta, 1987). Examples of goal statements are:

The learner will develop:

- basic math skills

- an appreciation of poetry

- an understanding of World War II

"Educational goals are changes in students toward which we want learning outcomes to lead" (Brookover, 1980). Rather than identifying specific skills, educational goals describe characteristics or attributes of what society considers to be a well-educated person. Goals are to be the result or cumulative effect of a series of learnings. Obviously, as defined, goals designate the desired outcome of instruction but lack the specificity to actually implement an instructional sequence (Kourilsky & Quaranta, 1987). That is where educational objectives come into play.

Educational Objectives

An *educational objective* is a clearly defined, observable, and measurable student behavior that indicates learner progress toward the achievement of a particular educational goal. Educational objectives also are referred to as instructional or behavioral objectives. An educational objective should meet the criteria listed in Figure 15.1.

Educational or instructional objectives are used to operationalize educational goals. Reference is often made to a more specific term, *behavioral objectives.* Unlike other types of educational objectives, behavioral objectives force the teacher to describe the learning outcomes from the learner's viewpoint. Behavioral objectives answer the questions "How do you know the learner has learned?" and "What is the learner to do to prove he/she has learned?" (Burns, 1977). Examples of behavioral objectives are shown in Figure 15.2.

Taxonomies of Educational Objectives

In the development of educational objectives, a taxonomy or classification system is needed. Benjamin S. Bloom has developed a widely used hierarchy of levels of intellectual behavior referred to in the literature as *Bloom's Taxonomy of Educational Objectives* (Bloom, 1956). The levels are listed in Figure 15.3. This hierarchy is helpful in delineating the increasingly complex levels of the intellectual process. It is also important when planning instruction to incorporate activities from the full range of levels in students' learning experiences to stimulate and develop their intellectual skills. This is especially true relative to helping students master what is popularly referred to as higher order thinking skills (HOTS). The higher order thinking skills in Bloom's Taxonomy are analysis, synthesis, and evaluation.

How can a teacher demonstrate democratic principles in the classroom?

Figure 15.1: Criteria for Educational Objectives

1. The place or condition for learning is established. Specific references should be made to the activity in which the goal is to be attained, i.e., test, game, laboratory experiment, recital, or report on an activity.

2. The learner's behavior is stated in measurable and observable terms. The types of evidence need to be stated clearly, i.e., completion of a specific test or experiment, completion of a recital, or submission of a written report.

3. The minimally acceptable level of performance is stated. Examples include the desired percentage of correct responses on the test, the maximum number of permissible errors in the recital, and the desired length of the report and number of permissible grammatical errors.

Source: Kourilsky, M., Quaranta, L. (1987). *Effective teaching: Principles and practice.* Glenview, IL: Scott, Foresman.

Figure 15.2: Examples of Educational or Behavioral Objectives

1. The student provides the correct answer for 90% or more of the items on the test.

2. The student places 50% or more of the arrows within six inches of the center of the target.

3. The student dissects the frog and correctly identifies and labels each part of the frog stipulated in the exercise.

4. The student is present for all rehearsals, arrives on time for the recital, and is error-free in the recital.

5. The student prepares a 10-page report on an activity with five or fewer spelling errors and no incomplete sentences.

Goals and objectives become the structure that schools and teachers use in determining how they will organize for instruction. As indicated in the following section, several different approaches are used.

Organizing for Instruction

Teachers and principals can be creative in organizing schools and students. Typically, students are treated as members of a group, but the group does not have to include the entire class; students may be clustered into smaller groups with similar interests or instructional needs. An alternative to group instruction is cooperative learning in which the teacher encourages students to work together in addressing problems; the teacher provides the initial leadership in defining the activity and functions as a resource person for the process. Another alternative is individualized instruction in which the teacher works with each student on a one-to-one basis diagnosing, prescribing, and evaluating progress. Independent learning can be viewed as an extension of individualized instruction, but the responsibility of the student is increased and the teacher is not as closely involved with the student. Additional descriptions of each of these types of instruction are found in the following discussion. Figure 15.4 summarizes the principal types of instruction with brief information about the teacher's role and an example of a typical activity. The description of the Montessori Method in the Historical Note on page 521 provides brief background information about a learning environment that focuses on sensory training and physical exercises.

Group Instruction

Much classroom teaching can be classified as *group instruction*. The teacher either views all students in the room as members of a single group or divides the class into subgroups. In the first instance, the setting is teacher dominated. Various instructional strategies may be used, but individualization often is sacrificed in an effort to accommodate the needs and interests of the group.

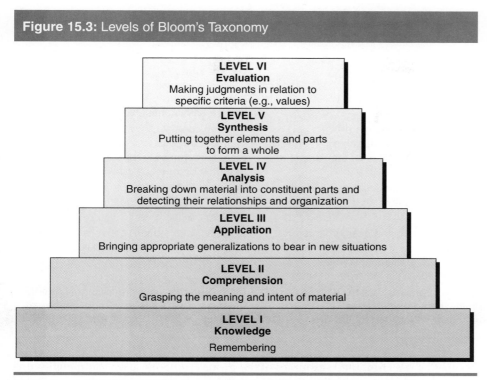

Figure 15.3: Levels of Bloom's Taxonomy

LEVEL VI
Evaluation
Making judgments in relation to
specific criteria (e.g., values)

LEVEL V
Synthesis
Putting together elements and parts
to form a whole

LEVEL IV
Analysis
Breaking down material into constituent parts and
detecting their relationships and organization

LEVEL III
Application
Bringing appropriate generalizations to bear in new situations

LEVEL II
Comprehension
Grasping the meaning and intent of material

LEVEL I
Knowledge
Remembering

Source: Kourilsky, M., & Quaranta, L. (1987). *Effective teaching: Principles and practice.* Glenview
IL: Scott, Foresman.

When subgroups are used, the role of the teacher changes. Major portions of the teacher's time are spent planning, coordinating, and monitoring the activities of the subgroups. For the groups to function, students must assume more responsibility for their learning. The capacity of the group to teach itself is enhanced because students typically are assigned to subgroups on the basis of special needs or interests.

A major challenge for the teacher in group instruction is to develop ways to organize teaching/learning activities for the entire group, while at the same time recognizing individual differences among students. Thus, in planning the group activities, the teacher also must be sensitive to the needs of individual students.

Cooperative Learning

In *cooperative learning*, the class consists of students working in small groups rather than as individuals. The groups often are considered to be heterogeneous in terms of contribution and/or classroom performance, and students have the opportunity to learn from their peers. The result of this interaction is a higher noise level in the classroom, sometimes referred to as the "busy hum of learning." Peers are rewarded for helping one another. Rather than being in competition with each other, students experience a sense of interdependence; they have a reduced likelihood of failure and an increased probability of success

Figure 15.4: Types of Instruction

Type of Instruction	Teacher's Role	Typical Activity
Group instruction	Provides formal instruction Monitors class activity	American history: Teacher gives formal lecture on historical facts.
Cooperative learning	Sets the stage for learning Facilitates groups of students Organizes the structure of the classroom	U.S. presidents: Class is divided into teams of three or four students. Each team is responsible for conducting research on one U.S. president.
Individualized instruction	Acts as resource person Guides and monitors student's learning	Reading: Each student is assigned a different short story according to his/her reading ability.
Independent instruction	Negotiates topics and assignments with students Consults and advises students Evaluates student's learning activities	English: Each student consults individually with the teacher and is given a special essay topic.
Mastery learning	Provides formal instruction Administers formative tests Provides feedback to students	Math: students work progressively through the basic math facts (e.g., addition before subtraction).

because of the combined resources of the group. Depending on the specific content, teachers can vary their instructional approach. The teacher still has responsibility for setting the stage and working with students, but students work in groups rather than as individuals (Brandt, 1989).

How can a teacher work with a group of students and still individualize instruction?

The positive effects of cooperative learning in elementary and secondary schools appear to be associated with two essential elements—group goals and individual accountability (Slavin, 1989). By working together, students have the opportunity to exercise leadership and also reap the benefits of other indicators of group success. As individuals, they are responsible for their personal performance and achievement. Peer tutors and support groups can be especially useful in breaking down some of the barriers found in multicultural schools.

For several reasons, the use of cooperative learning as the organizing scheme in the classroom is likely to increase. First, research findings are positive. Students who have had good experiences in cooperative learning are more willing to participate in the instructional approach and will have a higher level of confidence as they become involved. Second, the likelihood of cooperative learning becoming more commonplace also is enhanced because this approach is frequently employed in preservice and in-service education for teachers. Last, and possibly most important, students and teachers seem to enjoy this method of organizing the classroom for instruction (Slavin, 1989).

Individualized Instruction

Individualizing instruction for each student is a worthy but difficult goal. Traditionally, schools have been organized to provide instruction for groups of

Historical Note:
Maria Montessori and the Montessori Method

Maria Montessori was the first woman in Italy to receive a medical degree. Her early career involved working with retarded children at the University of Rome psychiatric clinic and pedagogical school that prepared teachers of the mentally retarded and emotionally disturbed. The methods she developed were extended to normal children at her first Casa dei Bambino (Children's House), opened in 1907 in a Roman slum area. This gave her an opportunity to test and perfect ideas, methods, and materials. The school proved so successful that other Montessori schools were established in Rome and other cities.

The Montessori Method, as it came to be called, emphasizes sensory training using a set of materials and physical exercises developed by Montessori. Intent and motivation are at the heart of the method. Materials are intended to arouse the student's inter-est, and interest provides the motivation for learning. Instruction is highly individualized and is designed to develop self-discipline and self-confidence.

Through numerous lectures and extensive writings, Dr. Montessori disseminated her ideas, and educators from throughout the world came to Italy to observe her program and be trained in her approach. By 1915, almost 100 Montessori schools were in operation in the United States. In 1929, the International Montessori Association was formed. Montessori fled fascist Italy for Spain in 1934, and worked in several places in Europe and Asia before her death in 1952. Although the Montessori Method has been considered controversial by many educators since its inception, today thousands of Montessori schools operate in virtually every country in the world.

students. When the group approach is not successful in addressing the specific instructional needs of a few students, *individualized instruction* often is used as an alternative. The teacher assumes the role of a resource person who guides and monitors the student's learning rather than providing formal instruction in a traditional class setting.

Individualized instruction also may be used to cope with teaching and/or learning differences in the classroom. The approach can be especially effective as teachers work with gifted and talented students or slow learners in the same classroom.

Independent Learning

In this organizational option, topics or assignments are negotiated between the student and the teacher on an individual basis. Then students assume personal responsibility for their learning; the role of the teacher is to facilitate the process. The teacher functions first as a consultant/adviser to the student and later as an evaluator of the student's learning activities.

Rather than being an option restricted to gifted and talented students, *independent learning* can be used with most students. As they work independently, students learn to set goals, plan their learning, and assume personal responsibility for their programs. Students thus assume an increased level of responsibility for their own schooling. The teacher's responsibilities are different with different students. Success is measured by the extent to which the student completes the topics or assignments in a timely manner at the predetermined level of quality.

Cooperative learning provides an opportunity for students to learn by working togeth-er with the teacher serving as a resource person. These experiences provide a model for lifelong learning.

Mastery Learning

Mastery learning is more than an organizational option; it is a process for teach-ing and learning. Benjamin S. Bloom of the University of Chicago is the person most commonly associated with mastery learning. The two basic assumptions of mastery learning are that (a) most learning units are sequential; thus, the con-cepts from one unit are built upon and extended by the next unit; and (b) all students can learn at the mastery level if the learning units are small enough. Mastery learning is generally taught through group instruction and, therefore, is primarily teacher centered. Table 15.1 shows the major differences between mastery learning and other systems of instruction (Guskey, 1985).

The mastery learning instructional format assumes that the teacher presents the learning unit and then administers what is called the first formative test. The purpose of the test is to check learning progress and provide the students with feedback and suggestions to help them overcome any difficulties they are expe-riencing. Following the test, students who have not mastered the material are provided corrective work for a few class periods. Then a second parallel test is administered to ensure that the students have achieved mastery before the class moves on to the next learning unit. Students who demonstrated mastery on the first formative test are given enrichment activities during the corrective phase of instruction. Figure 15.5 illustrates the mastery learning instructional process.

Table 15.1: Major Differences Between Mastery Learning and Personalized Systems of Instruction

	Model	
Characteristic	Mastery Learning	Personalized Systems of Instruction
Basis of instruction	Group	Individual
Pace of instruction	Teacher determined	Student determined
Primary source of instruction	Teacher, supplemented by materials	Materials, supplemented by the teacher
Standard of mastery	80–90%	100%
Number of retake tests per unit	One	As many as needed for mastery
Correctives	New and different approach	Repetition of original material
Major applications	Elementary and secondary levels	College level

Mastery learning as a process has been especially popular with researchers involved in effective schools research. The concept enables the teacher to address the special needs of students in multicultural environments. Critics, however, assert that the process has been oversimplified, that mastery of the individual units does not necessarily transfer to future learning, and that students cannot be expected to learn and achieve at the mastery level indefinitely.

Teaching Strategies

Effective teachers use different strategies, tactics, or methods depending on their personal talents, the content to be taught, and the interests and abilities of the students. As discussed in Chapter 1, teaching is often described as an art. This does not imply that teachers operate without design or planning; rather, it underscores the need for teachers to understand and be able to use a variety of strategies as they work with students.

Teaching has also been described as a craft or an applied science (Tom, 1984). In fact, it may be inappropriate to assume that teaching should take a single form. Adler (1984) refers to three types of teaching—didactic instruction, coaching, and Socratic questioning. In didactic teaching, students acquire knowledge by becoming actively engaged in instruction through question and answer strategies. Coaching calls on the teacher to prepare the student for exhibiting a skill in public. Socratic questioning does not assume that the teacher or the student knows all the answers; the goal is to develop an understanding of ideas and values. Adler's ideal teacher possesses a blend of instructional skills, judgment about student understanding of the material, expertise on

Figure 15.5: The Mastery Learning Instructional Process: (a) Instructional Sequence and (b) Achievement Distribution Curve in a Mastery Learning Classroom

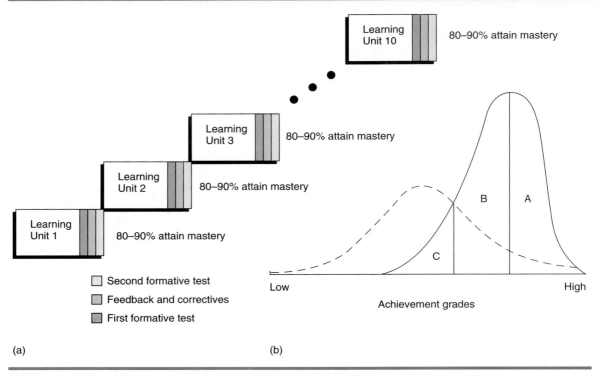

Source: Adapted from Guskey, T. (1985). *Implementing mastery learning.* Belmont, CA: Wadsworth.

the subject matter, and the capacity to communicate effectively with individuals and groups (Duke, 1984).

Models of instruction may be grouped into five categories: expository, demonstration, inquiry or discovery, critical thinking, and independent learning. Rather than selecting a single method of instruction, the effective teacher should be familiar with, and understand, how to use a variety of methods in response to different teaching/learning opportunities. Summary information on the models of instruction is presented in Figure 15.6.

Expository Instruction

Expository instruction, a teacher-centered method, gets its name from exposition, which is the discourse designed to convey information. The most common forms of expository instruction are formal lecture, informal lecture, and teacher-led discussion. Expository instruction is considered appropriate when (a) all students need to know an essential body of knowledge and (b) the students are relatively homogeneous in their ability and knowledge of the topic.

Through the use of modern technology in many of today's classrooms, teachers can provide students with access to a wide range of learning resources and activities.

Teacher Role

In expository instruction, the teacher controls and directs the learning process and determines the methods of presentation, the pace of instruction, the quantity of supervised practice or reinforcement, and the form of student evaluation. The role of the student is to "follow the leader." The student is expected to listen, read, and answer questions as the teacher directs.

Resources

Appropriate instructional resources for expository instruction include filmstrips, films, slides, videotapes, and guest speakers. These resources are used to summarize and reinforce information or skills already provided through teacher-centered instruction. The most common forms of evaluation are standardized tests or teacher-written criterion-referenced tests.

Potential Problems

Expository instruction works effectively in small segments. Several weaknesses emerge when this method is the primary method of instruction. First, expository or lecture instruction can result in the teacher being especially vulnerable to manipulation by students. For example, if the teacher is diverted, instruction

Figure 15.6: Models of Instruction

	Teacher's Role	Student's Role	Strengths
Expository instruction	• Teacher-centered • Controls and directs the learning process • Determines methods of presentation	• Follow the leader • Listens, reads, and answers teacher-directed questions	• Best method for students grouped homogeneously by ability
Demonstration instruction	• Plans, organizes, and conducts the demonstration	• Observes, listens, and participates as directed	• Retention is enhanced by active participation
Inquiry or discovery instruction	• Guides the learning process • Stimulates and challenges learners	• Student-centered activities • Self-directed critical thinking and problem solving	• Encourages higher order thinking skills • Challenges gifted/talented students
Critical thinking	• Facilitates the learning process • "Nondirected" • Stimulates and challenges learners • Empowers students	• Finds out information for themselves • Asks questions, rather than being asked questions	• Encourages higher order thinking skills and problem solving
Independent Instruction	• Provides the stage for learning • Provides resources • Provides individual instruction	• Exercises initiative and responsibility • Reports progress to teacher • Establishes own learning pace	• Frees teacher to work individually with students

ceases. Another weakness of expository teaching is that the second assumption associated with the method—homogeneity of the students—is seldom met.

The principles underlying this method are not consistent with the current emphasis on individualizing instruction to meet the diverse needs of students and to stem the tide of student dropouts. Causes of, and solutions for, the dropout problem are complex, but the consensus appears to be that overdependence on teacher-centered and teacher-dominated instruction contributes to students dropping out of school. One of the reasons is that expository teaching assumes that the student has a level of preknowledge that often is not present. Thus, the student is quickly frustrated and feels lost. These feelings compound

Weaknesses	Resources	Evaluation
• Principles not consistent with meeting the needs of individual students	• Filmstrips • Films • Slides • Video tapes • Guest speakers	• Standardized tests • Teacher-written criterion-referenced tests
• Students must have prior knowledge to benefit from demonstration	• Science labs • Computer labs • Drama classrooms • Specialized materials	• Written exams • Student products (e.g., lab reports, computer programs discussion, etc.)
• Takes a sophisticated learner to really be effective	• Topics and ideas for exploration • Research tools	• Oral and written student reports • Standardized tests that focus on higher order thinking skills and problem solving
• Many teachers find this method difficult	• Topics and ideas for exploration • Research tools	• Standardized tests that focus on higher order thinking skills and problem solving • Open-ended questions
• Difficult to orient students to work independently	• Learning packets • Teaching kits • Reading machines • Computers	• Written exams • Student products • Oral and written student reports

themselves until the learner simply gives up and drops out of school at the first opportunity (Barone, 1989; Cuban, 1989).

In elementary and secondary schools expository instruction can be effective. However, the teacher who uses the method should keep in mind that students differ in their levels of competence and that expository instruction requires more extensive and detailed daily lesson planning. Some would contend that lectures virtually need to be scripted. The structure and direction of the lecture or discussion should be obvious to the learner. Further, even with extensive preparation and a quality presentation, the teacher must realize that portions of the information contained in a lecture will have to be repeated or retaught.

Demonstration Instruction

In *demonstration instruction,* the student learns through doing and/or observing. This method includes laboratory experiments, dramatizations, constructions, recitations, and exhibitions. Demonstration instruction is assumed appropriate when (a) the student's level of understanding will be enhanced by observing or working with a functioning model or guide, and (b) the student has sufficient background and maturity to understand the value or relevance of the demonstration.

Teacher Role

The teacher's role is to plan, organize, and in most cases conduct the demonstration. Additional responsibilities include emphasizing and clarifying those portions of the demonstration activity especially related to the desired learning outcomes. For example, the teacher demonstrates to students how to dissect a frog. The student's role is to observe, listen, and participate as directed. Usually, the teacher will supervise closely the first cut with a scalpel. Then, after the demonstration and the initial supervised activity, the student becomes more independent. The merits of this method are that retention is enhanced if the student, in addition to observing, is able to become actively involved in the teaching/learning activity.

Resources

The required resources for demonstration instruction generally make this method relatively expensive. Fully equipped science laboratories, computer laboratories, and drama classrooms all require specialized equipment and instructional materials. Evaluation may be by written examination; however, it may be more appropriate to evaluate students' products in the form of laboratory reports, computer programs, discussion, or recitation because students can model what has been demonstrated.

Potential Problems

Properly conducted and supervised, this methodology can be most effective; however, the learner must have sufficient prior knowledge to benefit from the demonstration. For this reason, demonstration instruction is often preceded by expository instruction. The teacher's ability to teach skills is critical to the effectiveness of this methodology. The teacher must be capable of conducting the demonstration effectively. For example, the teacher who "cannot carry a tune" is not the teacher who should sing the scale in a vocal music class. The demonstration should relate directly to the specific instructional objectives; if it does not, the demonstration may be merely an effort to entertain students.

Inquiry Instruction

Inquiry instruction was first made popular in America by John Dewey at the beginning of this century. (See Chapter 5 for additional discussion.) Subsequently, other authors have referred to this method of instruction as problem solving, the inductive method, creative thinking, the scientific method, or conceptual learning. Irrespective of the title, the essential elements of each approach are basically the same as those identified by Dewey.

Reflective thinking or inquiry takes place when a person is faced with a problem or forced choice. The five phases of reflective thinking are (a) suggestion (selection of topic), (b) intellectualization (exploratory discussion), (c) hypothesis (educated or informed guess about the outcome), (d) reasoning (drawing of inferences or conclusions based on facts), and (e) testing of the hypothesis (Massialas & Zevin, 1983). Each phase is part of a well-designed *inquiry instruction*. The activity is student centered; the most common forms are oral and written student reports and nonmathematical problem-solving activities.

In contrast to other forms of instruction or teaching, the "transmission of the accumulated knowledge and wisdom of a culture" is not the primary role of inquiry instruction (Skinner, 1965). Students use the process to develop a better understanding of current knowledge and create new knowledge.

Teacher Role

In inquiry instruction, activities are student centered and the task for the teacher is to help the learner become a self-directed critical thinker and problem solver. Rather than imparting knowledge in a structured learning environment, the teacher guides students through the inquiry process and challenges them to develop the skills inherent in the inquiry process. The goal is for students to understand the discipline of the process and appreciate the rigor inherent in inquiry instruction.

Resources

The concept of inquiry instruction assumes that (a) students have the tools needed, i.e., sufficient reading ability to follow the directions and successfully complete the lesson; (b) students are self-directed enough to enjoy the process and not be frustrated; (c) the activity is student centered and thus gives additional responsibility to the student; and (d) students are sufficiently sophisticated in higher order thinking skills to progress from one inductive level to another.

Potential Problems

Successful inquiry instruction is dependent upon the effective interaction of sophisticated students and teachers in a supportive learning environment. Students and teachers must be comfortable with the challenges associated with the student-centered dimensions of the inquiry process. Successful inquiry instruction in today's educational environment requires that students have easy access to research tools and educational technology and be free to use them at their own pace.

Critical Thinking Instruction

With the development of *critical thinking* as the instructional goal, the student becomes more active and responsible and the teacher becomes less dominant. The teacher organizes and provides direction for student learning, but the student is an active rather than passive participant.

What different teaching styles have you encountered in your schooling?

Analytic or higher order thinking skills are the central elements in the process of critical thinking. Students who become critical thinkers can view problems in different dimensions and consider problems in a larger context. They seek maximum information before deciding on a course of action. Rather than finding quick and simple solutions to complex problems, critical thinkers not only examine the particular problem as an individual issue but also consider it in the larger dimension of related issues (Ellis, Mackey, & Glenn, 1988). Teachers and students become active in identifying and seeking solutions to problems. The process of critical thinking is illustrated in Figure 15.7.

Teacher Role

The teacher is no longer the center of activity. In the critical thinking or inquiry model, the teacher is a guide, facilitator, stimulator, even a cheerleader who challenges learners. In essence, the teacher abdicates his/her position and empowers students. By empowering students, the teacher no longer monopolizes the learning process; thus, the term *nondirected* is often applied to the teacher's role. To an extent this is a misnomer, for the teacher does direct, but in a less visible manner. The teacher must plan carefully the topics and ideas the class will explore, organize and time the various activities, and arrange to make available the resources the students will use. The teacher often assumes the role of devil's advocate; students are usually forced to defend and explain their positions. At the conclusion of the activity, the teacher summarizes, recaps, and asks students

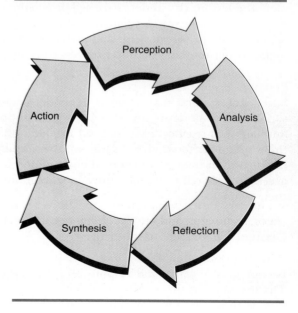

Figure 15.7: The Process of Critical Thinking

for clarification. Students are the focus of inquiry instruction; they take the initiative to find out for themselves, and they ask questions rather than being asked. Students are free to explore. Evaluation focuses on the students' ability to internalize and apply content to other situations. Options for evaluation include standardized tests that focus on higher order thinking skills, problem solving, and critical thinking as well as open-ended questions.

Resources

Critical thinking requires that students have independent access to the range of learning materials and research tools that they will need in their studies. In today's educational arena, this would require easy access to the full range of computer programs and information retrieval systems. Students likely will go beyond the school walls and secure resources and information from various community agencies and businesses.

Potential Problems

The problems associated with this mode of instruction are primarily an outgrowth of teachers' experiences as students; teachers tend to teach as they were taught. For this reason, teachers often have difficulty adapting to change. Most teachers were taught by expository instruction; to teach and help students learn differently requires a totally new orientation. Modeling of critical thinking or inquiry instruction is something few teachers have observed, let alone experienced as a method of learning.

Independent Learning

A range of student-centered teaching methodologies may be used in independent learning. They include programmed instruction, self-paced instruction, contract learning, and performance-based instruction, which are often collectively labeled personalized systems of instruction (PSI). These methodologies are individually based, student-paced instructional models in which students learn independently of their classmates. A PSI may be an appropriate mode of instruction if the following assumptions are held by the teacher: (a) students are not homogeneous; (b) as they mature, students' heterogeneity increases; and (c) most students will learn best if allowed to learn at their own pace.

Teacher Role

The teacher's role is to provide the stage for learning. This includes providing both the various instructional materials and a stress-free environment. Much as in inquiry instruction, the teacher using PSI assumes the role of learning facilitator, stimulator, and informational resource. The primary role of the teacher in a PSI classroom is to provide individual instruction. Whole class presentations are usually informational rather than an opportunity for instruction (Guskey, 1985). Optimally, the teacher sets goals and, with individual students, establishes the criteria and means for evaluating each student's learning. The student's role is crucial; the student must exercise initiative and responsibility. The student reports progress to the teacher at prescribed, regular intervals and establishes his/her own learning pace.

Resources

Instructional materials for PSI vary greatly. They include teacher-written learning packets, sophisticated programmed teaching kits, the spectrum of reading machines, and computer-programmed or assisted instruction. Ideally, a PSI classroom would resemble a mini instructional media center more than a classroom.

Potential Problems

Evaluation under most forms of PSI bears little resemblance to traditional forms of evaluation because the focus of instruction is on how well the students use the tools of learning—reading, writing, and speaking—to solve problems and think critically. The PSI setting may provide reward systems for purposes of providing motivation, feedback, and discipline (Womack, 1989).

A classroom operating exclusively under a PSI format is a rarity. One of the largest potential problems with the PSI format is that, once established, the system can run so smoothly that teachers feel they have nothing to do and end up behind their desks. Rightfully, under this mode of instruction, the teacher is liberated to work individually with students. Another potential problem is that administrators accustomed to the more traditional teacher-centered forms of instruction have difficulty evaluating both PSI instruction and the teacher using the methodology. A final problem is how to orient students effectively so that they can work independently and sustain their self-motivation.

How will you as a teacher determine the instructional strategy that you will use in the classroom?

Relationships Between Learning and Teaching

Various proposals to reform, reinvent, and restructure schools as ways to improve education have come from both public and private sources. Many of the recommendations have focused on the mandates and admonitions designed to change school operation or programs as a means to improve student performance. Major emphasis has been placed on modifying the structure or the decision making process. However, one of the problems with education reform is that the simplistic prescriptions are not consistent with what educational research says about teaching and learning. After a decade of school reform recommendations, questions are being raised about whether sufficient attention is being given to the most critical consideration—the relationship between how teachers teach and how children learn. Marzano (1992) has indicated that the challenge is to base school reform decisions on what is known about how children learn.

One teaching-learning model that incorporates virtually all of the types of instruction discussed earlier in this chapter has been presented by Marzano (1992). In proposing the concept of dimensions of learning, Marzano has relied on six basic assumptions. First, research about learning should be reflected in instruction. Second, learning is a complex process that involves five types of

If teaching and learning are active, participative processes, students will develop the higher order thinking skills needed to acquire and integrate knowledge in solving problems.

thinking—the five dimensions of learning. Third, large interdisciplinary themes are the most effective way to promote learning. Fourth, students should be explicitly taught higher-level attitudes and mental habits that facilitate learning. Fifth, two types of instruction should be used—teacher directed and student directed. Sixth, assessment should focus on students' use of knowledge and complex reasoning rather than on recall of low-level information. This process of learning involves five dimensions:

1. Positive attitudes and perceptions about learning

2. Thinking involved in acquiring and integrating knowledge

3. Thinking involved in extending and refining knowledge

4. Thinking involved in using knowledge meaningfully

5. Productive habits of mind

Planning models for utilizing the concept assume that dimensions 1 and 5 (positive attitudes and productive habits) will be addressed in all curricular units; they constitute the environment for learning. The concept's three broad planning models focus on acquisition and integration of knowledge, application of knowledge to an issue, and student exploration of issues and questions. Traditional student assessment procedures may not be sufficient indicators of student learning under this concept; consideration likely will be given to authentic assessment procedures based on successful completion of meaningful-use tasks and other evidence, such as portfolios (Marzano, 1992). As learning activities change, the teacher changes roles so that student learning opportunities are maximized. Thus, students are prepared for their days of independent learning when formal schooling has been completed.

Technology and Instruction

Recent and projected technological developments provide immense opportunities to expand the instructional capacities of teachers and learning opportunities for students. (See Chapter 16 for a further discussion of technologies.) Educators and policy makers face a series of opportunities and challenges as they search for effective uses of technology in learning and instruction, and for the resources required to implement technology in schools. The challenge is for schools to use technology as a tool that will open the doors to new ways of learning. Technology enhances opportunities for student growth and should be used to educate students who can think for themselves (Snider, 1992).

The challenge for decision makers is to create a vision that recognizes the potential uses of technology in education so that schools become informed and discriminating users of technology rather than captives of the latest fad. A second challenge is for teachers to view technology as a tool to improve current and future learning for all students. As this occurs, the traditional fears that the human element will be displaced by technology will be replaced by a recognition that human relations can be enhanced by the use of technology. Finally, technological tools are effective only to the degree that the users are trained and informed as to their potential. Installation of instructional technology in a school is expensive in terms of both dollars and staff time; therefore, decisions to acquire technology should include sufficient resources to train both student and teacher users (Apple, 1988).

Technology has the potential for expanding curricular opportunities and affecting classrooms in a variety of ways. Various national efforts have been made to expand the use of technology. Instructional television via satellite transmission brings outstanding instructors into classrooms in isolated areas. Both teachers and students have the opportunity to learn through this activity. Media such as videotapes may be used repeatedly to enhance the understanding of complex concepts. Significant advancements have been made in information retrieval systems through telephone linkages between computers. For example, a teacher can access research information (e.g., the ERIC system) related to the improvement of teaching and learning. The development of the compact disc and international electronic network technology brings to each student's desktop computer instantaneous access to information in libraries and other depositories throughout the world.

Teacher Uses of Technology

One of the continuing barriers to expanded use of technology in the classroom is that some teachers fail to recognize the ways in which technology can be used to increase their efficiency in the classroom. Rather than presenting information and issuing instructions in the traditional format, technology enables the teacher to devote more time to working with individual students and addressing their particular problems. Rather than speaking to the group of students, the teacher can use technology for the group instruction. The teacher then can function more as a guide or facilitator in working with individual students or groups of students in the teaching/learning process (Lemonick, 1992).

As more teachers who have had experience with technology as students enter the classroom, the classroom uses of technology likely will expand. Currently, some districts have automated many of the menial routine classroom tasks so that teachers can devote more time to working directly with students. This permits teachers to use their time more efficiently. The greater challenge is for all teachers, and especially those in isolated settings with limited resource materials, to recognize and use the resources available in the rapidly expanding information highway. Databases and literary works formerly available only in affluent schools can now be accessed in any school. Rather than being limited to print materials available in the local school, teachers now can use resources from throughout the world in planning their lessons and developing instructional materials for students. For these uses to become commonplace, it has become obvious that increased resources are needed to provide all teachers with comprehensive in-service training programs in the use of technology (Castor, 1993). If teachers are to maximize their use of computers, they should be available in their school workrooms, classrooms, and homes. Computers become tools for active learning and empower both students and teachers (Callister & Dunn, 1992).

Technology provides teachers with the opportunity to change the ways that they teach and enhance learning opportunities for students. Teachers can devote greater portions of their time to preparation of learning experiences for students. Instructional units can be prepared and stored so that students can access the information at their convenience. With technology, greater emphasis can be placed on small group learning activities rather than formal teacher lectures. Diverse students working together can share learning experiences. When teachers use technology as a teaching tool, students have the opportunity to access the original material rather than relying on lecture notes. As teachers become more proficient in the use of technology, they can become facilitators who address individual needs, gather materials, and structure learning opportunities for students (Solomon, 1993).

The expanding availability of CD-ROM products is providing teachers with access to information in a variety of forms other than print materials. The number of school districts using CD-ROMs has increased from 3% in 1989 to 43% in 1994; the number of buildings is estimated to be 29% ("Common Measures," 1994). Teachers and students can access songs, pictures, audio tapes of speeches, and interactive pictures of bodies moving in orbit. Research advancements have the potential of creating *virtual reality* through technology in the next few decades. With special goggles and bodysuits, technology will provide visual

As a teacher, what kinds of decisions would you like to make in the school in which you are teaching?

How did conditions in your school affect your performance as a student?

images, smells, and sounds that will make an indelible impression. The contention is that this technology will enable teachers to create learning experiences that give students the simulated experience of being transported to distant places such as Mount Everest or planets in space (Lemonick, 1992).

Effective use of these materials requires that old instructional habits will have to be broken. Rather than imparting information, the *good* teacher will pose questions and design challenging educational activities. As stated earlier, staff development activities are critical so that teachers can both develop a better understanding of how students learn and create effective learning opportunities for students (November, 1993).

Student Uses of Technology

Progress has been made in providing students with access to computers. Since 1984, the number of students per computer has dropped from 125 to 14 ("Common Measures," 1994). Picciano (1994) has classified student uses of computers into three broad applications: tutor, tool, and tutee. Tutorial applications include drill and practice, tutorials, simulation, and instructional games and problem solving. Tool applications include word processing, spreadsheets, and database software. Tutee applications include various programming languages.

Figure 15.8: Students Per Computer Per Year

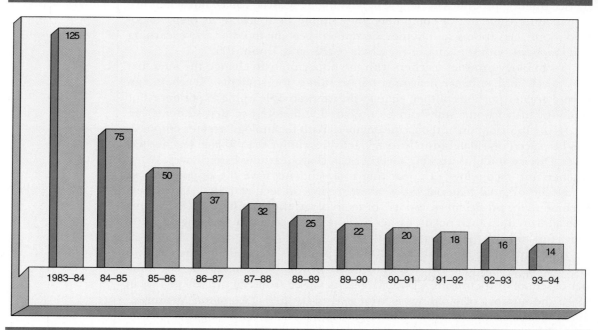

Tutor Applications

Tutor applications empower both the student and teacher by reducing the need for direct personal contact and providing opportunities for students to progress at different rates. In addition to supporting regular instructional activities, tutor applications also can be used for remedial or enrichment purposes.

The assumptions for *drill and practice* are that students have already received basic instruction and that the computer can be used for mastery learning. The computer applications reinforce a lesson or material that has been presented to the student. Students learn at different rates, and the computer provides the opportunity for individualized, self-paced learning. The computer provides immediate feedback, automatic adjustments to the student's rate of progress, and record keeping.

Tutorial programs are an extension of drill and practice, but the intent is to teach something new. Though limited by the instructions used in the program, tutorial programs provide an artificial person who responds to the student. The goal is to maximize the student's educational performance. One of the limitations is that typical tutorial programs assume an orderly progression in learning and have difficulty with the quantum leaps and reflective thinking of some students. However, tutorial programs are especially valuable when students are ill or live in isolated areas or when teachers of a specialized subject are not available.

Simulation provides the student with the potential to maximize the computer's capabilities and expand learning opportunities. Rather than being restricted by programs prepared by others, the student writes the instructions and uses the computer to solve problems. The student develops higher order thinking skills by becoming involved in the orderly progression of steps involved in addressing a problem. A major benefit of simulation is that efforts to address problems are made in a safe and artificial setting. The results of the simulation can then be used in determining the options to be considered in real-life situations.

Instructional games and problem solving provide students with the opportunity to compete among themselves or to compete with the computer. One of the reservations with this application is that some instructional games are poorly designed, but many are well done and have instructional value. Instructional games are especially useful as supplemental activities; they add some variety to the student's day. Many are more useful with elementary school students, but some are appropriate for secondary students. Obviously, teachers should preview the materials to verify their usefulness and relevance for the content area and the age group.

Tool Applications

Tool applications provide opportunities for students to expand their learning opportunities, improve their performance, and develop skills that will enhance their abilities as independent learners.

The initial uses of *word processing* typically are to teach writing as a process in which a student writes, revises, and rewrites until satisfied with the effort. Word processing software makes revisions easy by avoiding retyping; the result is a better written product without excessive effort. With spell check and grammar check programs, students can develop quality products. However, as with the hand calculator, some persons question if students should have access to the spell check and grammar check programs. As desktop publishing software has become available, students have the opportunity to produce visually stimulating quality material.

Spreadsheets also empower students and permit them to manipulate numbers in a manner that would be impossible with hand calculators or electronic adding machines. Spreadsheets take the drudgery out of hand calculations. The challenge is to ensure that students not only develop a sufficient level of basic competency in their mathematical skills, but also develop an understanding of alternative formulas as tools for problem solving. In many instances, the understanding of the formula is more important than expending energies on repetitive calculations.

Databases provide students with the opportunity to develop data storage and searching skills. National and international databases are expanding at an exponential rate; students can access information in libraries, public agencies, and private sources throughout the world. Students can use database software to build their own databases for class projects or continuing learning opportunities. Massive databases can be transmitted electronically for students to use in class projects. Kindergarten students can receive responses from scientists in such agencies as the National Aeronautical and Space Administration. With the federal emphasis on creating an *information highway,* classrooms and homes throughout the nation will have immediate access to information formerly available only in a few large research libraries or governmental agencies.

Tutee Applications

Tutee applications assume that students and teachers learn how to program a computer to do a particular task. Rather than being a tool or resource used to solve a problem in a given class, the goal is to learn how the computer functions. This requires that students develop an understanding of programming languages; programming requires that students learn rules, syntax, and logic constructs.

Given the pace at which knowledge about information processing and retrieval is expanding, the challenge for both teachers and students will not be to learn specific subject content, but to learn how to learn. By the time schools identify what technical information or skills to teach, the content often is obsolete. When confronted with a problem in the technological age, the student will not be expected to recall from memory the necessary information; rather, the student will be expected to secure the desired information by utilizing various data retrieval systems. The challenge will be for students to become critical and informed consumers of information.

Characteristics of Effective Schools

Implementation of many school reforms requires a change in the ways that schools operate. The challenge is for schools to become more effective as they are confronted with changes in the composition of their student bodies and the world scene, as well as changes in programs and output expectations. For over two decades, educational researchers have worked to identify the conditions that contribute to differences in effectiveness among schools (Edmonds, 1979; Edmonds, 1982; Westbrook, 1982; Clark, Lotto, & Astuto, 1984). In addition to the early work by Edmonds and others, other approaches may be found in Levin's concept of accelerated schools, Goodlad's league of schools, and Sizer's network of secondary schools. In this context, *school effectiveness* refers to the level at which students are performing in the basic skills. The typical characteristics of effective schools are summarized in Figure 15.9.

Strong Administrative Leadership

The consensus appears to be that schools are most effective when the principal and the instructional staff are in agreement about what they are doing, believe

Figure 15.9: Characteristics of an Effective School

Strong administrative leadership
- Principal has a clear vision about the desired direction for the school.
- Principal has a commitment to the improvement of instruction.

Safe and orderly environment
- Working conditions support the efforts of teachers to address specific problems of their students.
- Environment is conductive to teaching and learning.

Emphasis on instruction in the basic skills
- Commitment to the basic skills as instructional goals.
- Basic skills are the foundation for higher order thinking skills.

High teacher expectations of students
- Teachers set high performance standards for students.
- Teachers use clear and appropriate rewards to recognize student work.

Monitoring and reporting student performance
- Systematic assessment of student progress.
- Curriculum alignment.
- Curriculum, desired outcomes, and the assessment activities all match.

Necessary resources to meet objectives
- Sufficient personnel and materials.
- Sufficient time for instructional planning, staff development, and adapting new innovations.
- Opportunities provided for professional growth.

Culture of the school
- Positive human interactions among students and teachers.
- Continuous growth and development of students and teachers.
- State-of-the-art instructional practices and strategies for teaching and learning.

that they can accomplish their objectives, are committed to providing an environment in which they can accomplish the task, show a willingness to monitor and assess their effectiveness, and adjust their performance based on information.

In effective schools, two common elements are evidence of strong leadership from the principal or faculty leaders and participative decision making. Effective leaders exhibit self-confidence, articulate a clear vision about the direction for the school, and strive to integrate their aspirations with those of others (Nelson, 1986). The challenge is to communicate in word and deed a clear statement of direction for the school and ensure the integration of that vision with the direction being pursued by the school district. The importance of having a vision or clear goals seems obvious, but implementation often is difficult because of conflicting pressures and priorities from school board members, teachers, students, and parents (Rosenholtz, 1985).

Effective leadership comes in different forms (Peters & Waterman, 1982). Principals have different personal administrative behaviors, and the community and school board expectations vary with the school and the setting. Behaviors that succeed in one school may not succeed in another. The common elements are clear goals, willingness to take risks, appropriate skills, and a commitment to instructional leadership (Cawelti, 1987).

In effective schools, teachers have greater opportunity to participate in decision making about such matters as instructional materials, techniques, and policies. Thus, teachers have a greater stake in the school's goals and its future. The challenge for the principal is to work with staff and patrons in creating a supportive environment for school improvement. This climate is achieved by promoting collegiality and cooperative decision making.

Throughout the nation, many school districts have decentralized their management process and initiated school-site decision making to provide for greater teacher involvement and participation in decisions about the daily operation of schools. This is being done, for example, in Dade County, Florida; Hammond, Indiana; Richmond, Indiana; Adams County, Colorado; Edmonton, Alberta; and Santa Fe, New Mexico.

Safe and Orderly Environment

Another characteristic is that the school should provide a safe and orderly environment in which teachers and students can devote their time and energies to teaching and learning the basic skills. Teachers and students should not be diverted from their primary mission by disruptions or outside interference. One function of the principal is to ensure the safety of the school, but the principal is only one person. Teachers, students, and patrons also have responsibilities in maintaining a safe and orderly school environment. This characteristic of an effective school also is one of the National Education Goals. The recent Phi Delta Kappa poll indicated that fighting/violence/gangs and lack of discipline were perceived to be the two biggest problems in the public schools (Elam, Rose, & Gallup, 1994).

Teacher effectiveness can be enhanced by providing and encouraging the effective use of instructional technology to improve instruction and expand teaching and learning opportunities.

One of the principal's most important roles is to serve as a buffer for teachers. In this role, the principal stands between the teacher and various outside influences such as community organizers and other school and central office staff. The teacher is free to perform the primary task—helping students learn. The proportion of time devoted to the primary responsibility (i.e., teaching) increases the likelihood of producing the desired student outcome (i.e., learning). This buffering by the principal also includes minimizing such classroom interruptions as announcements and assemblies (Rosenholtz, 1985). This sense of security that the school is a safe place is critical so that students and teachers can pursue learning without fear of interference.

Emphasis on Basic Skills

Research findings at both the classroom and the school level emphasize the importance of commitment to basic skills as instructional goals. The assumption is that students must master the basic skills before they can succeed with higher order thinking skills or be successful at higher levels of education. The basic skills are the foundation that enables students to be more effective in abstract learning and critical thinking and to become discriminating consumers of knowledge and information. Additional impetus for schools concentrating on learning and academic achievement was provided by the recommendations in a recent report from the Committee for Economic Development (1994).

High Expectations of Students

Successful instruction also is related to the beliefs by teachers that they and their students can be successful. With this attitude, success rather than failure becomes the expectation. This requires teachers to be specific in their expectations of students and also to be sensitive to the individual differences of students and the various teaching approaches and materials that are most effective with different students. The importance of schools placing a strong emphasis on student achievement was endorsed by the Committee for Economic Development (1994) in its report entitled *Putting Learning First: Governing and Managing the Schools for High Achievement.*

Monitoring and Reporting Student Progress

The school reform movement has emphasized the importance of accountability and reports on school performance. Schools are placing greater emphasis on establishing procedures for determining school performance and using this information to enhance teacher and student performance and to inform patrons and district administrators (Blum, Butler, & Olson, 1987).

Monitoring and reporting student progress involves several elements. First, the systematic assessment of students allows teachers to gauge their success in working with students and gives students critical information about their progress. Teachers and principals have a range of options when they select measures to assess instructional effectiveness—measuring student performance on normed tests, comparing trends in student performance over a period of years, and analyzing scores for groups of students.

Measuring student performance on normed tests has certain limitations. Schools with high percentages of students from low socioeconomic backgrounds likely will have difficulty attaining "effective" levels of achievement when compared with national norms. Rather than using norms based on a student population different from the home school, school effectiveness can be measured in terms of improved performance of students. As an alternative, scores for groups of students can be predicted based on the school's demographic composition. Students can be considered to be performing better than predicted even when their actual scores are below average. Similar concerns are related to assessing effectiveness on the basis of trends in student performance over a period of years. If the membership and composition of the student body changes within and between years, these assessment approaches may not be appropriate.

A second consideration related to student assessment is *curriculum alignment,* the effort to ensure that what is assessed during the evaluation was both planned

Professional Reflections

"Know the difference between an instructor and a teacher. An instructor thinks the subject matter is the most important, the teacher thinks the students are the most important."

Cathy Pittman, Teacher of the Year, Georgia

"Teach significant things in significant ways."

M. Ignacio Timajero, Teacher of the Year, Texas

and taught. Significant amounts of classroom time are consumed by the administration of standardized tests to students. For assessment activities to be relevant, what is tested must have been taught and what is tested must be related to the curriculum that has been selected to produce the desired outcomes (Berliner, 1985). Thus, for the educational process to be successful, the challenge is for teachers and administrators to ensure that curriculum, desired outcomes, and assessment activities are carefully matched.

Necessary Resources

Adequate or sufficient human and material resources are critical considerations for effective schools. The number of personnel in the school must be sufficient to provide teachers with time for staff development and to plan new activities. Rather than having all of their time scheduled for necessary activities, teachers need some *slack time* during which they have some independence. They must have opportunities to experiment and invent or adapt innovations, which is not possible in settings where efficiency has a higher priority than flexibility and creativity. The concept of resources also refers to the materials, supplies, and equipment required to provide students with opportunities to learn.

Culture of the School

Even though not identified in the literature as one of the characteristics of an effective school, the *culture of the school* is a critical element in the creation of an effective school; however, school culture cannot be created by an edict from the school's leadership. The culture of the school is a result of both content and process. Content refers to the information in the curriculum as well as the structure, norms, values, and instructional techniques used in the school. Process refers to the human interactions that develop in a school. These relationships do not evolve in a vacuum; the school's leadership plays an important role in the creation of these political and social relationships.

In terms of the potential importance to school improvement, the culture of the school can be influential in different ways. It can be a supportive environment

How did the culture of your high school differ from the culture of the elementary school that you attended?

in which teachers cooperate and assist each other, or a competitive environment in which interaction and cooperative activities are limited to those that are required. School cultures also differ in the extent to which they are rule-oriented or laissez-faire. Acceptance of the premise that the culture of the school is influential assumes that human attitudes and behaviors and the administrative structure influence the extent to which the school is effective (Purkey & Smith, 1982).

The culture of the school can be improved by changing the attitudes and behaviors of the school staff as well as changing the school's organization and norms. Leadership is considered to be important, but consensus is considered to be more important than overt control. Positive changes are more likely to continue if they have become part of the culture of the school and its value system rather than being imposed by administrative edict. The culture of the effective school is illustrated by the ways in which its structure, process, values, and norms channel staff and students toward successful teaching and learning (Purkey & Smith, 1982).

To achieve the school's goals and objectives, emphasis needs to be placed on ensuring alignment of the curriculum with student assessment procedures and the school's goals. For this to be accomplished, continuing education programs or professional development of school staff should be a school priority. Illustrative activities include state-of-the-art instructional practices, strategies, and techniques to improve teaching. In this context, individual staff members are encouraged to develop an individualized professional growth program (Blum, Butler, & Olson, 1987).

School improvement efforts have given new hope for the capacity of the schools to educate disadvantaged youth. Two possible critical elements of improvement efforts are strong building-level leadership and educational standards with accountability. Even though many contend that education is more than the mastery of the basic skills, the effective schools movement has brought renewed attention to the importance of mastery of the basic skills for success in education.

Summary

The overall goal of education, free public instruction for all, is attained through the selection of educational goals and the implementation of instructional objectives for meeting the goals. These goals and objectives help teachers to determine how to organize for instruction. Teachers may use a variety of organizational options as they work with students, and often vary the strategies to recognize differences in students. Technology has the potential to provide teachers and students with opportunities to increase instruction capacity, but effective utilization of technology requires knowledgeable implementation.

In the next chapter, the focus is on social, political, and educational issues that affect projections for the future. The principal concern is on the different forces that will impact on schools and teachers as they seek to serve an increasingly diverse and multicultural pupil population.

Key Terms

Bloom's Taxonomy of Educational
  Objectives
Cooperative learning
Critical thinking
Culture of the school
Curriculum alignment
Databases
Demonstration instruction
Drill and practice
Educational goals
Educational objectives
Expository instruction
Group instruction
Independent learning

Individualized instruction
Information highway
Inquiry instruction
Mastery learning
Reflective thinking
School effectiveness
Simulation
Slack time
Spreadsheet
Tutorial programs
Virtual reality
Word processing

Discussion Questions

1. What is lost when a teacher does not get to know a student? How can you ensure that the quiet, average student is not neglected in your classroom? How does a teacher go about building a positive relationship with each student?

2. What are the most important goals of American public education?

3. How will a well designed system of goals, objectives, and outcomes affect the ways in which a teacher organizes instruction and works with students?

4. How does the role of the teacher change in the various ways in which schools and classrooms may be organized for instruction?

5. How can the teacher determine if certain strategies would be more appropriate with particular subjects or groups of students?

6. How has technology affected the role of the teacher? How can the teacher use technology to improve instruction and student performance?

7. How will the interest in national goals and standards for American education affect the daily activities of teachers in the classroom?

8. How can the characteristics of the effective schools concept be made more relevant in suburban, rural, and inner-city schools?

9. Given the importance of educational leadership in developing an effective school, what action can teachers take when the principal fails to provide active instructional leadership for the school?

10. How have schools changed in their day-to-day operation and decision making styles compared to early days in American education discussed in Chapter 4?

References

Adler, M. (1984). *The Paideia program.* New York: Macmillan.

Apple, M. W. (1988). Teaching and technology: The hidden effects of computers on teachers and students. In L. E. Beyer and M. W. Apple (Eds.), *The curriculum: Problems, politics, and possibilities* (pp. 289–311). Albany, NY: State University of New York Press.

Barone, T. (1989). Ways of being at-risk: The case of Billy Charles Barnett. *Phi Delta Kappan, 71,* 147–151.

Berliner, D. (1985). Effective classroom teaching: The necessary but not sufficient condition for developing exemplary schools. In G. R. Austin & H. Garber (Eds.), *Research in exemplary schools* (pp. 127–154). New York: Academic Press.

Bloom, B. (1956). *Taxonomy of educational objectives 1: Cognitive domain.* New York: David McKay.

Blum, R., Butler, J., & Olson, N. (1987). Leadership for excellence: Research-based training for principals. *Educational Leadership, 45*(1), 25–29.

Brandt, R. (1989). On cooperative learning: A conversation with Spencer Kagan. *Educational Leadership, 47*(4), 8–11.

Brookover, W. (1980). *Measuring and attaining the goals of education.* Alexandria, VA: Association for Supervision and Curriculum Development, Committee on Research and Theory.

Burns, R. (1977). *New approaches to behavioral objectives.* Dubuque, IA: Wm. C. Brown.

Castor, B. (1993). A technology-ready state. *Electronic Learning, 13*(2), 58.

Cawelti, G. (1987). Why instructional leaders are so scarce. *Educational Leadership, 45*(1), 3.

Clark, D., Lotto, L., & Astuto, T. (1984). Effective schools and school improvement. *Educational Administration Quarterly, 20*(3), 41–86.

Committee for Economic Development. (1994). *Putting learning first: Governing and managing the schools for high achievement.* New York: Committee for Economic Development.

Common measures. (1994). *Executive Educator, 16*(12), A11–A14 (December).

Cuban, L. (1989). The "at-risk" label and the problem of school reform. *Phi Delta Kappan, 70,* 780–784.

Duke, D. L. (1984). *Teaching: The imperiled profession.* Albany, NY: State University of New York.

Edmonds, R. (1979). Some schools work and more can. *Social Policy, 9*(5), 28–32.

Edmonds, R. (1982). Programs of school improvement: An overview. *Educational Leadership, 40,* 5–11.

Elam, S., Rose, L., & Gallup, A. (1994). The 26th annual Gallup Poll of the public's attitudes toward the public schools. *Phi Delta Kappan, 76*(1), 41–56.

Ellis, A. K., Mackey, J. A., & Glenn, A. D. (1988). *The school curriculum.* Boston, MA: Allyn and Bacon.

Guskey, T. (1985). *Implementing mastery learning.* Belmont, CA: Wadsworth Publishing Co.

Kourilsky, M., & Quaranta, L. (1987). *Effective teaching: Principles and practice.* Glenview, IL: Scott, Foresman.

Lemonick, M. D. (1992). Tomorrow's lesson: Learn or perish. *Time.* Special edition, fall, 59-60.

Marzano, R. (1992). *A different kind of classroom: Teaching with dimensions of learning.* Alexandria, VA: Association for Supervision and Curriculum Development.

Massialas, B., & Zevin, J. (1983). *Teaching creatively: Learning through discovery.* Malabar, FL: Robert E. Krieger.

Nelson, H. (1986). *The principal as an instructional leader: A research synthesis.* Springfield, IL: Illinois State Board of Education, Illinois Renewal Institute.

November, A. C. (1993). Of fiberglass hulls, and CD-ROMS. *Electronic Learning, 13*(2), 26.

Peters, T., & Waterman, R. (1982). *In search of excellence: Lessons from America's best-run companies.* New York: Harper and Row.

Picciano, A. G. (1994). *Computers in schools: A guide to planning and administration.* New York: Macmillan.

Purkey, S., & Smith, M. (1982). Too soon to cheer? Synthesis of research on effective schools. *Educational Leadership, 40,* 64–69.

Rosenholtz, S. (1985). Effective schools: Interpreting the evidence. *American Journal of Education, 93,* 352–388.

Skinner, B. (1965). Why teachers fail. *Saturday Review, 67,* 101.

Slavin, R. (1989). Research on cooperative learning: Consensus and controversy. *Educational Leadership, 47*(4), 52–54.

Snider, R. (1992). The machine in the classroom. *Phi Delta Kappan, 74,* 316–323.

Solomon, G. (1993). Making a difference. *Electronic Learning, 13*(2), 18–19.

Tom, A. (1984). *Teaching as a moral craft.* New York: Longman.

Westbrook, J. (1982). *Considering the research: What makes an effective school?* Austin, TX: Southwest Educational Development Laboratory.

Womack, S. (1989). Mode of instruction. *The Clearing House, 62,* 205–210.

PART SEVEN

Projections for the Future

Education for the Twenty-First Century   **Chapter 16**

Education for the Twenty-First Century

For the future to be bright, it must be lit by the lamp of learning, the true Olympic torch.

William A. Henry III (1992)

A Critical Incident in My Teaching Career . . .

Many years ago I had a little girl in my 5th grade class who was almost a feral child. Before the age of five she had been subjected to physical and sexual abuse.

After the child's father shot her mother while she stood watching, the child was placed in the foster care system. The trauma that she had experienced, coupled with moderate retardation, handicapped this child until she could barely function.

This child was a nightmare to deal with in a classroom setting. Her problems went far beyond what a classroom teacher is "trained to handle." She told me that "The good Frances stays at home and the bad Frances comes to school."

Frances ate from garbage cans and hoarded food and other things in her desk. Many nights I went home and cried because I didn't know what to do to help her.

Two months ago at an orientation meeting for the new students in my gifted program, a slim young lady who looked familiar approached me. "Mrs. G, do you remember me?" It was Frances. Her cousin was in my new program and Frances had come along just so she could say hello to me.

Frances' foster mother had adopted her. She never gave up on Frances and had given her back her life. Frances holds a full-time job with Goodwill Industries and is a productive, self-supporting citizen. She came to tell me that she still loves me for loving her. She has given me the courage never to give up on any child.

Judith Schefkind Gross
Teacher of the Year, Connecticut

The intriguing curiosity of the future is the unknown; each person has a vision and a dream of the world of tomorrow. Rather than being an endless cycle of repetition of the past, the future is a journey into the unknown. The one constant is change. We will learn to live with and capitalize upon the explosive increases in knowledge, the expanding capacity of technology, the growing potential for travel, and the ways that electronic advancements give us access to cultures throughout the world (Henry, 1992).

This chapter examines projected technological advances and societal trends for the next century and their potential impact on education. These trends include projected demographic, socioeconomic, and demographic changes and their implications for education. Trends and challenges confronting education are identified, and questions and issues are raised about the future of the schools in the context of these trends. The information in the chapter will enable you to:

- Discuss what schools must do to meet the needs of school-age youth.
- Describe how the future economy may influence the educational enterprise.
- Discuss the changing workplace and the worker of the future.
- Identify how schools can accommodate the changing workplace.
- Describe how the school can accommodate the lifestyles of the families of tomorrow.
- Speculate on how technological advances might influence schools and learning.

Few would argue that we live in a global society that has experienced unprecedented change. Those changes have included transitions from an agricultural world to an industrial world and, during the twentieth century, to an information-oriented world. What will the world of the twenty-first century look like? What will its educational system look like? Numerous hypotheses attempt to answer these questions. One way to glimpse the education of the next millennium is to study projected societal trends. The Historical Note on page 553 discusses an early "futurist's" attempt to answer similar questions.

Societal Trends and Educational Developments for the Twenty-First Century

In the following discussion, initial attention is given to socioeconomic and demographic changes that will influence education in the twenty-first century. Areas of interest include the changing demographics of school-age youth, the aging of the population, changes in the economy and the workforce, and the shrinking world or globalization. Also discussed are the effects of technological advances on the operation of schools and the simultaneous movements toward nationalization and decentralization in education. The following section describes various approaches to the study of the future that can be integrated into the existing curriculum.

The Changing Demographics of School-Age Youth

America's schools will face greater challenges as their student populations become more diverse. Student populations will become more diverse as the minority population in the United States increases at a faster rate than the general population. The most rapid growth likely will be among Asian and Pacific Islanders; annual growth rates for the 1990s are projected to be about 4%, with this sector of the population increasing from 3% of the total to 11% by 2050. The Hispanic population is expected to increase from 24 million in 1992 (9% of the total) to 81 million in 2050 (21% of the total.). A large portion of the growth of these two groups will be related to immigration ("How We're Changing," 1993). If these trends continue, events will validate Boyer's (1988) prediction that by the year 2000 approximately one-third of all students will be minorities and a sizable number of them will be from socially and economically disadvantaged families. Figure 16.1 shows the population changes anticipated from 1980 to 2030 by ethnicity and race.

Social problems appear to be increasing because of the interaction resulting from increases in immigration and the proportion of the population in poverty. Immigration is greatest in the sunbelt states, and most of the immigrants are Hispanics and Asian-Americans. Not only have many of these immigrants not had access to adequate educational opportunities, but many also are from homes

Historical Note:
Nostradamus—Astrologer, Physician, and Futurist

Nostradamus (Michel de Nostredame) was born in 1503 at St. Remy in Provence and died in 1566. An astrologer, physician, and adviser to Henry II and Charles IX, as well as Catherine de Medici, Nostradamus was well known for his predictions of the future. In 1555 and in subsequent years he published 10 "Centuries" or books, each containing 100 rhymed quatrains of predictions of the future. For example, he predicted with accuracy the fatal death of Henri II, the decline of the Catholic Church, and the details of the French revolution and the Napoleonic period.

During his lifetime, futuristic prophecy was considered taboo and was condemned. As a result, he was forced to disguise his prophecies by using symbolism, hidden meanings, and terminology from several languages including French, Spanish, Portuguese, Italian, Latin, Greek, and Hebrew.

The fame of Nostradamus continued beyond his lifetime. Generations of followers have regarded his quatrains as serious prophetic messages. For example, several contemporary commentators have alleged that he foresaw World War II in great detail. As we anticipate the next millennium, Nostradamus enthusiasts will no doubt be particularly interested in his predictions and visions for tomorrow.

Source: Cavendish, R. (Ed.) (1983). *Man, myth and magic.* New York: Marshall Cavendish.

Figure 16.1: Projected Population Growth, 1980–2030 (percent by race)

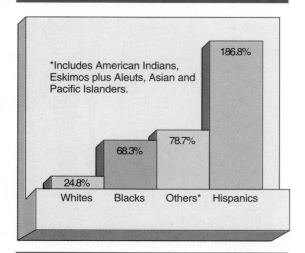

*Includes American Indians, Eskimos plus Aleuts, Asian and Pacific Islanders.

186.8%

78.7%

68.3%

24.8%

Whites   Blacks   Others*   Hispanics

Source: Footlick, J. K. (Winter/Spring, 1980). What happened to the family? (p. 16). *Newsweek.* Reprinted with permission.

in which English is not the first language. Thus, the education deficit is even more severe.

The trends in the proportion of the population in poverty are distressing. In 1992, 14.5% of the population was living in poverty. After several years of modest increases, the proportion stayed constant from the 1991 level. For schools, the disturbing fact was that 21.9% of the persons under 18 were living in poverty; this was the highest percentage since 1975. The rate for persons 18 to 64 was 11.4% and for persons over 65 was 12.4%. The data also suggest that the incidence of poverty no longer is a minority problem; in fact, poverty rates for whites increased significantly from 1990 to 1991. In the same period, blacks, Hispanics, elderly persons, or persons in married couple families did not experience significant increases in the percentages in poverty ("How We're Changing," 1993; "How We're Changing," 1994).

Poverty rates for school-age whites were less than for school-age blacks and Hispanics. For the total population in 1992, the proportion was 21.9% for children under 18 years; for whites, the under 18 proportion was 16.9%; for blacks it was 46.6%; and for Hispanics it was 39.9% ("How We're Changing," 1993).

Figure 16.2: Poverty Rate by Race and Ethnicity: 1992.

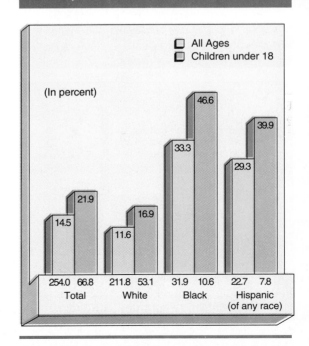

Source: U.S. Bureau of the Census. *How we're changing.* (1994). Current population reports, Special studies, Series p–23, no 187. Washington, DC: U.S. Department of Commerce, Bureau of the Census.

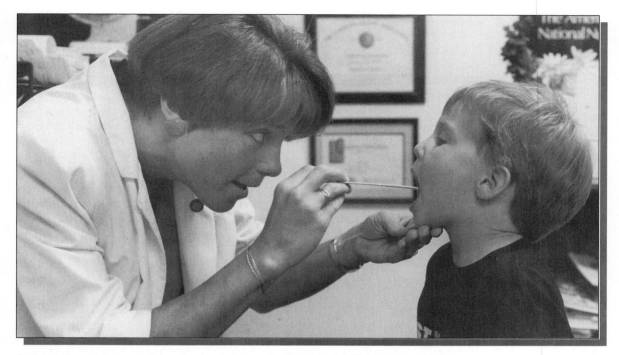

Policymakers are recognizing the importance of adequate healthcare to a child's success in school and are proposing that the full range of social services be available in schools.

Even though a reduced dropout rate was among the national goals for education, absenteeism and dropouts continue to plague urban high schools. Educational attainment rates appear to be stabilizing; the proportion of persons 25 to 29 years old who have completed high school in 1993 was not greatly different from the proportion in 1983. However, the proportion of persons with a bachelor's degree or more is increasing. As noted in chapter 8, the problem is that the proportion of whites with a bachelor's degree or more in 1993 was 22.6% while the percentage for blacks was 12.2% and for Hispanics was 9.0% ("How We're Changing," 1994).

Educational Implications

As these demographic changes take place, the educational needs of youth are changing. Programs will need to be reexamined, and greater resources will be required to provide meaningful programs for a more heterogeneous student body. Special programs will be needed to help many students develop proficiency in English. In addition, supplementary educational experiences will be needed to help some students from disadvantaged environments.

The quality of the nation's educational system must be improved if America is to maintain its leadership position in the world economic community. In an earlier era when nations were isolated, disparities in the quality of education among nations were of little concern so long as the nation produced sufficient

What are the advantages and disadvantages of one-stop social service programs in which social and medical services are available in local schools?

goods and services for its economy. However, that luxury no longer exists with the emergence of a global economy and free trade. In a world that relies upon an educated workforce with technological understanding and specialized skills, America's educational system must be improved if the nation is to continue to be a world economic power. A skilled workforce will be essential to prevent the export of high-paying jobs. This need for a skilled workforce extends beyond production workers, for the nation also will need scientists and engineers to respond to the need for additional investments in civilian research and development (Henry, 1992).

The challenge is greater than merely devoting attention to the basic skills and good work habits. To meet the demands of a more diverse student body, educational personnel will need to be well versed in a variety of forms of multicultural, multiethnic, and bilingual education. The research on mentoring and modeling behavior tells us that teachers, administrators, support personnel, and school governing bodies will need to be sensitive to the problems of students from different cultural and linguistic backgrounds. Further, professional and support personnel also should be representative of those diverse backgrounds.

As the population increases in urban areas, heavier demands will be made on the limited resources of older, inner-city school districts. In the 1950s and 1960s, many of these districts had the reputation that they provided exemplary education programs. For a variety of reasons, these districts do not enjoy the same reputation as we approach the turn of the century. As the baby boomers begin to retire and represent the same proportion of the population as school-age youth, these two age groups will compete for federal and state revenues for medical care and other services (Footlick, 1990). This competition may result in more creative ways to finance education; districts may consider district consolidation or the sharing of tax bases.

To serve students from single parent and double-income homes, schools will be asked to develop or expand before-school and after-school programs and supervision for school-age children whose parents are working. The need for safe, affordable, and quality care for infants and children whose parents are working continues to plague families, in particular poor families. Numerous legislators continue to work toward the development and implementation of a comprehensive child care policy at the national level.

The Aging of America

The proportion of the United States population that will be aging, or "graying," will increase as yesterday's baby boomers reach 65 years old and as improved health care and nutrition bring increased life expectancy. In 1992, 32 million Americans were 65 years of age or older ("How We're Changing," 1993). Demographers project that by the year 2010, 13% of the population will be 65 years and over. By 2030 the percentage is projected to increase to 32%, where it is expected to level off to the year 2050 (see Figure 16.3).

It is also projected that as the population ages, people will opt for later retirement and/or second careers. The federal government's changes in the mandatory retirement age may result in a growing number of senior citizens remaining in or reentering the labor force.

Figure 16.3: Percentage Distribution of the Population, by Age: 1992–2050.

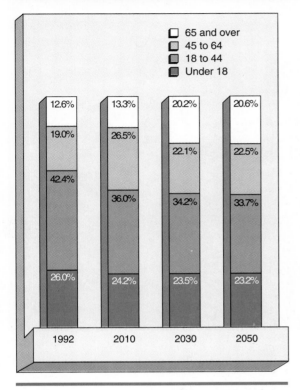

□ 65 and over
■ 45 to 64
■ 18 to 44
■ Under 18

	1992	2010	2030	2050
65 and over	12.6%	13.3%	20.2%	20.6%
45 to 64	19.0%	26.5%	22.1%	22.5%
18 to 44	42.4%	36.0%	34.2%	33.7%
Under 18	26.0%	24.2%	23.5%	23.2%

Source: U.S. Bureau of the Census. *How we're changing.* (1993). Current population reports, Special studies, Series p–23, no 184. Washington, DC: U.S. Department of Commerce, Bureau of the Census.

Educational Implications

The extraordinary growth of our elderly population is not without economic and educational consequences. The increase in funds required to meet the social security and medical needs of tomorrow's elderly population will probably have a deleterious effect on the financing of education. Not only will there be competition for limited resources, but an aged population that does not have children enrolled in school tends to be less supportive of education (Elam, Rose, & Gallup, 1994). The challenge will be to renew the interest and support that this group has for education.

On a more positive note, a significant number of these senior citizens may take advantage of occupational and postsecondary educational opportunities to prepare for second careers or enhance avocational opportunities. Tomorrow's postsecondary institutions may witness an entirely new group of students in many schools, the septuagenarians.

What implications does elimination of mandatory retirement at age 70 have for education and the teaching profession?

The aging American population presents a variety of social problems and opportunities.

Economic Transformation

Carnevale (1992) contends that the structure of the American economy is undergoing significant changes as the emphasis on volume associated with mass production shifts to an emphasis on efficiency; the goal is to produce higher volume at lower costs. Besides efficiency, performance in the new economy is being measured on five additional standards. The first is quality, or the matching of products and services to human needs while maintaining standards in production. The second is variety, or providing choices in response to diverse needs. The third is customization, an extension of variety, in which goods and services are tailored to individual clientele. The fourth is convenience, in which user-friendly products and services are delivered in ways that satisfy customers. The fifth is timeliness, which is accomplished by innovations, continuous improvement, and quick development of new applications.

The unknown about the future of the American economy is the effect of changing economic relations among nations. The world is moving toward the development of an international economy with the signing of the North American Free Trade Agreement with Canada and Mexico and the congressional approval of the GATT agreement for international free trade. These agreements open new markets for America's goods, but the unknown is the effect that they will have on certain manufacturing jobs in the American economy. These events are taking place when the major economic trend in jobs is the shift from an industrial/manufacturing-based economy to a service/information/technology-based economy. By 2005, it is estimated that service workers and administrative support workers will comprise more than one-third of the nation's workforce. Job creation will be greatest in health, education, childcare, protective services, computer systems analysis, and government occupations (Leftwich, 1994). This major shift will have profound implications on the future workforce, as will be discussed later in this chapter.

Educational Implications

As the nature of the American economy shifts, skills that once were demanded only of the white-collar elite are being required of all workers (Carnevale, 1992). These new skills for all students can be grouped into six categories. The first is the academic basics, including reading, writing, and computation. The second is adaptability skills such as learning to learn, creative thinking, and problem solving. Personal considerations are emphasized in the third group of skills; these self-management skills include self-esteem, goal setting, motivation, employability, and career development. The fourth group includes social skills such as interpersonal relations, negotiation, and teamwork. Another group focuses on communication skills such as listening and oral communication. Consistent with the human emphasis in these skills, the last group of influencing skills includes organizational effectiveness and leadership. These skills reflect the changing workplace and the changing values of management. Many of these skills are required in workplaces that emphasize total quality management and customer satisfaction.

Students of the next millennium will need to be able to process information about complex systems, think holistically and abstractly, and above all, be creative. In short, higher cognitive skill development will be a necessary component of education. Since tomorrow's economic forecast emphasizes a shift to a service-oriented global society, we probably will experience more active involvement of students in service/learning experiences. Volunteerism in hospitals, museums, and community service across the globe will become an integral aspect of the teaching/learning process. This movement toward community service has been incorporated into high school completion requirements in some communities and has given impetus to the enactment and implementation of a national youth service program during the Clinton Administration.

If you had the opportunity to volunteer for a particular social service activity, what would it be?

Changing Workforce

Each of the future trends described in this chapter will have profound implications for the changing workforce. Similarly, the changing workforce will influence the trends of tomorrow in significant ways. The structure of jobs will continue to evolve throughout the coming decades. About 25% of the jobs will be in human services, and some of these jobs, like childcare and home health care, pay little more than a minimum wage (Leftwich, 1994). Approximately 45% of the workforce is currently involved in information processing as a result of computer technology. The dilemma is that wages for many of these newly-created jobs are not as high as in the previous industrial manufacturing economy.

In the industrial-manufacturing workforce many positions have been eliminated by the increased use of *robotics*. And, as the science of robotics becomes more advanced, futurists predict that robots will become capable of reproducing themselves, with the smarter ones improving on the original pattern with each new robot produced. Humans will relate to robots in the same manner as they relate to domestic animals (Elmer-Dewitt, 1992).

In part a result of robotics and other methods and systems that have increased productivity while decreasing the number of workers engaged in the production process, tomorrow's workforce will continue to shift from manufacturing or industrial employment to service or information processing. Many of these persons will be employed in jobs that will be vulnerable to changing job requirements due to continually advancing technology. As a result, retraining of employees will become commonplace, and the worker who is most receptive to retraining will be the most valued employee of tomorrow.

In the future more women will enter and remain in the workforce, a trend that has increased steadily in recent decades (see Figure 16.4). Minorities (see Figure 16.4) and elderly workers will constitute the majority of tomorrow's workforce. It is estimated that this trend will continue beyond the turn of the century. As the age increases at which a person can receive maximum Social Security benefits, the workforce will include much older and more experienced employees.

Educational Implications

The discouraging news for students looking forward to employment is that some of the fastest growing occupations pay low wages. However, for students and for

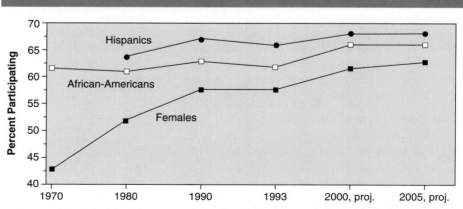

Figure 16.4: Female and Minority Participation in the Workforce, with Projections: 1970–2005.

Source: U.S. Bureau of the Census. (1994). *Statistical abstract of the United States 1994.* Washington, DC: U.S. Government Printing Office.

education, the encouraging news is that there is a positive correlation between education and earnings. Occupation groups with the highest median earnings have the largest proportions of workers with post-high school education (Leftwich, 1994).

Leaders in the American private sector have called for schools to place increased emphasis on the basic skills (Committee on Economic Development, 1994). Policymakers and educators also recognize that to prepare a workforce for tomorrow, the schools will need to do a better job of teaching basic skills such as verbal, mathematical, and scientific literacy in addition to logical reasoning (Carnevale, 1992). In addition, for students to function in an information age, the school curriculum should help students develop higher order cognitive skills, such as creativity, flexibility, decision making with incomplete data, complex pattern recognition, information evaluation/synthesis, and holistic thinking (Dede, 1990; Muller, 1993).

Schools will also need to change their curricula to reflect the technology in the workplace. As a result of technology, a greater emphasis will be placed on group task performances, collaborative learning, and solving real-world problems using concepts and skills from multiple subject areas rather than from a single–subject-centered discipline. New types of interpersonal skills also will be needed for the coming decades; therefore, the school curriculum and instructional practice will need to place a greater emphasis on a variety of forms of communication, both verbal and nonverbal (Dede, 1990).

Globalization

One of the most challenging trends projected for the future is the possibility of global interdependence. As our nation plans for the twenty-first century, we no longer have the luxury of geographical and economic isolation from other nations. International economic competition, international politics, and the interaction among peoples and nations emphasize the importance of students being informed about the world. Relationships among nations will be based more on cooperation than confrontation. Competition among nations in the twenty-first century will be played out using the weapons of commerce–growth rates, investments, imports and exports—not aggression or war. Through the United Nations, efforts will be made to address worldwide environmental problems that cannot be addressed piecemeal (Nelan, 1992). International trade agreements, which provide other evidence of global interdependence, will grow in size and number.

Advances in telecommunication satellites and fiber optics, which already have provided almost instantaneous communication between nations, are eroding the meaning of nationality, ethnicity, and boundaries (Henry, 1992). These advanced telecommunication technologies will make it possible for us to expand our knowledge of the world in significant ways. In short, we have the capability of creating a new twenty-first century world citizen. In this science–technology-society, we will need knowledge that is global in scope (Merryfield, 1991).

As the economic system of the United States becomes increasingly linked to the economic systems of other nations, the English language probably will emerge as the global language. Naisbitt and Auburdene (1990) contend that more than 1 billion individuals around the globe currently speak English; two-thirds of all scientific papers are published in English; and an increasing number of Chinese are mastering English, a trend that is expected to continue. As the international boundaries become more permeable and a global identity emerges, having mastery of English in addition to other languages will be an asset.

In the coming decade we will witness the expansion of multinational corporations and industries in unprecedented numbers. These new industries will reflect a more cooperative model of doing business, compared to the competitive model that has persisted for decades. We also will experience more collaborative projects and joint ventures between countries in manufacturing, marketing, banking, law, agriculture, research and development, science and technology, education, medicine, and the arts.

Educational Implications

As the world shrinks, schools will need to rethink their curriculum and plan for a global society. Developing an understanding of our fellow world citizens will require study of such areas as differences among nations. Case (1993) has identified five affective and cognitive elements essential for a global perspective—open-mindedness, anticipation of complexity, resistance to stereotyping, inclination to emphasize, and nonchauvinism. Case indicates that these elements are intertwined and cannot be taught in isolation. Thus, a global perspective emerges from the interaction of the elements. An understanding of language and cultural differences is an essential part of developing an overall global understanding.

How should schools respond to the shrinking world and development of a global society?

Global issues change over time with the expansion of knowledge, changes in political alignments, and advancements in transportation and communication. Accordingly, schools of tomorrow will have to redesign and reconceptualize their view of the world and the curriculum. In place of the classical curriculum that features the history and culture of Western civilization, we will need a new interdisciplinary approach that focuses on world cultures, world history, world geography, and the humanities, taught from a global perspective. Rather than consisting of a set of accepted premises, instruction should emphasize different points of view; comparisons of different times, geographical areas, and cultures; and the possible impact of alternative actions. A critical consideration in this area is to balance the presentation of different frames of reference and points of view (Case, 1993).

Preparing the world citizen for the information age will necessitate different instructional strategies, new learning methods, and the application of technology to the schools. Schools no longer will be defined by their four walls. Rather, geographic and cultural boundaries will be penetrated and the students of the future will have an opportunity to experience other cultures firsthand.

Different approaches may be used in selecting materials and working with students in these areas. Issues and concepts often overlap. Additional attention needs to be given to refinement of materials and processes of instruction. Few would question the critical importance of students having a broader perspective of the world, but the wide differences in the values of different cultures present a challenge for the teacher in organizing and presenting materials (Merryfield, 1991).

Technological Advances

When considering the impact of technology, the tendency is to consider large-scale programs such as the space program and scientific or medical research. These programs are significant, but the range of effects that likely will accrue from technological advances extend beyond the dramatic research projects and the speed with which information and data can be processed and accessed to a variety of social effects. This increased access to information can help to break down barriers between nations and bridge cultural differences. The rate of change in the field of technology is contributing to a shrinking world in which children can sit in their own home or in a schoolroom and communicate with others throughout the world. Opportunities and access that previously have been restricted to economically privileged youth will become available to a much broader range of the population.

There is general recognition that electronic technologies will continue to have a dramatic impact on the economy, the workforce, the media, and the school. One of the most advanced technologies of the future is *artificial intelligence*. Artificial intelligence research began approximately 30 years ago and has produced artificially intelligent neural network computer programs that have the capacity to learn how to learn (Ward Systems Group, 1993). Artificial intelligence is not intended to compete with human intelligence, but to supplement and enhance our ability to think, create, and solve problems.

What effect have technological advances had on your education?

Among the numerous projections of how technology will transform our planet in the years to come that have particular relevance to education are the following:

- New developments in advanced computer technology will provide future robots with improved interactive multisensory capabilities (Elmer-Dewitt, 1992).

- By the year 2000 a new system of communication by satellite network will make it possible to transmit audio, video, or computer data and will serve as an interactive communication system with isolated areas (Picciano, 1994).

- Telecommunications systems that link telephone networks, cable-TV systems, satellite broadcasts, and multimedia libraries will not only provide easy access to remote parts of the world, but spur the rapid growth of "virtual communities" (Elmer-Dewitt, 1992).

- Interconnected communications systems will serve as home/work/school stations. This technology will incorporate a variety of computer interface devices such as microphones, video cameras, video disc recorders, biofeedback units, etc. (Lemonick, 1992).

Educational Implications

Since World War II, the technological revolution has improved the quality of life immensely, but the full potential for education has not been realized. Advanced technology has opened the door to new opportunities for teaching and learning. Integrated learning systems (ILS) are being developed in which students are test-

Learning is an active process in which children develop human relations skills as well as develop an appreciation for, and understanding of, their peers.

ed, records of progress are maintained, and lesson materials are adjusted in accord with student progress. However, while some of the major vendors have the technical and pedagogical expertise needed for ILS to be successful, many school districts have not acquired ILS because of the initial costs and the annual costs of upgrades and maintenance. In addition, the teaching staff need extensive training to assume this new role as managers of instruction (Picciano, 1994).

Video technology is a less dramatic recent development that can expand the resources available to students and teachers. At the advanced levels, the videos can be interactive using programs that have been added to the discs. As with ILS, cost is one of the barriers to extensive use of this technology. A less extensive application is available through HyperCard that permits the teacher to develop programs to control a videodisc presentation (Picciano, 1994).

Developments in data communications provide access to a variety of international databases. Currently, teachers and students can access traditional databases such as encyclopedias, research databases, information exchanges, and technical information, but the true potential of data communications will be realized when data sources have been tailored to the needs of individual elementary and secondary students. Projections for the future of education see the computer as bringing about a fundamental change in the grade–level-based educational system. "This will be replaced by instruction tailored to the individual student, with computers acting both as tutors and libraries, interacting with students individually and giving them access to a universe of information so vast that it will make today's Library of Congress look like a small-town facility" (Lemonick, 1992, p. 59).

With the assistance of electronic technologies, learning and instruction can be *transdisciplinary education* or *holistic education* (Muller, 1993); the focus is on broad-based ideas and problems, not fragmented or discrete subjects. Students have the opportunity to draw solutions from their knowledge of a variety of disciplines or fields of study. Such an integrated view of learning will be compatible with the complex, interdependent, and global nature of the world.

The concept of the information highway has the potential of providing public schools throughout the nation with dramatic increases in the access to data and information. Effective implementation will require significant investments in both hardware and software as well as orientation and training for teachers. Simply developing an understanding of the magnitude of this resource will be a significant challenge, much less promoting its effective use (Pearlman, 1994). The public policy challenge will be to ensure that all students and teachers have access to this valuable resource (Boehjle, 1994).

To augment transdisciplinary education, all students will need to be computer literate. Knowledge of word processing and information retrieval will be pivotal to providing real-world contexts and real-world problems for students to solve. Student learning opportunities can be enhanced through video writing assignments in language arts, micro-based laboratories (MBLs) in science, microcomputer simulations, and computer-based experiences. Applications can be found in social studies, database management software for organizing student research projects in a variety of subjects, synthesizers in music, computer graphics in art, *CD-ROM* (compact disc, read-only memory) laser disk systems in science, voice-activated keyboards, and interactive television. With special goggles and bodysuits, technology will enable teachers to provide simulated experiences of being in distant places or in space (Lemonick, 1992).

Increasingly, applications of computer technology are becoming available beyond historical tutorials, remedial exercises, and early computer-assisted-instruction (CAI). Through exploratory learning, students can direct their own learning and develop higher order thinking skills as they utilize technology in the identification and solution of problems. Video exploratory application will enable them to bridge the traditional boundaries of disciplines in learning exercises (Means, Blando, Olson, & Middleton, 1993).

If students are to keep pace with the expanding knowledge base during and after their school years, the curriculum will have to place greater emphasis on development and enhancement of thinking and communication skills. *Electronic books* and CD-ROMs may replace many of the print materials that have been the principal source of information for the past few centuries; new techniques for teaching and learning can emerge from language learning software (Hill, 1992).

Educators will find it increasingly difficult to remain current in their discipline or field because of the rapid increase of knowledge and information. Like their students of the next millennium, they will look to advanced technology for

What examples of transdisciplinary education can you envision that include your discipline?

part of the solution to the knowledge explosion. However, technology also likely will result in changes in the instructional process and in the role of the teacher. Rather than their primary role being to dispense information, teachers will become managers of information and mentors or guides for students in their quest for information (Berliner, 1992). The contributions of technology to education will be determined by the ways in which it empowers students and teachers, not by the information that is transmitted or processed (Saffo, 1994).

Effective use of technology in the classroom cannot be achieved through the *quick fixes* of purchasing a computer with related software and providing in-service training for teachers. Attention needs to be given to curriculum integration and planning. The entire instructional staff needs to develop a basic understanding of the potential and limitations of technology as an instructional resource. Teachers need to develop an understanding of the multiple uses of technology. Long-term effective use is dependent upon sufficient resources for training, facilities, and staffing as well as the acquisition of quality hardware and software (Picciano, 1994).

Many of today's schools are entering a new phase in the use of instructional technology. They have made the first investment; students are becoming increasingly familiar with technology; and teachers are recognizing the potential of technology as an instructional resource. Suppliers are making major investments in the development of compatible hardware and software for educational applications. With the experience of both successes and failures, educators have a better understanding of their current capability; however, today's state-of-the-art applications are often outdated tomorrow. The challenge is to keep pace with emerging developments and introduce them into the schools as soon as teachers, students, and technology will permit (Picciano, 1994). Careful planning is required if schools are to maximize the use of technology. Figure 16.5 enumer-

---

Figure 16.5: Technological Principles for Schools

1. To select appropriate hardware and software, schools must decide on the desired uses and purposes of technology. Effective software can help retrieve and sort information, solve problems, dramatize events or issues, or assure mastery of skills. The first step is to establish where technology can accomplish tasks more efficiently or effectively than humans.

2. In planning for broader implementation of technology, careful provision must be made for the time and expense involved in training personnel in its use.

3. In the computer field, early attention is given in selecting programs to assure balance between instructional applications that provide "drill and practice" and those that make more open-ended, creative uses of the technology.

4. Care is taken to provide equity in access to technology as a learning tool in order to assure that neither teachers nor students are denied the opportunity to learn in this manner.

5. Students receive training in how to access, synthesize, and present information, and they participate regularly in assisting teachers in the presentation of such information to other students.

Source: Cawelti, G. (1989). Designing high schools for future. *Educational Leadership, 47*(1), 30–35. Reprinted with permission of the Association for Supervision and Curriculum Development Copyright 1989 by ASCD. All rights reserved.

ates five basic principles that schools should consider as they plan for the use of advanced technology in the classroom.

Private Contractors for Public Education

One of the most controversial developments in public education in the 1990s has been the emergence of private for-profit firms that are contracting for the operation of individual schools and entire school districts. Private providers are not new for public education; for decades, many school districts have contracted for pupil transportation, food services, and custodial services. In addition, in the past few years, new private firms have been formed that contract to provide remedial assistance for groups of students or to provide components in the instructional program. These relatively new entrepreneurs include a variety of firms such as Josten's Learning, Huntington Learning Centers, Brittannica Learning Centers, Kaplan Educational Centers, and Kumon Educational Institute (McLaughlin, 1994). The critical difference between these prior contracts and this new development is that the new efforts involve the complete operation of one or more schools, and possibly the entire school district.

Current contracts include a variety of arrangements. In Minneapolis, a private firm has an employee who is serving as the superintendent of schools. Contractors are operating groups of schools in Baltimore (Schmidt, 1994; Blackshear, 1993), Wichita, and Miami ("Privatization Update," 1994; McCarthy, 1994). Education Alternatives, the Baltimore firm, has recently contracted to operate the entire school district in Hartford, Connecticut. Many of the current contract schools are located in disadvantaged urban areas. The details of the contracts vary among the different school districts, but the expectation is that student performance will improve (Golle, 1994).

Another example of privatization is the Edison Project; the goals of this well publicized effort are to invent, develop, and operate 1,000 new schools. These schools will be privately operated on a for-profit basis; the annual expenditures are to be equivalent to the per-pupil expenditures in public schools. Seed money for the effort has come from various private communications and electronic firms. The momentum for this effort was reduced with the election of President Clinton in 1992 (Brodinsky, 1993), but interest may be renewed as a result of the shift in power that came after the 1994 national election.

Educational Implications

Privatization has the potential of impacting the educational system in two primary areas—staffing and program emphasis. From the staffing perspective, both of the major teachers' organizations have expressed concerns about privatization. Their reservations may be related to one of the reasons for privatization of services in both public and private enterprises—the desire to reduce employee costs and avoid restrictive employee relations statutes or contractual commitments related to hiring, job security, and fringe benefits.

As indicated earlier, much of the interest in privatization can be traced to low student performance in schools serving disadvantaged communities. As the private firms work to improve performance, they likely will focus their efforts on specific learning activities that will improve student performance in the desired

How might the focus of privatization efforts in suburban schools differ from the current focus on student performance in urban schools?

areas. Thus, one issue is the extent to which student enrichment activities and supplemental programs are sacrificed in the quest for improved student performance in the basic skills. However, if privatization extends to suburban schools with a different clientele, the contractor likely will encounter a different set of interests in those communities.

In contrast to traditional public schools that are expected to respond to a variety of external pressures (often without additional resources), these entrepreneurial efforts can restrict their programs to the provisions of the contract. The emergence of the private alternative may result in public schools reexamining their staffing structures, program offerings, and school calendars. School officials may be forced to review such items as student activities, teacher tenure, and year-round schools. As in the private sector of the economy, this new source of competition may force the public schools to subject their operation to a serious critique (Lemonick, 1992).

The public policy dilemma is whether the same set of regulations and rules should apply to ensure that the private contractors are held to the same level of accountability as would have existed if the schools were being operated in the traditional manner. An early analysis of the Baltimore contract found that student performance had declined, class size had increased, and that the district was having compliance problems related to special education programs and the federal Chapter 1 program for the educationally disadvantaged (American Federation of Teachers, 1994).

Private providers do not become involved in operating schools or school districts because of altruistic motives; they view this field as an important component in the service economy. Given the economic values of private providers, they likely will behave in the same manner as any entrepreneur—respond to the interest of the client.

Nationalization and Decentralization of Education

Public policy pressures for reform of public elementary and secondary education in the 1980s and 1990s have been paradoxical. Simultaneous pressures have developed for both the nationalization and decentralization of education. The traditional governance structure of local school boards has been characterized as unresponsive to the changing needs of students and society. Pressures for national standards for curriculum content and student assessment have been accompanied by calls for decentralized decision making, teacher empowerment, and parental choice.

By 2010, historians may view the development and endorsement of the National Goals for Education by the National Governors Association in 1990 as the first step in the nationalization of public education in the United States. This action contributed to federal education reform proposals being presented by both the Bush and Clinton Administrations, and the eventual enactment of the *Goals 2000: Educate America Act* in 1994. Various professional education groups are actively involved in the development of curriculum and education standards for the various subjects taught in the schools. The assumption is that textbook developers will utilize the standards in the development of new textbooks. With funding from the U.S. Department of Education for the development of the

Professional Reflections

"We are in a profession where the investment outlives the investor—a profession which affects and impacts the future of our nation more so than any other endeavor. . . . what happens in the twenty-first century depends on what happens in our classrooms today . . . "

Majorie West, Teacher of the Year, Colorado

standards, provisions are being made for widespread dissemination through free-access computer networks (Diegmueller, 1994).

Much of the impetus for the decentralization movement can be traced to the school reform reports and the subsequent actions of state legislatures. In contrast to the nationalization movement that is projected as being voluntary even though the public pressures for participation likely will be great, the decentralization movement has been mandatory in some states, such as the requirement for school-site decision making in Kentucky (Kentucky Education Reform Act, 1990). Other decentralization efforts are illustrated in the legislation authorizing the creation of *charter schools* in Arizona, California, Colorado, Georgia, Hawaii, Kansas, Massachusetts, Michigan, Minnesota, New Mexico, and Wisconsin (Bierlein & Mulholland, 1994). Typically, charter school legislation is accompanied by some efforts to decrease state regulatory authority on these schools. The potential effect of these movements is national standardization of some facets of education such as curriculum and assessment, but opportunities for diversification in structure and decision making in local schools. The unknown is whether this seeming intellectual contradiction will contribute to improvement of education for youth.

Educational Implications

This movement toward a national education system may represent only a formalization of what has been occurring for over 100 years. Even though states and localities have taken great pride in their individuality and have valued local control, structural differences have not been great among the nation's schools. Grade levels are the same; graduation requirements are rather similar; basic curricular offerings do not vary greatly; and teacher qualifications permit the interstate movement of teachers. Thus, the major differences resulting from education reform may well be in the informal acceptance and ratification of the national goals and standards, and the process to be used in assessing the degree to which schools are achieving the national goals and standards. The critical issues then become the participants in, and the process for, developing and adopting the goals and standards, assessment techniques, and expected performance levels.

The public policy dilemma confronting state and national leaders likely will be what action should be taken when students in localities, states, or the nations do not perform at the expected level. For example, if the national standards are not attained, will legislation be enacted that will be punitive on the underperforming states, local school districts, schools, teachers, or students? The 1990

Ask Yourself:
Are You a Futurist?

KEY: (High) 5, 4, 3, 2, 1, 0 (Low). The larger numbers should be used to indicate a high degree of agreement with the statement or tendency to act a certain way.

Circle response that most nearly reflects *how you feel about yourself:*

5 4 3 2 1 0/   1. I am interested in emerging ideas and information about most things.
5 4 3 2 1 0/   2. I am flexible and adaptable in most situations.
5 4 3 2 1 0/   3. I think of myself as being in relative control of my life now and in the future.
5 4 3 2 1 0/   4. I am generally confident of my powers to analyze, synthesize, interpret, and apply myself to new facts, conditions, and events.

Circle response that most nearly describes *your work behavior:*

5 4 3 2 1 0/   5. I regularly and systematically examine broad goals and specific objectives to assure responsiveness to emerging conditions.
5 4 3 2 1 0/   6. I periodically reassess professional goals and growth relative to changes in my field.
5 4 3 2 1 0/   7. I keep an open mind to the possibility that may choose to retread myself professionally or be nudged/forced to do so.
5 4 3 2 1 0/   8. I regularly read a variety of published materials to update my work-related knowledge, skills, and attitudes. My reading includes materials directly related to my field and at least some infields not commonly thought to be relevant (but which *may* directly or indirectly yield information or ideas which are mindstretching or adaptable/useful).
5 4 3 2 1 0/   9. I periodically participate in seminars, workshops, conferences, and/or courses directly related to my field or indirectly useful, in the sense noted in #8.

Circle response that most nearly *describes your personal life:*

5 4 3 2 1 0/   10. I commonly reflect on my personal values and seek to revitalize them.
5 4 3 2 1 0/   11. I read a variety of books, journals, and magazines which collectively stimulate creative imagination and thinking about myself and others, for example, through science fiction, poems, novels, travel books and articles, materials on the arts, scholarly articles on alternative futures, etc.

What specific changes do you forsee in the next decade as a result of the push for both nationalism and decentralization of education?

Kentucky Education Reform Act contains provision for takeover of deficient local school districts, for the removal of the school board and superintendent, for teachers to lose their tenure rights, and for the state to appoint an outside person to administer the school district.

One major effect of the decentralization and the school reform movements has been the reduction of the discretion of local school boards with the increased state regulation and requirements for schools, and the transfer of different types of powers to individual schools. The interaction of national standards and decentralization provide professional educators with the opportunity to have greater influence and authority over education. The unanswered questions are whether the interests of the individual disciplines can be balanced against the broader collective needs of education at the national level and whether a sufficient number of teachers and parents have the time and energies that will be required for successful decentralization and charter schools.

5 4 3 2 1 0/   12. I engage in a variety of leisure-time and cultural activities that are pursued for personal enjoyment and growth, that are not directly work-related and that have no predetermined objective.

5 4 3 2 1 0/   13. I cultivate and maintain a variety of friendships—not just persons who are work-related, within the "expected" friendships based on socioeconomic class, neighborhood, college ties, etc.

5 4 3 2 1 0/   14. I feel comfortable about my lifestyle, my values, and my aspirations—and neither feel threatened by those who are different nor inclined to pressure others to become more like me.

Circle response that most nearly describes *your behavior as a citizen, parent, or member of groups:*

5 4 3 2 1 0/   15. I tend to encourage others to think about the possible future, which starts in the next minute—and the aspects of it that we should prepare ourselves for, adapt to, or block.

5 4 3 2 1 0/   16. I stimulate others to learn the processes by which they can develop and continually revitalize personally meaningful values and to use those processes with discretion.

5 4 3 2 1 0/   17. I stimulate other's futuristic thinking and behaving, for example, through various types of rewards, praise, and recognition.

5 4 3 2 1 0/   18. I try to provide a role model of an informed, rational person who is guided in part by futuristic knowledge and processes.

5 4 3 2 1 0/   19. I participate in futuristic group activities, in futures-oriented groups and in groups with occasional emphases on alternative futures, and try to create a societal receptivity toward futurism as a means of improving the quality of life and attaining positive social goals.

5 4 3 2 1 0/   20. I demonstrate the values of futuristic thinking in my roles as a citizen, parent, and/or group member.

Your "score": Add up the numbers you have circled. The closer you are to a score of 100, the more likely you are to be a "futurist."

Source: Copyright by Joel L. Burdin, November 6, 1979. Used with permission.

The thrust of the various education reforms suggests the possibility that the true professionalization of teaching may have begun. Significant advances are being made in certification standards for teachers, content standards for students, and efforts to reform teacher preparation and licensing. The effective interaction of these activities can substantially increase the probability that all children will learn (Wise, 1994).

Futures Education

Futures education, or futurism, has grown in popularity during the past 30 years. Today both the corporate and governmental establishments devote considerable attention to the systematic study of trends and to predicting the future. The majority of formal courses in futurism, however, have been found primarily at the university level rather than the elementary or secondary levels. For those elementary and secondary educators who want to introduce their students to the study of the future, there are a variety of program formats that can be used in the classroom. Pulliam (1991) describes five approaches to the study of the future that can be integrated easily into the existing educational curriculum.

1. *Interdisciplinary approach.* The focus is on an interdisciplinary core curriculum and the relationship between a variety of subjects or disciplines, such as the relationship between biology and economics or science and social studies. The application in an elementary school might include a combined science and social studies unit that focuses on the anticipated impact of the greenhouse effect on the natural ecological balance of the future, and its relationship to economic development. Synergetic, integrated, holistic, core, and interdisciplinary studies are basic to a futures curriculum.

2. *Problem-analysis approach.* Students analyze and solve problems and probe for underlying cause-and-effect relationships. The application of such a problem-analysis approach in a secondary school might include an exploration of the moral and ethical considerations of genetic engineering. Emphasis is placed on the power of the individual or group to alter the environment.

3. *Optimistic locus of control.* In spite of the skepticism of today's society, futures education typically takes an optimistic world view and stresses the positive and empowering capabilities of the human race. Studying the future in an elementary school might include a unit in language arts in which students write science fiction stories that exemplify current technological solutions to global problems.

4. *Open-ended, inquiry-based methodology.* Rather than disseminating mere facts and information, curriculum includes hypothetical simulations or scenarios that pose probable alternative solutions. The application of an open-ended, inquiry-based methodology in a secondary school might include the development of exploratory predictions of the future through attitude surveys, brainstorming techniques, future games, or the Delphi technique. The Delphi technique offers a means of forecasting or polling based on group consensus. Such a methodology might be best suited for a course in journalism, political science, history, or sociology. Students are encouraged to project themselves into a variety of probable future scenarios and to extrapolate creative solutions to problems. The major goal is to teach creative thinking skills.

5. *Values tracking in the futures.* Most futures courses emphasize values and the choice among future alternatives. Futurism requires students to reexamine the values of society, the nation, and the world, as well as their personal convictions. The application of a values component in an elementary school might include a unit in social studies that grapples with

What other problem/issues might you recommend for problem analysis by secondary students?

the question "What might the ideal education be in the future?" The futures curriculum examines the nature of choice and decision making and offers the type of classroom interchange that leads to values identification and clarification—prerequisites for creative problem solving.

As educators, our challenge is to prepare students so that they can cope with the complexity of change. In spite of the uncertainty of the future, there is much we can do to aid our students in preparing for it by helping them develop the skills needed to analyze, clarify, generalize, and make critical judgments. In addition, the study of the future offers numerous creative opportunities for imagining and designing the best possible alternatives and visions for tomorrow.

"Ask Yourself" on pages 570–571 presents an informal personal assessment to help you determine the extent to which you yourself think, believe, or act as a *futurist*.

Summary

Projecting the future is never without its risks. A number of societal trends are so marked, however, that there is reason to believe that they will extend into the next century. Each of these trends will affect education in significant ways. Two of the trends that will affect education the most are the growing minority student body and the aging population. Both have the potential of placing a heavy financial burden on the economy, which in turn may have a deleterious effect on the financing of education. As discussed in Chapter 13, the great debate of this and future decades may concern the competition between the needs of youth and those of the aging population.

One of the most visible trends is the advances in technology. Of the projected technological advances, artificial intelligence is one of the most innovative and has the greatest potential to enhance our ability to solve problems creatively. Yet, while the educational implications of technology are limitless, they are not going to be the panacea for curing all the ills of education. A total redesign of the educational enterprise, including the curriculum, may be necessary for the technology to be most effective.

The complexity of tomorrow's world requires a certain type of knowledge and skill that enables one to adapt and cope with ongoing change. A futures curriculum can help develop the necessary skills to cope with the uncertainty of tomorrow's future.

Key Terms

Artificial intelligence
CD-ROM
Charter schools
Electronic book
Futures education
Futurist
Robotics
Transdisciplinary (holistic) education

Discussion Questions

 1. What teacher has had a long-term impact on your life? In what way? What are the challenges and responsibilities for the regular classroom teacher in dealing with special children in an inclusive classroom? What resources are available to teachers who are experiencing difficulties with children in their classroom?

2. Much of the conjecture about the future centers around global interdependence. What effect will the recently signed international trade agreements have on the need for various educational programs and services?

3. What elementary, secondary, and postsecondary curriculum recommendations would you advance to best prepare the world citizen for tomorrow's global society?

4. It is hypothesized that the technology of the future, in particular electronic technologies, will have a profound impact on the school. Design a home/work/school station of the future that integrates the use of advanced technology in your subject matter discipline.

5. If you were designing a curriculum for the study of the future, which of Pulliam's five approaches would you choose and why?

6. Approximately twenty-five years ago the renowned psychologist Carl R. Roger (1970) wrote an essay entitled "From Interpersonal Relationships: U.S.A. 2000" for a symposium sponsored by the Esalen Institute. In his essay he discussed such topics as relationships between men and women, parents and children, individuals in the workplace, and religion as interpersonal living. If you were invited to write an essay on "Interpersonal Relationships in the Next Millennium," what key points would your essay include?

7. In 1966, John R. Platt wrote the following for the American Association for the Advancement of Science: "A lifetime ago we made the transformation to education for a living. It is time now to make the transformation to education for wholeness, for delight, and for diversity" (p. 1139). What do you think Platt meant by this statement? Does the quote still apply for the future (i.e., the year 2010)? If yes, how? If no, why not?

References

American Federation of Teachers (AFT). (1994). *The private management of public schools: An analysis of the EAI experience in Baltimore.* Washington: AFT.

Benjamin, S. (1989). An ideascope for education: What futurists recommend. *Educational Leadership, 40*(1), 8–14.

Berliner, D. (1992). Redesigning classroom activities for the future. *Educational Technology, 32*(10), 7–13.

Bierlein, L., & Mulholland, L. (1994). *Comparing charter school laws: The issue of autonomy.* Tempe, AZ: Morrison Institute of Public Policy, Arizona State University.

Blackshear, P. (1993). The tides of change: Privatization in education. *School Business Affairs,* (June), 26–30.

Boehjle, B. (1994, June 7). Information superhighway must be open to all students. *School Board News, 7.*

Boyer, E. L. (1988). The future of American education: New realities, making connections. *Kappa Delta Pi Record, 25*(1), 6–12.

Brodinsky, B. (1993). How "new" will the "new" Whittle American School be? A case study in privatization. *Phi Delta Kappan, 74,* 540–547.

Carnevale, A. (1992). Skills for the new world order. *American School Board Journal, 179*(5), 28–30.

Case, R. (1993). Key elements of a global perspective. *Social Education, 57,* 318–325.

Dede, C. (1990). What will the future hold for schools and technology? *School Administrator, Special Issue: Computer Technology Report,* 39–40.

Diegmueller, K. (1994, September 28). Standards-setters hoping to publish best sellers. *Education Week, 1,* 15.

Elam, S., Rose, L., & Gallup, A. (1994). The 26th annual Gallup Poll of the public's attitudes toward the public schools. *Phi Delta Kappan, 76,* 41–56.

Elmer-Dewitt, P. (1992). Dream machines. *Time.* Special edition, fall, 41.

Footlick, J. K. (Winter/Spring, 1990). What happened to the family? *Newsweek,* 14–18, 20.

Golle, J. T. (1994, June 22). You must take care of your customer. *Education Week,* 44.

Henry, W. A. III. (1992). Ready or not, here it comes. *Time.* Special edition, fall, 34.

How we're changing. (1993). Current population reports, Special studies, Series p-23, no. 184. Washington: Bureau of the Census, U.S. Department of Commerce.

How we're changing. (1994). Current population reports, Special studies, Series p-23, no. 187. Washington: Bureau of the Census, U.S. Department of Commerce.

Kentucky Education Reform Act. (1990). Frankfort: General Assembly of the Commonwealth of Kentucky.

Leftwich, K. (1994). Job outlook 2005: Where to find the good jobs. *Vocational Education Journal, 69*(7), 27–29.

Lemonick, M. D. (1992). Tomorrow's lesson: Learn or perish. *Time.* Special edition, fall, 59–60.

McCarthy, M. M. (1994). External challenges to public education: Values in conflict. Paper presented at the Annual Meeting of the American Educational Research Association, New Orleans, LA, April, 1994.

McLaughlin, J. M. (1994, June 7). Privatization trend likely to continue. *School Board News,* 4–5.

Means, B., Blando, J., Olson, K., & Middleton, T. (1993). *Using technology to support education reform.* Santa Monica, CA: SRI International.

Merryfield, M. (1991). Science-technology-society and global perspectives. *Theory Into Practice, 30,* 288–293.

Muller, R. (1993). A world core curriculum. *The NAMTA Journal, 18*(3), 93–102.

Naisbitt, J., & Auburdene, P. (1990). *Megatrends 2000: Ten new directions for the 1990s.* New York: William Morrow.

Nelan, B. W. (1992). How the world will look in 50 years. *Time.* Special edition, fall, 37.

Pearlman, R. (1994, May 25). Can K–12 education drive on the information superhighway? *Education Week,* 48.

Picciano, A. G. (1994). *Computers in schools: A guide to planning and administration.* New York: Macmillan.

Platt, J. R. (1966). Diversity. *Science, 154,* 1139.

Privatization update. (1994, June 7). *School Board News,* 4.

Pulliam, J. D. (1991). *History of education in America.* Columbus, OH: Merrill.

Rogers, C. R. (1970). From interpersonal relationships: USA 2000. In M. Dunston & P. W. Garden (Eds.), *Worlds in the making: Probes for students of the future* (pp. 320–325). Englewood Cliffs, NJ: Prentice-Hall.

Saffo, P. (1994). The soul of a social machine. *Electronic Learning, 13*(5), 16–17.

Ward Systems Group. (1993). *NeuroShell.* Frederick, MD: Ward Systems Group.

Wise, A. (1994, June 1). Professionalization and standards: A 'unified system of quality assurance.' *Education Week,* 38, 47.

Appendix

Selected Federal Legislation Supporting Education

1785   Northwest Ordinance—Reserved the sixteenth section of each township for the support of education.

1787   Northwest Ordinance—Endowed public institutions of higher education with public lands.

1802   First federal institution of higher education established—the U.S. Military Academy at West Point (the Naval Academy was established in 1845, the Coast Guard Academy in 1915, and the Air Force Academy in 1954).

1862   First Morrill Act—Provided land grants to the states for the support of agriculture and industrial colleges.

1867   Federal Department of Education established.

1890   Second Morrill Act—Provided money grants to each state to support land grant colleges; no grant would be provided to any state that denied admission to the land grant college on the basis of race unless it provided for separate institutions.

1917   Smith-Hughes Act—Provided grants to support teachers' salaries in vocational education at precollege level.

1918   Vocational Rehabilitation Act—Provided grants for rehabilitation training of World War I veterans.

1920   Smith-Bankhead Act—Authorized grants to states for vocational rehabilitation.

1933   Civilian Conservation Corps—Provided vocational and basic skills training to youth 18 to 25 enrolled in the corps.

1935   National Youth Administration—Provided part-time employment to high school and college students to help them remain in school

1935   Bankhead-Jones Act—Provided grants to land-grant colleges.

1941   Lanham Act—Provided aid to school districts affected by the location of federal tax exempt property.

1943   Vocational Rehabilitation Act—Provided rehabilitation assistance to disabled veterans.

1944   Servicemen's Readjustment Act (G.I. Bill)—Provided financial assistance to veterans to continue their education.

1944   Surplus Property Act—Authorized transfer of surplus government property to educational institutions.

1946   Fullbright Act—Provided for international educational exchange.

1950   National Science Foundation (NSF) Act—Established the National Science Foundation to promote basic research and education in the sciences.

1950   Public Law 815—Provided funds for school construction to districts in which federal tax exempt property was located within the district.

1950   Public Law 874—Provided funds for operating expenses to school districts in which federal tax exempt property was located within the district.

1958   National Defense Education Act—Provided financial assistance to state and local education agencies to strengthen instruction in areas deemed critical to national defense (e.g., mathematics, science, and foreign languages); for the improvement of guidance counseling and testing service; educational media; and student loans and scholarships.

1962   Manpower Development and Training Act—Provided training for unemployed and underemployed persons to enable them to become wage earners.

1963   Higher Education Facilities Act—Provided funds to institutions of higher education to construct classrooms, laboratories, and libraries.

1964   Economic Opportunity Act—Established the Job Corps and Project Head Start as part of its antipoverty program.

1965   Elementary and Secondary Education Act—Provided assistance to local school districts for children in low-income families, for library and instructional materials, for supplemental educational centers, and for research and training.

1965   Higher Education Act—Provided funds to institutions of higher education for construction and improvement of facilities and for student loans and scholarships. Established National Teacher Corps.

1965   National Foundation on the Arts and the Humanities (NFAH) Act—Established the NFAH and authorized grants and loans to encourage production and scholarships in the arts and humanities.

1966   Adult Education Act—Authorized grants to states to establish and expand educational programs for adults, including the training of adult education teachers.

1967   Education Professions Development Act—Provided grants to improve the equality of teaching and meet shortage of trained education personnel in specific areas.

1968   Bilingual Education Act—Provided funds to school districts to provide bilingual education to students with limited English proficiency.

1972   Education Amendments of 1972—Provided support for a number of postsecondary education programs; established the National Institute of Education, a Bureau of Occupational and Adult Education, and a bureau level Office of Indian Education; prohibited sex discrimination in admissions to institutions of higher education.

1975   Indian Self-Determination and Education Assistance Act—Mandated increased participation of Native Americans in the operation of their educational programs.

1975   Education of the Handicapped Act—Required that all handicapped children ages 5 to 18 be provided a free appropriate education designed to meet their unique needs.

1978   Career Education Incentive Act—Authorized the creation of a career education program for elementary and secondary schools.

1979   Department of Education Organization Act—Established a Department of Education.

1981   Education Consolidation and Improvement Act—Consolidated 42 federal programs into 7 block grants.

1984   Carl D. Perkins Vocational Education Act—Provided grants to states to make vocational education accessible to all persons, including the disadvantaged, the handicapped, single parents and homemakers.

1986   Handicapped Children's Protection Act—Allowed courts to award attorneys' fees to parents of disabled students who are successful in challenging district actions under the Education of the Handicapped Act.

1986   Drug Free Schools and Communities Act—Provided support for drug abuse education and prevention programs.

1988   Education and Training for a Competitive America Act—Authorized new and expanded programs in literacy, math-science, foreign languages, vocational education, international education, and technology training and transfer.

1990   Individuals With Disabilities Education Act—Revised and extended programs established under the Education of the Handicapped Act, changed the name of the Act and all references from handicapped children to children with disabilities.

1990   Displaced Homemakers Self-Sufficiency Assistance Act—Provided assistance to states to provide employment training programs and referral support services to displaced homemakers.

1990   School Dropout Prevention and Basic Skills Improvement Act—Extended support to secondary education programs for basic skills improvement and dropout prevention and reentry.

1990   National Environmental Education Act—Provided support for environmental education programs and training of professionals in environmental fields.

1990   Americans With Disabilities Act of 1990—Prohibited discrimination against persons with disabilities, required greater access to public facilities and accommodations for persons with disabilities.

1991   Civil Rights Act of 1991—Amended the Civil Rights Act of 1964, the Age Discrimination Act of 1967, and the Americans With Disabilities Act of 1990 with regard to employment discrimination and related regulations.

1993   National and Community Service Trust Act of 1993—Provided education grants for two years for persons 17 years or older who perform community service before, during, or after postsecondary education.

1993   Student Loan Reform Act—Reformed the student aid process by allowing students to receive loans directly from the institution of higher education, eliminating banks as the middle men.

1993   School-to-Work Opportunities Act—Provided support for the development of school-to-work programs that match noncollege bound youth with employers who can provide work-based learning experiences and assist in finding future employment.

1993   Goals 2000: Educate America Act—Formalized a set of eight national education goals, established the Education Standards and Improvement Council to develop model standards for all major academic areas and the National Skills Standards Board to develop entry-level standards for clusters of vocational-technical occupations.

1994   Improving America's Schools Act—Reauthorized the Elementary and Secondary Act for five years and made eligibility for Title 1 funds dependent upon the development of school improvement plans that include high content and performance standards.

Glossary

Academic freedom. The teacher's freedom to determine the most appropriate instructional materials and the most appropriate teaching strategies without censorship, interference, or fear of reprisal.

Academy. A type of private secondary school operating in the 1800s, designed to teach subjects useful in trade and commerce.

Acculturation. The process of becoming conditioned to the cultural patterns of the dominant group.

Accountability. A concept in which the schools and teachers are held responsible for the accomplishment of expressed educational goals.

Acquired immune deficiency syndrome (AIDS). A serious health condition caused by a virus that destroys the immune system and leaves the body incapable of fighting disease.

Activity curriculum. A curriculum that is determined to a large extent by student interest and that emphasizes self-expression through games, singing, or other creative and spontaneous activities.

Adequacy. The extent to which funding for programs and learning opportunities is sufficient.

Administrative law. The formal regulations and decisions of state or federal agencies.

Adult education. Education, for credit and noncredit, provided to individuals who are beyond the age of compulsory attendance, who have either completed or interrupted their formal education.

Aesthetics. The branch of philosophy concerned with values in beauty, especially in the fine arts.

Affirmative action. Affirmative steps to recruit and hire, or recruit and retain, individuals from groups who are underrepresented in the workplace or the classroom.

Alternative certification. State provisions or regulations for awarding a teaching license to a person who has not followed the traditional teacher education program; exceptions typically are related to completion of a concentrated professional education sequence, teaching internships or prior experience, or credits for work experience.

Alternative schools. Schools that offer specialized programs and learning experiences not normally found in the public schools, or that provide greater individual attention for students who are not making normal progress.

Amalgamation. A form of diversity that supports the "melting pot" notion and envisions American culture as emerging from the best elements of many cultures.

Apparent reality. The reality made up of day-to-day experiences and life events.

Artificial intelligence. Technology that allows the computer to perform functions that traditionally have been the realm of human intelligence, such as thinking and problem solving.

Assimilation. A response to population diversity that requires conformity to a single model, which is largely defined by traditional British political, social, cultural, and religious institutions.

At risk. A term used to describe students who are achieving below grade level expectations or are likely to experience educational problems in the future, as well as students who are likely to experience physical and mental health problems.

Attorney general. The chief legal officer of the state who serves as legal advisor to official agencies of the state.

Axiology. The branch of philosophy concerned with the nature of values.

Back-to-basics movement. A revival of essentialism begun in the 1970s and echoed in education reform reports of the 1980s that emphasizes the three R's, a core curriculum, and more rigorous academic program requirements.

Behavioral objectives. Action-oriented statements that indicate specific behaviors or knowledge that students are expected to learn or demonstrate upon completion of an instructional sequence.

Behaviorism. An educational theory predicated on the belief that human behavior can be explained in terms of responses to external stimuli. The basic principle underlying behaviorism in education is that behaviors can be modified in a socially acceptable manner through the arrangement of the conditions for learning.

Bibliotherapy. The use of books as a therapeutic intervention.

Bilingual education. Instruction to non-English-speaking students in their native language while teaching them English.

Bloom's Taxonomy of Educational Objectives. List and organizing scheme containing expected learnings for students.

Board certified. Certification awarded by the assessment board of a profession acknowledging the recipient's qualifications in specified areas.

Building principal. The person responsible for the administration and management of a school.

Career ladder. A career development plan that provides differential recognition and rewards for teachers at steps of the plan, which coincide with increased experience and expertise.

Cartesian method. A process proposed by Descartes that involves the derivation of axioms upon which theories can be based by the purposeful and progressive elimination of all interpretations of experience except those that are absolutely certain.

Categorical funding. The practice of state funding of specific educational programs or activities (e.g., bilingual education, education of handicapped pupils, pupil transportation, or in-service programs).

Categorical imperatives. Universal moral laws that guide our actions and behaviors.

CD-ROM. A compact disc with read-only memory used for the storage of audio, visual, and textual data.

Certification. The authorization of an individual by the state to teach in an area where the state has determined he or she has met established state standards.

Charity (pauper) schools. Schools in colonial New England designed for children who could not afford to attend other fee-charging schools.

Charter schools. Publicly supported schools established upon the issuance of a charter from the state, local school board, or other entity and designed to provide greater autonomy to individual schools and greater choice in educational programs to parents and students.

Chief state school officer. The elected or appointed executive officer of the state department of education, responsible for elementary and secondary education, and sometimes for higher education; often referred to as the superintendent of public instruction or the commissioner of education.

Child abuse. The repeated mistreatment or neglect of a child, which can result in physical, emotional, verbal, or sexual injury or harm.

Child benefit theory. The legal theory that supports providing state aid to private education when the aid benefits the private school child rather than the private school itself.

Child (student)-centered curriculum. Curriculum designed with the child's interest and needs at the center of the learning process; learning takes place through experience and problem solving.

Choice. Power or authority of (1) a local school board to select the instructional program and level of funding to be provided students in the school district, or (2) parents to select the school that their child can attend.

Classical conditioning. A type of behaviorism that demonstrates that a natural stimulus that produces a certain type of response can be replaced by a conditioned stimulus.

Clinical depression. A serious depression with persistent symptoms that typically last for at least two or more weeks.

Cluster suicides. A series of suicides that are closely related in time and place.

Cognitive styles. The alternative processes by which learners acquire knowledge.

Cooperative educational service agency. An educational service agency established by a group of school districts for the purpose of providing a specified service or services to constituent school districts.

Common schools. Publicly supported schools started during the mid-1800s attended in common by all children.

Compensatory education. Special educational programs designed to overcome the educational deficiencies associated with the socioeconomic, cultural, or minority group disadvantages of youth.

Competency testing. Testing designed to assess basic skills and knowledge.

Comprehensive high school. A public secondary school that offers curricula in vocational education, general education, and college preparation.

Constitution. A written contract for the establishment of a government; the highest level of law.

Continuing education program. Postsecondary education programs for adults, including career development programs, degree programs, and vocational offerings.

Continuity. The repetition of major curriculum elements to ensure that skills can be practiced and developed.

Cooperative learning. Instructional system that assumes that students will study and work together in a supportive relationship rather than competitively.

Core curriculum. A curriculum design that emphasizes the required minimum subjects and topics within subjects that all students are expected to learn.

Cosmology. The branch of philosophy concerned about the nature of the universe or cosmos.

County superintendent. The chief educational officer of a county. The office of the county superintendent typically delivers specific programs and provides specific services to the local school districts located in the county.

Crisis intervention team. Volunteer teachers, counselors, administrators, social workers, school nurses, and school psychologists who network with each other and identify the student who appears to be overwhelmed by stress, or displays suicidal gestures or suicidal threats.

Critical literacy. A type of curriculum that challenges all unequal power relationships and denounces any form of exclusion.

Critical pedagogy. The art or science of applying the principles of social reconstructionism to create a better society.

Critical theory. A set of principles that reflect the melding of the philosophies of Kant, Hegel, Freud, and Marx.

Critical thinking. The process of thinking and problem solving that involves the examination and validation of assumptions and evidence and the application of logic to the formulation of conclusions.

Cultural literacy. Assumed body of knowledge about which persons should be able to demonstrate mastery if they are to function at an optimal level in society.

Cultural pluralism. A form of diversity that emphasizes the multiple cultures in the larger society.

Culture. The behavioral patterns, ideas, values, religions and moral beliefs, customs, laws, language, institutions, art, and all other material things and artifacts characteristic of a given people at a given period of time.

Culture of the school. Social interactions of the students and adults in the school environment and the ways in which their behavior is influenced by the official rules and established mores of the school.

Curriculum. All the educational experiences of students that take place in the school.

Curriculum alignment. The correlation between what is assessed and what was planned and taught.

Dame school. The elementary school in the New England colonies, usually held in a kitchen or living room and taught by women with minimal education.

Database software. Computer software designed to facilitate the construction and management of databases.

Database. A large collection of facts or figures stored on a computer in such a way that specific information can be accessed upon demand.

***De Facto* segregation.** Segregation existing as a matter of fact, regardless of the law.

***De Jure* segregation.** Segregation sanctioned by law.

Deductive logic. Logic that deduces concrete applications from a general principle or general rule.

Demonstration instruction. Instructional technique in which students learn through doing and/or observing.

Deschooling curriculum. A curriculum based on the belief that the values promoted by formal educational institutions are unhealthy and harmful, that the public school system should be discontinued, and that the curriculum should be determined by what the learner likes, not what will be useful to someone else.

Desegregation. The abolition of racial, ethnic, or gender segregation.

Disparate impact. The situation that exists when a policy or practice has a differential impact on individuals in a protected class.

Discrimination. Showing bias or prejudice in the treatment of individuals because of their race, ethnicity, gender, or handicapping condition.

Distance education. Education delivery system characterized by a separation in space and time for teaching and learning activities. Teaching takes place mostly through audio, video, computer, and print technologies, and learning is through independent study.

Drill and practice. Instructional technique in which the assumption is that learning is enhanced through repetitious activities, i.e., memorizing and reciting the multiplication tables.

Dropout. A pupil who leaves school for any reason except death, before graduation or completion of a program of studies and without transferring to another school or institution.

Due process. The process by which individuals are provided fair and equitable procedures in a matter affecting their welfare (procedural due process) and are protected from unfair deprivation of their property.

Economic distortions. Instances when the impact of a tax contributes to a change in consumer decisions concerning such actions as the site at which they secure services or purchases or their place of residence.

Educational foundations. Charitable or not-for-profit entities established to receive and/or distribute funds that can be used to enrich the educational opportunities for students.

Educational goals. Broad general statements of desired learning outcomes.

Educational objective. A clearly defined, observable, and measurable student behavior that indicates learner progress toward the achievement of a particular educational goal.

Educational overburden. A condition that exists in many urban districts because of the relatively larger number of pupils in these districts who require high-cost educational programs and the fact that the costs of goods and services to provide instruction are higher.

Educational malpractice. Failure on the part of a professional to render a reasonable amount of care in the exercise of his/her duties with resultant injury or loss to another.

Electronic books. Content formerly available only through print material that can be accessed through commercially available CD-ROM and other software as well as through on-line networks.

Emergency (temporary) certificate. A certificate issued to a person who does not meet the specified degree, course, or other requirements for regular certification; issued with the presumption that the recipient teacher will obtain the necessary credentials for regular certification.

Eminent domain. The right of the government to take private property for public use.

Emotional abuse. Nonphysical abuse such as blaming, rejecting, or withholding security and affection.

English as a second language (ESL). A form of bilingual education in which standard English is taught to limited-English-proficient students.

Epistemology. The branch of philosophy concerned with the investigation of the nature of knowledge.

Equal opportunity. A legal principle that when applied to education requires school districts and other agencies to develop policies and procedures to ensure that the rights of employees and students are protected and that they are given equal treatment in employment practices, access to programs, or other educational opportunities.

Equity. The equal treatment of persons/students in equal circumstances.

Essentialism. An educational theory that focuses on an essential set of learnings that prepare individuals for life, by concentration on the culture and traditions of the past.

Ethics. The branch of philosophy concerned with the study of the human conduct and what is right and wrong or good and bad.

Ethnic group. A subgroup of the population distinguished by having a common heritage (language, customs, history, etc.).

Ex post facto **law.** A law passed after the fact or after the event.

Existentialism. A philosophic belief that focuses on personal and subjective existence; the world of choice and responsibility is primary.

Expository instruction. A teacher-centered instructional method designed to convey information through formal lecture, informal lecture, and teacher-led discussion.

Expulsion. Exclusion of students from school for periods of time in excess of 10 days.

Fair use doctrine. The rules that govern the reproduction and use of copyrighted materials.

Field (clinical) experience. Applied learning experiences of education students provided prior to and in addition to the internship or student teaching experience.

Flat grants. A method for allocation of educational funds based on the allocation of a uniform amount per student, per teacher, per classroom, or other unit.

For-profit enterprise activities. The profit-making activities engaged in by school districts to enhance state and local revenues.

Formative evaluation. Form of evaluation designed to provide feedback while an activity is underway to improve the manner in which the activity is conducted.

Foundation plan. State school finance system that provides a base amount per pupil to local school districts from a combination of state and local tax sources with the amount of state funds per pupil received by a local school district being in inverse relation to the fiscal capacity per pupil of the local school district.

Free schools. Private schools, popular during the 1960s and 1970s, which promoted the value of out-of-state activities, informal study in the community, and students discovering for themselves what they want to learn.

Full state funding. School finance system whereby all funds for the support of the public schools come from the state and from state-level taxes.

Futures education (futurism). The study of the future.

Futurist. An individual concerned with the study of the future and the projection of trends for the future.

Gateway drugs. Substances such as alcohol, tobacco, and marijuana, which may serve as stepping-stones for a child's later use of hard drugs.

Gender equity. In education, this term refers to the concepts of equal treatment and equal opportunity for all students, regardless of their gender.

Grammar school. A secondary school, originating in ancient Rome and continuing into the nineteenth century, which emphasized a classical education; forerunner of the high school; in current usage, an elementary school.

Great Books. The great works of the past including literature, philosophy, history, and science, which represent absolute truth according to perennialist theory.

Group instruction. Instructional system in which teachers divide the class into groups of students (often five to eight students) and structure instruction and learning activities for this smaller number of students.

Hermeneutics. The art or science of the interpretation of lived experience.

Hidden curriculum. The rules, regulations, rituals, and interactions that are part of the everyday life of the school.

Homophobic harassment. A form of intimidation against gay, lesbian, and bisexual individuals.

Home schooling. The education of children outside the school setting and in the home; a form of private education.

Horizontal equity. In the financing of schools or the treatment of individuals, the principle that states that those who are alike should be treated the same; the equal treatment of equals.

Hornbook. Wooden board on which a sheet of parchment was placed and covered with a thin sheath of cow's horn; used in colonial New England primary schools.

Human immunodeficiency virus (HIV). Any of several retroviruses that cause AIDS.

Humanism. The dominant philosophy of the Renaissance that emphasized the importance of human beings and promoted literature and art of classical Rome and Greece.

Humanistic education. An educational program reflecting the philosophy of humanism.

Idealism. The oldest philosophic belief which views the world of the mind and ideas as fundamental.

In loco parentis. In the place of a parent.

Incentive pay. Paying teachers more for different kinds or amounts of work (e.g., master teacher plans or career ladder plans).

Incompetence. Lack of legal qualification, inability or capacity to discharge the required duty. In regard to teachers' incompetence, falls into four general categories: (1) inadequate teaching; (2) poor discipline; (3) physical or mental incapacity; (4) counterproductive personality traits.

Independent learning. A range of student-centered teaching methodologies that include programmed instruction, self-paced instruction, contract learning, and performance-based instruction.

Indian education. Term used to refer to educational programs specifically designed for Native Americans.

Indirect compensation. Payments or fringe benefits that employees receive in addition to payments in the form of money; classified as either employee benefits or employee services, such as health and life insurance, long-term disability protection, or leaves with pay.

Individualized education program (IEP). Program designed by a team of educators, parents, and at times the student to meet the unique needs of the child for whom it is developed.

Individualized instruction. Instructional system in which teachers work with students on a one-on-one basis and structure instruction and learning activities for each student.

Inductive logic. Logic that begins with a combination of facts and from those facts a general principle or rule is formulated.

Infant school. A type of public elementary school introduced in the United States in the nineteenth century to prepare children aged four to seven for elementary school.

Information highway. A series of electronic networks for communication and information sharing that are potentially accessible by telecommunication links to all schools, homes, and offices.

Inquiry instruction. Problem-oriented instructional system in which students assume major responsibility for designing and structuring their learning activities and teachers serve as resource persons and facilitators.

Insubordination. The persistent and willful violation of a reasonable rule or direct order from a recognized authority.

Integrated curriculum. A curriculum design that combines separate subjects from within the same discipline, and in some instances content from two or more branches of study.

Integration. The coordination of skills and knowledge across disciplines in the curriculum.

Intelligence quotient (IQ). A number intended to indicate an individual's level of mental development or intelligence.

Intermediate education service agency (IESA). State-authorized governmental entity that serves one or more local school districts; the functions of such entities vary by state. In individual states, the entities perform a variety of functions, i.e., providing special education and vocational education programs, in-service training, or financial accounting and reporting services between local school districts and the state.

Intervention programs. Programs or strategies directed at providing assistance to children and adolescents who are already at risk.

Junior college. An educational institution that offers courses for two years beyond high school. These courses may transfer to a four-year institution or may be complete career or vocational programs.

Junior high school. An intermediate school between elementary and high school that includes grades 7 and 8 or 7, 8, and 9.

Law. A body of rules of action or conduct prescribed by controlling authority and having binding legal force.

Learning disability. Having a disorder or delayed development in one or more of the processes of thinking, speaking, reading, writing, listening, or doing arithmetic operations.

Least restrictive environment. The educational setting that enables the handicapped child to have an educational experience most like that of a nonhandicapped child.

Lemon test. A tripartite test used by the courts to evaluate claims under the establishment clause. Asks three questions: Does the action or policy (1) have a primarily secular purpose, (2) have the primary effect of advancing or inhibiting religion, or (3) foster an excessive entanglement between the state and religion?

Life adjustment education. An educational program, popular in the mid-twentieth century, which focused on youth who did not attend college, rejected traditional academic studies, and stressed functional objectives, such as vocation and health.

Limited open forum. The condition said to exist when schools provide noncurriculum student groups the opportunity to meet on school premises during noninstructional time.

Linguistic minority. Nonnative English speakers and others who are native speakers of English, but have been exposed to another language in the home since birth.

Logical positivism (logical empiricism). The view that no proposition can be considered scientifically valid unless it can be verified on logical or empirical grounds.

Local property tax. A tax on real property (land and buildings) levied by a local governmental unit such as a school district.

Magnet school. A school offering specialized and unique programs designed to attract students from throughout the district, thereby promoting racial integration.

Mainstreaming. The placing of handicapped children, to the maximum extent possible, into the regular classroom where they have contact with nonhandicapped children.

Master teacher. A teacher who is given special status, pay, and recognition, but remains in the classroom as a role model for other teachers, or is released from a portion of the regular classroom assignment to work with other teachers in a supportive, nonsupervisory role.

Mastery learning. Instructional system in which the desired learning and performance levels are identified and teachers work with students until they attain the desired level of performance.

Mentoring. Formal and informal relationships between a beginning teacher and an experienced teacher(s) that are sources of information and support for the beginning teacher.

Metaphysics. The branch of philosophy concerned with the nature of reality and existence.

Multicultural education. An educational strategy that provides for those students whose cultural and linguistic backgrounds may prevent them from succeeding in the traditional school setting that historically reflects the dominant Anglo-Saxon culture.

Municipal overburden. A burden caused by the need for a greater range of social services in urban areas that must be paid for by the same taxpayers who support the schools.

National Assessment of Educational Progress (NAEP). A series of tests that are given to a sample of school children throughout the nation to provide national information about the general level of performance of elementary and secondary school students.

National curriculum. A single standardized curriculum for all schools in the nation.

National goals for education. General achievement or performance targets for America's elementary and secondary schools adopted by the National Governors Association.

Naturalism. A philosophic or educational philosophy that emphasizes the natural world, the freedom of the individual, and the development of that which is natural in humans.

Neglect. One of the most severe forms of child abuse that includes an unwillingness to provide for the basic needs of the child.

Negligence. A failure to do (or not do) what a reasonable and prudent person would do under the same or similar circumstances, the result of which is injury to another.

Neo-Thomism. A traditional philosophy that bridges the dualism of idealism and realism and emphasizes the existence of God, which can be known by both faith and reason.

New basics. A curriculum composed of English, mathematics, science, social studies, computer sciences, and foreign languages for those aspiring to college.

Nongraded school. A school in which grade divisions are eliminated for a sequence of two or more years.

Normal school. Institutions established in the 1800s for the purpose of training teachers.

Null curriculum. Those things that are not included in the formal curriculum because of their controversial nature, because they represent different values, or because of the lack of resources or information.

Object lesson. An instructional activity that centers on concrete materials within the child's experience and involves discussion and oral presentation.

Ontology. The branch of metaphysics that is concerned about the nature of existence and what it means for anything "to be."

Open classroom. An architectural design for elementary schools popular during the 1960s that consisted of large open instructional spaces not divided into traditional walled classrooms.

Operant conditioning. A type of behaviorism in which any response to any stimulus can be conditioned by immediate reinforcement or reward.

Paideia. The general body of knowledge that all educated individuals should possess.

Parochial school. A private elementary or secondary school supported or affiliated with a church or religious organization.

Peer-to-peer sexual harassment. A form of sexual abuse that includes having been verbally harassed or touched, pinched, or grabbed in a sexual gesture by a classmate or peer.

Perennialism. An educational theory that focuses on the past, namely the universal truths and such absolutes as reason and faith. Perennialists believe the purpose of the school is to cultivate the rational intellect and search for the truth.

Phenomenology. The study of the consciousness and experiencing of phenomena in philosophy.

Philosophical analysis. The process of systematic questioning of assumptions, values, theories, procedures, and methods designed to help formulate and clarify beliefs about teaching and learning.

Philosophy of education. The theory of philosophic thought that defines our views about the learner, the teacher, and the school.

Plenary. Absolute, as the power of the state legislature to enact any legislation controlling the schools that is not contrary to the Federal Constitution or the state constitution.

Policies. Guidelines or principles for action adopted by a local school board to provide direction for administrative rules and regulations used in administering a local school district.

Postmodernism. A philosophical movement that emphasizes innovation, change, and diversity. Such a movement is reflected in architecture, art, dance, music, and literature.

Postvention programs. Strategies or programs designed to help the school return to normal in the aftermath of a crisis, which include grief counseling, support groups, interacting with the media, and follow-up care.

Power equalization. State school finance system in which the governing board of each local school district determines its spending level per pupil. For each unit of local tax rate, the state will provide sufficient funds to ensure a guaranteed amount; state funds will be in inverse relation to the fiscal capacity per pupil of the local school district.

Pragmatism. A philosophy that focuses on the things that work; the world of experience is central.

Premack principle. The principle that states that because organisms freely choose to engage in certain behaviors rather than others, providing access to the preferred activities will serve as a reinforcement for engaging in nonpreferred activities.

Prevention programs. Strategies including programs, activities, and services designed to reduce the occurrence of at-risk behaviors in children and adolescents.

Profession. An occupation involving relatively long and specialized preparation on the level of higher education and governed by its own code of ethics.

Professional development. Activities designed to build the personal strengths and creative talents of individuals and thus create human resources necessary for organizational productivity.

Programmed instruction. A teaching method that enables individual students to answer questions about a unit of study at their own rate, checking their own answers and advancing only after answering correctly.

Progressivism. A theory of education that is concerned with "learning by doing" and purports that children learn best when pursuing their own interests and satisfying their own needs.

Project method. An instructional methodology that attempts to make education as "life-like" as possible through the use of educative activities that are consistent with the child's own goals.

Property right. The right to specific real or personal property, tangible and intangible; e.g., the right to continued employment or the use of one's name.

Proprietary school. School operated by an individual, group, or corporation for profit to serve the educational needs of a particular clientele.

Proximate cause. The primary act or mission that produces an injury and without which the injury would not have occurred. A standard used to determine a teacher's liability in the cause of an injury.

Rate bill. A tuition fee based on the number of children paid by the parents during the mid-1800s.

Real reality. A form of reality that includes the realm of ideas, eternal truths, and perfect order in the philosophy of idealism.

Realism. A philosophy in which the world of nature and physical matter is superior to the world of ideas. Matter exists whether the mind perceives it or not.

Reduction in force (RIF). A reduction in the total number of employees needed by a school district because of enrollment declines, curriculum changes, or other occurrences.

Reflective thinking. Thinking that is characterized by deliberate inquiry into all assumptions, claims of knowledge, evidence, and one's own thought processes.

Restructuring. A buzzword of the 1990s, connoting a number of prescriptions for education: parental choice, year-round schools, longer days and longer years, recast modes of governance, alternative funding patterns, and all-out commitments to technology.

Revenue elasticity. Capacity of a tax source (i.e., sales, income, or property tax) to yield more or less revenue as the economy expands or contracts.

Reverse discrimination. Discrimination or bias against members of one class in an attempt to correct past discrimination against members of another class.

Robotics. The technology involving the use of robots in business and industry, usually for performing repetitive tasks.

Scholasticism. The philosophy of Thomas Aquinas that serves as the foundation for Catholic education and holds that man is a rational being who possesses both a spiritual nature and a physical nature, that truth can be arrived at through the deductive process, and that when reason fails, man must rely on faith.

School board. As created by the state, the governing body for a local school district, with members generally selected by popular vote.

School effectiveness. The level at which students are performing in the basic skills.

Scientific method. The systematic reporting and analysis of what is observed and retesting of hypotheses formulated from the observations.

Secondary school. A program of study that follows elementary school, such as junior high school, middle school, or high school.

Secretary of education. The executive officer of the U.S. Department of Education; a member of the president's cabinet.

Secular humanism. Allegedly a faith that denies God, deifies man, and glorifies reason.

Sense realism. The belief that learning must come through the senses.

Separatism. A form of diversity that suggests that by maintaining a separatist position, minority groups can build strength, maintain their identity, and gain power.

Sequence. The arrangement of learning experiences in curriculum to ensure that successive experiences build upon preceding ones.

Seven liberal arts. The curriculum that includes the trivium (grammar, rhetoric, and logic) and the quadrivium (arithmetic, geometry, music, and astronomy).

Sex bias. The biased behavior that results from believing in sex role stereotypes.

Sex discrimination. Any action that denies opportunities, privileges, or rewards to a person or persons because of their gender, in violation of the law.

Sex role stereotyping. The attribution of specific behaviors, abilities, personality characteristics, and interests to one's gender.

Sexual abuse. Contact or interaction between a child and an adult when the child is being used for the sexual stimulation of the perpetrator or another person.

Simulation. In teaching and learning, making the educational environment and experiences resemble the situation in which the learning will be applied as near as possible.

Single salary schedule. A salary schedule for teachers that provides equivalent salaries for equivalent preparation and experience.

Site-based management. Delegation by a school board of certain decision-making responsibilities about educational program and school operations to individual schools. Usually provides that teachers, parents, and the principal serve as the decision-making group.

Skinheads. Neo-Nazi gang members.

Slack time. Time for teachers that is not scheduled for necessary activities, but during which they have some independence.

Social class. A social stratum in which the members share similar characteristics, such as income, occupation, status, education, etc.

Social mobility. The movement upward or downward among social classes.

Social reconstructionism. An educational theory that advocates change, improvement, and the reforming of the school and society.

Social reconstruction curriculum. A curriculum design that aims to engage students in a critical analysis of society and prepare them to effect change and create a more equitable society.

Social selection. A position that suggests schools serve the wealthy and powerful at the expense of the poor.

Socialization. The process by which persons are conditioned to the customs or patterns of a particular culture.

Society. A group of persons who share a common culture, government, institutions, land, or set of social relationships.

Socioeconomic status. The social and economic standing of an individual or group.

Socratic Method. A dialectical teaching method employed by Socrates using a questioning process based on the student's experiences and analyzing the consequences of responses, leading the student to a better understanding of the problem.

Sovereign immunity. The government's freedom from being sued for money damages without its consent.

Special district. An agency established by the state legislature that functions between the state education agency and a collection of local school districts to provide various services to the state education agency and the school districts.

Spiral curriculum. Curriculum in which a subject matter is presented over a number of grades with increasing complexity and abstraction.

Spreadsheet. A computer program designed to facilitate the organization, manipulation, and display of data.

Stare decisis. Let the decision stand; a legal rule that states that once a court has laid down a principle of law as applicable to a certain set of facts, it will apply it to all future cases where the facts are substantially the same and that other courts of equal or lesser rank will similarly apply the principle.

State board of education. A state agency charged with adopting regulations and monitoring local school districts to ensure implementation of the constitutional and statutory mandates related to the operation of the state system of schools.

State department of education. The operating arm for the administration of state education activities and functions.

Statutory law. That body of law consisting of the written enactments of a legislative body.

Strategic planning. A planning process that involves the establishment of a mission statement, the specification of goals and objectives, and the linking of funding priorities to the accomplishment of program priorities.

Subculture. A group of people distinguished by ethnic, racial, religious, geographic, social, economic, or lifestyle traits.

Subject-centered curriculum. Curriculum designed with the acquisition of certain knowledge as the primary goal. The learning process usually involves rote memorization and learning is measured using objective test scores.

Subject-area curriculum. A curriculum design that views the curriculum as a group of subjects or a body of that subject matter which has survived the test of time.

Suicide gesture. A behavior that suggests a willingness to commit suicide.

Suicide ideation. Thoughts about suicide.

Suicide threat. An expression of an intention to commit suicide.

Sunday schools. Educational programs of the later 1700s and early 1800s offering the rudiments of reading and writing on Sunday to children who worked during the week.

Superintendent of schools. The chief executive officer of the local school district whose educational program and related responsibilities include planning, staffing, coordinating, budgeting, administering, evaluating, and reporting. This person informs and works with the local school board.

Suspension. Exclusion of students from school for a period of time of 10 days or less.

Tabula rasa. Literally, blank slate: applied to the concept of the human mind which says that children come into the world with their minds a blank slate.

Tax benefits. Tax deductions and tax credits designed to benefit patrons and nonpublic schools.

Teachers' institute. A teacher training activity begun in the nineteenth century, lasting from a few days to several weeks, where teachers met to be instructed in new techniques, informed of modern materials, and inspired by noted educators.

Tenure. The status conferred on teachers who have served a specific period that guarantees them continuation of employment, subject to the requirements of good behavior and financial necessity.

Theory. A hypothesis or set of hypotheses that have been verified by observation or experiment, or a general synonym for systematic thinking or a set of coherent thoughts.

Theory of education. Systematic thinking or generalization about schooling.

Tort. A civil wrong that leads to injury to another and for which a court will provide a remedy in the form of an action for damages.

Transdisciplinary (holistic) education. Method of instruction that involves a variety of disciplines that focus on broad-based ideas rather than on discrete subjects.

Tutorial program. Instructional system in which one person is assigned to assist, instruct, and/or examine a student; may be a professional employee of the school district, a fellow student, or an out-of-school volunteer adult.

Vernacular schools. Elementary schools originating in Germany in the sixteenth century that offered instruction in the mother tongue or vernacular, and a basic curriculum of reading, writing, mathematics, and religion.

Vertical equity. The assumption that groups that have different needs should be treated differently and also that those within each group should be treated in the same way.

Virtual reality. Multi-sensory electronic systems in which the user is placed in a simulated environment and given the opportunity to make choices that create multi-sensory experiences resembling reality.

Vocational education. Secondary and postsecondary programs of education designed to provide an alternative to college preparation and to prepare students for employment in all occupations except those requiring at least a baccalaureate degree.

Voucher. A grant or payment made to a parent or child to be used to pay the cost of the child's education in a private or public school.

Whole-child movement. An educational movement emphasizing totality of the child as the composite of the social, emotional, physical, and mental dimensions.

White flight. The exodus of middle and upper class white families from urban school districts to avoid desegregation.

Word processing. The manipulation of written text through the use of computer programs that facilitate the typing, editing, and rearranging of text material.

Author Index

Subject Index